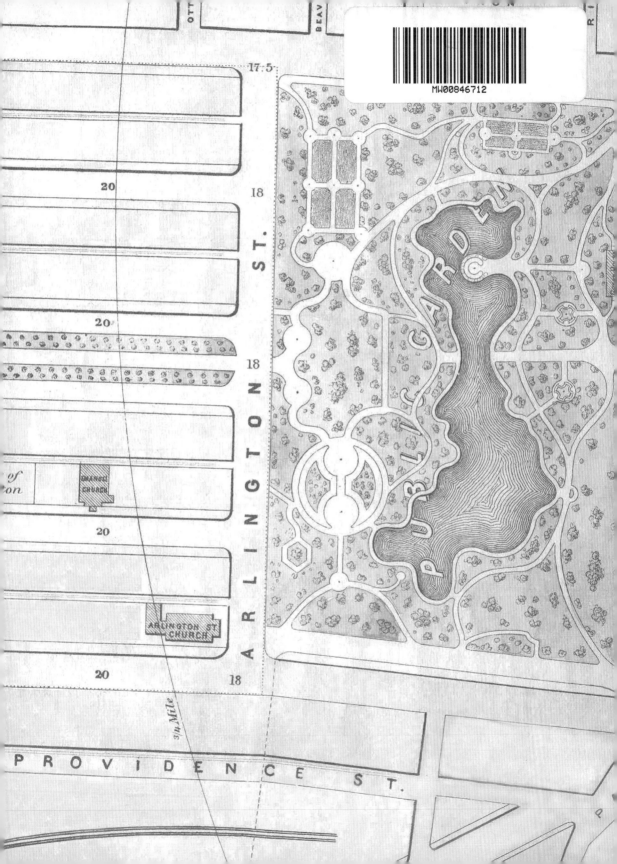

Mind and Hand

—◦◦◦—

"The massive building stood out, sharply defined against the sky, for there was nothing beyond it to the south save a broad expanse of water."
— William Hoyt (class of 1868)

First "permanent" home, opened in 1866 on newly reclaimed land in the Back Bay, Boston

Mind and Hand

The Birth of
MIT

Julius A. Stratton

Loretta H. Mannix

The MIT Press
Cambridge, Massachusetts
London, England

MIT Press books may be purchased at special quantity discounts for business or sales promotional use. For information, please email special_sales@mitpress.mit.edu or write to Special Sales Department, The MIT Press, 5 Cambridge Center, Cambridge, MA 02142.

This book was set in Bembo by the MIT Press
Printed and bound in the United States of America.

Library of Congress Cataloging-in-Publication Data

Stratton, Julius Adams, 1901–
    Mind and hand : the birth of MIT / Julius A. Stratton, Loretta H. Mannix.
        p. cm.
    Includes bibliographical references and index.
    ISBN 0-262-19524-0 (alk. paper)
1. Massachusetts Institute of Technology—History. I. Mannix, Loretta H. II. Title

T171.M428S77 2005
378.744'4—dc22

                                                                    2004056688

A work

initiated by Julius A. Stratton

continued by Loretta H. Mannix

completed by Philip N. Alexander

Contents

Foreword

———✦———

This book provides a thorough, well-documented treatment of the early history of the Massachusetts Institute of Technology through about 1870, and of the European and American antecedents and influences that are central to an understanding of the Institute's origins.

Because the book developed over a period of more than three decades, it has had three authors. The original concept was Julius A. Stratton's. Dr. Stratton was an alumnus, faculty member, provost, chancellor, and the Institute's eleventh president (1959–1966). While his interest in MIT's history began early in his career, it deepened during the mid- to late 1950s with the approach of the Institute's Centennial in 1961. He worked hard with a few others on the faculty—especially John Burchard, dean of the School of Humanities and Social Science—to identify someone to prepare a comprehensive, scholarly history in time for the Centennial. These efforts did not work out, but Dr. Stratton's enthusiasm continued to grow. His President's Report for 1961, for example, alluded to key published sources on the founding and early development of MIT—including Emma Rogers's *Life and Letters of William Barton Rogers* (1896) and Samuel C. Prescott's *When M.I.T. Was "Boston Tech"* (1953)—and outlined his larger, unrealized vision:

> Some day we must add to these [published sources] a coherent account of the flow of ideas that have influenced academic aims and the methods of teaching at the Institute throughout the century. They can be understood only when

placed in the context of the great industrial and intellectual movements of the times. The Industrial Revolution in Britain, and to a lesser degree on the Continent, had a profound impact upon the social and political thought of the nineteenth century. Out of this ferment emerged radically novel views on the purposes of education. In many countries technical institutions appeared, each a model expressing local and national interpretations of new ideas. It was the great virtue of Rogers that he was able to draw deeply from these fresh currents of thought, to profit from British, French, and German example and experience, and to fashion a wholly new institution in harmony with American attitudes and character, and responsive to national needs.

This vision captures Dr. Stratton's approach to the writing of history—not as a mere chronicle of events, but as a reflection on how ideas are born, cross-fertilize, and lead to innovation.

Following his retirement from the MIT presidency, Dr. Stratton moved to New York City to serve as chairman of the Ford Foundation, and during those years his ideas for the history coalesced further. Upon his return to Cambridge in 1971, he began research for the book. He was ably assisted in this work by his administrative assistant, Loretta H. Mannix. Miss Mannix had worked with him since the early 1950s.

During the 1970s I was the chancellor, or principal deputy, to the MIT president. Because Dr. Stratton and I were the only ones who up until that time had held the title of chancellor, a bond that had begun about a decade earlier between a very junior faculty member and a president grew into a friendship strengthened by regular luncheon meetings at which we discussed the affairs of the Institute and occasionally touched on issues relating to his book. I shall always be grateful for Dr. Stratton's friendship, interest, and encouragement, which began in 1971 and continued until his death in 1994.

Miss Mannix's involvement in the book project evolved over the years from library and archival research to participation in the writing. And, following Dr. Stratton's death, she carried on in an effort to finish the work. Because their relationship had been one of close collaboration from the outset, and because portions of the book prepared by one author were reviewed and revised by the other, it is impossible to credit either with specific sections—in that sense, it was a true collaboration.

Early in this decade, Miss Mannix's health declined, and by late 2002 it became clear that she was unable to finish the task. Consequently, I sought another writer to complete the work, for which it was necessary to undertake additional archival research, to write all of three chapters and complete several others, and to assemble the whole in a seamless fashion. Philip N. Alexander, research associate in the MIT Program in Writing and Humanistic Studies, graciously undertook this task in 2003, thereby making possible the publication of this book. Working closely with him was Lois Beattie, administrative assistant in the Institute Archives and Special Collections, who had worked for many years with Dr. Stratton and Miss Mannix on technical issues relating to the manuscript, and whose keen editorial insights and advice have been invaluable.

All those at MIT who have long awaited completion of this book will join me in expressing gratitude to Mr. Alexander.

Paul E. Gray
President Emeritus
MIT

$\mathscr{P}\,r\,e\,f\,a\,c\,e$

long the banks of the Charles River, reaching back into the heart of
Cambridge, rise the buildings of an impressive institution.[1] Today at the
Massachusetts Institute of Technology, more than five thousand students pursue interests that range from soil mechanics to meson physics, from industrial dynamics to existentialism, and include much in between. A faculty of
nearly a thousand is here to guide, to teach, to add some contribution large or small to
our understanding of the world in which we live.[2]

But MIT is more than classrooms and laboratories, more than the sum of particular groups of students, professors, and researchers at any moment in time. Embedded
within us is an intellectual heritage, a cluster of ideas that inspired the founders and that
has shaped the character of the institution over more than a century. Several generations of faculty, students, staff, alumni, and trustees have built on these ideas to mold a
great center of teaching and research.

The coherence and continuity of any cluster of ideas find expression in personal
and social goals, in concepts of progress, in reflections on the meaning of life. With the
passing of centuries, philosophies have come and gone. Sometimes they have grown
powerful, sometimes endured, sometimes transmuted into different forms, sometimes
disappeared. Often they stem from a perception of needed change, of goals not yet
achieved, of aspirations to be fulfilled. Philosophies take shape through the dedicated
work of disciples, partisans, and advocates, followed by a widening public influence, the
emergence of schools of thought and political and social movements, the establishment
of new institutions and the reshaping of old ones.

So what is this cluster of ideas that has imparted to MIT its own special character and helped define its mission? The roots are in the Enlightenment of the late eighteenth century, when as a result of the influence of the new science—originating with Newton, Locke, and others—people began to believe that through human effort *this* world could be made a better place to live, and that we need not wait for the next. Out of this emerged the idea of progress, which led to the rapid advance of technology through the Industrial Revolution. This in turn encouraged yet more forward-thinking movements: representative democracy as a form of government, the utilitarian philosophy of Bentham, the conviction that "the greatest happiness for the greatest number" should be a key human goal.

The Industrial Revolution was born in Europe, but quickly crossed the Atlantic. With this migration came also an impetus for the study of science in America, which gradually transformed views on the nature and role of higher education. Tension between the old (classical) and the new (scientific) stimulated opportunities for reform, and for the rise of innovative, diverse institutions. MIT emerged, thus, as an experiment in scientific and technical education in the middle of the nineteenth century. It was not the first such experiment—Rensselaer Polytechnic, for example, predated it by three decades—but it was among the most successful.

Among the people profoundly influenced by the intellectual trends of their age—by this cluster of ideas—was MIT's founder, William Barton Rogers. In many respects it is difficult to talk about him as *the* founder, as others who contributed to the experiment played key roles as well—members of his own family, friends, colleagues, other scientists, local benefactors, a whole range of people swept up by the notion of progress. And, while they came from different backgrounds, they shared a sense of the importance of education for useful work.

But how much of the driving force for their experiment was derived from political and social convictions, how much from dedication to teaching the new technology for application in industry, and how much from the pursuit of career plans by energetic, imaginative individuals? Samuel Prescott, whose book on MIT is the only full-length history to date,[3] touches on some of these issues, but his work is more a chronicle than a study of the intersection between intellectual traditions, social and political forces, and personal goals. It tells much about external events but little about the heart and mind beneath.

Our goal here, in contrast to Prescott's, is to explore the ideas that shaped the institution as it emerged and as we know it today. As time has passed, how true have we remained to the original philosophy? What other factors have come into play? What can the process of drawing together sometimes disparate intellectual elements tell us about where we are now? Does MIT still hold meaning as a special kind of institution? The MIT we know today is vastly different from what it looked like fifty or a hundred years ago. But underneath the surface change lies an intellectual heritage with remarkable relevance and staying power.

I have been at MIT for more than half a century. I have seen it from the vantage point of a student, of a faculty member in two departments, and of an administrator. I have watched it grow from a rather small institution focused on the preparation of engineers into an institution with broad research and educational interests in engineering, the sciences (natural and social), the humanities, and related disciplines. The changes that have taken place here are a reflection of our common need to adapt to new circumstances, knowledge, and experience.

The more I think about MIT, the more it presents itself not as a collection of buildings, of professors, of students, of courses, of papers and catalogues, but as a living vital entity—a being with a character, a personality, a philosophy, a mode of action, a heritage of ideas and methods that have made a deep impression on all who come to know it. And like other living beings, MIT has a history—the story of where and how it was founded, its struggle for survival, its growth and innovations, its evolving position in the nation and the world.

MIT was established because the time and the place were right, because a group of citizens, teachers, scientists, and prospective students were ready to make it work. Through the years, while remaining true to its initial purpose, it has evolved in ideas, in approach, in reach, and in material development and numbers. Faculty and administrators with philosophies of their own have come and gone, science and industry have undergone dramatic shifts, and society as a whole is in many respects unrecognizable compared to what it was in the mid-nineteenth century. Yet MIT's core values remain—its cluster of ideas, its bedrock principles—even as adjustments are made over time in response to new ideas, demands, and needs.

This is a study that I have pondered for many years. It relates to philosophical questions that interested me as a graduate student in France and at MIT, and to which I have always wished to return. This is not a history, therefore, in the usual sense, but more a reflection on the emergence of an institution. The narrative begins with our European heritage; proceeds to trace the continuum between this heritage, American higher education, and the founding of MIT; and concludes with an account of the Institute feeling its way in the early years.[4]

I am reminded, finally, of what Samuel Eliot Morison confided to readers in his preface to *The Founding of Harvard College* (1935), about the process of writing institutional history:

> It has been an exciting cruise for an American historian, who now invites the reader to glide downstream with him and enjoy the sights. You may join the trip if you wish, where the movement becomes rapid and the bottle-neck begins; but you must not expect me to carry you through the gorge into calm reaches in the space of a single volume. Although warned by the horrid example of Thomas Prince (A.B. 1707), who began his "Chronological History of New-England" with the Creation, and died before he reached the year 1631, I have been unable to get beyond 1650 in the present tome.

In other words, it is virtually impossible to capture and convey in a single volume the essence of a complex, varied institution such as MIT or Harvard. But even though this narrative goes only as far as 1870, I hope that it will contribute to a deeper understanding of our origins, of where we are today, and of where we may go in the future. I also hope that others will pick up the story from where we have left off.

Julius A. Stratton

otes

1. Adapted from Julius A. Stratton's drafts and notes for a preface, written in the 1970s.
2. As much of this text was drafted in the 1970s, the figures cited are not accurate in "today's" terms. The faculty has remained steady at about a thousand, but the student body has almost doubled to around ten thousand.
3. Samuel C. Prescott, *When M.I.T. Was "Boston Tech," 1861-1916* (Cambridge, Mass.: Technology Press, 1954).
4. Dr. Stratton planned to publish this work in two volumes. The present book, conceived as volume 1, carries the narrative through 1870; volume 2 was intended to proceed through 1900.

Prologue

———⊱⋅⊰———

On April 10, 1861, Governor John A. Andrew of Massachusetts signed into law an act of the General Court granting a charter to the Massachusetts Institute of Technology and reserving from sale forever one square of state land, "namely the second square westwardly from the Public Garden between Newbury and Boylston streets, according to the plan reported by the Commissioners on the Back Bay, February twenty-one, eighteen hundred and fifty-seven," for the use of the new Institute and for the Boston Society of Natural History, the latter to have one third of the square granted.[1]

In its initial concept, the Massachusetts Institute of Technology was not a school. It was a three-part educational institution designed to consist of a "society of arts, a museum of arts, and a school of industrial science," to aid "generally, by suitable means, the advancement, development and practical application of science in connection with arts, agriculture, manufactures and commerce."[2] The proposed institution was patterned after British and European models, and its founders expected that all three components would develop as planned and contribute significantly to the diffusion of useful knowledge, the advancement of the industrial classes, and the strengthening of the region's economy. It was not their original intention to compete with existing institutions of higher learning, a point they were careful to emphasize on a number of occasions.

It was as a Society of Arts, and a Society of Arts *only*, that the Institute functioned from its formal organization in May 1862 until a preliminary session of the School of Industrial Science opened in February 1865. The society was intended as a "department of investigation and publication . . . to promote research in connection with industrial science, by the exhibition, at the meetings of the Society, of new mechanical inventions, products and processes; by written and oral communications and discussions, as well as by more elaborate treatises on special subjects of inquiry; and by the preparation and publication, statedly, of Reports exhibiting the condition of the various departments of industry, the progress of practical discovery in each, and the bearings of the scientific and other questions which are found to be associated with their advancement." The society's members were to be organized into several committees relating to the industrial arts, and there would be committees responsible for a proposed journal and for the supervision of the museum and the school.[3]

The meetings of the society would consist chiefly of oral presentations and demonstrations. The mid-nineteenth century was the heyday of the public lecture; in Boston, for example, the Lowell Institute lectures had been enormously popular. It was a time, too, when people in all walks of life were keenly interested in natural history and when their fancy had been caught by the promise of science and technology redounding to the benefit of commerce, industry, and individual prosperity. As an educational medium, the public lecture would soon be overtaken by programs of formal study and by the availability of schools established in response to rising aspirations. Eventually it would be outmoded by changes in the character of life brought about by the very scientific and technical developments that at first had been the magnet for its popularity. But in its prime, the public lecture served a useful purpose and was highly valued.

The museum, termed the "central feature" of the Institute, was designed to extend its educational influence through exhibition facilities for raw materials, working models of machinery and mechanical inventions, and industrial products. The emphasis was to be on the "practical instruction" it afforded, and the "great purpose of *instruction*" was not to "be lost sight of in the multitudinous gathering of materials."[4]

Finally, the School of Industrial Science promised "*systematic training in the applied sciences*, which can alone give to the industrial classes a sure mastery over the materials and processes with which they are concerned" through "regular courses of instruction . . . by lectures and other teachings, in the various branches of the applied sciences and the arts" so that "persons destined for any of the industrial pursuits might, at small expense, secure such training and instruction as would enable them to bring to their profession the increased efficiency due to enlarged views and a sure knowledge of fundamental principles, together with adequate practice in observation and experiment, and in the delineation of objects, processes, and machinery."[5]

Among the most interesting aspects of MIT's founding is the manner in which its initial form and purposes emerged through the refinement of an amorphous, ill-defined, and unsuccessful effort in 1859 for the establishment of a Conservatory of Art and Science. And an important aspect of its early development, following the granting of the charter in 1861, is the way in which the founders wisely adapted their original plan in response to the growing need for scientific and technical education of the highest order. That the Institute did emerge, with a groundswell of support that sharpened its focus, testifies to an awakening in the community to the need for educational change. There was a conviction, too, on the part of a number of influential and knowledgeable citizens that in an age that was becoming increasingly dependent upon the fruits of advancing science and technology, the future of Boston—and indeed New England—lay in an enlightened response to the needs of the times. The apprenticeship system of Colonial times was not only unwieldy and complicated to manage, but also unsuitable for an expanding economy. The promise for the future lay in the systematic training of young people in the useful arts and in those scientific and technical principles which could provide a base for improving the welfare of all citizens. For a long time science had been largely a preoccupation of the amateur. But now, from this haphazard approach, science was moving toward professionalization and specialization, and its aspirants sought sound, fundamental training in scientific principles and in the arts of manufacture.

The traditional, classical system of higher education found itself under increasing scrutiny. The Lawrence Scientific School at Harvard had been the only local response to the perceived need for educational reform since its inception in 1847, the same year in which Yale's Sheffield Scientific School was inaugurated, but it had fallen short of expectations in the area of technical education and its integration into the larger fabric of the university was a fundamental problem. Indeed, the question of whether technical education could achieve its highest aims within the context of a university would become the focus of a debate between Harvard and the new Massachusetts Institute of Technology that would extend over the next half century, threatening the Institute's very existence on more than one occasion.

By the midpoint of the nineteenth century, however, circumstances and currents of thought combined to create a favorable climate for educational reform. In an age of expansion, science and technology were fostering change in ways of doing things, and New England, unable to prosper on an agricultural base, had little alternative but to capitalize on its growing manufacturing and industrial expertise. Further agents of change were the public's thirst for new knowledge, the expanding functions and activities of learned societies, New England's traditional bent toward institutions for the public good, and the availability for development of new land created by the filling of Boston's Back Bay.

The Antecedents

Chapter 1

———⋅≻●≺⋅———

European Origins

T his is the story of an institute of technology, of how it came to be founded and how it grew. But what is technology? Few words are more familiar today. We live in a technological age. Technology is the key to material progress and imparts the dominant character to our modern culture. It shapes the world about us and the lives we lead. Yet from the very fact that technology encompasses such a diversity of human skills and achievements, it appears to defy clear and concise definition. How does technology differ from science, and indeed is technology not merely applied science? What is its relation to engineering? And in this complex world, can one understand the evolution and history of technology without some insight into economic, political, and social conditions?

Technology is the product of man's striving through the ages to master the problems of his physical environment and to alter and control the resources of nature. From the beginning of civilization man has displayed a creative talent in his endeavors to improve the conditions of life, to provide food and shelter, protection against cold and hunger, and defense against beasts and men. He was impelled by a desire to make things. He learned by doing. So it was that prehistoric man created knives and arrows and axes by the chipping and flaking of stones. So, too, by experiment and experience, he built shelters, lighted fires by the rubbing of sticks, and shaped and baked clay into pottery.

This was technology in its most primitive form. Technological accomplishments, passed on from generation to generation, shaped the culture of the tribe—even as today. As time went on and skills broadened, man progressed from hunter and gatherer to food producer—a grower of harvests and herder of cattle. The wandering tribesman settled down on the land and tilled the soil with tools devised by an advancing technology. Then villages were formed where artisans and craftsmen might live and work. As man increased his power to shape the forces and materials of nature according to his will, monuments and temples appeared, villages grew into cities, walls and fortresses, roads and bridges were constructed, and the foundations were laid for modern civilization.

Thus the origin and early progress of technology came through discovery and invention, inspired by an urge to meet the material needs of life. But our view of technology, whether in the past or the present, must not be limited to its utilitarian orientation, for the artisan shares with the inventor the same creative desire to design and make things, blurring the line between invention and fabrication. The scientist, on the other hand, seeks to understand rather than to fabricate, and by observation, measurement, and analysis to determine the laws that govern the universe in which we live.

In the beginning, theory played little if any part in the advance of technology. Purely empirical, technical knowledge was passed on from generation to generation of artisans. Science began to emerge in the ancient world long after technology. As the philosophy of Nature, it became one of the great cultural achievements of Greece, and as an exercise of the intellect was deemed essentially unrelated to the useful arts and crafts. Indeed, the philosophers of ancient Greece brushed aside the utilitarian potentials of science as unworthy of their attention. Yet the contributions of that same age to architecture, to the erection of buildings and monuments, and to many a technological innovation can never be overestimated. It is true that the manual practice of the useful arts was relegated to servants and slaves. But those who directed them in new enterprises had technical knowledge and experience—the foundations of engineering. Even among the philosophers there were a few brilliant exceptions—among them Archimedes, a great mathematician who displayed also a genius for invention. In an endeavor to formulate the basic laws of mechanics, he applied mathematics to the results of physical experiment and was led thereby to a number of practical inventions—a by-product of long-standing usefulness demonstrating how technology may derive from science.

But apart from the work of a few early pioneers such as Archimedes, science remained a branch of philosophy and made little progress throughout the Middle Ages and into the late Renaissance. By contrast, technology experienced revolutionary advances. The development of water wheels and windmills supplied new sources of energy. The invention of the wheeled plough did much to improve the practice of agriculture. The discovery of gunpowder transformed the art of war. The production of iron and steel increased, and metals were skillfully shaped into countless artifacts of practical use. Great advances were made in the fabrication of textiles, and the spinning wheel was introduced into the home. With the invention of printing began the wider diffusion of knowledge that was soon to have an impact on the development of Western civilization.

These are no more than a few illustrations of the success of man's continued efforts during those mid-centuries to master his environment and to improve the conditions of life. Nevertheless, technology remained largely empirical and pragmatic. It was the work of artisans and craftsmen, who learned their trade through apprenticeship and practice without benefit of theory. But their labor and inventions contributed to a broad rise in material welfare and the passage of Europe from medieval to modern times. The period known as the Renaissance, from the fourteenth century into the seventeenth, saw a flourishing of fine art and literature and a quest for knowledge as well. The power of such great minds as Copernicus, Kepler, Galileo, Descartes, Pascal, and Bacon gave birth to modern science.[1]

It was Francis Bacon (1561–1626) who most clearly expressed the transition of ideas and perspective that marked the advent of a new era of material progress in Western Europe. Eloquently he set forth his belief in the utilitarian role of science and its relation to what we know today as technology. "Human knowledge," he wrote, "and human power meet in one; for where the cause is not known the effect cannot be produced."[2] And again: "Now the true and lawful goal of the sciences is none other than this: that human life be endowed with new discoveries and powers."[3] The advance of scientific knowledge, according to Bacon, was to be achieved only through a disposition to seek out and explore new paths through experiment and unbiased observation. From the cumulative results of such observations, the scientist would arrive step by step, through the process of induction, at the laws that govern nature. An understanding of the laws of nature, in turn, would enhance the power of man's control over his environment and guide him to fruitful discoveries and inventions.

Here science and technology appear clearly as parts of a whole. Science is the search for knowledge and understanding; technology is the practical application of that knowledge to useful ends. And progress in each should sustain and nurture the other. Bacon cautioned: "Let no man look for much progress in the sciences—especially in the practical part of them—unless natural philosophy be carried on and applied to particular sciences, and particular sciences be carried back again to natural philosophy."[4]

The time was ripe for change. From the works of a few great leaders such as Bacon, a new philosophy of life emerged that was to dominate thought throughout much of the eighteenth century. The Enlightenment took form in England but spread rapidly to Western Europe, and it was in France that its influence was perhaps most profound. It was an era marked by a breaking away from many of the established doctrines and dogmas of the past, a readiness to rely on observation and experience as a primary road to truth, and a deep faith in the power of human reason and common sense. Most fundamental to the period of the Enlightenment was a belief in progress, a conviction that man with the help of knowledge and reason might learn to master his environment and to improve life on this earth without limit. A tremendous impetus was imparted to the study of science as the source of knowledge and to technology as the means of progress.

It is to France that we must look for the earliest models of professional technical education. As far back as the thirteenth century a royal corps was concerned with the construction of bridges, roads, and waterways, the members known as *ingénieurs*,[5] the word coming from *engins*, referring to the military machines used for the construction and maintenance of fortifications. Until 1676, when a *corps du génie* was formed, these engineers were part of the infantry, their professional skill derived from experience and tradition rather than from formal theory and training. Later, as the term began to be applied to individuals involved in nonmilitary construction, the term "civil engineer" was devised to distinguish them from their military counterparts.[6] They built many monumental structures throughout the land, some of which survive to this day. But with the growth of trade and commerce and the spirit of progress that stirred the country in the age of Enlightenment, it became evident that learning by experience was not enough. The magnitude and complexity of new projects and the need for some degree of order in design and practice called for builders with a common knowledge of basic principles, conversant with the advances in the fields of mathematics and physics which could now be applied with advantage to engineering projects.

In 1716 a Corps des Ponts et Chaussées was formed to oversee government construction projects. A quarter of a century later, Jean-Rodolphe Perronet (1708–1794), then its leader, who has been called the father of engineering education, established an instructional program within the Corps. The year 1747 is generally cited as the founding date of the École des Ponts et Chaussées, though it was not officially so named until 1775, after which, with a more formal organization, it has been characterized as a "full-fledged engineering school."[7]

In these early days there was no formal faculty. Lectures were given by leading engineers engaged in active practice, and a system of "mutual instruction" was developed whereby the older students taught their juniors. Private tutors were often employed by those students who wished to delve deeper into such subjects as mathematics, physics, chemistry, and architecture. The curriculum extended over a three-year period, with the summers devoted to field assignments for work in progress, enabling the student to relate theory to practice. From a twentieth-century point of view the École des Ponts et Chaussées had many shortcomings. It must be honored, however, as the first organized school of civil engineering in the modern sense of the word, one which set patterns of instruction—such as the intermingling of study and work—that were to influence technical schools of the Western world for a century to come.[8]

Throughout the eighteenth century, and well into the nineteenth, France remained the center of educational change and innovation. Much of this initiative was directed toward technical training because of rapid industrialization and the growing military and civil needs of the government. Confusion and disorder accompanied the French Revolution, yet it was in that era that a step was taken which proved to be a landmark in the history of higher technical education.

In 1794 the École des Travaux Publics was established in Paris, intended to be a central school for the preparation of professional engineers for the military and civil service as well as for private industry. The plan initially envisioned the eventual abandonment of the existing special schools of engineering. In the following year this School of Public Works became the École Polytechnique.

The dominant figure in this new institution was Gaspard Monge (1746–1818), the mathematician and inventor of descriptive geometry, who believed firmly that the proper education of an engineer must rest on a solid foundation of science. He attracted to the faculty some of the most illustrious chemists, physicists, and mathematicians of the time, and the Polytechnique soon became the most renowned center of scientific study in all Europe. Admission was by a rigorous, highly competitive system of examinations. Though weighted toward the mathematical and theoretical, the curriculum in the beginning was supplemented by laboratory work, by exercises in drawing, and by some instruction in practical application.

In 1795, however, the original goal of providing complete training of students in any one of several branches of engineering—civil, mechanical, mining, artillery, and others—was set aside in favor of fundamental scientific training for all students. The curriculum was reduced from three years to two and henceforth comprised a unified group of scientific studies considered basic to the profession of engineering. Upon completion of the highly disciplined preparatory course, the student was free to pursue the field of his choice in one of the special schools, such as the École des Ponts et Chaussées, the École des Mines,[9] and a number of others. These, in turn, were reorganized, becoming advanced "schools of application" for graduates of the École Polytechnique. Despite the latter's orientation toward mathematics and science, it is credited with having a greater influence on higher technical education than any other institution, its example extending beyond Europe to the United States.[10]

The École des Ponts et Chaussées and the École Polytechnique are but two of the large number and variety of technical institutions that emerged in France during the period 1750 to 1850. Two others—the Conservatoire des Arts et Métiers and the École Centrale des Arts et Manufactures—are also of special interest in relation to the founding of the Massachusetts Institute of Technology.

René Descartes (1596–1650) had been an early advocate in France of technical museums and schools "for the perfecting of the arts." In the middle of the seventeenth century he proposed the establishment of such institutions where rooms would be set aside for each trade group with adjacent space for collections of "all the mechanical instruments necessary or useful to the craft taught." He called for funds for conducting experiments and professors "skilled in mathematics and physics so as to be able to answer all questions" and able also to instruct the artisans in the procedures they must daily put into practice. More than a century would pass before an institution of this character would become a reality.[11]

The Conservatoire des Arts et Métiers was another creation of the revolutionary period. Founded in 1794, it soon became the "greatest industrial museum in Europe . . . indeed the 'Solomon's House' of Francis Bacon and Descartes' museum of machines come true."[12] Its purpose was to "diffuse useful knowledge and awaken among French artisans and workers that spirit of invention in the mechanical arts that had given Britain such a lead in industrial technology."[13] Its organization was fourfold: an extensive museum of applied science, the collections stemming from a bequest to the state of an inventor, Jacques de Vaucanson (1709–1782), supplemented by additional collections obtained during the Revolution and later; a large scientific and technical library; laboratories for testing and research; and an instructional program, some of the courses of a popular nature, including physical sciences, engineering, and practical subjects, attracting over the years large numbers of artisans, mechanics, industrialists, and the general public. General Arthur Morin (1795–1880), a professor at the Conservatoire beginning in 1839, became director in 1852 and has been credited with establishing the first teaching laboratory of engineering. As with the École Polytechnique, some of the best scientists and engineers of the time were associated with this institution.[14]

The Conservatoire exerted widespread influence. It may have inspired the creation of the Royal Institution of Great Britain,[15] and was also very likely an important source of inspiration for a proposal in the late 1850s for a Conservatory of Art and Science in Boston that preceded the effort to found the Massachusetts Institute of Technology.[16]

The École Centrale des Arts et Manufactures was established in Paris in 1829 as a private institution in response to the growing demands of industry for trained engineers. The founders were three scientists, an engineer, and a wealthy gentleman named Alphonse Lavallée, who provided the initial funds and became the proprietor.[17] The majority of Polytechnique graduates were then being absorbed into military or government service, and there was a dearth of civilian engineers at a time when France was endeavoring to improve its competitive position with respect to British manufactures. Described as an "idea whose time had come," École Centrale was an immediate success. In 1857, when Lavallée retired as its director, he donated the school to the state, and it became a public institution.

Its organization and methods of instruction reflected in many ways the influence of the École Polytechnique, though the mathematics and science subjects were oriented toward the practical rather than the abstract. The highest standards of scholarship were required of the students in a three-year curriculum, the first two of which were designed to ensure a general scientific background, with the third devoted to various fields of specialization, according to individual interests:

> Courses were given in descriptive geometry, general applied physics and industrial mechanics, steam engines, machine construction, industrial chemistry, building construction, mining methods, metallurgy, business methods and management, drawing, and, after 1834, railroads. Shopwork . . . was not much used, but models of machines were taken apart, drawn, and then reconstructed, and laboratory exercises were given in physics and chemistry.[18]

The course work was supplemented by visits to industrial laboratories and factories, as well as to museums, and by individual student projects.

The École Centrale was the first school of "civilian" engineering,[19] and its founders looked upon it as a direct response to the needs of the times. Their graduates were to be the "bearers of *la science industrielle*," trained through a curriculum marked by "strict academic accountability, and, above all, by intense effort" to "unify theory and practice" toward useful ends.[20] Beyond the accomplishments of these graduates, the school and its program exerted a large influence upon engineering education, extending to America and certainly to the School of Industrial Science of the Massachusetts Institute of Technology.[21]

❧

The technical schools of France set the pattern and were soon copied in most of the countries of Europe. Mathematics and science were recognized as the essential foundation, and engineering progressed from the work of the artisan or craftsman to the level of a learned profession. Although the Polytechnique maintained the highest standards of scholarship, it evolved separately and independently from any university. In this, too, it was the forerunner of many of the most distinguished technical institutes in Europe in the early nineteenth century. According to the classical tradition prevailing at that time, universities were dedicated to learning for learning's sake, and any course of study directed toward practical or material ends was alien to their treasured ideals. And so it came about that the technical schools made their independent way, beginning with the trade schools for craftsmen and rising to the Polytechnique and the *écoles d'application* of France, as well as the Technische Hochschulen of Germany, Austria, Switzerland, and those of Scandinavia, a number of which were ultimately to achieve the status of a technical university.

It was in Germany that the conflict between university tradition and the industrial needs of the country came most clearly to the fore. In the eighteenth century little was accomplished apart from the founding of a pioneer mining academy at Freiberg in Saxony in 1765 and an academy of construction in Berlin in 1799. Both were rather elementary but combined classroom theory with practical experiments in laboratories and visits to mines and construction projects.

With the ending of the Napoleonic wars, however, the German states entered upon a new and vital period. Political unity was achieved and the transition begun from an economy largely dependent on farming and handicrafts to one dominated by modern industry and commerce. There was a growing need for competent engineers and technicians—a need not to be met by craftsmen bound to the job for which they had been apprenticed. The example of France was clear and convincing. The progress of industry, as well as public works, was dependent upon leaders in engineering, properly educated for their profession. In the beginning, several attempts were made to incorporate the necessary courses into the curricula of the classical German universities. But such studies as had immediate practical utility as an objective were rejected as unworthy, and the efforts failed. The only alternative, as in France, was the establishment of independent polytechnic schools of professional rank and breadth.

The first such school marking the birth of a new industrial era in Germany was created at Karlsruhe by Karl Friedrich Nebenius in 1825. Initially the plan envisaged the training of technicians and the higher education of engineers in one and the same institution. The incompatibility of these two objectives was soon recognized, and in 1832 the school was reorganized to focus wholly upon the basic needs of the engineering profession. First came a preparatory period of two years at the level of our secondary schools, but with an emphasis on mathematics and related studies rather than on Latin and Greek. There followed next two years of intensive study in science and mathematics, with a curriculum modeled upon the example set by the École Polytechnique in Paris.

But whereas a graduate of the Polytechnique had to turn to a separate "school of application" to complete his education in the special field of his choice, at Karlsruhe this culminating stage of professional training was incorporated into a final two or three years. In the beginning the choices were limited to architecture, civil engineering, and forestry, but departments were soon added to include mechanical engineering, chemistry, building construction, and more as time went on. Later, too, the two-year preparatory section was abandoned, its role being fulfilled by the establishment of Realschulen throughout Germany.[22]

The movement leading to the founding and subsequent evolution of the polytechnic at Karlsruhe gave rise to a number of others throughout the German states which were to attain international renown. Later in the century, as already noted, many of these polytechnic schools were designated as Technische Hochschulen, or advanced schools of technology, with a greater breadth of curriculum and degree-granting powers comparable to those of a university. Of all these it was the school at Berlin-Charlottenburg that was destined to take the lead, yet it is to Karlsruhe that credit must go for being the first to embrace the principles of the École Polytechnique and the École Centrale and in the formative years to adapt them to the needs of the German state and industry. Not only did Karlsruhe serve as a model for the many technical schools that were emerging throughout the homeland, but it would also exert a powerful influence on the form of early technical schools in the United States.

On the continent of Europe the Industrial Revolution awakened broad concern for technology and stimulated national desires to provide sources of sound professional education for engineers. The term "Revolution," as has frequently been pointed out, is to some degree misleading. The movement was neither sudden nor violent, nor can one define sharply either the beginning or the end, although it is convenient to designate the years from 1750 to 1850 as the era of transition to the modern world. Within that hundred years, first Great Britain and then much of Western Europe experienced truly revolutionary changes in the style and character of life, the transformation of societies predominantly rural and agrarian into societies ever more urban and industrial, with profound effects upon the economics, politics, and cultural institutions of the lands involved.

From the beginning until well into the nineteenth century Britain was the undisputed industrial leader of the world.[23] The factors contributing to this industrial preeminence were many and diverse, but a perception of the ultimate need for a system of higher technical education based on science was hardly to be numbered among them. Rather, it was a leadership that stemmed from individual enterprise and a talent for ingenious invention. There was no counterpart in Britain to the École Polytechnique, the École Centrale, or the German higher technical schools. The pioneers of British industry were for the most part workingmen, trained by apprenticeship, and with a minimal knowledge of elementary science.

Technological education first appeared in Britain not as a necessary and organized preparation for the leaders of industry but rather as a humanitarian movement to improve both the welfare and the effectiveness of the workers and the idle youth of the growing cities. To John Anderson (1726–1796) of the University of Glasgow goes the credit for being among the first to respond to the needs of the artisans and mechanics. A member of the university's faculty beginning in 1754 as professor of oriental languages, he was appointed to the chair of natural philosophy in 1757. After studying various industrial processes at nearby workshops, he added to his regular course in physics an evening course of lectures and laboratory demonstrations in "Experimental Philosophy," open to both regular students and what would prove to be large numbers of "operative mechanics and artisans," thus making available to these workers instruction in the basic scientific principles of their arts.

Anderson attached great importance to the laboratory demonstrations involved "because theories without experiments have been the great bane of philosophy in every age and in every country." In support he cited Bacon's admonition that "we must not suppose, nor feign; but we must find out what it is that nature does and brings forth." He published *A Compendium of Experimental Philosophy* in 1760, and, between 1786 and 1795, several editions of *Institutes of Physics*, providing students with a general outline of the course and a record of the experiments carried out. A wide range of subjects was treated, among them physics, chemistry, mineralogy, botany, electricity, and the principles of mechanics, heat, hydraulics, and pneumatics, along with their application to the arts and manufactures. Lectures were accompanied by experimental demonstrations whenever possible. This course was the forerunner of the mechanics' institutes that were to spread over Britain and on to the United States.[24]

Anderson died in 1796, leaving a bequest for the establishment of an institution "for the good of Mankind and the improvement of Science," to be known as Anderson's University, instruction in which was to be open to both sexes. A plan of organization was outlined in full detail in his will, including the exact composition of a large board of trustees, comprising "representatives of trade, manufacture, agriculture, art, as well as the learned professions."[25] The university would be managed by a committee, elected annually, of nine board members. Not to be represented, however, were the professors:

> They shall never be Trustees nor Ordinary Managers at the same time that they are Professors. Their whole power shall consist in meeting with their respective Colleges . . . and in the Senate of the University, for the giving of Degrees, and Rewards to the Students, and in giving Lectures and holding Examinations of the Students as to their progress in Learning. . . . And if additions shall be made to the salaries of any of the Professors it shall be with prudence and in order to encourage merit; it being well known that where Professors have great independent Salaries and the Power of increasing their own Salaries, they, in general, become either perfectly idle or Execute only part of their duty, or become so negligent of it as by their Conduct to lead the Students to be idle and dissipated.[26]

Anderson's bequest included an extensive library and a large collection of apparatus and models but insufficient funds for the immediate fulfillment of his ambitious dream. Through a subscription, however, enough money was obtained for a modest start in the fall of 1796, advertised as "PROFESSOR ANDERSON'S INSTITUTION OR NEW SCHOOL OF ARTS AND MANUFACTURES ETC." Three courses were offered—Lectures on the Arts and Manufactures connected with Natural Philosophy and Chemistry; a Popular Course of Lectures on Natural Philosophy and Experimental Philosophy; and a Popular Course of Lectures on Chemistry. The emphasis was on "useful knowledge," and the response of citizens, of managers, and of young people preparing for careers in industry was immediate. Though the notice emphasized that the two popular courses would be "particularly interesting to the Ladies," women would also be admitted to the course on arts and manufactures in accordance with the terms of Anderson's will. Thomas Garnett (1766–1802), a physician and the first holder of the chair of natural philosophy, in commenting on the encouraging response of women, deemed it "an era in the annals of female education which posterity may contemplate with peculiar pleasure."[27] He would move to London in 1799 to become the first professor appointed in the Royal Institution.

One of the earliest and most popular teachers at Anderson's Institution was George Birkbeck (1776–1841), also a physician, appointed professor of natural philosophy and science in 1799 to succeed Garnett. In the fall of 1800 he organized morning and evening courses for mechanics and other working tradesmen. Birkbeck believed that men should be taught "the principles of the arts they practise," the basic laws of science which had been brushed aside as irrelevant in the preparatory years of apprenticeship. He resigned his professorship in 1804, moved to London, and resumed the practice of medicine. His interest in the task of imparting technical knowledge to working people continued, however, and apparently through correspondence, he advised and encouraged the Glasgow workingmen in the establishment in 1823 of the Glasgow Mechanics' Institution.[28]

Anderson's Institution, said to be the first technical college in the English-speaking world,[29] and the Glasgow Mechanics' Institution would come together in 1886 as the Glasgow and West of Scotland Technical College and, with other changes over the years, would finally become in 1964 the University of Strathclyde. At one time it was known as the Royal Technical College, and the latter's emblem and motto, "Mente et Manu," appear on the cover of James Muir's book on John Anderson. In our fruitless search for documentation of the selection of "Mens et Manus" as the motto of MIT, this discovery at last promised some hope. Unhappily, an inquiry to the University of Strathclyde librarian revealed that exactly the reverse was a more likely answer:

It was in 1912 that the Chairman's Committee approved and adopted the motto "Mente et Manu." I have no source material to assist me in the appraisal of the circumstances of that adoption. I can guess this much: that the Director of the College . . . had undertaken a U.S. itinerary which included M.I.T. and other similar institutes. Since the Royal Technical College had but recently changed its name from the Glasgow and West of Scotland Technical College, it is probable that he was motivated to recommend an emblem for his expanding Institution and it is not impossible that M.I.T.'s "Mens et Manus" triggered the sequence of events which resulted in our own Latin motto![30]

Public interest in London had been slow to awaken, but changes of perspective on the needs of education were beginning to emerge early in the nineteenth century. The utilitarian philosophy of such men as John Stuart Mill, Jeremy Bentham, and Lord Brougham began to exercise a profound influence on the social views of Britain. A new thirst for knowledge seemed to have arisen, along with a fresh spirit of inquiry and a growing belief in science as the means of advancing the arts and manufactures. The demand for skilled workers with some scientific knowledge was rising, along with a general interest in science and popular education. In the background also was a movement of the working class seeking to better their lot in life.

In 1816 Jeremy Bentham (1748–1832) published in great detail a proposal for a "Chrestomathic School," designed for the "extension of the new system of instruction to the higher branches of learning, for the use of the middling and higher ranks in life."[31] The name, taken from the Greek, refers to "useful learning" or the "study of useful things." The plan of proposed studies began with an "elementary stage" of reading, writing, and "common arithmetic," continuing with mathematics, natural history, and natural philosophy—including mechanics and chemistry, "appropriate drawing," and "Technology, or Arts and Manufactures in general." There would also be "grammatical exercises" and "historical and biographical chronology." Lack of space, the age of students, and "utility not sufficiently general" were grounds for the omission of gymnastic exercises, fine arts, *belles lettres*, moral arts and sciences, and logic. "Applications of mechanics and chemistry" were also not included. To Bentham, however, this "branch of instruction" covered gunnery, fortification, navigation, and the art of war.[32] In describing his proposed institution he stressed the utility of learning and the need to emphasize that which was most likely to be of service to the student in his subsequent life and career, to impart some useful skill, as well as intellectual knowledge. This ambitious plan never became a reality.

In 1817 Timothy Claxton (1790–?), a London mechanic who had been denied membership in a philosophical society, organized, with other mechanics, the Mechanical Institution for "the mutual instruction of each other on all subjects connected with the arts, sciences, manufactures and commerce; but more particularly on such matters as lead, or may seem to lead, to any improvement in the mechanical arts."[33] Plans for a library and collection of models and machinery were never carried forward. Meetings of the association continued, however, until Claxton left London in 1820. He emigrated to Boston, Massachusetts, in 1823 and became an important figure in the organization of mechanics' institutes in America.[34]

In 1823, shortly after the inauguration of the Glasgow Mechanics' Institution, an article appeared in the *Mechanics' Magazine* of London in which the editors urged the local mechanics to establish a similar institution, designed to provide artisans and working men an opportunity to acquire a basic knowledge and understanding of science as it applied to the technical operations which they performed. The time was apparently favorable, for the idea quickly caught on. Among those who responded was George Birkbeck, who took the lead in the movement, with the support of Bentham, Brougham, and other prominent utilitarians of the day. In referring to the London

Mechanics' Institution, Birkbeck's entry in the *Dictionary of National Biography* states that "neither the ridicule of its enemies nor the quarrels of its promoters sufficed to prevent its eventual establishment."[35]

Opposition to the movement came from several sources—from those who distrusted the social reformers who were promoting it, those who questioned the value and necessity of including such subjects as mathematics in the curriculum, and those who questioned as a matter of principle the wisdom of providing instruction in science to the working classes. Some held the view that a knowledge of science imparted to other than the upper classes could lead only to "strange views and dangerous social tendencies."[36] Indeed, the editors who set the idea in motion did hope that the institution would endeavor to impart some understanding "of the science of the creation and distribution of wealth" and were firm in the opinion that the institution should be entirely controlled by the mechanics themselves and not beholden to benevolent persons for financial and other assistance.[37] This proved to be a divisive issue, posing fundamental questions about the organization and conduct of the proposed institution. In the end the editors would withdraw, and the mechanics, appearing to welcome financial help, would be represented on the Committee of Managers. The London Mechanics' Institution came into being in December 1823. Birkbeck was elected president, with John Millington of the Royal Institution as a vice president.[38]

With Birkbeck in charge as director, classes opened in February 1824, offering to the public popular lectures on mechanics, chemistry, geometry, hydrostatics, electricity, optics, and similar topics. The emphasis was to be on basic scientific principles and their applications, with experimental demonstrations using the institution's collection of "philosophical" apparatus. A chemical laboratory, a geological museum, and a collection of models of machinery enriched the lecture program.[39] A new periodical, the *London Mechanics' Register*, established by supporters of the institution, reported regularly to its readership on the lectures and other items of interest. A prefatory statement to Volume II of the *Register* gives a contemporary view of the aims:

> Amongst the distinguishing features which characterize the present state of society, the most striking and the most gratifying is the universal thirst for knowledge, so pre-eminently conspicuous in that numerous and important class of individuals, to whom, till within a few years, the stores of literature were almost inaccessible. Hitherto, the humble mechanic has witnessed the effects produced by his manual exertions, without inquiring into the principles upon which his operations depended; or, if his curiosity has been occasionally awakened to an investigation of the philosophical facts connected

with his occupation, his intention has been frustrated, and his researches have ended in disappointment, from the want of that scientific instruction which could alone conduct his inquiries to a satisfactory result. Happily for this country, the mist that has so long shrouded the latent talent of the "operative artisan" is at length dispelled, and the establishment of mechanics' institutions has given an irresistible impetus to those mental energies, of the very existence of which he was almost unconscious.[40]

The concern for new sources of technical education adapted to the needs of industrial workers spread rapidly, and the London Mechanics' Institution became the model for mechanics' institutes throughout Britain. By 1840 more than two hundred had been established. For thirty or forty years they fulfilled a popular need, and although eventually many evolved into little more than social clubs, in a number of instances they provided the foundation for the subsequent rise of important technical colleges.[41] The London Institution itself evolved over the years, becoming in 1866 the Birkbeck Literary and Scientific Institution and eventually, in 1926, Birkbeck College of the University of London. It still exists today with an enrollment largely of part-time students.[42]

The concerted effort to improve the lot of workers and artisans and to teach them "the principles of the Arts they practise" and "the various branches of science and useful Knowledge"[43] was a major step forward, though severely handicapped by the almost total absence of adequate preparatory schooling. But Britain moved only slowly to meet the educational needs of those who were destined to lead in the establishment and development of industry. The old traditions of practical training through apprenticeship were vigilantly preserved. Through the first half of the century England, in marked contrast to the Continental view, declined to look upon engineering as a profession based not alone upon experience and inventive genius—upon "hard heads and clever fingers"[44]—but also upon a systematic education in the principles of science and mathematics and the methods of their application to the tangible problems of industry. Sentiments still prevailed that industry should receive "the fertilizing power of science through the 'education of hands rather than heads.'" There was a clear and important distinction between "technical" education and "university" education. Not until about 1840 were chairs of civil engineering established in a few university colleges.[45]

The Great Exhibition held in London in 1851—the Crystal Palace Exhibition—and other major international exhibitions that followed are commonly credited with giving rise to a national awakening in Britain to the hard reality. After holding for almost a century a position of undisputed dominance in the Industrial Revolution, Britain was rapidly being overtaken, not only by advancements on the Continent, but also, somewhat to its chagrin, by developments in America. By the Paris Exhibition of 1867 the signs were clear. Many now attributed this loss of leadership to the extraordinary progress of scientific and technological education in France and neighboring continental countries. America's progress could largely be attributed to ingenuity and inventiveness, spurred on by necessity.[46]

A spontaneous movement to rectify this national weakness took form and gathered momentum over the next decades. Courses in science and engineering were incorporated into the curricula of many of the newer urban colleges which were soon to become universities, among them Manchester, Birmingham, and Liverpool. Oxford and Cambridge, the pillars of liberal education founded on the classics, were slow to embrace these new disciplines once judged hardly worthy of a scholar. It was James Clerk Maxwell who firmly established the physical sciences at Cambridge. When in 1871 the Duke of Devonshire, head of the Cavendish family and then chancellor of the university, provided the funds for the establishment of a physical laboratory, Maxwell was appointed the university's first professor of experimental physics and set about immediately to plan and supervise the construction of the new Cavendish Laboratory.[47] Soon thereafter lectures were offered in applied mechanics, workshops and laboratories were established, and engineering studies were accepted and flourished. At Oxford, however, interest in the utilitarian values of science lagged far behind, and it was not until early in the twentieth century that the first chair of engineering was established.

This brief retrospect touches upon only the major thrusts in the development of higher technical education throughout Europe. In each country the pattern followed was influenced by economic need, the political environment, and markedly by the traditions of the people.

Britain made major contributions to the progress of modern science and thought through such men as Bacon, Boyle, and Newton, but the great universities of Oxford and Cambridge were but little involved. Science was a leisure-time occupation of gentlemen of substance, and technology was to be learned by doing.

By contrast, France recognized the import of the ideas of Bacon as well as the immense significance of Newton's work. It was in France that the scientific spirit of the Enlightenment first took hold in education and that research in science was first systematically organized. The Academy of Sciences promoted study and research on a national level, and science was accepted and pursued by the universities. Under the economic threat of British dominance in the Industrial Revolution, the conviction grew that the key to technological progress lay in the mastery of the principles of science. To educate students with this end in view was not, according to the French belief, the function of the university. But special institutions were established for the specific purpose, such as the École des Ponts et Chaussées and the École Polytechnique. These were schools of the highest standing, attended by an intellectual elite and serving as a model to other countries of Europe and, later, to the United States.

In Germany early efforts to introduce the study of engineering into the old established universities were totally rejected. Knowledge, according to the cherished academic tradition, was to be pursued for its own sake, not as a necessary preparation for a useful profession. And so, as in France, higher technical education developed through institutions wholly independent of the classical universities.

Austria, Switzerland, Holland, and Scandinavia followed comparable paths in the creation of highly respected polytechnics. Only Britain lagged behind, and when tardily she hastened to catch up, it was the universities which responded to the need. No great polytechnic emerged.

Chapter 2

Migration of a Heritage

M any a page of history has been written to tell of the transfer of beliefs and cultures from the Old World to the New. The early settlers in America brought with them the customs and patterns of thought that prevailed in the lands from which they had come. Each colony bore the imprint of its origins, the place and the circumstances which had led to the westward journey. Thus was imparted the Puritan character of New England; the relative freedom of thought in Pennsylvania, with its mixture of Quakers, Huguenots, Scots, Irish, and Germans; and the influence of the Church of England upon the planters of Virginia.

But America was indeed a new world, and the modes of life and thought had now to be reshaped and adjusted to meet the demands or conditions of a new environment, both physical and social. The contrast in climates, the vast untouched lands, the need for food and the struggle for survival, the governance of their settlements—all gave birth among these pioneers to new perspectives on nature and human existence. And in this pioneer land, where life could be hard and the tasks ahead loomed large, these new settlers were fortunate in their lack of entrenched institutions and traditions. Dissenters in their native land, their courage in coming to America and their openness to new ways and new ideas could find expression in a place of new beginnings. They were ready for change, the land and the opportunities were immense, and it was almost inevitable that a new and independent nation would one day emerge. Henry Steele Commager has said:

The Old World imagined, invented, and formulated the Enlightenment, the New World—certainly the Anglo-American part of it—realized it and fulfilled it. It was Newton and Locke, and their eighteenth-century successors in Britain and on the Continent . . . who launched the Enlightenment, gave it respectability and, somewhat tentatively, experimented with it. But it was Americans who not only embraced the body of Enlightenment principles, but wrote them into law, crystallized them into institutions, and put them to work. That, as much as the winning of independence and the creation of the nation, *was* the American Revolution.[1]

While it is true that many of the early settlers were motivated by a desire for religious and political freedom, it was primarily the hope for a better material and economic life that impelled them to undertake this great adventure. Many were craftsmen who brought with them the tools and skills common to the practical arts of the time. Their knowledge and talents had now to be applied to new problems under new conditions—the production of materials for the construction of homes and buildings, the provision of clothing, the preparation of land for the growing of food. With the passage of the first difficult years and continued isolation from Europe, the colonists began to develop a characteristic ingenuity for the solution of their technical problems as well as a sense of independence and self-sufficiency. Carpenters, blacksmiths, artisans, and craftsmen of every sort established shops, usually as part of their own households. Small factories emerged to meet the essential needs of the people. These signs of a coming industrial movement were most prominent in New England, where soil and climate were less favorable to the pursuit of agriculture and the new settlers tended to congregate in small towns and villages.

Despite the pressing needs, the ample supply of raw materials, and plentiful talent, Colonial manufacturing industry failed to flourish in the years before the Revolution. The primary barrier to progress was the mercantile policy pursued by Britain, a policy designed to ensure a favorable balance of trade for the mother country and to divert Colonial energies away from the development of competitive manufacturing industries. The mercantile policy also provided England with raw materials that might be resold directly on the Continent, used to manufacture goods for their Continental trade, and supply needs within the empire without recourse to purchase on foreign markets. All manufacturing in the Colonies that might compete with British industry was prohibited, and British imports naturally became the prime source of Colonial supply of manufactured goods of major importance.[2]

Where British interests could best be served, however, some manufactures in the Colonies were actually encouraged. For example, Britain was dependent on outside sources for pig and bar iron since it lacked an adequate supply of timber, then the only available source of fuel for the production of this commodity. The timber stock of the Colonies was ample, and iron production was therefore encouraged. In eliminating import duties on iron in 1750, however, Parliament also banned further development in the Colonies of fabricating shops, a prohibition difficult to enforce and virtually ignored.[3]

Though iron had been made earlier on a small scale in Greenland, Canada, and Virginia, the iron works of Massachusetts can claim priority for projects of an entirely different magnitude and complexity, involving "joint financing, a complicated technology, specially imported workmen, and heavy capital risk."[4] In Braintree work was completed in 1645 on the "first successful blast furnace set up within the present limits of the United States," and Hammersmith, dating from 1646 on the Saugus River in what was then Lynn, is considered to be "America's first successful integrated ironworks." Beyond its achievements in the production of iron, however, Hammersmith is important historically for the men it trained who moved on and made major contributions to the development of the early American iron industry.[5] Associated with this project as the principal promoter and manager was the son of Governor Winthrop, John Winthrop the younger, a man of many talents, a consuming interest in science, and a practical turn of mind, and his successor as manager, Richard Leader, who built Hammersmith and later large sawmills in Berwick, Maine. Of these two E. Neal Hartley has written in his *Ironworks on the Saugus*:

> If to Winthrop must go the credit for the initial impetus to New England iron-works, to Richard Leader, scientist, merchant, and engineering genius, is due the credit for their really effective start in the little industrial community of Hammersmith. If Winthrop may be called "America's First Scientist," Leader has, thanks to what he wrought on the banks of the Saugus and Great Works rivers, good claim to the designation, "America's First Engineer."[6]

The American Colonies enjoyed the freedom of unrestricted trade until the middle of the seventeenth century, when several British Navigation Acts imposed severe limitations. Direct importation of Continental manufactured goods was prohibited, certain Colonial goods could be shipped only to British ports, and transport between ports of the British empire was confined to British or Colonial vessels, a provision that had much to do with the birth and growth of the shipbuilding industry in New

England. Under these conditions, however, it was possible to continue free trade among themselves and to develop some trade routes with the West Indies, where the British also had colonies, and with southern Europe for the exportation of such provisions as bread, flour, beef, and pork, and the importation of rum, sugar, molasses, salt, and wine. The major portion of the agricultural output of the Colonies, however, was for home consumption. The effects of the Navigation Acts were not wholly negative, for Colonial shipping benefitted from British naval protection, and the northern colonies, for whom the sea was a prime economic concern, were spared competition with foreign vessels.[7]

Although the mercantile system imposed certain restraints on industrial development, the spirit of technological inventiveness and the desire for independence were very much alive. The Colonial governments took steps to encourage manufactures and to assist in their development through bounties, premiums, and subsidies. Bounties, most often used, were applied to specific articles in the hope of increasing production, while premiums, aimed at elevating manufacturing standards, were occasionally granted for certain quality goods. Subsidies were sometimes provided to individuals in support of the manufacture of particular products. Other forms of individual assistance included loans, lotteries, monopoly rights, and even grants of land. Such industrial development inevitably capitalized on the abundant natural resources of the land.[8] Blacksmiths, tanners, wheelwrights, printers, masons, and millers were self-reliant and ingenious in the practice of their arts. Many took on apprentices, a system for which there were regulatory laws and statutes, not so much as a vehicle of education, as in Britain, but as a means of ensuring the availability of needed labor. Inducements to immigrate to America, such as the payment of passage, were offered by masters eager for additional workers, and various laws were passed for teaching children the arts of spinning, weaving, and other "useful" skills.[9]

The interests and the philosophy of Americans were predominantly utilitarian. Science was by no means ignored in Colonial times, however, which saw significant contributions in such fields as astronomy, botany, medicine, meteorology, and natural history.[10] In botany and natural history, in particular, scientific curiosity led to the assimilation of knowledge about the vast reaches of the new world. Identification, classification, and nomenclature were important goals of these inquiries, but some did lead to scientific ideas going beyond the mere collection of data and specimens.[11]

As a rule, scientific inquiry was the preserve of the amateur and the man of means, with the pressure for professionalization and specialization emerging only in the nineteenth century. Popular interest in science centered on applied science, however, and science was pursued largely for the light it might shed on the solution of practical problems. Though Benjamin Franklin's (1706–1790) work on electricity has been widely recognized as a distinguished scientific achievement, the life and work of this creative man are marked also by his many contributions to useful knowledge and its practical applications, and above all by his firm belief that scientific progress was fundamental to improvement in the quality of life.

As early as 1727 Franklin had formed a club called the "Junto," the members of which were to meet once a week for "their Improvement of Useful Knowledge." Out of the Junto grew the Library Company of Philadelphia, started with the personal books of the members as a nucleus and enlarged through its conversion into a subscription library. The Library Company eventually expanded its activities to include cabinets of "philosophical" instruments and apparatus, public lectures, and a laboratory.[12]

The first Philadelphian to propose an American organization such as the Royal Society of London was John Bartram (1699–1777), the botanist, who in 1739 suggested that a society be formed for the "study of natural secrets, arts, and syances" and for the dissemination of its "discoveries, freely." His ambitious plan was not then considered viable, but within a few years he, together with Benjamin Franklin and Thomas Bond (1712–1784), a physician, succeeded in bringing such a society into being.[13] It was called the American Philosophical Society, and the founding document, "A Proposal for Promoting Useful Knowledge among the British Plantations in America," was written and printed by Franklin in May of 1743:

> The English are possess'd of a long Tract of Continent, from Nova Scotia to Georgia, extending North and South thro' different Climates, having different Soils, producing different Plants, Mines and Minerals, and capable of different Improvements, Manufactures, &c.
>
> The first Drudgery of Settling new Colonies, which confines the Attention of People to mere Necessaries, is now pretty well over; and there are many in every Province in Circumstances that set them at Ease, and afford Leisure to cultivate the finer Arts, and improve the common Stock of Knowledge. To such of these who are Men of Speculation, many Hints must from time to time arise, many Observations occur, which if well-examined, pursued and improved, might produce Discoveries to the Advantage of some or all of the British Plantations, or to the Benefit of Mankind in general.
>
> But as from the Extent of the Country, such Persons are widely separated, and seldom can see and converse, or be acquainted with each other, so that

many useful Particulars remain uncommunicated, die with the Discoverers, and are lost to Mankind; it is, to remedy this Inconvenience for the future, proposed,

That One Society be formed of Virtuosi or ingenious Men residing in the several Colonies, to be called The American Philosophical Society who are to maintain a constant Correspondence.

That Philadelphia being the City nearest the Centre of the Continent-Colonies, communicating with all of them northward and southward by Post, and with all the Islands by Sea, and having the Advantage of a good growing Library, be the Centre of the Society.

That at Philadelphia there be always at least seven Members, viz. a Physician, a Botanist, a Mathematician, a Chemist, a Mechanician, a Geographer, and a general Natural Philosopher, besides a President, Treasurer and Secretary.[14]

The society so founded, organized in 1744, did not survive much beyond its initial year, but the desire for such an organization remained. Later a group similar to Franklin's Junto was formed, becoming in 1766, with prospects for sustained interest and success, The American Society for Promoting and Propagating Useful Knowledge.[15] But the exclusion from membership of several distinguished citizens gave rise to the reappearance, with Bond as leader, of the old American Philosophical Society. In 1769 a union of the two was agreed upon, and The American Philosophical Society, Held at Philadelphia, for Promoting Useful Knowledge became the focal point of scientific concerns in the Colonies.[16]

The first volume of the society's *Transactions* made clear its early intentions to contribute earnestly to the advancement of "useful knowledge":

Knowledge is of little use, when confined to mere speculation: But when speculative truths are reduced to practice, when theories, grounded upon experiments, are applied to the common purposes of life; and when, by these, agriculture is improved, trade enlarged, the arts of living made more easy and comfortable, and, of course, the increase and happiness of mankind promoted; knowledge then becomes really useful. That this Society, therefore, may, in some degree, answer the ends of its institution, the members propose to confine their disquisitions, principally, to such subjects as tend to the improvement of their country, and advancement of its interest and prosperity.[17]

Benjamin Franklin was the first president, serving from 1769 until his death in 1790, to be followed by David Rittenhouse (1732–1796), astronomer and mathematician, and Thomas Jefferson, who served from 1797 to 1814,[18] the years 1801 to 1809 coinciding with his years as president of the United States.

Faith in the importance of "useful knowledge," a direct heritage of the European Enlightenment, was to become a major force in the shaping of American education. And the city of Philadelphia, with its diversity of ideas, interests, and people was to become, as the "port of entry of the Enlightenment," a major force in the intellectual, social, and political development of the new country.[19]

With the onset of the Revolution, the consequences of mercantilism and of the damper it had imposed upon the development of Colonial industry had become all too apparent. The normal flow of manufactured goods from Britain was immediately cut off, though the ingenious Americans did find ways of obtaining British shipments by way of other countries, such as Holland. Privateering became a successful business for many, and armed merchant ships carried on trade with Europe and the West Indies. A surge of industrial activity began throughout the northern colonies to meet the needs of war and to supply some of the necessities of life. Iron works were busy with the production of tools, firearms, and cannon. Mills were established for the manufacture of gunpowder. The production of leather and a variety of other goods for domestic consumption increased, and the textile industry grew to fill the need for clothing.

It was a vigorous beginning. With the conclusion of the war, however, British manufactures again flooded the American market, and for a few years the young industrial movement failed to prosper. In many instances British goods were preferred by the Americans, a factor that had contributed greatly to wartime illicit trade with British firms. The influx of foreign goods produced an outflow of cash and a depletion of commercial credit on the foreign market, problems which tended to force a renewed interest in domestic goods.[20]

In 1807 the need for self-sufficiency was further underscored when Britain and the United States were again on the verge of war. Britain, then at war with France, had instituted measures and carried out acts of aggression against the United States with respect to neutral trade with her enemies and had insisted on the right to impress deserters from the British Navy serving on American merchant ships. Jefferson's final response to these measures, the Embargo of 1807, had been preceded by the Non-Importation Act of 1806, which would refuse admission to certain British manufactures beginning on November 15 of that year. As a retaliatory measure the act was a controversial step, and shortly after it became effective, Jefferson, probably for diplomatic reasons, had recommended, and Congress had authorized, its suspension until December 1807.[21]

Anglo-American relations were sorely strained, and the situation was not helped on June 22, 1807, when H.M.S. *Leopard* summarily fired on the American frigate *Chesapeake*, bound for the Mediterranean and not far out of port. The attack, causing loss of American life and damage to American property, succeeded in the recovery of British seamen, a goal the British would continue to pursue.[22] The situation was complicated further when it became clear in December of that year that a Napoleonic decree aimed at barring British products from the Continent would be applied to the products of other nations as well.[23]

At odds with both the English and the French, Jefferson faced a difficult decision—do nothing, declare war, or institute an embargo. Considering the latter to be the "lesser evil," he recommended to Congress the immediate adoption of an embargo, and an Embargo Act was quickly passed. It prohibited all exports from America and forbade all ships in American ports, including foreign vessels, to sail for foreign ports. Though the Non-Importation Act came into effect at this time, its provisions were essentially overtaken by the Embargo Act, which promised a greater degree of hardship for the American people than Jefferson had foreseen, along with its intended message of displeasure for the two powers abroad. To Jefferson it also promised freedom from attack for American shipping and thereby from the risk of having to declare war, and it bought time in the hope that further negotiations would prove successful.[24]

The embargo proved difficult to enforce, particularly in New England, where commerce and shipping had been the principal sources of wealth and economic prosperity, and enforcement acts passed in the hope of tightening up the restrictions provoked strong protests from town meetings and even threats of secession. On March 1, 1809, three days before the end of his second term as president, Thomas Jefferson signed the Non-Intercourse Act expressly prohibiting trade only with Great Britain and France and repealing the existing embargo laws.[25]

Though his experiment in commercial restrictions as an alternative to war had not been successful, it did have a salutary effect upon the development of American manufactures. The embargo had been very unpopular with many, particularly in New England, but some of the middle states had appeared to welcome it because of the manufactures it had fostered in their own areas. Still others felt that the embargo was actually an attempt to enlarge manufactures at the expense of commerce.[26] Jefferson's attitude toward those who held the latter opinion has been described as follows:

It can hardly be claimed that this lover of the land was greeting the industrial age with enthusiasm, but in his concern for national independence he had come to embrace the concept of economic nationalism. As an advocate of economic self-sufficiency he was quite out of sympathy with commercial men who were jealous of manufacturing. They had some ground for believing him relatively indifferent to them, for he undoubtedly regarded those engaged in the carrying trade as the main cause of the international difficulties which had beset the country. But he was chiefly grieved with them at this moment for not taking a national view of things.[27]

Jefferson's view of manufactures shifted during the course of his life from early misgivings about the development of an industrial population, as opposed to an agrarian culture, to an appreciation of manufacturing in the further growth of the new nation. In the 1780s his *Notes on the State of Virginia* included a rather firm stand against industrial development. Though he did not rule out domestic workshops for home consumption, he believed at that time that America should concentrate on the land, cultivate the raw materials, engage in free trade, and "for the general operations of manufacture, let our work-shops remain in Europe." The *Notes* was not originally intended for publication, and he never carried out a later hope of revising it.[28] His view still held in 1791 when Alexander Hamilton's extensive "Report on the Subject of Manufactures" was presented to Congress, strongly supporting industrialism and the encouragement of American manufactures as basic to financial and economic growth. Jefferson did not approve of this report, nor was the prospect of an industrial nation well received by Congress. Conditions for foreign commerce became more favorable in 1792, and no action was taken on Hamilton's proposals.[29] It should be noted, however, that in mid-1791, while still holding that agriculture would best serve the interests of the country, Jefferson came to feel that manufactures would have to be "seriously" pursued should British and European trade policies then in force be continued.[30]

By the end of his first term as president, Jefferson had softened his view of industrial employment, and he acknowledged at the end of his second term that the country had gained an "inestimable advantage" through the promotion of manufactures engendered by the embargo laws.[31] The need for industrial independence had been made forcefully clear. After the War of 1812, which provided further, conclusive evidence of that need, Jefferson would venture to accord the manufacturer a place beside the agriculturist. But beyond economic self-sufficiency, he was not prepared to say for certain how extensive industrial development should become, believing that "in so complicated a science as political economy, no one axiom can be laid down as wise and expedient for all times and circumstances."[32] He never abandoned his reservations about the rise of large industrial cities with their attendant problems, such as the Industrial Revolution had produced in England.

As the nation grew and its needs broadened, pursuits other than agriculture would assume a growing importance in the economy. This trend was enhanced by the War of 1812, fueled by the military's requirements and the demand for consumer goods no longer being imported.[33]

The end of the war found the United States poised for a great migration to the West and a new era of industrial progress. From the earliest days of the new nation the useful arts and invention had been encouraged, and a variety of technological developments were already at hand. A Federal Patent Act had been in place since 1790, the same year which saw the beginnings of the factory system in Providence, Rhode Island. The cotton gin and other inventions had aided the expansion of the textile industry, which in turn called for the production of textile machinery. Interchangeable parts and steam power provided a significant advance, while improvements in transportation and capital growth were important factors in launching a period of economic prosperity. Small shops and work at home gave way to the factory system and the beginnings of mass production. Because of the shortage of labor, machines were welcomed by the workers. Ingenious inventions proliferated throughout the land, new industries emerged, numerous towns and cities in the East developed into manufacturing centers, and for many Americans this industrial revolution brought major changes in their way of life.

Chapter 3

The Rise of Technical Education in America

The spirit of independence and progress in America gave rise to a widespread desire for more and better education. In part the movement expressed the will of the people to improve their social and economic condition. But no less important was the growing awareness on the part of industrial leaders of the need for workers with a breadth of technical knowledge as well as manual skills. Public libraries, popular lectures, societies, and institutes of many sorts sprang up throughout the country, with the intent of "diffusing useful knowledge to the people."

The Industrial Revolution had evoked in Great Britain a comparable demand for a more general access to practical education. Prominent utilitarians such as Jeremy Bentham, George Birkbeck, and Lord Brougham led the way in establishing new approaches and new institutions for the diffusion of useful knowledge among the workers. Soon many of their ideas were transported across the Atlantic, here to be reshaped to harmonize with a vastly different environment.

In 1826 Josiah Holbrook, a graduate of Yale and a former student of Benjamin Silliman, one of the pioneers of natural science in America, published a comprehensive plan of popular education to which he gave the title "American Lyceum of Science and Arts." According to the plan, meetings would be held "for the purpose of investigating and discussing subjects of knowledge, and may choose for discussion any branch of Natural Philosophy, such as Mechanics, Hydraulics, Pneumatics, Optics, Chemistry, Mineralogy, Botany, the Mathematics, History, Geography, Astronomy, Agriculture, Morals, Domestic or Political Economy, or any other subject of useful information."[1]

The first branch of the American Lyceum was established in the town of Millbury near Worcester, Massachusetts, by Holbrook, who, after a course of lectures, succeeded in organizing a group of farmers and mechanics into a "society for mutual improvement."[2] The idea took hold with phenomenal rapidity. Within the year lyceums had been organized in more than ten neighboring villages. Holbrook continued energetically to promote the plan through lectures and journal articles. The lyceum movement spread throughout New England and into a number of other states. In 1831 delegates representing some 1,000 town and village lyceums gathered in New York City to discuss problems and procedures in popular education and to organize the National American Lyceum with Stephen Van Rensselaer as its first president.

Van Rensselaer, a Harvard graduate in 1782, was a large landowner in upper New York State. He had served in the New York Assembly and state Senate and also as lieutenant governor, and had been a member of Congress. He was a member of the first Erie Canal Commission in 1810 and the second in 1816, being president of the latter until he died in 1839. Vitally interested in agriculture and education, he was first a member and then chancellor of the Board of Regents of the University of the State of New York, and would later found the first nonmilitary engineering school in the United States, the Rensselaer Polytechnic Institute.[3]

The National Lyceum survived only a few years, but many of the local organizations carried on effectively until the time of the Civil War. The original plan of discussion and mutual instruction was eventually largely abandoned, and in its place programs of lectures were initiated to be conducted for a fee by gentlemen of national renown. With all its shortcomings, the lyceum movement constituted a major step forward in the process of disseminating practical knowledge and democratizing education.

A further manifestation of the need and desire for self-improvement among the working people became evident in the establishment of mechanics' institutes in a number of industrial centers throughout the country. These institutes emerged almost simultaneously with those in Britain and were of the same general character and purpose. Each was a voluntary association of mechanics, often encouraged and supported by industrial leaders of the community and organized to provide instruction in the basic principles of science applied to the mechanic arts. As might have been foreseen, however, given the wide variations in social and economic conditions throughout the new United States, the American institutes displayed a far greater diversity of approach to their common objectives than did their counterparts in Scotland and England.

In the 1820s mechanics' institutes of one form or another were established in New York City, Philadelphia, Boston, Baltimore, and Cincinnati. The most illustrious and successful of all was the Franklin Institute, incorporated in 1824 through the initiative and zeal of two young men of Philadelphia, Samuel V. Merrick and William H. Keating. Neither was an artisan or craftsman by occupation. Merrick, a member of a large mercantile family, had recently assumed responsibility for the management of a factory. Keating, the newly appointed professor of chemistry and mineralogy at the University of Pennsylvania, had completed his studies in the scientific and technical schools of France and Switzerland and was well informed on the objectives and plan of Anderson's Institution in Glasgow. Both were inspired by ideas that were emerging throughout much of the country: that the wide diffusion of useful knowledge was essential to the continued progress of America; that learning, at whatever level, should be accessible to all, independent of social rank; and that if industry were to grow and prosper, the work of the mechanic in any art must be guided by a knowledge and understanding of the underlying, basic scientific principles, rather than by mere dependence on traditional practice inherited through apprenticeship.

Merrick and Keating were doers. They stirred the interest of a number of prominent Philadelphians, prepared a constitution, and successfully launched the Franklin Institute of the State of Pennsylvania for the Promotion of the Mechanic Arts, so named in honor of Benjamin Franklin.[4] According to its charter, the purpose of the institute was "the promotion and encouragement of manufactures and the mechanic and useful arts, by the establishment of popular lectures on the sciences connected with them, by the formation of a cabinet of models and minerals and a library, by offering premiums on all objects deemed worthy of encouragement, by examining all new inventions submitted to them, and by such other measures as they may judge expedient."[5]

The scope of the institute's interests expanded rapidly, but the predominant aim from the very beginning was instruction. At the outset lack of funds prevented the hiring of lecturers, a common practice of mechanics' institutes, but evening lectures on various aspects of science and technology of popular interest were offered by volunteers from the membership. Within a short time, however, steps were taken to employ a more professional faculty, offering systematic instruction in natural philosophy and mechanics, applied chemistry and mineralogy, architecture and engineering. It was the participation of able and illustrious figures in the programs of lectures, laboratories, research, and teaching that distinguished the Franklin Institute and ensured its success in the years to come.[6]

Few mechanics or artisans of the early 1800s had enjoyed the advantages of an education beyond the most elementary schooling. Without some prior introduction to basic principles it was difficult, or even impossible, for many to grasp the full meaning of popular lectures on scientific topics. In response to this situation, early in 1826 the institute's Committee on Instruction was asked to determine whether the educational program should be extended to reach those whose education was insufficient for an understanding of the branches of knowledge that were becoming increasingly important and useful, and a general plan was laid out to meet the needs of the "rising generation."[7]

At the same time Peter A. Browne, the institute's corresponding secretary, was urging the board of managers to establish a technical school where artisans might be trained as "scientific mechanics or manufacturers," unencumbered by requirements for the study of useless dead languages and at a cost accessible to all. A meeting of citizens of Philadelphia, which he had convened in an attempt to garner public support, approved of his idea, a report containing a plan of instruction was prepared, and a board of trustees for the proposed "Polytechnic and Scientific College" was appointed.[8]

In considering these two proposals the board faced fundamental questions about the nature of the institute's goals and reponsibilities with respect to its educational program. Opposition to Browne's plan arose from several quarters, with strong differences of opinion developing within the board, the Committee on Instruction, and the membership. Many, with ties to the University of Pennsylvania, resented what they looked upon as implied criticism of their institution.[9]

In the end the institute's board of managers decided in favor of its own plan, aimed at the "rising generation," and in September 1826 opened a high school with the hope of broadening secondary education and making it available to all. And Browne's "college" failed to receive from Philadelphia citizens the assurance of financial support that might have permitted it to begin operation as an independent entity.

Historically, the discussion preceding the institute's decision on the establishment of the curriculum is most significant. Private schools, at that time the only ones available beyond the city schools for elementary instruction, concentrated on classical studies. Some, including Browne, argued that such subjects, particularly the classical languages, should be eliminated as worthless to anyone destined for a vocational career. However, the majority in the Committee on Instruction took the position that to exclude liberal studies was to limit the breadth of mind and view of the student and that in a democratic society all should have equal educational opportunities, independent of wealth or class. Secondary education should be neither purely vocational nor terminal.[10]

As finally agreed upon, the curriculum of the high school combined with mathematics, drawing, and "practical sciences" such courses as English, history, Latin, Greek, and modern languages. The ideas and philosophy underlying the curriculum were clearly set forth by Walter R. Johnson, a Harvard graduate and principal of the new school, in a series of papers published in 1828 entitled "On the Combination of a Practical with a Liberal Course of Education."[11]

For a brief time the school was strikingly successful, drawing large numbers of students. In 1829, however, the institute, encountering financial difficulties and beset by troubled relations with Johnson, withdrew its sponsorship. Renamed the Philadelphia High School, it continued for a few years, then quietly faded out of existence.[12] But a model had been set for a new era in the philosophy of American education—the joining together of practical and liberal studies. For the Franklin Institute the next step would be an endeavor in 1837 to establish a technical school.

The climate was favorable for the dissemination of "useful knowledge" among the manufacturers, mechanics, and citizens of the country. In 1825 John H. B. Latrobe, a lawyer and former student at West Point, and a group of prominent citizens of Baltimore, directly inspired by the example of Philadelphia's Franklin Institute, founded the Maryland Institute for the Promotion of Mechanic Arts. In addition to popular lectures, it held exhibitions of the products of local industry and offered prizes for excellence in various branches. A cabinet of architectural and mechanical models was organized, as well as a library and a drawing school. These initial efforts were an immediate success. Within two years there were some 540 members of the Institute, and 50 had registered as students, taking regular courses of instruction.[13] The industrial interests of the city and state were developed and stimulated, while the school, the public lectures, and the library served the educational needs of the entire community. Soon a high school, patterned after that of the Franklin Institute, was established.

The history of such institutes—particularly the Franklin and Maryland Institutes—has a strong bearing on the origins of the Massachusetts Institute of Technology. It was in Baltimore in 1827 that MIT's founder, William Barton Rogers, embarked upon a life-long career as a teacher and leader in education; and in Philadelphia a decade later he and his brother Henry were to draft a proposal for a technical school at the Franklin Institute.

Useful though they were, lyceums and mechanics' institutes fell far short of meeting the educational needs of the United States. Much progress had been made in industrial development, thanks to the ingenuity and inventiveness of American workers, but the construction of roads, canals, bridges, mills, and harbors called for a level of technical knowledge and leadership that was severely lacking. Many large projects, such as the Erie Canal, and later, the railroads, such as the Baltimore and Ohio, served as training schools for young men who were to become practical engineers, but the basic principles essential to the successful design and production of an increasingly sophisticated technology could not be acquired in this way. The influx of skilled Europeans was insufficient to meet the need. And so schools began to emerge whose aim was the preparation of professional engineers.

United States Military Academy at West Point

The United States Military Academy at West Point was the first institution in America designed to offer an engineering education based on scientific principles. The academy owes its origin to certain strong convictions that took form in the minds of such men as Washington, Adams, Jefferson, and Hamilton during the years of the Revolution and the period immediately following. First was the belief that the young republic should depend for its defense principally upon citizen soldiers or militia rather than upon the maintenance of a large regular or standing army as was common in most of the countries in Europe. Second was the understanding that leaders must be available to instruct and command these volunteer troops—professional officers thoroughly trained in the military arts and science. Included among these professional leaders must be highly skilled engineers, for the Revolution had made abundantly clear the American deficiencies in the design and construction of fortifications.

After much discussion and several futile attempts to organize a school for officers and cadets, the Congress in 1802 authorized the president, then Thomas Jefferson, to establish a Corps of Engineers which "shall be stationed at West Point . . . and shall constitute a military academy." The commander of the Corps, a chief engineer, was to be the superintendent of the academy.[14] This was the official date of founding, but for a number of years, because of lack of leadership and support, little or nothing was accomplished. It was the onset of the War of 1812 that highlighted the shortcomings of the academy and impressed again upon the nation the dire need for officers and engineers adequately prepared to plan and execute successful military operations.

In the spring of 1812 Congress succeeded in passing a bill providing for the reorganization of the academy, giving it degree-granting powers, adding professorships of natural and experimental philosophy, mathematics, and engineering to the faculty, and calling for rigorous officer training. The bill also increased the number of cadets and strengthened the entrance requirements. But there were still difficult problems and deficiencies, such as lack of equipment and buildings, and the result fell far short of the desired overall improvement in the academy's educational program and reputation.

In 1815 President James Madison decided that the institution needed a permanent superintendent, specially appointed and responsible to the secretary of war. To this newly independent post he named Captain Alden Partridge, an 1806 graduate of the academy who had previously studied at Dartmouth. He had taught mathematics at the academy since graduation and was then professor of engineering. He had also served as the officer in charge in the absence of General Joseph G. Swift, who was both commander of the Corps of Engineers and superintendent.

Partridge assumed control at a difficult time and under difficult circumstances, with Congress providing little financial support and the War Department generally disregarding his appeals for more stringent requirements for cadet appointments. But he brought his own difficult personality to the task. Though he was intelligent and made some improvements, particularly with respect to the life of the cadets, his administrative style caused a great deal of friction, and he was a controversial figure. Revered by the students, at war with the board and with the faculty, partly with respect to matters of curriculum, his period in office was stormy, as was his eventual departure.[15] By June of 1816 President Madison was convinced that Partridge would have to be replaced. He had in mind Sylvanus Thayer, who he believed could inject new life and meaning into the academy.[16] As the situation continued to worsen, Madison's term came to an end. The appointment of Thayer fell to President James Monroe, who finally relieved Partridge in 1817.[17]

Thayer was a fortunate choice. Born in Braintree, Massachusetts, in 1785, he had entered West Point as a Dartmouth graduate, was commissioned a lieutenant in 1808 after only one year of study, and joined the Corps of Engineers, serving in New England. In 1810 he taught mathematics at West Point. Following service in the War of 1812 he was sent abroad, as a brevet major, with a fellow officer to make a comprehensive investigation of European military schools, arsenals, and fortifications, and to purchase books and equipment for the academy.[18] Quite naturally he was drawn to the École Polytechnique, whose philosophy, methods, and curriculum he carefully studied. Upon his appointment as superintendent of the academy he initiated a complete system reform destined to succeed because of his clear perspective of what must be accomplished and because he had the strength of character to see it through.

Thayer designed a four-year curriculum, modeled after that of the French schools, including mathematics; civil engineering; natural and experimental philosophy; chemistry, mineralogy, and geology; drawing; French and English; history, geography, and ethics. To these were added, of course, military instruction. An excellent faculty, some trained abroad, was appointed. New texts, many available only in French editions, were used. Though Thayer did not abandon the classical textbook-recitation system, section sessions required student participation through questions, discussions, and oral presentations. Great emphasis was placed on the importance of daily work and on practical applications and illustrative demonstrations in connection with professorial lectures.[19]

In the sixteen years of Thayer's incumbency West Point evolved into an institution whose character and standards were unequalled in the United States. Its high quality as a military academy is evident in the Army officers it trained. But until the time of the Civil War, West Point was basically a school of engineering. Military architecture and fortifications were important in the curriculum, but great emphasis was placed on civil engineering—the design and construction of canals and harbors, of highways and bridges, of the burgeoning railroads. The country was entering a period of accelerating growth, of pushing west the frontiers. The need for civil engineers rose rapidly, and only West Point could supply them. Many graduates of the academy resigned from the military service to take up private engineering practice, and many students enrolled with that end solely in mind. New schools of technology, such as Rensselaer, began to emerge, and established universities introduced courses in civil engineering. But where were they to find teachers and textbooks? Only West Point and its graduates could supply that need, and until well into the 1840s it was the principal source of practitioners in this field. In addition, West Point was the first to introduce technical education at a professional level.

For all this, much credit goes to Sylvanus Thayer. With the advent of Andrew Jackson as president, circumstances changed. He and his followers looked upon West Point as an "aristocratic" institution, and some thought it unnecessary. When Jackson involved himself directly in student discipline, Thayer resigned early in 1833.[20] His influence persisted after his departure, however, largely through the faculty he had assembled, and engineering continued to be a primary concern. In 1833 71 percent of the classroom hours for the four years was devoted to science and engineering subjects. Twenty years later the same percentage held. Prior to 1851 the military engineering courses were "completely theoretical in orientation," but thereafter practical military engineering, with field experience, was included.[21] Of those who were graduated in the period 1833 to 1866, nearly 26 percent left the military service for civil positions. Almost a quarter of those worked in some field of engineering, some 11 percent became college professors in related fields, and 4 percent were college or university presidents.[22] Because of its strong emphasis on science and engineering, West Point "placed itself in the vanguard of educational reform in the ante-bellum era" and in doing so contributed significantly not only to the field of engineering, but also to the broadening aims of higher education.[23]

Thayer's own interest in engineering education would continue throughout his life. He saw clearly the need for more civilian engineering schools and in 1867, through an endowment to Dartmouth College, made possible the establishment on that campus of the Thayer School of Engineering.

Norwich University

Following his dismissal as superintendent at West Point, Alden Partridge resigned from the Army and in 1819 returned to the town of Norwich in his native Vermont, there founding the American Literary, Scientific and Military Academy, which opened in the fall of 1820 with 100 students. Four years later, with an enrollment of 162, he decided to move the school to Middletown, Connecticut.[24] The reasons for this change are not entirely clear, but it has been suggested that Partridge may have wished to relocate near the seashore in the hope of attracting naval officers and those seeking positions in the Navy, since there was no naval academy at that time.[25] With construction of a building under way, the school was incorporated by the state of Connecticut under the same name in May 1825, opened in August, and by the fall of 1826 reported an enrollment of 293.[26] That spring a petition to the legislature for degree-granting powers and permission to raise money for additional buildings through a lottery was denied, opposed by other educational institutions and by the clergy, who frowned upon the military training offered and the proposed lottery. The following year Partridge tried again, this time asking only for degree-granting powers. Facing continued opposition, he withdrew his request a year later. His active participation in the institution ceased at that time, though he retained the title of president in a reorganization. The academy continued briefly, but the property was eventually sold to the Methodist Church of New England for Wesleyan University.[27]

In June 1827 Partridge had opened a preparatory school in his old academy building in Norwich, "designed more particularly for preparing youths for admission into the institution at Middletown," but also for West Point and other colleges and universities. In 1829, however, when the school at Middletown finally foundered, he closed the preparatory school and reopened the academy in Norwich.[28] It would be reorganized and chartered in 1834 as Norwich University, with Partridge as president.[29]

Partridge had long been an outspoken advocate of reform in American education. He was strongly affected by the utilitarian spirit of the times and decried the absence of useful, practical instruction in schools and colleges. He shared also the citizen-soldier philosophy of national defense. To avoid the potential hazards of a large professional standing army, he proposed that practical and scientific military instruction be incorporated into the educational system to prepare citizens in the art of war, should they be called into the field in a time of national emergency.

A history of Norwich University states that a "full engineering course, with practical work in the field" and a "course in Agriculture" were included in the curriculum published in the first catalogue in 1821 and claims priority in the matter of agricultural instruction. The engineering work, following the example of West Point, appears to have been the first such instruction offered in a private institution in the United States.[30] In 1835, when the university consisted of four departments—Collegiate, Civil Engineering, Teachers', and Primary—with a "thorough course in Military Science" required of all students, the civil engineering curriculum included:

> Algebra, Geometry, construction and use of Logarithms, Plane and Spherical Trigonometry, Mensuration of Heights and Distances, Planometry, Stereometry, Practical Geometry generally, including particularly Surveying and Levelling, Descriptive Geometry, Conic Sections, Mechanics, Statics, Hydrostatics, Chemistry, Geology, Architecture, Construction of Common Roads and Railroads, Canals, Locks, Bridges, Aqueducts, Viaducts; also the English and French languages, Geography and History. Much practical field work was given. The students in this department were carefully trained in Declamation, weekly exercises in composition being required.[31]

In 1843 Partridge resigned in a difference with the trustees, but the institution continued and prospered. Although Norwich never achieved the national renown as a technical school that would come to Rensselaer and others at a later date, it was a pioneer among American engineering schools.

The Gardiner Lyceum

Robert Hallowell was born in England of Loyalist refugee parents, who had left Boston in 1776 but returned to the United States in 1792. When he was only five years old, he inherited the Maine estate of his maternal grandfather, Dr. Silvester Gardiner, and later, in accordance with the terms of the will, added Gardiner's surname to his own. Following graduation from Harvard in 1801, he spent two years abroad studying agricultural and manufacturing practices, developing also a strong interest in agricultural and technical education.[32] In 1822 he established a lyceum in Gardiner, Maine, for the higher instruction of young men who were contemplating careers in industry or agriculture.

Despite its name, the Gardiner Lyceum differed notably from the mechanics' institutes and lyceums that were spreading throughout the country in that the full time of students was required and an organized curriculum prescribed, although short courses were also offered for those desiring special studies. Its principal was Benjamin Hale, a graduate of Bowdoin College and at that time also a licensed Congregational Church preacher. In his address at the opening of the school in 1823 he emphasized the need for "instruction in those branches which are most intimately connected with the arts," providing a knowledge not simply of the laws of chemistry, physics, and mechanics, but also their practical applications.[33]

The regular curriculum differed but little from that of Partridge's academy:

First year
Arithmetic, Geography, Bookkeeping, Algebra, Geometry, Mensuration, and Linear Drawing.

Second year
Trigonometry, Surveying, Navigation, application of Algebra and Geometry, Differential and Integral Calculus, Mechanics, Perspective, Chemistry and Agricultural Chemistry. Instead of the last mentioned study, Civil Engineering is pursued by those who prefer it.

Third year
Natural Philosophy, Astronomy, Political Economy, the Federalist, History, Mineralogy, Natural History, Natural Theology.

Besides the above, Blair's Rhetoric is studied during the first and second years, and the Evidences of Christianity during the second and third years. The students in the two higher classes are also instructed in composition and declamation.

The short courses, of three- and four-months duration, included Civil Architecture, with Geometry, Architectural Drawing, and the mechanical principles of Carpentry; Surveying; Navigation; Chemistry; and Agriculture, with Agricultural Chemistry, Anatomy and diseases of domestic animals, and some Natural History.[34]

Teaching methods emphasized the practical:

It is a constant object in instruction at the Lyceum to familiarise the students' minds with the practical application of their lessons. Surveying and Levelling are taught not only in the recitation room but in the field; the pupil in chemistry is carried into the laboratory, and allowed to perform experiments; and the classes in Mechanics are exercised in calculating such problems as occur in the practice of the machinist or engineer. Habits are thus formed of great importance to the pupil; and he becomes familiar with those processes of thought which will be necessary to him in active life. His mind is not only stored with the abstract principles of science but he has learned the very distinct and no less difficult lesson, of bringing his knowledge to bear upon any subject, to which it is applicable.[35]

Funding for the school was derived from student tuition fees, from private sources—Gardiner prominent among them—and, most important, from legislative appropriations from the state. It was perhaps fortunate that Gardiner was a member of the Maine house of representatives in 1822! Unfortunately, state aid was discontinued in the early 1830s, and the school, with declining enrollments and financial difficulties, ceased to exist.

However, the Gardiner Lyceum had left its mark. It played an important early role in the development of American agricultural and engineering education, and as the first institution of its kind to receive grants of public money from a state legislature, it anticipated in some respects the Congressional Land-Grant Act of 1862, now widely known as the Morrill Act. An interesting connection to the school of the Massachusetts Institute of Technology would come through Gardiner's grandson, Robert Hallowell Richards, who was among the first students to enroll in February 1865 and the first class to be graduated in 1868.

Rensselaer Polytechnic Institute

The utilitarian turn of mind, the awakening to a need for practical education, and the desire to promote the application of science to useful purposes were spreading throughout the country, along with a recognition that engineering as a profession would require education at a superior level after the European model. In 1824, Stephen Van Rensselaer, mentioned previously in connection with the National American Lyceum, established a school in Troy, New York, the idea for which had originated with Amos Eaton.[36]

A graduate of Williams College in 1799 with a bachelor of arts degree, Amos Eaton turned to the law and was admitted to practice in New York in 1802. An earlier interest in science and in teaching prevailed, however, and he soon began to devote his energies to the fields of geology, mineralogy, botany, chemistry, and surveying, combining his broad interest in scientific matters with a practical desire to put science to work. In 1816 he went to Yale to study with Benjamin Silliman and the following year was invited to give a course of lectures on mineralogy and botany at Williams. From 1817 to 1824 he traveled throughout New England and New York as a public lecturer, concentrating on the natural sciences. During this period he completed geological surveys in New York, including the area surrounding the Erie Canal, these projects supported financially and in spirit by Stephen Van Rensselaer. In the spring of 1822 Eaton was at West Point giving a course in botany.[37]

During these years plans for opening a school for practical education began to take shape in his mind, and in 1824 he approached Van Rensselaer for financial help in equipping an experimental school for which he already had thirty prospective students:

> In addition to the benefit of the loan of apparatus (which I feel unable to purchase) I could then have the great additional benefit of announcing the School, as under your sanction and patronage. This will be the first attempt of the kind in the world. And I am very desirous that the plan should be fostered by the same patronage, which originated the most extensive geological survey in the world.[38]

Van Rensselaer agreed and by November 1824, having completed arrangements for the organization of the school, was ready to appoint a board of trustees. In a letter to the Reverend Samuel Blatchford, named as president of the board, he described the new venture and its plan of operation:

> A school . . . for the purpose of instructing persons, who may choose to apply themselves, in the *application of science to the common purposes of life*. My principal object is, to qualify teachers for instructing the sons and daughters of farmers and mechanics, by lectures or otherwise, in the application of experimental chemistry, philosophy, and natural history, to agriculture, domestic economy, the arts and manufactures.[39]

By training teachers of applied science and by preparing them to deliver popular lectures with experimental demonstrations in neighboring towns and villages, Amos Eaton hoped to diffuse a knowledge of science among those who might use it best. Though in the beginning the emphasis was on branches of science most closely related to agriculture, it was not long before the rapid expansion of roads, canals, and bridges, and even the birth of small industries, began to exert new needs. In 1826 instruction in land surveying was offered, and in 1828, lectures in civil engineering— a comprehensive term then employed to encompass engineering applied to civilian rather than military projects. Interest grew, and in 1835 the school's charter was amended to allow the granting of degrees and the creation of "a department of Mathematical

Arts . . . for the purpose of giving instruction in Engineering and Technology."[40] In the same year the first class in civil engineering was graduated, the first students in the United States to receive the degree of civil engineer.

In these early and sometimes difficult years, it was Amos Eaton, as senior professor with responsibility for the direction of the school, who provided leadership and gave the institution its distinctive character and purpose. His ideas on education were vigorous and innovative. He firmly believed that one must *learn by doing*. In his plan the student would in effect assume the role of a teacher and would "learn by preparing, lecturing, and demonstrating, precisely as the teacher did." He would "begin, in every branch of learning, with practical application, and acquire principles as his progress required, thereby combining the two effectively." And he would be required to participate in "corporeal exercise," which would improve his mind and would be derived from "land-surveying, general engineering, collecting and preserving specimens in botany, mineralogy, and zoology, examining workshops and factories."[41] He further placed great emphasis not only on laboratory instruction but also on individual student participation in experiments. It was a far cry from the methods of the classical colleges and universities.

An October 1835 announcement of the school, by then called the Rensselaer Institute, indicates that the normal duration of the course was one year, following which students who had been adequately prepared upon entrance and who successfully completed the required public final examinations, could receive the degree of bachelor of natural science or the degree of civil engineer, those in the latter group designated as the "Engineer Corps." A master of arts could later be conferred following two years of practical work.[42] At this time the Reverend Eliphalet Nott, president of Union College, was serving as president of the Rensselaer Board of Trustees.

Eaton's death in 1842 was followed by a period of financial difficulty and uncertain leadership and purpose. All this changed late in 1846 with the appointment of Benjamin Franklin Greene, then professor of mathematics and natural philosophy at Washington College in Maryland.[43] He was named senior professor, a title carrying from the beginning the responsibility for the direction of the school, which he completely reorganized. It has been said that "Greene, more than any other man, gave to engineering education in America its distinctive form and character."[44]

Greene had been graduated from Rensselaer in 1842 and was completely committed to the experimental and laboratory methods of teaching introduced by Eaton. But he recognized that the rapid advance of industry called for radical revisions in the teaching of science and engineering. He began an intensive study of the methods and curricula of French and German technical schools, traveling to the Continent to observe their operations. He returned to begin a full-scale revision of the curriculum, lengthening the program to three years.[45] A preliminary year, established as a preparation branch as early as 1826, was also available for students inadequately prepared in the basics of science and mathematics. Eventually this was incorporated as the first year of a regular four-year course.

In the design of the curriculum—which would soon serve as a model for other institutions in the United States—Greene drew heavily upon the École Polytechnique and the École Centrale des Arts et Manufactures of Paris. The École Polytechnique imposed severe requirements for admission and was focused principally on the fundamentals of science and mathematics. Graduates were then prepared to complete their technical education in a "school of application" specializing in some specific field of the arts or engineering. Of these, the École Centrale was one of the most renowned. It was Greene's plan to unite these two stages of a technical education into a single institution. The revised curriculum was adopted in 1849 and was fully in place by 1854.[46]

From the time of his installation as senior professor and director, Greene had insisted on calling Rensselaer a polytechnic institute, modeled upon those of Europe and of collegiate rank. The name appeared in the 1847 catalogue and won general acceptance, though it was not legalized until 1861. In 1849 Greene prepared a report for the board of trustees containing a review of the state of European technical education, his own concept of "The True Idea of a Polytechnic Institute," and a detailed description of Rensselaer's reorganized curriculum. This report was published in 1855 in a pamphlet entitled *The Rensselaer Polytechnic Institute; Its Reörganization in 1849–50; Its Condition at the Present time; Its Plans and Hopes for the Future*, a document that has been called a classic in the history of engineering education in the United States.[47] To judge by the curricula of a number of other engineering schools taking form in the latter half of the nineteenth century, including the Massachusetts Institute of Technology, its influence was substantial.[48]

For many years Rensselaer, along with West Point, ranked first among the engineering schools in America. Students, many of them graduates of other colleges, came to Troy from all parts of the country and a number of foreign lands to prepare for professional careers. Upon graduation they dispersed to fill many important positions in industry, government, and education.

Polytechnic College of the State of Pennsylvania

Though the need for an alternative to a classical education was becoming ever more apparent, a variety of proposals for technical schools put forward in the first half of the nineteenth century failed to receive the support necessary for a solid beginning.

Therefore, no strong movement toward independent institutions devoted solely to scientific and technical education developed prior to the Civil War. There was, however, the Polytechnic College of the State of Pennsylvania, termed "the missing school" by one historian of technical education because of the scant attention it has received.[49] It was brought into being largely through the efforts of Alfred L. Kennedy, who received a charter, with degree-granting powers, in April 1853. Its incorporation was greeted with "hearty approbation" by the *Scientific American*.[50]

Alfred Kennedy was a chemist with a medical degree from the University of Pennsylvania in 1848. He had served briefly as professor of chemistry at the Philadelphia College of Medicine and lectured also at the Franklin Institute. Peter Browne, whose plan for a "Polytechnic and Scientific College" had failed in 1826 to gain acceptance by the Institute, would be a member of the board of trustees of the new college. In 1849 Kennedy had opened a chemical laboratory for practical work but in 1850 went abroad for two years, during which he visited schools and laboratories in Great Britain and on the Continent, studying in Paris and working in the foremost laboratories of Germany. He also closely observed European methods of scientific and technical education.[51]

The Polytechnic College of Pennsylvania opened in the fall of 1853 aiming to provide facilities for professional education which would "compare favorably with those of the best Polytechnic Institutions of Europe."[52] It was "designed to supply a great want in American Education, to wit: THOROUGH COLLEGIATE TRAINING FOR THE PRACTICE OF Mine Engineering, Civil Engineering, Mechanical Engineering, Analytical and Industrial Chemistry, Metallurgy, and Architecture."[53] Military engineering was also offered. The curriculum was strictly technical, except for modern languages, a necessary adjunct to technical studies at that time. Admission was normally by examination, and each course was two years in length, leading to a bachelor's degree, with a master's degree in civil engineering available for graduates providing evidence of "three successful years of practice."[54] An 1855 advertisement in the *Scientific American* called it the "only college in the Union in which gentlemen graduate in the industrial professions," and several years later it was described as the "Ecole Polytechnique of America."[55]

As president of the faculty, Alfred Kennedy strove to maintain the highest standards of an independent, professional school. For a time the institution prospered, but slowly the financial problems worsened. Kennedy committed his entire personal fortune to no avail, and the college ceased to exist after a productive life span of some thirty-five years. The college's *Historical Record* contains brief biographical accounts of its graduates, and the majority appear to have had authentic professional engineering careers.

❧

The foregoing presents a brief account of the early rise of independent technological institutions in the United States in response to the growing national need for engineers fortified with a knowledge of the scientific principles basic to their arts as well as practical experience. At the same time a number of established colleges and universities were beginning to enlarge their fields of study to meet the popular demand for more "useful learning."

The slow incorporation of science into the curricula of early American colleges reflects the lethargy of academic thought in a rapidly changing world. Harvard in its first years, following the example of Cambridge University, had considered even mathematics a subject "fit for mechanics rather than men of learning."[56] There was little to offer in physics, or natural philosophy, as it was then called. A comparable state of affairs prevailed at Yale. By the middle of the eighteenth century, however, conditions had begun to change. In 1712 the College of William and Mary had created a chair of natural philosophy and mathematics, and the Hollis Professorship of Mathematics and Natural Philosophy was established at Harvard in 1727.[57] But the teaching of science was not on a level comparable to that of Europe and experimental equipment was largely lacking, though both institutions, along with Yale, were developing collections of instruments and "philosophical apparatus" for demonstration purposes. With the founding of a number of institutions in the mid-1700s, including the University of Pennsylvania, Princeton, Columbia, and Brown, there were signs of changing educational values as scientific subjects found wider acceptance.[58]

Following the Revolution and the War of 1812 a new spirit enveloped the academic community. The dedication to the classics, to Greek and Latin, began to weaken, foreshadowing a broader view of what constituted a liberal education. Study of modern literature and modern languages was introduced, and the range of scientific subjects gradually increased. Education entered a new era in response to the needs and demands of a free and independent America.

Along with more science, a few institutions began to offer subjects bearing upon practical applications. In 1835, for example, the College of William and Mary offered a course in civil engineering,[59] and in 1833 the Board of Visitors of the University of Virginia added a similar course to the duties of the mathematics professor. He was able to fulfill this obligation only through a series of lectures, but by 1836 it seemed possible, with the help of the professor of natural philosophy, who happened to be MIT's founder, William Barton Rogers, to establish a "School of Civil Engineering," with each sharing a very limited amount of instruction.[60]

These two institutions present rather special cases. With priority belonging to William and Mary, they operated under a limited form of elective system, and a "School" at the University of Virginia was at that time actually no more than a department, often with but one professor. Because of Professor Rogers's association with both, they bear directly on the founding of the school of the Massachusetts Institute of Technology.

In these decades when expectations were high for social and economic progress, a number of factors combined to force a reconsideration of educational practice. Among these were the increasing age and preparation of incoming students in comparison with earlier days, the popular demand for more "useful learning" and the practical applications of science, together with better educational opportunity for the working classes, and college enrollments that failed to increase despite population growth. Advances in Europe had rendered obsolete much of the scientific instruction available, and the apparatus and instrumentation needed were expensive. In addition, despite declining interest in the classics, the response of most colleges to these changing times had been largely the addition of new subjects to the regular classical program, thus creating a crowded schedule of required subjects and limiting the time that could be devoted to each. Curricular studies became the order of the day, and thus began the long and crucial debate on what constituted a liberal education and on the virtues and weaknesses of a curriculum allowing for free electives.[61]

The president of Brown University, Francis Wayland, was one of the pioneer proponents of change. A graduate of Union College in 1813 and a clergyman, he had served as a tutor at Union from 1817 to 1821, and briefly in 1826 as professor of mathematics and natural philosophy before becoming president of Brown University in 1827.[62] At Brown he exerted every effort to broaden and modernize the academic base, to adopt an elective system, and to bring more science, both pure and applied, into the curriculum. In 1842 his *Thoughts on the Present Collegiate System in the United States* called for a reappraisal of the aims of higher education in the light of America's needs.

Wayland's extensive report to Brown's Corporation in 1850 spoke again to this problem. In attempting to respond to the need within the confines of "the common prejudice in favor of a four years' course, and of the universality of degrees," the colleges and their students now faced an impossible situation. None of the disciplines, he said, was well served:

We have now in the United States, according to the American Almanac of the present year, one hundred and twenty colleges pursuing in general this course. All of them teach Greek and Latin, but where are our classical scholars? All teach mathematics, but where are our mathematicians? We might ask the same questions concerning the other sciences taught among us. There has existed for the last twenty years a great demand for civil engineers. Has this demand been supplied from our colleges? We presume the single academy at West Point, graduating annually a smaller number than many of our colleges, has done more towards the construction of railroads than all our one hundred twenty colleges united.[63]

It was time, he felt, to recognize that "new studies cannot be introduced without curtailing the old" and that the problem would not be solved "by the system of instruction which we inherited from our English ancestors."[64]

Wayland gained approval for changes in admissions policies to attract both greater numbers and a wider spectrum of students, for curricular reform, and for flexibility to resolve the problem of enlarging fields of study. Four years would be required for a master of arts degree, a shorter period for the bachelor of arts, and a three-year program in practical subjects would lead to a bachelor of philosophy. In the reforms thus instituted, with funds raised by the Corporation, Wayland encountered both support and opposition. He won the approval of the Rhode Island General Assembly and the Providence Association of Mechanics and Manufacturers. But the faculty did not take kindly to the new and less rigid arrangement of the curriculum, and though enrollments did increase for a time, the qualifications of the students admitted were not as high as they liked.

In the end Wayland resigned, and Brown retreated for a while to the status quo. His views were slightly ahead of his time and the days of those who opposed him were numbered.[65] The idea of reform was in the air, demand was increasing for a more practical education in keeping with the spirit of the day, and change was inevitable. In due course, Wayland's 1842 and 1850 statements came to be seen as prophetic, influential documents in the literature of American higher education.[66]

The establishment of schools of engineering attached to the older colleges and universities also came about through a process of slow evolution, beginning with courses in "natural philosophy" added to Greek, Latin, history, and literature, as already noted, followed by the sciences, and in some instances their useful application. The final—though by no means inevitable—step was the organization of a complete curriculum as an optional course leading to a degree. In time, separate "schools" were established, attached to and yet largely independent of the basic central college, as with schools of theology, law, and medicine, thus forming a university. Years were to pass before engineering would be ranked with these "learned professions," but progress was on the way. Even before Francis Wayland attempted a radical reform of the Brown curriculum, his alma mater, Union College, had successfully launched a complete course in civil engineering, and Harvard, Yale, and Dartmouth had already established scientific schools.[67]

Union College

Union, founded in 1795 at Schenectady, New York, was one of the earliest colleges to provide instruction in science and engineering. In 1804 Eliphalet Nott, in many ways the most innovative and distinguished American academic leader of the first half of the nineteenth century, was named president, a position which he held for sixty-two years. As was true of most college presidents of that period, Nott was both a classical scholar and a clergyman. But to this orthodox background he added skill and interest in practical mechanics. For his innovative design of stoves and his work to improve the safety of steam boilers he was awarded some thirty patents.[68] This breadth of mind and outlook was slowly but inevitably reflected in changes in the Union curriculum, and by 1824 mathematics and science courses would comprise nearly half of the required subjects in the final three years of the program leading to a bachelor of arts degree.[69]

In 1828 Nott also became president of the Board of Trustees of the Rensselaer Institute, a relationship which no doubt broadened his perspective. That same year two curricular options were offered to students at Union in their sophomore, junior, and senior years. One, a revised classical program, emphasized modern languages rather than Greek and Latin and devoted more time to mathematics and science. The other, leading to a separate degree, was scientific, with 33% of the time allotted to science, 30% to mathematics, 30% to social studies and English, and 7% to modern languages.[70] This parallel, elective course plan was strongly criticized by those who felt that the very "foundations of sound learning" were under attack. But the idea appealed to many, and for a time Union's enrollment was second only to Yale's.[71]

In 1845 Nott resigned from the board of Rensselaer and established at Union a complete course of civil engineering, a first step toward a school of engineering. As the first institution of its sort to make such a move, Union College must be ranked as yet another kind of pioneer in American engineering education. To build and lead the new school Nott chose William M. Gillespie, a graduate of Columbia College and a former student at L'École des Ponts et Chaussées. As a civil engineer, as well as a teacher, he gained recognition in America and abroad. He believed strongly that for the proper training of an engineer, practical experience must be matched by a thorough knowledge of underlying scientific principles. He was convinced further that engineers should be exposed also to liberal studies and that a liberal arts curriculum, in turn, should include some scientific subjects.

Gillespie remained at Union until his death in January 1868. Under his leadership the courses in engineering grew and prospered, and many graduates became prominent contributors to the developing industrial era.[72]

The Sheffield Scientific School at Yale

The development of science and engineering at Yale began with the appointment in 1802 of Benjamin Silliman as professor of chemistry and natural history, an appointment that Silliman described as "a cause of wonder to all, and of cavil to political enemies of the College."[73] He was no less surprised himself, for he had never studied the disciplines of which he would now become the sole professor. A Yale graduate with a bachelor of arts in 1796, he had taught briefly in a private school, entered a New Haven office in the fall of 1798 for the study of law, and in 1799 was appointed a tutor at Yale, a position that allowed him to continue to study for his chosen profession. He passed the Connecticut Bar examination in the spring of 1802. He had, however, in the summer of 1801, privately accepted President Timothy Dwight's astonishing proposal that he allow his name to be placed before the Yale Corporation for a chair which had been approved in 1798 for establishment when funds became available.

Dwight's selection of a twenty-two-year-old nonscientist for this important post is testimony not only to his confidence in Silliman and his willingness to accept risk, but also to the scarcity of qualified science teachers in America at that time. He had rejected the possibility of seeking a candidate abroad "who, however able he might be in point of science, he would not understand our college system, and might therefore not act in harmony with his colleagues":

> He said, however, that it was at present impossible to find among us a man properly qualified to discharge the duties of the office.... He saw no way but to select a young man worthy of confidence, and allow him time, opportunity, and pecuniary aid to enable him to acquire the requisite science and skill, and wait for him until he should be prepared to begin. He decidedly preferred one of our own young men born and trained among us, and possessed of our habits and sympathies.[74]

Following the confirmation of his appointment in September 1802, Silliman spent the next two years preparing for his new teaching responsibilities, mainly through study at the Medical School in Philadelphia, where he came to know many important men of science. On April 4, 1804, he delivered his first lecture in chemistry at Yale, and soon plans were made to send him abroad with $10,000 to purchase books and chemical and physical apparatus. At his suggestion the trip was arranged to provide also an opportunity for further study to, as he said, "improve in my profession."

Silliman left in March 1805 for a very productive year in Europe, chiefly in England and Scotland, again enlarging his acquaintance among important scientists of the day and spending the winter in Edinburgh studying chemistry, geology, and medicine. The trip, long a "cherished desire," fulfilled all of his expectations. He would later say:

> In relation to professional improvement, I trust it has been already rendered evident that a much higher standard of excellence than I had before seen was presented to me, especially in Edinburgh. Upon that scale I endeavored to form my professional character, to imitate what I saw and heard, and afterwards to introduce such improvements as I might be able to hit upon or invent. It is obvious that, had I rested content with the Philadelphia standard, except what I learned from my early friend, Robert Hare, the chemistry of Yale College would have been comparatively an humble affair. In mineralogy, my opportunities at home had been very limited. As to geology, the science did not exist among us, except in the minds of a very few individuals, and instruction was not attainable in any public institution. . . . Here my mind was enlightened, interested, and excited to efforts which, through half a century were sustained and increased. Had I remained at home, I should probably never have reached a high standard of attainment in geology, nor given whatever impulse has emanated from New Haven as one of the centres of scientific labor and influence.[75]

Thus began in earnest the career of one who would become one of the most influential scientists of his day, playing an important role in the professionalization of American science, in the organization of a growing scientific community, and in promoting the cause of scientific, technical, and medical education and research at Yale.

Silliman proved to be a teacher of extraordinary ability. His knowledge of European methods and progress, his dramatic power as a public lecturer and in the classroom, his textbooks and the *American Journal of Science and Arts*, which he published, all combined in a most striking manner to excite an interest in science on the part not only of his students, but also of a wider audience. For many years there were no facilities at Yale for systematic laboratory work of any kind. Only one small room was available for Silliman's own use, and there, with limited available laboratory assistance, he was able to carry out a variety of notable experiments. In addition, he gave private laboratory instruction both to the assistants who helped him prepare his demonstration lectures and to others with a commitment to natural science. During those early years he served as professor of geology, mineralogy, and pharmacy as well as chemistry, and he carried out all of these duties with distinction.[76]

At last, in 1846, two additional appointments to the faculty were made: Silliman's son, Benjamin, Jr., in practical chemistry, and John Pitkin Norton, in agricultural chemistry and animal and vegetable physiology. Young Silliman had been working since graduation from Yale in 1837 as an assistant to his father in chemistry and mineralogy while serving also as associate editor of the *American Journal of Science and Arts*. He was much interested in teaching, and during this period, like his father, also gave private laboratory instruction in chemistry and mineralogy to students not enrolled in the college. A number of these would have illustrious careers as teachers and men of science, and one of them was John Pitkin Norton. Norton had just returned from two successful years of work in the laboratory of the Agricultural Chemical Association in Edinburgh, and immediately following his appointment he went abroad to Utrecht for further study in preparation for his teaching duties.[77]

In August 1847, the same year in which Harvard opened its Lawrence Scientific School, the Yale Corporation established a Department of Philosophy and the Arts, which included a School of Applied Chemistry. Its principal aim was to provide advanced instruction in "philosophy, literature, history, the moral sciences other than law and theology, the natural sciences excepting medicine, and their application to the arts." College graduates and "other young men of fair moral character" would be admitted for whatever studies they might wish to pursue, and Yale undergraduates would be allowed to take courses only with permission from the "academical faculty." Individuals who had been "dismissed" from Yale or other institutions would not be admitted.[78]

At this time Norton, who refused to take on responsibility for instruction in animal and vegetable physiology, became simply "professor of agricultural chemistry," and Silliman, "professor of chemistry and the kindred sciences as applied to the arts." And it was in this direction that student interest would prove to lie. Eight of the eleven students in the first year, four of whom had already earned bachelor's or master's degrees, were enrolled in the School of Applied Chemistry.[79] Enrollment increased, and instruction, except for two courses of lectures given by Norton and Silliman, consisted mainly of individual work in the laboratory under their guidance.[80] Neither entrance requirements nor final examinations were established, and no formal curriculum had been devised.

One provision with respect to the establishment of the department would inevitably lead to problems, especially as enrollments increased. The Yale Corporation had specified that no college funds could be used for its support. The appointments of Silliman and Norton in 1846 had permitted no salary, and the two were forced to rely mainly on student fees and personal resources for all expenses, including compensation for their services and the rent exacted by the Corporation for the building in which they were allowed to develop and equip their laboratory.[81] Silliman resigned in 1849 to take up a professorship in the Medical School of the University of Louisville but would later rejoin the Yale faculty.[82]

With the departure of Silliman, Norton assumed sole responsibility for the school. He was anxious to set up a regular curriculum leading to a degree and late in 1850, citing the example of other institutions beginning to offer such programs, urged the Corporation to establish a degree "as a strong stimulus to the scientific students" and "a direct inducement to the pursuit of full & lengthened courses of study," a move that he felt would also "greatly conduce to the welfare & reputation" of the Department of Philosophy and the Arts. The Corporation did not act favorably on this proposal until July 27, 1852, when it authorized a bachelor of philosophy degree for students at least twenty-one years old, in residence for two years, and successfully completing examinations in at least three branches of study. For students in the physical sciences, the requirements specified proficiency in two departments of physical or mathematical science and either French or German. Six men had already successfully completed the requirements thus established and were granted degrees later in the same year.[83] They have been characterized as "up to that time, the best prepared group of young chemists graduating from an institution of higher learning in the United States."[84]

The July 27, 1852, meeting of the Corporation was important for yet another significant step in the growth of scientific and technical education at Yale, for on that day it established a professorship of civil engineering and appointed William A. Norton (no relation to John Norton) to this chair with the provision that no existing college funds be used for this purpose. Norton, then professor of civil engineering at Brown University, was graduated from West Point in 1827 and had taught at the academy, at the University of the City of New York, and at Delaware College in Newark, Delaware. He had been at Brown since 1850.[85]

At the request of the elder Silliman, William Norton had prepared a proposal for the establishment of a School of Engineering in connection with the Department of

Philosophy and the Arts, and Silliman urged that it be approved by the Corporation: "The addition of so important a branch of instruction to those already included in the department of applied science will contribute to draw the attention of the country more and more to Yale College and to New Haven as a place where, in due time, every demand for useful knowledge may be satisfied without interfering with the regular course of instruction & mental training as already established."[86] Norton was prepared to pay all of the expenses and provide all the apparatus needed, the income to be derived solely from student fees and whatever contributions he might be able to secure without conflicting with the college's own fund-raising efforts. The program would cover two years, but students would be free to enroll for partial courses. The curriculum would include surveying, drawing, descriptive geometry and its applications to civil and mechanical engineering, principles of architecture, analytical geometry and calculus, mechanics and its applications to machinery and engineering, the science of construction, and field-engineering. Twenty-six students enrolled for the first year, 1852–53, among them the members of Professor Norton's previous class at Brown.[87]

In September 1852 John Norton died. With Benjamin Silliman, Jr., he had succeeded not only in securing a permanent place for the School of Applied Chemistry, but also in advancing the cause of science at Yale. His successor was John Addison Porter, professor of chemistry as applied to the arts at Brown University, who agreed to take charge of the laboratory instruction in 1852–53, an arrangement soon made permanent by his appointment as professor of analytical and agricultural chemistry. A graduate of Yale in 1842 and a former student of Justus Liebig in Giessen, Germany, he had served briefly as an assistant to Eben S. Horsford at the Lawrence Scientific School at Harvard. He had been teaching at Brown since 1850 and was admirably suited to carry on the work which John Norton had begun.[88]

In 1854 Benjamin Silliman, Jr., rejoined the Yale faculty as successor to his father, who had retired in 1853. His appointment at that time specified that he would be responsible for instruction in chemistry in the college as well as the Medical Department, but would also have some connection with the Department of Philosophy and the Arts.[89]

The appointments of William Norton and Porter, together with the inauguration of a "School of Engineering" and regularization of the course of study in chemistry by Porter, marked a turning point for scientific study at Yale. Enrollments grew and by 1854 the chemical and engineering schools were combined under the title "Yale Scientific School." Though this step appears to have been a merger in name only, it did signify a desire to accord science and engineering a legitimate and more prominent place in the curriculum.[90]

The rapid development of the material resources of the country and the growing demand for scientific and technical instruction would soon convince the Corporation of the need for better organization, an expanded faculty, and a broader range of studies. The difficulty, of course, was money. A fund-raising effort was initiated to which a number of the alumni and friends of Yale contributed. But it was the donations of Joseph E. Sheffield, beginning in 1858, when he provided a building and a fund for professorships, that promised to endow the future for science and engineering at Yale.

Sheffield, a native of Connecticut and the father-in-law of Professor John Porter, had made his fortune first as a cotton merchant in the South and then in the development of canals and railroads in New England and the West, and knew at firsthand of the great need for adequately trained engineers. By 1861 his contributions to the Scientific School had amounted to $100,000, in gratitude for which the Yale Corporation announced that henceforth the school would be called the Sheffield Scientific School. When Sheffield died in 1882, his gifts over the years and his bequests amounted to some $1,100,000.[91]

In 1859 a degree of civil engineer was established as a higher degree for those already holding the bachelor of philosophy, the requirements for which were strengthened at the same time. Distinguished members joined the faculty, many basic subjects in science and engineering were added to the curriculum, and necessary laboratory equipment was purchased abroad. Soon Sheffield was ranked among the leaders of scientific instruction and research. Yet despite a growing national need and importance, there was a tendency in those early days at Yale—and at other institutions as well—to look with some condescension upon the students of the Scientific School. Partly this was due to lower admission standards, partly because the course of study was completed in three years rather than the normal four, and partly, no doubt, to vestiges of the old belief that courses centered on "useful knowledge" had no place in a true university. In any event, it is interesting to note that in those days Sheffield students were not allowed to sit with the regular academic students in chapel![92]

In 1863 the school—the only institution to apply—was designated by the Connecticut legislature to receive the income from the fund to be derived from the Land-Grant Act of 1862. In accepting the designation, Yale agreed to award free scholarships annually to Connecticut students, the total to equal one-half of the payment to be received from the state. Responding to the intent of the law, a course in "Industrial Mechanics or Mechanical Engineering" was organized, evening lectures for mechanics were arranged, and faculty appointments were made in fields related to agriculture. Yale publications often referred to Sheffield as the "Connecticut College of Agriculture and the Mechanic Arts." In the early 1870s Sheffield was receiving $8,100 a year from the state fund.[93]

In July 1863 the Yale Corporation had established a governing board for Sheffield to be composed of faculty members associated with the school and formally organized with a chairman and a secretary-treasurer, this board to be responsible for its financial management. But in 1871, when Joseph Sheffield was preparing to make further gifts of securities and a new building, he stipulated that a separate board of trustees be legally incorporated. The Articles of Incorporation, effective February 8, 1871, included the following statement: "The object and purpose of said corporation is to promote the study of physical, natural and mathematical sciences in the college or school of science known as the Sheffield Scientific School located at said city of New Haven."[94]

This board would consist of nine directors, among them the governor of Connecticut, the president of Yale College, the chairman of the Trustees of the Peabody Museum of Natural History in the college, and at least three professors of the Scientific School. Its creation would one day lead to strains between the school and the college. Of particular concern would be the growth in the school of a "General Course," for students not wishing to concentrate on one special field, raising serious questions about ways in which the classical colleges and universities might effectively respond to the growing demand for "useful" knowledge without compromising what many considered to be their essential mission.

The first half of the nineteenth century was a time of vigorous educational debate, as established institutions endeavored to find a balance between the classical and the practical and to make way for freedom of choice. Against this background, Sheffield commanded a distinguished reputation. It made major contributions to the advancement of technical education, and it developed more surely than the Lawrence Scientific School at Harvard. There would be many similarities between its curriculum and that of the School of Industrial Science of the Massachusetts Institute of Technology, at least one faculty member of which looked upon Sheffield in 1871 as a most worthy competitor: "Our only real rival thus far is the Sheffield, and with them we are on the most cordial terms; but I wish we had two or three more men of the weight and standing and mature ability as some of theirs."[95] Later it would be among those men of "weight and standing and mature ability" that MIT's third president would be found—Francis Amasa Walker, Sheffield's professor of political economy.

The Chandler School of Science and the Arts at Dartmouth College

As was true for both Harvard and Yale, Dartmouth College owed the development of a school of science and the arts to a benefactor who had come to appreciate the need for a higher level of technical education. His name was Abiel Chandler, and when he died in 1851 he bequeathed $50,000 to the college for the establishment and support of a scientific department or school.

A native of New Hampshire, Chandler had worked on a farm before attending Harvard College, from which he was graduated in 1806. He taught school in Salem and Newburyport over a period of eleven years before deciding to abandon teaching for a mercantile career. In his transition from teacher to merchant he soon discovered that, despite his education, he possessed little of the knowledge basic to his new profession. Through experience, however, he achieved considerable success and retired in 1845 from the Boston firm of Chandler, Howard & Company with the means and determination to help others.[96]

For the proposed school Chandler specified a separate board of visitors, whom he named, with power to appoint their successors, to ensure that the faculty and trustees of Dartmouth, charged with direct management responsibility, would faithfully carry out the strict provisions of his will. He was equally specific about the instruction to be offered:

> In the practical or useful arts of life composed chiefly in the branches of mechanics and civil engineering, the invention and manufacture of machinery, carpentry, masonry, architecture and drawing, the investigation of the properties and uses of the materials employed in the arts, the modern languages and English literature, together with bookkeeping and such other branches of knowledge as may best qualify young persons for the duties and employments of active life: but first of all and above all I would enjoin in connection with the above branches the careful inculcation of the principles of pure morality, piety and religion, without introducing topics of controversial theology, that the benefits of said department or school may be equally enjoyed by all religious denominations without distinction. No other or higher preparatory studies are to be required in order to enter said department or school than are pursued in the common schools of New England.[97]

These conditions were rather difficult for the trustees of Dartmouth to accept in their entirety, but so also would be the refusal of this generous donation. At their annual meeting in 1851 they voted to accept the bequest and to establish "The Chandler School of Science and the Arts," thus creating what has been termed "the most troublesome problem" confronting Nathan Lord, then president, during the latter part of his administration.

By the fall of 1852 a curriculum had been laid out and seventeen students were enrolled, their preparation amounting to little more than an ordinary grammar-school training. The degree of bachelor of science was to be awarded after the successful completion of a three-year course, and all teaching responsibilities were to be fulfilled by members of the existing Dartmouth faculty, without, in the first years, any addition to their number. In 1856 John S. Woodman, professor of mathematics in the college, was placed in charge of the school as professor of civil engineering, and a year later the program was increased to four years with a revised curriculum. Mathematics, natural science, modern languages, and graphics, along with some English, history, moral science, and political economy, were included in the first three years. In the fourth year, in addition to required continuing studies, the students were allowed to elect subjects in civil engineering, business, or English literature and philosophy. Although every effort was made to design a program in accord with the specifications of Chandler's will, in no way was it possible to cover fully the range of subjects which he initially proposed.[98]

The intimate connection between the new school and the college proper was a source of bitter resentment and controversy on the part of many of the faculty, hard feelings that persisted as long as the school endured. The primary cause of the conflict was the low level of admission requirements to be met by students at Chandler. It was naturally difficult for such students to attain within four years the level of intellectual maturity of their classmates at the college, and consequently the degrees they received represented a lower level of achievement. Members of the faculty, especially those with no teaching duties in the school, maintained that this would ultimately weaken the academic standing of Dartmouth itself and bring it into disrepute. Differences of opinion on how the school should be related to the college proved also to be a source of friction among the trustees as the faculty pressed for the separation of Chandler as an independent entity with its own faculty and funds. As was the case in the early days at Sheffield, the regular students of Dartmouth tended, moreover, to look down on those enrolled at Chandler as failing to meet the standards of a classical education.[99]

The organizational and structural problems of a science school incorporated within a traditional college naturally differed in many ways from those of a wholly independent school of technology. With attendance at the Chandler School between 1869 and 1876 averaging seventy-two per year, a few faculty members were added. But the school continued to be a source of controversy. In 1865 Dartmouth's trustees succeeded in changing its name to the Chandler Scientific Department despite strong opposition from the academic faculty on the grounds that its goals and standards did not merit such status.[100]

But there were still other developments in science and engineering studies at Dartmouth. In 1867, through generous gifts from Sylvanus Thayer, the Thayer School of Civil Engineering was founded. As Chandler had done before him, Thayer called for a self-perpetuating board of overseers, with four members, whom he would appoint. The fifth, and president of the board, would be the president of Dartmouth.[101] This arrangement and other provisions appear to have been carefully worked out, thus largely eliminating the risk of the controversies that had beset Chandler. The Thayer School soon won national recognition and became the Thayer School of Engineering, combining a graduate professional school and the undergraduate Engineering Sciences Department of Dartmouth College.[102]

The University of Michigan

Shortly after Michigan's admission to the Union in 1837, a legislative act established the University of Michigan as a state institution to be located in Ann Arbor, and it opened in 1841. Its corporate predecessor, the Catholespistemiad, or University of Michigania, in Detroit had been chartered by a territorial act in 1817, its name changed to the University of Michigan in 1821.[103] Although the original charter specified that seven of the thirteen professorships be in scientific fields, mathematics included, this predecessor institution has been characterized as "not, in practice, much more than a classical academy."[104]

The act of 1837 also called for substantial representation for science, and in 1846 the legislature transferred to the university the state's scientific collections to be added to the mineral and other collections already being assembled for its "cabinet" or museum. Though provision had been made for a professor of civil engineering and architecture if it were felt desirable, in these early years the curriculum adhered largely to the traditional classical pattern.[105] During this period the governance of the institution rested with the board of regents, chaired by the governor of the state, and an annually elected president of the faculty, and there would be no chief executive officer until the election in 1852 of Henry P. Tappan as the first president of the university, an appointment that would bring significant change.[106]

Tappan, a graduate of Nott's Union College and a clergyman and philosopher, immediately proposed the establishment of a scientific course, mentioning particularly "Civil Engineering, Astronomy . . . and the application of Chemistry and other Sciences to Agriculture and the industrial arts generally." Plans were made for a scientific course to include civil engineering in the third and fourth years, and the first lecture in civil engineering was given early in 1854. Two bachelor of science degrees were awarded in 1855, and the first in engineering in 1857. A four-year course leading to the degree of civil engineer was included in the catalogue for 1855–56. It was based on a common curriculum for both science and engineering in the first three years and specialization in the fourth. Completion in four years was possible for the "industrious student," but a "longer time" might be spent with "advantage and profit." Students would be admitted for partial courses if properly prepared but would not be eligible for the degree. The studies included "Mathematics, Graphics, Physics, Natural Science, Elements of Astronomy, Language, Philosophy, . . . Plane Geodetics, Railroad and Mining Surveying, Leveling, Nature and Strength of Materials, Theory of Construction, Architecture, Machines (particularly the steam engine and locomotive), and Motors (particularly steam and water)."[107] Two students received the civil engineer degree in 1860.

A Department of Engineering and a four-year engineering curriculum were established in 1858 but remained under the jurisdiction of the Department of Literature, Science, and the Arts. In 1871 a proposal to establish a full-fledged scientific school, "to be called SCHOOL OF TECHNOLOGY, or, INDUSTRIAL SCHOOL, or, SCHOOL OF ART AND TRADES, or some other suitable name," failed to find adequate financial support. In 1895 the Department of Engineering and its courses became a separate entity, with Charles E. Greene, a member of the first graduating class of the Massachusetts Institute of Technology and professor of civil engineering at Michigan since 1872, as dean of the college.[108]

In the years immediately preceding the Civil War, the idea of scientific and technical education at the college and university level received increasing attention, and several institutions took steps, some tentative, to move in this direction.[109] With the coming of peace, however, conditions rapidly changed. The development of industry and the West brought great pressure for improvements in technical training, and schools of engineering proliferated throughout the country—as divisions of established colleges and universities, as independent institutions, and as integral parts of the movement toward state colleges and universities to which the Land-Grant Act of 1862 gave such powerful support.

The schools just described, together with the Lawrence Scientific School at Harvard, were among the American antecedents of the school of the Massachusetts Institute of Technology, and the example of both French and German scientific schools would also play a role. In its initial concept, however, MIT looked primarily to European examples very different in organization and aims. How and why it joined the mainstream, with the School of Industrial Science becoming its central feature and an immediate success, may be one of the most interesting stories in the history of technical education in the United States.

The Rogers Brothers and the Boston Scene

Chapter 4

A Family Affair

Intellectual and professional traditions come down through history in various ways. One is the family unit: in music, Scarlatti (father and son), Bach (father and sons), Haydn (brothers), Mozart (father and son), Mendelssohn (brother and sister), and Strauss (father and sons) are among the best known; in literature, Brontë (sisters and brother), Grimm (brothers), and Dumas (father and son). A similar phenomenon occurs in science and technology. The Bernoulli clan of mathematicians, based in Switzerland, consisted of two brothers, Jakob (1654–1705) and Johann (1667–1748); their nephew, Nikolaus (1687–1759); Johann's sons, Nikolaus II (1695–1726), Daniel (1700–1782), and Johann II (1710–1790); and Johann II's sons, Johann III (1744–1807) and Jakob II (1759–1789). John Herschel (1792–1871) followed in the footsteps of his father, William (1738–1822), and William's sister Caroline (1750–1848), as an innovator in the field of astronomy. Charles Darwin's grandfather Erasmus (1731–1802) was a medical practitioner and botanist; his first cousin Francis Galton (1822–1911), a geneticist and statistician; two of his sons, George (1845–1912) and Francis (1848–1925), astronomer and botanist, respectively; and his grandson Charles (1887–1962), mathematician and physicist. Benjamin Silliman (1779–1864) and his son Benjamin, Jr. (1816–1885) were distinguished authorities in chemistry and geology attached to Yale University for much of their careers. Yet another father-son pairing—Louis Agassiz (1807–1873) and Alexander (1835–1910)—were naturalist-zoologists connected to Harvard University. The Baldwins of Massachusetts—Loammi, Sr. (1745–1807) and Loammi, Jr. (1780–1838)—made a significant mark in civil engineering.

William Barton Rogers

The list could go on and on, but our focus here will be on a family whose destiny was closely tied to the founding of the Massachusetts Institute of Technology. The Rogers family included Patrick Kerr Rogers (1776–1828), his wife Hannah (Blythe) Rogers (ca. 1775–1820), and sons James Blythe Rogers (1802–1852), William Barton Rogers (1804–1882), Henry Darwin Rogers (1808–1866), and Robert Empie Rogers (1813–1884). Patrick was a physician, chemist, and popular science lecturer; William and Henry made their marks in the field of geology and as university educators; James and Robert were physicians who went on to careers as professors of chemistry. Two of the brothers—William, primarily, but Henry as well—played an important role in the process that led to the founding of the Institute and helped shape its early character and mission.[1]

Patrick Rogers, an Irish nationalist who fled Ireland for the United States in 1798 to escape prosecution by the British authorities, studied medicine at the University of Pennsylvania, where his interests tended more toward science than clinical practice. His thesis for the M.D. degree (1802) was a study of the chemical and therapeutic properties of *Liriodendron tulipifera*, the tulip or yellow poplar tree, as determined by experimental observations.[2] When the chair of chemistry became vacant at the University of Pennsylvania, he applied without success, whereupon he turned to lecturing on science to popular audiences. He offered two series, one on chemistry and the other on natural philosophy (physics). In a pamphlet dated March 12, 1811, under the heading of "Lyceum," he laid out the premises for these courses and outlined the plan of the natural philosophy course. Of special note, in light of Patrick's progressive political views, was his openness to the participation of women. The venture, he said, would take "the form of a popular school of general Physics,

Henry Darwin Rogers

James Blythe Rogers

where both sexes, as long as it will receive an adequate patronage, shall enjoy an equality of opportunity."[3]

By this time, three of his four sons had been born: James, William, and Henry; Robert followed soon afterwards. All four would follow their father as scientists and teachers of science. William Barton Rogers was named in part after Benjamin Smith Barton, professor of materia medica, natural history, and botany, Patrick's mentor at the University of Pennsylvania; Henry Darwin Rogers for Erasmus Darwin, for whom Patrick had enormous admiration.

After a period as an apothecary and physician in Baltimore, where he also "home-schooled" his sons, Patrick assumed the chair of natural philosophy and chemistry at the College of William and Mary. James, William, Henry, and Robert all attended the college.[4] The earliest of William's surviving letters, one that he wrote to his brother James in December 1819, touches on classwork at the college, particularly in science subjects:

It were fortunate if the students were as remarkable for their talents as good nature, but it is not so; with the exception of about eight, there was perhaps never an assemblage of young men so totally destitute of genius and so miserably deficient in understanding. Yesterday (as Mr. Hawes tells me) Dr. Smith[5] inquired of a student what was the nature of a material substance, the answer was, "One which affects our senses and exerts reason!" Father asked the same person for a definition of a solid; after much hesitation, a good deal of muttering, and abundance of broken sentences, the gentleman answered with great philosophical gravity that it was "A – a – a body which was solid." The chemical class, however, advance as well as could be expected, and will no doubt bear a good examination.[6]

Robert Empie Rogers

The earliest evidence, however, of the brothers' deepening scientific and pedagogical interests is a letter that James, writing from Baltimore where he had gone to study medicine, sent to William two years later:

> I now sit down to write you a short letter, in which you may not calculate on anything new, except a new and in my opinion a rather singular opinion advanced by Dr. De Butts[7], which he delivered this evening, one which I think is wholly unsupported by any evidence. It is this, that no two bodies of heterogeneous character are presented to each other without thereby chemical union being produced; for instance, a drop of water applied to a plate of glass adheres to it by virtue of chemical attraction, or affinity; and that the different forces of this attraction are to be observed in all degrees, from the simple case I have mentioned to those in which the most powerful chemical attraction exerts its influence. In a word, what Father denominates "heterogeneous adhesion" is with him really a chemical union. I believe this opinion to be erroneous, inasmuch as there is in this case to be observed none of those changes which are said to be characteristic of chemical affinity. When you write me (which do soon) give me your opinion on this point. Dr. De Butts seems to have considerably improved as a lecturer since I last heard him, but yet he falls far short of Father. However, I think his lectures are sufficiently full for his class, for very few of the members of it that I know are capable of comprehending one half of what he says. I have often, while listening to the Doctor, wished the students could hear one of Father's lectures on the subject, for they as far surpass the Doctor's in point of correctness, science and elegance, as the meridian sun does the evening star in brilliancy.[8]

This was sharp criticism, coming from a student under twenty years old, but it reflected the kind of challenge to authority—both political and intellectual—that exemplified Patrick's own life and his approach to bringing up his sons.

Patrick's style of pedagogy—demanding yet invariably geared to the level of his audience—led him to publish an introductory physics text, *An Introduction to the Mathematical Principles of Natural Philosophy*, intended to fill gaps in the science preparation of students entering college.[9] This text, divided into four parts (Dynamics, Doctrine of the Free Motion of Masses, On the Laws of Impulse, and On the Laws of Pressure), was also in a sense young William's first appearance in print. Patrick observed in a letter to Thomas Jefferson that William, with his "very extraordinary passion for physico-mathematical sciences," had supplied proofs of the 14th, 35th, 68th, and 93rd propositions.[10] Most of the proofs were Patrick's, of course, sometimes with the guidance of writings by Isaac Newton, Thomas Young, Gaspard Monge, and other mathematicians and natural philosophers.

Jefferson apparently liked Patrick's book enough to invite him to Monticello and to enter into a brief discourse with him. Patrick, as usual, stood his ground on certain principles, even as he agreed in general with Jefferson's opinion about the relative strength of French scientific treatises over English ones:

> Your comparative view of the merits of the French and English writers on mathematical and physical science is that which I have long entertained. Two great works, however, in the English language, those of Young and Robinson,[11] may be regarded as exceptions to the general standard of the English writers on the various branches of mechanical philosophy. Yet, I confess, I am not a convert to the theory of light and heat which is so ably defended by the former,—the theory of undulations in a diffused universal medium. The latter, in his system of mechanical philosophy, which is delivered in the happiest style of an experienced teacher, avails himself of the best and latest investigations of his contemporaries of every country.
>
> The fluxional notation and idea must undoubtedly give place to the differential, in England and in this country, at no distant period. The clearness and facility of the latter, compared with the obscurity and difficulty of the former, in the hands of beginners, will soon fix the destiny of the two methods. The best Scotch mathematicians have already decided in favour of the differential method. . . . Although we have a pretty large library in this place, we have very few books of real use to the profession, unless those on metaphysics, or what has been pompously denominated the philosophy of the mind, are to be considered as such. We have indeed the works of Bézout and Laplace,[12] with several of the best treatises on chemistry, and the systems of natural and mechanical philosophy. . . . And of course we have access to most of the old writers on physics and mechanics, from Archimedes to Newton.[13]

In this same letter, Patrick again extolled William's scientific initiatives, which now included a complete translation of Bézout's *Éléments du calcul différentiel* (so that his youngest brother Robert would have access to a basic text on the theory of infinitesimals) and deep study of the "more abstruse" parts of the *Edinburgh Encyclopedia*, a multivolume work edited by the Scottish mathematician and natural philosopher, David Brewster, from 1807 to 1830.[14]

୧ଵ୧

In October 1825 William and his younger brother Henry, feeling the need to establish a degree of financial independence, returned to Baltimore. Patrick, writing to William from Williamsburg, indicates that both sons had found teaching positions, probably in the same elementary or grade school:

> I am anxious to know how you and Henry come on in your new engagement [teaching], and how the business consists with the health of both. If you are able to continue with those duties it will be a very important circumstance; you may, by a dignified and kind comportment to the boys, lay a sure foundation for an independent establishment for yourselves at some future day, should it suit in respect to your health.[15]

And in the autumn of 1826, with Patrick's encouragement, William and Henry together opened "an independent establishment" in Windsor, a small town about fourteen miles from Baltimore. The establishment was likely high-school level, with offerings that included Latin, Greek, and mathematics. The youngest Rogers brother, Robert, aged thirteen at the time, joined his older siblings in Windsor and attended their school.

The school did not take off as quickly as the brothers hoped, however, and William soon complained to his father about lack of progress:

> Our school has been nearly stationary since we saw you. We cannot expect to make much more than a support in our present situation. The profits of the school would be sufficient to satisfy one of us, as it would enable him to lay by something for the future; but, as by the present arrangement they must be divided between us, they will not enable us to improve our circumstances. However delightful the place and society, we therefore cannot regard the situation as a permanent one, at least for both of us.[16]

William added that he had declined to apply for a position that his father had recently brought to his attention, as home tutor to three sons of "Mr. W. Garnett, the husband of the lady who teaches a very celebrated school in Virginia." And again he bemoaned the bleak financial outlook, while simultaneously expressing enthusiasm about the work itself:

My present situation is truly delightful in every respect but one: it is not sufficiently lucrative. But for this I would not change my abode, with the same
employment, for any other in the world. . . . Teaching is much less profitable
in Maryland than in Virginia. There, a classical teacher may in a few years lay
up what will enable him to obtain a profession and begin the practice of it;
here, unless he is so fortunate as to become fashionable in the city, he can only
realize a support. You may, perhaps, hear of some situation in Virginia that
would be desirable. If you should, please inform us. . . . Do not from this letter infer that I am displeased with our present situation. I am highly pleased
with it, but I feel that I ought to look to the future.[17]

Patrick might well have advised patience, considering that the school had been open
just a few weeks.

William, however, continued to look farther afield. In January 1827 he started giving lectures at the Maryland Institute for the Promotion of Mechanic Arts, in
Baltimore. John Latrobe and other prominent citizens of Baltimore had established the
institute in 1825, inspired by the example of Philadelphia's Franklin Institute as a venue
for practical learning. Limited funds impeded the institute's early growth; a few professorships were established, but instruction was largely given by part-time lecturers, some
appointed with modest compensation, others simply as volunteers.[18] An excerpt from
William's inaugural lecture reads:

I need not in this place enlarge upon the usefulness of popular courses of scientific instruction . . . Of late years, the public mind, both in this country and
abroad, has been much interested in this subject. In many places institutions
calculated to render useful science attainable by the mass of society have been
established; and such is the growing impression of their value that their number continues yearly to increase. Our own city has not been backward in this
career of improvement. The Maryland Institute is, I believe, the second in
point of seniority in the United States, and has now been upwards of a year in
successful operation.[19]

This is one of the earliest surviving indications that his approach to science and science
teaching was evolving along the lines of practical applications. But the managers of the
institute were in no hurry to offer him a full-time post, even though the chair in natural philosophy opened up in the spring.

By this time William was a confident, experienced teacher who assumed a willing audience, and the Maryland Institute allowed him not merely to put this talent on display, but also to immerse himself in science. In January 1827 he wrote to his father in evident exhilaration over the demonstrations he had been giving in astronomy:

> My lectures continue to be well attended. On Monday night the room was crowded. I am at present engaged with the subject of astronomy, and have already delivered four lectures upon it, in which I have been assisted by an admirable tellurian which has been loaned to me. It would be difficult to give you an idea of the beauty of this instrument. It was constructed by an ingenious young mechanic in this place a few years ago, and has since been in the possession of a teacher of a female school. It has suffered much from the ill-usage it has received, but is still of great value in illustrating many important points in astronomy. It exhibits with great precision the relative motions of the earth, the moon, and Venus around the sun. . . . As a means of illustration, I think it is infinitely more useful than an orrery or planetarium of the same magnitude. Embracing but a few planetary bodies, it is simple, and the movements it exhibits are conspicuous at a distance. I wish you could see it in operation. I am sure you would desire to have one among your apparatus.[20]

William's use of the tellurian—an apparatus for illustrating, among other things, diurnal and seasonal changes caused by the earth's rotation—underscored his interest in the demonstrable, the practical, and the useful in science teaching. He had also made the acquaintance of two local men of science (one of whom was with the U.S. Corps of Engineers) and been "surprised by the crudeness of their scientific knowledge on some subjects." He added, "I have the vanity to think that I could sometimes set them right."[21]

The Windsor school, meanwhile, was still not living up to expectations. Henry wrote to his father in April 1827, echoing William's pessimism and the desire of both to move into a better situation:

> The school yields us at present about five hundred and fifty dollars, and we may calculate on an average of five hundred. This, it is true, is ample for every present expense, but the future is also to be thought of. Our duties are light and our leisure considerable; we think, therefore, that were we once entered upon the study of a profession we might prosecute it with considerable facility and but little expense. . . . We would be glad . . . to have some certain and

definite object in view, but it is difficult to fix upon the choice of a profession, both law and medicine are so greatly overdone.[22]

If law and medicine were out, that essentially left the ministry, agriculture, or education—and education, already focused on science in William's case, was something in which they had both found satisfaction.

Although lacking the necessary apparatus (the tellurian excepted) for practical demonstrations, William appears to have been highly successful in teaching natural philosophy at the Maryland Institute. As he wrote to his father just after Christmas, 1827:

> I am progressing with my lectures in the Institute, and I believe the class is well pleased with them. . . . As it is, though I do not possess a single philosophical instrument, my lectures are very well attended. . . . I make great use of the blackboard, and manage to communicate the more obvious principles of the science pretty clearly by means of drawings and diagrams. My last lecture treated of uniformly accelerated and retarded motion and projectiles. In the preceding lecture I exhibited the experiment of the guinea and feather by means of a small air-pump.[23]

Thus, William's ability to captivate an audience continued to emerge, alongside his love for science and science teaching. Within a year he received a permanent appointment as lecturer at the institute, with compensation amounting to two hundred dollars for two lectures a week over each three-month period. His hopes for a professorship failed to materialize right away, however, possibly because the institute's finances compelled caution in the handing out of such appointments.

Early in 1828 a technical high school—"an English and Mathematical School," as William described it to his father[24]—was projected as part of the Maryland Institute. William was asked to plan, organize, and direct this school, and he submitted the following proposal:

TO THE COMMITTEE OF THE INSTITUTE:
Gentlemen, —In obedience to your request, I submit the following hints towards a plan and regulations for the High School about to be established in the Maryland Institute. . . .

1. The aim of the school being to impart such knowledge and to induce such habits of mind as may be most beneficial to youth engaging in mechanical and mercantile employments, the study of mathematics will be an object

of primary attention, and will, it is expected, be pursued to a considerable extent. The earlier classes will be instructed in arithmetic, reading, writing, grammar and geography; the more advanced, in algebra, geometry, mensuration, surveying, navigation, perspective, etc., and perhaps in English composition. The latter grade of scholars, after having made a certain proficiency in their mathematical studies, will be taught the elementary principles of astronomy, mechanics, natural philosophy and chemistry, and will be permitted to attend the lectures in the Institute in aid of their scientific studies, as a reward for their diligence and improvement.

2. Classical studies are not within the scope of the school.

3. The number will be limited to fifty.

4. To obtain admission into the school, the pupil must be able to spell correctly, read with facility, write a fair hand, and perform arithmetical computations at least as far as the rule of three.

5. The price of instruction will be eight dollars per quarter, in which the expense of fuel, pens, slate-pencils and other stationery, and books, is not included.[25]

This proposal is of special interest, as it appears to be the first of a sequence of plans for technical schools that William had a hand in, culminating, more than three decades later, with the *Scope and Plan of the School of Industrial Science of the Massachusetts Institute of Technology*.

Meanwhile, he continued to sharpen the focus of his teaching along the lines of applied science and engineering. About a week after his proposal was submitted, he delivered a much-acclaimed public lecture on railroads, particularly the technical aspects of construction and machinery. The lecture was advertised in the local newspapers: "The editors of the American are requested to give notice that Professor Rogers will give a public lecture on Rail Roads, at the Maryland Institute, on TUESDAY EVENING, 22d inst. at half past 7 o'clock; and to assist him in illustrating his subject, the Rail Road Company have politely offered him the use of their models."[26] Henry reported to his father a couple of weeks later that William "has lately delivered to very crowded assemblies on the subject of Railroads, which have greatly roused the attention and gained the interest of the people here. . . . Indeed, such was the eagerness displayed by the populace to become better acquainted with the principles of an undertaking in which they are all interested, that the lecture-room could not contain more than half of those who endeavoured to gain admission."[27] The railroad industry, as it turned out, would become a key source of employment for graduates of technical schools, secondary and collegiate alike.

The proposal for a technical high school was accepted by the Maryland Institute trustees, and William, now with the rank of professor, took joint charge with Henry. The school at Windsor was abandoned, with Robert moving to Baltimore to become one of the first students at the new school. James, who had worked for a time as a physician and industrial chemist, now came as a lecturer to the Maryland Institute. Once again the brothers Rogers were together, each striving to support himself, each seeking an appealing and profitable career related to science and science education.

The school opened in May 1828 as reported in the local press:

> THE HIGH SCHOOL of the Maryland Institute will be opened on Monday the 12th of May, under the superintendence of WILLIAM and HENRY ROGERS. The aim of the School being to impart such knowledge, and to induce such habits of mind as may be most beneficial to youth engaging in mechanical and mercantile pursuits, the study of mathematics will be an object of primary attention. The earlier classes will be instructed in arithmetic, reading, writing, grammar and geography:—the more advanced in algebra, geometry, mensuration, surveying, perspective, &c. and in history and English composition. The latter grade of pupils, after having made a certain proficiency in their mathematical studies, will be taught the elementary principles of astronomy, mechanics, natural philosophy and chemistry, and, in aid of their scientific studies and as a reward for their diligence and improvement, will be permitted to attend the lectures in the Institute. Classical studies are not within the scope of the School.[28]

Ten students enrolled the first day, and seven more by the end of the first week. "I have no doubt," William wrote to his father, "that in less than six months our school will be in a very flourishing condition."[29]

In August 1828 Patrick Kerr Rogers died of malarial fever, at the age of 52. William lost little time in seeking to succeed him as professor at the College of William and Mary. Through the efforts of his brothers, a number of letters were addressed to the president and trustees of the college, testifying to William's fine character and exceptional ability. Two of those who submitted testimonials, both Army engineers in Baltimore, were privately less than enthusiastic about the wisdom of this move: "It is [their] opinion," Henry wrote to William, "that your ultimate advancement would be more promoted by your remaining here. They state that there is now opening in this country an extensive field for highly respectable and lucrative exertion in the growing spirit for works of internal improvement demanding the superintendence of scientific men."[30] But while the early nineteenth century was indeed the dawn of an age when men of science would find themselves in increasing demand, the demand could not be fully met until higher education responded more systematically. The trend had already begun, with the opening of Rensselaer Polytechnic Institute just four years earlier, but much remained to be done.

William was appointed professor of natural philosophy and chemistry at William and Mary on October 13, 1828, and soon thereafter moved to Williamsburg. Henry and James remained at the Maryland Institute as lecturers, respectively, in natural philosophy and chemistry. *Life and Letters* suggests, somewhat cryptically, that "a chain of natural causes" led to William's succession to Patrick's post.[31] What this chain was is unclear; certainly a son would not "naturally" succeed to his father's professorship, and although William was well known as a teacher and lecturer in Baltimore, his experience had been in a mechanics institute and its associated high school, not in a college. It is possible that since Patrick died just over a month before the start of classes, the trustees were hard pressed to come up with another prospect in time.

Following the customary introductory address, William continued his teaching with renewed zeal. In his second year the number of students in natural philosophy was the highest in ten years and exceeded the enrollment of all other classes. He captivated his students not only with his eloquence, but also, as at Maryland, with his skill in practical demonstrations. As he wrote to Henry:

> I have just concluded my lectures on caloric, to my own satisfaction, and, I am well assured, in a manner agreeable to the class. No little difficulties arising from want of instruments, or from imperfection in those we possess, or any other trivial circumstances connected with my duties, give me the slightest uneasiness or perplexity. I employ every accessible means of illustrating my subject in an intelligible manner, and, when instruments fail me, I have recourse to explanations. The want of apparatus is certainly a serious difficulty in the way of a lecturer. But I believe that one course delivered under these circumstances is of more real value as an exercise to the professor than half a dozen assisted by the usual auxiliaries.[32]

An extract from the college catalogue of 1829–30 conveys a sense of what courses in chemistry and natural philosophy looked like at the time. The junior chemical course comprised:

Inorganic and Organic Chemistry, the application of Chemistry to the Arts of
Bleaching, Dyeing, Tanning, Metallurgy, Brewing, Distillation, the manufacture
of Glass and Porcelain, etc., together with the Elements of Botany and
Mineralogy. The senior natural philosophy course embraces Dynamics,
Mechanics, Hydrodynamics, Pneumatics, Acoustics, Optics, Magnetism,
Electricity, Meteorology, Physical Geography, etc., together with the practical
subjects of the strength of Materials, the construction of Watch and Clock work,
of Roofs, Arches, Bridges, Roads, the Steam Engine, and elementary principles
of Architecture. . . . The studies in all the Scientific Departments are conducted
by means of Lectures and Recitations, from appropriate text books.[33]

William's pedagogical interests and abilities, however, extended beyond chemistry
and natural philosophy into other areas of science. When the professorship of mathematics became vacant in 1830, he was asked to assume those duties until a replacement
could be found. Despite the heavy burden, he relished teaching in this new field and
appears to have both stimulated interest and raised standards among the students. In a
letter to his father's brother, James Rogers, he wrote:

Our classes are now fully under way, and though I have double duty to perform (lecturing 12 times a week), I find that my labours fatigue me much less
than I had anticipated. In order to place the mathematical department on a
more elevated and scientific footing than it has hitherto occupied, I have
organized evening conversaziones of my classes who meet me twice a week
for the purpose of consulting me on the difficult points which they meet with
in their progress, and of obtaining those familiar and colloquial explanations
which are frequently necessary to a perfect understanding of their studies.
These meetings are likely to prove highly useful. They have already led a
majority of my class to take an interest in their mathematical studies which has
never before been evinced in our institution. So that you perceive I am doing
even superrogatory duty![34]

So immersed was he that he sometimes literally added himself and his students to
the mix of experimental demonstration, observation, and analysis:

I exhibited nitrous oxide to several of my students, and in some instances with
the most powerful effects. I have myself inhaled it twice in private, and found
its operation upon my system to be somewhat peculiar. It imparts to me a

sense of omnipresence. I lose all feeling of relation to the earth or sublunary things, and seem winged away through boundless space, the only sentient being in existence. My emotions are pleasurable, but their characteristics are vastness, grandeur, sublimity and solitude. The influence of the aerial draught continues for a long time, and as it subsides I become gradually sensible of my presence upon the ground, and look around me with the haughty disdain and towering importance of the Great Mogul.[35]

William clearly took delight in teaching, and conveyed a spirit of excitement that would have been advantageous to a man of science at the time. The nineteenth century was the era of the popular lecture. The public was eager to learn of recent advances in science and technology, and the popular lecture and its close relation, the lyceum movement, were the means by which much new knowledge was transmitted. This mode appealed to the Rogers brothers, partly because of the opportunity it offered for public exposure and partly as an outlet for their own enthusiasm for discovery in a burgeoning field. In Baltimore, William's public discourse on the new, exciting topic of railroads had been well received. Given the restrictions placed on outside activities among the faculty, it is unlikely that he would have been able to do much along these lines at William and Mary, but he apparently elicited a similar response from his students.

Henry Rogers, meanwhile, had assumed the chair of chemistry and natural philosophy at Dickinson College, Carlisle, Pennsylvania. While he only remained at Dickinson a year and a half (autumn 1829 to spring 1831), he continued to broaden his scientific horizons by editing a popular science magazine, *The Messenger of Useful Knowledge.* He and William often shared ideas about science education, with William particularly forceful in his advocacy of the lecture-demonstration method over the textbook-recitation method. The latter he saw as a crutch, with students

habitually leaning upon the thoughts, and repeating the words of others, accustomed to be satisfied with whatever stand *in verbis magistri*, their powers of thought are but imperfectly developed, and whatever of invention they may have had is enfeebled and paralyzed by disuse. Inured to influences such as these, and scarcely permitted to walk alone, how little is the mind prepared for that vigorous and independent exercise of its powers demanded in the pursuits of life, and how utterly unfit for the hardy achievements of original and inventive genius!

From their youngest days the Rogers brothers had been trained by their father to work with their hands and to make apparatus or search it out elsewhere for use in their scientific investigations. This method of creative thinking about solutions to practical problems was the *modus operandi* that William and Henry hoped to instill in their students.

Shortly after leaving Dickinson in the spring of 1831, Henry with his brother Robert joined a surveying party laying out plans for railroad track between Boston and Providence—the first indication, beyond William's popular lectures at the Maryland Institute, of the Rogers brothers' engineering interests. But by this time Henry had also become fascinated with the socialist theories of Robert Owen, and in May 1832 he sailed for England with Owen's son (Robert Dale Owen) to give scientific lectures to working-class men. While in England he was introduced into scientific circles—he was especially fascinated by the geologists—and on his return to the United States in 1833, stimulated William's interest in geology. He also started a series of lectures at the Franklin Institute, the first of which would deal with "Physical Geology, or the present existing causes modifying the earth's structure."[36]

It was an auspicious time because states were just beginning to launch large-scale geological surveys. As William's own interest in geology grew, his summers became occupied with field work and the investigation of mineral springs. By 1834 it was apparent to him that a systematic geological survey of Virginia was greatly to be desired and that every effort should be made to persuade the legislature to initiate and support one. William and Henry hoped, in fact, to work together on the survey if it materialized. As Henry wrote to their Uncle James in July 1834:

> I think from present appearances that a brief course on Geology which I think of giving some time late next winter in Richmond will succeed, all of whom we have mentioned it to are much in glee with it. Bye & Bye we may be able to awake sufficient zeal in the subject in Virginia to [?] at least a partial survey of the State. Some gentlemen of high standing seemed to think so. Everything will depend on the vigor with which we present the subject to public notice by our voluntary exertions, in the mean time. And William is certainly on the right road to awaken a very general attention to its importance.[37]

A lengthy debate ensued, during which William appeared before the House of Delegates in Richmond to lay out the whys and wherefores. In characteristic fashion, he emphasized the practical utility of the subject—partly, no doubt, because of the political appeal such an argument would have, but also because of his own deep appreciation for science as a useful discipline:

All are willing to admit the great extent and value and diversity of our mineral wealth, and at the same time to confess that its distribution through our territory, its precise boundaries in any one locality, its exact nature as ascertained by science, and its susceptibility of economical and profitable application to the purposes of commerce, manufactures, and the arts of life, are matters of which scarcely anything as yet has been accurately determined. ... [Y]our committee have felt it incumbent to enquire more particularly into the specific bearing which enquiries of this nature would have upon all the great divisions of our territory ... which confirm them in the belief that such a survey as the one in question, cannot fail to prove eminently advantageous to our state.[38]

The arguments in favor were eventually successful, and on March 6, 1835, an act was passed establishing the Geological Survey of the State of Virginia. William was appointed state geologist in August 1835, and meanwhile was publishing on geological topics in *Silliman's Journal* and *Farmer's Register*. By then Henry had already begun work on a geological survey of New Jersey, and was appointed state geologist in 1836. The Rogers brothers and their assistants went on to map New Jersey, Pennsylvania, and Virginia, and although public support for these labor-intensive efforts waned by the late 1830s, both William and Henry sustained their geological research interests in the decades to come.[39]

The geological projects coincided with a new phase of scientific activity in the lives of both William and Henry. William became professor of natural philosophy at the University of Virginia in August 1835,[40] and also that year was elected to membership in both the Virginia Historical and Philosophical Society and the American Philosophical Society. Henry became professor of geology and mineralogy at the University of Pennsylvania in 1835.

Several factors likely stimulated these moves. One was William's health. His somewhat fragile constitution compelled him to consider leaving the swampy, malarial climate of Williamsburg. Another factor—a central theme in the correspondence between William and Henry during this period—was the possibility that one day they might work together on a venture requiring a broader range of knowledge and experience than was available in backwaters such as Williamsburg and Carlisle. Probably the watershed, however, was the productive time that Henry had had in England, meeting prominent British scientists and developing a focal interest in geology; thereafter, William grew more restless and chafed at his own isolation from the latest developments in the world of science. The University of Virginia—one of Thomas Jefferson's crowning achievements, an institution free of sectarian control and supported by the state, where science and other subjects useful in the modern world stood on an equal footing with the classics—promised a high level of exposure to progressive trends in science and science education; the University of Pennsylvania had already proved itself a favorable environment for science, as the boys' father, Patrick Rogers, discovered during his student days there.

Also during this period, around 1837, William and Henry presented "a memorial" to the Pennsylvania state legislature for the establishment of a school of arts—a polytechnic school, in other words—at the Franklin Institute. This was the second in the series of proposals—the first had been submitted to the board of the Maryland Institute in 1828—that would eventually coalesce and emerge as a plan for the Massachusetts Institute of Technology.

Focused on the practical trades and professions, the brothers' proposal for the Franklin Institute outlined the scientific principles and techniques essential for those seeking to become (or to further their proficiency as) mining engineers, mineralogists, geologists, carpenters, architects, and mechanics. It discussed the differences between this kind of education and the kind—"preparing young men for the learned professions"—practiced at most colleges and universities. In contrast to the latter, it laid out "the importance of adopting a system of education which while it embraced a full & concrete developement [*sic*] of the principles of physical sciences should carry those principles out in their applications to the Arts, by detailed practical lessons & especially by actual discipline in the workshop." The proposal concluded:

> Such with many other branches of instruction of a like character are proposed to be embraced in the plan of practical education now submitted. And who can doubt that the mechanical, manufacturing & agricultural classes of the community would derive the highest advantages from the establishment of an institution directed by these views. With a mind stored with a knowledge of the principles as well as the details of his own and other associated pursuits— disciplined to careful inquiry, minute accuracy of calculation & just modes of reasoning upon his operations—the young Mechanic, Artisan or Manufacturer—would enter upon his career—with the sure prospect of a high degree of usefulness to himself & Society—and in the certainty of having the respect of his fellow citizens. . . .

Thus trained in the details of the Science as well as the practice of the Useful Arts—the Mechanic would be placed on a level in point of professional education with the Lawyer & the physician. Proudly conscious that the companion of knowledge may be labour—he would be but little likely to feel humiliated by a comparison of his accurate & substantial attainments—with the more superficial because necessarily more general acquirements of the pupils of any of our higher Institutions of Learning. Thus thoroughly prepared for practical usefulness as well as dignified respectability in his profession, he would command that station in Society to which the high value of his exertions give him just claim.[41]

The Franklin Institute proposal did not get very far, however, and William went on to spend eighteen years as professor of natural philosophy at the University of Virginia, an experience that profoundly influenced his ideas on education. The university, opened in 1825, reflected Jefferson's Enlightenment principles—faith in progress, devotion to science, and commitment to the diffusion of useful, practical knowledge. In both structure and subject orientation, it marked a radical departure from academic traditions of the time. Jefferson was of a strongly utilitarian turn of mind. His vision for the university included an emphasis on science, not only science per se but science focused on "those branches . . . that are useful to us"—mechanics, hydraulics, acoustics, optics, chemistry, mineralogy, botany, and zoology, among others (in essence, all subjects "useful to modern times"). One of his further innovations was the offering of instruction in modern languages, as well as modern history and geography. Yet for all his devotion to the practical and the relevant, he did not regard education as a mere training ground for a particular profession or calling; it must also, he believed, build intellectual and moral character, partly by achieving an appropriate balance between science, engineering, and the humanities. Freedom of inquiry, however, the right of a student to select fields of study most in harmony with his own interests and that would best prepare him for a future vocation, was one of Jefferson's core principles.

When he assumed his appointment at the University of Virginia, William had already been crafting a philosophy of education along these same lines—a philosophy that evolved during the course of the next two decades, that eventually made its way with him to Boston, and that played a key role in the early development of MIT's School of Industrial Science. As professor of natural philosophy at Virginia, he offered instruction in general physics and celestial mechanics, and later added a course in geology and mineralogy. Physics was open to students in their junior and senior years, and, according to contemporary catalogues, encompassed the study of statics, dynamics, mechanics (solids, liquids, and airs), strength of materials, acoustics, heat (including meteorology and the steam engine), electricity and galvanism, magnetism, electro-magnetism, and optics. To classes in descriptive astronomy William lectured on the nature of celestial phenomena, the theory of celestial motions, and methods of observing and computing planetary motion and position. A more advanced course that he offered on physical astronomy dealt with gravitation, tides, and other natural forces.

William offered geology for the first time in 1841–42, in a form and with content clearly influenced by his work on the state survey. The practical and descriptive aspects of geology were emphasized, with special attention to the structure and mineral products of the United States. William outlined the mineral zones and the order of stratification, displayed specimens to illustrate the nature of materials under study, and analyzed the relationship of rock and other geological formations to the nation's mineral resources. Methods of exploration were discussed, as well as ways to interpret the content of ores, rocks, and soils. In mineralogy, matters with economic value received special attention.

William felt quite at home with the University of Virginia's educational style, innovative as it was and representing such a marked departure from the practice of most classical institutions. Particularly appealing to him was instruction by lectures and demonstrations, followed by oral examinations and written exercises. This stood in contrast to the usual didactic methods, confined to recitations based on textbook assignments. William was convinced, like Jefferson before him, that teaching by lecture and demonstration would bring the subject matter to life, motivate students to independent thought, and discourage mere rote memorization.

From the testimony of former students and friends, it is clear that William was a gifted speaker and teacher. His lucid explanations clarified difficult concepts, even for the novice. Francis Smith, William's successor in the chair of natural philosophy at Virginia, praised his ability in this regard: "Who can forget that stream of English undefiled, so smooth, so deep, and yet so clear, that passed from point to point with gentle touch, that commonly flowed along with the quiet of conscious power, yet sometimes became tumultuous with feeling, and then came the music of the cataract and the glory of the rainbow!"[42] William's appeal to listeners was evidently enormous, and students are said to have crowded into his classes for an unparalleled experience in learning. He was to make excellent use of this oratorical power—both inside and outside the classroom—in his later career.

William was chosen by his colleagues as chairman of the faculty in the fall of 1844, and in this position he exhibited the administrative acumen later put to fine use in Boston. He accepted the post at a difficult time: students were often in open rebellion, a professor was murdered. These and similar events stirred a widening degree of public distrust and animosity toward the university. The Virginia House of Delegates instructed its Committee on Schools and Colleges to investigate the situation, with a view toward possibly rescinding financial support for the university. The task of defending the institution fell to William, who prepared a statement outlining the objectives and methods of instruction, the university's success and immense value to the state, and its vital need for public support. This statement, appended to the committee's final report, illustrated the breadth and depth of William's understanding of higher education, and it was a vital element in the legislature's decision to continue financial support for the university.

By this time both William and Henry were becoming more involved in science from the organizational standpoint, particularly the founding and early development of professional and learned societies. Henry was a charter member and helped to organize the first meeting (April 1840) of the Association of American Geologists and Naturalists,[43] which a decade later became the American Association for the Advancement of Science; in August 1840, William was elected to the newly established National Institution for the Promotion of Science. The brothers read a paper written jointly— "Observations on the Geology of Western Peninsula of Upper Canada and the Western Part of Ohio"—at the December 1841 meeting of the American Philosophical Society in Philadelphia. They presented another coauthored piece—this one on the physical structure of the Appalachian mountain chain—at the Boston meeting of the Geologists and Naturalists in April 1842. One observer later recalled this as "the most lucid and elegant effort of oral statement" that he had ever heard, adding that the Rogers brothers, "in their peculiar field of exploration . . . have made the most original and brilliant generalizations recorded in the annals of American geology."[44] The paper made such an impact, in fact, that the brothers were named "honorary members" of the Boston Society of Natural History in June 1842. In 1843 William served on the Geologists and Naturalists' Committee on Drift; in April of that year Henry chaired the Geologists and Naturalists' Fourth Annual Meeting (Albany, New York) and a month later delivered two papers at the centennial meeting of the American Philosophical Society. The brothers' reputation was spreading internationally, too: in June 1844 they were elected "foreign members" of the Geological Society of London, and in August William learned of his election to the Royal Society of Northern Antiquaries, headquartered in Copenhagen.[45]

William and Henry had spent much time on geological excursions in New England, among other places, in 1840–41, and William in particular was becoming increasingly attached to the place; he yearned for its "highly cultivated nature and society," as contrasted with Virginia's sectarian narrowness and conservatism.[46] Henry, however, was the first of the brothers to establish a close connection to the area. John Pickering, who traveled with him to Albany for the Geologists and Naturalists' convention in April 1843, encouraged him to move to Boston as a free-lance lecturer on geology.[47] In December, at the suggestion of the president of the Boston Society of Natural History, George B. Emerson, Henry gave a course on American geology at the Masonic Temple in Boston. The first lecture in the series, delivered December 5, was advertised in the newspapers as covering "Means of Geological Investigation; Different Classes of Rocks; Series of Stratified Formations; Scale of Geological Time; Central Heat; Fluidity of the Interior of the Globe; Thinness of the Earth's Crust."[48]

The course went so well that in May 1844 John Amory Lowell invited Henry to give a series of lectures at the Lowell Institute, an experiment in public education established a few years earlier by the terms of the will of John Lowell, Jr., who died in 1836; John Amory Lowell, the benefactor's cousin, served as the institute's first "trustee" (administrator). Henry accepted the invitation and set up temporary residence in Boston, where he prepared and delivered twelve lectures (twice!) in 1844–45; spoke before the Lyceum in Portsmouth, New Hampshire, with a thousand in attendance (January 1845); gave talks to various private groups; and, in 1845–46, delivered yet another series of lectures at the Lowell Institute. He settled into the Boston scene so comfortably, in fact, that he soon resigned his post at the University of Pennsylvania, and in 1846 was considered for the Rumford Professorship at Harvard. He would lecture again at the Lowell Institute in 1848–49, this time a series on the "Application of Science to the Useful Arts." Because his lectures were so popular, each set of twelve was given twice in the same year. In 1853–54 Henry was among ten fellows of the American Academy of Arts and Sciences presenting individual lectures for the Lowell Institute—his subject, "The Arctic Regions."

William visited Henry in Boston from time to time, and in summer 1845 joined him on a tour through the White Mountains of New Hampshire. On this trip he met the family of James Savage; his relationship with them grew over the next four years, and in June 1849 he married James's daughter Emma in Boston.

Boston had already become a more than desirable (even ideal) place in his mind. When Henry wrote him in March 1846 outlining the possibility of a polytechnic institute connected to the Lowell Institute, his interest was piqued even further. Henry's letter says, in part:

A family portrait—William Barton Rogers with the Savage family; standing, Rogers and his wife Emma Savage Rogers; seated, his father-in-law James Savage and brother-in-law James Savage, Jr.

Mr. Lowell, with whom I have been talking, after mentioning the feature in the Lowell will which enjoins the creation of classes in the [Lowell] Institute to receive exact instruction in useful knowledge, requested me to give him, in writing, the views I had just been unfolding of the value of a School of Arts as a branch to the Lowell Institute. . . . He is a very cautious man, desires never to make a mis-move, fears to expand his Institute too fast, and has had doubts of the practicability of attaching this sort of practical College to the Institute, lest it might be too large an affair to build; but he sees its value and now is a fine occasion to inspire him to the zeal which he is quite capable of feeling in its behalf. His plan would be to teach the operative classes of society,— builders, engineers, practical chemists, manufacturers, etc.; to admit in the first year only in limited numbers, and to teach them regularly; to have, perhaps, two permanent and salaried professors at the head of it, and to make up the rest of the instruction by assistants and by teachers, who would give courses of instruction occasionally on special branches. How much I want you near me at this time to aid me in digesting and submitting my views on this important scheme to Mr. Lowell! If you and myself could be at the head of this Polytechnic School of the Useful Arts, it would be pleasanter for us than any college professorship.[49]

He concluded by asking William to send him a copy of the proposal that they had prepared and presented to the Franklin Institute in 1837.

William's response was enthusiastic:

Were this or any other promotion of your views to lead hereafter to a closer union of our labours by placing me also in the congenial air of Boston, I would indeed rejoice. Under circumstances so auspicious for effort in teaching and research we could, I am sure, both of us be more productive and far happier in our labours than can be now. Ever since I have known something of the knowledge-seeking spirit, and the intellectual capabilities of the community in and around Boston, I have felt persuaded that of all places in the world it was the one most certain to derive the highest benefits from a Polytechnic Institution. The occupations and interests of the great mass of the people are immediately connected with the applications of physical science, and their quick intelligence has already impressed them with just ideas of the value of scientific teaching in their daily pursuits.[50]

He was unable to find a copy of the brothers' memorial on behalf of the Franklin Institute, which was unfortunate, he said, because "it contained a clear and forcible exposition of the subject."[51] But he produced something even better—a detailed, updated proposal for a polytechnic school that he hoped Henry could use in his discussions with Lowell and others.

This was the third in the series of proposals that anticipated the establishment of the Massachusetts Institute of Technology, still more than a decade away. William's outline for the "school of practical science," as he called it, envisaged two departments: one to lay "a broad and solid foundation" in scientific principles, the other to provide "instruction in chemical manipulation and the analysis of chemical products, ores, metals and other materials used in the arts, as well as of soils and manures." The intention was not merely to accommodate students pursuing formal coursework in the practical branches, but also, in the style of the Royal Institution of London and similar European models, to be "acceptable and useful to the public at large" through course offerings that would "draw all the lovers of knowledge of both sexes to the halls of the Institute."[52]

William identified fields and professions toward which the educational program of the school would be primarily directed—engineering, architecture, machinery, mining, and manufacturing—and he cited examples of ways in which a solid underpinning in scientific principles was essential to the development of practical knowledge and skills. One example, the application of chemical standards to the dye and print works of Lowell, Massachusetts, may have been selected to demonstrate his familiarity with local industry. William closed with a statement about science as a broadening, deepening, and, above all, *useful* influence on technical education:

> There is no branch of practical industry, whether in the arts of construction, manufactures or agriculture, which is not capable of being better practised, and even of being improved in its processes, through the knowledge of its connections with physical truths and laws, and therefore we would add that there is no class of operatives to whom the teaching of science may not become of direct and substantial utility and material usefulness. It would, I think, be especially adapted to fulfil another, and in some respects a higher purpose by leading the thoughts of the practical student into those wide and elevated regions of reflection to which the study of Nature's laws never fails to conduct the mind. Thus linking the daily details of his profession with the grander physi-

cal agencies around him, and with much of what is agreeable and ennobling in the contemplation of external things, it would insensibly elevate and refine his character and contribute to the cheerfulness as it aided the proficiency of his labours. In this respect it is, I think, demonstrated that physical studies are better capable of being useful to the operative classes than the study of literature or morals, because their truths are more readily and eagerly seized upon by such minds and form the strong staple of practical usefulness thus firmly infixed. It is easy to extend the golden chain of relations until these may embrace every realm of nature and of thought.[53]

The proposal exuded William's characteristic blend of idealism and realism, which kept surfacing as plans for the "polytechnic" evolved.

He kept pushing the subject. In October 1847 he urged Henry "to sound some of the leading practical men in Boston on the subject of our scheme." "I look forward," he said, "with unmixed happiness to the time now approaching when I shall be able to join you in preparing for our common effort and our common engagement in the ample and grand theatre which Boston offers."[54] And a few months later: "I confidently believe we can soon get up a Franklin Institute, or School of Arts, which will be a source of great pleasure as well as profit. Could we not count certainly on large classes from among the mechanics and merchants to patronize lectures such as we could give on applied science, and science itself in its more elevated bearings? I am sure of it."[55]

The fact is, he was feeling more and more isolated in Virginia and wanted to move north. In December 1846 he had declined a lucrative professorship in mineralogy, geology, and agricultural chemistry at the University of Alabama. He resigned his post at the University of Virginia in 1848, hoping to establish himself elsewhere, but withdrew his resignation on the advice of friends. Nevertheless, his time away from Virginia was increasingly spent in Boston, Pennsylvania, New York, and Europe (England, Germany, and Switzerland in the summer of 1849). Much of this travel was professional: he played an important role in 1847, for example, in events leading to the establishment of the American Association for the Advancement of Science (as it emerged out of the Association of American Geologists and Naturalists) and he attended AAAS meetings in Philadelphia (1848), possibly New Haven (1850), and Albany (1851). Some of the time, particularly in the summer months, was spent at his wife Emma's family home in Lunenburg, Massachusetts. But while his marriage to Emma Savage in 1849 had cemented his link to Boston, he did not move there permanently until the summer of 1853.

As William's ties to Boston strengthened, his brother's began to weaken. By 1850 Henry was complaining that "[f]or a man of any brains whatever, Boston has no peace or quiet, all is restless excitement and unproductive change of thought and of pursuit."[56] Even though he was busy on the lecture circuit and in the organizational side of the major professional associations, his efforts to establish himself in a secure academic post, such as the Rumford Professorship at Harvard, had turned up nothing. He envied his brothers' situations in a "calmer studious atmosphere": James as professor of chemistry at the University of Pennsylvania, and the other two—William and Robert—as professors at the University of Virginia. Robert had held the chair in chemistry and materia medica at Virginia since 1842; James had become professor of chemistry at the University of Pennsylvania in 1847 after more than a decade in the chemistry chair at a medical school in Cincinnati.

The eldest and youngest brothers were as close a pairing, in the sense of shared intellectual and professional interests, as the middle two. James and Robert collaborated on a new edition of a popular college-level textbook—*Elements of Chemistry*[57]—and when James died in 1852, Robert succeeded him as professor of chemistry at the University of Pennsylvania. The textbook appeared at just about the time William and Henry began hatching plans for their Boston "polytechnic school." As the polytechnic idea gradually evolved into the Massachusetts Institute of Technology, however, it was without Henry in the kind of partnership the brothers had envisioned. Henry spent more and more time overseas—particularly in Scotland and England—beginning in 1855, and in 1857 he became Regius Professor of Natural History and Geology at the University of Glasgow. While he continued to correspond with William on scientific and educational matters, the remainder of his career unfolded across the Atlantic. It was left to William, then, to pursue their dream of a Boston polytechnic.

Chapter 5

Harvard

The evolution of science and engineering studies at Harvard in the mid-nineteenth century was partly shaped by the growing interest in science itself and partly in response to the rising public demand for greater attention to "useful learning" at the collegiate level, a story of critical importance to the history of MIT. In 1847 Harvard would become one more in a succession of institutions that were adding such instruction to existing curricula or that were establishing separate schools solely for formal scientific and technical education, providing further evidence of a movement already under way when the Institute of Technology was founded in Boston in 1861. Harvard, however, calls for more extensive treatment than other predecessor institutions not only because of its location and the view it offers of the local scientific community, but also because of its relations with the Institute over the years, particularly in its attempts to annex the school of the Institute in 1863 even before it had opened, and because of later efforts to merge the two institutions in 1870, 1897, and 1904. An agreement reached in 1914 called for a joint venture involving the courses in engineering, with the Institute providing the instruction and Harvard the financial support, using a large bequest intended for instruction in applied science. This arrangement was terminated in 1917 when the courts ruled against Harvard's diversion of the funds in this way.

Bound up with the progress of Harvard as it attempted to accommodate new educational demands, and with the later struggle of a rival Institute of Technology to fulfill its promise, were the lives of several prominent individuals of the day, members of a scientific and technological community itself reaching for professional stature. The force of academic politics and the interplay of strong personalities, able and ambitious, offer a rich combination of human relationships and institutional aims played out against a background of national advancement, industrial growth, and educational reform.

Had certain alternative choices been made at Harvard as early as the 1840s and had state legislative decisions in the 1860s with respect to an important educational measure—the Congressional Land-Grant Act of 1862, also known as the Morrill Act—been made in Harvard's favor, it is altogether likely that the Massachusetts Institute of Technology might not exist today. Over the years some have speculated that the course of scientific and engineering education in Boston might have taken a very different turn if the geologist Henry Darwin Rogers, first, and later his brother William Barton Rogers had not failed to secure Harvard faculty appointments.[1]

From the time the Institute was chartered in 1861, however, the specter of Harvard would haunt every president in the nineteenth century and reach into the early twentieth as well. But the continuing rivalries and recurring confrontations of that period aside, the circumstances of the founding of Harvard's Lawrence Scientific School and its subsequent development are important as Boston's first serious response to the need for higher technical education.

Harvard College, the first such institution in the English colonies, was founded in 1636 and established in the tradition of the English universities. Its early curriculum, with textbooks and instruction largely in Latin, was "well adapted for a general education in the seventeenth and early eighteenth centuries" and included logic and rhetoric, Greek and Hebrew, ethics and metaphysics, with some mathematics and physics, or natural science. There was also astronomy, oriented toward the mathematical and the practical, and the beginnings of a collection of "philosophical apparatus," a collection that by the late eighteenth century had grown to be the best among colleges in the New World and equal to many in Europe.[2]

In 1728 Isaac Greenwood, a 1721 Harvard graduate, was appointed to a newly endowed Hollis Professorship of Mathematics and Natural Philosophy. For a while he was "an ornament to the College, and a great stimulus to science in the colonies" and is said to have done "much to bring the College in tune with the age, and to arrest the trend of practically inclined young men to private schools and to business." By 1738, however, his abilities had been overshadowed by his thirst for drink, and he was, after appropriate warnings, discharged.[3]

Greenwood was replaced by John Winthrop of the class of 1732, the "first important scientist or productive scholar on the teaching staff of Harvard College." He was an excellent teacher and has been credited with "introducing four decades of undergraduates to the scientific point of view." He has, in addition, been compared favorably with Benjamin Franklin for the range of his interests, including the practical applications of his investigations carried out in the "first laboratory of experimental physics in this country." Looked upon as the founder of American astronomy, he made significant contributions to that field and was elected to membership in the Royal Society of London.[4]

Natural philosophy, including astronomy and physics and the relevant mathematics, was the earliest scientific department of the college. Other sciences, such as chemistry and biology, might be treated briefly as part of natural philosophy but did not become independent components of the curriculum until the late eighteenth or early nineteenth centuries. During this period the teaching of such disciplines was "closely aligned with that of theology . . . they were, to varying degrees, conceived not merely as areas of exact knowledge but handmaidens of theology and moral philosophy."[5]

By the early nineteenth century, scientific subjects occupied an important place in the curriculum, with regular courses required of all students. The approach was broad, in the belief that the well-educated young man should have some understanding of all fields, including natural history, chemistry, physics, and astronomy. Instruction was by textbook and recitation, with some lectures, and demonstrations in chemistry and physics.[6] The application of science to the "useful arts" was touched upon, yet no organized study of the practical applications of science was attempted. But times were changing. An industrial revolution was under way, particularly in New England, and the need for new approaches to education began to be more widely appreciated.

One of the first significant steps in the enlargement of academic perspective at Harvard came with the founding in 1816 of the Rumford Professorship through a bequest from a New Englander who had spent much of his life in Europe, dramatically immersed in the social and political activities of the time, yet always with a dominating interest in the practical uses of science and invention. Benjamin Thompson, Count Rumford, was born in 1753 in Woburn, Massachusetts, and at the age of thirteen was apprenticed to merchants, first in Salem and then in Boston, where he took advantage of evening classes offered for working people in a variety of proprietary schools.[7] Back in Woburn by 1770, he soon apprenticed himself to a physician for the study of medicine. He shared a common interest in scientific matters with his friend and neighbor, Loammi Baldwin, who would later superintend the construction of the Middlesex Canal, and in June 1771 the two attended John Winthrop's natural philosophy lectures at Harvard, though neither appears to have had any official connection with the college.[8]

In 1772, Thompson, nineteen years old, became a schoolmaster in Concord, New Hampshire, earlier called Rumford and then still generally known by that name. Here he established close relations with the Loyalist governor, John Wentworth, who named him a major in the Fifteenth Regiment of Militia. Two years later, suspected of Toryism, Thompson fled to Woburn and Boston, engaging in undercover activities leading to a further flight to London in the spring of 1776, when the British troops and large numbers who favored their cause left for Nova Scotia.

Through his audacity and venturesome spirit he managed to attach himself to influential people, increased his fortune, became undersecretary of state for the Colonies, and then, at a price of £4500, lieutenant colonel commandant of the King's American Dragoons, which saw service in South Carolina and in New York. In 1783, while on a tour of the Continent, he secured an invitation from Carl Theodor, the elector of Bavaria, to join his court. With permission to do so from George III, he remained in Bavaria for eleven years and in 1792 was promoted to the rank and dignity of the Imperial Counts of the Holy Roman Empire, choosing for himself the title of Count of Rumford.

During this long period Benjamin Thompson accomplished much by way of encouragement of industrial development, mechanical innovation, economic organization, and care for the poor. Through it all his concern for the basic elements of science never weakened. He published a multitude of papers dealing with the conduction and convection of heat, the relation of heat, light, and mechanical motion, military technology, and such practical subjects as the efficient design of stoves and fireplaces. Although his theories and proposals by no means attained universal acclaim, he was widely recognized as a leading scientist of his day. At the age of twenty-seven he was made a Fellow of the Royal Society, then largely an assemblage of amateurs with interests in science and natural philosophy, and in succeeding years received similar honors from other European societies. Rumford responded in turn with generous donations for the advancement of science and its applications. In 1796 he made gifts to the Royal Society of London and to the American Academy of Arts and Sciences for the establishment of the Rumford Premiums, to be awarded to "the Author of the most Important Discovery or useful Improvement . . . on Heat or on Light, the preference always being given to such Discoveries as shall in the Opinion of the Academy tend most to promote the good of Mankind."[9]

Late in 1798 the count, obviously hoping for a government appointment, informed Rufus King, the American minister in London, that he was considering returning to America. It would take a while, but by June 1799 President John Adams had given his approval of an offer, though he pointed out that others who had left the country under similar circumstances had encountered difficulties upon their return. On September 7 King informed the secretary of war that he had "had some conversations" with Rumford and felt that he would "wisely decline." A formal letter on the following day offered him an appointment as superintendent of the proposed Military Academy and inspector general of artillery. Count Rumford declined on September 12 because of "engagements which great obligations have rendered sacred and inviolable."[10]

A prime reason for this decision was his involvement in an effort which, in concert with others, would lead to the founding in London in 1799 of the Royal Institution "for diffusing the knowledge and facilitating the general introduction of useful mechanical improvements, and for *teaching* by means of regular Courses of Philosophical Lectures and Experiments the application of Science to the common purposes of life."[11] Some historians have asserted that Rumford had looked to the Conservatoire des Arts et Métiers in Paris as a model, and others, that his inspiration had come from Anderson's Institution in Glasgow.[12] Rumford had indeed obtained from the latter information about its organization and instructional program, and Thomas Garnett, the first holder of its chair of philosophy, would become the Royal Institution's first professor when it opened in March 1800.[13]

Rumford was a difficult man. The early days were stormy as his original plan met some opposition, and the institution never developed as he had hoped, its character eventually being shaped by Humphry Davy and Michael Faraday, two early and distinguished participants. The idea of a technical school for artisans and a museum was abandoned in favor of popular lectures and scientific courses, the publication of a journal, and the establishment of a laboratory for the promotion of knowledge through scientific research.

Count Rumford left London in 1802 for France, where he died in 1814. His bequest to Harvard carried a clear statement of his intentions:

> For the purpose of founding, under the direction and government of the Corporation, Overseers, and governors of that University, a new institution and professorship, in order to teach by regular courses of academical and public Lectures, accompanied with proper experiments, the utility of the physical and mathematical sciences for the improvement of the useful arts, and for the extension of the industry, prosperity, happiness, and well-being of Society.[14]

❦

The goals and purposes set forth so incisively by Rumford were hardly compatible with the traditional perspectives of an old and classical college. That they were so promptly accepted is again evidence of changing times and a growing sense of the need for a new type of education. In 1816, two years after his death, the Rumford Professorship and Lectureship on the Application of Science to the Useful Arts was established as a part-time position.

The first appointment to this chair was Jacob Bigelow, a prominent figure in the later founding of the Massachusetts Institute of Technology. Only twenty-nine years of age, Bigelow was already on his way to a most distinguished career. He was then a lecturer at the Harvard Medical School and professor of materia medica, a post he would continue to hold.[15]

Following graduation from Harvard in 1806, Bigelow began immediately to prepare for the medical profession as a student in the office of a physician, first in Worcester and then in Boston, where he also attended medical lectures at Harvard. Licensed to practice in 1809, he entered the Medical School of the University of Pennsylvania for further study. He enrolled also as a private pupil with Dr. Benjamin Smith Barton, the same scientist who a decade earlier had been Patrick Rogers's mentor in chemistry. Under Barton's tutelage Bigelow developed a particular interest in botany. He received his medical degree in 1810 and returned to Boston for private practice.

Jacob Bigelow was a remarkable man. In a memorial following his death in 1879, Oliver Wendell Holmes paid tribute to him as an enthusiastic botanist, an accomplished scholar, an eminent practitioner, a reformer of medical opinion and practice, a social innovator, and a philosopher. And he cited as "the last great movement" of his life his avid espousal of a "change in the educational system by which the classical languages should cease to be the exclusive or chief tests of a liberal training."[16] It was this deep interest in educational reform which led to his support of the Massachusetts Institute of Technology and his active participation as an officer of its governing board.

Bigelow won wide recognition for his many contributions to the fields of medicine and botanical science, but he was also praised for his "mechanical ingenuity" and "shrewd eye for the practical." Drawn to the work of the hand as well as of the mind, he was an excellent craftsman. For his distinguished series of volumes entitled *American Medical Botany*, for example, he devised a method of printing in colors from copper plates and prepared all of the engravings himself.

The Rumford Lectures by Bigelow, a requirement for all students of the college, were delivered also to large audiences in Boston and appear to have been a tremendous success. From careful observation and questioning of local artisans—mechanics, blacksmiths, glassblowers, clock makers, and printers among them—he had familiarized himself with their trades and methods.[17] All appreciated his clear exposition of the relation of basic scientific principles to practical invention, together with demonstrations with the aid of drawings, models, and apparatus constructed by his own hand. After ten years of lectures, he resigned the Rumford Professorship, retaining until 1855 his faculty position at the Medical School. He served also as an overseer of Harvard from 1846 to 1854.

In 1829 Bigelow published "for the use of Seminaries and Students" a volume of some five hundred pages entitled *Elements of Technology, taken chiefly from a Course of Lectures delivered at Cambridge on the Application of the Sciences to the Useful Arts.*[18] He presented it as an "elementary volume . . . composed for the instruction of the uninitiated, rather than for the perfection of adepts," intended to respond to a "want, not yet provided for, in our courses of elementary education," at a time when the practical applications of science were becoming ever more important:

> There has probably never been an age in which the practical applications of science have employed so large a portion of the talent and enterprise of the community, as in the present; nor one in which their cultivation has yielded such abundant rewards. And it is not the least of the distinctions of our own country, to have contributed to the advancement of this branch of improvement, by many splendid instances of inventive genius and successful perseverance.[19]

Bigelow made a special point of relating the sciences and the arts, in the belief that drawing a line between the two created only "comparative, rather than absolute" distinctions:

> In common language we apply the name of sciences, to those departments of knowledge which are more speculative, or abstract, in their nature, and which are conversant with truths or with phenomena, that are in existence at the time we contemplate them. The arts, on the contrary, are considered as departments of knowledge, which have their origin in human ingenuity, which depend on the active, or formative processes of the human mind, and which without these, would not have existed. . . . Discovery is the process of science;

invention is the work of art. So common, however, is the connexion of the two with each other, that we find both a science and an art involved in the same branch of study.[20]

A book of twenty-one chapters, *Elements of Technology* dealt with such subjects as the Materials used in the Arts, the Arts of Printing, Engraving, Casting, Architecture and Building, Heating and Ventilation, Illumination, Locomotion, and Metallurgy. A list at the end of each chapter included works to which students might turn for a fuller treatment of particular subjects. A second edition, with additions, appeared in 1831, and the work was later expanded and published in two volumes as *The Useful Arts*.[21]

Despite many erroneous statements to the contrary, Bigelow was not the originator of the word "technology," a fact made plain in his first edition:

> I have adopted the general name of Technology, a word sufficiently expressive, which is found in some of the older dictionaries, and is beginning to be revived in the literature of practical men at the present day. Under this title it is attempted to include such an account as the limits of the volume permit, of the principles, processes, and nomenclatures of the more conspicuous arts, particularly those which involve applications of science, and which may be considered useful, by promoting the benefit of society, together with the emolument of those who pursue them.[22]

Yet there can be little doubt that his adoption of the general term was instrumental in bringing about its rapid and widespread use in America. In particular, it seems likely that he was responsible for the name of the Massachusetts Institute of Technology.[23]

In ancient Greece the basic root, τεχνη (*techne* or art), appears to have been in common use. As today, it embraced many shades of meaning, but all pertained in some way to an art or craft or skill, a system or method of making or doing, whether of the useful arts or the fine arts. Hence were derived such words as "technic," "technical," and "technician." By the addition of λογια (*logia*, a combining form meaning "words" or "discourse"), "technology," a discourse or treatise on an art or arts, is derived.[24]

The word was adopted in Latin, but how early it was incorporated into the English language is not certain. It is listed, however, in several English dictionaries of the seventeenth and eighteenth centuries. In the *Glossographia*, published by Thomas Blount in 1674, and in the dictionary of E. Coles, published in 1685, "technology" is defined as "a treating or description of Crafts, Arts, or Workmanship."[25] Similar definitions appear in the works of Cocker in 1704, Kersey in 1708, and the well-known dictionary of Nathan Bailey in 1730.[26] Bailey defined "technology" as "a Description of Arts, especially Mechanical Ones," adding:

> Under Mechanical Arts are such arts wherein the Hand and Body are more concerned than the Mind, and which are generally cultivated for the sake of the Gain or Profit that accrues from them, such as Trades, Weaving, Turnery, Masonry, etc.
>
> Science, as opposed to Art, is a formed system of any Branch of Knowledge, comprehending the Doctrine, Reasons, or Theory of the Thing, without any immediate Application of it to any Uses or Offices of Life.

There, in clear and concise language, Bailey set forth the gulf which had separated science and the arts since the time of Aristotle.

But a change of view and spirit was approaching. From Francis Bacon had come the belief that the true goal of science was to serve useful ends. That philosophy opened the way for the Enlightenment of the eighteenth century—the faith in progress, the conviction that man by organized effort could fashion a better world. Slowly, throughout Western Europe, there was an awakening to the fact that material progress in the arts and crafts depended not only upon human skill and experience, but fundamentally upon a comprehension of the laws of nature and how they might be applied to practical purposes. The mind and the hand (*mens et manus*) became partners in a common cause.

Although the word "technology" is as old as the Greeks, it was used but rarely before the mid-1700s and only in reference to some process of the manual arts. Then in a series of books and papers beginning in 1769, Johann Beckmann (1739–1811), a professor of economics at the University of Göttingen, prepared the first systematic and comprehensive treatment of some thirty or more arts and crafts. He endeavored to set forth the basic principles which governed these diverse arts and to establish a field of study comparable to medicine or law. To designate the sum of all knowledge relating to machines or mechanical processes, Beckmann chose the word "technology," and he became known as the "founder of scientific technology."[27]

The word soon came into frequent use throughout Europe. By the beginning of the nineteenth century, with the Industrial Revolution in full swing, the interdependence of science and technology was broadly recognized. As noted earlier, in 1816—the same year in which the Rumford Professorship was inaugurated—Jeremy Bentham proposed the establishment of a "Chrestomathic School," or one "conducive to useful learning," in a description of which he included a "Sketch of the Field of Technology" with a definition of the word: "To a course such as that here proposed, a not unapt conclusion may, it should seem, be afforded by a view of what has been termed *Technology*,— General Technology,—the aggregate body of the several sorts of manual operations directed to the purposes of art, and having, for their common and ultimate end, the production and preparation of the several necessaries and conveniences of life."[28]

The word's transfer to America took place much more slowly. During the very early years of the nineteenth century it appears to have been practically unknown to Americans and seldom if ever used even by those up-to-date on European developments. It did not appear in Noah Webster's *Compendious Dictionary of the English Language* published in 1806, though "technical," defined as "belonging to arts and sciences," was included.[29] By 1828, when Webster published his more extensive two-volume work, *An American Dictionary of the English Language*, "technology" was there, along with "technical" and "technological," with a reference to technological institutions, and "technologist." Webster defined technology as "a description of arts; or a treatise on the arts" and as "an explanation of the terms of the arts."[30] This was a year before Bigelow's *Elements of Technology* in which he acknowledged that the word had already appeared occasionally in technical literature, and no doubt through his own lectures and writings it began to find more common use and general acceptance.

A successor to Bigelow as Harvard's Rumford Professor was not named until 1834, when Daniel Treadwell was appointed.[31] Born in 1791, Treadwell had received a very limited formal education but possessed an inventive and inquisitive mind and great mechanical aptitude. He was an avid reader, had taken instruction in French, and had studied physics and mathematics on his own while serving an apprenticeship with a Boston silversmith in whose firm he became a partner in 1812. During this period he was also busy with the design and construction of a machine for making wrought iron nails and, in partnership with another, one for making screws of metallic wire, or wood screws, a business that might have prospered had not the end of the War of 1812 made British screws once more available in America. By 1817, weary from these endeavors, he changed course and began to study medicine under Dr. John Ware of Boston, through this association coming to know Jacob Bigelow and other young medical men, who became life-long friends. The appeal of mechanical invention was strong, however, and a year and a half later he turned his talents again in this direction, producing a foot-lever printing press and then a press powered by a steam engine. The latter found wide application in American book publishing and was first used for newspapers by the *Boston Daily Advertiser* in 1829.

Over the years Treadwell became involved with city water supplies and railroading and invented a machine, known as "The Gypsey," for spinning cordage. His invention led to the formation of the Boston Hemp and Cordage Manufacturing Company, a venture in which he was associated with Francis Calley Gray, a fellow of the Harvard Corporation from 1826 to 1836.

In 1828, when Sylvanus Thayer was superintendent of West Point, Treadwell declined to serve on its board of visitors for lack of time, but in 1829 and 1830 he agreed to present a series of lectures for Harvard students on engineering and practical mechanics, with particular emphasis on the steam engine, railroads, and road construction. Harvard granted him an honorary master of arts degree in 1829. It is reasonable to assume that both Jacob Bigelow and Francis Gray supported his appointment to the Rumford chair. He accepted the post with some reservations about his qualifications, but his attainments and his deep interest in the applications of science to the useful arts were admirably suited to the task.

Before commencing his lectures, Treadwell journeyed to England to observe manufacturing processes, visit institutions devoted to the useful arts, and purchase models and apparatus to be used in illustrating his lectures. A letter to President Josiah Quincy prior to his departure set forth his understanding of the duties of the professorship and the terms of appointment. He would be required to deliver forty lectures annually on the "philosophy of the arts, particularly those which are of practical importance in the business of life." The Corporation would purchase with Rumford funds the apparatus and models necessary for the illustration of his lectures by "direct experiments." His salary would be $800 a year, with the remainder of the Rumford fund's interest to be used for additions to the apparatus and keeping it in repair. He agreed to reside in Cambridge, but, his salary representing only a part-time commitment, he would "have leave of absence when not engaged in lecturing, for the purpose of attending to engineering, or any branch of industry the pursuit of which will enable me to render my lectures more immediately practical and instructive."[32] The part-time nature of the position, with freedom to attend to other professional interests, is an important point to remember in relation to later appointments to the Rumford chair, to which both Henry and William Rogers aspired—Henry in the mid-1840s, William in the early 1860s.

Treadwell resigned his professorship in 1845 but remained professionally active for many years. He had already, in 1840, become interested in a subject earlier pursued by

Count Rumford—the design of cannon. After preliminary experimental work, he was convinced that the use of wrought iron and steel would produce cannon of greater strength than those currently in use, and in 1843 he secured a contract from the Ordnance Department to devise machinery and processes for their manufacture, forming with Jacob Bigelow and others the Steel Cannon Company. Though he failed to gain government acceptance of his invention, either in the United States or abroad, his scientific work would be recognized in May 1865, when the American Academy of Arts and Sciences awarded him the Rumford Premium "for improvements in the management of heat, embodied in his investigations and inventions relating to the construction of cannon of large calibre, and of great strength and endurance."[33] The Steel Cannon Company lost money and failed, but a number of cannon had been manufactured. One of these, a thirty-two pounder, weighing 1800 pounds, bearing the inscription "Daniel Treadwell, Inventor and Maker, 1844," was, after his death in 1872, presented by his wife to the Massachusetts Institute of Technology.[34]

Yet another bequest to Harvard exemplifying the growing desire for "useful learning" became marginally involved with the establishment and survival of the Massachusetts Institute of Technology. The will of Benjamin Bussey of Roxbury, probated in March 1842, named Harvard College as the residual beneficiary after the expiration of certain life income and tenancy provisions for his family. It was his desire to "benefit my fellow-citizens and posterity, according to my ability, by devoting ultimately a large portion of my fortune to promote those branches of education which I deem most important and best calculated to advance the prosperity and happiness of our common country."[35] Half of the endowment was designated for the Schools of Law and Theology. Harvard was instructed further to retain Bussey's two-hundred-acre estate called "Woodland Hill" in Roxbury and to establish there, supported by the remaining half of the endowment, "a course of instruction in practical agriculture, in useful and ornamental gardening, in botany, and in such other branches of natural science as may tend to promote a knowledge of practical agriculture and the various arts subservient thereto and connected therewith . . . the institution so established shall be called the 'Bussey Institution.'" The funds were also to be used for the support of instruction, there or at Harvard College, in related branches of the physical sciences.[36] An historical account of the institution praises Bussey for his "remarkable foresight" in the matter of agricultural and horticultural education, an important element twenty years later in the Congressional Land-Grant Act of 1862.

Harvard did not gain full responsibility for administering the bequest until 1861, when the portions for Law and Divinity were put to immediate use. Because a member of the family still lived at Woodland Hill, however, the funds for the proposed Bussey Institution were invested against the day when this Roxbury property would become available. Though a decade would pass before the institution could begin operations, Harvard had gained control of these funds for this practical purpose at precisely the time when the new Institute of Technology in Boston was struggling to become a reality, and very soon thereafter Harvard would be a vigorous contender for the funds to be derived in Massachusetts through the Land-Grant Act. When the president of Harvard in his report for 1867–68 called attention to discussions then under way for the establishment of the Bussey Institution, he expected that it would be an "Agricultural College of the highest class . . . recognizing the high and difficult character of the art of husbandry, which lays all the mechanical, chemical, and physical sciences, including botany and zoölogy, and even comparative psychology, under contribution," a college "which can only exist in close connection with a university richly endowed with chairs of pure science."[37] In this statement he was raising an argument used in 1863 in the competition for the state's land-grant fund, and he was doing so at a time when the Institute of Technology might be vulnerable to acquisition.

Further support for agricultural and horticultural education would come to Harvard through a bequest of James Arnold, a wealthy whaling merchant of New Bedford, who died in December 1868, his will specifying that part of his residuary estate be set aside as a trust to be used for the "promotion of Agricultural or Horticultural improvements, or other Philosophical, or Philanthropic purposes." He named three trustees for this fund, among them his brother-in-law, George B. Emerson, a Harvard graduate and prominent educator with strong interests in natural history, and an important figure in the founding of the Massachusetts Institute of Technology. In 1872 the trustees transferred the fund to Harvard College to establish the Arnold Arboretum in connection with the Bussey Institution, along with an endowed Arnold Professorship of Botany.[38]

In August 1838 a proposal that Harvard consider the "propriety of establishing a school for the instruction of civil engineers" had been put forward by Benjamin Peirce, then University Professor of Mathematics and Natural Philosophy and later Perkins Professor of Astronomy and Mathematics. Acting on the suggestion of an engineer whom he did not identify, Peirce wrote to President Josiah Quincy:

Benjamin Peirce

The class of young men, fitting themselves to become engineers, is so rapidly increasing, that I have thought it my duty to address you upon a subject suggested to me by an engineer; the propriety of establishing a school for the instruction of civil engineers similar in its plan to that which has been so eminently successful in the law-school. Many practical men will, I am confident, oppose the plan and yet I am inclined to the belief that it would meet with great favour from the public, and would be much frequented, and would do much good. Even the most practical admit that a thorough mathematical education gives a young engineer great command over the details of his profession, and to mention a single name, we know that Mr. Storrow arose at once to the top of his profession on account of the great theoretical knowledge which he acquired at the Polytechnic school, where he saw no practice out of the lecture room. Indeed, from the nature of many of the engineer's studies, they can be better taught in such a school than amidst the hurry of active business, precisely as a lawyer or physician can acquire the general principles of his profession better, before attempting to practise; and if he begins his practise too soon he is sure to lament it. But perhaps I am wrong and am arguing too theoretically, and my only object is to suggest the subject to you hoping that you would think it worth while to put it in a proper train for being thoroughly discussed.[39]

The ambiguity of the source prompts speculation as to his identity. One might assume that the "engineer" was the same "Mr. Storrow" cited as an example of one who had profited greatly from European study. Charles Storer Storrow and Peirce were Harvard classmates, receiving their degrees in 1829, and Storrow has been prominently mentioned as influential later in Abbott Lawrence's decision to support a scientific school at Harvard.[40] But if Storrow had indeed been Peirce's source, it seems likely that Peirce would have so indicated in his opening sentence. Possible alternatives are Samuel Morse Felton, a Harvard graduate in 1834, and Loammi Baldwin the younger, of the class of 1800 and the son of Count Rumford's old friend.

Loammi Baldwin the younger, who would one day be referred to as the "father of Civil Engineering in America," possessed a natural aptitude in mechanics and practical science but initially chose to become a lawyer, a profession he soon abandoned. In 1807 he traveled to England to observe internal improvements, a subject in which he was keenly interested, dating back to his father's work on the Middlesex Canal. He had hoped to visit France and the Continent as well but could not because of the British blockade of French ports then in force.[41] Returning home in 1808, he opened an office in Charlestown, and became actively engaged on a national scale in canals, surveys, water power projects, naval dry docks, railroads, development of industrial sites, city water supplies, and other civil engineering projects.

Baldwin also became a spokesman in support of engineering education, stressing the need for trained engineers well grounded in scientific principles, and the absolute necessity for such education if America was to prosper and grow economically, capitalize on its natural resources, and increase the well-being of its citizens. He applauded the practice of the canal companies in taking on student engineers, who paid for the privilege of learning by doing, and he recommended that state boards responsible for public improvements associate with their projects formal instructional programs in engineering subjects. But he was well aware that this would be only a beginning and that as the nation grew and developed, the American college must soon recognize and respond to the need for adequately trained engineers far beyond the numbers that West Point could supply. He accepted students in his own office in Charlestown for a fee of $200 for two years and paid them for work they did in the field.[42] Storrow was one of these students for a short time.[43] Available to them in Baldwin's office was "the largest and best professional library of engineering works" in the United States.[44]

About the year 1835 Baldwin asked Samuel Felton, then in charge of a school for boys in Charlestown, to provide instruction in "physics, mathematics, surveying, and kindred subjects" to the students, or apprentices, associated with his office. This Felton agreed to do on a part-time basis. In the process he developed a genuine interest in engineering and became a student there himself. He would later pay tribute to Baldwin's efforts to advance the profession of civil engineering, which he regarded as "a high and honorable calling, and deserving recognition as such, equally with those of medicine, divinity, or law."[45]

Baldwin died in June 1838, and Felton assumed responsibility for the business. He, too, surely had come to appreciate the need for formally trained engineers and may well have approached Benjamin Peirce, whom he had certainly known as a student, with the idea that Harvard might make a contribution in this regard—if Baldwin had not already done so before his death.

Chapter 5

Speculation aside, Peirce's proposal of 1838 was immediately referred to a committee of the Harvard Corporation to consider both the possibility and advisability of offering such instruction.[46] A year later Peirce was having second thoughts. His earlier plan, he said, "appears to me, on further examination, to require a greater apparatus of instructors and instruments, than it might appear prudent to provide, in the uncertainty which there must be concerning its final success." He therefore suggested that it be "publicly announced, that University students, who may join the College, shall have the liberty of studying any branch of Practical or Theoretical Mathematics which they may desire to study, and shall be entitled to certificates upon the same principles as the regular students of the College." He was sure that "in some of the departments, the instructors would, no doubt, be glad to avail themselves of an opportunity to obtain higher classes of students; and would be ambitious to do all in their power to increase in this way the numbers of the College; and if they were successful, their success would appear to themselves and would do more than anything else to stimulate them to new efforts."[47] This, too, was referred to the Corporation,[48] but it appears that no action was taken.

The idea of a school persisted, however, and by late April 1840 President Quincy and his committee reported that "such a school would be useful and ought to be established provided it can be done without the appointment of any other Professors or incurring any important additional expense to the College." Benjamin Peirce, Daniel Treadwell, Joseph C. Lovering, the Hollis Professor of Mathematics and Natural Philosophy, and John W. Webster, then Erving Professor of Chemistry and Mineralogy—who later was to become renowned for a wholly nonacademic affair, committing murder—were appointed to work out a plan similar to the Law School and self-supporting.[49] Given the restrictions attached to the committee's recommendation, it is not surprising that no progress was made at that time. Five more years would pass without definitive action on the part of the Corporation. In 1842 word of the Bussey bequest was received, but, as earlier noted, these funds would not become available for many years.

There appears to have been support within the faculty for the establishment of a new school, but little consensus on its scope and purpose. Some felt the need for a source of special training for professional careers other than divinity, law, and medicine after the regular college years, or, in other words, a graduate school. Others acknowledged that many young students had little desire to spend three or four years immersed in the classics, but sought preparation for work in the "useful arts." For their part, Peirce

106

and Asa Gray advocated an advanced school in science and literature,[50] both for college graduates and for any other students who might prove themselves adequately qualified, a proposal wherein the term "science" may be presumed to have included its practical as well as its theoretical aspects.

By 1845, a year in which both Daniel Treadwell and Josiah Quincy would resign, Harvard College had become well awakened to the call for higher scientific and technical education. The vacancy in the Rumford chair and the advent of a new president provided an opportunity for further consideration, with the Rumford taking on even more significance. In December, a few weeks before the final confirmation of Quincy's successor by the Board of Overseers, the Corporation appointed yet another committee, this time to study the organization and duties of the college's scientific department. The chairman was Acting President James Walker, Alford Professor of Natural Religion, Moral Philosophy, and Civil Polity and also a fellow of the Corporation, with Samuel A. Eliot, the treasurer, and John Amory Lowell, Trustee of the Lowell Institute and a fellow of the Corporation since 1837, as members. Within a few days the committee, citing the impending change in the presidency, decided that it was not the moment to go into the details of a new organization of this department, nor would it be expedient to take up the question of instituting a school of engineering or of practical science. They did suggest the appointment of a tutor in mathematics and chemistry, citing knowledge of chemistry as prerequisite to progress in the sciences generally. Finally, in the committee's judgment, an appointment should be made to the Rumford Professorship.[51]

Josiah Quincy, who had been president since 1829, was in his early seventies and still vigorous when he presented his resignation to the Corporation, effective immediately following the commencement exercises scheduled for August 1845. He had been determined to leave "before there could be the faintest suspicion that his powers were beginning to fail him," but more important, he wished to step aside in favor of Edward Everett.[52]

Everett had entered Harvard at the age of thirteen, graduated in 1811 with high honors, remained to study for the ministry, and early in 1814 became pastor of the Brattle Square Church in Boston,[53] where he served until his appointment in 1815 to a newly founded professorship at Harvard. The endowment was sufficient to allow immediate leave at full salary for two years of study abroad. He earned his Ph.D. from Göttingen in 1817, applied for an extension of leave, and spent the following two years on the Continent and in England before returning to take up his duties as Eliot

Professor of Greek Literature. Though he was an excellent and inspiring teacher, his thoughts turned toward political life, and when he was elected to Congress in 1824, Harvard insisted upon compliance with the university's requirement of professorial residence in Cambridge if he were to hold his chair, and he was forced out in March 1825.[54] Shortly thereafter, in 1827, he began a long period of service as a Harvard overseer, and in 1828, when President Kirkland retired, he was on the list of candidates for the presidency, a list from which he promptly withdrew his name.[55]

An orator of great repute, Everett served for ten years in Congress, four terms as governor of Massachusetts, and finally as ambassador to the Court of St. James during the administration of President John Tyler. Though he was not officially informed until July 1845 that his appointment would not be renewed by President James Knox Polk, the news was not unexpected. During the previous winter and spring there had been rumors and speculation, along with overtures from friends, about the presidency of Harvard. After Quincy's resignation, there was further pressure for favorable consideration, but he was loath to entertain the prospect of a position fraught with details and disciplinary problems. Immediately following his return to Boston in September, he received formal word of the Corporation's wish to appoint him to the presidency. He finally accepted in late November with "great misgivings," recording in his diary the feeling that he was making "an experiment of a most perilous nature to my reputation and happiness."[56] He was formally elected by the Corporation on January 3, 1846, confirmed by the Overseers on February 5, and immediately took office, though the inauguration ceremonies were not held until April.[57]

Everett proved to be the first of what Samuel Eliot Morison has termed the "minor prophets" of the Harvard presidency after the resignation of Quincy, and with his formal confirmation by the Overseers began "the three most wretched years of a life which, though crowded with honors, was singularly unhappy. For never did Everett obtain the consideration to which he believed he was entitled by his dignity and parts."[58] It was a brief and stormy presidency. He was a brilliant scholar, had profited greatly from his travels abroad and his study in Germany, and no doubt he wished to develop at Harvard a university on the order of the great European institutions. But he was incapable of controlling a disruptive student body which "proceeded to make his life a hell,"[59] and his relations with the Corporation, which had been so anxious to have him, proved troublesome as well. Life in Cambridge bore out all the misgivings and forebodings which he had initially expressed about the post. He considered resignation early in 1847, made it official later in 1848, and "to the relief of all" it was accepted early in 1849, when Jared Sparks was quickly chosen to succeed him, assuming office on February 1 of that year.[60]

A significant achievement for Everett, however, was the establishment of the Lawrence Scientific School. From the beginning of his administration, he tried to promote a broader view of the purposes of a university and the need for a new curriculum. On April 30, 1846, in his inaugural address as president of what he insisted must be called the "University at Cambridge," he stated:

> It is a question well worthy to be entertained, whether the time is not arrived when a considerable expansion may be given to our system, of a twofold character; first, by establishing a philosophical faculty, in which the various branches of science and literature should be cultivated, beyond the limits of an academical course, with a view to a complete liberal education, and secondly, by organizing a school of theoretical and practical science, for the purpose especially of teaching its application to the arts of life, and of furnishing a supply of skilful engineers, and of persons well qualified to explore and bring to light the inexhaustible natural treasures of the country and to guide its vast industrial energies in their rapid development.[61]

He was setting as a goal of his presidency an enlargement of Harvard's educational mission, adding to the existing "academical and professional" programs a division for extended education beyond the baccalaureate—a graduate school—as well as a "school of theoretical and practical science."

The urgent need for better education in science and the principles of its application to the useful arts was not a new theme for him. On several earlier occasions he had spoken on the importance of the mechanical arts, on the advantage of scientific knowledge to working men, and on the advancement of American manufactures. In 1835, for example, in addressing the literary societies of Amherst College on "Education Favorable to Liberty, Knowledge, and Morals," he had said:

> When we consider the laws of the human mind, and the path by which the understanding marches to the discovery of truth, we must see that it is the necessary consequence of the general extension of education that it should promote the progress of science. . . . We are confirmed in the conclusion that the popular diffusion of knowledge is favorable to the growth of science by the reflection that, vast as the domain of learning is, and extraordinary as is the

progress which has been made in almost every branch, it may be assumed as certain,—I will not say that we are in its infancy, but as truth is as various as nature, and as boundless as creation,—that the discoveries already made, wonderful as they are, bear but a small proportion to those that will hereafter be effected.[62]

When Everett spoke in his inaugural of a School of Practical and Theoretical Science, a plan prepared by Benjamin Peirce had been in the hands of the Corporation since late February. It began by laying out the object of the proposed school:

> to bring the University into more immediate and intimate connexion with the community to which it belongs, by supplying the public demand for scientific education of various kinds. It is intended to subserve the purpose of organizing the different scientific professorships, and enabling the professors to cooperate in an efficient system of instruction, distinct from that given in the present academical course. It is not to be regarded as an institution for general and liberal education, but as designed to furnish one of a particular and professional character.[63]

The proposal promised to furnish a "complete and thorough scientific education" for the profession of civil engineering comparable to that offered in law and medicine. And for those interested in "art or manufacture," it promised the "elementary knowledge" essential for success. It was expected to draw upon a wide spectrum—college graduates seeking general or specialized training in science; civil engineers, surveyors, and architects, as well as astronomical observers; railroad superintendents, factory agents and overseers, manufacturers, merchants, and mechanics. While the complete course would require two years, students who wished to enroll only for a particular branch of special interest would be permitted to do so. It stressed an advantage over West Point, "the only school of the kind in this country," Peirce said, where discipline was "excessively rigid," the course longer, and the students subject to "great exposure during encampment, which is often destructive to their health," as well as a year's commitment to military service upon graduation.

The president and five professors would constitute the faculty. The Rumford Professor, heading the list, was expected to cover a wide range of subjects—civil and naval architecture, applications of heat and moving forces, vaporization, illumination, the arts of locomotion and manufactures among them. Next were the Erving Professor of Chemistry and Mineralogy, responsible also for geology, metallurgy, and agricultural chemistry; the Hollis Professor of Natural Philosophy, including physics, with mechanics, hydrostatics, hydrodynamics, electricity, magnetism, and optics; the Fisher Professor of Natural History, including botany, gardening, and animal physiology; the Perkins Professor of Mathematics and Astronomy, covering theoretical and practical mathematics, studies at the Observatory, surveying, and practical engineering in the field; and design taught by a drawing master, including drawing from models and nature, and architectural and topographical drawing. From the college would come instruction in French and German, history, geography, and rhetoric. If the faculty consented, a student might elect "other branches in the collegiate course." The fee would be $50 per term or $25 for half a term or less, entitling the student to use the college library and attend the university's Public Lectures, a privilege already granted to the Law School students. Peirce proposed the establishment of an endowment fund of one-third of the net income after expenses. A second third would go to the Observatory, and the remainder would be divided among the instructing staff "in such proportion as the corporation may from time to time decide."

Though the details and arrangement of the curriculum were not laid out, Peirce's plan represented the first formal proposal for higher technical education in Boston. He described it as "imperfect" and acknowledged that it would "undoubtedly require some changes with the growth of the school, the improvement of the arts and the progress of science if from no other cause." And he was confident that it would "meet with just and impartial criticism."[64]

There had been no immediate action on the part of the Corporation. Apparently they had not been inclined to alter their December decision, in view of the change in administration, to delay any serious consideration of a reorganization of the scientific department. They had, however, urged that an appointment to the Rumford Professorship should go forward. Before Peirce's plan could be carefully considered, therefore, a worthy successor to Daniel Treadwell must be found. Against the rising demands for "more useful learning" and increasing calls for curricular revision, the Rumford was caught up in the developing plans for a scientific school.

Chapter 6

The Lawrence Scientific School at Harvard

The effort to fill the vacant Rumford chair was already under way when Edward Everett's appointment to the presidency was confirmed by the Board of Overseers on February 5, 1846. Indeed, he noted in his diary on that same day a "desultory" Corporation discussion of candidates for the post.[1] He did not record who these candidates were, but there is ample evidence to point to Henry Darwin Rogers as one of the leading applicants in a situation wherein personal animosities and scientific controversies would reach an unusually high level, bringing into full play the politics of the academic profession along with a tangle of conflicting and interwoven interests of a variety of personalities.

Rogers's friend George Stillman Hillard, a lawyer and author, suggested that he apply for the Rumford chair. A graduate of Harvard and its Law School, Hillard has been described as "learned, scholarly, witty, agreeable, ironic, a conservative to the end." He shared an office with Charles Sumner, and the prominent literary figures of the day—Nathaniel Hawthorne and others—were among his circle of friends.[2] Into this society Henry Darwin Rogers moved with enthusiasm, staying with Hillard and his wife in their Pinckney Street home. His decision to settle in Boston was reached at just about the time that Treadwell was contemplating resignation, and Henry's name was soon before the Corporation as a candidate for the Rumford chair.

In considering the competition for this post it is well to keep in mind the scarcity of available academic positions for men of science during that period. At times it seemed as if candidates and their supporters were mounting well-orchestrated campaigns for political office. Existing scientific rivalries were heightened, and cliques solidified. At this particular moment at Harvard, the situation was made more complex by the change in administration and by the unresolved discussions on whether and how to establish a school of theoretical and practical science. Complicating the matter further was the beginning of a protracted and heated controversy over the theory of evolution, with the Boston scientific community eventually lining up on both sides.

Rogers at first seemed confident of success. But opposing factions quickly rallied, and for differing reasons. The opposition came from three quarters, simultaneously working against him for their own purposes, all three claiming credit for his elimination, and each often being given sole credit in later accounts.

First there was Asa Gray, the distinguished Fisher Professor of Natural History, at the time a vigorous opponent of the theory of evolution. In 1844 Robert Chambers, an Edinburgh publisher and amateur scientist, had published anonymously a volume entitled *Vestiges of the Natural History of Creation*,[3] wherein he "affirmed his belief in the spontaneous generation of organisms and the transmutation of species."[4] The book generated wide popular appeal, though it was denounced as no less than a scandal, unscientific, irreligious, and untrue, and rejected by many of the most prominent specialists in geology and natural history. Many, but not all. Henry Rogers was receptive to the idea. Gray was vehemently opposed and "considered the idea of the transmutation of species instead of special creation most objectionable both theologically and philosophically." Yet he is said to have looked upon it as "an attack on the integrity of science as much as a disturber of religion."[5]

That Henry Rogers had expressed support for the *Vestiges* was no help to his candidacy.[6] Asa Gray considered him a "Vestiges heretic" and took immediate steps to block his appointment, communicating his concern to his colleagues on the faculty as well as to the Corporation, most likely through Charles Greely Loring, his father-in-law, then a fellow. Writing to John Torrey of the Medical College of New York on January 26, 1846, Gray added a parenthetical note:

(*Entre nous*, from what I learned yesterday from one [of] our Corporation, I have no doubt but that Rogers—thanks to our prompt and decided action—is thrown out of the question for the Rumford Professorship.—So his friends must look elsewhere for him.)[7]

Gray's biographer has termed this a "questionable victory," stating that "Rogers's coming might very well have changed the history of science in Boston in important ways."[8]

Gray, however, was not the only one at work, and his reference to "our prompt action" leads to speculation that he may have told Benjamin Peirce that a Corporation vote was imminent. Peirce, however, seemed not as sure as Gray that Rogers was completely out of the running and wrote confidentially to his friend Alexander Dallas Bache, Superintendent of the Coast Survey in Washington, for an opinion of Rogers's qualifications. Bache had known Rogers in Philadelphia and had written a paper with him in 1834 on the coals of Pennsylvania. Both had been members of a small club of scientists, nearly all of whom had some involvement with higher education, an informal group meeting occasionally for "mutual support and instruction."[9]

Peirce informed Bache that a last-minute warning had enabled him to obtain a week's delay of the election. He described the vacancy as an opportunity "to make the professorship the head and center of a new school to be attached to the university for instruction in practical science; and upon this school I hope to concentrate all the scientific ability attached to the university"—a step that would convert the Rumford from a part-time occupation to a full-time position with added responsibilities. This could be accomplished only if the "right man" could be secured. Henry Rogers, with "strong personal friends" among the Corporation, had come "very near obtaining the appointment through the exertions of his literary friends." But Peirce argued that he was "deficient in accuracy" and known as a geologist, even considered by some in that field to be "vague and extravagant."

While deprecating the value of Rogers's ability as a lecturer, he praised the "power of clear explanation" of his personal candidate for the position, Morrill Wyman, about whose knowledge of chemistry the chemists were doubtful. He added, however, that Wyman would withdraw "if an engineer of known eminence were to apply, or any man whose claims were undoubtedly of a high order."[10] A practicing physician in Cambridge, Wyman was a graduate of Harvard College in 1833 and the Medical School in 1837, and whether he was a serious candidate for the Rumford is not at all clear.[11]

Emphasizing that the post required "an authority among engineers, mechanics, etc.," Peirce urgently needed Bache's "real opinion" of Rogers:

> The subject of new inventions is especially enjoined as a branch of his instruction. If you give me your opinion, as I hope you will, it will ensure Rogers's election if it is in his favor; and it shall not be used, if it is against him, unless it is *absolutely necessary*.[12]

The response was immediate. Bache had seen Rogers less frequently in recent years but recalled that he was "reasonably well grounded" in mathematics, "very well trained in general physics," and "well acquainted with the chemistry of the day and pursued analysis with some success." He termed his career as a geologist "distinguished" but added that "the boldness of his theories have more recently surprised (& often captivated) me." In praising him as a "precise" and "brilliant" lecturer, he added that he "shines more as a lecturer than as a teacher." He judged that he should be "prepared, for some branches of analytical chemistry" and mining, and "could easily prepare himself" for general chemistry:

> For a Professorship of Geology I would take him in preference to anyone, *perhaps*. . . . Mechanics and its applications, machines, inventions, civil engineering, the application of mathematics to machines and to engineering seem to me to require most special study, so with technical chemistry, the processes of the arts & trades & their history. I cannot imagine a mind capable of acquiring these things as a by play and while engaged primarily in other studies. While then I would not hesitate to take Rogers as a geological teacher & might even prefer him to others in mining, etc. I could not support his pretensions to a chair of the applications of science to the arts.[13]

The letter was used promptly by Peirce.

Throughout January and February 1846 the campaign for Rogers was carried forward by Hillard and Amos Binney, a well-known conchologist and one of the founders of the Boston Society of Natural History. Through their efforts, and particularly through those of the Rogers brothers, laudatory letters of support—often speaking directly to points raised in opposition—were obtained and transmitted to the Corporation.[14]

Though he would later be a member of the Board of Overseers, Hillard had no formal association with the institution in 1846. His Harvard connections, however, were many and strong and his access to information direct. His uncle, James Savage, Harvard class of 1803, was an overseer, and there were other friends among that board. He certainly knew the Fellows of the Corporation at that time: Charles Loring, John Amory Lowell, Lemuel Shaw, James Walker, and Benjamin Robbins Curtis, who had been a classmate at Harvard Law.

Word of Bache's response obviously reached Hillard and Rogers, for a letter from Hillard to Benjamin Curtis in February mentioned opposition from Philadelphia:

> The men of science there are rent into cliques and factions. There is all manner of unkindness and bitterness among them. . . . Mr. Rogers has some per-

sonal enemies, or at least, de-wishers among the scientific men of Philadelphia. . . . I have reason to think Mr. Bache is to be included. Any opinion, therefore, directly or indirectly proceeding from him should be received with caution.[15]

Hillard also confirmed that Rogers, "a member of my family, since last June," had applied for the Rumford at his suggestion.[16] Citing his eminence as a geologist as unquestioned, he stated that Rogers was "a thinker, a student, and an observer," with "an accurate eye and a dexterous hand." He called attention, too, to his "winning, persuasive, and gentlemanly" manners, his clarity of expression, and his reputation as a public speaker. And he expressed "confidence approaching conviction" that he would be a "vital and a life-giving teacher":

> Above all, he has a fresh, salient and growing mind, with a deep-seated principle of progress. . . . To put such a man into our University would be opening a fountain of fertilizing influences there. And is there not need of that? Is the scientific department there a very fruitful fig tree? . . . the scientific department of the college does not produce results satisfactory to its friends. In the name of those friends, let me beg of you to select a man in whose veins the warm blood of intellectual life freely runs. What we want in those "trim gardens" of learning is trees that will germinate and bear fruit, and not frosts that will do nothing but rot. Do not select a man who is safe because he is dead.[17]

Hillard enclosed a letter addressed to him by Henry's brother William, a "man of truth," he said, who "would speak as conscientiously in this case as in that of any other person."[18] It was designed to establish Henry's "pretensions on a just foundation," and was obviously composed with full knowledge of the opposition. William had left to Hillard, however, the task of an open response to Bache's opinions. It was a vintage Rogers piece, admirably demonstrating the eloquence that this elder brother could marshal on behalf of a cause he wished to further—in this case, an appointment to the Rumford Professorship, which he called "the chair of Technology in Harvard."

William cited Henry's early education, his productive experiences abroad, and most recent twelve-year concentration on "researches or teachings connected with Geology & all its allied practical & theoretical Chemistry Mechanics & Agriculture." And he presented a veritable catalogue of interests and accomplishments, always emphasizing their "applications" and "applied forms" and underscoring an "inventive genius" and a "habit of thought" both "precise and mathematical." In summary, he said:

With so wide a range of study & experience in Applied Science it would indeed be strange had he not made large attainments. . . . I think I am uttering a judgment unbiased by affection when I say that I know of no one who by the natural tendency of his genius & by the whole course of his studies & active scientific pursuits is so capable of filling worthily the vacant chair, by giving the largest scope & the strongest interest to its practical instructions. Indeed it seems to me as if by accident his entire career had been but a series of preparations for precisely such a place.[19]

When William solicited a supporting letter from his friend J. W. Bailey, professor of chemistry and mineralogy at West Point, he attacked the opposition:

Until today I had supposed that no letters would have been called for to sustain his pretensions. Nor would they have been, but for some efforts made by parties not in Boston to thwart his wishes by raising the old cry of his *love of Theory* & insinuating thus that he was unsound in Science. *We* know whence this ungenerous I will not say envious movement proceeds—for we have witnessed like manifestations from the same quarter on former occasions. Henry has been *independent* & has spurned all patronage from *cliques*—& for this even now, the attempt is made to depreciate him. I mention these matters, that should you think proper to express your opinion of his qualifications you may give such form to your letter as may best promote his views. His great merit as a geologist & as a lecturer, even his maligners do not of course deny— Indeed they *praise* him in this particular, but *then* refer to the disqualification of a love of Theory. You know as well as I that no man in this country has been a more diligent & minute *observer* than my brother. And this has been his course in Mechanics, Chemistry & the Applied Sciences as well as in Geology.

In a marginal note, he added:

This cry of *Theory* amuses me. Does any believe that Dumas & Liebig are the less various, minute & accurate in their science *because* they have *generalized*? Is it not quite the *reverse*?[20]

A third source of opposition now added to the complexity of the Rumford decision. One of those most bitterly opposed to Rogers was John W. Webster, who in
February 1846 launched a very effective effort for the
candidate of his choice. It was Webster who first
informed Eben N. Horsford of the vacancy and then
proceeded to campaign vigorously on his behalf, aided
by James Hall, geologist of New York State.

Horsford, born in 1818 in Moscow, New York, had,
after the usual preparatory education, entered Rensselaer
Polytechnic Institute in Troy, where he studied under
Amos Eaton. After one year he was graduated in 1838
with the degree of civil engineer. Ironically, he had
hoped at that time to secure a place with William Barton
Rogers in connection with his geological survey of
Virginia. Rogers had filled all the openings his funds
would allow but indicated that should his appropriation

Eben Norton Horsford

be increased, he would be happy to take him on.[21] Instead, Horsford found a situation
with the New York geological survey under James Hall, and not long after, in 1840, he
was appointed professor of mathematics and natural science at the Albany Female
Academy. During his period there he also presented a series of lectures in chemistry at
Newark College in Delaware. In the fall of 1844 Horsford left for Germany to study
chemistry with the renowned Baron Justus von Liebig, whose laboratory at Giessen had
earned worldwide fame, and he was still there in February 1846, unaware of the opening at Harvard and of Webster's suggestion that he be appointed.[22]

In nominating Horsford, Webster spoke of his own interest in the establishment of
a scientific school, stating that he had raised the question on earlier occasions, and ventured an opinion that Treadwell, whom he considered admirably qualified to head such
a school, might be persuaded to return. Failing that, however, he wished to present the
name of Eben N. Horsford, "a gentleman who will after one year, return home, every
way qualified for the duties of the Rumford chair, & to be the head of a school of science." He portrayed him as a "thorough geologist, an engineer, a capital draughtsman
. . . an excellent chemist, mineralogist, &c." with a "familiarity with all the prominent
manufacturing processes & operations." He hoped that he would be seriously considered and prophesied that Harvard would regret a failure to secure his services.[23]

In a letter to Edward Everett, Webster reviewed in more detail his thoughts about
the need for a scientific school. He mentioned his periodic suggestions over the years

for improvements to the chemical laboratory, which he described as "inconvenient" and with equipment "quite inferior to that of almost every other college in our country," for allowing the substitution of chemistry for other courses in the college curriculum, for more extended and practical courses, and for laboratory space to afford opportunity for the students to carry out experiments and research. He had even proposed a course that would be useful to law students, "embracing all points of evidence which require some knowledge of chemistry, as cases of poisoning, &c."—an especially interesting proposal coming from one who would soon be convicted of murder. He expressed great pleasure at the prospect of a scientific school to be headed by the Rumford Professor and urged the appointment of Horsford, enclosing several letters of support.[24] Though no firm decision had been made by the Corporation with respect either to the inauguration of a scientific school or to placing the Rumford Professor in charge of it, Peirce's proposal was obviously well known to his fellow faculty members.

Henry Rogers was still under consideration when that proposal was presented to the Corporation in late February 1846. At the same time Bache's letter, which they had already discussed, was forwarded by Everett to Samuel Eliot, with an indication that he agreed that "we are hardly ready to come to the choice of a Rumford Professor."[25]

Henry kept his brothers informed, and they continued to express confidence even as they decried the "cliques" working against them. Regrettably, most of his letters on this subject have not survived, those that have, only in edited versions in the *Life and Letters of William Barton Rogers*. The first mention there of his candidacy appears in a March 8, 1846, letter to William containing a paragraph, carefully edited by Emma Rogers, relating to the professorship:

> A few days ago I mentioned how my affairs were looking, and promised to write again whenever I should gather any further knowledge of the intentions of the Corporation [of Harvard University]. . . . It has been Peirce's darling wish for a long time past to reorganize the Scientific Corps of the Faculty; but this they cannot do, with _____ in the way, and he fears that if the Rumford Chair is filled without other changes being made, a golden occasion will be lost for the more thorough reform which he desires. . . . If they can effect what they desire, they will make a sort of extra-faculty school of science for the use of young men who desire a scientific education without the diploma of the college and without the classics, etc., and who would not even be undergraduates of the college. And they would place the Rumford Professor at the head, in the central position in this corps, and select him for his practical familiarity with the useful arts,—a man such as Treadwell might have been if

he had given himself to the chair only. Whether this is a feasible plan, I am not quite prepared to say, so difficult would it be to find a mechanician, an accomplished engineer in the wider sense, who would also be an able teacher; but if successful, it would be a good thing for this community and for the college.[26]

A letter from James Rogers identifies Webster as the faculty member standing in the way of a reorganization of the scientific corps:

> This scheme originated with Pearce [*sic*], who would prefer a practical engineer in the Rumford, and would not oppose Henry for the Chair of Webster, *could he be removed.* Whatever may be the changes he writes in confident hope of at no distant day obtaining some permanent berth in Cambridge. It delights me to know that he will at last come off more than conqueror, of the jealous enemies of his just claims to advancement.[27]

William, too, seemed to feel that Henry's "prospects of some acceptable place in Harvard" were "almost as good as could be wished" and that he would be successful "should the proposed change be effected."[28]

Without benefit of the full text of Henry's letter, it is difficult to judge accurately his state of mind with respect to the Rumford. His description of the qualifications necessary, were the post to entail also the headship of a new school, allows speculation that he did not consider himself to be a viable candidate for that position. On the other hand, all three brothers seemed confident that "some" place would be made for him. His inclusion among those to be especially invited to the inauguration of Edward Everett on April 30 may also indicate that he had not been removed from the candidate list.[29]

William Rogers spent the summer of 1846 in Boston. Correspondence for that period is thus scarce, and there is little record of what was going on with respect to Harvard from his and Henry's points of view. A letter to Henry, who spent some time at Lake Superior, revealed that William had spent a day at Cambridge in the company of Charles Sumner, where he heard the closing class oration, followed by a dinner with the Longfellows. He reported that Peirce and Gray had asked after Henry, but if he made any reference to the Rumford, it was presumably excised prior to publication in *Life and Letters*.[30]

The entry of Eben Horsford into the competition for the Rumford had brought the consideration of a successor to Treadwell essentially to a halt. Enthusiastic supporting letters were received even before he knew he was a candidate. When he finally learned that his name had been proposed, he informed Everett and the Corporation that he approved of the efforts on his behalf. Through Webster he forwarded testimonials from his associates at Giessen, including a glowing account from Liebig, and promised others from individuals known to the faculty and the Corporation. Everett's acknowledgment, indicating that the professorship would probably not be filled immediately, included a letter of thanks to Liebig, whom he knew, saying that Liebig's statement had been the most important one received.[31]

Horsford, too, had some opposition, chiefly Benjamin Peirce, who expected the faculty member in charge of the school to be well versed in engineering and mechanics, in which he felt Horsford lacked preparation and experience. Webster and Hall were diligent in securing assurances for the Corporation that their candidate's qualifications in this respect were impeccable.[32] Such assurances and other letters of support continued to arrive throughout the spring. William A. Norton, then of Delaware College, supplied letters written in 1843 when Horsford applied for a professorship at the University of Pennsylvania. Among them was a recommendation from Henry Rogers, who, Webster said, had spoken of him "in the strongest terms as every way qualified for the office" and predicted "from an acquaintance of several years that he will become highly distinguished in the scientific annals of our country," an opinion in which, according to Webster, William Barton Rogers concurred. Webster did not forward the letter to Everett, thinking it not "quite proper" to do so, since Henry was an applicant for the Rumford.[33] At the end of June 1846 Horsford withdrew his name from the competition. Months would pass before an appointment would be made.

Though the Rumford activity was quiet for a time, Peirce and Everett were discussing the scientific school during the summer of 1846.[34] By the fall, pressure for more help for the existing science courses was mounting, with Joseph Lovering pleading for money for equipment for his courses in mathematics and natural philosophy, ascribing their deficiencies to "the extension of the physical sciences by the discoveries of the present century," and urging that the department "now begin to take a wider range commensurate with the progress of science."[35] At the same time the faculty was debating the elimination of the rather limited elective system then in effect, and, in accord with Everett's inaugural statement, discussing the extension of the collegiate course beyond the baccalaureate program. On these issues Peirce had firm opinions, and in sending them to Everett he also pressed gently for the proposed scientific school, a "thorough revision of the scientific course of instruction," and consideration of the "expediency of widening the field of the natural sciences."[36]

Late in November the Corporation was moved to appoint yet another committee—Everett, Walker, and Lowell—to report a plan for a School of Science and Literature as a separate department of the university and to present a list of candidates for the Rumford. On the same day Everett, writing to Liebig on a different subject, asked to be remembered to Horsford if he was still at Giessen and commented that the professorship was still vacant.[37]

There is some question whether Horsford's withdrawal in June was genuine or part of the strategy of his supporters, and his return to America followed immediately by a trip to Cambridge early in 1847 was timely. On January 6 he and Webster called on Everett, and on the following evening the two dined with Everett and his family. A few days later, Everett and Horsford attended a class in physics, and Horsford again dined with the Everetts.[38]

On January 27 James Rogers expressed pleasure at Henry's "bright prospects," but on the same day Lowell, Walker, and Everett, meeting to consider a plan for the scientific school, agreed that Horsford should be recommended for the Rumford.[39] By mid-February the Corporation and the Overseers had approved both the plan and the Horsford appointment, and James Rogers had already written again to Henry saying, "What claim has he? or is his success to be attributed to the little Giessen reputation he may have gained. I am mortified, that such a thing should have so much weight."[40] The answer may be that, in light of Everett's stated goal to create in Cambridge a university that could match the best of the European institutions, Horsford's training abroad and his letters of support from Germany—particularly that of Liebig, whose opinion he valued highly—carried the day. It is not surprising that Horsford would emerge in his mind as the one candidate who could bring to bear on his project the background and prestige that would ensure success. At least so he thought at the time.

Though Henry Rogers was once a major contender, his prospects diminished considerably when Horsford was nominated. With both Peirce and Gray against him, his chances for election were lessened, and even if the Corporation had decided in his favor, any hope of harmony in the fledgling school would have been severely compromised.

Still another significant figure in the history of the Lawrence Scientific School was at that time beginning to make his mark on the local scene. Louis Agassiz had arrived in Boston in October 1846. He had come with letters of introduction to Edward

Everett and had been in touch with him soon after his arrival. He was an immediate social and scientific success. An entry in Everett's diary for January 12, 1847, reveals that he was in the audience that evening, when Agassiz, as part of a series of Lowell Institute lectures, delivered "decisive blows at the *Vestiges*."[41] How greatly his presentation tipped the scales against Rogers—at a time when Horsford was in town—is not clear, but Asa Gray reported to John Torrey in February:

> Rogers & his friends are grievously disappointed at the filling up of our Rumford Chair. Lately, since Agassiz has so unsparingly & thoroughly cut up Lamarckian Vestiges theories, Rogers & friends have found it was high time to disclaim them, and something, we know not what, induced them to think that, on *privately* renewing him as a candidate, they were to succeed in carrying on without our knowledge till all was done. But "it was the dog that died," as the song runs. It was *they* who were taken aback by the sudden appointment of another man.[42]

In the late 1850s Darwin's *Origin of Species* would lead Gray to change his views on evolution and also generate heated debates on the subject in both the Boston Society of Natural History and the American Academy of Arts and Sciences. As Agassiz continued to denounce roundly Darwin's theory, Gray found a true ally in William Rogers and would refer to him as "perhaps the most distinguished geologist and physicist of the United States, the elder brother of a most distinguished family of savants who have made the name illustrious."[43]

Late in January 1847 the committee on the establishment of a scientific school presented its report, and by mid-February a general plan was approved by the Corporation and Overseers for an "advanced School of Instruction in Theoretical and practical Science and in the other usual branches of Academic Learning, to be called the Scientific School of the University at Cambridge." The president and university faculty members providing instruction in the school would constitute the faculty. Admission would be granted not only to college graduates, but also to persons eighteen or older deemed to be qualified. Good moral character was a requisite, and bonds were to be furnished for the annual fee of $100, this income to be used for faculty compensation, a library and cabinet, and the general expenses. Requirements for a "suitable diploma" were to be decided by the faculty.[44]

Only a first step had been taken for an undertaking with no supporting funds except the income from the Rumford and with the curriculum still to be worked out. A final program would not be accepted by the Corporation until January 1848.[45] It is not clear how closely the committee wished to follow Peirce's proposal, which included languages, geography, and rhetoric from the "collegiate department." One member, James Walker, differed with Everett even before their report was submitted, for he was under the impression that they were expected to present a complete scientific curriculum, with no languages or history for the first classes of the proposed school.[46] The question of the inclusion of the humanities, a debate that would occupy educational circles well into the twentieth century, seemed, therefore, to be an early problem, significantly at an institution which had heretofore concentrated on the classics and a traditional curriculum.

When the Corporation named the faculty of the school, the five professors envisioned by Peirce in 1846 were included, along with the director and assistant observer of the Astronomical Observatory. Soon, however, professors of Latin and Greek literature were added.[47] And Everett invited Jared Sparks, McLean Professor of American and Modern History, to offer a course. "Although we call it 'Scientific,'" he said, "we have made provisions for students of Classical learning, and should be glad to increase the attractions for young men desirous of spending a year in finishing their education."[48] But Sparks did not "see how history can be taken into the plan with any prospect of success," for he doubted that those "desirous of pursuing an extended course in other branches" would be "sufficient to compensate the lecturers by any reasonable fees, or to excite the degree of interest so essential to every one, who would labor successfully in the field of instruction." He was not willing to "engage at present to prepare an extended historical course," and was, therefore, "not encouraged to believe that any aid from me can be made available for attaining the main object."[49]

When Everett proposed further appointments in mechanics (Treadwell, the late Rumford Professor), architecture, and history, the nominations were opposed by Samuel Eliot and laid on the table by the Corporation, causing Everett to complain in his diary that he was wanted only to "keep the books of the faculty and discipline."[50] That he still hoped to create a graduate school is evident in a letter to a British friend. "My wish," he said, "is to add a literary department for philological studies," making the school, "as far as the very different circumstances of the country demand & admit, a kind of German university. The experiment (for such of course it is) is undertaken in pursuance of an idea thrown out in my inaugural address."[51]

When Everett informed Horsford of his election to the Rumford, he indicated that the salary would be $1,500, holding out the hope of an opportunity to give some

Lowell lectures. He promised two hours a day at most of teaching in one term and one in the other, with the remainder to be lecturing or hearing recitations. He promised also a good, well-furnished laboratory and as much time as possible for the pursuit of investigations. Horsford would be expected to "take a leading part" in the "projected Scientific School," which Everett hoped would open in the fall, and would "receive a proportionate share of what may accrue from it." Everett added that it was "impossible to say how much this expectation may be worth, or whether it be worth anything."[52]

Soon after Horsford formally accepted the appointment, the Corporation approved the necessary transfer to him of the instruction in chemistry. Everett, Samuel Eliot, and Lowell were appointed a committee on the improvement of the chemical laboratory as well as the need for extended courses in geology and mineralogy, for which Webster would now be responsible.[53]

As Everett faced the urgent need for funds, particularly the problem of financial support for the laboratory promised to Horsford, he came to believe that his friend Abbott Lawrence, a major contributor in 1843 to a fund for the establishment of the Astronomical Observatory at Harvard, might be willing to help. A formal proposal was forwarded by Samuel Eliot, and by June 7, 1847, a special meeting of the Corporation was held to consider an offer of $50,000 from Lawrence for the support of a scientific school.[54] The donation was an amount almost unprecedented in those times, and the offer was promptly accepted. Everett immediately wrote Lawrence, praising him as a "benefactor of the first class" and promising to confer with him at length on "our Scientific School, which had before only a paper existence."[55]

Everett was naturally pleased, but a diary entry reveals a measure of concern. He had "taken all the responsibility of organizing the Scientific School" and of "procuring the appointment of Mr. Horsford, whom not a member of the Corporation knew." He had encouraged Horsford to "propose the erection of a laboratory, which no one had thought of" and "suggested to Mr. Eliot the possibility that Mr. Lawrence would endow it, which had not entered into his head." Now he found "the endowment of Mr. Lawrence—in which seemingly the entire Organization of the School will for the present merge—brought out to the public in a manner to connect with it every name but mine."[56]

Abbott Lawrence was a prominent merchant and manufacturer who played a leading role in the development of the textile industry and in the founding of the city named in his honor. He was a prominent public figure as well, active in politics, had served two terms in Congress, and would, in 1849, be appointed United States minister to the Court of St. James.[57] His letter to Eliot dated June 7, 1847, contained more than an offer of money. It was a detailed discussion of the need for engineering and scientific education, with specific instructions about how the funds were to be used.

This proposal was prepared with the aid of Charles S. Storrow, chief engineer and treasurer of the Essex Company, of which Lawrence was president.[58] Storrow, whom Peirce had briefly mentioned in his 1838 letter to President Quincy concerning a school for civil engineers, was born in 1809, the son of a commission merchant of an old Boston family. His early education was obtained largely in France, where his father was engaged in business. He was graduated from Harvard in 1829 with a bachelor of arts degree, ranking first in his class. Like his classmate Benjamin Peirce, he had demonstrated an exceptional ability in mathematics. Most graduates of that time entered the ministry or the law, with some choosing medicine or business, but Storrow was an exception. He intended to become "a civil engineer," and he would return to France for training,[59] after a brief association with the office in Charlestown of Loammi Baldwin the younger.

Early in 1830 Storrow entered the École des Ponts et Chaussées, where he developed a special interest in the subject of hydraulics, not only in its theoretical aspects, but also in its practical applications. From France he went on to England to learn by observation the elements of construction and operation of railways. Back in Boston in 1832 he joined the engineering staff of the Boston & Lowell Railroad, the first steam railroad in New England. He must have been a very valuable addition, for it appears that he was the only staff member who had ever seen a locomotive. He was soon placed in charge as agent.

Next he became engaged in the planning and development of a new textile town below Lowell on the Merrimac River that would bear the name of Lawrence. The project was sponsored by the Essex Company, organized by the Bostonians who had first established mills in Lowell and built the Boston & Lowell Railroad. Storrow, now a member of the company, undertook the design of dams, canals, locks, and mill buildings, and as chief engineer directed their construction. Moreover, he planned streets and parks, schools and churches. To this new city of Lawrence Storrow devoted much of his active life, serving with vision, integrity, and wisdom, and thus transpired his long and close relationship with Abbott Lawrence, as well as his clear insight into the urgent need for trained engineers.[60]

The original impetus of the Lawrence proposal was the need for education in the applications of science to useful purpose. Our inherited "sterile soil," he felt, provided "perhaps stronger motives in New England than in any other part of the country to encourage scientific pursuits, from the fact that we must hereafter look for our main support to the pursuit of commerce, manufactures, and the mechanic arts." Citing deficiencies in higher education relating to "certain branches of knowledge," he asked:

> Where can we send those who intend to devote themselves to the practical applications of science? How educate our engineers, our miners, machinists, and mechanics? Our country abounds in men of action. Hard hands are ready to work upon our hard materials; and where shall sagacious heads be taught to direct those hands? . . . We need, then, a school, not for boys, but for young men whose early education is completed either in college or elsewhere, and who intend to enter upon an active life as engineers or chemists, or in general, as men of science, applying their attainments to practical purposes.[61]

Lawrence called for a first-rate faculty, physical facilities, philosophical apparatus, cabinets of ores and metals, as well as "the most thorough instruction in Engineering, Geology, Chemistry, Mineralogy, Natural Philosophy, and Natural History." He suggested "three permanent professors"—chemistry, engineering, and geology—with "eminent men from the practical walks of life" brought in at "stated periods," for "this School of Science should number among its teachers men who have practised, and are practising the arts they are called to teach. Let theory be proved by practical results." He believed that the faculty "should depend to a considerable extent upon fees," as the "best guarantee to exertion and fidelity, and the permanent prosperity of the institution." Finally, he asked that "the whole income of this school be devoted to the acquisition, illustration, and dissemination of the practical sciences forever."[62]

In the weeks that followed there were a number of meetings and "little perplexities," as Everett called them, and it became clear that Abbott Lawrence intended to participate actively in decisions concerning the proposed school.[63] Late in June 1847 Everett sent Samuel Eliot a copy of the program drawn up prior to Lawrence's offer, calling it "only a *project*," since it had never been submitted to the scientific faculty for formal approval. He pointed out also that it was a time for decisions, but "considering the great division of responsibility and agency which exists among us I have doubts whether we actually get to work in September."[64] Eliot believed the entire program did not have to begin "at once like a great exhibition" and suggested a partial opening, prompting Everett to complain that "our worthy Treasurer regards me in the light of a Proctor and treats me on all occasions with about as much consideration."[65]

Lawrence expected to be consulted before any faculty appointments were made, and though Eliot and Horsford could settle on building plans, he, Lawrence, would select the builder. He requested that suitable buildings be erected at once for the chemical, engineering, and geological departments—not, however, to include dwellings for the professors. The accounts of the school were to be kept separate from all other funds, and the Corporation was to establish tuition fees distinct from the college fees, with current expenses to be paid from those fees. And he laid out a plan whereby remaining funds were to be invested to achieve an eventual endowment for the engineering and geology professorships. Thereafter the income was to be devoted "to the teaching and diffusion of scientific knowledge as *then* applied to the practical Arts." Beyond the right to extend "the School, by combining some other branches of science whenever I may deem it expedient," he proposed to "leave the matter in your hands, with the hope that you may be successful in procuring the services of *able heads* and *devoted hearts* to the cause of science."[66]

The discussions continued, with impatience on the part of Lawrence and frustration on that of Everett, who noted that Lawrence was dissatisfied with "poor Professor P," urging Everett to get rid of him—not, said Everett, "an easy process."[67] Sensing that Samuel Eliot had offended Lawrence by referring to Peirce as the "father of the Scientific School," Everett explained that Peirce had been calling for such a school for several years and had, in fact, prepared a plan prior to the decision of the Corporation and Overseers to establish one. Speaking not only for himself, but also for the Corporation, he assured Lawrence that they were fully aware of the importance of his donation:

> I shall make it a special duty, now and hereafter, (and this, whether my connection with the University be long or short) to see, as far as depends on me, that full justice is done to this rare act of liberality. Your name will be connected with the School, in the manner most acceptable to yourself; not to be forgotten while anything belonging to Cambridge is remembered.[68]

Late in August the Corporation voted to name the Scientific School for Lawrence, a decision received with "great applause."[69] They had recently voted to begin only with chemistry, deferring the full opening until professors were secured for geology and engineering, a decision for which they really had no alternative. Six students enrolled in the fall.[70]

There were more "perplexities" ahead, however, arising partly from the concept of the school in the minds of its proponents. Everett still cherished the idea of the German university and the extension of the collegiate curriculum beyond the baccalaureate. Peirce's proposal had envisioned an engineering school with a well-rounded curriculum, while Lawrence proposed that they concentrate initially on chemistry, engineering, and geology. Horsford would prove to be interested chiefly in his chemistry, and the engineering post would be difficult to fill. It happened that the geology chair would fall easily into place, perhaps too easily. It was an appointment that would profoundly influence the character and future of the Lawrence Scientific School.

In mid-June 1847 Everett had mentioned the prospect of a very competent professor of geology.[71] When Henry Rogers, still up to date on Harvard affairs, informed his brother William of Abbott Lawrence's donation, he indicated that Lawrence was discussing the geology professorship with Louis Agassiz.[72] Agassiz had captured Boston's fancy from the moment of his arrival in the fall of 1846, and Lawrence, Lowell, and Everett had been no less captivated than the general public. With his European background and training in science, his considerable reputation and charismatic personality, his boundless energy and persuasive eloquence, who could be a more obvious candidate for the geology professorship of the new scientific school?

As a naturalist, Agassiz's interests were by no means limited to the "animal kingdom." He had made extensive studies of glaciers and the ice age in Switzerland and had published significant works on the subject. But he was not a well-rounded geologist, and there were several Americans, the Rogers brothers among them, who might well and profitably have been considered. However, the inclusion of a chair of geology in Lawrence's proposal and his reservation of the right to combine "some other branches of science whenever I may deem it expedient" may well have been made with Agassiz in mind.

With the approval and encouragement of Lawrence—an approval he was later greatly to regret—Agassiz was invited to become a member of the faculty. His wishes with respect to title were followed, and on September 25, 1847, the Corporation formally elected him "Professor of Zoology and Geology in the Lawrence Scientific School in the University at Cambridge."[73] In some ways it was a fortunate choice for the cause of graduate education and the advancement of research at Harvard, as well as for the cause of science for its own sake in the United States, but it was hardly in harmony with the ideas and objectives of Lawrence and the school he had endowed.

Nearly two years would pass before an engineering professor could be secured. One candidate had presented himself as early as November 1846. William M. Gillespie, who only the year before had been appointed professor of engineering at Union College, expressed an interest in a similar post if a scientific school were to be established. But despite letters of support, material relating to his course at Union, and personal calls between November 1846 and August 1847, he seems not to have been seriously considered.[74]

In June 1847 Everett had also expected an early appointment for engineering. The first choice had been Charles Storrow, whom Lawrence wanted not only for that post, but also as head of the school. Storrow declined, however, electing to remain with the new city of Lawrence, where there was much to be done. John Freeman, who considered Storrow the "best educated engineer in America," would later say that Storrow "felt that he should enjoy himself better in the actual direction of a large engineering enterprise than he should to settle down into a professorship."[75]

Next Sylvanus Thayer was called on for help. He suggested Edward H. Courtenay, professor of mathematics since 1842 at the University of Virginia, where he had been a colleague of William Barton Rogers. An honor graduate of West Point, he had taught natural and experimental philosophy and engineering there, as well as mathematics at the University of Pennsylvania. He had been an engineer with the New York & Erie Railroad and was associated with several construction projects, among them Fort Independence in Boston Harbor.[76] He also declined, partly for financial reasons and partly because he had been away from practical engineering for several years. An offer from Abbott Lawrence for an additional salary payment did not change his mind.[77]

Two who might have placed a different stamp on the school about to be launched had now declined, and the search went on, with Thayer continuing to explore possibilities among graduates of West Point. Despite suggestions from several sources, a few applications, some directly to Abbott Lawrence, as well as some prominent names who declined to be considered or to accept appointment, the post remained unfilled. It appears that Thayer declined it himself. In the fall of 1848 the Corporation elected Captain Henry W. Halleck, a West Point graduate then stationed in California, who refused to accept it.[78] Supposedly created for the advancement of practical technical education, the Scientific School had been notably unsuccessful in attracting a suitable engineering professor. The difficulty highlighted the urgent need for trained engineers and engineering professors beyond those that could be supplied by West Point.

When the program for the Scientific School was finally accepted late in January 1848, the Corporation voted to limit it to the "department of Physical and exact Science," thus eliminating classical studies and architecture, which Everett had wanted to include and for which he had a candidate. The decision was influenced by the "judgment and wish" of Abbott Lawrence, according to Everett, who hoped a way might still be found to fulfill "the original plan in its full extent." The school's faculty also adopted the program and elected Horsford as dean.[79]

Everett looked upon the new venture as "an attempt to introduce a supplementary course of Scientific instruction to be pursued without the restraint of Academic Discipline." He considered it "an experiment, at least as an appendage to an Institution, of which the most prominent department is subject to a purely academic organization."[80] This experiment, however, already had problems. Soon after the chemical course opened in the fall of 1847, Everett noted in his diary that Horsford was "not yet a popular teacher,"[81] a situation duly reported by Henry Rogers to his friend George Hillard then in Rome. Hillard felt "a sort of savage satisfaction" in Horsford's "failure as a lecturer":

It is no more than just retribution to them for taking a pig in a poke in that manner, though it is mournful to think of the fate of our best endowed University in such hands. I feel more and more reason for being content with your not being there.[82]

There were financial problems as well. The administration considered petitioning the legislature for aid from the state's School Fund for a library and scientific apparatus and were advised by the chief justice not to do so at that time, but to move slowly and perhaps try to interest other institutions in joining with them in an appeal.[83] To Everett the school was "a slender affair without endowment (effective), without hello, without life. I would fain do what little I can to remedy the evil but I want both influence and power; to say nothing of health."[84] He noted the difficulty of building up an "institution wholly without funds for any purpose of general expenditure." And by August 1848 he was referring to the Lawrence Scientific School as "really in a poor way" because of an "entire absence of funds."[85]

Even before Agassiz delivered his first lecture in the spring of 1848, he had asked the Corporation for a museum.[86] By fall he was complaining about his salary, became embroiled in a controversy involving Horsford and his assistant, and expressed doubts about the condition of the school, claiming that Horsford was promoting that which was "economically useful" rather than pure science.[87]

Early in July Everett notified the Corporation of his intention to resign, effective at the end of the next term.[88] He bowed out on February 1, 1849, to be succeeded by Jared Sparks, another of Samuel Eliot Morison's "minor prophets." In acknowledging a letter from the faculty on his resignation, Everett commented on the Lawrence Scientific School:

> I have been influenced by the persuasion that superior culture in Natural and exact Sciences and in their application to the arts of life is among the urgent wants of our country. I have felt confident that without encroaching upon time and means sacred to the academic departments, there is an amount of talent and learning at command in Cambridge, capable . . . of being called into action for the object alluded to, with signal benefit to the country and credit to the University.[89]

Agassiz continued to complain and in the summer of 1849 sent Lawrence a some-what tactless reminder of the need he had pointed out two years before and now confirmed by experience—a regular appropriation of funds:

> If your object is still such as you repeatedly expressed to me, to promote science at the same time you educate practical men, you must place your professors in a position in which they can devote the greater part of their time to original investigations. . . . Do not object, as you once did, that if the School can not sustain itself, it would only show that it is in advance of the age and that you must wait.[90]

He guaranteed that if given what he asked for, there would be "a Museum worth looking at which shall do more to increase the reputation of the Scientific School and attract pupils than several more buildings." And he added: "As it may be of very little consequence to the Scientific School whether I remain connected with it or not, I cannot expect that my view should have great influence with you."[91]

Abbott Lawrence, about to take up his duties as minister to the Court of St. James, was moved to set the record straight. A September 1849 letter to Samuel Eliot, to be substituted for his July 1847 communication, set forth his intentions with respect to the school in the light of two years' experience. He had reservations about views expressed in Agassiz's letter and a document received from the school's faculty "that it is necessary, or important, or even desirable that the Scientific man should be raised above the necessity of taking care for himself, and his household, in order that he may devote his whole soul to scientific investigations":

Neither the history of the most important scientific discoveries, nor the facilities for the prosecution of scientific investigations afforded by any institution in the world with which I am acquainted, justifies the belief that such provision is best for the professor, or for the science to which he devotes himself. His mind is stimulated to more valuable effort by sharing with the rest of mankind, in a degree of uncertainty as to the future. If a portion, therefore, of his means of support be provided with as much security as human life allows, the rest may well be left to his own exertions.[92]

Lawrence now proposed that the three professorships—chemistry, engineering, and geology—be "placed financially on a separate foundation." Current expenses should come from student fees, and "if the students are not prepared to pay the cost of such a portion of an education which has an immediate pecuniary value, the attempt to give it had better be discontinued." The letter reveals that his $50,000 donation was under his control, and he intended now that the remainder be used to fund the engineering professorship. The college would have to find elsewhere the funds for buildings and collections that he once hoped to support.

Lawrence continued to believe in the importance of geology and was impressed "with the eminent attainments, and the admirable powers, both intellectual and moral," of Agassiz. But students had not enrolled for this subject, and he would not now provide a permanent fund for this post, believing that "the time for its immediate usefulness in the way of instruction has not arrived." As evidence of his "estimate of the value of Mr. Agassiz's services to the cause of science," he promised $1,500 a year for five years "with the wish that it may enable him to do, if not so much as he hoped, yet something not unimportant for the progress of Science," the Corporation to decide what duties might be required of him. The message was clear. Lawrence expected the Corporation "to provide good instruction in Chemistry, and Civil Engineering, in the manner which has been all along contemplated by them and myself, and which seems demanded by the present state of the knowledge and wants of the community in which we live."[93]

Shortly, President Sparks offered the engineering professorship to Lieutenant Henry L. Eustis of West Point and informed him about the arrangements now proposed by Lawrence. Eustis was elected by the Corporation on September 29, 1849, and accepted early in October. The son of a brigadier general in the United States Army, he was born at Fort Independence in Boston in 1819. After graduation from Harvard College with honors in 1838, he entered the Military Academy. Ranking first in his class, he was commissioned as second lieutenant in 1842 and joined the Engineer

Corps. Following service as assistant engineer on the construction of sea-walls in Boston Harbor and then as engineer in charge of projects for the improvement of Newport Harbor, he returned to West Point in 1847 as assistant professor of engineering. His Harvard tenure would last for many years, and he served as dean of the Lawrence School in 1862-63 and from 1871 to 1885.[94]

As the year 1849 drew to a close, Harvard was rocked by a scandalous event. On November 23, Professor John W. Webster murdered Dr. George Parkman of Boston, who was pursuing him for repayment of a loan. Parkman had called on him at his laboratory at the Medical School and was never seen again. Webster had fatally struck his creditor, and, himself a doctor, had used his talents in a systematic effort to dispose of the body, parts of which were discovered by the janitor in the brick vaults of the building. Webster's trial was sensational. He was convicted and hanged in August of 1850.[95] Soon after the discovery of the killing, James Rogers suggested that Henry might seek Webster's chair, the Erving Professorship of Chemistry and Mineralogy.[96] There is no evidence that he did so. The post went to Josiah P. Cooke, then instructor in chemistry and mineralogy, early in 1851.

The Webster-Parkman incident occurred during a period when Harvard was suffering from what Samuel Eliot Morison has called a "fresh political assault." The attack stemmed from a complicated set of issues touching upon Harvard's governance, the control of the Corporation by Unitarians, the elective system, academic freedom, and the nature of the curriculum. It was a stormy period, with sharp political differences exacerbated by equally sharp differences of opinion with respect to abolition, and a perception on the part of some that the institution was "the haven of a smug aristocracy."[97]

In January 1850 the state legislature appointed a special committee, chaired by George Boutwell, then a representative from Groton, "to consider and report what legislation, if any, is necessary to render Harvard University more beneficial to all the people of the Commonwealth." Their report in April concluded that despite "its early history, its great reputation, its central position, and, when compared with other American institutions, its unequalled resources. . . . *the college fails to answer the just expectations of the people of the State.*" They attributed this failure partly to Harvard's reluctance to acknowledge that times had changed, and though there was still some interest in "general learning, for its own sake," there was now far greater demand for "specific learning for a specific purpose." Many, they said, "would gladly resort to an institution of the higher class, for a limited period of time, if they could there obtain instruction which would make them better farmers, or mechanics, or engineers, or merchants."[98]

The committee identified as a basic problem the life tenure and self-perpetuating nature of the Corporation, which "leads to the perpetuity of particular opinions in education and religion."[99] It is interesting to note in this connection that during the search surrounding the Rumford Professorship questions had been raised about the theological opinions of Henry Rogers; Webster had emphasized the Unitarian beliefs of Horsford; and President Eliphalet Nott of Union College had mentioned that William Gillespie's religious ideas were not in tune with those of New York, but would provide no obstacle in Boston.[100] The committee recommended that legislative action be taken to increase the Corporation's membership to fifteen. Except for the president and treasurer, the members would be elected by the legislature for limited terms.[101] A minority report was also filed, objecting mainly to the proposal that would radically change the election and tenure of the Corporation.[102] No immediate action ensued, and a very different General Court elected in the fall enabled Harvard to preserve the status quo.[103]

This was a time, says Samuel Eliot Morison, "when most things were tested by utilitarian values."[104] These values, however, would endure. They had inspired Peirce's proposal and Lawrence's intentions with respect to the school, and they would find expression later in an effort to found an Institute of Technology in Boston.

With a new set of instructions from Abbott Lawrence and the addition of Eustis as professor of engineering, the school appeared to be on its way. It was not exactly what Everett had hoped for, since it was to be narrowly focused on the scientific side, the extension of the regular academic course into a graduate year having been set aside. Discussions about the arrangement of the school continued, and further committees were appointed to consider the problems. Horsford and Agassiz were on opposite sides with respect to many educational issues, and the treasurer, complaining that the school's funds were in an "irregular condition," commented that "heedless professors seem to think they have a rich college and a richer founder to spend for them as much as they want. They'll swamp our Treasury and bankrupt Lawrence."[105]

The school evolved, too, in a manner quite contrary to the hopes and plans of its early proponents. The appointment of Agassiz had been widely hailed, but Lawrence and others initially failed to grasp that he was guided by a philosophy at odds with the beliefs and purposes fundamental to practical technical education. He was dedicated to the view that only pure science had a place in a university. He scorned the teaching of practical science or those subjects designed to qualify students for the active pursuits of life. As a geologist he was concerned with the ice age and the shaping of the earth, but knew nothing, nor cared, about mining or mineralogy. Though he could be difficult, he was yet a man of personal charm and certainly of persuasive eloquence. He was a dynamic lecturer for general audiences and an avid teacher of teachers. For a number of years the school became identified in the public mind with his presence and initiative. In short, he had "stolen the show."[106]

The school awarded its first bachelor of science degrees in 1851 on the basis of attendance for at least one year and passing an examination on subjects chosen by the student and approved by the faculty.[107] Of the four graduates that year, two had been studying with Agassiz, who approached them in June about taking a degree in the Lawrence Scientific School. One, the eminent naturalist Joseph LeConte, later said he was not particularly interested but that Harvard wished to have something to show for its first year of full operation, and he consented: "I was already a much graduated man, having the degrees of A.B., A.M., and M.D. . . . and had had no idea up to that time of becoming a student in the Scientific School, or indeed of having any official connection with Harvard at all, having come simply to study with Agassiz."[108] John D. Runkle of New York, also one of the four, had been enrolled since 1848, and in December 1851 was also awarded an honorary master of arts degree.[109] He would later become directly involved in the organization of the Massachusetts Institute of Technology and serve as both a long-term member of its faculty and its second president.

During the early days the Lawrence Scientific School did not function as a cohesive unit but consisted rather of small, separate groups, each comprising a professor and his students—in effect, a tutorial system well suited to the wide divergences in the degree of student preparation.[110] For a time chemistry was the best situated. A substantial portion of Lawrence's funds was applied to the construction of a chemical laboratory. It was one of the first in the United States organized and equipped for teaching analytical chemistry to individual students and is said to have exerted a profound influence on the development of analytical chemistry in America. In the conduct of laboratory instruction Eben Horsford was a pioneer in bringing European methods to the New World, but his interests lay more in the direction of graduate instruction and research than in elementary teaching, and his fiscal management of the laboratory left much to be desired. The students enrolled for chemistry were not as many as he had originally hoped to attract, nor did their degree of preparation or commitment to long-term study meet his expectations. His income not only fell far short of his needs, but also, he felt, was entirely out of proportion to the amount of work he was required to do.[111] Increasingly he turned his attention to practical research that might lead to financial gain.

Horsford was not alone in his complaints. Agassiz, determined to establish at Harvard a great museum of natural history comparable to the French Jardin des Plantes, continued to press for financial help and also demanded from the Corporation an indication of their plans with respect to his "means of existence."[112] There were recurring questions about the relation of the Harvard Observatory to the Scientific School,[113] and repeated suggestions from the visiting committees that the usefulness of the Scientific School might be improved if instruction were to be limited to practical science, pure science being "classed as a separate department."[114]

When Abbott Lawrence died in 1855, the school to which he had given his support was plagued by financial, organizational, and personality problems, and even his bequest of an additional $50,000 did not solve the difficulties. A clear set of institutional goals had not yet emerged, and the school's relations to the university were ill-defined. Despite all its problems, however, many of its students became distinguished leaders in their respective fields.[115]

No story of the early days of the Massachusetts Institute of Technology would be complete without due recognition of the Lawrence Scientific School as a forerunner of higher scientific and technical education in Boston, as a powerful neighbor, as a potentially threatening rival, and, along with Harvard College, as the principal source of MIT's earliest faculty. But one thing is clear: neither William nor Henry Rogers believed that Harvard had preempted their own ideas for a polytechnic school in Boston.

In February 1848 Henry told William that Joseph Lovering, Hollis Professor of Mathematics and Natural Philosophy, did not expect large numbers to enroll in the Lawrence Scientific School. Agassiz, Henry said, would attract some but his "general attractiveness" would not be particularly helpful, as the enterprise was intended "for professional young men, or those aiming at a career in Science or the useful arts. . . . The real opening here is among the mechanical classes, etc."[116] The brothers, evidently, were determined to forge ahead.

The Founding of MIT

Chapter 7

---

*Pre-Historic Annals
of the Institute*

By the late 1850s several societies in Boston, reflecting in part the general growth of the city and its surrounding communities, had reached the point where their accommodations were either too small for their purposes or no longer suitable for their developing and changing activities. This pressure for additional space combined with the imminent availability of new land in the Back Bay provided the impetus for a movement which sought from the state a reservation of a portion of this land for the use of these institutions.

At the same time a man named William Emerson Baker was beginning to promote a "comprehensive project, namely, the erection of a building, for the accommodation of the various historical and kindred societies having their seat in Boston."[1] Though his plan for a Conservatory of Art, Science, and Historical Relics has often been cited as the source of the effort that eventually led to the founding of the Massachusetts Institute of Technology, Baker actually took no part at all in the Institute's establishment. It is true, however, that his plan did serve initially as a catalyst in bringing together for possible concerted action three organizations seeking solutions to their space problems—the New England Historic Genealogical Society, the Boston Society of Natural History, and the Massachusetts Horticultural Society. Soon individuals with broader interests in popular education and technical instruction would be drawn in, supporting a proposal to set aside some of the newly developing Back Bay lands for philanthropic and educational purposes. Though strains would develop within this loose confederation, leading to Baker's withdrawal, his ability in the early stages to capture the public attention was critical to the success of the final venture.

Baker was a wealthy manufacturer of sewing machines for domestic and commercial use, a gregarious and flamboyant individual with a penchant for grandiose schemes. Born in Roxbury in 1828, he left high school at the age of sixteen because of straitened family circumstances. He proved to be an avid salesman for a wool-jobbing firm, developed an interest in the sewing machine, and early in the 1850s joined forces with William O. Grover, a Boston tailor who had bought manufacturing rights to the sewing machine from Elias Howe. They soon organized the Grover and Baker Sewing Machine Company, with a salesroom in the Mercantile Building at 18 Summer Street, where the Massachusetts Institute of Technology would later rent space to begin operations. The company was successful, and branch offices were opened in New York, Philadelphia, Baltimore, and other cities. Many valuable patents with applications to commercial use were issued to Grover and Baker, as well as a patent for the first portable sewing machine. A series of suits eventually resulted in the joining together of the Isaac M. Singer Company, Wheeler & Wilson, and Grover & Baker in a so-called "trust," which reputedly monopolized the sewing machine market for more than twenty years. Between 1854 and 1856 Baker was in Europe, selling sewing machines, overseeing their manufacture under license, and involved in litigation to protect the Grover & Baker patent rights. By the time he returned to the United States, the business was making money despite legal costs abroad, and his own fortune was advancing rapidly.

With the business on a firm footing, Baker found time to turn his attention and energies to a large, ambitious project such as his proposed conservatory. It is quite likely that the Conservatoire des Arts et Métiers in Paris and similar European institutions with which he had become familiar provided inspiration for the plan, which he began to promote in the late 1850s.[2]

The New England Historic Genealogical Society, with quarters at 13 Bromfield Street, was already contemplating the construction of a building of its own when Baker became an active member in 1857. It was a project of which he heartily approved. Soon he brought before the society his conservatory plan, and by February 1859, a special committee having given it favorable consideration "in general," a further committee was appointed to confer with representatives of other societies. The Genealogical Society did not continue for long as a part of this effort, and it would be 1871 before it was able to relocate through purchase of a building on Somerset Street. Some of its members, however, were active in the promotion of the conservatory and in succeeding proposals by virtue of their particular interests and connection with other organizations.[3]

In the fall of 1858 the Massachusetts Horticultural Society was considering whether to move, alter their building at School Street, construct a new one elsewhere, or rebuild at their present site. They cooperated on the conservatory plan and continued through later proposals, though in a rather half-hearted manner, marked by misgivings and many doubts. They would remain in the picture until the spring of 1861 and withdraw at the final moment. As in the case of the Genealogical Society, some members had other compelling reasons to support the developing plans for the Back Bay and were active in their promotion. Baker also approached the Board of Trade for support, but consideration of his plan was postponed "on the ground principally that, wanting a distinct commercial feature, the project belonged to institutions of a literary and scientific nature, rather than to one exclusively devoted to trade."[4]

Finally, there was the Boston Society of Natural History, founded in 1830. Its quarters on Mason Street had for a long time been unsatisfactory. Each year the mounting problems strengthened the resolve of the members to find better accommodations, leading to consideration in 1857 of a site in the south part of the city, then being developed, but "the mercantile disasters of that season prevented any immediate action."[5] By 1859 the need was urgent. As the society joined with others as a major participant in a larger effort, it continued to maintain its independent goals and identity as a separate institution.

The year 1859 saw the first formal approach to the legislature for space on the Back Bay for the Natural History Society and other associations. Central to an understanding of the events of 1859 and the two succeeding years is an address by Governor Nathaniel P. Banks at the opening of the legislative session in January. In his annual report on the accomplishments of the previous year, the financial condition of the state, and problems for consideration in the ensuing months, the governor raised two important issues that would bear directly on the fate of projects not yet before the legislature: the disposition of the proceeds of the sale of the Back Bay land, to which the Commonwealth had been given title by the Supreme Court, and the need for study and illustration of the natural history of the state.

Moderate expectations forecast that the Back Bay land sales could bring in from three to five million dollars within five years. With admonitions that "an overflowing treasury is prolific of unwise legislation," and in the absence of large public debts, Governor Banks presented a proposal for the use of the anticipated funds: "I trust the legislature will be able to make provision for the application of this property to such public educational improvements as will keep the name of the Commonwealth forever green in the memory of her children;—and to this end I earnestly recommend, for reasons already stated, that the first public charge to be made upon this property shall be for the enlargement of the public school fund until it net the sum of THREE MILLION DOLLARS."[6] The figure of three million dollars had been recommended by the Board of Education and its secretary, George Boutwell, a former governor, "as a measure indispensable to the full success of the common school system."[7] In support of his proposal, the governor reminded the legislature that "there are a half million persons in the Commonwealth, under twenty-one years of age, who must seek their scholastic training in the Public Schools alone."[8]

In January 1828 a report of the Committee on Education of the House of Representatives had "declared that means should be devised for the establishment of a fund having in view not the support, but the encouragement, of the common schools, and the instruction of school-teachers."[9] A permanent fund was again suggested in 1833, with some of the proceeds of the sale of Commonwealth lands to be invested and the interest made available annually for this purpose. The committee report at that time made its intentions clear:

> It is not intended, in establishing a school fund, to relieve towns and parents from the principal expense of education, but to manifest our interest in, and to give direction, energy, and stability to, institutions essential to individual happiness and the public welfare. . . . Therefore we recommend that a fund be constituted, and the distribution of the income so ordered as to open a direct intercourse with the schools; that their wants may be better understood and supplied, the advantages of education be more highly appreciated, and the blessings of wisdom, virtue, and knowledge, carried home to the fireside of every family, to the bosom of every child.[10]

Chapter 169 of the Acts of 1834 finally established the Massachusetts School Fund, effective January 1, 1835, using unappropriated funds already in the treasury.[11]

The fund functioned in this way: one half of the annual income was distributed among the cities and towns according to the number in each of children between the ages of five and fifteen, with the proviso that no money would be granted to "any town or city which had not sent in a report, and which had not raised by taxation for the support of schools, during the previous school-year," the equivalent initially of at least $1.50 for every child in the above age bracket, a sum which would double by 1869. From the School Fund a town apparently received twenty or twenty-five cents per child, a seemingly small sum, but important for the incentive it provided to raise by taxation the ever-increasing amounts needed for education.[12] The remaining half of the income from the School Fund went to the normal schools for teacher training, and "schools for the blind, for the deaf and dumb, for feeble-minded persons, &c."[13] It was inevitable that costs would continue to rise, increasing the importance in the minds of state legislators and town officials of the enlargement of the School Fund, both as a source of additional support for public education and as an incentive for communities to assume responsibility for the basic funds needed for this purpose. Any threat, no matter how small, to the increase of this fund loomed large as a potential evil demanding the most rigorous opposition.

With respect to the natural history of the state, the governor, in his 1859 address to the legislature, pointed to the efforts of Charles L. Flint, the secretary of the State Board of Agriculture, to form a collection of illustrative specimens:

> The idea, creditable alike in conception and execution, is suggestive of scientific enterprises of greater moment, than a chance collection crowded into the vacant rooms of the capitol. Ought not Massachusetts, in the flush of wealth and power, to provide for the most complete illustration of her own natural history, or at least blend her efforts with the co-operative power of individuals, associations and institutions, partially or altogether devoted to natural science, for the initiation of a work, the commencement of which would shed additional lustre on her name. . . . Neither the means, the occasion, nor the agents are wanting for its complete success. . . . We have also private and public associations devoted to science, collections of specimens that would honor European cabinets, not publicly exhibited; young men of energy to follow the career of Humboldt, and Audubon, in pursuing wisely directed inquiry; and among individual devotees of science, we have the first naturalist of the age, to direct their labors. . . . The world would wish such an enterprise success.[14]

Clearly it was Louis Agassiz and his plans for a great museum in Cambridge that the governor had in mind, lending support to Agassiz's hopes that the legislature would see fit to finance, at least partially, his proposed Museum of Comparative Zoology at Harvard.[15] He had long dreamed of a teaching museum, loosely associated with Harvard but with a separate faculty independent of the university and the Lawrence

Scientific School. He envisioned a great establishment along the lines of the Jardin des Plantes in France and had been actively seeking ways to achieve this goal since his unsuccessful appeal to Abbott Lawrence in 1854. When Lawrence died in 1855, though he left Harvard sufficient funds to ensure a permanent faculty appointment for Agassiz, he made no provision for the much-desired museum. Agassiz did manage, however, to arouse the interest of Francis Calley Gray, an industrialist and former fellow of the Harvard Corporation, who died in December 1856, leaving a bequest of $50,000 for the founding of a museum, the money to go to Harvard or some other institution for the support of its scientific operations but not for buildings or salaries. Agassiz was determined that Harvard should administer this bequest, and he set about gaining the support of his visiting committee and making plans for the necessary fund raising. In December 1858, when the Corporation recorded Gray's letter of intent, the effort was under way. James Lawrence, Abbott's son, convened thirty influential friends of Harvard to hear of Agassiz's plans, and some fifteen of them formed a permanent committee, headed by Dr. Jacob Bigelow and Samuel Hooper, to raise a private subscription.

In March 1859 Agassiz is said to have stormed the State House, acknowledging that private funds would support the building but asserting that the state should also support the project, thereby providing permanence for the institution. Despite his preference for pure science, his statements laid particular emphasis on recent advances in *applied* geology and scientific *agriculture*, in deference no doubt to the practical tenor of the times. Agassiz brought his appeal for state funds to the legislature at precisely the time when the memorials by the Boston Society of Natural History and the committee concerned with a conservatory proposal were under consideration.

It is difficult to believe that the Natural History Society would either consider becoming a satellite of a new museum or relinquish its independence to Louis Agassiz. It is possible, however, that the governor's favorable comments concerning efforts in the field of natural science might have influenced their decision, despite his strong support for Agassiz, to ask for a grant of land in the Back Bay. As for William Baker and those beginning to show an interest in the conservatory proposal, other statements by Governor Banks might well have provided encouragement:

> THE STATE is the unit of our industrial system, and nothing should be disregarded which enlarges its resources, develops its wealth, or concentrates and controls its trade, in which lie the secrets of its power and prosperity.

The manufacturing interest, so heavily oppressed during the late financial crisis, and which has failed to receive that direct recognition which every branch of American industry may justly demand, though paralyzed by partial losses, is steadily advancing, and the energy and skill which planted it upon soil so far from the staple commodities which it works, will, I trust, at no distant day, re-establish something of its ancient prosperity. I recommend to you a favorable consideration of all measures which are designed to promote the interests of those who by investment of capital or labor are dependent upon its success. It may be expedient to inquire what improvement can be made in legislation relating to other industrial interests.[16]

When the proponents of the conservatory finally submitted to the legislature a memorial asking simply for a grant of land, a statement of their aims included a perhaps convenient misinterpretation of what the governor had really said: "To second and aid in carrying out the wise and liberal suggestion of his excellency the governor, in his Address alluding to the propriety of appropriating for Educational purposes the proceeds of sales of the Back Bay lands belonging to the Commonwealth, lying near the Public Garden in the City of Boston."[17] Certainly he had referred to "educational purposes" in his remarks, but it was the School Fund and the public school system that he identified as the beneficiaries of the proceeds of the Back Bay land sales. A later recollection of Matthias Denman Ross, a prominent participant in the conservatory effort, reveals that the governor was not wholly receptive to their ideas when they sought his support during the legislative session:

> We asked him to give us his co-operation in influencing the Legislature then in session to set apart, or reserve from sale, about twenty acres of space on the Back Bay. . . . Our purpose was to procure ample space for the educational institutions which the committee represented. . . . Governor Banks asked us what axe we had to grind, and our reply was, "The broad-axe of the State of Massachusetts, your Excellency; and we want you with the Legislature to turn the grindstone." . . . Our zeal was somewhat chilled, but we were not discouraged by the Governor's somewhat adverse attitude.[18]

The state's commitment to increase the principal of the School Fund, the appeal of Agassiz for financial support, and the governor's cold reception of the conservatory committee's ideas were three interrelated deterrents to successful passage of any proposal that could conceivably result in the lessening of money flowing into the School

Fund. A further deterrent would be the possible creation of an institution that, if successful, might eventually compete for both public interest and public money with the plan for a replica in Cambridge of the famed Jardin des Plantes. Such fears had ramifications beyond the simple decision to remove a few squares of land from sale.

The governor had clearly stated an intention to increase the principal of the School Fund. It is safe to say that he had not at all in mind the segregation of a few squares of the Back Bay for educational purposes. Nor was he recommending the expansion of existing societies or their coming together in a plan of grand proportions designed for the edification of the masses. As the conservatory idea was refined and developed, however, a proposal would be placed on the legislative agenda at every session until the end of Banks's term and fall to his successor, Governor John A. Andrew, to sign into law not only a grant of land, but also a charter for an institution intended to respond to the demands of a new age. Though Governor Andrew was favorably disposed toward the aims of the final proposal and supported its passage, he eventually expended every effort to combine the formal teaching functions of this new institution—the Massachusetts Institute of Technology—with Harvard University, the educational mecca already existing in Cambridge.

In January 1859 William Baker brought his conservatory plan before the Boston Society of Natural History. It was received with interest and apparently some skepticism. It did, however, serve to highlight an opportunity to petition the legislature for a portion of the Back Bay lands, and his proposal was referred to a committee under the chairmanship of Dr. Samuel Cabot, Jr., a well-known Boston surgeon and naturalist. The committee was soon empowered to add to their membership and to meet with representatives of other societies for the purpose of joint action in a petition to the legislature.[19]

In the meantime, Baker and Ross, a manufacturer vitally interested in the development of the Back Bay, were elected to membership, thus bringing in two individuals with special interests in the larger plan.[20] Both appear as committee members in the memorial finally submitted to the legislature by the society on February 25. In addition to Dr. Cabot as chairman, the petitioning committee also included Thomas T. Bouvé, William Barton Rogers, Thomas J. Whittemore, and Dr. Samuel Kneeland, Jr., secretary of the society.[21] Though a very active member of the society, Rogers was away from the city for much of the spring of 1859 and is said to have taken "but little part" in this effort.[22]

The first large-scale meeting on the project was held on February 18 at the Natural History Society, attended by "gentlemen representing the associations of Agriculture, Art and Science, and various industrial, educational and moral interests of the city."[23] This was an organizational gathering, at which Marshall P. Wilder, a merchant and horticulturist, was chosen as chairman and Kneeland, secretary:

> The object of the meeting was to take steps for memorializing the present legislature for a grant of land belonging to the Commonwealth, in aid of a plan for a conservatory of art and science. . . . A reading of a portion of the Governor's message, in which he refers to the value of the public land, and advises a certain disposition to be made of a portion of it, brought the subject fairly before the meeting.[24]

The record of the discussion reveals both support for the plan and the vagueness of its conception. Each supporter in turn viewed the proposal in the light of his own special interests—from the extension of knowledge and the elevation of "the intellectual standard of the community" to the furtherance of mercantile interests, the advancement of science and the arts, the development of agriculture, and exhibition space for both the fine arts and agricultural products and machinery. European examples, such as the Museum of Practical Geology and Kew Gardens in London, were cited. There was a perception that America was lagging behind Europe in the creation of such institutions, and a conviction that the existence of new land on the Back Bay presented a golden opportunity for the development of "some purposes of public improvement."

The Honorable Alexander H. Rice, a member of Congress and former mayor of Boston, "considered that some such plan as the one presented, for the enlargement and practical application of science in its various branches to the useful and ornamental arts of life, was imperatively demanded as an educational measure. Boston must have it; he considered it not a question of fact, but merely a question of time."

Louis Agassiz, "the first naturalist of the age," as referred to by Governor Banks and very much in the legislative eye at that moment, thought it was of "great importance, as occupying the middle ground between abstract science and its practical application. Science, in the abstract, must go alone, not hampered with any considerations of practical application, assisting but not interfering with each other; the moment they are combined in the same association, science must languish. Hence the importance of some institution occupying the ground of an interpreter between the two, which he thought the proposed plan would do."

Ross announced that "his own pursuits led him more especially to favor the section which would form a kind of Polytechnic Institute; the utility of this could not be questioned, and its probable success he thought merely a question of time." In responding, Agassiz referred to the "Polytechnic School," reiterating his belief that "such an institution, intermediate between trade and science, was vitally important; they could not be combined in the same association—this he likened to the high schools, which are the necessary medium between the primary school and the university."

John D. Philbrick, superintendent of the Boston Public Schools and president of the American Institute of Instruction, spoke also to the point of a polytechnic institution, saying that there was none "in America worthy of the name" and expressing the hope that Boston would take the lead in this respect as it had with primary and high schools. Terming it an "educational agent," he spoke specifically about the value of "a collection of objects illustrating education, from the primary school to the university" as being a "most desirable thing," and he also thought a "department of drawing and design patterns, almost entirely neglected here, was of great interest to the manufacturers of the country." Seemingly, at least the germ of an idea for a school was here.[25]

Marshall Wilder, highlighting his interest in agriculture, alluded to the "land bill now before Congress, which, if passed, would give the income of 220,000 acres of government land to Massachusetts to be devoted to an agricultural college if the State would erect the building." He hoped that perhaps this income might be devoted to the agricultural department of the proposed plan. The bill to which he referred was eventually vetoed by President Buchanan, but a persistent senator from Vermont named Justin Morrill would try again and succeed in obtaining passage in 1862 of a Land-Grant Act which would have a profound effect upon technical education in the United States.

The February 1859 meeting was rounded out by the presence of two nineteenth-century environmentalists. George H. Snelling and the Honorable Alexander Everett, taking a cue no doubt from a reference to "God's great gifts of light and air" in the governor's address, pleaded for more open space in the Back Bay to provide the fresh air and comfort that the citizens of Boston both needed and wanted, these benefits to be heightened by the ennobling effects of the "glorious prospect of the setting sun." In April, Snelling would carry his cause to the point of a memorial to the legislature, urging that a basin of water seven hundred feet wide be substituted for the planned Commonwealth Avenue. He was against filling the Back Bay, pointing out the advantages of retaining a body of water renewed twice a day, apparently neglecting to take into consideration the effects of the mud flats at low tide, a situation which the filling was precisely designed to alleviate.[26]

Certain that support would come from the Back Bay Commissioners, William Emerson Baker moved that a committee be appointed to prepare a memorial for a reservation of "sufficient space of the Commonwealth land for the purpose of the contemplated Conservatory of Art, Science, and Historical Relics." As finally constituted, the committee, which would act with power, consisted of himself, along with Benjamin F. Edmands, a dry goods merchant and retired major general of the Massachusetts militia; Samuel H. Gookin, also a dry goods merchant; George W. Pratt of the Horticultural Society; Alfred Ordway, president of the Boston Art Club and in charge of the Fine Art Gallery of the Boston Athenaeum; and Marshall P. Wilder as chairman.

The various interested societies were asked to prepare memorials in support of the project. In this connection Ross raised an important point. No doubt sensing that the varied interests were hardly prepared to formulate a definite plan at this time, he suggested that the main goal be to secure the land, at least four blocks of 600 x 200 feet each, for he feared that another opportunity to obtain ample space would never present itself again. Public support should be sought, and the plans "matured afterwards." It would not be too many years before Ross's foresight in the matter of the amount of land required could be viewed in hindsight with the deepest envy.

The committee of the Boston Society of Natural History was ready. On February 25, 1859, Samuel Cabot, as chairman, submitted a memorial setting forth the society's needs and asking for a grant of land on the Back Bay for itself and "other kindred Associations."[27]

Early in March the Massachusetts Horticultural Society voted to appoint a committee with its president, Joseph Breck, as chairman, to unite with the Natural History Society in the petition for a grant of land. Marshall P. Wilder and George W. Pratt of the large committee were among its members.[28] On March 9 the committee appointed by the citizens of the Commonwealth, as they then identified themselves, submitted a memorial to the legislature.[29] A copy of a printed version contains a notation by William Rogers that this document was drawn up by Samuel Kneeland.

The memorial was presented "in concert with a Committee representing the Boston Society of Natural History." It sought a grant of land so that existing organizations might associate themselves in proximity with one another, thus enlarging the usefulness of their collections, bringing together conveniently "a few leading Institutions, which, if once established on the ground, would form a nucleus around which would cluster kindred Associations of immense value to the people of the State." Each would retain its identity, but when gathered together, they "might be known" collectively "as the Massachusetts Conservatory of Art and Science." By this time the phrase "historical relics" had disappeared from the proposed title. Nor did it appear in the printed record of the meetings which culminated in this approach to the legislature.

The memorial suggested four squares and proposed that no legal title be conveyed, the land to revert to the state should the grantees in the future not continue to use it for the stated purpose. Though no detailed plan had yet been devised, the four squares "might be" divided into four sections: agriculture, horticulture, and pomology; natural history, practical geology, and chemistry, with "museums of specimens"; mechanics, manufactures, and commerce; and fine arts, history, and ethnology. Each should have sufficient space to accommodate institutions which "the future progress of the State may develop." The final paragraph acknowledged the efforts of Professor Agassiz toward the establishment of a museum in Cambridge "for the development of abstract science," and emphasized the "desire to co-operate with such labors in the building up of Institutions of a more directly practical character, which will enable the masses of the people, engaged in industrial occupations, more effectually to avail themselves of the advantages to be derived from the labors of those who are wholly devoted to purely scientific research."[30]

The memorial was referred to the legislature's Committee on the Back Bay Lands, and the testimony at two hearings in March 1859 bears witness to the all-encompassing nature of the proposal and its lack of definition. At the first hearing there were statements on the space needs of the Natural History and Horticultural societies, the State Board of Agriculture, and the Charitable Mechanics' Association. Ross mentioned a movement to establish an organization to promote manufactures, similar to an agricultural society. He was also confident that means could be found to erect buildings, referring to an unnamed gentleman ready to furnish $25,000. He was sure that at least $50,000 could be raised for buildings and a like amount for endowment.[31]

Immediately following the first hearing, a meeting was held to make further plans. There was much discussion, with repeated references to practical education and the benefits to be derived by manufactures, commerce, and trade. The value to the "State and to the Country" was emphasized, and the proposal was praised as "the most important movement that has ever been agitated in this community: There is a necessity for it; the time has passed when a mere college education is considered as sufficient to fit a man for the active duties of life; we now want and must have *practical* education, such as Institutions like the one proposed alone can give us."[32]

The Board of Trade, which had earlier declined to consider Baker's proposal, now appeared ready to do so, since "the interests of commerce and manufactures were made so prominent." There were gestures toward Agassiz, with reassurances that the effort "was not antagonistic to the Cambridge Museum plan":

> The Cambridge collection, as part of the educational apparatus of the University, did not in any way conflict with our Boston collection, which would be of more direct practical utility to the masses of the people. There seem to be insuperable objections to their union, but there was not a shadow of a reason for their opposition; they could work together in different parts of the same great field of Nature, for the good of all.[33]

Philbrick spoke to the "vast importance of our system of education":

> We had originated the first Normal School, which he considered the greatest step yet made in the method of instruction; let us go a step farther, and establish the first truly Polytechnic School, which shall bring within the reach and understanding of all the results of abstract science.[34]

Ross felt certain that the plan would come before the committees on education and on finance in addition to the Back Bay Lands Committee, and urged all to sustain it through powerful supporting testimony. On Baker's motion the committee was enlarged by the addition of Edward S. Tobey, president of the Boston Board of Trade; James M. Beebe, a jobbing merchant and importer; Benjamin S. Rotch, a Boston merchant, founder of the New Bedford Cordage Company, chairman of the Fine Arts Committee of the Boston Athenaeum, and son-in-law of the late Abbott Lawrence; Samuel Cabot, Jr.; Amos Binney, Jr., of the Natural History Society; Samuel Kneeland, Charles L. Flint, and John D. Philbrick.

An impressive array of people appeared before the second hearing of the Back Bay Committee, where the increased value of the lands was stressed, along with benefits which would accrue to the people of every part of the state, to commerce in general, to art and American culture. Popular education was characterized as the bulwark of free institutions, and the legislature was urged "to crown the glorious educational system of Massachusetts." Baker cited Kew Gardens, and Ross presented a catalogue of the Museum of Practical Geology and a description of the South Kensington Museum in London, as well as of the polytechnic school in Paris. Tobey expressed approval that commerce would be fully represented, as in Europe, and stressed the importance of naval architecture and exhibition space for "models of ships, marine engines, and the numerous inventions connected with naval matters and commerce."[35]

The *Boston Journal's* rather full report on this hearing cited the testimony of the Reverend Mr. Waterston, whose theme was also the great institutions of Europe and the lack of similar instruments of education in America. In addition he emphasized that all they were really asking for was a piece of land:

> Now the state was asked to improve an opportunity which might not again occur in a century. They were not asked for endowments or for collections but for a spot where rich collections may be placed for the good of the country. They did not ask for a levy but only a place to stand on.[36]

Throughout March 1859 large numbers of petitions signed by hundreds of citizens from cities and towns all over the state in support of the reservation of Back Bay land flowed into the legislature, largely through the efforts of William Baker. The form which he circulated for their signature expressed hearty approval of the plan: "There is a pressing need of Institutions where the people of the State may become acquainted with the applications of Science to the Agricultural, Mechanic, and Fine Arts . . . [through] various Scientific, Industrial, and Art collections, to be freely opened to the public for their pleasure and instruction."[37] The *Traveller* reported that one such petition had been received from Mrs. Harrison Gray Otis and some five hundred other ladies.[38]

During the period when the legislature was in session, public meetings were often held in the evening on a topic of general interest, usually one closely connected to pending bills. At such an occasion on March 17, 1859, the governor spoke briefly in support of the conservatory proposal. But the principal speaker of the evening was Louis Agassiz. Hundreds were turned away as an "immense audience of respectable citizens came to hear the greatest naturalist on this continent." He chose for his topic the training of young people from their earliest years to observe and study nature as the best means of disciplining their intellectual faculties. And he favored a practical rather than a theoretical education, knowing that at this time practical considerations could weigh heavily in the fate of his museum plans then before the legislature.[39]

The Senate became embroiled in heated debate on this bill, which also covered aid for Tufts College, Williams College, Amherst College, and the Wesleyan Academy at Wilbraham. A senator from Middlesex County denounced Harvard as an aristocratic institution from which the people were excluded and suggested that the museum be located in the Back Bay.[40] A member of the House termed the bill legislative logrolling—one of a series of measures of legislative extravagance that must stop somewhere. He proposed removing everything except the Agassiz appropriation. He believed that in nine cases out of ten the four years spent in college were four years thrown away and that in many cases a college education was like embroidery on a flapjack about to be eaten. Yet, so that his own Hampden County might not be left behind in grasping at the public treasury should the bill pass, he moved that the appropriation for Wesleyan Academy be doubled![41]

The bill was finally redrafted and on April 2, 1859, the governor signed an act providing for aid to Agassiz's museum and the institutions included in the original bill. The incorporation of the museum, with the governor as the president and other public officials as trustees, followed a few days later. George Boutwell, the Board of Education secretary, had termed the museum a noble and generous proposition that should not be withheld from the people of the state.[42]

This legislation, Chapter 154 of the Acts and Resolves of 1859, was rather complicated. Its central focus was the Bay Lands Fund, which had been established in 1857 to receive the proceeds of the sales of that land. The first section stated that all of the proceeds up to $300,000 must be used to redeem the scrip which had been issued in 1856 in connection with the project. Thereafter one-half of the sales proceeds was to be added to the principal of the School Fund. The grants to the institutions involved were to come from the remainder but would be paid on an annual basis up to a specific limit. For Agassiz's museum the share was 20 per cent of this remainder up to a limit of $100,000 and would be paid only if the institution had raised by subscription an equivalent sum. The commissioners of the Back Bay were also instructed to reserve $100,000 for purposes of improvement, such as roads and bridges. Ultimately, when all obligations had been met, everything else would go to the School Fund.

The governor had been granted his wish, as expressed in his annual message, that the School Fund would eventually benefit from the Back Bay sales. Agassiz's grant, however, would come only gradually and after other commitments had been fulfilled. In the future, therefore, Agassiz, too, would be wary of any action that might lessen the proceeds of the sale of the new land on the Back Bay.[43]

To return to the conservatory proposal, on March 30, 1859, a joint special committee issued a glowing report, much stronger and with the arguments more clearly presented than the memorial with which it was concerned. It emphasized the advantages of one location for "a variety of scientific and industrial institutions . . . of practical utility to all classes in the Commonwealth," and the need for practical education and the diffusion of knowledge. It included a much more detailed account of the proposed sections, was sanguine about support from the "private munificence of Boston," certain of its "great importance as an educational measure," and confident of its economic advantages for the state:

> Her future industrial progress will be greatly influenced by the practical educational facilities which these institutions by their union are designed to afford. The existence of such grand practical schools in Europe requires of us to take all possible advantage of our resources in this direction, under the penalty of taking a second rate position among the nations; and this no true American will be content to do, without a struggle for the supremacy.[44]

Despite the brief reference to "practical schools," neither in the report nor in the original memorial was any organization as a medium of formal education proposed. The report did, however, refer to European educational museums, and with respect to natural history and practical geology mentioned Agassiz's March 17 address and his Museum of Comparative Zoology: "The fact that the people appreciate the value of purely abstract investigations in science as distinct from and equally important with those designed to develop more directly our material wealth, we consider one of the most striking evidences that, as a community, we possess the true elements of progress, both in intellectual and material prosperity."[45] The prevailing view of museums as a means of informing and educating the public was emphasized:

> In this age of invention, the importance of an institution where the people may see models of machines, witness the processes of manufacture from the raw material to the perfect fabric, and examine the practical application of science to the arts and to navigation, cannot be overestimated. Institutions of this polytechnic character have been found, in Europe, to be of the greatest advantage in stimulating the inventive spirit of the people, and have led to some of the most important discoveries by persons who otherwise would have remained obscure and comparatively useless....
>
> For popular education in these departments we must have representations of the things studied, for the masses of the people learn from observation and experience and not by abstract study. Increased educational advantages in this direction would not only add to the material prosperity of our own State, but by drawing strangers from all parts of the country would become the means of diffusing knowledge to an extent which can hardly be estimated at the present time.[46]

Committee members were not concerned about the effect on the School Fund of the reservation of land from sale:

> The Committee are of the decided opinion that the reservation from sale of the land asked for in this memorial will tend greatly to enhance the value of the remaining lands, and in their judgment this increase will equal the sum which the State would receive from the sale of the reserved portion. . . . every county of the State should there have a space for the display of its products in every department of industry; so vastly superior would this advantage be to each county, compared to the small sum of money each would receive from the sale of the proposed reservation, that could the people of the State be made to understand this, not one foot of the whole tract would probably be sold except for such educational and industrial purposes.[47]

And their conclusion was favorable. From "an educational and financial point of view," the petition should be granted. But a final, abrupt paragraph spelled doom for the proposal in that session: "The Committee, however, notwithstanding an entire unanimity in these views, are united in the feeling that the present is not a propitious time for action in the premises, and therefore request to be discharged from the further consideration of the subject."[48]

The newspapers in the days preceding the issuance of this report seemed uncertain of its tenor, first saying that the committee would report unfavorably, then retracting the statement. Finally, an editorial in the *Boston Traveller* predicted that the House would probably instruct the committee to report a bill. But the report was simply accepted and the committee discharged as requested on April 6. Senator George Odiorne of Suffolk County, later to be numbered among the incorporators of the Massachusetts Institute of Technology, introduced a bill for the appointment of a commission to consider the conservatory proposal but was not able to secure its passage.[49]

Certainly the legislature had been much taken up with the Agassiz bill and also with end-of-the-session business as they prepared for adjournment. Baker later claimed that he had "received an impression some time previous to the report of the Legislative Committee" that it would be "favorable, yet that action would be deferred until the Back Bay Land—Public Garden Bill—was disposed of."[50] But it is also true that the proposal, despite laudatory aims, was exceedingly broad and lacked focus. Even the definite request of the Natural History Society for space for a flourishing institution seemed lost in the welter of ideas and idealistic language of both the memorial and the testimony.

The Reservation Committee, as they now called themselves, met again at the Natural History Society on April 8. Unhappily, a newspaper account provides the only available record of this meeting at which Ross explained the memorial's fate. Determined to continue, they voted to hold meetings monthly or oftener if required. In the hope of securing public support for a renewed effort, they voted also to print for circulation both the memorial and the report, with added comments to dispel the public impression of an unfavorable legislative view.[51]

It is not clear when this pamphlet was issued or to whom it was distributed. It included the joint committee report, the memorial of March 9 without date or the names of the seven original committee members, and appended undated comments. "Representing the interests of various Scientific, Commercial, Industrial, Educational and Art Associations," they asked for the "attention of the friends of these interests" and the "co-operation of the citizens of the Commonwealth, to enable them to present a more completely organized plan at the next session of the legislature." The plan had not failed. They had simply considered it "inexpedient to press so important a subject at the close of the session" since in any event the land would not be immediately available. Appended to these comments were the names of a reconstituted committee, with Marshall P. Wilder still chairman. Though the committee as enlarged in March did not include Alexander H. Rice or William Barton Rogers, both were now among those listed, while the names of Benjamin F. Edmands and William Emerson Baker had disappeared.[52]

A brewing controversy would become public by May 1859 and end in a division among the proponents of the conservatory. Perhaps in a very constructive way this contributed to the sharpening of the proposal.

On the day following the April 8 meeting of the Reservation Committee, there had appeared in Boston the first issue of a newspaper called the *Conservatory Journal*, with Baker as editor, proprietor, and publisher, to be devoted to the cause of establishing a Massachusetts Conservatory of Art, Science, and Historical Relics. The disappearance of the latter term in the preparation of the March memorial may well have been an early sign of dissension. Baker cited nearly ten thousand signatories to supporting petitions from people all over the state. He reported on the hearings, printed statements of support, and hinted that other, but unspecified, land might be available if the legislature did not approve the reservation in the Back Bay. Promising plans by April 15, Baker appealed for articles for the collections to be displayed and for funds.

He cited the inventive genius of the citizens of New England, labeled the time as the *practical* age, and foresaw the elevation of the masses through the activities of the proposed conservatory:

> We need, then, a Polytechnic Institute, where the advancement of the useful arts may be noticed and practically described. Where may be properly organized a school of design to increase our supremacy as a manufacturing State. Wherein could be opened a Conversazione which would tend to disseminate useful knowledge upon subjects of every day life, upon domestic and political economy, etc.[53]

Baker had at first planned to have an art festival and exhibition in the Music Hall, but settled on leased space in the Sears Building at the corner of Chauncy and Summer Streets, where more room would be available for displays to be arranged in various departments, "free from all *exclusiveness*." These departments, with the exception of "Historical Relics," were essentially those included in the March memorial. The office of the "Massachusetts Conservatory of Art and Science" was at 16 Summer Street, next to the Grover & Baker Sewing Machine Company in the Mercantile Building. Baker referred to several unnamed "distinguished gentlemen" who had volunteered to deliver lectures related to the exhibits, and the public was invited to contribute both money and articles for display. The Worcester Railroad had offered to transport without charge items destined for the conservatory, and adequate security was promised. John Sears, who was interested in the establishment of a zoological garden as part of the conservatory, had offered to contribute, for certain financial considerations, a collection he was then exhibiting on Portland Street in Boston, including "six African Lions, one Leopard, one Jackall, Lynx, Coyote, Wild Cat, Ant-Eater, two Limas, one Hyena, Civit, two Alpaccas, Prairie Wolf, twenty varieties of Monkeys, Anaconda from Congo River, Crocodile from Egypt, Mountain Cat from California, and various other small animals and birds."[54]

Baker's proposal was immediately discussed, and favorably, on the editorial page of the *Boston Journal*:

> Petitions to the city government praying that the proposed Conservatory of Art, Science and Historical Relics be located in the Public Garden are at the Merchants Exchange and in circulation for signature. The petitions are accompanied by an engraved plan which conveys an idea of the prospective appearance of the new portion of the city. It locates the Conservatory near the center

of the Public Garden and directly opposite Commonwealth Avenue. Improvements look very fine on paper, and we trust it will be fully realized. ... We believe that William E. Baker, Esquire, of the Grover and Baker Sewing Machine Company is entitled to the credit of getting up this plan, and he is entirely entitled to the thanks of all friends of this enterprise and for the efforts which he is making to promote the success of the Conservatory.[55]

But the ideas of the flamboyant Mr. Baker, though they had initially helped to stir the several societies to action, were clearly incompatible with the aims of those with whom he had attempted to associate himself. His plan, even in its initial presentation, went far beyond the interests of any one of the institutions that had joined in the project, and it is apparent that his enthusiasm for the idea was now carrying him even further beyond their earnest hopes for a few squares of land on the Back Bay. A later report of the Building Committee of the Natural History Society termed it "altogether too fanciful and impractical to succeed."[56] Though the institutions very much needed public support, their leaders were also conscious of mission and protective of institutional identity. Above all, their vision of what could be accomplished was both sophisticated and practical. Men of substance and attainment, they were very much aware of the industrial and commercial needs of the state, and fully cognizant of the growing need for better education in a variety of disciplines. It was virtually inevitable that their views and Baker's dream would not find common ground and that their relations would deteriorate.

By early May 1859 the committee representing what they now called the Massachusetts Conservatory of Art and Science were ready to divorce themselves publicly from his activities. A meeting of the Reservation Committee on May 4 resulted in a special notice in the newspapers, the wording unequivocal in its renunciation of Baker and his plans. It stated that they "find themselves compelled, by the course adopted by Mr. W. E. Baker, a former member of the committee, to publish the following statement: They wish it to be distinctly understood that Mr. Baker long since ceased to be a member of this committee; and that the publication of the so-called 'Conservatory Journal,' the leasing of a large building, and the solicitation of specimens to fill it—the plan of a single structure to be located on the Public Garden, or elsewhere—and all the steps recently taken by Mr. Baker, by festival or otherwise, to advocate or promote the success of any such scheme as is sketched in the above-mentioned Journal—are prosecuted without the sanction of the Committee, and wholly on his own responsibility."[57] The committee named was, as already noted, minus Baker and Benjamin Edmands, replaced by Alexander Rice and William Rogers. Why Edmands was dropped is unknown. Perhaps he was on Baker's side. He would later, however, become a supporter of MIT and a member of its Government from 1864 to 1869.

The *Boston Journal* carried a small item calling attention to the special notice, commenting: "Mr. Baker has entered upon the work of securing the establishment of the Conservatory with a zeal and enthusiasm which his former colleagues evidently think is carrying him beyond the limits of prudence."[58] The newspapers also contained a disclaimer by Baker to eliminate any confusion that the original group might be directly involved in the establishment of the preliminary conservatory or in the publication of the *Conservatory Journal*, joining with them "in stating that they are not as a Committee engaged in this mode of aiding the cause. . . . it may not be generally known that he resigned and withdrew himself of his own free will from that Committee (on March 21st.) that he might not compromise his associates by working in other ways to aid the cause, than the one for which the Committee was especially appointed."[59]

This statement may very well have been exacted from Baker in the hope of avoiding a protracted public dispute that might seriously affect the Reservation Committee's plans to pursue their own aims. But on the same day, the *Conservatory Journal* revealed that Baker was not planning to retreat without further word: "We have to contend against various petty jealousies. . . . These petty objections incite us on, for no one can work with much zeal until there comes opposition. We would, however, caution the public to look for the 'MOTIVE,' when any ingenious objections are raised."[60] This issue included a sketch of the proposed "Massachusetts Conservatory of Art, Science, and Historical Relics, by William Waud, Architect, from suggestions by Wm. E. Baker." The advantages of a Public Garden site were emphasized, and an announcement was made that the temporary location in the Sears Building was now ready to receive articles for display.[61]

Baker took his case to the newspapers again on May 9 with a signed statement reviewing the history of his proposal. He complained that he had not been able to get the committee together as often as he had an idea and that two or three of the group never approved of his suggestions. He firmly believed that there should be but one building with accommodations for many societies rather than a site where only those with means could erect structures of their own. He released a copy of his letter of resignation, claiming that the committee did not approve of his methods of "agitating the whole State," that they had at first refused to accept his withdrawal but that he had submitted it a second time so that he could proceed to carry out his plans. He noted that some of the committee would learn these facts for the first time, since Rogers and Rice had been absent from the city and had only been added since his resignation, and he expressed regrets that he had been forced to make a public issue of the problem.[62]

Later in May the *Conservatory Journal* contained an editorial entitled "Concentration is Strength" in which Baker expressed gratification at the widespread commendation of the plan of the structure proposed and of the location in the Public Garden, citing two thousand prominent citizens as having signed petitions in favor of this location. He had expected unanimity of sentiment when he embarked upon this project, but such had not been realized among the historical and scientific associations involved. The people's favorable opinion he looked upon as conclusive; but there were differences of opinion about the details of the establishment. He had concluded, with the advice of judicious friends, that the interim establishment on Summer Street was unnecessary and that it would be better to concentrate his efforts on the ultimate goal. Baker looked to the *Conservatory Journal* as a means of keeping fresh in the minds of the people a project that would be an honor, he said, for the city of Boston.[63]

A major factor in the demise of Baker's proposal for a conservatory in the Public Garden was the passage by the Legislature in 1859 (Chapter 210) of an act prohibiting the construction of anything on the land between Charles and Arlington Streets but a possible city hall, which was later built, in 1862, on School Street. In the view of Walter Muir Whitehill, this legislation "blocked the way for such contraptions as the cruciform glass house designed by William Waud that was injudiciously proposed in the same year as a Massachusetts Conservatory of Art, Science and Historical Relics."[64] Baker appears to have made an attempt at reconciliation in a letter to Marshall Wilder dated May 30, 1859, intimating a willingness to compromise for the good of the cause and stating that if a location could be decided upon, a great step toward success would have been taken.[65] No response to this letter has been found, nor is there any indication that Baker participated in the efforts that followed.[66]

Baker's role in the events leading eventually to the founding of the Institute of Technology was not a substantive one. He never envisioned a scholarly institution for formal education in the principles and practice of science and technology, but neither is it clear, for that matter, that the early supporters of the Institute envisioned such an institution. Baker did serve initially to bring together a few institutions with housing problems, and his short-lived *Conservatory Journal* helped to arouse public interest. The disagreement about his approach for the conservatory set the stage for a proposal that would in time crystallize the thinking of those with a genuine interest in an alternative to classical studies and a stake in the increased availability of young people trained in new ways for the era ahead.

Why did this first memorial fail? Certainly Baker and his activities proved to be a complicating factor. The controversy over the future of the Public Garden, Snelling's appeals for the preservation of a basin of water in the Back Bay, and Agassiz's solicitation of state funds for the Museum of Comparative Zoology, with implications for the revenue from the sale of the Back Bay lands and the financial status of the School Fund, also contributed to a very confusing picture. The joint committee's favorable statements were undoubtedly heavily influenced by Samuel Kneeland, while the newspaper accounts in the days before the presentation of the memorial reflected indecision and serious questions. It was late in the session to debate thoroughly a plan that was admittedly vague, too broad, and lacking in concrete details. The need to "elevate the masses" was a goal of undisputed merit, but a much more resolute and cohesive plan would be required to garner unconditional favor with the public's elected representatives.

The real loser for the moment was the Boston Society of Natural History, which knew exactly what it wanted and why, and which had been completely engulfed by a visionary idea not easily committed to paper. The seed of something greater was there, however, and it was Matthias Ross who produced for the legislative committee concrete examples of what he at least had in mind, though these ideas could hardly be found in the proposal in definite form. It was he who urged that advocates of the proposal get the land first and mature their plans afterwards, suggesting that he understood better than most that raising the specter of new and amorphous institutions was not helping the cause. The sanctity of the School Fund was perhaps the most significant element of all and would continue over the next two years to be a powerful political obstacle.

As one of the earliest proponents of the use of a portion of the Back Bay land for educational purposes, Matthias Denman Ross would be a key figure in the successful outcome of the developing plans. He was born in Hamilton County, Ohio, near Cincinnati, in November 1819, one of eleven children. He undoubtedly received a common school education and was taught surveying and map-making on the family farm by his father. He worked briefly at surveying, studied some law, and taught school before becoming interested in cotton machinery, an interest that led him in 1846 from a cotton mill in Ohio to Lawrence, Massachusetts, and the Bay State Mills, the construction of which he supervised and of which he was agent for several years. In 1855 he came to Boston and, with John B. Pearce, founded the firm of Ross & Pearce, later to be Ross, Turner & Co., for the production of linen thread for fishing lines and nets. Like many Boston businessmen of the time, he was involved in a number of commercial and civic activities

Matthias Denman Ross

simultaneously—member of the original Board of Directors of the Boston Safe Deposit and Trust Company, later president of the Mercantile Wharf Corporation, and director of the Quincy Market Cold Storage Company among them. He served as a member of the Boston Harbor Commission and Boston's Commission on the Back Bay Lands, as well as the Boston School Committee. He was also chairman of the Board of Trustees of the Eliot School.

Described as an individual of "towering presence" and "strong individuality," Ross was considered "a man of the people." Successful in business, he found time to work for a number of public-spirited causes, with the Massachusetts Institute of Technology chief among them. As an active force in the Reservation Committee, in the founding of MIT, and as a member of its governing board from 1862 to 1892, he was a tireless worker, playing a role for which he has never received adequate recognition. A resolution upon his death in 1892 emphasized the "earnest and active part" he took in "all the preliminary discussions which led to the establishment of the Institute of Technology":

> As early as 1857, a small party of gentlemen, interested in the filling and the developing of the Back Bay district of the city, held frequent meetings at his house, and one of the earliest suggestions made by Mr. Ross, was, that a series of squares of this newly made land should be reserved from sale and devoted to the use of such scientific and educational institutions as already existed or were likely in the near future to be established in the city. . . . In all the long years of his service . . . but few members have been more constant in their attendance and more prompt in the performance of such duties as fell to their lot.[67]

Over the years other statements have underscored Ross's role, at the same time clarifying where William Rogers was positioned with respect to these earliest efforts. In 1917 John M. Ordway, Professor of Chemistry from 1869 to 1884, whose brother, Alfred Ordway, was a member of the Committee of Associated Institutions, as the Reservation Committee came to be known, spoke very definitely on this point:

The idea of an Institute for scientific education was suggested by M. D. Ross before 1860, and while the present site was still under water. He associated himself with other business men having a rather indefinite idea as to what they wanted; and they set to work to secure from the State a donation of the land still to be made. After much effort they succeeded in getting a reservation of one square for the Institute and the Natural History Society. Meanwhile, they had brought in Prof. Rogers to co-operate and give a definite shape to their plans.[68]

From this account of the conservatory proposal, it is evident that William Barton Rogers was not actively involved in the appeal of 1859 and that his name was associated with the effort only as a representative of the Natural History Society. Even in that capacity he was not included in the Reservation Committee which submitted the March memorial. And *Life and Letters* states that Rogers "took but little part" at that time.[69]

Early in February, writing to his brother Henry, since 1857 Regius Professor of Natural History at the University of Glasgow, William reported on a forthcoming lecture trip to Virginia and mentioned that friends of Agassiz were working hard to secure a large appropriation from the state for his museum project. William mentioned also that the Natural History Society and other groups were "agitating a plan" to ask for land on the Back Bay for "an extensive building for the united accommodation of them all."[70] He spoke of it again on February 14:

> The application will be made by the Natural History Society and other parties here, to induce the Legislature to set aside a large lot in the Back Bay improvement for the reception of a grand cruciform structure for the museum and libraries of the various societies and for a grand polytechnic depository.[71]

And later, writing from Richmond, Virginia:

> There is quite a stir in Boston on the subject of setting apart a large space in the Back Bay lands for a polytechnic museum and other scientific uses. From what I learn, I conclude that the Legislature will favor the movement. This will be important for the Natural History Society.[72]

Nowhere in these letters is there mention of his own relation to these efforts through the Natural History Society, and indeed one can detect a certain degree of detachment. Rogers had been in Washington before going on to lecture at the YMCA in Richmond, where he also presented a benefit lecture for the College of William and Mary, whose building had been destroyed by fire. He went on to Petersburg, Lynchburg, and Norfolk for a series of eight lectures and spent some time in Williamsburg as well, stopping in Philadelphia on the way home. By April 4 he was back in Boston, reporting to Henry on his recent trip and mentioning that during his absence the legislature had granted $100,000 from the income of the Back Bay lands to Agassiz. This was just two days after the act had been signed, and it is not clear whether he realized that the $100,000 would not be received immediately. He noted also that the plan of the Natural History Society had been favorably received but would not be acted upon at that time by the legislature.[73]

If Rogers ever referred to the developing disagreements with Baker, no correspondence has survived. His own name appeared in the papers as a member of the Reservation Committee when the division with Baker occurred, and on June 15 he was named, along with Cabot, Binney, and Kneeland to a Natural History Society "reservation" committee to continue to work with and serve as a member of the larger group. *Life and Letters* does not refer again to the effort to secure land until the fall of 1859, with the first mention of his active participation in the project not occurring until January 2, 1860.[74]

Events relating to other institutions during this period are also relevant. The minutes of the Board of Visitors of the University of Virginia for June 30, 1859, show that an election took place on that day for a professorship of physical geology and agricultural science. Two names were placed in nomination—Commander Matthew F. Maury and William B. Rogers. Maury was elected by a vote of five to three.[75] The professorship, said to be "on a footing of equal dignity with the other chairs," was to cover also meteorology and climatology and was planned to include subjects related to agricultural science not already taught at the university, the course of study being designed for those planning to become farmers. Maury was not able to accept the proffered post, and the "professorship never advanced beyond the stage of nominal creation."[76]

It seems unlikely that Rogers's name would have been placed in nomination at Virginia without his knowledge so soon after his visit there. It is, of course, entirely possible that six years of lecturing and private research based in Boston had not brought the reward or inner satisfaction that he might once have anticipated and that he may have mentioned while in Virginia a desire to find a permanent place. But it is equally probable that he could not have been seriously contemplating a return to the South, given the need for his wife to remain close to her widowed father, one factor leading to their move to Boston in 1853, along with his strong feelings about the developing strains between North and South over the issues of slavery, secession, and the survival of the Union.

During the summer Henry wrote from London of a conversation with Agassiz, then also abroad, who indicated that he hoped to appoint William as professor of geology in the Lawrence Scientific School or in the new museum:

> He told me in confidence of his wish and purpose to make room for you in the scientific school or new museum as professor of Geology, he wishing to relinquish it and retain the Zoology, as soon as the museum affairs are organized. If this should suit you, I do sincerely trust it will be done. . . . But beware of hard work of the brain, in any form. There is something particularly noxious to cerebral health in the climate and stimulating life of New England. I have been made painfully conscious of this on meeting our fellow countrymen and women this year here in England.[77]

Before departing for Europe that summer, Agassiz had indeed sent to President James L. Walker of Harvard his "views respecting the best mode of carrying out the plans now only sketched, in case I should be removed from the sphere of my activity before I return to Cambridge next autumn." He recommended that Henry J. Clark[78] be appointed to carry out the plans for the Museum of Comparative Zoology and to succeed him "in the professorship of Zoology, which I believe cannot hereafter remain coupled with that of Geology. I hold that Professor William B. Rogers is the man most competent to fill the professorship of Geology, next to him Mr. James Hall of Albany."[79] Agassiz survived, however, and his recommendations did not require implementation, the matter of splitting geology and zoology held in abeyance.

There is only fragmentary evidence of what Samuel Kneeland called the "pre-Rogers history of the Institute." Kneeland would later be a member of the instructing staff of MIT, secretary of its governing board from 1866 to 1878, and secretary of the faculty from 1871 to 1878. As he left the Institute in 1878, he would refer to himself in a letter to Rogers as "one of the workers in its interest, even before your services were enlisted in its behalf." And to the board Kneeland cited his "efforts to advance the interest of the Institute (years before any of its present members except Messrs. Wilder & Ross, dreamed of its establishment)."[80]

In 1885, as Professor Silas W. Holman was preparing a brief history of the Massachusetts Institute of Technology, he sought information about the early days from Kneeland, who responded in part:

All the pre-historic, or pre-Rogers history of the Institute is unknown, or at least unwritten. An interesting history, which will soon be impossible, might & should be written from materials collected by me—the hard, necessary, and never appreciated nor paid work of the days of small things—and now in the hands of M. D. Ross, Esq., a member of the Corporation, on Devonshire St. He and I were the chief and almost the only living workers, with Hon. Marshall P. Wilder, in the days when there were 20 feet of water where the Institute is now. The history of the Institute as given in Prof. Runkle's sketch, on the occasion of Prof. Rogers' death, is much like a history of England beginning with William the Conqueror, or that of N. America beginning with the Declaration of Independence. I have neither the time, disposition, nor ability to do justice to this period of the Institute's history; Prof. Rogers found a field well prepared for the Technological seed which he so well planted and which has produced such good fruit though grafted with some unnatural and unprofitable stocks—but he knew not who had prepared it, and received much credit which belonged to workers in the field before he came to Boston. . . . There is no one in the Corporation, except the two mentioned, who knows anything, or probably cares anything, about the pre-historic annals of the Institute.[81]

Nevertheless, another stage would be added to the "pre-historic annals of the Institute" before a final proposal for an Institute of Technology would emerge. William Barton Rogers would play an important role in both.

Chapter 8

—◦◦◦—

An Auxiliary to the Cause of Education

T
he concerted effort of 1860 to secure land on the Back Bay actually began late in 1859, when early in November the Natural History Society reviewed a plan for a double building connected by an arcade to accommodate both the Natural History and Horticultural societies. It was "approved by the Society as satisfactory, but was not adopted as a definite plan." At this time the curators of the various departments were asked to prepare estimates of requirements, and work went forward by the Reservation Committee on a memorial seeking two squares of land, the second square for the purposes suggested in the conservatory proposal.[1]

William Rogers's air of detachment continued into that fall, when he again mentioned the project to Henry and with no indication of a significant involvement on his part:

> The Natural History, Horticultural, and other societies are making great efforts to secure a long parallelogram of the new-made land west of the Public Garden and parallel with the lower part of the Milldam, about the Toll-gate, and they have good hopes of succeeding. They have already prepared plans for large and elegant structures for their accommodations severally.[2]

By early January 1860, however, his tone had changed, and he had been drawn into the project in a meaningful way:

A Memorial prepared by me in behalf of the Natural History, Horticultural, and other societies will be presented to the Legislature erelong and it is thought the grant of land on the Back Bay will be made for their benefit. My Memorial has been highly approved.[3]

It was his habit to affix his initials to a copy of any piece he had authored when the published version did not so indicate, and he followed this practice in this instance. At least one copy is available of the document, which became House no. 13, on which he firmly planted "W.B.R." both at the beginning and at the end.[4]

If the committee records for this period were available, they might reveal why and when the Reservation Committee was increased to eighteen members through the addition of George B. Emerson, the Reverend Dr. Robert C. Waterston, and Erastus B. Bigelow.[5] Waterston was a Unitarian minister at New North Church from 1859 to 1861 and an active member of the Natural History Society. He had testified on behalf of the conservatory proposal and was among those credited with "great efforts" in early 1860 in support of the memorial recently submitted. He was convinced that the reservation would be of "immense advantage to the city and the Commonwealth . . . and then we shall have something to be proud of and the advantages will be felt through coming generations."[6] He was evidently interested in educational matters, later urging the society to establish a series of lectures for teachers.[7] The addition of George Emerson, though probably initiated to strengthen the claims of the Natural History and Horticultural societies, would prove ultimately to be of great benefit in the early development of the Institute of Technology. And the addition of Erastus Bigelow signified an important further step in a gradual change in orientation of the project.

Erastus Brigham Bigelow was keenly aware of the critical need for scientific and technical education and well qualified to speak for the industrial interests of the state. Described as "one of the great inventors of his time," with a "rare faculty in the application of science to the useful arts," as well as a "sagacious man of business,"[8] he is best known for his invention of power looms for carpeting, but he also made significant contributions through inventions for the manufacture of fabrics. He was born in 1814 in West Boylston, Massachusetts, the son of a farmer and wheelwright with little money, who later owned a small factory for the manufacture of cotton. Beginning at the age of ten, he worked at a variety of jobs, studied briefly at the Leicester Academy, but for lack of funds never fulfilled an ambition to attend Harvard and become a doctor.

Bigelow was fourteen when he invented an automatic machine for piping cord. His invention of a loom for the manufacture of coach lace was followed by a power loom for the Lowell Manufacturing Company, then the largest American carpet firm, for whom he supervised the construction of the machinery and the building in which it was housed. Later he founded the Bigelow Carpet Company for the weaving of Brussels, Jacquard, and Wilton carpets. His Brussels carpeting was exhibited at the London Exposition of 1851 to very favorable notice, and he was a member of the London Society for the Encouragement of the Arts, Manufactures, and Commerce.

A founder, with his brother, of the town of Clinton, where the Bigelow Carpet Company flourished, he was thoroughly convinced that the economic health of New England depended upon the establishment of a sound system of manufactures:

> The endowments, no less than the necessities, of Massachusetts, indicate this as the path for her. Her climate, if severe, is yet invigorating. She has the needed facilities for travel and transportation largely provided; she has abundant water-power; and above all, an intelligent population of remarkable industry and energy.[9]

Erastus Brigham Bigelow

In 1864 he was a founder of the National Association of Wool Manufacturers. He ran for Congress in 1860 and was narrowly defeated by Alexander H. Rice, a fellow member of the Committee of Associated Institutions.

Bigelow was a member of the Institute's governing board from 1862 until his death in 1879, when he was identified in a resolution presented by William Rogers as "one of the honored band of associates whose active zeal contributed to the foundation of this Institute" and "its most valued early counsellor." Acknowledging his "inventive genius," which had "wrought such great industrial results," the resolution emphasized the value of Bigelow's efforts "in behalf of scientific technical education during his long connection with the Institute." It testified also to "the urbanity and modesty of character which united with rare intellectual gifts and earnestness of purpose, gave so often a gentle and winning charm to his companionship."[10]

Just as the phrase "Historical Relics" had disappeared by the time the first memorial was submitted to the legislature, the title "Conservatory of Art and Science" disappeared from the second. No longer "a Committee appointed by citizens of the Commonwealth," the petitioners were now "a Committee representing various associations devoted to Agriculture, Horticulture, Natural History, Mechanics, Manufactures, Commerce, the Fine Arts, and Public Education." Again they said that their plan would "effectually assist in carrying out the wise suggestion of His Excellency the Governor, in his Message of 1859."[11]

Rogers's memorial of 1860 drew heavily on the original appeal to the legislature and the joint special committee report. Still not sure how many organizations would be participating, he described the four departments whose interests were represented on the petitioning committee, all of these functioning essentially as museums.

The Horticultural Society and the Natural History Society would be responsible for the first two departments: agriculture, including horticulture and pomology; and natural history, geology, and chemistry. It was expected that the first would have a laboratory "equipped for every branch of chemico-agricultural experiment," which would not only furnish "reliable reports" on various products and soils, but also "might by its larger researches help to advance the theory as well as the practice of agricultural processes." The Horticultural Society would also be responsible for landscaping and care of the grounds.[12]

Particular emphasis was placed on the urgent space needs of the Natural History Society, "desiring to make their labors more extensively useful, and at the same time to secure for themselves a more efficient equipment for scientific research." Also stressed were the "educational and practical benefits" that would accrue to the public from "collections properly systematized, and freely thrown open to general study and inspection":

> Such comprehensive exemplars of nature are recognized by the great leaders in popular education as among the most efficient means of diffusing useful knowledge throughout a community, and of promoting the yet higher ends of a general intellectual and moral culture, where truth is valued for its own intrinsic beauty and grandeur as well as for its material applications, and where the discipline of the faculties of mind and heart accompanying the study of natural objects and laws is no less regarded than the treasures of knowledge to be amassed.[13]

Due mention was made of Agassiz and his new museum, "which must still be fresh in the minds of the Legislature. . . . The interests as well as the honorable distinction of the Commonwealth must in some degree be influenced by the labors of those of her citizens who devote themselves to science, and whose unbought ardor of research may from time to time bear them on to observations and discoveries of value in the affairs of life as well as in advancing the boundaries of knowledge."[14] Two further repositories under this department would enhance its own usefulness and that of the third section relating to the industrial arts: a museum for organic and mineral products similar to the Museum of Economic Botany at Kew, and one for mineral substances and geological specimens, such as that of the School of Mines and Economic Geology, also in London.[15]

The third department would cover mechanics, manufactures and commerce, and technology in general—a first mention of the latter—presenting "most weighty claims to the consideration of the legislature." A comprehensive institution devoted to these areas was urgently needed, its proceedings and exhibitions promising to attract a "throng of visitors, not more by the large treasure of knowledge which it placed within their reach, than by its thousand suggestions to stimulate invention and assist discovery."[16]

Finally, a department of fine arts and education including a gallery for the exhibition of works of art, for "the cultivation of the fine arts must be regarded as a *necessary* supplement, in every wise system of education, to the teachings of practical science and the more purely logical exercises of thought." There would be an educational museum, "exhibiting the materials and equipment proper to each grade of school instruction, and exemplifying practically the latest improvements at home and abroad in the apparatus of intellectual and physical training."[17] Such a museum was mentioned in the joint committee report and was, in fact, a suggestion made earlier by John D. Philbrick.

The Natural History Society and the Horticultural Society were both ready, having "matured, in a great degree, building plans," and able to proceed as soon as the land was in condition. The value of proximity to all of these existing and proposed institutions was underscored. There was great confidence that support and ample collections would be forthcoming and that other associations would in time wish to join in a plan of such "far-reaching and weighty importance as connected with the interests of education, science, and the industrial arts throughout the Commonwealth."

This was basically an outline for a collocation of educational museums, some not even in existence, which would lay out their collections for the inspection and elevation of the public. An important addition, however, was a brief statement expressing the hope that "at an early day" courses of public lectures and demonstrations might be offered, such as those at the London Polytechnic, which "while aiming at a familiar exposition of science and the arts, would exhibit in practical operation by working models, or otherwise, the more important discoveries and inventions as they arise." There was a hope also that interests representing the fine arts and "other branches of liberal culture" might introduce series of public lectures.[18]

Most important of all, however, was yet another hope, only briefly touched upon, suggesting that the "educational value" of the museum relating to the industrial arts might one day be enhanced by the establishment of "a comprehensive Polytechnic College":

> Indeed, considering how greatly the educational value of museums is augmented by connecting with them an organized system of oral teachings, your memorialists are persuaded that ere long the public liberality would not only provide in this connection for popular lectures on the various branches of industrial science, on the plan of those of Morin, Payen and other eminent professors of the Conservatoire of Paris, but would establish a comprehensive Polytechnic College, which like the "Central School of Arts and Manufactures," of the same city or the great "Trades Institute of Berlin," would put in practice *a complete system of industrial education* supplementary to the general training of other institutions, and fitted to equip its students with every scientific and technical principle applicable to the leading industrial pursuits of the age.[19]

It is interesting to note that when the *Boston Advertiser* printed the memorial in full on January 28, 1860, the column was entitled, "A Polytechnic School."

Stating at the outset that there was no desire to "dictate as to the position or extent of space to be reserved," the memorial nevertheless suggested that "the area between Boylston and Newbury, Berkely [*sic*] and Exeter Streets, and a fraction next westerly" would be "admirably suited to the object in view, as well from its position and convenient shape as from the ample space it would offer." In closing, it was sanguine about the financial effects of a reservation from sale of the desired land:

> The magnitude of the public interests involved . . . so greatly overshadows any financial considerations . . . that [the petitioners] deem it needless, if not unworthy the occasion, to dwell on the direct profit which would probably accrue to the State treasury from the measure suggested. . . . Such an appropriation of part of the land would in a few years more than repay the treasury by the increased value which it would give to the adjoining tracts, while by the better knowledge and wiser practical guidance which it would be the means of imparting to the public, it would return to the Commonwealth, even in money value, an amount almost incalculably beyond its cost.[20]

This memorial was certainly an improvement in clarity over its predecessor, but only two established institutions were represented. At the annual meeting of the Horticultural Society in January 1860, Marshall Wilder reported on the Natural History Society's plans, and President Breck reported on the sale of the Horticultural building, the funds invested against the day when a permanent location might be found. He stressed caution: "I hope no hasty action will be taken on this subject, but recommend that the Society take time, and wait patiently for a favorable opportunity, which, no doubt, will present itself in the course of a few months, or in a year or two."[21] A month later they had leased Amory Hall at the corner of Washington and West Streets for three years, with a possible extension of two more. In the meantime they had forwarded to the legislature a petition in aid of the memorial of the Associated Institutions.[22]

Petitions were also submitted by the Boston Board of Trade, the Massachusetts Charitable Mechanics' Association, the Natural History Society, the New England Society for the Promotion of Manufactures and Mechanic Arts, and the State Teachers' Association. The American Academy of Arts and Sciences also submitted one, the result of a meeting at which both Rogers and Josiah Quincy spoke in behalf of the proposal.[23]

Rogers perceived strong sentiment in their favor, according to letters to Henry. On January 17 he sent him a copy of the plan, "which I have laid out in behalf of the Commission," referring to its "wide scope" and "the number of important public interests which are concerned":

> Our (or rather my) Memorial is before the Legislature, and will probably be acted on next week. Thus far the sentiment is strongly in its favour. We ask for from eight to ten acres of the Back Bay land for buildings to accommodate the Natural History, Horticultural, Agricultural, Technological, etc., societies. The plan is magnificent, and if carried out will do great service.[24]

The Committee on Education began a series of hearings at which members of the petitioning committee and others testified, all reported briefly in the papers. William's letter to Henry on January 30, however, implies that he was carrying a large share of the burden:

> Thus far much of the talking, as well as writing, has fallen to me. We have a good prospect of success. But you know that the course of legislation is not to

be inferred from the action or report of a committee. Our open opponent, thus far, has been the Secretary of the State Board of Education,—the former Governor, Boutwell. . . . Until lately I did not imagine that any jealousy could be felt towards a plan which contemplates almost entirely popular and economic objects.[25]

On January 31 the *Traveller* confirmed that Boutwell was opposed.

During that winter the topic of the legislative educational meetings open to the public was "Education as related to the Natural Sciences." Rogers spoke on the evening of February 16. As reported by the *Boston Journal*, his hour-long address was presented "in his most happy and elegant manner" before a "small but appreciative audience, who braved the storm to secure what they knew would be a rich intellectual treat." He first pointed out the value of the study of natural science in "strengthening the mind, cultivating the memory and the senses of observation, and of forming habits of accurate examination." This was not to be achieved "by books alone, but by the actual objects, frequently displayed, explained, and handled."

Rogers naturally took the opportunity to discuss the memorial then before the legislature and the advantages of the "educational museum" it promised. As reported in the *Boston Journal*, he made a strong plea for legislative acceptance of the proposal:

Here, if anywhere in this country, we have the elements for the establishment of such an educational museum; the centre of manufacturing industry, the seat of the highest social refinement, the beneficent patron of everything good, beautiful and elevated, Boston is, of all places in this country, and perhaps in the world, the proper place for this all-important and much-needed auxiliary to the cause of education. Having neither the splendor of Paris, nor the population of London or New York, Boston, in the general intelligence, wealth, munificence and refinement of her people, can compare favorably with any of the cities of the globe. He would scorn the narrow idea that the establishment of these institutions in Boston would be for the sole advantage of the city and its surroundings. Boston is intimately and indissolubly connected with every town in the State; her interests are theirs; and theirs cannot be separated from her own; it would be suicidal in this matter for the country to array itself against the city. . . . He showed conclusively that this is no Utopian and visionary scheme, but an eminently useful and entirely practical and practicable plan; not the mere whim of a paroxysm of enthusiasm, but the long studied and carefully elaborated convictions of a committee of the most intelligent citizens, who have freely contributed their time, their money, their best judgment, and unremitting efforts, for many months, in bringing this plan to the greatest possible perfection. An examination of the memorial must convince every intelligent and thinking mind that this is the greatest educational movement which has ever been brought to their notice; and that the Legislature which grants the petition of those who seek this opportunity to advance the interests of the State will deserve and will obtain the grateful thanks of the present and all future generations in this Commonwealth. It is an opportunity which can never occur again in Massachusetts, and he hoped that every member of the Senate and House of Representatives would fully examine the memorial. If this were done, he was confident that not a dissenting voice would be heard when that truly noble and entirely disinterested plan was brought before the Legislature for its final approval.[26]

Rogers's emphasis in this talk, following the principal focus of the memorial, was on the collections that would be brought together and exhibited for the benefit of the farmer, the miner, the mechanic, the manufacturer, the student of science, and the lover of the beautiful in art.

By February 23 the Joint Standing Committee on Education presented a report, signed and written, according to a Rogers notation, by Charles U. Upham. The statement opened by stressing the responsibility to keep the School Fund inviolate—"a right, vested, sacred, and never to be alienated or impaired"—and emphasized that the petitioners had been informed that the "Committee could not be brought by any considerations whatever to favor any proposition that would involve a diminution of the prospective receipts into the treasury of the proceeds of a property thus pledged to the schools of the Commonwealth."[27] They were not, however, opposed to the proposal itself: "They have heard the parties now before them with the deepest interest in the objects they have at heart, and with a full appreciation of the just claim of those objects upon the patronage of an enlightened government."[28] And, "as the guardians and trustees of the rights and interests of the common school fund," they had focused their deliberations on whether the requested reservation of land would increase the value of the remaining property and ultimately benefit the School Fund even as it might "improve the character and embellish the appearance of that section of the city."

More than the appeal and importance of the proposal may have spoken to them, however, for there is some indication that the developing lands were not selling as rapidly and land values not rising as high as had been originally hoped. It was just possible that the requested reservation might indeed be helpful. The only lots then in demand were those opposite the Public Garden and Commonwealth Avenue, both of which were to be "embellished with ornamental grounds." To open a few squares in the center of the area might well result in increased values and higher rates. The legislative committee could find some justification for their conjecture among the Commissioners on the Back Bay, whose 1859 report stated that "upwards of 2 million square feet" had yet to be sold but that they had not in the previous year made "any extraordinary effort" to do so, feeling that as more of the Bay was filled, "greater disposition to purchase lands will be evinced." A year later some sales, producing mortgage notes as well as cash, had been achieved "at a time of great depression in real estate," resulting in prices lower than those obtained previously for lots in similar locations. The commissioners looked upon these sales, however, as "highly beneficial . . . and auspicious of the speedy completion of the improvements in the Back Bay."[29]

Considerations of land values and increments to the School Fund were to be of prime importance in the future debates about the requested reservation of land. In this case the legislative committee was using the issue to promote favorable action on the memorial. Soon, however, the issue would be used against the reservation and persist until the granting of a charter for an institution which in early 1860 was still only a vague possibility.

The committee did not believe that the petitioners were "prepared to occupy" as many as the three squares of land for which they had asked. Since the Natural History and Horticultural societies had "the means in hand to establish elegant structures" on one square, they finally recommended the reservation from sale of the second square between Newbury and Boylston Streets west of the Public Garden, provided that the petitioners would complete the buildings and landscaping within one year after the land was made available to them. There would be no charge for the use of the land but "said buildings and land, if perverted to other purposes," would "revert wholly and directly, without delay, to the Commonwealth." The committee's suggested resolve would impose restrictions on the price of lots opposite to this reserved square as well as on the method of payment, and further restrictions were placed on the sales of other land in the area.[30]

Rogers, Ross, Waterston, and others had testified before the Committee on Education and were undoubtedly much encouraged when the House passed the reservation bill on March 15, ordering it to be engrossed. The Senate, however, would prove to be a more difficult hurdle.[31]

Meanwhile, the Committee on Public Lands was conducting hearings on the 1859 petition of George Snelling asking for a change in the Back Bay plans to secure air for the Common.[32] In testimony Snelling wished to make clear that he was not against the original conservatory proposal. He felt that he had been unfairly blamed for its failure at the last session, but felt also that it was a project that could be established anywhere. Somewhat later he published a pamphlet with his plan and testimonials in favor of it from a variety of people, including several interested in the conservatory and its successor plan. He underscored the dire consequences of the Back Bay land fill and posed the "great question":

> Whether the millions that are to live on this peninsula shall have the privilege of breathing the pure air of heaven, freshened by the water from the ocean, or be forever deprived of such a blessing, that the treasury may be enriched. . . . One of our most intelligent citizens . . . had no doubt that the moral and intellectual elevation of Boston was, in a good degree, owing to the inspiring and refining influences of the scenery. . . . You cannot say to the toil-worn mechanic, panting for the fresh air of which you have deprived him and his family, "Go to Nahant or Newport!" . . . There can be no question but that the act of 1857 is virtually an act to increase the mortality of the capital; and Boston, hitherto, so healthy a city, will figure in vital statistics as a warning for wise and humane administrators in other parts of the world and in other ages.

Further, it was Snelling's belief that if the filling were allowed to progress, much of the land would remain unsold for up to fifty years:

> There are not now, and will not be for some years to come, a hundred men in Boston who are prepared to build those "first-class houses," to which the plan is exclusively adapted.
>
> So far from the millions being realized which have been promised from high official sources, it is not unlikely that, if the present plan be persisted in, it will end in a drain on the treasury.[33]

But in the end neither Snelling nor his predictions prevailed.

The House resolve became stalled in the Senate late in March 1860 despite an impassioned speech in its favor by the chairman of the Committee on Education, Senator Reed of Plymouth.[34] The bill was refused a third reading and laid on the table, became involved in motions to reconsider, and finally, on April 3, when the legislature prorogued until January 1861, was referred to the next General Court.[35]

Acknowledging the opposition, William Rogers had at first expressed confidence but at the end of March 1860 informed Henry that the resolve had failed to receive final approval:

This result we had not dreamed of while the matter was pending in the lower House, and its great success there made us at first quite confident that it would encounter no serious opposition in the Senate. But meanwhile some enemies of the bill were quietly preoccupying the minds of the senators, so that when the time for the action drew near we found that the narrow financial views instilled into them could not be corrected. Unluckily, the Back Bay lands were last year pledged to the increase of the common-school fund, and we were driven to the narrow basis of argument that our improvement would double the market value of the adjacent lots, and thus not take from the prospective school fund. We brought evidence to show that this would be the effect, but the majority of the senators refused to be convinced. In another year no doubt the measure can be carried, as now its merits are pretty well understood through the State, and we shall have a legislature uncommitted, to operate on.[36]

Newspaper accounts attest to the difficulties, centered chiefly on the matter of the School Fund. On the one hand, it was said that the proposal would be an aid to its enhancement; on the other, that it would result in a loss to the state. Some said that the projected increase in the value of the land was visionary; others thought Boston, which was intimately involved, should contribute. Still others questioned the right of the state to preempt the means of securing income which rightfully belonged to the common schools. Those who supported the bill cited the encouragement it would give to the arts and sciences, and the benefits it would bring to agriculture, manufactures, and the mechanic arts, for the institutions seeking the use of the land were educational in the highest sense of the word. The latter sentiments came from Senator Amasa Walker of Norfolk County, whose son, Francis Amasa Walker, would become the third president of the Massachusetts Institute of Technology.[37]

An editorial in the *Boston Transcript* commented at length on the Senate's refusal to pass the House bill, saying that in the debate, "a disgrace to the State," some of the reasons offered against passage showed "dullness of perception and ignorance of the subject. . . . not calculated to impress an outsider with a high idea of the boasted intelligence of Massachusetts." If the Senate planned to reject "all matters requiring some measure of intellect to be comprehended," then they should "keep their reasons to themselves."[38]

The records of the Natural History Society's Building Committee sum up the effort for that year, citing the "great efforts" of Rogers, Ross, Emerson, Waterston, and Binney, along with opposition from "country members, ex-Governor Boutwell, Sec. of education, and other interests" concerned about the School Fund. To engender "public interest in its welfare," the society decided to revive the discontinued practice of an annual address, a convenient excuse afforded by its thirtieth anniversary. Rogers was asked to be the speaker for what proved to be a "successful and brilliant revival" of an old custom.[39]

The affair was held on May 11, 1860, and Rogers proved to be a happy choice. The *Traveller* identified him as coming from Cambridge, which, as will shortly be apparent, he undoubtedly wished that he did. It reported that he had reviewed briefly the condition of the natural sciences in earlier times and cited the need for an organization such as the Boston Society of Natural History as it was founded in 1830. He cited the accomplishments of the scientific world in the previous thirty years and ended with an appeal on behalf of the society, which had "asked the Legislature for the privilege of doing the state a service by occupying some of its land upon the Back Bay for a museum that should be a benefit to all, and that privilege had been refused." He asked for "cooperation and hearty support" when the application would come again before the legislature.

The *Traveller* went beyond the substance of the talk to describe in some detail Rogers's approach and manner of delivery, giving further testimony to his legendary powers of oratory. Noting his "modest naturalness of manner" and "deep earnestness of feeling," the writer termed his address "electrifying" and a "great success," with "passages of glowing beauty," marked by "clear fluency of accurate diction," a "generous catholicity of temper . . . uttermost loyalty to truth," and an "assured mastery of knowledge."[40] High praise, even taking into account the florid flavor of much journalistic expression in the mid-nineteenth century. A comment on Rogers's inclusion of "effective humor here and there" provides a glimpse, too, into a seldom-seen side of his personality.

The Committee of Associated Institutions met on May 28 and resolved to press their case again, confident of ultimate success for what they continued to feel was the "greatest educational movement ever agitated in the state." Other than the founding of Harvard College in 1636, it may well have been. At this time Marshall Wilder, because of the press of other business, resigned as chairman of the committee but remained as a member, while William Rogers was elected to succeed him. Though a newspaper account reported the appointment of Rogers as final action, he informed his brother Henry on May 29 that he had "conditionally agreed" to accept the chairmanship.[41] No formal record of this meeting has been found, and Rogers himself later seemed unclear on the sequence of events. An 1861 letter from Samuel Kneeland, however, informed him that on May 28, 1860, George B. Emerson proposed a committee of three "to mature a plan for a Polytechnic Institution," that Rogers, Erastus B. Bigelow, and James M. Beebe had been chosen, with power to add to their ranks either from within or outside the general committee, and that "Messrs. Ross and Dalton were accordingly added some time in the summer."[42] Beebe had been a member of the general committee since March 11, 1859, when its numbers had been increased, and Charles H. Dalton had no formal connection with the effort until his appointment to this subcommittee.

George Barrell Emerson

George Barrell Emerson had presumably been added to the Committee of Associated Institutions as a representative of the interests of the Horticultural and Natural History societies, but no doubt also with an eye to his standing as a respected educational leader. And it is altogether fitting that he was the one to propose that the focus of the proposal before the legislature be sharpened through the preparation of a plan for a "polytechnic institution." Following his retirement in 1855 as proprietor of a school for "young ladies," which he had established in 1823, he had traveled to Europe to pursue both his botanical and educational interests, the latter particularly in Germany. An 1817 graduate of Harvard, his teaching experience had begun as principal of a private school in Lancaster, Massachusetts, and included a brief period as tutor in mathematics at Harvard and service as the first headmaster, from 1821 to 1823, of the English High School in Boston. He had been active in the founding of the Boston Mechanics' Institute in 1827 and the American Institute of Instruction in 1830.

The son of a physician, he had grown up on the family farm in Wells, Maine, where he was born in 1797, and where he developed a lifelong interest in natural science. He was active in the founding of the Boston Society of Natural History in 1830, serving as its second president for several years beginning in 1837. He is particularly well known for his extensive *Report on the Trees and Shrubs Growing Naturally in the Forests of Massachusetts*, first published in 1846. It was he who brought to Harvard the bequest of James Arnold of New Bedford that led to the establishment of the Arnold Arboretum. He would become an active member of the governing board of the Institute of Technology, serving from 1862 until his death in 1881, when his "earnest sympathy and support" dating from his appointment to the Committee of Associated Institutions were gratefully acknowledged, along with "his zealous labor in behalf of education in general . . . his varied intellectual culture, his wisdom as a counsellor, his sympathy and kindness as a teacher, and his urbanity and frankness as a gentleman," as well as "the enthusiasm with which, almost to the close of his fruitful life, he entered into whatever thought and purpose might tend to the spread of sound knowledge and to the intellectual and moral benefit of the community."[43]

James Madison Beebe was born in Pittsfield in 1809 and educated in the schools of that town and Stockbridge Academy. At the age of sixteen he became a clerk in a dry goods firm in Boston and at twenty-one was in business for himself, eventually becoming the second largest importer in the United States. He served as chairman of the family trust of banker and philanthropist George Peabody, and was once in business partnership with James Pierpont Morgan's son Junius, who left in 1855 to join the Peabody banking house in London. Beebe was a director of the Boston & Albany Railroad and Provident and Webster banks, and president of the Chicopee Manufacturing Company as well. He was also a trustee of the Massachusetts General Hospital, and from 1856 to 1858 had been president of the Boston Board of Trade. In 1862 he would become a member of the board of the Institute of Technology and serve until his death in 1875.[44]

Charles Henry Dalton, the son of a physician, was born in Chelmsford in 1826, and grew up in the new city of Lowell. His selection for the committee to plan a polytechnic undoubtedly rested on his experience with the textile industry, though his demonstrated organizational and administrative abilities, as well as his financial acumen, could not have been ignored. An auspicious beginning as a clerk in a Boston commission house led to an assignment to settle a strike at the Hamilton Woolen Company in Southbridge, where he remained in charge for several years. In 1854 he became a partner in the firm of J. C. Howe of Boston, also commission merchants, and was active in the reorganization of the Manchester Print Works in New Hampshire. During the Civil War he represented Governor Andrew in Washington, concerned with the recruitment and arming of the Massachusetts regiments. Like many of his Bostonian peers, he was a trustee or director of a number of institutions, serving as a trustee and president of the Massachusetts General Hospital, vice president of the New England Trust Company, and treasurer of several manufacturing companies. He was chairman of the Boston Park Commission during the development of the city's park system and also of the Boston Transit Commission, responsible for the construction of the subway. He would serve as MIT's first treasurer, from 1862 to 1866, and a member of its board until 1879. A memorial tribute following his death in 1908 emphasized his "excellent judgment" and "well-balanced mind," capable of "clear-headed" decisions "justified by subsequent results."[45]

The idea of a "technological institution" had begun to take hold, and the group was aware that the most recent memorial might have suffered "in part at least, due to the incompleteness and vagueness" of their initial statement with respect to the "claims of Industrial Science and Practical Education as leading objects in the plan of collocated institutions." Finding, however, that, "in spite of their ill success, an earnest and increasing interest was very generally felt for the establishment of an Institution devoted to Industrial Science and Education,—the Committee determined on taking such steps as were practicable towards the organization, in a preliminary form, of an Institution of this character."[46] William Rogers described their new effort to Henry and asked for some help:

> Among our present purposes is that of framing a plan for a Technological department, with which some of our leading men, as Erastus Bigelow, Ignatius Sargent, etc., think they can secure a subscription of $100,000 from the manufacturers and merchants, and that being assured, we can come before the Legislature with an irresistible claim.
>
> Now can you not, while in London, gather up all documents relating to the Kensington Museum, that in Jermyn Street, etc., which might be of assistance in digesting such a plan? You will do us a great service by sending me such as you collect.[47]

It is important to note the kind of institution to which he looked as examples.

Rogers's commitment to the plan continued to deepen. It had been a busy spring. During February, March, and April 1860, he was engaged in lively debates with Louis Agassiz at the Natural History Society on Charles Darwin's recently published work, *On the Origin of Species*, a review of which he had prepared for the *Boston Courier* of March 5.[48] He informed Henry that he did not "intend entering upon any general discussion with Agassiz in regard to Darwin's views," but would limit himself to "a fair exposition of such collateral geological ideas as may be introduced."[49] On this score he appears to have been very successful, entangling Agassiz in his own arguments and clearly winning the confrontation. Characterizing the Boston debates as "unique," one historian has asserted that "William Barton Rogers has not received justice in the history of the controversy."[50]

Rogers left the field to Asa Gray for similar debates with Agassiz at the American Academy. He shared with Gray the belief that Darwin's theories should not be rejected out of hand and deserved careful consideration by the scientific community, a decided change for Gray, who had bitterly opposed evolutionary ideas in the 1840s. Rogers was particularly upset by a report indicating that he had "followed Agassiz in *denouncing* Darwin's doctrine as unfounded and unphilosophical":

> I at once called for the correction, saying that I *denounced* no doctrine which aimed at honesty and truth, whatever might be its character, and that "I thought no man of science would for a moment think of denouncing any scientific opinion whatever, much less the calm and candid arguments of so fair minded a philosopher as Darwin." This, though unintentional, was a hard hit.[51]

An extract from a later letter to Henry sets forth his position:

> You will I suppose meet with Mr. Darwin at Oxford. Please say to him how much I have enjoyed his book & how proud I have been to enrol myself if not among his disciples in all respects, at least among the defenders of his leading doctrine, & of the broad philosophy which he exemplifies. . . .
>
> In New England & I believe elsewhere in this country the cause of liberal thought has been greatly secured by the publication of Darwin's book. Since a few of us stood up for fair play in regard to it, it is pleasant to see how many who would otherwise have kept sealed mouths have shewed their sympathy for unfettered inquiries.[52]

A rare description of Rogers in action stems from the Agassiz-Rogers discussions. Nathaniel Southgate Shaler, then a student of Agassiz and a member of the Natural History Society, has told of the delight he and his friends took in raising questions that would pit one against the other to the enjoyment of all:

> Agassiz was admirable in discourse, when at his best the most simply eloquent speaker I have ever heard, but his capacity for debate was small. Rogers, on the other hand, was not only an able and learned geologist, but very skilful in argument, with a keen sense of the logic which should control statements. . . . I can see before me now the noble shape and brilliant countenance of my master, as

he eagerly, often incautiously, set forth his hypothesis, while Rogers, keen-faced and alert, prepared himself for his attack. When his turn came, with an odd gesture by which he seemed to turn his eagle eyes "hard aport," he would launch on a task of mingled criticism and construction, in both of which he was most effective.[53]

In a lighter vein, and much later, Rogers engaged in an exchange on Darwin with Delia Rogers, his sister-in-law, who had written:

See Nature's secret is unveiled
Great Science's aim an end
A tadpole in the girl we love
A Jackass in a friend.
            as viewed by Dely Rogers, March 25, 1870

His reply:

Think what we will of Darwin's plan
It has this charm at any rate
An onward March is better than
A movement that's degenerate.
            W.B.R.[54]

More than the Darwinian controversy, of course, called for Rogers's attention. He was doing some geological work and was also much interested at this time in binocular vision. More than thirty geological or other scientific papers authored by him appeared between 1859 and 1861.[55] He planned a course of five or six lectures at New Bedford in 1860 but no speaking engagements in distant places.

The prospect of an appointment at Harvard, too, was very much on his mind. At the end of March 1860, he reported to Henry on the possibility:

Some days ago Hillard showed me part of a letter just received from Felton, now, you know, President of Harvard, in which he expresses the strong wish of himself and others to have me in Cambridge. They are proposing to establish a Professorship of Geology and Mining in connection with the Lawrence School, at least for the present; and when they have made such financial arrangements as will enable them to offer a respectable salary they will, I suppose, invite me to take the place.... If I enter Cambridge I can do so without in the slightest degree relinquishing the individuality I have heretofore maintained. So, at least, I think and on no other terms would I be willing to connect myself with the college. Probably no final step will be taken in this matter for two or three months. Hillard thinks they would not offer a less salary than $1,500, and that I should be able to continue to reside in Boston. For the present, of course, the matter is wholly between ourselves.[56]

Two individuals close to Agassiz later indicated that he was responsible for the failure of Rogers to secure the Harvard appointment, one saying that "it would have been politic on his part if he had offered the chair of geology to William B. Rogers, then a resident of Boston. But Agassiz did not like to have any one so near, who might overshadow him."[57] And Nathaniel Shaler, who would be graduated from the Lawrence Scientific School in 1862 and serve as dean from 1891 to 1906, agreed, even attributing to this personal conflict Rogers's growing dedication to the concept of an independent polytechnic institute:

> It was well known even to Agassiz's students that Rogers desired to have a place in Harvard College as professor of geology. He was admirably well fitted for this position, a man of distinguished general ability, well informed in the science and an admirable teacher. Agassiz was at once professor of zoology and geology, though I believe that I was the only person who ever took the degree in geology while he taught at Harvard, and I had mainly to depend on outside help and fight hard for my training.... Large-minded as my master was in most of his contacts with men, he could not be persuaded to allow Rogers beside him. Presuming, it may be, on our relations, which had become rather those of man with man than pupil with teacher, I tried to debate the proposition with him, only to find that it was not debatable. It was a pity, for from this refusal to give him the place in the School to which he was entitled by his quality and station, Rogers was in a way compelled to turn his energy to the creation of a rival institution, the Massachusetts Institute of Technology, with the result that Boston supports two rival schools in a field which has fair place for but one.[58]

Whether Rogers became more interested in the efforts of the Committee of Associated Institutions because a Harvard appointment was not immediately forthcoming is unclear, and the opinion of one man is not sufficient proof. A Harvard appointment, however, was a hope that Rogers did not abandon until some time after the Institute of Technology was founded. In the meantime, as a member of the sub-committee on a "technological department," he turned his attention to the preparation of a proposal that might find acceptance in the legislature.

Chapter 9

Facts of the Founding

During the summer of 1860, and into the early fall, William Rogers was at Sunny Hill, the Lunenburg (Massachusetts) summer home of his father-in-law, in not very good health but writing to his brother Henry on scientific matters, with occasional remarks about the political situation in the United States and the problems of secession and slavery. In August he attended the meeting of the American Association for the Advancement of Science at Newport, where he read two papers relating to geology, two on binocular vision, and one on the electric discharge in vacuum tubes.[1] He was working as well on the plan for a "technological department" for presentation to the legislature.

He was still at Sunny Hill when he informed Henry on September 24 that on a recent visit to Boston he had read a "pretty full outline" of a "*very large*" plan to the committee appointed in May. It had been "much liked" and would soon be presented to a "meeting of leading persons." It was a plan for an "Institute of Technology, to comprise a Society of Arts, an Industrial Museum, and a School of Industrial Science," and he believed that its "educational feature . . . ought most to recommend it" and that it would be "well appreciated":

> It provides for regular systematic teaching in Drawing and Design, Mathematics, general and applied Physics, Practical Chemistry, Geology and Mining, and would require at least five fully equipped professorships, besides laboratories, even at the beginning. It contemplates two classes of pupils— those who go through a regular and continuous course of practical studies, and those who attend the lectures on Practical Science and Art.[2]

When appointed in May, the committee had been asked to prepare a plan for a "Polytechnic Institution." Rogers's outline called it a "Technological Institute," but at some point prior to September 24, perhaps when he presented it to the committee, it became an "Institute of Technology." And later, when it was printed for wider circulation, the text indicated that it would be called the "Massachusetts Institute of Technology." Adding "Massachusetts" surely was done to gain broad acceptance from the public and legislators outside the city but also because the memorialists genuinely did look upon their project as beneficial to the entire state.

In 1890 Augustus Lowell, then a member of the Institute's governing board, stated that "technology" was included in the name of the new institution at the suggestion of Dr. Jacob Bigelow, "one of its earliest advocates, to represent a new departure in the history of instruction."[3] There is no manuscript evidence to support this attribution, and a resolution at the time of Bigelow's death in 1879 contains no reference to his part in the naming of the organization.[4] Lowell's source could well have been his father, John Amory Lowell, also an early supporter and, along with Bigelow, a vice president of the Institute in its earliest days. Rogers was of course no stranger to the word "technology." In 1846 he had referred to the Rumford Professorship at Harvard as the "Chair of Technology." He owned a copy of Bigelow's *Elements of Technology*, and he had added "Technology" to the title of Section III in the January 1860 memorial, the first which he had prepared and basically an extended version of the original petition related to the Conservatory of Art and Science. Whatever the source, it was a name that would endure.

On October 5, 1860, the plan was presented to a group of "leading citizens" and the Committee of Associated Institutions of Science and Arts at the rooms of the Boston Board of Trade in the Merchants' Exchange on State Street. The call to the meeting had announced that an effort would be made "at an early day, to organize an INSTITUTE OF TECHNOLOGY . . . to be established, if practicable, upon the land of the Commonwealth, on the Back Bay, in Boston." The committee, believing that their goal was "one of great importance to the business interests of the State," asked for the "sympathy and counsel of those who take an active interest in industrial progress."[5] Samuel H. Gookin, a dry goods importer and a director of the Board of Trade, presided in the absence of Erastus Bigelow, identified by the *Boston Advertiser* as "chairman of the sub-committee having the matter in charge." Letters to Rogers from Erastus Bigelow during this period indeed confirm that Bigelow was responsible for the arrangements with help from M. D. Ross. They particularly emphasize a desire to

BOSTON, Oct. 1, 1860.

Sir,

It is proposed to make an effort, at an early day, to organize an INSTITUTE OF TECHNOLOGY, — embracing a Society of Arts, a Museum of Technology, and a School of Industrial Science, for the promotion of Mechanics, Manufactures, and Commerce, — to be established, if practicable, upon the land of the Commonwealth, on the Back Bay, in Boston.

An outline of the objects and plan of the Institute, prepared at the suggestion of the "Committee of Associated Institutions of Science and Arts," will be read by Prof. WILLIAM B. ROGERS, at a meeting to be held on Friday, October 5, at eleven o'clock, A.M., at the Rooms of the Board of Trade, No. 55, Merchants Exchange.

Anxious to have the sympathy and counsel of those who take an active interest in industrial progress, and believing the object to be one of great importance to the business interests of the State, the Committee ask as an especial favor that you will be present on the occasion.

WILLIAM B. ROGERS,	AMOS BINNEY,
MARSHALL P. WILDER,	Dr. S. KNEELAND, jun.
SAMUEL H. GOOKIN,	CHARLES L. FLINT,
ALFRED ORDWAY,	B. S. ROTCH,
M. D. ROSS,	J. D. PHILBRICK,
ALEX. H. RICE,	GEO. B. EMERSON,
E. S. TOBEY,	R. C. WATERSTON,
JAMES M. BEEBE,	ERASTUS B. BIGELOW,
Dr. S. CABOT, jun.	CHARLES H. DALTON,

Committee.

"conform" these arrangements to Rogers's "wishes" and expressed the hope that he was "rapidly gaining in health."[6]

Rogers called his report, which was well received and highly praised, a mere outline of a broad plan, truly practical in nature and educational in the highest sense, in which the committee hoped to "interest those representing the material prosperity of the Commonwealth and directing its great mechanical, mercantile, and manufacturing energies." He pointed out the "advantages that would accrue to any state from the establishment of such an institute peculiarly within reach of the people of Massachusetts, the great manufacturing and commercial hive of New England."[7]

Alderman Otis Clapp was pleased that there would be another approach to the legislature, especially "with this additional and definite element in their educational plan." Massachusetts must have an Institute like this one, he said, to maintain its position as a manufacturing state and to compete. He emphasized the moral influence it would exert: "Many, and perhaps the majority of our people, are uninterested in useful knowledge, and he thought this plan promised to elevate the masses from low and sensuous pleasures to pursuits and aims at once noble, practical, and of public utility."[8]

Erastus Bigelow and M. D. Ross followed up immediately with letters which serve to clarify their position with respect to the developing plans. Both were happy with the outcome of the meeting. Bigelow believed that to gain maximum public support and political advantage the society should be organized as soon as possible and "members . . . admitted from every county in the State," a move calculated to "inspire general confidence, a condition indispensable to the procurement of legislative or financial aid."[9] The plan, Ross said, should not appear in the newspapers until it was available in pamphlet form, after which it should be distributed "all over the State . . . as the plan *actually* [adopted] by a society *actually organized*, but not able to go into operation until the land is reserved for its use by the Legislature."[10] Though it was prepared immediately for printing, its distribution and the attempt to organize the society were delayed until after the forthcoming presidential election.

Late in October William wrote to Henry about a variety of matters, including the probable success of Lincoln and Hamlin, sending him copies of the pamphlet for possible distribution abroad:

> After the elections are over, and the public ready for other thoughts, we shall try to interest parties here and in the other larger towns, so as to effect a preliminary organization. Then this Institute will join the Natural History Society, Horticultural Society, etc., in a renewed application to the Legislature for a grant of land on the Back Bay. I think you will find the plan of the

Institute to include all the features which we used to talk of, and to be at least broad enough for any practical result.[11]

Correspondence between the brothers at this time is notable for the absence of any indication that Henry might participate in the new venture. It is highly unlikely that he would relinquish his professorship in Scotland, where he appeared to be well settled. Nor is there any surviving discussion between the two of the role that William might play if the proposal should succeed. Obviously, however, his commitment was increasing.

Following the November election, the *Objects and Plan of an Institute of Technology*, addressed to "Manufacturers, Merchants, Mechanics, Agriculturists, and Other Friends of Enlightened Industry in the Commonwealth," was "distributed through the City and State among persons who were thought most likely to be interested in the subjects to which it relates; and in order to elicit the opinions and invite the co-operation of those best qualified to judge of the practical merits of the plan."[12] An accompanying circular letter signed by Rogers as chairman of the Committee of Associated Institutions of Science and Arts indicated that a meeting would soon be held to adopt "measures preliminary to the organization of the Institute." A copy of the pamphlet in the MIT Archives contains the characteristic "by W.B.R.," but some draft pages appear to have been written by others and later copied by him. One of these sections was prepared by M. D. Ross.[13]

The *Objects and Plan* is the first published statement about the proposed "Institution devoted to the Practical Arts and Sciences, to be called the MASSACHUSETTS INSTITUTE OF TECHNOLOGY, having the triple organization of a Society of Arts, a Museum or Conservatory of Arts, and a School of Industrial Science and Art."[14] As a Society of Arts, the Institute "would form itself into a department of investigation and publication":

> to promote research in connection with industrial science, by the exhibition, at the meetings of the Society, of new mechanical inventions, products, and processes; by written and oral communications and discussions, as well as by more elaborate treatises on special subjects of inquiry; and by the preparation and publication, statedly, of Reports exhibiting the condition of the various departments of industry, the progress of practical discovery in each, and the bearings of the scientific and other questions which are found to be associated with their advancement.[15]

Objects and Plan

of

An Institute of Technology

including

A Society of Arts, a Museum of Arts

and

A School of Industrial Science.

Proposed to be established in Boston.

Prepared by direction of the Committee of Associated
Institutions of Science & Arts,

and

Addressed to Manufacturers, Merchants, Mechanics
Agriculturists and other friends of enlightened Industry
in the Commonwealth.

A plan of action—draft of the title page and cover letter for a pamphlet, Objects and Plan of an Institute of
Technology, *by William Barton Rogers, ca. September 1860*

Dear Sir,

In sending you the accompanying pamphlet setting forth the objects and plan of an Institute of Technology proposed to be established if practicable on the Back Bay lands in Boston. We beg to request that you will give it your early and thoughtful attention.

In our view of the great advantages which the industrial interests and practical education of the Commonwealth would derive from such an Institution we cannot but hope that our plan will so approve itself to your judgement as to win your sympathy and active co-operation.

It is proposed at an early day to hold a meeting in this city for the purpose (of (formally organising) adopting measures preliminary to the organisation of) the Institute. Of this you will be duly notified; and we trust that your interest in the subject will secure us the benefit of your presence on the occasion. Meanwhile it will give us great pleasure to be allowed to number you among the prospective Members and to have the influence and authority of your name as well as the advantage of your counsel in connexion with the undertaking.

Should you (wish to be enrolled) and to write with as a Member) please indicate the class of subjects, as mentioned under the heads of "Committees of Arts", in which you would feel most directly interested.

for the Committee

William B Rogers
Ch:

A *Journal of Industrial Science and Art* would, the committee hoped, provide a record of the society's proceedings and the "condition and progress of the Museum and School," as well as a "faithful record of the advance of the Arts and Practical Sciences at home and abroad."[16]

Though the document was not intended to present a detailed outline of the proposed organization of the "Institute, in its character of a Society of Arts," it did indicate that its plan of government would be much like that of "similar societies elsewhere."[17] Twelve Committees of Arts were described in some detail, several relating to the various industrial arts, plus engineering and architecture, commerce, navigation and inland transport, and graphic and fine arts. There would also be separate committees on the Museum of Industrial Art and Science, or Conservatory of Arts—the word "Conservatory" now appearing again but in a minor way—the School of Industrial Science, and Publications.[18]

Of first importance for the museum would be the "extent of practical instruction to be derived. . . . A mere miscellaneous collection of objects, however vast, has little power to instruct, or even to incite to inquiry."[19] Possible arrangements of some departments were outlined, and the section closed with a caveat concerning the fluidity and flexibility of the proposal:

> Such is an imperfect sketch of the Museum of Industrial Science and Art, which we would desire to see established as the central feature of our proposed Institute of Technology. . . . We know, that, even under the happy auspices which seem to be gathering around our enterprise, the early development of the Museum must fall very far short of the imposing organization which our anticipations have traced; but it is the nature of such a plan to be susceptible of indefinite expansion.[20]

Important as these two segments were "as instruments for diffusing practical knowledge, and affording incentives and suggestions tending to the improvement of the industrial arts," the third component—the School of Industrial Science and Art—would provide "that *systematic training in the applied sciences*, which can alone give to the industrial classes a sure mastery over the materials and processes with which they are concerned":

> Such a training, forming what may be called the intellectual element of production, has, we believe, become indispensable to fit us for successful competition with other nations in the race of industrial activity, in which we are so

deeply interested. In the communities abroad, where manufactures and the mechanic arts have attained the greatest proficiency, and are now making the most rapid advances, such an education in practical science is recognized as the chief instrument in their extension and improvement; and the Schools of Practical Science, and the Polytechnic Institutes, designed to form an industrial class thus thoroughly trained in the principles of their respective arts, are highly honored, as well as liberally, and even munificently, endowed.[21]

The proposed School of Industrial Science and Art would thus offer "regular courses . . . in the various branches of the applied sciences and the arts." Here "persons destined for any of the industrial pursuits might, at small expense, secure such training and instruction as would enable them to bring to their profession the increased efficiency due to enlarged views and a sure knowledge of fundamental principles, together with adequate practice in observation and experiment, and in the delineation of objects, processes, and machinery."[22]

Rogers did not lay out a definite organization for the proposed school but did include a brief description of the several expected branches of instruction: design; mathematics; physics, both general and applied; applied chemistry, requiring an "ample and well-appointed *Laboratory*"; and geology, including "*Physical Geology and Mining*." Each of these would be designated as a "SCHOOL," with the teaching oriented toward the needs of the mechanic arts, engineering, architecture, manufacturing, and agriculture. The instruction in the "SCHOOL OF DESIGN" might also be a "valuable help to general education." In this connection Rogers mentioned also the "higher culture of the Fine Arts," the latter a remnant of the conservatory proposal that would eventually disappear.[23]

There would be two classes of students:

those who enter the school with the view of a progressive systematic training in applied science, and who have the preliminary knowledge, as well as time, for a continuous prosecution of its studies; and the far more numerous class, who may be expected to resort to its lecture-rooms for such useful knowledge of scientific principles as they can acquire without methodical study, and in hours not occupied by active labor.[24]

Instruction would not be free, but it was hoped that the "entire systematic training" might be "within reach of aspiring students of humble means, and that the lecture-room instructions might be made accessible to all at only an inconsiderable expense."[25]

"Merely popular lecturing in its usual form" was regarded as "inconsistent with the grave practical purposes which we have in view" and "could not be recognized in connection with our plan." There was the possibility, however, of "much valuable aid from courses of lectures on subjects not directly provided for in the School, but of a nature to be conducive to the general objects of the Institute."[26]

The final paragraphs captured the overall educational mission:

It will be apparent that the education which we seek to provide, although eminently practical in its aims, has no affinity with that instruction in mere empirical routine which has sometimes been vaunted as the proper education for the industrial classes. We believe, on the contrary, that the most truly practical education, even in an industrial point of view, is one founded on a thorough knowledge of scientific laws and principles, and which unites with habits of close observation and exact reasoning a large general cultivation. We believe that the highest grade of scientific culture would not be too high as a preparation for the labors of the mechanic and manufacturer; and we read in the history of social progress ample proofs that the abstract studies and researches of the philosopher are often the most beneficent sources of practical discovery and improvement.

But such complete and comprehensive training can, in the nature of things, be accessible to only comparatively few; while the limited and special education which our plan proposes, would, we hope, fall within the reach of a large number whom the scantiness of time, means, and opportunity, would exclude from the great seats of classical and scientific education in the Commonwealth.

It will thus be seen, from the peculiar character and objects of this Department of the Institute, that it could not interfere with the interests of the established schools of learning devoted to general literary and scientific education. Aiming to supply the industrial classes with a knowledge and training of which they are specially in need, and which it would be incompatible with the purpose and organization of the universities and colleges to attempt to provide, it would, we feel assured, command the good wishes and active sympathies of the scholars, and men of science, who dispense the high instruction of these schools. Nor can we doubt that it would be gladly welcomed by all those who are practically occupied in the Arts, as a new source of success and enjoyment in their labors; while, by the large-minded manufacturers, merchants, mechanics, and agriculturalists, who control the material fortunes of the Commonwealth, it would be heartily and liberally recognized as a needed and truly momentous addition to our means of industrial as well as of educational prosperity.[27]

The *Objects and Plan* was circulated locally to many Harvard faculty members, prominent Boston clergy, the newspapers, all the members of the General Court, Daniel Treadwell, people from the New Bedford, Bridgewater, and Worcester areas, and even Nathaniel Hawthorne, Ralph Waldo Emerson, and A. B. Alcott of Concord. Copies were sent also to the president of Columbia and to Peter Cooper in New York, Benjamin Silliman at Yale, and Joseph Henry at the Smithsonian, among others. A long list of various categories of manufacturers, bankers, educators, architects, artisans, engineers, and government officials prepared by M. D. Ross as prospective recipients brought the estimated total of copies needed to 5,655. Whether such a large distribution was ever made is not known, but a second edition was printed in 1861.[28]

The response was gratifying. Someone called the plan "the most important plan ever set in motion in Massachusetts," and there were offers of help, support for the inclusion of mining and geology, and special praise from the president of the Mechanics' Institute.[29] Several individuals indicated particular interest in one or more of the Committees of Arts. Thomas Sherwin, headmaster of the Boston English High School, wisely sensed the amount of money needed to put the plan in full operation:

> No department of human life demands and appropriates a greater amount of genius and of accumulated knowledge than the industrial. . . . The best interests, not only of our community, but of our whole country and even of the entire world, require that the supply should be as nearly as possible commensurate with the demand. With these convictions, I am sincerely grateful to you for the very able manner in which you have shown how the desiderata may be attained. The plan is magnificent and will demand magnificent means. I hope that, after the present political and financial disturbance shall have subsided, the requisite means will be forthcoming.[30]

Sherwin would become a member of the Government of the new Institute of Technology and its Committee on Instruction in 1863, serving until his death in 1869. He came quite naturally to the support of the proposed institute, as it gave promise of extending the aims and opportunities for which his own institution had been founded in 1821.[31]

In October 1860 the Natural History Society learned of a bequest of $10,000, and this tangible encouragement provided new vigor for their effort to obtain a grant of land on the Back Bay. In December Rogers moved that a "statement of the wants and claims of the Society and the necessity for a larger building" be prepared for publication. He, Dr. Augustus A. Gould, and Amos Binney were chosen to do so. A pamphlet, based on reports of the various curators and entitled *Objects and Claims of the Boston Society of Natural History*, was issued early in January 1861. It followed very closely the format of the Institute's *Objects and Plan* and was distributed to members of both houses of the legislature.[32]

The Horticultural Society's space problems had been solved, at least for the short term, through their five-year leasing arrangement for Amory Hall. In December 1860, following a meeting at which Rogers informed them of the plan to memorialize the legislature once again, a previously appointed committee recommended that the society proceed with a petition, promising to erect within five years "a crystal palace or conservatory for its use and for the growth of plants commensurate with the wants of the society, the progress of horticultural science, and honorable alike to the city and Commonwealth." But doubts were expressed about the expediency of the whole idea, a vote was postponed, and more information was requested on what was expected of them.[33]

When the Committee of Associated Institutions met again on December 31, Marshall Wilder reported on the society's hesitation. Rogers worried that since the governor planned to speak favorably of the entire plan in his annual message, "any hesitating or backward movement" on the society's part "might prove embarrassing." George Emerson questioned petitioning the legislature at all without their participation, for they alone could provide a "beautiful and attractive plan" for the site. Rogers agreed that "imparting external beauty" and thus perhaps adding "pecuniary value to the land" might be of some importance, and was sure that the "Natural History and Technological Societies" would erect "handsome buildings" with "attractive surroundings." Most important, however, they would offer benefits to the "scientific, industrial, commercial, and educational interests" of the state "worthy of the attention and generous assistance" of a legislative body very likely "as much interested in science and industrial progress as in agriculture and horticulture." Rogers added, however, that he hoped the Horticultural Society would submit a petition without asking for any particular plot of land, leaving its division to be decided later among the societies themselves. Erastus Bigelow hoped that "unity of purpose and a distinct plan, even to the details, would be adhered to; without these he had very little hope of success."[34]

❧

The final attempt to secure the reservation of land and the first effort to obtain a charter for the proposed Institute of Technology were launched with the opening of the legislative session of 1861 and a new governor, John A. Andrew, in office. The *Boston Journal* printed a favorable editorial on the project, saying in part:

> This noble project is worthy of our Commonwealth, and, setting aside the claims and great advantages to science, the pecuniary interests of Boston demand it. While other cities are planning princely parks and other projects too costly for our ability, it behooves Boston to see that it loses not its fair name and its power to retain our men of science and culture, as well as to elevate and refine the masses, and to attract strangers.[35]

Governor Andrew's address to the opening session of the legislature on January 5, 1861, contained a section on "Practical Scientific Institutions":

> The wise foresight which has secured such large provision for the education of the children of the Commonwealth, enjoins us to use all reasonable means to promote the spread of useful knowledge, and especially to facilitate such practical scientific instruction as shall elevate while it invigorates the industrial arts.
>
> A favorable opportunity is now afforded to advance this desirable object by setting apart a suitable portion of the Back Bay lands for the accommodation and collocation of institutions devoted to practical branches of art and science. In this connection, the views and wishes of the Boston Society of Natural History, the Massachusetts Horticultural Society, and the Institute of Technology have already to some extent been presented to the Legislature, and will, it is understood, be submitted to you during your present session, in detail. The valuable contributions which the two first named societies have rendered, the enlarged sphere of usefulness which under these new conditions they would be enabled to fill, and the material benefits which the proposed Institute of Technology is adapted to confer, are considerations which commend the purposes of the petitioners to the favorable attention of all friends of education and industry, and will, I doubt not, receive at your hands such liberal appreciation as they deserve.[36]

Having made this encouraging statement and despite the land fill already in progress, Governor Andrew nevertheless raised the question of whether there might be some way to create the basin of water proposed by George Snelling and supported by Josiah Quincy, a bill still before the legislature.[37]

The petition by the Boston Society of Natural History, dated January 1, 1861, and signed by Jeffries Wyman as president, asked for a grant of land on the Back Bay for its use in accordance with the petition of the Committee of Associated Institutions of Science and Arts.[38] The Horticultural Society, however, still wavered. In his address to its annual meeting on January 5, President Joseph Breck reviewed the history of the appeals to the legislature since 1859 and once more urged caution:

> The whole scheme may, perhaps, appear to some Quixotic; but if we have a continuation of the unexampled increase and prosperity of our country, we may reasonably believe that the Back Bay will, in a few years, become the most prominent and attractive part of the city; and when these sections we desire to be reserved are surrounded with elegant residences, no doubt liberal subscriptions will be readily made, if needed, to sustain the institutions which we hope will be established there.
>
> The present aspect of the affairs of our country have so affected my own mind, that I must confess I have some misgivings about the rapid settlement of the Back Bay lands; for, if our worst fears should be realized, there may be such a depreciation of the value of this land, as well as of all other property, that it might about as well have remained from whence the soil or gravel was taken, where the possessor of a farm composed of it was the poorer the more he had of it. God grant that we may have a speedy settlement of all our difficulties. Yet, with the present existing uncertainty of public affairs, my courage rather fails me, and I feel almost inclined to recede from the stand I have hitherto taken. No doubt our Society will be disposed to use all their influence in aiding and assisting the other associations, but I trust we shall not commit ourselves to any course that will involve us in any very heavy expense.[39]

The gloomy problems to which Breck referred were those leading up to the outbreak of the Civil War. Certainly the political climate influenced the time and attention that could be devoted to consideration of a subject in many ways remote from the fundamental issues tearing the country apart, though the Institute of Technology and its orientation toward the industrial arts might well have been cited as an aid to the economic health of a region that could be sorely hampered by the lack of Southern cotton should war break out.

Preoccupation with the presidential election had already delayed the distribution of the *Objects and Plan* in the hope of a more tranquil moment. As the citizens of Boston—and friends and members of families—lined up on opposite sides of the national debate, strains developed in the fabric of a community with no clear and set-tled view about the implications of slavery, the dangers of secession, the preservation of the Union, the competency of President Lincoln, and the effects of all of these prob-lems on the manufacturing interests of the region. It was hardly the most propitious time to garner solid support for a new venture.

Despite President Breck's misgivings, however, and after much discussion and some amendments to their committee's recommendation, the Horticultural Society finally voted to ask for a grant of a portion of the land between Berkeley and Clarendon Streets, "to be used for the promotion of horticulture and the legitimate objects of the society and for no other purpose."[40] Asking for a specific piece of land was contrary to the expressed wish of Rogers, who was no doubt responsible for the altered wording when the society's petition was submitted on January 14 asking only for "a section of land in the Back Bay."[41]

Early in January 1861 a circular notified all who had received the *Objects and Plan* of a meeting on January 11 to organize an association to petition for an act of incorpora-tion for the Institute of Technology. This would constitute the final phase in the devel-opment of this proposal. A section for return provided an opportunity for those unable to attend to indicate their willingness to be placed on a "List of Prospective Members" of the proposed Institute.[42]

An editorial in the evening edition of the *Boston Transcript* on January 10 praised the plan for the "largeness of its general views, and the homely sagacity of its practical suggestions," adding:

We can afford to laugh at the vaporing of Southern secessionists as long as we feel conscious that our system of labor is such as to enable us to compete with other nations in the markets of the world. To do this, we need not only indus-try, but intelligent industry; and the success of the present plan for the estab-lishment of an Institute of Technology would tend greatly to make and keep our industry intelligent. Every dollar given for this purpose by manufacturers and men of business and capital, will be returned a hundred fold.[43]

When the "friends of the Institute" gathered on January 11 at Mercantile Hall, 16 Summer Street, they chose Rogers as chairman for the evening and as secretary, John D. Runkle, an 1857 graduate of the Lawrence Scientific School who was currently an assistant to Benjamin Peirce, then the consulting astronomer for the *American Ephemeris and Nautical Almanac*, based in Cambridge. For Runkle, whose name had been placed on the list to receive a copy of the *Objects and Plan* by M. D. Ross, that evening was the beginning of a long association with the Institute.[44]

Several pages of undated handwritten notes by Rogers appear to be an outline of his presentation to those called together "to assure ourselves that the plan in which we are interested has won the approving sympathy & kindled the friendly zeal of the community to such a degree as may encourage us to persevere," and "to frame a preliminary organization or association by the formal record of membership in the proposed Institute of Technology of such as heartily approve its objects & plans." Believing that the formation of this association would lead to favorable legislative action, he proposed the preparation of a plan of government to be put into operation as soon as the Institute was legally chartered. The nearly one hundred persons who had indicated interest represented many walks of industry, science, and the professions, and he asked those friends present to aid in the extension of this list to other interested persons.[45]

As reported in the *Boston Transcript*, Benjamin Peirce spoke in favor of the proposed Institute, citing "a great want of such practical education among our mechanics. . . . This Institute, he believed, was a public necessity for this purpose, that the mechanic may accomplish intelligently and from a knowledge of principles what he is now apt to do solely from a routine manual dexterity. . . . He believed a beginning had now been made, and in the right way to accomplish a good thing."[46] The Reverend Ezra S. Gannett expressed thanks "in behalf of religion for this great educational movement" and praised the committee "for their disinterested and so far successful labors in the face of so many obstructions and under so dark a political horizon":

> Whatever educates and refines the laboring classes, brings them nearer to God . . . a knowledge of God's works, and the principles which govern the material universe, is conducive to the highest piety. . . . The education of the laboring classes in the direction of their employments was a good measure politically as well as morally: a people wisely at work are free from the temptations to do mischief which indolent and ignorant communities are so apt to fall in with and yield to.[47]

An "Act of Association of an Institute of Technology" was adopted:

We the subscribers, feeling a deep interest in promoting the Industrial Arts & Sciences as well as practical education, heartily approve the objects & plan of an Institute of Technology embracing a Society of Arts, a Museum of Arts, and a School of Industrial Science, as set forth in the Report of "the Committee of Associated Institutions, etc.," and we hereby associate ourselves for the purpose of endeavoring to organize & establish in the city of Boston such an Institution under the title of the Mass: Institute of Technology, whensoever we may be legally empowered & properly prepared to carry these objects into effect.[48]

Thirty-seven signatures were appended to the document, including those of Eben N. Horsford and Benjamin Peirce of Harvard.

A Committee of Twenty was appointed "with power to increase their number . . . to represent the interests and objects of the Association, and to act generally in its behalf, until it shall be legally incorporated and regularly organized under the title, and according to the purposes, of the Massachusetts Institute of Technology."[49] They were instructed to work with the Committee of Associated Institutions of Science and Arts to secure from the legislature both a charter for the Institute and a grant of land for its own use and that of "other institutions devoted to the Practical Sciences," and to prepare a "Constitution and By-laws for the government of said Institute in its several departments."[50]

Ross had apparently drawn up a tentative list for the Committee of Twenty, identifying some by profession and some by the sections of the school with which he thought they might become associated. Not all of these were appointed, the final membership including nine members of the Committee of Associated Institutions: James M. Beebe, Erastus B. Bigelow, Charles H. Dalton (marked on Ross's list for the School of Design), Charles L. Flint, Samuel H. Gookin, John D. Philbrick, M. D. Ross, Edward S. Tobey, and Marshall P. Wilder. Among the remainder were Thomas Aspinwall, a lawyer; Edward Clarke Cabot, an architect; John Chase, a contractor from Chicopee; James A. Dupee, a stock and exchange broker; James B. Francis, a hydraulic engineer; John C. Hoadley, an engineer and manufacturer; Frederic W. Lincoln, a nautical instrument maker and mayor of Boston from 1858 to 1860; Thomas Rice, a paper manufacturer, member of the Massachusetts legislature from 1857 to 1860, and chairman of the joint special committee on the petition of the conservatory in 1859; John P. Robinson, a commission merchant; John D. Runkle, listed by Ross for the School of Mathematics; and Francis H. Storer, a chemist with a degree from the Lawrence Scientific School in

We the subscribers, feeling a deep interest in promoting the Industrial Arts & Sciences as well as practical education, heartily approve the objects & plan of an Institute of Technology embracing a Society of Arts, a Museum of Arts and a School of Industrial Science, as set forth in the Report of "the Committee of Associated Institutions, &c." and do hereby associate ourselves, for the purpose of endeavoring to organize & establish, in the city of Boston, and an Institution under the title of the Mass: Institute of Technology, whensoever we may be legally empowered & properly prepared to carry these objects into effect

William B Rogers

Chs. E. Ware

T. Russell Jencks

Carlos Pierce

Nath. B. Shurtleff

John T. Heard

Jas. C. Converse

Joel Parker

Jona Preston

Francis Alger

Geo. L. Garrett

C. Allen Browne

E. S. Ritchie

Aug. A. Hayes

Sidney Homer

Amos Williams

Thomas Boyd

Geo. W. Tuxbury

Hen. Bigelow

Jno. C. Dalton

Samuel A. Green

Geo Odiorne

Levi L. Willcutt

E. B. Ellis

Chas. Nowell

John D. Philbrick

E. N. Horsford

Benjamin Peirce

Wm. P. Parrott

H. Dalton

Wm. E. Coale

J. D. Runkle

Daniel Bryant

R. Morris Copeland

James Slade

Chas. W. Folsom

Chas. B. Kittle

1855, listed by Ross for the School of Chemistry.[51] On a motion by Gookin, Rogers was added as chairman of the Committee of Twenty, the designation of which was not altered to reflect an additional member. It is inconceivable that his appointment could have been an afterthought. He was at the top of Ross's list, identified as a scientist, and by now, having been responsible for the preparation of the *Objects and Plan*, his further active participation and leadership were clearly essential.

Within a few days two separate memorials were presented to the legislature, both in the hand of Rogers and signed by him as chairman of the respective committees, their names listed. The Committee of Twenty sought a charter and a grant of land:

> for an Institution to be entitled the Mass: Institute of Technology having for its objects the advancement of the Mechanic Arts, Manufactures, Commerce, Agriculture & the Applied Sciences generally together with the promotion of the practical education of the Industrial Classes;—and proposing to attain these ends by the threefold agency of discussions & publications relating to industrial art & science,—by a Museum of Technology embracing the materials, implements & products of the practical arts & sciences,—and by a School of Industrial Science for instruction by lectures, laboratories & other teachings in these several departments.
>
> They also respectfully pray that a section of land on the Back Bay may be reserved & granted to the use of said Institute on such terms and conditions as may be deemed most conducive to the objects of the Institute and the industrial & educational interests of the Commonwealth.[52]

The memorial of the Committee of Associated Institutions of Science and Arts asked first that the legislature grant a charter to the proposed Institute and, second, that a continuous piece of land be set aside in the Back Bay for its use and for the Horticultural and Natural History societies, pointing to "the amplest evidences of public approbation and sympathy":

> Your memorialists, therefore, feel no hesitation in renewing their application to your honorable body in a modified and more perfect form; trusting the issue to your wise judgment of the merits of their plan, and to the ever-recognized claims of education, industry, and science upon the fostering favor of the State.[53]

On January 16, 1861, the Boston Board of Trade decided to support the proposals, feeling that the Institute, with provision for "material prosperity as well as for intellectual progress," was now more in keeping with their own goals than the earlier proposal, which they had declined to support:

> In the departments which concern us as merchants we find that due attention is intended to commerce and manufacturers, to maritime and inland transport, to statistics of foreign and domestic trade, to the improvement of harbors and the construction of docks and piers, to the model equipment and propelling power of vessels, and naval architecture generally. This development of the original design has caused the active cooperation of our committee.[54]

Hearings before the Joint Standing Committee on Education were soon under way and fully reported in the papers. The proponents emphasized the educational advantages and the benefits to industry and the economic viability of the state. The opponents focused on the financial aspects—losses in revenue to the state, and, in turn, to the principal of the School Fund.

Speaking for the entire plan at the first hearing, Rogers emphasized that "the application is a united one, and does not represent a multitude of diverse interests, as might at first appear." He cited the interlocking nature of the purposes of the petitioning institutions and the mutual benefit to be derived, with a resulting economy of expenditure. He described the Boston Society of Natural History as "a great adult school whose means of instruction in the science of nature are widely availed of," mentioning its contributions over thirty years to the "education of the public mind and to the promotion of the material interests of the community." He spoke of the "beneficial influence" of the Horticultural Society. The Institute of Technology, with as "yet no positive existence," he termed a necessity for a state whose natural resources were poor—"it is only through the force of intelligence concentrated upon industry that the position of the Commonwealth can be sustained." The petitioners, he stressed, "only ask for space to carry out this beneficent system of co-partnership at their own expense."[55]

Erastus Bigelow was the chief spokesman for the Institute of Technology and was followed at the second hearing by M. D. Ross on the financial effect of the requested reservation. No prepared text for Bigelow has been found, but the newspapers presented a full report of his strong and lengthy statement. Pointing out that the Institute was "designed to connect theoretical or school education with the practical pursuits and necessaries of life," and that the United States had no institution to respond to this need, he said:

> The application of science to the arts of life, theoretically taught in some of
> our universities, is not practically cared for in this country, as it is in Europe.
> The managers of such an institution . . . must be practical business men . . .
> from their experience able to direct the stream of useful knowledge in the
> proper channels. The Society of Arts . . . will be composed of business men,
> who will direct the affairs of the Museum and the Industrial school.

Bigelow suggested "about 82,000 feet of land, or two-thirds of a square," and assumed that under the worst circumstances the state would lose no more than $100,000 as a result of the reservation from sale, almost certain to be lessened by an increase in the value of the adjacent land. "Such an Institute is a *necessity*," he said, bringing forth the now familiar argument that "manufacturing must be the business of Massachusetts" and adding that "in many departments she sees business tending to other localities, in spite of the education, intelligence, enterprise, and thrift of her people." From his own early experience when "instruction even in the principles of practical science" was not available, he had come to appreciate the "proper value" of "such schools as the Institute will be." He emphasized that "this is not a Boston, but a State Institution" to which the "State was bound to offer a helping hand . . . for the sake of her citizens in all coming time, that they may not be forced to struggle against unnecessary obstacles in their business pursuits, which in the aggregate must form the wealth and determine the position of this commonwealth among her sister States."[56]

M. D. Ross had been convinced from the beginning that the state would not suffer financially through the requested grant of land, and was confident of the force of his arguments presented in a pamphlet entitled *Estimate of the Financial Effect of the Proposed Reservation of Back-Bay Lands*.[57] An accompanying testimonial signed by twelve individuals identified as "architects, builders, and dealers in real estate in Boston" supported his contention that a reservation of land for the educational purposes outlined would lead to the enhancement of the value of the adjacent property.[58]

This was a vital part of the testimony as it became increasingly evident that opposition was centered around the money that might be lost to the School Fund. Reserving from sale a small amount of land hardly seems to have called for such concentrated opposition, but the School Fund was a "sacred" item. It must also be remembered that the legislators were being importuned constantly by Agassiz for money in the name of pure science. The 1859 legislative grant for his museum was to come from the School Fund in annual installments, but the state's Back Bay Commissioners had indicated late in 1860 that an initial distribution would not be made until August 1861, at which time he would probably receive $20,000.[59]

Succeeding testimony by George Emerson dealt principally with the petitions of the Natural History and Horticultural societies, their relation to the larger plan and their value to the public. President Breck, speaking for the Horticultural Society, concurred in the belief that a "collection of the native trees and shrubs of the state would be of great value to the agricultural interests of the Commonwealth" and promised to develop such a collection, while Mr. Strong, a vice president of the society, indicated that in time a conservatory would be added, "making a winter as well as a summer garden for the citizens of the state visiting Boston."[60]

Rogers had a final word:

It would be humiliating indeed if a great state could not grant the reservation asked for on account of higher grounds than the question of dollars and cents. He considered that he was advocating a grand educational plan of the highest range and a benefit for all time to the state, and he should consider his time ill spent in pressing the financial aspect of the plan prominently before the committee. It is something that cannot be estimated in money value that this committee are working for, namely, the education of the people of the state in those principles of knowledge of daily application for which common schools and colleges make no provision.[61]

Shortly after these hearings, Ross informed Rogers of a conversation with Joseph White, then secretary of the State Board of Education, who, he said, labored "under the grossest ignorance of the facts" about the sales prices of the Back Bay lands:

I expressed a wish that we might have the *cooperation* of the Board of Education. He remarked in reply that he did *not* regard our plans as *Educational* and added that Prof. Rogers seemed to have some fears that the public would not so estimate them and that consequently the scheme would lack sufficient "dignity" to suit you. I think he is a *contemptable* [*sic*] specimen of an Educational man. Just as he (White) made this remark our friend Parker of Worcester came along, shook me by the hand warmly and expressed his delight at seeing us again in the field pursuing our plans. I gave him a copy of the Estimate. It will be a pleasure to me now to see that Board of Education (alias ignorance) well raked down as they deserve.[62]

Among the members of that board in 1861 was Cornelius C. Felton, president of Harvard University![63]

When Rogers prepared a list of those in favor and opposed, he identified White as a "great enemy,"—"Log rolling," he noted. He felt, however, that they would prevail even without White's support:

> A newly appointed officer of little influence. I think we shall succeed, though movements of opposition, of which we know nothing, may defeat us. The interest excited by the Technological plan among the intelligent and liberal-minded is rapidly extending. . . . John A. Lowell takes a lively interest in the matter, and I think will help it substantially.[64]

The affair was moving slowly, however, the *Traveller* reporting on February 6 that the Committee on Education "are still hammering on the Back Bay land reservation, and are not, judging from appearances, very near the end of the hearing."[65]

Early in February Ross informed Governor Andrew of a suggestion by a Board of Education member that a meeting with the Committee of Associated Institutions might help to clear up the board's misapprehension about the plan in relation to the School Fund. And he reminded him that the memorial indeed represented a "State Educational movement" that should receive the Board's "full cooperation."[66] This would not happen for more than a month and only after further prodding from Rogers himself. In the meantime, Ross urged Rogers to "see White and feel his pulse a little."[67]

When John D. Philbrick testified before the fourth hearing of the legislative committee, he addressed the question of the School Fund, of which, as superintendent of the Boston Public Schools, he had firsthand knowledge. Stating first that he was not opposed either to an increase in the fund or the fund itself, he asked by how much it would be diminished and what the benefits of the reservation plan might be in comparison with the "trifling addition which the sale of the land would make to the School Fund." And he pointed out that from the beginning the fund's stated object was the encouragement rather than the support of education. Even if $100,000 could be added, "the average increase to the educational advantages of the children of the State . . . would be less than one cent apiece. It would be a waste of time to dwell upon the comparison further."[68]

George S. Boutwell replied that the Board of Education had never taken a position on the plan though some members favored it, adding that the "School Fund must stand on its merits." The legislature's committee "must judge of the limits within which its usefulness should be circumscribed. . . . Weigh well the evidence, and see that the cause of education was properly cared for."[69]

In response Rogers stressed the "educational capital" that would accrue to the Commonwealth:

Education is not for children alone, nor does instruction cease with the school and college; it was the duty of a State to educate not only the young in the rudiments of knowledge, but to instruct the adults in the principles and practice of intelligent industry. . . . nearly two hundred individuals, representing the wealth, intelligence, and industrial energy of various parts of the State had signified a wish to become members. . . . Such assurances of approbation and of earnest sympathy . . . gave evidence of the fitness of the enterprise to the wants and aspirations of the community, and furnished a happy augury of the success of the new instrument of practical education which it is proposed to set in action for the benefit of the Commonwealth.[70]

He spoke also of the Boston Society of Natural History, its "service to the State for the last thirty years," and its readiness to "go on and build at once." And finally:

The committee ask not a *boon*, but only an *opportunity*, from the State, in requesting this reservation; they consider that the institutions they propose to develop there will confer, in all future time, benefits upon the intellectual and material interests of the State, compared with which the pittance which some fear may be taken from the School Fund sinks into utter insignificance.[71]

During the course of his remarks Rogers had already mentioned for the first time that the petitioners for the Institute of Technology would request that any grant of land by the Commonwealth be accompanied by a condition that they raise a guarantee fund for the "proper carrying out of the plan."

As the legislative deliberations continued, the Boston newspapers provided coverage and favorable editorial commentary. In mid-February 1861 Rogers was rather hopeful, though he informed Henry that the "public mind" was in "advance" of the legislature and the "fear of entrenching upon the fund devoted to the common schools is an obstacle to our success. The fund is of course a darling of the demagogues, as well as with the well-meaning who are imperfectly informed." The newspapers also were reporting and commenting on a similar effort in New York, where Rogers said his pamphlet was "exciting much attention." It had been "highly extolled" in the *Evening Post*, the editor of which was William Cullen Bryant. It was quoted as well in the *Tribune*, the author of the latter piece having made special note of the failure of the

Massachusetts legislature to act favorably at an earlier session, stating that since the country did not need two such institutions, New York was the better location.[72] On February 6 a bill had indeed been filed in the New York Legislature for the incorporation of an Institute of Technology to be located in Central Park, where the establishment of a zoological and botanical garden had already been authorized. It was referred to the Committee on Literature, and its legislative history appears to have ended there.[73] Ross immediately called the relevant articles to the attention of Rogers:

> The enterprising people of New York are being "waked up" by the Institute of Technology. Between N.Y. and Cambridge—we may have bidders enough for our knowledge of the subject to be in demand even if we are not appreciated by our own Legislature.[74]

A most flattering form of response, stemming from the copy of the *Objects and Plan* sent to Peter Cooper, deserves particular mention. In 1857 the New York Legislature had passed an act to "enable Peter Cooper to found a Scientific Institution in the City of New York," a building for which was already under construction. As a youth Peter Cooper had had little opportunity for education, but his natural inventiveness and mechanical ingenuity enabled him to take full advantage of an apprenticeship to a coach-maker and, aided as well by a keen business sense, to move on to succeed handsomely as a manufacturer. His business interests ranged from cloth-shearing machines to glue, to blast furnaces, rolling mills, and iron mines, to railroads and telegraphy. It has been said that "as an inventor, Cooper possessed genius which might have made him an earlier Edison, had it been joined to the necessary technical training."[75] He was keenly aware that the days had passed when apprenticeship training could suffice, understood very clearly that changing circumstances underscored the need for formal technical education, and had long thought about establishing a workingman's institute. He was particularly interested in supporting young people who lacked adequate financial means for education and therefore the opportunity not only to enjoy a better life, but also to contribute to the improvement and advancement of the community and the country.

In April 1859, with the building completed, the original legislation was formally amended and specific goals were laid out. Six trustees were named, with Cooper as president of the board. The aim of the school was "to offer free to the laboring classes of both sexes the training in the mechanical arts and in the sciences that he had never had." But the intent was larger than that of a purely vocational school. There were to be free evening courses in applied, social, and political science; a free reading room, art galleries, and scientific collections; and a school of design and "other useful arts" for "respectable females."[76]

In addition, there were plans for a society to be called the Associates of the Cooper Union for the Advancement of Science and Art, the purposes described as follows:

> The encouragement of science, arts, manufactures and commerce; the bestowal of rewards for such productions, inventions and improvements as tend to the useful employment of the poor, the increase of trade, and the riches and honor of the country; for meritorious works in the various departments of the fine arts; for discoveries, inventions, and improvements; and generally, by lectures, papers, and discussions thereon, and other suitable means, to assist in the advancement, development, and practical application of every department of science in connection with the arts, manufactures and commerce of the country.[77]

Finally, when funds became available, a "thorough polytechnic school" would be established.[78]

On several counts the *Objects and Plan* would be of interest to Peter Cooper, as the Cooper Union, part of which was already in operation, and the proposed Institute of Technology shared some similar goals. Rogers no doubt knew that Cooper's institution was under way in New York when he sent him a copy. Its opening ceremonies had been reported in the *Scientific American* in the fall of 1859 and an item concerning its large enrollment appeared early in 1860.[79]

In March 1861 the *Boston Transcript* called attention to an annual report of the Cooper Union trustees covering those portions of its program already under way and the two which had not yet been organized—the Society of the Associates, which never did materialize, and the Polytechnic School, for which funds were not yet available. Praising the "accustomed spirit and liberality" of the citizens of Boston and the "very able report of Professor Rogers," the trustees omitted only a short introductory paragraph to Section III of the *Objects and Plan* and quoted the entire description of the Institute's school as it was expected to develop. In this way they hoped to "awaken the attention" of citizens who might "aid in the immediate establishment of such a school in this city, where the rooms and the apparatus are already provided, and a guarantee of a comparatively small sum annually would be adequate for the purpose."[80] Though public support was not aroused at that time, the institution persevered and the Cooper Union for the Advancement of Science and Art went on to include degree-granting Schools of Art, Architecture, and Engineering, and a Faculty of Humanities and Social Sciences.

Meanwhile, Louis Agassiz, busy courting the legislature for funds, invited the governor to join the members in a scheduled visit to his museum. Bringing his institution to first rank depended, he said, upon their liberality at that moment, when one of his "highest aims" was "to free science in America from the dependent position in which it still stands with reference to Europe":

> In fact scientific men in America have now to fight for their independence & they will never take the standing to which they are entitled before the scientific institutions of the country are on a level with those of Europe, and we ought if possible to raise them higher. You can urge this argument for me; if I do it myself it would appear presumptuous, and yet I know that this is the bitter state of things under which every devotee of science is now sighing in this country.[81]

Reporting on the Committee on Education hearings on the Museum of Comparative Zoology, the newspapers covered Agassiz's appeals for money to carry him through until the state funds became available. He predicted "disastrous" consequences if the bill then under consideration were passed without changes. His means had been exhausted, he received no salary from the museum, and he would have to discontinue his voluntary instruction to teachers.[82] Reputedly, however, he was able to charm the legislature into giving him money even when they professed to have none, and he was, therefore, a competitor for attention and a constant reminder of the linkage of the Back Bay Lands Fund and the School Fund. Certainly his state of mind agitated those who clung to the belief that the School Fund would be harmed by the grant of a square of land to the Institute of Technology and the Natural History and Horticultural societies, whose petitions were also proceeding through the legislative process.

While Agassiz was urging Governor Andrew to visit his museum, Rogers was urging the governor to convene the Board of Education for a hearing.[83] This time the appeal succeeded, and Andrew, apparently believing that too many voices might be harmful, sent a little advice to Rogers along with an invitation to meet with the board on March 16, 1861. His letter was signed "Yours faithfully and fervently":

> I hope you will come & advocate the claims of the Nat. Hist. & Inst. of Tech.—but, no one else should speak. Be thou the advocate. Take time enough. Cover

the ground to suit yourself. Several speakers wd. do harm. At least I fear they wd. And you may say from *me*, that I wish *one* complete argument, & that no other be made.

Between ourselves I know *you* wd. have a powerful effect, left to yr. self.— & I fear someone else might come in, & weaken it.[84]

The bill concerning the Boston Society of Natural History having been ordered to be engrossed by the Senate on March 15, 1861, the society was sufficiently confident to appoint a Building Committee. Rogers was one of the members. The Institute of Technology, however, could not then be as certain of success.

The Joint Committee on Education scheduled a public hearing for the morning of March 19. Because of high citizen interest, it was held in the large hall of the House of Representatives, with Rogers addressing the meeting. Bearing the same date, House Document 171 contains the joint committee's report, signed individually by the members, according to a Rogers notation. A draft of the document is in Rogers's hand, as is the original copy of the final report in the State Archives.[85]

In his report Rogers briefly stated the case for the Natural History Society and the Institute, reiterating points made throughout much of the testimony since the introduction of the bill and citing its wide appeal across the state. He pointed out that the memorialists for the Institute had promised to raise a guarantee fund of $100,000 as assurance of good faith in carrying out their plans, were fully confident of their ability to attract financial support, and already had pledges, if the state granted the land, of "a munificent endowment to be devoted to the School of Industrial Science, and of a liberal appropriation from a different quarter for building purposes." He did not mention that the endowment to which he referred would not support the Institute's principal operations or that the appropriation for building purposes would not be received until the prospective donor had died.

In summing up the plan, he stated that the Society of Arts would stimulate "the already skilled and cultivated practical talent of the State"; the museum would "offer a large treasure of knowledge for the instruction of the general public"; and the school, "while providing a systematic training in the applied sciences and arts of design, for its regular students, will open the instructions of ample lecture rooms to the large class of artisans, merchants and others seeking for such teachings in practical science as they can acquire in the intervals of labor and without methodical study." The Institute would "fill an important gap in the present educational plans of the Commonwealth" since such training "could not be effectually provided in any of the existing institutions of the State." Rogers added that it planned to "encourage the formation of local societies of arts in different towns of the Commonwealth, whose correspondence and interchange with the central institution in Boston may carry the working activities of the latter into every part of the State," an idea mentioned for the first time and never again. He revealed plans for lectures to be arranged every year for teachers which, combined with their visits to the museums, would "conduce to more thorough practical teaching in the common schools." In conclusion, he implied that the public advantages of the proposal were such that the state might even be wise to consider granting funds for the purpose.[86] But he did not press that point:

> Such, however, is not the kind of aid craved by the petitioners. The land for the use of which they apply, has already, indirectly and in part at least been dedicated to public education. They do not propose to withdraw it from this object, but on the contrary to give it a new and vastly increased value for educational purposes. The character and extent of their plans, as well as their formal assurances to this effect, show that in carrying out their objects they will bring together *in the services of education* on the proposed grant, a wealth of funds and of all the machinery of practical instruction, far exceeding the entire money value of the land, and compared with which the dividend accruing from it to the school fund when applied in the same service, would be utterly insignificant.[87]

By the time Rogers prepared House No. 171 for the Committee on Education, the amount of land that the memorialists could reasonably expect to receive was undoubtedly clear. Early in the report he specified "the first section of land lying west of Berkeley and between Newbury and Boylston Streets, extending to Clarendon Street." The Natural History Society would occupy "about one-third" and the remainder would be for the Massachusetts Institute of Technology. And apparently still under the impression that the Horticultural Society would carry through its plans, Rogers indicated that the memorialists also sought the "next section of land lying west of Clarendon Street in the same range" for their use.[88]

Though their petition seems not to have been formally withdrawn, the Horticultural Society's misgivings were somehow conveyed in time to alter the report through an inserted paragraph in another hand: "The Committee unanimously came to the conclusion that there was no immediate urgency in their case, and, as there is a doubt existing in some minds as to the propriety of making the grant, it was deemed advisable to dismiss this branch of the petition, and leave it to future developments for legislative action, should it be desired."[89] The record of the Natural History's Building

Committee states that the Horticultural Society made no effort to obtain a grant "on account of the opposition of some of its members, who were afraid their 25-cent annual show would not be so well attended if their hall were situated so far from the center of business."[90] In the final paragraph "your Committee" expressed themselves in favor of the bill.[91]

The preparation of favorable legislative reports and resolutions by a petitioner no doubt would have been called into question in later years, but Rogers's participation on both sides of the memorial was certainly an important factor in presenting a strong case in the best light. Nor was he above preparing an unsigned editorial in praise of his own memorial. Such a piece, found among his clippings, had already appeared in the *Boston Journal* for March 2 and covered familiar ground.

Rogers's point of departure this time was the recent publication of *An Account of the Proceedings Preliminary to the Organization of the Massachusetts Institute of Technology*, including a brief summary of the effort, beginning with the 1860 memorial of the Committee of Associated Institutions, with no mention of the conservatory proposal, and a copy of the 1861 petition. It contained a list of some 170 individuals who had already become members of the Institute—largely from Boston and the immediate area, but some from Clinton, New Bedford, Springfield, Lowell, and Salem. It included the Act of Association signed on January 11, as well as the petition of the Natural History Society, and supporting memorials from the Boston Board of Trade, the American Academy of Arts and Sciences, the Massachusetts Charitable Mechanics' Association, the New England Society for the Promotion of Manufactures and Mechanic Arts, and the State Teachers' Association.[92]

The distribution of this pamphlet is not known. Rogers had already sent a copy to Henry: "You will be almost inclined to laugh at my becoming such a pamphleteer, but in truth to do anything with the public or the Legislature, definite printed plans, stationery, and arguments are indispensable."[93] As an anonymous editorialist, Rogers began, "We have been reading the pamphlet recently published," and ended with a call for legislative support:

> It is therefore greatly to be desired that our Legislature should make ample provision on the Back Bay for the accommodation of this and the other associated institutions—looking not merely to the immediate needs of the Institute as regards space, but to that large development of its different departments which, in the course of a few years, will most assuredly call for the amplest means of expansion.[94]

After the presentation of his report and the bill which he had also prepared, he wrote Henry that "the crisis of our Technological plan is now approaching." He expected "no serious opposition in the House," but "obstruction in the Senate":

> The Secretary of the Board of Education, recently appointed, has opposed us in Committee. But the Board itself has not sustained his opposition. Some of the Professors at Harvard have shown sympathy with us, among them Peirce, Bowen, Judge Parker, etc. The "Transcript," "Journal," etc., have been warm in commendation. The plan I have set forth, if carried out, will be grand enough in its practical, educational and moral bearings to claim no little of that public interest and support which now goes so exclusively to the neighbouring city beyond the bridge. The feeling in favour of our plan is daily widening and deepening, and I am quite hopeful of success. The Report, preceding the Bill, gives the argument so clearly and fully as to make us almost independent of public advocates.[95]

Rogers was supremely self-assured with respect to everything he did, and his commanding presence and powers of oratory were strong factors in his favor. But confident though he was, a crisis did indeed lie ahead. A good deal of debate would be heard on Beacon Hill and much pressure would have to be exerted on individual legislators before the bill would finally pass.

When the House took up the question of engrossment on March 22, it was refused, 74 to 63,[96] despite a long speech by Mr. John Q. Hammond, repeating all of the arguments heard before and warning that Massachusetts could easily be left behind if the bill were defeated:

> The proposed Institute of Technology cannot fail of providing a most valuable adjunct to every interest in the Commonwealth indirectly and directly. . . . We have the military school at West Point for our army officers instruction and the naval school at Annapolis for the Navy. But sir, "Peace, peace, hath its trophies as well as war." Or at least it ought to have, and for the promotion and encouragement of agriculture, commerce, and the arts schools of preparatory and practical instruction in all of these departments are necessary.[97]

A vote to reject was followed by one to reconsider, the papers reporting that the principal argument in opposition was that the proposed grant would be detrimental to the School Fund. It was finally recommitted with amendments, requiring the Natural History Society and the Institute of Technology to accept the proposed act within a year and pay into the School Fund any difference between the current appraisal of the adjacent land and its value in ten years.[98] Rogers was busy writing letters to influential people and legislators, using his considerable persuasive powers and political instincts, and urging others to write as well. And he kept in close touch with Governor Andrew.[99]

Though it was reported on March 29 that the House bill had been ordered engrossed and the proposed amendments adopted, the debate still went on, the newspapers bringing out once more the issue of the School Fund. One legislator was convinced that the grant would divert funds for the support of the public schools and was willing to make a special appropriation for it, but another was equally convinced that the fund would not be hurt. Another complicated the problem by offering an amendment, finally rejected, that one-half of the income of one square of the Back Bay lands in three equal divisions be appropriated for the academies at Monson, New Salem, and the Young Ladies Collegiate Institute at Worcester.[100]

As the House and Senate attempted in conference to produce a final version, Rogers seemed confident of its passage in a letter to Henry:

> Our Bill has required continual watching. Not only had I to write the Report of the Committee, but by personal interviews and correspondence, assisted by others interested in the cause, I have been continually occupied in trying to make members understand our plan and objects. I now feel so sure of success that I am quite relieved. What may be the progress of the Institute in obtaining funds to carry out its purposes, it is difficult to foresee. But I believe it will secure the necessary means for a handsome beginning within the time limited.[101]

Finally, on April 8, 1861, the bill was passed by the House, followed by the Senate on April 9.[102] It was approved by Governor Andrew on April 10, and appears as Chapter 183 in the *Acts and Resolves of Massachusetts* for the year 1860–61.

The act covered the incorporation of the Massachusetts Institute of Technology and the granting of "Aid to Said Institute and to the Boston Society of Natural History," the aid being the reservation of one square of land on the Back Bay. Both institutions were

COMMONWEALTH OF MASSACHUSETTS.

In the year One Thousand Eight Hundred and Sixty-one.

AN ACT *to incorporate the Massachusetts Institute of Technology, and to grant aid to said Institute and to the Boston Society of Natural History.*

Be it enacted by the Senate and House of Representatives in General Court assembled, and by the authority of the same, as follows: *Section 1. William B. Rogers, James M. Beebe, E. S. Toby, D. H. Gookin, E. B. Bigelow, M. D. Ross, J. D. Philbrick, F. W. Storer, J. D. Runkle, C. H. Dalton, J. B. Francis, J. C. Hoadley, M. P. Wilder, C. L. Flint, Thomas Rice, John Chase, J. P. Robinson, F. W. Lincoln Jun., Thomas Aspinwall, E. A. Dupee, E. C. Cabot, their associates and successors, are hereby made a body corporate, by the name of the Massachusetts Institute of Technology; for the purpose of instituting and maintaining a society of arts, a museum of arts, and a school of industrial science, and aiding generally, by suitable means, the advancement, development and practical application of science in connection with arts, agriculture, manufactures and commerce with all the powers and privileges, and subject to all the duties, restrictions and liabilities, set forth in the sixty-eighth chapter of the General Statutes. Section 2. Said corporation, for the purposes aforesaid, shall have authority to hold real and personal estate to an amount not exceeding two hundred thousand dollars. Section 3. One certain square of State land on the Back Bay, namely, the second square westwardly from the Public Garden, between Newbury and Boylston streets, according to the plan reported by the Commissioners on the Back Bay, February twenty-one, eighteen hundred and fifty-seven, shall be reserved from sale forever, and kept as an open space, or for the use of such educational institutions of science and art as are hereinafter provided for. Section 4. If at any time within one year after the passage of this act, the said Institute of Technology shall furnish satisfactory evidence to the Governor and Council that it is duly organized under the aforesaid charter, and has funds subscribed, or otherwise guaranteed, for the prosecution of its objects, to an amount at least of one hundred thousand dollars, it shall be entitled to a perpetual right to hold, occupy and control, for the purposes herein before mentioned the westerly portion of said second square, to the extent of two-third parts thereof, free of rent or charge by the Commonwealth, subject nevertheless, to the following stipulations, namely: persons from all parts of the Commonwealth shall be alike eligible as members of said institute, or as pupils for its instruction; and its museum or conservatory of arts, at all reasonable times, and under reasonable regulations, shall be open to the public; and within two years from the time when said land is placed at its disposal for occupation, filled and graded, said institute shall erect and complete a building suitable to its said* purposes, appropriately enclose, adorn and cultivate the open ground around said buildings, and shall thereafter keep said grounds and building in a sightly condition. ....

Section 5. The Boston Society of Natural History shall be entitled to hold, occupy and control, for the objects and purposes for which said society was incorporated, and which are more fully set forth in its constitution and by-laws, the easterly portion of said second square, to the extent of one-third part thereof: provided, that the said society shall, within two years from the time when said portion of land is placed at its disposal for occupation, filled and graded, erect a building suit-able to said objects and purposes, and appropriately enclose, plant and adorn the open ground around said building, and shall thereafter keep said grounds and building in a neat and ornamental condition.

Section 6. The rights and privileges given in the last two sections, are granted subject to these further conditions following, namely: All buildings whatsoever, which may be erected by either of the herein named institutions up-on any portion of said second square, shall be designed and completed, the grounds surrounding said buildings enclosed, laid out and ornamented, and the said buildings and grounds kept and maintained in a manner sat-isfactory to the Governor and Council; and in case either of the said institutions shall, after due notice given, neglect to comply with the requirements of this section, or fail to use its portion of said square, or at any time appropriate said portion, or any part thereof, to any purpose or use foreign to its legit-imate objects, then the right of said delinquent institution to the use, occupation or control of its por-tion of said square shall cease, and the Commonwealth, by its proper officers and agents, shall have the right forthwith to enter and take possession of the portion of land so forfeited.

Section 7. The above named societies shall not cover with their buildings more than one third of the area granted to them respectively. Section 8. The Commissioners on the Back Bay are hereby instructed to reserve from sale the lots fronting on said square on Boylston, Clarendon and Newbury streets, until said so-cieties shall, by enclosure and improvements, put said square in a sightly and attractive condition. Section 9. Upon the passage of this act, the Governor, with the advice and consent of the Council, shall ap-point three disinterested persons, who shall appraise the value of all the lands specified in the third and eighth sections of this act, and make a return of said appraisal to the Governor and Council, and if when the lands mentioned in section eight shall have been sold, the proceeds of such sales shall not be equal to the whole amount of the appraisal above mentioned, then the societies named in this act shall pay the amount of such deficit into the treasury of the Commonwealth, for the school fund, in proportion to the area granted to them respectively. Section 10. This act shall be null and void, unless its provisions shall be ac-cepted within one year, by the Massachusetts Institute of Technology, and the Boston Society of Natural History, so far as they apply to those societies respectively.

House of Representatives, April 8, 1861. Passed to be enacted John A. Goodwin, Speaker.

In Senate, April 9th 1861. Passed to be enacted William Claflin President

April 10th 1861. Approved.

John A. Andrew

required to accept the provisions of the act within one year, and would be required to pay any difference between the appraised value of the adjacent land and the amount received in the eventual sale of that land, which was not to be sold until the two societies had erected their buildings and improved the area. This provision, termed "ungracious" by Rogers, bears out his statement that the only real opposition to their cause had come "from friends of the School Fund who were worried about land values"; happily, this provision was repealed on April 29, 1863. In addition, the Institute of Technology was required to show evidence within one year of having raised a guarantee fund of $100,000.[103] The previous few months had been a constant struggle, but the aims and purposes of the proposed Institute seem never to have been seriously in question.

The Natural History Society was ready to go. On July 18, 1861, it held a special meeting to accept the terms of the Act of the General Court, make plans for the sale to the city of its Mason Street property, and authorize negotiations for the filling of the Back Bay land to the height necessary to build. M. D. Ross was asked to participate in these negotiations.[104]

The road was not as clear for the new Institute of Technology. On April 12, 1861, Fort Sumter was attacked and surrendered to the Confederacy on April 14. With the country plunged into civil war, the times were far from favorable for the raising of money for peaceful purposes, however worthy, and the launching of new enterprises, however badly needed. Although on April 16 Rogers wrote Henry that plans were to be made for collecting the necessary funds, he said too that it might be wise to defer the project until later, and the major part of his letter was devoted to news of the war and the condition of the country. By May 7 he was saying clearly that the Back Bay plans "must wait for the restoration of tranquillity."[105] While the plans for the Institute of Technology were held in abeyance, he devoted himself to the efforts of the Natural History Society as a member of its Building Committee.

The Struggle
to Get Under Way

Chapter 10

———————————

Persistent Perseverance

he square of land in the Back Bay and the charter for the Massachusetts
Institute of Technology had barely become official when the country was
plunged into civil war. The surviving letters of William Rogers for this period reflect his preoccupation with the war as well as his unquestioned loyalty
to the Union and his sorrow and disappointment that so many friends and
former pupils in Virginia were on the secessionist side. How strongly he felt is apparent
in an unsigned editorial that he prepared for the *Evening Transcript* published on May 1,
1861. Entitled "No Armistice with Rebels," it was a rousing call to reject "proposals for
armistice, or other devices of timidity or of treacherous scheming to gain time":

> Let us hope that no disastrous parleying with piracy, no misguided tolerance
> of those who are acting secession without daring to proclaim it, shall arrest the
> progress of that thorough and overwhelming chastisement which is needed to
> crush out the hopes of treason, and to vindicate the worth and dignity of
> republican freedom before the world. The government can now command the
> entire colossal energy of the free states—millions of freemen, glowing with the
> awakened fire, are impatient to lend their arms and their treasure to the sup-
> pression of treason and the establishment everywhere throughout the land of
> constitutional liberty. . . . They and the whole civilized world with them, call
> upon our government for such a tremendous demonstration of physical and
> moral energy, as shall leave no hope for rebellion, and as shall put down for-
> ever the arrogant pretensions with which the Cottonocracy has presumed to
> insult the free states, and freemen throughout the world.[1]

Along with many others who supported the Institute, Rogers was associated with several war efforts throughout a trying period, when sharply divided views in Boston sorely tested long-standing friendships and relationships, and events were not going well for the Union. When the Somerset and other clubs proved too solidly conservative for the more liberal so-called Radical Republicans, other organizations were formed to show support and attempt to influence public opinion. In the fall of 1862 Rogers withdrew from the Friday Club, saying that neither "health, nor purse, nor taste" allowed him to remain.[2] It is highly possible that he did so in part because the conservative views and opposition to the war of most of the members were certainly not to his "taste,"[3] for in 1863 he was active in the newly formed Union Club:

> Among my multifarious affairs at this time is the organization of the Union Club, of which Mr. Everett is President, and I am one of the four Vice-Presidents. We are making thorough republicanism and loyalty to the government, proclamation and all, quite the fashion even with many who used to be terribly conservative. We are also busy with a society for distributing interesting patriotic documents at home and abroad. I mail you a little pamphlet containing our constitution and by-laws.[4]

Organized in March 1863 by John Murray Forbes, a wealthy China trade merchant and railroad man, the New England Loyal Publication Society was designed to promote the dissemination to the public of pro-Union views through the distribution of broadside reprints of articles and speeches to local and other Northern newspapers and to papers in Great Britain as well. Rogers was a member of its executive committee. Among others actively engaged in its activities were Edward Atkinson, Henry Bromfield Rogers, a Boston lawyer of no relation to William, and William Endicott, Jr., names then or later to be associated with MIT. Forbes would become a member of the Institute's Government in 1866. It appears that most or all of these, including probably William Rogers, provided financial support to the project, which was said to be effective beyond the measure of its financial resources in comparison with a national society and local groups in other areas, who operated chiefly through the medium of pamphleteering.[5]

In 1863 Rogers was a member of a large committee appointed by Governor Andrew to raise $50,000 to supplement available Government funds in meeting the expenses of recruiting fifty thousand acclimated colored soldiers.[6] Rogers was also a member of the organizing committee of the Protective War Claim Association in 1862, and after the war he was associated with the New England Branch of the Freedmen's Union Commission.[7] Exactly how much time he devoted to all of these associations is difficult to tell. It is clear, however, where his sentiments lay and what public image he wanted to project.

For Rogers the war proved to mean more than eloquent statements and good works. Early in August 1862 his brother-in-law, Major James Savage, Jr., a member of the Second Massachusetts Regiment, fell wounded at the battle of Cedar Mountain in Virginia. William and his youngest brother, Robert, set off for the battlefield only to learn that James had been taken prisoner and sent to the Confederate Hospital at Charlottesville, a destination that the two could not reach. William reported to Henry on August 22:

> I returned on Monday night from my visit to Washington, Culpepper, and the
> battlefield near Cedar Mountain, where so many of our Second Regiment
> were killed or wounded. . . . While in Washington I wrote a number of open
> letters to be sent by flag of truce from Fortress Monroe to influential old
> friends and physicians in Richmond and Charlottesville, in the hope that they
> might exert themselves to better the condition of the wounded prisoners. . . .
> My visit to the field gave me a view of Bull Run, Manassas and other scenes
> of blood, and of the desolation which blasts this region in which the dreadful
> drama of war is enacted. . . . The public mind has become more strongly
> impressed with the necessity of making the war one in which slavery is to be
> sternly dealt with instead of being, as at first, petted and indulged. At the close
> of the war that oligarchy which has ruled and well-nigh demoralized the
> nation will be no more.[8]

Though in September James wrote that old friends of the university were treating him well and kindly, he died on October 22.[9] Manuscript evidence suggests that Rogers, through Southern friends, attempted to help others seeking injured kin behind the battle lines.[10]

There was little time for scientific work in those days, but Rogers's bibliography shows thirteen publications from 1861 to 1864, mostly in the *Proceedings* of the Boston Society of Natural History, covering brief presentations at their meetings. There was an occasional presentation at the American Academy of Arts and Sciences, of which he was elected corresponding secretary in 1863. In that year also he was appointed to the Academy's committee on the Rumford Premium.[11]

More time-consuming perhaps than anything else was a totally unexpected appointment which Rogers accepted in the summer of 1861 only after many protestations and with great reluctance, but to which he gave his very best attention. The same session of the legislature which passed the act of incorporation for the Institute of Technology also enacted a bill creating a state office of inspector of gas meters and illuminating gas. Late in June Rogers was greatly surprised to read in the newspapers of his appointment by the governor and council as the first holder of this office—unbelieving all the more because the governor had already discussed the post with him, presumably after he had been approached by mutual friends, and from the outset he had refused to be considered.[12] He had suggested Augustus A. Hayes, a distinguished consulting chemist and a man of general scientific culture, as better qualified.[13] And he had informed John R. Rollins of Lawrence, who was interested in the post, that he felt bound to recommend Hayes but would be happy to support his candidacy should the authorities "look to other qualifications." On two occasions he did present Rollins's name to the governor for consideration if the choice were to "range beyond those who have had actual scientific experience in connexion with the subject of gas." He owed Rollins this much, for in the spring Rollins had sent a glowing letter in support of the Institute's cause to a member of the House of Representatives from his district known to be opposed to the pending bill.[14]

With his own appointment publicly announced, Rogers wrote immediately to the governor and declined for the second time. The announcement, however, soon brought forth "such letters of encouragement and satisfaction from various quarters" that he felt bound to reconsider. With some embarrassment he informed both Rollins and Hayes of the situation, indicating that he might, after looking further into the duties and responsibilities of the position, change his mind.[15] He finally accepted on the grounds that he would have to give only one or two hours a day, with a promise of help from Hayes; that the necessary travel around the state would be good for his health, which was, as nearly always, precarious; and that perhaps the public exposure might even help in furthering plans for the Institute of Technology. He wrote at once to Henry seeking information on "any subject connected with illuminating gas." By September 10 he was collecting information about gas-holders and test-meters across the state, using his home, 1 Temple Place, as his office, with the title of state inspector of gas-meters and gas. Soon an office was opened on Washington Street.[16]

It is possible that Governor Andrew was exacting a little *quid pro quo* for his support for the grant of land. He was a friend of Rogers, saw him socially, knew that he had no day-to-day responsibilities, and recognized that it would be some time before the Institute could be organized. Rogers himself said that "from the beginning the Governor & others have been impressed with the importance of selecting for the place some one who is known to the public professionally as a man of science."[17] During the long protracted effort to secure the Back Bay land he had talked a good deal about the *practical* aspects of science and its *useful* applications. Here was a problem calling for just such a protagonist. Louis Agassiz could hardly be approached for such a mundane position as gas inspector, and in any case he was much occupied with the new Museum of Comparative Zoology. Rogers's scientific reputation was good. He was persuasive, knew how to deal with the legislature, would take the problem seriously, and get the office off to a good start.

Andrew had been helpful as the Back Bay proposal faced the final countdown. Who urged Rogers to accede to the appointment is not known. Perhaps some of the practical merchants of the Committee of Twenty sensed that Andrew could be, or might have to be pressed to be, helpful in the future.

That fall John Amory Lowell asked Rogers to give a course of lectures on the application of science to the useful arts for the Lowell Institute in January 1862. Though Rogers accepted this request with a feeling that the public mind would be preoccupied with national events and therefore not particularly interested in scientific discourses, he did so also with the hope that his talks might further the interests of the Institute of Technology.[18]

All who had worked so long and hard for legislative approval of the Back Bay project were rightly apprehensive about the war's effect on their plans and recognized that for the Institute of Technology, at least, conditions were not favorable for the raising of funds or for the inauguration of a wholly new institution, the magnitude of which was only beginning to come clearly into focus for its proponents. For the time being, these problems were virtually set aside as the Natural History Society, an organization in place and sorely pressed for space, moved ahead, with Rogers and Ross very much involved.

It has been said that Rogers was interested in the Natural History Society project "as a component in his own effort to secure land for a technical school."[19] This is a misreading of his role and of the chronology of the entire development, for he was drawn into the plans of those who were seeking to establish some kind of polytechnic institute mostly through his association with the society's plans for relocation. An honorary member since 1842, when he was still in Virginia, he had taken a prominent part in its activities since his arrival in Boston in 1853. Though his travels during the spring of 1859 had prevented his active participation in the first committee appointed by the society to obtain land on the Back Bay, he was reappointed to that committee, remaining a member even after he assumed the chairmanship of the larger Committee of Associated Institutions and became intimately involved with the developing plans for the Institute of Technology. As the effort to obtain the land drew to a close in the spring of 1861, he had come to feel that it was the plan for the Institute that gave added force to the society's appeal: "They will owe this noble opportunity of enlargement wholly to myself and others of the *Institute*; for this latter, by its practical purpose, has been the only cause of our success with the Legislature."[20] With the Institute's plans now held in abeyance, however, he could direct his attention to the Natural History Society as a member of its Building Committee and in support of its need for additional funds.

About the Institute he was characteristically optimistic:

> The Technological Institute has not yet collected a fund, but with the dawn of better times, in the spring probably, we shall be preparing to put a part of our plan in operation.[21]

One of the chief deterrents was the requirement that within one year satisfactory evidence be furnished to the governor and council that a fund of at least $100,000 had been "subscribed or otherwise guaranteed" to the new organization before its right to occupy its share of the square of land could be affirmed. It also had to be "duly organized," which called for something beyond the existence of the Committee of Twenty, with Rogers as chairman, whose names, although not identified as such, appear in section 1 of the act.

Though it was generally agreed that the Institute's plans must be deferred, there had been some attempt to secure the guarantee fund. As early as the summer of 1861, M. D. Ross informed Rogers of a conversation with Ralph Huntington:

> He voluntarily expressed a hope that we would soon mature our plans for the Institute of Technology—as he wished to see them with reference to his intention to give us aid. The recent death of an old domestic in his family—the feeble health of his daughter Mrs. James—and his own advanced age—reminds him of the other world—in view of all these things it is wisdom in us to lose no time in getting our plans matured for Huntington Hall—which will probably cost $50,000—and possibly more in order to accommodate the *Lowell School of Industrial Science*. If when you come down to the city you can spend a day and evening with us in consultation about plans ... we can make a sketch sufficient to carry to Mr. Huntington a distinct idea of the Hall and its uses. ... I hope you will find time soon to frame a formula for the organization of the Institute—preliminary to accepting of the charter and terms of the grant, &c &c.[22]

Shortly thereafter Ross presented the Institute's case to Huntington and once again pressed Rogers for concrete plans:

Being somewhat disappointed in not having you go with me to meet Mr. Huntington yesterday P.M. I buckled on an extra coat of mail—and charged him to the tune of $75,000 instead of $50,000. . . . he told me all about his property and invited me to come and see him often, wants to meet you and says he will think favourably of going ahead immediately if the plans can be matured. The Harvard College people have been trying very hard to get him to aid them but he says Harvard has never done anything for him and he don't mean to help them—but anything on the Back Bay he regards as a legitimate object for him to give to, etc. etc. Now my dear Sir he is our man, and good for $75,000 I think. We must have plans of building, constitution & By-Laws, etc. all ready as soon as possible and call the Committee of 20 together.[23]

In responding, Rogers found Huntington's interest "an earnest of the general aid we have a right to expect from the friends of liberal progress who like himself have the power to help us," and he was confident that "*further reflexion on the permanent & grand utility of the plan* will impel him *early* to take a leading part in promoting its execution." He fervently hoped that Huntington would "*not postpone* his wise liberality, but secure at once the harvest of satisfaction and grateful regard which will sweeten and brighten the remainder of his years":

There could arise no nobler opportunity than is offered in these opening plans of our Institute. Of all the forms of generosity, that which connects itself with the education & improvement of the practical classes is the one which commands the highest reverence of the philanthropist and the most lasting gratitude & honor of the community.[24]

Ralph Huntington

For Huntington Rogers envisioned great joy in seeing "crowds gathered for instruction in a spacious Hall of his erection—& which throughout all parts of the land & in succeeding times should connect his name with public education & the best interests of humanity." But he could promise more: "How much real satisfaction might he draw day after day from marking the good effect of his generosity & how much strength as well as pleasure might he derive from the kindly relations in which in his declining years he would be placed to the officers of the Institute & the hundreds of others recognising him gratefully as one of the founders of the Institution!"[25]

But Huntington did not hurry, and it would be April 4, 1862, before Rogers could place on the record a memorandum of "Conversation with R. H. Esq. in presence of M.D.R.," in which Huntington "renewed the statement . . . that he had provided in his will to give $50,000 to the Inst. of Technology," intimating, but not promising, "other help at an earlier day for our building."[26] A few days later, following a request from Rogers, Huntington confirmed his intention in writing, at the same time clarifying how the funds were to be paid: "$20,000 at my decease, and the remainder at a subsequent period should the continued usefulness of the enterprise be then apparent to my Trustees."[27] Rogers may not have been happy with the written confirmation, for the prospect of an initial payment of only $20,000 upon the death of the donor, with the remainder at the discretion of his trustees at some later time, would be a much less impressive sum in the eyes of the legislature. Herein may lie the reason for a remark in 1865, responding to a reference to "Huntington Hall," that he was not in favor of attaching any individual's name to the hall, "at the present, if at any time."[28]

The correspondence between Ross and Rogers at this time is interesting on several counts, among them an indication that there were early discussions about naming the Institute's building and hall for Huntington in return for a major gift. In pressing Rogers for the immediate preparation of a definite plan for the organization, at the same time apologizing for making demands upon his time, Ross had provided further evidence of Rogers's position with respect to the project. Finally, in making his case for the virtues and rewards of philanthropy at great length, Rogers's enthusiasm led him to make the rather exaggerated statement that the "Institute is something new in this country & in some respects even the world. . . this will make its foundation an event particularly remarkable & clothe its leading patrons with more than usual distinction & honorable remembrance."[29]

Early in January 1862, when submitting his report as gas inspector, Rogers indicated that he had been "so very unwell" that he had been unable to prepare anything on the progress of the Natural History Society and the Institute of Technology for the governor's annual message. He was still, however, working hard for the society, and the meetings of its Building Committee were normally held at his house. It is clear that he was taking a major part in the planning of that project and was a member of a subcommittee charged with signing the contracts approved by the main committee.[30] He was busy raising funds as well, in March turning over to Thomas T. Bouvé, the society's treasurer, a thousand dollars each from Nathaniel Thayer and Henry Bromfield Rogers. He was especially pleased about these gifts as evidence that "Boston people, in spite of the war and its many demands, do not forget their wonted liberality to education and science."[31]

Rogers continued to take an optimistic view and hoped that, with the funds for the Natural History building virtually assured, financial support would be forthcoming for the Institute and its own building. Early in 1861, he had informed his brother Henry that John Amory Lowell might provide substantial help, as he was taking "a lively interest in the matter."[32] Now, late in March 1862, he wrote to Lowell, seeking a definite commitment: "Should you be inclined to carry out the munificent purpose which you intimated last year in regard to our school of industrial science by permitting us to state that you are prepared to appropriate to the active uses of the proposed school the annual amount to which you referred on that occasion, we think that this assurance, together with the prospective gift from Mr. Huntington, would be accepted by the Governor and Council as a substantial compliance with the condition of the Legislative Act."[33] Referring to his long-standing "intention, when the funds of the Lowell Institute should have sufficiently accumulated, to establish a school for the instruction of mechanics in the sciences connected with their trades," Lowell responded: "Should your Institute of Technology be successfully established, I shall avail myself of its advantages, if permitted, by opening this school on their premises, and devote to this object a sum not less than $3,000 a year."[34]

Life and Letters states that Lowell's "reply is of especial interest not only intrinsically" but because it represented the "formal beginning" of relations between the Lowell Institute and the Institute of Technology. This is true, but it is even more interesting because it made very clear that the funds promised by Lowell, though undoubtedly to be used to pay for the use of lecture rooms and faculty compensation, were intended at that time to support an independent operation of the Lowell Institute. On his part, Huntington had made a commitment solely for a bequest, only a portion of which would be received immediately upon the death of the donor. The Institute of Technology was a long way from $100,000 in hand.

As April 10, 1862, approached, they were compelled to move toward some form of organization. In addition, the reality of their financial situation offered no alternative but to ask the legislature for an extension of time for the procurement of the guarantee fund, hoping that the extenuating circumstances of the war would favorably dispose the members to allow perhaps another year. Rogers had wanted to avoid this step, one "never exempt from annoyance & uncertainty."[35] Yet it had to be done, and some evidence of progress and public support would have to be shown, even if only inadequate "prospective means" could be offered.

Those who had signified their intention of becoming members of the Institute were, therefore, called to a meeting at the rooms of the Board of Trade in the Merchants' Exchange on the morning of April 8, with the Committee of Twenty meeting beforehand to hear a report of an unnamed subcommittee on constitution and bylaws. Rogers may have been a committee of one on these bylaws, though he did consult with Lowell during their preparation.[36]

Frederic W. Lincoln, Jr., was chosen chairman of this first Institute meeting and John D. Runkle, secretary pro tem. The Act of Incorporation of 1861 was read and accepted, the governor and council to be notified. The bylaws were discussed section by section, modified to some extent, and adopted. They were to be printed for general distribution, along with excerpts from the Act of 1861 and the *Objects and Plan*.[37]

In looking closely at the first organizational structure of the Institute and the bylaws which were to govern its operations, it is important to keep in mind that the Massachusetts Institute of Technology was chartered as a corporate body with three components—"a society of arts, a museum of arts, and a school of industrial science."[38] William Rogers would say that the Museum was to be the central feature, but it was also clear that he expected the organization to function through the Society of Arts, though the society is not mentioned at all in these bylaws, through which "control" of the Institute was delegated to a body called the "Government":

> The general direction, management, and control of the Institute shall be vested in a body, to be called the "Government of the Institute," to consist of the President, Vice-Presidents, Secretary, and Treasurer, and the Chairmen of the several Committees of Arts hereinafter mentioned, together with the members of the Committees on the Museum, on Instruction, on Publication, and on Finance. The Government shall have power to institute from time to time such standing rules and orders, not inconsistent with the By-laws, for regulating the action of the several Committees, the choice of subjects for investigation and discussion, and reports on the same, as it may deem expedient; and shall have power to fill all vacancies occurring in its own body during the current year, except those of Chairmen of the Committees of Arts.[39]

First Meeting of the
Massachusetts Institute of Technology.

Boston April 8th. 1862.

In accordance with a notice issued
by Prof. William B. Rogers, the individual
first named in the Act of Incorporation, and
the Chairman of the Committee of twenty, appointed at a meeting held, January 11th. 1861,
in Mercantile Hall, Boston, charged, among
other duties, with the framing of By-Laws
for the government of the Institute, a meeting was held at the Rooms of the Boston
Board of Trade, at eleven o'clock A.M. this day

The meeting was organized by the
choice of F. W. Lincoln Jr., as Chairman,
and J. D. Runkle, as Secretary.

Prof. Rogers presented the Act of
Incorporation passed by the Massachusetts
Legislature, and approved by the Governor
April 10th. 1861, which is in the words following;
to wit:

An Act
To Incorporate The Massachusetts Institute
Of Technology, And To Grant Aid To Said
Institute, And To The Boston Society Of
Natural History.

Met at the
Rooms of the
Board of Trade.

Act of In-
corporation

The Institute itself would be comprised of associate, corresponding, and honorary members, the associate members being those who signed the January 11, 1861, Act of Association and those who had agreed to join by April 8, 1862. Though they were sometimes referred to as the "Original or Foundation Members," the bylaws identify them as associates, the class to which future members would also be elected. Thereafter, candidates for associate membership, with Massachusetts citizenship required, were to be nominated by at least two members and elected by ballot at a regular meeting, with three-fourths in the affirmative required for election. An admission fee of $2, an annual assessment not to exceed $5, and a $50 life membership fee were specified. Corresponding and honorary members could be nominated by the Government and need not be citizens of the state, with no fees apparently assessed.[40]

The officers were to be "a President, four Vice-Presidents, a Secretary, a Treasurer, and such Officers connected with the School of Industrial Science and the Museum of Technology as it may hereafter be found expedient to appoint." Except for the secretary, who would be elected annually by the Government, the officers and principal standing committees, after nomination by a committee of three from the Government and four from the Institute at large, would be elected annually by the members of the Institute. An Auditing Committee of three members would be elected in the same way but would not be members of the Government.[41]

There were to be thirteen Standing Committees of Arts, and every member of the Institute was expected to enroll in at least one. Membership in more than one was allowed, though the chairmanship of more than one was not. Those committees with a membership of ten or more were entitled to frame their own bylaws, provided they did not conflict with those of the Institute, and to elect a chairman to represent them as a member of the Government. There was no mention of the duties and responsibilities of these groups. The mandate of the principal standing committees was clear, all "subject to the direction of the Government."[42]

The president's charge was simply to preside at the meetings of the Institute and the Government, with "one of the Vice-Presidents, in the order of their numbers," to stand in for him in his absence. Though these duties were hardly onerous, his position with respect to the Government in practice represented executive responsibility for the conduct of the Institute's business.

The treasurer was to keep an account of all moneys received and expended, could disburse money only with the approval of the Finance Committee, and was to report to the Government semiannually or oftener when required. No money could be expended "in behalf of the Corporation [the Institute as a corporate body], unless appropriated by the Government; and all contracts shall be approved in writing by the President and the Treasurer."

The secretary's duties were spelled out more fully:

It shall be the duty of the Secretary to give notice of, and attend, all meetings of the Institute and of the Government; to keep a record of the business and orders of each meeting, and read the same at the next meeting; to conduct the correspondence of the Institute, when not otherwise ordered; to keep a list of the members of the Institute; to collect the assessments and other dues, and pay them over to the Treasurer; to notify officers and members of their election, and of their appointment on committees; to prepare, under the direction of the Government, an Annual Report of the transactions and condition of the Institute; and generally to devote his best efforts to forwarding the business and advancing the interests of the Institute.[43]

A relatively large order.

The annual meeting of the Institute was to be held each year in May for the election of officers, presentation of annual reports, and other business. Ordinary meetings were to be held semimonthly for the reading of minutes and correspondence, the transaction of current Institute business, and the presentation of written and oral communications relating to the practical arts and sciences followed by discussion.[44]

On April 8, 1862, an interim Government was elected, with William Barton Rogers, president, and John A. Lowell, Jacob Bigelow, Marshall P. Wilder, and John Chase as vice presidents. All would be reelected at the first annual meeting in May.[45]

John Chase of Chicopee, an early member of the Institute, was undoubtedly chosen to underscore the state-wide orientation of the institution, an aspect repeatedly stressed in testimony and public statements. A wealthy and prominent builder and contractor, he had been closely associated with engineering projects for manufacturing establishments in New England and other parts of the country. He served as vice president for one year only, appears not to have taken an active part, and died in the spring of 1866.[46]

The selection of William Rogers as president was a foregone conclusion. No other could possibly have been chosen, provided he was willing to serve. He had become indispensable to the success of the entire effort. It was he who had taken an amorphous and ill-defined appeal and shaped it into a proposal sufficiently clear and persuasive to convince the public and the legislature that it was worthy of support. That the details of the organization had never been fully considered seems not to have been a concern

Cr.   Cash.

1862						
May	5	To Mass. Institute Technology. For Gift of Wm Minot & Wm Minot Jr Executors of will of Mary P Townsend as per contra		x	3000	
"	6	" Interest a/c Six months interest of Charles Money on mortgage to May 1/62		√	90	
Nov.	1	" Interest a/c Six months interest of Charles Money on mortgage to Nov 1/62		√	90	
1863						
Jan.	3	" Mass. Institute Technology. For Gift of Henry B. Rogers		x	1.000	
Mch	16	" Mass. Institute Technology. From Robert Forbes		x	100	
Apr.	29	" Expense From Back Bay Commissioners 6 mos. Office rent to May 1/63 7500 " for Gas fuel &c 3533			11033	
May	4	" Interest a/c Six mos interest of Charles Money on mortgage to May 1/6		√	90	
"	5	" Mass. Institute Technology. From Wm Minot & Wm Minot Jr Trustee Mary P Townsend Estate		√	500	
"	"	" Admission Fees Enrolled members to date 350 Elected 38			388	
"	22	" Mass. Institute Technology. Subscription of Charles L. Dalton		√	500	
"	27	" Mass. Institute Technology. Subscription of S.P. Ruggles		√	500	
"	28	" Mass. Institute Technology. Subscription of Ralph B. Forbes		√	1.000	
Jun	4	" Mass. Institute Technology. Subscription of Edward Atkinson		√	200	
"	18	" Mass. Institute Technology. Subscription of James Savage		√	500	
"	23	" Mass. Institute Technology. Subscription of Thomas N. Greenleaf		√	500	
		Forward		√	8.568.33	

at that time. As the Institute developed, however, and the school achieved prominence, he could provide the required background and experience.

President-elect Rogers addressed the gathering, thanking them first for the honor bestowed upon him, referring to their "labors and anxieties," and emphasizing the "responsibility which now rested on all to aid in successfully developing the great scheme of Practical Education and Industrial Improvement to which they had in a measure become pledged to the community:—should they succeed, as present indications assured him they would, they might well claim the enduring thanks of the State, and of the friends of progress everywhere."[47] And he took great pleasure in announcing that "the Institute can even now point to prospective *contributions* equivalent in utility to *more than One Hundred Thousand Dollars*." He based this figure partly on the intended $50,000 bequest of Ralph Huntington (then still living), and an annual amount of at least $3,000 "for the Educational Department of the Institute from a Trust Fund well known for ... the beneficence of its application in the direction, and for the advancement and improvement of Public Instruction." This was the Lowell Institute.

Rogers announced further that at least $3,000 would be coming from the "Executors of the late venerable lady," Miss Mary P. Townsend. William Minot, one of the executors, had informed him in January that they were "inclined to aid the Institute," but had specified no amount, promising to see what could be given "in money & what in funds yielding income." The first entry in the treasurer's cash book no. 1 reveals that on May 5, 1862, $3,000 was received from the estate of Miss Townsend. The same ledger reveals, however, that the $3,000 came in the form of a transferred mortgage. An additional contribution of $500, this time in cash, would be received on May 5 of the following year. Though she was not the originator of the idea and had no way of knowing that it was to be done, the late Miss Townsend had the distinction of providing the first gift entry for the Institute's books.[48]

Based on these expectations, the total of "over" $100,000 was a very rosy projection. Nevertheless, a resolution was passed noting that the Institute was "greatly cheered" by this amount, with a further resolution that the Government be "directed forthwith" to petition the legislature for more time to raise the guarantee fund, inasmuch as "this prospective contribution is not in a shape literally complying with the stipulations of the Act of April 10, 1861."[49]

Thus it was that the Massachusetts Institute of Technology was finally organized in the rooms of the Boston Board of Trade in the Merchants' Exchange at 55 State Street, and it would continue to hold its meetings there until suitable quarters could be found.

Rogers immediately prepared a statement for the legislature, claiming that the funds secured for the Natural History Society building then under construction, representing "one part of the general improvement . . . ought to be regarded as an assurance that the Institute will be able within another year to appropriate its share of the legislative grant." In closing he indicated that they had until only a few days before considered that their prospective contributions would suffice but had just learned that "these resources were not likely to be accepted by the Gov. & Council as Complying with the requirement of the Act." They therefore asked for "an extension of the time for making up the prescribed amount in a shape so guaranteed as to be unquestionably accordant with the conditions of the Act."[50]

When the Institute and Government met again on April 22, 1862, Rogers could report that the Committee on Public Lands, without any opposition, would allow them another year. The necessary charter amendment was approved a few days later.[51] On May 6 the first annual meeting was held at the Board of Trade, the amendment to the charter was accepted, and the interim officers and the four principal committees—instruction, finance, museum, and publication—chosen in April were elected to serve for the ensuing year. Except for the secretary, the first Government of the Institute was in place. On July 15, 1862, the list of officers was complete with the election by the Government of Thomas H. Webb as "Permanent Secretary of the Institute."[52]

President
    William B. Rogers
Vice-Presidents
    John A. Lowell
    Jacob Bigelow
    Marshall P. Wilder
    John Chase
Secretary
    Thomas H. Webb
Treasurer
    Charles H. Dalton
Committee on Instruction
    William B. Rogers
    J. D. Philbrick
    Henry B. Rogers
    G. W. Tuxbury
    John A. Lowell

A. A. Hayes
J. B. Francis
Committee on Publication
    J. D. Runkle
    Lorenzo Sabine
    C. L. Flint
    George B. Emerson
    J. C. Hoadley
Committee on Museum
    Erastus B. Bigelow
    Fred W. Lincoln, Jr.
    Jonathan Preston
    S. P. Ruggles
    Ralph Huntington
    Alexander H. Rice
    R. C. Greenleaf
Committee on Finance
    M. D. Ross
    Edward Atkinson
    James M. Beebe
    E. S. Tobey
    E. H. Eldridge[53]

Additions to this roster were expected as the Committees of Arts were organized and chairmen elected, but, with a few exceptions, the concept of these committees never took hold.

Born in Providence, Rhode Island, Thomas Hopkins Webb was graduated from Brown University in 1821 and the Harvard Medical School, with an M.D. degree, in 1825. He appears not to have enjoyed success as a physician and is said in any event to have been more interested in science and in history. He was associated with the Franklin Society in Providence for a number of years, editor at one time of the *Providence Journal*, a founder of the Providence Athenaeum, and its first librarian. In 1850 he served as secretary of a United States commission on the Mexican boundary.[54]

Thomas Hopkins Webb

Webb's most recent post was that of secretary to the New England Emigrant Aid Company, chartered in Massachusetts to encourage Northern colonization of Kansas shortly before final passage by Congress in 1854 of the Kansas-Nebraska Bill. The development of the Western territories at that time was very much bound up with the question of slavery, and this piece of legislation called for popular sovereignty, ensuring that the people of Kansas would have the right to decide whether or not slavery would be permitted. The goal of the New England Emigrant Aid Company, initially known as the Massachusetts Emigrant Aid Company, was to facilitate emigration to Kansas and to give tangible support to the development of the territory so that Northerners, with antislavery views, would outnumber Southerners in that area. Similar organizations were soon founded in other parts of the North. Webb once described their goals as "to advance the cause of justice and humanity by extending and securing the blessings of freedom to our territorial possessions."[55]

The company suffered a number of difficulties, some internal, and was beset by many financial problems, even though Amos A. Lawrence, for whom Lawrence, Kansas, is named, contributed much in financial aid and leadership. Despite problems which persisted throughout its existence, the company is said to have doggedly carried on "the battle against slavery, in the face of obstacles and discouragements that would have driven most people to give up in despair."[56] As secretary, Webb worked extremely hard, apparently to the detriment of his health. Responsible for managing company headquarters at 3 Winter Street, Boston, he kept the records, carried on the correspondence, helped with fund-raising, arranged transportation for settlers and organized parties of such recruits for the journey, and visited Kansas settlements to assess their condition and progress. In 1855 his *Information for Kansas Emigrants* was issued, "regarded at the time as the most thorough and reliable of the numerous settlers' handbooks."[57] He even made time to collect books in order that Lawrence, Kansas, might have a library, a concern he would later show for the Institute of Technology.

With the onset of the Civil War the activities in Kansas were gradually phased out, and Webb's position became part-time and without salary as plans proceeded for the liquidation of the company's property. The Institute of Technology's need for a secretary came, therefore, at a propitious time. Undoubtedly Webb was well known to many supporters of the Institute, but he may have been suggested by Jonathan Preston, his brother-in-law, a member of the Government who would soon be responsible, with his son, for the design and construction of the Institute's first building on Boylston Street.

Of the twenty-nine individuals constituting the first governing body of the Institute, the youngest was thirty-five and the eldest, seventy-eight. The majority were in the range of forty to sixty-five. William Rogers was fifty-eight. Thirteen of the Committee of Twenty were included, as well as George B. Emerson and Alexander H. Rice, signatories to the January 1860 memorial. Marshall P. Wilder and M. D. Ross were the only survivors of the original committee relating to William Emerson Baker's plan for a Conservatory of Art and Science. The largest number were manufacturers, commission merchants, or businessmen, as Erastus Bigelow had foreseen. There were several inventors and engineers, one chemist, and two lawyers. Jacob Bigelow, George Emerson, John Philbrick, and William Rogers represented the field of education, and John Runkle could also be included in this category. Seven were Harvard graduates, including Jacob Bigelow, who was also a former faculty member, and John Amory Lowell, a fellow of the Harvard Corporation from 1837 to 1877. Two additional members had been granted honorary master of arts degrees by Harvard.

The first challenge to the Institute's existence came almost immediately and from within. How serious this was is difficult to determine from the minutes, but the fact that such a question arose at all and so soon is worthy of note. The immediate cause was the problem of finding suitable space until a building could be constructed on the Back Bay, the land for which could not be taken up until the guarantee fund had been raised.

At the first annual meeting in May 1862 a Committee on Rooms was appointed, consisting of Dalton, Ross, Ruggles, and William Rogers, with Erastus Bigelow as chairman. Jonathan Preston was later added.[58] Shortly they reported a decision to seek space, probably for two years, at the Boston Public Library, then located on Boylston Street across from the Boston Common. They already had in mind alterations to an unoccupied reading room on the first floor and were hopeful that a favorable response would be forthcoming. Rogers had written to Edward Everett, then president of the library's board of trustees, and had spoken with his friend George Ticknor, also a member of the board. A letter had been sent to the city council and to the chairman of the Committee on the Public Library.[59]

On August 5 they were greatly disappointed to be informed that "though highly favoring the objects of the Institute of Technology, and desirous in every proper way to contribute to its prosperity," the trustees could not accede to the request. Their reasons ranged from having declined similar requests from other organizations, the inherent problems of divided control over a large space, and the restrictions that would have to be placed on its use, to their conviction that they could not in good conscience divert to other purposes library space that would soon be needed for books. When this decision was reported to the Government meeting on September 23, 1862, the committee emphasized that "they were all actively engaged" in seeking a solution to the problem, and the discussion centered on securing quarters suitable for the preservation and exhibition of the models and other items they hoped to collect and display.[60]

A week later Erastus Bigelow was able to report that, after considering several different locations, they had concluded that space in the Mercantile Building on Summer Street would be the best solution. For a probable annual rental of $572 they could secure a hall for meetings and exhibition space, an office for Secretary Webb, and an adjoining smaller room under a two-year lease with an option to relinquish the space or extend the arrangement for a similar period, notice to be required three months before the end of the first year. Fitting up the space for their use would cost in the neighborhood of $600. Though the committee had been appointed to act with power, they were reluctant to "incur such a heavy expense" without taking counsel with the Government and raising a question about the wisdom of continuing in view of their "limited means" and the unsettled condition of the country.[61]

The record does not say who of the committee suggested a general discussion of the wisdom of proceeding. But one can well imagine that Dalton, the treasurer, would be most anxious for the entire Government to consider carefully what they were about to set in motion. Known as a man with a remarkable capacity for organization and administration, he would naturally have been somewhat alarmed at the immediate prospect of more than $1,000 in expenses, which would represent only an initial outlay for a venture that would prove to be more costly than anyone had thought, if they had ever thought much about it at all. Erastus Bigelow, too, though enthusiastic about the Institute's plans, was an astute businessman who could clearly appreciate the financial problems that lay ahead. In any event, it was prudent to remind the Government of their fiscal responsibilities. The record contains no remarks by Bigelow beyond opening the discussion and no statements by Dalton.

At least two members of the Committee on Rooms were not worried. Rogers was, as usual, confident that the Institute would be "suitably sustained by the Public," and stressed the importance of an immediate beginning, fearing that any delay would "inflict a serious injury, if not a death blow, upon the enterprize." According to the record, Jonathan Preston agreed. The Institute's purposes were of "too vital importance" to be "outweighed by a mere dollar and cent consideration":

> This is a *Peace* measure; and therefore the prevalence of a civil war, so far from dampening our ardor, or being suffered to arrest our progress, should stimulate us with new vigor to urge onward this great work.

To "withdraw" or "become lukewarm" at this juncture would be "disgraceful," a failure of "duty to the community," and furthermore:

> basely ungrateful to those gentlemen who labored so unceasingly in the infancy of this movement, and struggled against and successfully overcame truly serious obstacles, in comparison with which the present money question is of no account;—obstacles of such a nature as would have discouraged ordinary individuals,—indeed any save such as those whose heart and mind were so completely absorbed in the enterprize.[62]

An impassioned statement, perhaps embellished by the secretary, the logic of which might very well escape the man who would ultimately be responsible for paying the bills. But what could Dalton say, for the recent acceptance of the charter and legislative support for an extension of time on the guarantee fund rendered it politically inopportune to retreat even if only briefly.

Both Edward Tobey and Ralph Huntington offered to do their share toward meeting the expenses that might be incurred, and M. D. Ross, identified in the minutes as "one of the originators of the Institute," urged "persistent perseverance." The president deemed that there was "but one opinion on the subject" and hoped that the Committee on Rooms would "as speedily as practicable, consummate the business entrusted to them."[63]

In his first annual report, dated May 1863, the secretary commented on the implications of this discussion:

> This was an important juncture in the history of the Institute, as upon the decision then arrived at mainly depended, its vitality and progressive advance-

A makeshift home—the Mercantile Building on Summer Street, Boston, where MIT rented rooms from 1862 until the opening of its own quarters on Boylston Street in 1866

ment, or its death throe and extinction, evincing in the latter case the truth of certain unfriendly predictions that the project would prove an abortion. Fortunately there were among those present some of the earliest laborers in the field; persons who had viewed the subject under various aspects, & in all its bearings & dependencies,—who had encountered many difficulties, & met with some rebuffs, but still unswervingly persevered, in despite of discouragements; having followed the Scriptural inculcation of first counting the cost, they felt confident that, if they steadily pushed forward, they would make the foundation sure.[64]

Curiously, there were no meetings of the Government between September 30 and December 5, 1862, when they gathered in the secretary's office, No. 1 Mercantile Building, 16 Summer Street. What William Rogers later described as "a long and perplexing search" had ended.[65]

The December 5 meeting was important for the discussion of several organizational matters and especially for the presentation of the first semiannual report of the treasurer. As of that date, he had paid out no monies, and he had received in two semi-annual payments a total of $180, now deposited in the Revere Bank, representing one year's interest on the mortgage from the estate of Miss Townsend. The rent for Summer Street was obviously going to be paid by someone else. A little help came through Jonathan Preston, who indicated that the Commissioners on the Back Bay would be happy to pay at the rate of $150 per year for the use of the secretary's office for their meetings. That offer was gratefully accepted.[66]

President Rogers reminded the Government of its duty to set the schedule for the ordinary meetings of the Institute and proposed that a circular be sent to all of the associate members inviting them to attend. Wednesday, December 17, was chosen for the first meeting, with meetings thereafter to be held regularly twice a month in the evening. Jacob Bigelow, who had been absent from the two meetings in September, asked if any rules and regulations had been laid out for these ordinary meetings:

> How and by whom the business preparations were to be made—through what channels communications must pass—the course to be adopted by those desirous of exhibiting Plans, Models, etc.—the manner of conducting discussions, etc.—
>
> He deemed it highly important, in order to obviate difficulties liable to occur from time to time, to start aright and understandingly.[67]

For this practical and perceptive observation he was rewarded with the chairmanship of a committee to answer the questions he had posed, with Erastus Bigelow, John Philbrick, and William Rogers to work with him.

The subject of the ordinary meetings inspired what the secretary called "an interesting discussion and a free interchange of views and opinions . . . in relation to the objects and purposes of the Institute, the true sphere of its action, the wisest policy to be pursued, etc."[68] Exactly what was said during this discussion, however, he did not record.

It seems clear, in reviewing the events and the recorded meetings during this period, that not only had the actual cost of the Institute's activities never been carefully assessed, but also how the membership would achieve their stated aims and what their ultimate focus would be had never been thoughtfully considered. William Rogers had turned out the *Objects and Plan* as a document for the benefit of the legislature and for gaining public support, producing a statement with sufficient appeal to secure the grant of land and the charter. Had the legislature been asked for money, it is conceivable that these important considerations would have been addressed, enabling the Institute to reach the point of organization with a better idea of the financial and programmatic realities. The Institute in 1862 was hardly more than a "project," as Edward Everett had termed his proposal for a scientific school at Harvard in 1847.[69]

The brief moment of uncertainty in September was not a major agitation for withdrawal, but it was a warning that beneath the enthusiasm of the Institute's proponents lay some serious questions about the magnitude of the plans and how great an expenditure of time and money would be necessary for their fulfillment. If it was not yet clear, however, how the Institute would develop, an Act of Congress in 1862 would unwittingly supply the answer.

Chapter 11

The Land-Grant Act of 1862

he Massachusetts Institute of Technology is a land-grant institution but not, as many people believe, by virtue of the 1861 grant of land on the Back Bay by the Commonwealth of Massachusetts. It achieved land-grant status in 1863, two years after the receipt of its charter, when the legislature decided that its School of Industrial Science should receive a portion annually of the money that the state would derive from the Land-Grant Act of 1862, signed into law by President Lincoln on July 2 of that year.

On December 5, 1862, when M. D. Ross called the Government's attention to this important act, no official notice had yet been received from the governor of its impending availability. A committee consisting of President Rogers and Secretary Webb, with Charles Flint later added, was appointed to investigate whether the Institute might secure some of its advantages, "including as it does within its scope most of the objects embraced in the Act."[1] If the September doubts about the wisdom of continuing, soon put aside, can be looked upon as a slight threat to the Institute's existence, the prospect of participating in the Land-Grant Act brought a second, more serious, threat and the first in which Harvard would press for the consolidation of the two institutions.

Under the terms of the Land-Grant Act, each state received thirty thousand acres of federal land then available for public sale for each congressional member to which it was entitled under the census of 1860. States with such land within their borders were to claim the acreage within their own territory, while those without—and Massachusetts was one of these—were issued scrip for sale, the purchaser to locate such land in other parts of the country, principally in the West. Mineral lands were to be excluded. The funds thus obtained were to be safely invested by the individual states, the capital to remain intact and the interest devoted to the specified purposes: "the endowment, support, and maintenance of at least one college where the leading object shall be, without excluding other scientific and classical studies, and including military tactics, to teach such branches of learning as are related to agriculture and the mechanic arts, in such manner as the legislatures of the States may respectively prescribe, in order to promote the liberal and practical education of the industrial classes in the several pursuits and professions in life."[2]

Further provisions specified that the various states must signify their acceptance of the act within two years of its signing into law by President Lincoln, a deadline later extended; that none of the funds be "applied, directly or indirectly, under any pretense whatever, to the purchase, erection, preservation, or repair of any building or buildings"; that none of the money be used for expenses of the management of the fund; that the institutions provided for be in operation within five years; and that no state in rebellion be entitled to its benefits. When the Civil War ended, the latter provision was repealed so that all states could participate. Scrip issued could not be used for the location of lands until after January 1, 1863, and no state could on its own behalf use scrip to locate land in another state. Only individuals who purchased the scrip were eligible to do so.[3]

The act has been known generally as the Morrill Act, after Justin Smith Morrill, Republican member of Congress from Vermont, who first introduced a land-grant bill in December 1857. A revised bill submitted in April 1858 succeeded in passing the House on a roll-call vote of 105 to 100, and with some amendments, in which the House concurred, finally passed the Senate, 25 to 22, in February 1859, only to be vetoed on February 24 by President Buchanan.[4] Its passage through Congress had not been serene, with considerable opposition from the Southern states and a definite recommendation against passage by the Committee on Public Lands, which had been hostile to the idea from the outset. The president explained his veto: "The bill would: cost too much; confuse the relationship between the states and Federal governments; injure the newer states by putting vast amounts of their lands into the hands of outside speculators; compete unfairly with established colleges and universities, and violate the constitution, since Congress was not empowered to appropriate money for education."[5] This was the bill to which Marshall Wilder had referred on February 18, 1859, when he informed those interested in the Conservatory proposal that the "agricultural departments" of the plan might possibly benefit from a bill then under consideration by Congress.

Morrill introduced another land-grant bill on December 16, 1861, believing that passage might be more likely with Southern opposition removed from the scene. He made some changes in the earlier version, notably in excluding the seceded states and in mandating that institutions receiving aid under the act be required to include military tactics in the curriculum. At a time when the war was not going at all well for the Union, the need for more and better trained military officers was much on the public mind, and Morrill, a shrewd politician, was not unmindful that this requirement might add immeasurably to the appeal of the bill.

As before, the Committee on Public Lands, to which the bill had again been referred rather than to the favorably disposed Committee on Agriculture, recommended against passage. Meanwhile, at Morrill's request, Benjamin F. Wade of Ohio introduced it in the Senate in May 1862, and with some amendments it passed on a 32 to 7 roll-call vote in mid-June. On June 17 Morrill finally succeeded in having the Senate bill brought before the House for action. It passed on a 91 to 25 roll-call vote and was sent to President Lincoln.[6]

Over the years there have been some claims that Morrill has been given too much credit for the conception of the land-grant bill. The name most prominently put forward as an innovator in this area—and that many years after the passage of the act—was Jonathan Baldwin Turner, a Yale graduate who had taught at Illinois College from 1833 to 1848 before turning to experimental farming. Early in the 1850s he had proposed "A Plan for a State University for the Industrial Classes" using funds that had come to Illinois through federal government sales of public lands, expressing also the need for such an institution in all the states. At that time the Illinois legislature asked Congress, without success, to give "each state in the Union an amount of public lands not less in value than $500,000 for liberal endowment of a system of industrial universities, one in each state in the Union."[7]

Morrill, however, never set himself up as an innovator in education. He was very much aware of European efforts and of colleges oriented toward the practical pursuits of life already under way in America. He was aware, too, of previous recommendations for support through government aid. "He was not, therefore," according to his biographer, "proposing anything revolutionary, but a moderate, reasonable and practical extension of the educational equipment of the country."[8]

What is very clear is that Morrill was responsible for the preparation and introduction of the bill leading to the Land-Grant Act with which his name has become popularly associated, and that he persisted over a period of several years until his goal had been achieved.[9] Against the background of steadily mounting pressures for a more practical education as opposed to the strictly classical studies of the early colleges, an idea that had been steadily gaining ground since the middle of the eighteenth century and which he fully understood, Morrill fashioned a proposal using public lands as a medium of support for education, an idea that can be traced back to the late eighteenth century in the United States. Most discussions of the question of the provenance of the Land-Grant Act dismiss as inconclusive the claims of those who believe that Turner was the originator of the idea and give proper credit to Morrill for the Act of 1862, with the added note that it was an idea whose time had finally come.[10]

In 1867 Daniel Coit Gilman, then a professor at Yale's Sheffield Scientific School, to which Connecticut initially assigned its land-grant funds, published a long article related to the Morrill Act, entitled "Our National Schools of Science." In it he referred to scientific schools already in place when the bill was passed and to an emerging "Institute of Technology" in Boston. There are seeming inconsistencies in some of his statements. For example, he was "not sure" that each state should be allowed to solve "the problem of what to do with the public grant in its own way, with reference to its own wants, and according to its own understanding of the Congressional intent." Yet later he would cite as an attribute that the "people of every State are left free to determine how the scientific education of the industrial classes may be most efficiently promoted within their several limits." And at the outset he decried the lack prior to the act's passage of any thorough discussion of the "changes which are possible and desirable in the national education" through a "public conference of scholars or statesmen respecting the legitimate scope of the institutions . . . the wants of this country or the experience of others."[11]

To a faculty member of a scientific school, such as Gilman, the lack of discussion of educational issues surrounding the act might have been a legitimate point to criticize, but with all the opposition to the bill relating to questions on the use of public lands and the possible usurpation of states' rights that delayed its passage for five years, this omission may be looked upon in retrospect not only as fortunate but as evidence of Morrill's political instincts. Who knows how long the debates might have persisted if educational philosophy and curriculum content had been involved! Ironically, Gilman himself heartily approved the bill's omission of many ideas that might have come forward if public discussion and prior consultation had preceded the legislation:

> Many persons, aiming to benefit the industrial classes, would have insisted on some particular form of institution to be adopted in every State, and would have hampered the bill with objectionable features. . . . It would not have been surprising if a spite had been shown against Latin and Greek, or a predilection for manual labor, or a determination that a farm should in all cases be secured.

Some advisers would have thought it essential that the general government, in providing the endowment, should perpetually exercise the right of inspection or direction. Military men might have been tempted to insist on a military organization for the discipline of students. But all such objectionable restrictions are happily omitted from the act of Congress. It contains everything which is essential, and nothing which is unessential, to the end in view.[12]

And he was, therefore, confident that the Morrill Act would lead to positive results:

The land has been granted, the schools must begin. . . . The people hold the power, the people will decide upon the methods. They will blunder, they will experiment, they will try exploded notions, but they will never lose sight of the end in view. They will secure "the liberal and practical education of the industrial classes." When that is accomplished, and not till then, universal education will be the characteristic of the continent, as in earlier days it has already been of some portions of New England.[13]

Gilman did not misread the basic intent of the legislation, for he criticized "a popular misapprehension, even among intelligent men" that it would support only agricultural education, "an injurious and dangerous error, likely to lead to many popular complaints respecting the institutions established":

No birthright, no entailed estate, no aristocratic title, no official position, exempts the American from laboring with brain or hand, or with brain and hand, for the benefit of his fellow-men and the promotion of the general civilization. It is the comprehensiveness of the Morrill bill which constitutes its highest excellence. At the same time, while we insist upon the catholicity of this measure, we cannot and would not overlook another fact which is just as clear. Scientific schools, not classical colleges, are established by the act. The terms of the law, the explanations of its author, the intent of its supporters, unite in showing this beyond a doubt. Mathematical, physical, and natural science, the investigation of the laws of nature, are to be the predominant study, rather than language, literature, and history. The latter may be, the former must be, included. No slight is cast upon the classics, the venerated means of human culture, the acknowledged instruments of high intellectual discipline. They may hold their place; but other studies must predominate in the new institutions.[14]

Gilman's notes of a conversation with Justin Morrill in 1867 indicate that "he himself did not intend the schools to be merely agricultural schools; that title was not his but was given by the clerk who engrossed the bill. He did not intend it for class legislation, for farmers alone; he wished the teaching of science to be the leading idea, and instanced the vast importance of this to the manufacturers of New England. He expected the schools to be schools of science; not classical colleges, but colleges rather than academies or high schools. The bill was very carefully planned so that both old-established colleges and newly organized ones might use the fund."[15]

Even though Gilman was at that time concerned about the popular tendency to think of the land-grant schools simply as agricultural schools, the major pressures which led to the bill were indeed those of the agricultural interests, and Morrill himself often stressed agriculture in his own discussions. Of particular interest is Morrill's regard for Marshall Wilder, an important figure in the history of the Institute:

> Thirteen States had instructed their members to support this bill, and petitions from national and state agricultural societies and from large numbers of the people had shown the wide interest the measure had excited. All over the country many gentlemen interested in the subject of education favored me with their correspondence. The name of one, a foremost and influential friend, Colonel Marshall P. Wilder, must at least be recorded. His sympathy and support were unflagging.[16]

An interesting sidelight to this account is that some thirty years later Gilman would be offered but decline the presidency of the Massachusetts Institute of Technology.[17]

In addition to his keen business ability, responsible for the success of the firm of Parker & Wilder, commission agents and advisers to textile mills, Marshall Wilder possessed a consuming interest in horticulture and agriculture and was a devoted worker during all of his life in the promotion of these fields. At various times he served as president of the Massachusetts Horticultural Society, the American Pomological Society, the United States Agricultural Society, as well as the New England Historic Genealogical Society, which had an early but brief interest in the Back Bay project. He had served in the Massachusetts legislature as a representative from Dorchester, where he had a large estate on which he cultivated fruit and conducted experiments in the hybridization of flowers. Both locally and nationally he was a powerful force in the movement for the

improvement of agriculture, for the application of scientific principles to agriculture, and for better, more formal-
ized agricultural education.

Wilder was president also of the Norfolk County
Agricultural Society, and his first annual address to that
group concerning agricultural education is credited with
awakening local public interest in this subject.
Massachusetts had a commissioner of agriculture briefly in
the 1830s, and later, in March 1851, a volunteer group,
known as the Central Board of Agriculture, was organized
with Wilder as president. By 1852 this group had succeeded in convincing the legislature of the need for a State
Board of Agriculture. Charles Flint, another Institute supporter, was appointed secretary in 1853 upon the strong
recommendation of Edward Everett.[18]

Marshall Pinckney Wilder

Wilder, in a report on the first twenty-five years of
the Agricultural Board, called to mind the time of its
organization and a particular problem: "the great prejudice which existed against what
was then termed 'book farming'; and there were but few papers or periodicals that
would boldly stand forth as champions of the cause."[19] The attitude to which he
referred was particularly evident in the reception of a bill before the legislature in
1850 for the establishment of an agricultural college. The bill passed in the Senate, but
in the House of Representatives, whose membership included a greater number of
farmers, it was firmly rejected, leading its supporters to redouble their efforts. By 1856
a private group succeeded in obtaining an act of incorporation for an institution to
be called the Massachusetts School of Agriculture, with Wilder as president of the
board of trustees. His support for Justin Morrill's first land-grant bill of 1857
undoubtedly stemmed from his interest in this project.[20]

With the passage of the Morrill Act in 1862, the problem, as far as Massachusetts
was concerned, assumed a new dimension. The Board of Agriculture strongly supported the establishment of a state institution, and the Massachusetts Agricultural College
was chartered in 1863. The towns of Lexington, Springfield, Northampton, and
Amherst offered to comply with the terms of the enabling legislation, requiring them
to "raise by subscription or otherwise, the sum of seventy-five thousand dollars for
building purposes." Amherst was selected in a "nearly unanimous decision," mainly
because the land offered was better suited to the purposes of the new school.[21]

Chapter 11

While the Massachusetts Institute of Technology was preparing to ask for money from the expected land-grant fund, Governor Andrew was working on a plan to combine its School of Industrial Science, not yet organized and with no specific plan prepared, with Harvard's Lawrence Scientific School and Bussey Institution, the latter also not yet organized. Under Harvard's governance at that time, the governor was *ex officio* president of its Board of Overseers and closely informed about that institution's activities. A relatively new president, the Reverend Thomas Hill, was then in place at Harvard, a candidate whom Louis Agassiz and Benjamin Peirce had worked hard to promote and one who could be counted on to share their hopes—particularly Agassiz's hopes—to develop Harvard into a great university.

Hill, a mathematician and amateur naturalist, had graduated from Harvard in 1843 and the Divinity School in 1845, after which he had accepted a call as Unitarian minister in Waltham. When President Felton died in 1862, Hill was president of Antioch College in Ohio. Discouraged, however, by the lack of funds necessary to carry out his plans for that institution, he was considering a return to the ministry.[22] His election to the Harvard post on April 26, 1862, has been credited not only to the campaign on his behalf by Agassiz and Peirce, who were convinced that his election would lead to a real improvement in the scientific life of the college, but also to the influence of John Amory Lowell, the senior fellow of the Harvard Corporation: "Mr. Lowell decided that the University needed as President a clergyman to quiet the religious element, a Republican (or at least a strong Union man) to placate the politicians, an administrator to build up the professional schools, and a scientist to give new subjects their due place in the collegiate sun."[23] Opposition to Hill developed in the Board of Overseers because of a perceived lack of "business talent" and the feeling that he might "use Harvard for educational experiments,"[24] with a resulting delay in his confirmation until the fall, when he took up his duties on October 6. Early in his presidency Hill joined with Agassiz in urging the governor to support Harvard's claim to the land-grant funds.

In December 1862 Agassiz sent Governor Andrew a first outline of a "great University in Cambridge," describing privately and confidentially the inefficient condition of "our institutions of learning":

> The undergraduate department forms at present the essential part of our University; while the Law School, the Medical School, the Divinity School, the Scientific School and the Observatory are generally considered as acces-

sories and by some called excrescences of the College proper. The fact is that at this moment the College has more the character of a high school than of a University & the special Schools have in no instance yet reached the true character of University faculties. It would not be too severe to say that the Medical & Law Schools are only mills to turn out physicians & lawyers & the Divinity School a sectarian Seminary. The Scientific School is not yet sufficiently settled to have a fixed character & the Observatory is so shut up that outsiders hardly know what is going on there. Such a state of things is unworthy of a State in which public instruction is regarded as the most important concern of the community; & the present state of things in the whole country demands that our highest institutions of learning should be raised to a level commensurate to the aspirations of the nation. . . .

In the faculty of sciences should be combined mathematicians, astronomers, physicists, chemists, mineralogists, botanists, zoologists, geologists devoting themselves chiefly to the scientific pursuit of their study with men distinguished for their eminence in the application of the sciences to the useful arts, civil engineers, architects, mining engineers, military engineers, agriculturalists, etc., etc.[25]

He estimated that a fund of $2,000,000 would be sufficient, and he felt that the time would be right to convince the people of the need and the advantages of his proposed refashioning of Harvard into a great university.[26] He suggested also that a good beginning might be made by combining the contemplated Bussey Institution with the resources to become available to the state for an agricultural college.[27]

By December 22 Agassiz had a further suggestion. He informed Andrew that the faculties of the Lawrence Scientific School and the undergraduate department of the college had been considering the establishment of a military department. Whether they were doing this with an eye to the land-grant money or as a gesture toward the Civil War is not known, but since they had not been able to agree on a suitable plan, he asked, "Would it not be advisable under the circumstances that you take the wind out of their sails and make the proposition yourself?"[28] Perhaps his principal reason for writing, however, was to suggest that since those who planned to establish a polytechnic school were "going to press their scheme this winter," why not combine all into one institution?[29]

On the same day, Governor Andrew sent William Rogers an extract of the Morrill Act and suggested the consolidation proposed by Agassiz, not mentioning the source of the idea:

Now it seems to me we ought to begin now "on a broad gauge." Why could not a great plan, looking to the long future of the Commonwealth, be inaugurated. A mere model farm won't do, nor a model machine shop. This section of the Act hints the idea. You have gifts of divination in such matters, which I, not an academician, have not. You, as a professor of science, can plan, where I can only dream. Now, why might not the Bussey farm & fund, the land grant of the U.S., the Institute of Technology, the College at Cambridge, its Scientific School, Museum, Observatory, &c, &c, all be made parts, or colleges, or adjuncts, or complements of a system of higher education with its practical & experimental ramifications—and all tending to raise our standard of learning, increase its influence, render our industry more scientific & better taught, therefore more productive, and helping to popularize science without lowering its flight?—I wish I might have the instruction which I should derive from your reflections & views before writing my address to the Legislature. It meets the first Wednesday in Jany.[30]

Life and Letters editorially refers to Andrew's scheme as "magnificent, if impracticable."[31] It is difficult to believe that Rogers would ever have described the idea as "magnificent," for his "gifts of divination" did not permit him to envision such a combined institution. No doubt he responded in person, probably at once, but certainly when the two were together on the evening of December 29.

The following day Andrew wrote to say that he had forgotten on the previous evening to ask for a statement about the Institute's progress as he wanted to "say a good word for it" in his annual message, and he added, "The more I think of it, the more I feel that the national grant, the 'Bussey Institute,' & your Inst. of Technology might, without invading any necessary individuality of either (so far as its preservation may be needed to preserve devises, or what not) be safely & wisely combined into a great affair."[32]

Andrew had already sent a request for advice to Harvard. President Hill's response, oriented heavily toward agricultural education, was a resounding appeal that the land-grant money be concentrated in support of one strong institution—Harvard—claiming that in the Bussey Institution, though not yet in operation, Massachusetts already had a well-endowed "Agricultural School" connected with the college and the Lawrence Scientific School. Hill outlined the departments that should be organized and the professors that would be needed—a rare species that could not be duplicated in countless institutions all over the country. The program would be a model for other states to emulate, and it presented a "most glorious opportunity" to Massachusetts, of benefit not only to the state, but also to "our country and to mankind."[33]

Hill's response was transmitted by Agassiz with a cover letter, emphasizing the urgency of the moment and pressing the need for the organization of a "great University" even though "the one department of Agriculture should alone be carried into active operation at the outset."[34] Agassiz urged Andrew to include in his annual message to the legislature a "distinct declaration" of the need for a "real University . . . offering information of the highest character upon every topic of human knowledge" and a "distinct statement that the country has nothing of the kind yet, though many inferior establishments bear the name":

> We shall not be a nation, or as a nation shall not do our duty to the people before such institutions are founded. . . . Now is the time, Massachusetts the State to lead. . . . Be not afraid to offend the friends of Harvard. Those who love this university but will feel the truth of the statement and those who dis-like it join in the sneer. So you will please all.[35]

The governor took up the banner with a section of his January 1863 message entitled "School of Agriculture and the Arts.—University System." Much of the message repeated word for word President Hill's recent letter and drew also on Agassiz's outline for a university. Andrew opened with a description of the act and its provisions and followed with an account of the bequest of Benjamin Bussey to Harvard, moving on to agricultural education in Europe and efforts at such instruction in America. As examples of the state's interest in agriculture and practical education, he cited reports of the Commission on Agriculture and the establishment of the State Board of Agriculture, and made special note of an 1851 report by Edward Hitchcock on agricultural education.[36]

Hitchcock was a clergyman, who had been state geologist, his interest in that field influenced by Amos Eaton, and from 1825 to 1845 he was professor of chemistry and natural history at Amherst College. He was appointed president of the college in 1845 and served in that capacity for ten years before returning to teaching as professor of geology and natural theology. He had been a member of the State Agricultural Board, for which he prepared a report in 1851 on agricultural schools based on a survey of such institutions in Europe. In that report Hitchcock had advanced the possibility that through the "addition of a single professorship of technology" and the extension of "the collection of instruments to those of every art, this school might become a school of sciences, as well as of commerce and manufactures, and thus afford an education to the son of the mechanic and merchant, as well as the farmer."[37] A suggestion of just the kind of institution called for by the Morrill Act, said Andrew.

Andrew altered a Hill statement to include Agassiz's earlier suggestion, thus combining the "Bussey Institution and the means and instrumentalities of the Institute of Technology, as well as those accumulated at Cambridge."[38] In this way, he firmly believed, the "true idea of a University" could be achieved:

> I cannot doubt that the people of the Commonwealth have a right to those benefits; the prevention of all the waste of means, the weakening of resources, the repetitions of professorships, libraries, apparatus and other material, consequent on scattering instead of concentration. . . . The object should be to centralize and economise means and power, while distributing and popularizing education and its fruits.[39]

His plan "would give to Massachusetts a University worthy the dream of the fathers, the history of the State, and the capacity of her people," and he threw out a warning, perhaps to the Institute of Technology:

> Let no friend of any local institution, actual or proposed, avert his eyes. When we shall have obtained one central school, or a combination of schools interchangeably working each with and for the others, devoted to the grandest development of knowledge for agricultural, mechanical and military uses, and to the enlargement of the domain of science and art, to the discovery and encouragement of their true prophets and teachers, and to the widest diffusion of all their influences, then you will find the local seminaries springing up and distributing the results,—just as our town and district schools today disseminate the elementary lessons of science of which every boy and girl would be left in ignorance, were it not for the higher institutions, the original thinkers and the life-long students.[40]

The governor closed by recommending not only that the grant from Congress be secured, but also that steps be taken to purchase "if possible for a reasonable price, the life estate which now encumbers Woodland Hill," in order that the Bussey Institution funds "may not be allowed to slumber as they now do."[41] Could President Hill and Professor Agassiz have wished for anything more?

At least MIT was not written off completely. In a very brief section entitled "The Boston Society of Natural History and the Institute of Technology," Governor Andrew indicated some progress in securing funds for a building for the latter, suggesting "further indulgence," given the "peculiar circumstances of the times, and the great practical importance of its objects." He announced that the Institute had "begun its operations as a Society of Arts" and was preparing to open "some branches of the School of Industrial Science" and to collect objects for the museum.[42]

If implemented, Andrew's one-institution concept would certainly have absorbed the School of Industrial Science, and even the possibility of an amalgamation could have cast a pall on fund-raising efforts for a building. The fate of the museum, the Institute's central feature, and the Society of Arts under such an arrangement was not mentioned and probably not even considered. The Institute might have been able to continue for a time with an amended charter, but, realistically, not for long.

The matter of the Land-Grant Act was referred to a Joint Special Committee of the legislature. Andrew was thoroughly convinced of the merits of the proposal as an opportunity to realize Agassiz's ideal of a great university. If the Morrill Act could be criticized for lack of serious educational content, the governor had certainly injected into the legislative and academic debates to come a fundamental educational issue—whether scientific and technical education could best be pursued in a traditional university setting or whether an independent, distinctive type of institution was needed.

Peirce and Agassiz seemed confident of success, with Peirce writing often to Alexander Dallas Bache, saying on three separate occasions:

> Our governor in his message day after tomorrow will call upon [the] Legislature to found a great and real university, such as all American students shall seek to attend.

> Our governor, notwithstanding his scatterbrain mode of action, is fully awake here and will exert all his influence to bring the legislature to his opinion and the strongest members of the legislature are said to be fully sympathetic with him.

> Agassiz says with reference to the State Agricultural School, that he is informed the Committees of the Legislature are going to report all right, and that the opponents of the Governor's plan are rather getting smashed—a little smashed.[43]

Bache was delighted and wrote, "In regard to making the Alma Mater a great University Center, as proposed by the Governor of Massachusetts, my head and heart go with the plan, and I look to the Presidency of the present incumbent as the time, and to him as the man for the execution of this splendid scheme."[44]

But they underestimated the persuasive powers of Rogers and the force of the arguments that he and his associates could present. Once again the Institute would press its case diligently. Whether or not they realized it, they were taking a fateful step that would give major prominence to the School of Industrial Science, for which they still had no organizational plan and no definitive academic program. Once they succeeded in convincing a legislative committee of its need and importance, however, they virtually ensured that it was to this component of the Institute of Technology that their major attention would be devoted.

Early in February 1863 the governor invited representatives of the Institute, the Lawrence Scientific School, and the State Board of Agriculture to a meeting at his home. Agassiz's response to this invitation reveals that Hill and Peirce had also been asked to attend.[45] Henry Greenleaf Pearson, Andrew's biographer, states incorrectly that no "commanding person in a position of authority" was on hand to speak for Harvard because Hill "was not yet installed in office."[46] While it is true that his formal inauguration did not take place until April 1863, Hill had assumed office immediately upon his confirmation by the Overseers in October 1862, and was fully in charge from that date. Furthermore, he and Agassiz had been actively campaigning for the land-grant funds and supplying Andrew with words for his own statements in support of joining the institutions together, facts not mentioned by Pearson, who states that the "possibility occurred to Andrew." Rogers, for his part, did not agree that his "own scheme for a technical school of the highest efficiency did not need perfect independence to develop in" and that the members of the Board of Agriculture, considering the land-grant their "particular plum, would not consent either that it should be divided, or that it should be contributed to the common educational pudding."[47]

The undercurrents in this competition for the Morrill funds were many. A degree of personal rivalry persisted between Agassiz and Rogers, and many accounts stress their opposite views on Darwin and Rogers's low opinion of the Lawrence Scientific School as reason to take up the challenge. Rogers, who a year or two earlier had been added, at the request of Professor Charles W. Eliot, to the visiting committee for the Lawrence Scientific School, knew very well that the school was beset by problems, was in the throes of a rather bitter debate over curriculum change, and could not at that time respond precisely to the desired educational goals of the act.[48] He was certain also that though the Institute wanted and needed the funds, its independence was a prime consideration. His letters to Henry show him geared up for battle:

> Of course all the colleges, Harvard included, are rushing in to claim a slice of the loaf which comes to the State from the land grant. But the Legislature will

probably be deaf to them all. I trust that the fund will be divided between a School of Agriculture and our Institute of Technology.[49]

The Academy meets to-night, but I shall probably be detained by a committee of conference on the project of an agricultural college and other matters now before the Legislature.[50]

The need for financial support was urgent, as once again the Institute faced a deadline for producing evidence that it had raised the guarantee fund of $100,000. In presenting the Finance Committee's report to the Government on February 21, 1863, M. D. Ross, referring with hope to the prospects of a share of the land-grant fund, emphasized that no part of this could be used for bricks and mortar: "The Institute can hardly hope to avail itself of the favorable disposition of the Legislature toward its objects, unless it can give assurance of its ability either now, or within the coming year, to provide the Building or Buildings, necessary to carry its active purposes into effect."[51]

Rogers continued to look on the bright side. By mid-March he was hoping that "one half, or at least one third of the proceeds" would be granted.[52] And by the end of the month he wrote, "My efforts before the Legislative Committee have led to a favourable report, and unless certain secret opponents continue to avert present action, we shall receive one third of the benefit of the donation of land scrip from the United States, amounting to upwards of $100,000."[53] No doubt he knew that among these "certain secret opponents" were Agassiz, Peirce, and Hill.

The report of the Joint Special Committee, dated March 26, 1863, included a detailed consideration of all aspects of the act and a variety of proposed ways in which it might best be used by the state. The 360,000 acres granted to the state, if sold as expected for $1.25 per acre, the price at which other government lands were then being offered for sale, should yield a fund of $450,000, but the committee cautioned at the outset that the realities of the land market did not offer much hope of this potential amount.[54] More than eight million acres of land would be coming on the market for immediate sale and would obviously depress the price. The picture would be further complicated by the Homestead Act of 1862, which under certain circumstances offered free land to settlers, and the system under which pensions were paid to soldiers in the form of land scrip had already made large amounts of land in the West available for sale. These lands had not sold well and were on the market at reduced prices.

The committee's assessment was correct, for the record shows that Massachusetts eventually sold its allotted acres for a total of $236,287,[55] far less than originally hoped. There was good reason to be cautious, therefore, in planning for the use of the fund, and the committee recommended first of all that the scrip be sold as soon as possible in order that the amount of money with which they had to work would be known, expressing the hope also that other sources might be encouraged to lend support to whatever projects would be undertaken with its proceeds.

The report took great pains to emphasize the act's intent to support not only agriculture, but also the mechanic arts and the teaching of those sciences on which the industrial arts depended for advancement. Granting the certain need of an agricultural school for Massachusetts, the report stressed the parallel need for a school in support of industrial pursuits:

It may be said in opposition to this view, that the common opinion of this grant has been that it was for "agricultural colleges," and that no prominence has been given to the provision for "the mechanic arts," by any State that has heretofore acted on the subject, or by any who have heretofore examined the subject. This does not affect the fact. The intention of the law is transparent. All industry is or ought to be useful. It is not singular that Massachusetts, with her millions of dollars invested in so many branches of industry, and with her thousands of minds and hands employed in the use of tools and machinery, should be prompt to respond to a noble offer, to meet a serious want, which many of her wisest men have long felt and deplored.[56]

The report included a series of resolutions prepared by a group of merchants and industrialists who had met at the Board of Trade on February 16, 1863, with Edward S. Tobey presiding. Among those appointed to present these resolutions to the committee were Edward Atkinson, J. B. Francis, Henry Bromfield Rogers, and Tobey, all members of the Institute's Government.[57] While they refrained from specifying "any particular plan" for the distribution of the fund, they did register an "earnest recommendation":

that the legislature in appropriating the grant shall devote an adequate share through the Massachusetts Institute of Technology to those teachings in the mechanical and manufacturing sciences and arts which are the express object for which the institute was founded, and one of the leading purposes to which the national gift was intended to be applied.[58]

That William Rogers prepared these resolutions is clear from surviving drafts in his hand. A statement to his brother Henry in March 1863 that he had just "returned from the State House, where I have been in conference with a committee for some hours on the subject of an appropriation in which the Institute is interested," may indicate that he had a hand in the preparation of the committee's report as well.[59]

The report was firm that the fund should be used for truly professional education related to agriculture and the mechanic arts, citing such institutions abroad as "*professional*—open only to persons mature enough to decide definitely upon the calling they intend to pursue." In short, they should be schools "for young men and not for boys"[60]—a phrase used by Abbott Lawrence in offering to provide funds for the establishment of the Scientific School at Harvard in 1847: "We need, then, a school, not for boys, but for young men whose early education is completed either in college or elsewhere."[61]

The committee did consider the governor's recommendation that Harvard and the Institute of Technology be united, making use of the Bussey property as an experimental farm and creating in the process "a grand university," a "true university of the people, open to all and furnishing advantages to all."[62] The Massachusetts Board of Agriculture, however, wanted an agricultural college to be established independently and in another part of the state. Their committee, of which Marshall Wilder was an influential member, carried great weight with the legislative committee, which concluded that no connection be made with the Bussey Institution. Amherst College and Williams College were also anxious to have the funds, and some even proposed that the money be divided among all the colleges in the state. But the committee felt that if it were to be divided, the fund should not be split more than two ways, with the agricultural college in some rural area and the mechanic arts college near Boston.

A minority report by William D. Swan, dated March 30, 1863, held that the fund should be awarded to a single institution situated near the "great educational facilities of Boston and Cambridge." Among these facilities he included "the rapidly growing Institute of Technology." Already in place, "providentially," he said, was an "agricultural institution" connected with Harvard which "must finally be put in operation"—the Bussey Institution, offering an opportunity to "draw upon all the intellectual resources of Cambridge," and with an endowment and land already available. Its location was an added advantage—"at a sufficient distance" from Harvard "to prevent any possible danger which might be feared from the attempt to bring students from the farm and from the workshop into daily social contact with those pursuing a scholastic course."[63] This statement provides further evidence of an undercurrent of thought in mid-nineteenth-century Boston, reflected in early testimony on behalf of the Institute as an important "moral influence" that might help to "elevate the masses from low and sensuous pleasures." And it recalls also the separation at chapel of regular Yale students from those of its Sheffield School.

In the end the income of the fund derived from the Morrill Act would be shared by the Institute of Technology and a college to be patterned after the Agricultural College of Pennsylvania, which a subcommittee of the Joint Committee had carefully studied. In this way Massachusetts became the only state to select two institutions for support. As allowed by the Morrill Act, one-tenth of the total amount was set aside for the purchase of land for the agricultural college, leaving nine-tenths to be invested—one-third of the interest annually for the Institute of Technology and two-thirds for the agricultural college.[64] Marshall Wilder and Charles Flint, both members of the Government of the Institute and obviously placed in a difficult position in this matter, were to be among the trustees of the new Massachusetts Agricultural College.[65]

With respect to the mechanic arts, the Joint Committee's report had said:

> So far as a college for the mechanic arts is concerned, the State is fortunate in having already in the city of Boston an institution directly designed to accomplish the desired end. This is the Institute of Technology. If this should receive a part of this grant it should consent to a proper supervision and control by the State.[66]

Whether a March 21, 1863, partial draft of a Rogers letter, presumably to the chairman of the Joint Committee, was ever completed is not known, but it is clear that he wished to discuss with them the "*form* in which the state shall be represented in the Govt. of the Institute. As all *merely political influence* should be excluded."[67] The committee's recommended bill covering the grant to be made to the Institute specified that the governor, the chief justice of the Supreme Judicial Court, and the secretary of the Board of Education were to become members, *ex officio*, of the board of trustees—representation that Rogers would accept. But there was an added unwelcome provision:

> The legislature may appoint or establish overseers, or visitors of the said institute, with all necessary powers for the better aid, preservation, and government thereof.[68]

Rogers would prevail, however, for when the bill passed, the state's representation was limited to three *ex officio* members, a provision which remains to this day.

Chapter 186 of the Acts of 1863, "An Act in Addition to an Act to Incorporate the Massachusetts Institute of Technology," approved April 27, 1863, covered the grant to the Institute and specified the terms, including a requirement to provide military instruction:

> SECTION 2: Said institute of technology, in addition to the objects set forth in its act of incorporation . . . shall provide for instruction in military tactics; and in consideration of this grant, the governor, the chief justice of the supreme judicial court, and the secretary of the board of education, shall be each a member, ex-officio, of the government of the institute.[69]

Notably absent was the right of the legislature to appoint "overseers or visitors." This favorable outcome had required the same kind of political skill and persistence that had secured the small piece of Back Bay land which the Institute had only recently been able to take up through proof of having finally raised the required guarantee fund of $100,000.[70]

In a brief account of the effort to obtain a share of the funds, Rogers cited the limited representation of the state on the Institute's Government and reinforced his stand on independence and opposition to Harvard's "grand plan":

> The latter proposition . . . met with the instant reply from myself and others that the Institute had from the beginning determined to stand alone, that its independence was essential to its success, and that it would accept no grant from the State, or from any other quarter, which should in the slightest particular interfere with this independence. After hearing our statements and canvassing the subject very fully on several occasions, the committee abandoned their original purpose.[71]

On May 6, 1863, he formally reported to the Government that the Institute would receive one-third of the income of the land-grant fund, with acceptance required before July 1. The act was formally accepted in June and the secretary of the Commonwealth so notified.[72]

Boston Ap: 10. 1863

Satisfactory evidence having been
furnished that the Mass: Ins: of Technology
is duly Organized & has funds
subscribed for the prosec.~ of its
Objects to the Ext of One hund: thous:
Doll, it is hereby Ordered that
the said Ins: be allowed to take
possess: of s~ Land res:d for its
use by Chap: 183 of s~ acts
of 1861 & to hold Occupy &
Control the same Subject
to the Stipulat ~ & Conditions
cont:d in said act~

A plot in the Back Bay—official notification of land award prepared by Massachusetts secretary of state Oliver Warner, April 10, 1863

The Institute was now a land-grant institution. The subject was not raised again at a Government meeting until March 17, 1864, when Thomas Webb suggested that it might be wise for the Institute to purchase the scrip from the state and hold it for a favorable price instead of forcing its immediate sale. By this procedure a large additional sum might be gained. The matter was referred to the Finance Committee with power.[73]

Governor Andrew attended the Government meeting on April 4, explaining fully the Morrill Act and offering his opinions with respect to the management and disposition of the scrip. The details of a "considerable discussion" were not recorded, but later evidence indicates that he apparently believed that the scrip could be divided. Since the matter had been referred to the Finance Committee with power, no action was taken.[74] Following this meeting, Secretary Webb wrote to Brown University and the secretaries of several states for information on how their fund was being handled and the terms under which it was being assigned to those selected for participation.[75] Clearly, he was convinced that Massachusetts should move wisely and carefully in selling the scrip and in the implementation of the resulting fund, with a view to maximizing its benefits. The replies to his inquiries have not been found.

Henry F. French, the Massachusetts attorney general, soon to be appointed commissioner to sell the scrip, did not believe that the act of Congress would allow its division, and he hoped very much that the Institute of Technology would not insist on it. He further believed that seeking legislative permission would reopen the entire matter and could result in unfavorable amendments to the legislation. Even if such a procedure were to be allowed, he felt it would place the Institute and the Agricultural College into competition in the sale. He suggested that a company be formed to take the whole land, put it into stock, and sell it, a move in which he would be happy to cooperate.[76]

When Rogers and Ross turned to the governor on the matter of the division of the scrip, they found that he agreed with the opinion of Judge French, who would in 1864 become the first president of the Agricultural College:

> I have examined the law very carefully myself, and have had personal conferences with the Attorney General concerning it, and have taken his written opinion. The result with me, is,—although I did not see it clearly at the first,— that the principal of the fund is not divisible, although the income may be, and that the proceeds of any sales which may be made must go to the credit of the principal of *one common fund*.[77]

Upon hearing this, the Institute's Government voted that the Finance Committee meet with representatives of the Agricultural College to consider "how the end proposed in making the grant may best be accomplished."[78]

The annual report of the Institute secretary for the year 1864 summarized the events surrounding the decision of "persons 'learned in the law'" that the scrip could not be divided, pointing out that the Institute's movement to petition the legislature to set apart its share of the scrip "was arrested." So unless some arrangement not yet thought of were to arise, the Institute "will scarcely realize from this source more than $4,000 per annum, instead of $8,000 or $10,000, as some of our sanguine friends have anticipated would eventually be the case."[79]

The sale of the scrip for 324,000 acres was begun by notice of June 23, 1864. In February 1865 a preliminary session of the Institute's School would be opened, with full operation beginning in the fall. By May the commissioner had sold scrip for only 99,200 acres at 80 cents an acre. In his annual report, Webb again urged another approach:

> It may be worthy of consideration whether it is not advisable for the Institute, through the medium of some of its friends, to make an effort to obtain by purchase, at the present low market value, a portion of the unsold Scrip, under a reasonable expectation of deriving a material pecuniary benefit from the eventual sale of the lands whereon the same may be located.[80]

This whole problem worried along, and by March 2, 1867, a committee appointed to confer once again with a committee of the Agricultural College reported a unanimous opinion that the remaining scrip should be sold. An offer of 53 cents per acre had been made. Whether the Institute should attempt to arrange to buy its share for $38,000 and hold it in the hope of a better price later was again raised, but "an interchange of opinions" resulted in a prevailing Government view that it should be sold immediately.[81]

Had Massachusetts followed the example of the state of New York, and specifically Cornell University, the Morrill Land-Grant Act of 1862 would have provided a far greater fund than the $236,287 that the sale of the scrip finally totaled. Earle D. Ross, in *Democracy's College*, cites Massachusetts as one of the "larger scrip-holding states in the North" whose handling of the scrip was "inexcusably inefficient."[82]

The debate over the use of the land-grant funds in New York in some ways paralleled the debate in Massachusetts. There were two institutions anxious for the funds—

the Agricultural College in Ovid and the People's College in Havana. Both of these were chartered but neither at the time had any students, and neither was in operation. A counterpoint to their demands was the dream of a young state senator named Andrew Dickson White, on leave of absence as professor of history at the University of Michigan, for the creation of a great university. But the key component here was another senator named Ezra Cornell.

The long and complicated route by which Cornell University was established and awarded the proceeds of the Land-Grant Act is beyond the scope of this history, but in the light of recurring suggestions at Institute Government meetings that the scrip be purchased and held, it is worth noting that through the generosity and efforts of Ezra Cornell, the 990,000 acres of land for New York—roughly three times the acreage that came to Massachusetts—eventually yielded for Cornell University a fund of $5,460,038, beyond the initial proceeds of $688,576.[83] Through a plan authorized by the legislature on April 10, 1866, Senator Cornell, who had already purchased some scrip at fifty cents an acre, was able to buy the remaining 813,920 acres at thirty cents, and the proceeds of this sale were added to those already received for the College Land Scrip Fund, the interest on which would go annually to Cornell University. Ezra Cornell held the scrip, selling it later as land prices increased and paying the proceeds to the state under an arrangement through which a separate Cornell University Endowment Fund was established by the state. It is this fund which eventually produced an endowment of over $5 million.[84]

Ezra Cornell's enterprise—not without problems along the way—was centered around the pine lands of Wisconsin. It was not simply a matter of selling off some land; it required the time and attention that any business with a view to maximum profits would entail. In Boston no such benefactor with the requisite imagination, time, and money stepped forward, and the scrip was sold in routine fashion.

The decision to sell at once rather than wait for better prices was forced in part by short-term financial considerations. Money at the Institute was going out much faster than it was coming in, and the prospect of investing a large sum against future cash was perhaps not appealing to the Finance Committee, which was having a hard time raising funds for current expenses.

There was also continued apprehension about seeking approval for a step that might raise again the issue of the use of the Morrill funds. The Agricultural College people were nervous that their share might be taken away, or the conditions altered, and they wished to keep a low profile. They had some reason to be wary, for Harvard did not quietly disappear from the scene when the money was awarded elsewhere. As Harvard attempted to get its Bussey Institution under way, President Hill continued to press for the Agricultural College to be located near Harvard and closely connected with it.[85]

Governor Andrew continued to believe that the idea of a great university with the combined institutions participating in the venture would have been the ideal use of the funds, and it is certain that Hill and Agassiz restated their views in this respect after the legislative decision of 1863. In his annual address in January 1865, Andrew made his position clear when referring to the new agricultural college:

> Although overruled by the better judgment of the Legislature as to the views which I had the honor to present at length in the Annual Address of 1863, and although I remain more fully convinced than ever, after the reflection of two intervening years, of their substantial soundness, I have felt it to be my official duty cordially to co-operate in endeavoring to give vitality and efficient action to the college under the auspices determined by the law of its creation. . . .
>
> My own idea of a college likely to be useful in the largest way to the people, most vigorous in its growth, promotive of the progress of thrifty and intelligent farming, productive of scientific and exact knowledge (which is the true basis of prosperity), worthy of Massachusetts, and able to command the respect while it challenges the pride of her agricultural community—is one perhaps not yet to be realized. But I beg to commend the subject of Agricultural Education, and the patronage of this institution of the State, to your liberality.[86]

He opened his report on the Institute of Technology, "to which the legislature of 1863 assigned one-third of the Agricultural College fund," with the straightforward report of progress supplied to him, as usual, by Rogers. It mentioned the well-attended meetings of the Society of Arts, the plan for the School, its building under construction and some courses soon to be offered, and the hope for a second building for the museum. It cited the promise of a further contribution on a matching basis from a "generous donor" and expressed satisfaction that the "liberality already shown to the Institute by its friends continues actively regardful of its interests." But Andrew made no effort to speak of what the Institute, if successful, might contribute to the general welfare and reputation of the Commonwealth.[87]

The Institute would never receive from the state's land-grant fund as much as hoped or anticipated. The Cash Book records the first payment on December 30, 1865, amounting to $3,409.56. The next, in April 1867, brought $1,057.96. Thereafter, payments were generally made two or three times during the fiscal year. From 1865 to September 30, 1900, a total of $194,587.96 was received, representing an average of approximately $5,560 per year, closer to Webb's projected estimate of $4,000 than the $8,000 to $10,000 expectations of others.[88]

In 1930 an Office of Education survey of the land-grant colleges and universities attributed the establishment of the Massachusetts Institute of Technology to the "first Morrill Act," pointing out that it "had been previously chartered" but was not open to students until after it had been named in 1863 to receive a share of the state's land-grant fund.[89] Given that by 1930 the "Institute" and its "School" had long been synonymous, this statement can be taken at face value. The Institute began operations as a Society of Arts in 1862, but the final plan for the School was not laid out until 1864 and students were not admitted until 1865. A strong case can be made that the Morrill Act not only exerted a major influence on the nature of the school that finally emerged, which differed greatly from that initially projected, but also became an important factor in the development of the entire institution.[90]

Chapter 12

Harvard Again

When Louis Agassiz informed Governor Andrew in December 1862 that the Lawrence Scientific School was "not yet sufficiently settled to have a fixed character,"[1] he was identifying a problem that he had helped to create. And while he, Benjamin Peirce, and President Hill were campaigning for sole participation in the land-grant fund and the opportunity to create at Harvard a "great university," events there relating to the Rumford Professorship and the academic program of the Scientific School reflected this unsettled nature and at the same time bore directly on the plans of the Institute of Technology.

Eben Horsford's appointment to the Rumford Professorship in 1847 carried with it the expectation that he would play a prominent role in the new Scientific School, and soon thereafter he was given responsibility for the instruction in chemistry and supervision of the laboratory that Abbott Lawrence's donation would provide. In this way the Rumford became a full-time position linked with the Scientific School, of which Horsford was chosen dean in 1848.[2]

But within a few years he was complaining about the burden of his teaching duties, particularly the elementary instruction he was required to give, and the lack of funds to sustain the laboratory. By 1861 the situation had deteriorated to the point where the Corporation was also disenchanted, disturbed by the financial condition of his department and the lax way in which he had been administering its affairs, as well as by the extent of the outside work in which he was engaged using the facilities of the laboratory. At that time he was relieved of responsibility for the chemical instruction but continued as Rumford Professor, the post now essentially restored to its original part-time nature as in the days of Jacob Bigelow and Daniel Treadwell. Horsford resigned as dean of the Scientific School and was succeeded by Henry L. Eustis, professor of engineering. His replacement in chemistry was Charles W. Eliot.[3]

Charles William Eliot was born in 1834, the son of Samuel A. Eliot, treasurer of Harvard from 1842 to 1853, and was graduated from Harvard College in 1853 with a bachelor of arts degree. As an undergraduate he had participated in geological and mineralogical trips with Josiah P. Cooke, a young professor of chemistry, and Francis H. Storer, then Cooke's assistant. There were no chemistry laboratories for students in the college at that time, but Cooke's private laboratory was open to him. In the last term of his senior year he was able to take mechanics with Peirce, electricity with Lovering, and embryology with Agassiz. Following graduation he took a year to define his professional goals, studying languages and accounting and teaching an evening class at the Pitts Street School for working men and boys. Tending to like best the natural sciences and practical subjects, he decided upon "the profession of a student and teacher of science."[4]

In the fall of 1854 Eliot was appointed a tutor in mathematics at Harvard, an appointment carrying with it a seat on the faculty, in whose deliberations he took an active part. Since he was not married, he was required to live in one of the dormitories in the Harvard Yard and was responsible, with other members of a "parietal board," for maintaining order. At the same time he did some work in Cooke's laboratory and in the fall of 1856 was assigned to take over Cooke's chemistry class at the Medical School for the remainder of the academic year. He also served as an aide to then President Walker, assisting in the scheduling of classes, supervising the construction of buildings, and preparing material for the Corporation meetings. He was appointed assistant professor of mathematics and chemistry in 1858, his responsibilities limited to chemistry in 1861.[5]

Charles William Eliot

Eliot was an orderly man, and as assistant professor of chemistry in the Scientific School, he soon reorganized the teaching program and restored the affairs of the laboratory to a point where new apparatus could be purchased. He was also developing firm ideas about scientific and technical education.

On November 5, 1861, the Scientific School faculty appointed a committee consisting of Agassiz, Eliot, and Eustis to consider changes in the curriculum. Whether this effort was inspired partly by a perceived threat of competition from the Institute of Technology, not yet organized, is a matter of speculation. In December, though Agassiz "presented their report," it was read by Eliot, and referred to the Corporation as a plan "for the enlargement and improvement of the course of instruction," involving "important changes in the organization of the School."[6]

Eliot prepared this plan for the "Faculty in the winter of 1861–62." It proposed that "the School should thereafter 'provide a Course of Instruction extending through two years, and comprising a regular system of required recitations and exercises in Mathematics, Chemistry, Physics, Physiology, Botany, Zoölogy, Physical Geography, Rhetoric, French, German, & Drawing, preparatory to the prescribed studies of the special Departments of the School.'" A radical challenge to the status quo, it called for broader preparatory training before specialization, stronger admissions requirements, and entrance examinations. Degrees would be offered for four years of study—two of the general course and two specialized years—and special students would be admitted for particular studies, subject to faculty approval. The draft contained a note by Eliot that "the Institute of Technology was started very much after this plan."[7]

The Corporation referred the proposal to President Felton and John Amory Lowell, but no sweeping reorganization followed. Felton died on February 26, 1862, and Thomas Hill did not take office until October 6.[8]

The change in administration provided another opportunity for the Lawrence Scientific School to review its purposes and goals, an important step at a time when Governor Andrew was beginning to consider the disposition of the funds that would be derived through the Land-Grant Act. On September 30, 1862, Eliot was appointed to serve as acting dean while Eustis was on leave for active duty in the war, and the 1861 committee on the reorganization of the curriculum was asked to take up the problem again, Professor Joseph Lovering replacing Eustis.[9] A preliminary report soon presented by Agassiz as chairman was accepted as "embodying the views of the Faculty on the subject," and Eliot was asked to prepare a complete statement for a two-year preparatory course to be followed by two years in a special department leading to a bachelor's degree. By mid-November the proposal was ready for final approval before submission to the Corporation. At the request of several faculty members, Eliot asked Hill to attend this final meeting on a program they hoped to inaugurate at the beginning of the next academic year, cautioning that any "delay will materially affect its success." They had already asked the Corporation, perhaps with an eye to the requirements of the Morrill Act, to consider the establishment of a professorship of military instruction and to appeal for state aid.[10]

President Hill was there on November 18, 1862, when Agassiz and Peirce rose in opposition to the curriculum reorganization proposal. Professors Gray, Lovering, Wyman, and Eliot supported the plan. The faculty adjourned without ever taking a vote.[11] Reporting soon thereafter to the Corporation on the state of the Scientific School, Eliot emphasized the "present unsatisfactory status" of the departments of engineering and chemistry:

> There is in the community a strong demand for scientific education, which these Departments, each in its own one-sided fashion, partially meet. I believe that the University now possesses the means of meeting this demand fully and thoroughly and with profit to itself and the community.[12]

In early December, with Hill in attendance, the faculty met again to discuss the subject. Peirce announced that the absent Agassiz had a better plan.[13] It involved the inauguration of a series of University Lectures as a step in the creation of a great university and also, as already noted, the annexation of the proposed school of the Institute of Technology with the land-grant funds applied to this noble purpose. President Hill supported the idea, and once again a reorganization of the Scientific School was set aside. Two letters of Hill late in 1863 reflect the fundamental educational issues raised by the Eliot plan, issues that had figured prominently in William Rogers's defense of independence for his own institution.

In the first letter, written in response to an inquiry about the Scientific School, Hill emphasized the difference between the school and the college, where, through daily lessons and recitations, "an education is given in a variety of branches to every student," each "subject to discipline" and required to attend morning prayers. In the Scientific School, however, "we teach by single departments, and only encourage the students by persuasives to carry on collateral branches." Hill recommended the completion of the college course first, followed by that of the Scientific School. On that basis he felt that the school had no equal. He did grant, however, that for beginners not wanting to study Latin and Greek and seeking a "prescribed range of various scientific studies, to give them a general education, there may be better scientific schools," citing the school at Yale "which is well endowed and which stands in some sense as the rival of the College itself."[14]

The second letter was addressed to the Reverend George Putnam, a fellow of the Corporation, who had questioned a statement by a Scientific School professor that "things at the Yale Sc. School are on sounder principles than at Cambridge." Though Hill could understand how the professor had come to "*think* so," he did not "know why he should *say* so," and he proceeded to review the local situation in detail. One would think that Putnam, a fellow since 1853, would be entirely familiar with the background, but Hill's account sets forth the opposing views, and it highlights a basic difference in educational philosophy.

Pointing out that a "debate had been going on for 18 months in the Faculty of the Scientific School" when he assumed the presidency, Hill described the two sides of the argument:

> One party, this Professor among them, advocated the introduction of a *general course* of scientific study, in which boys might receive a knowledge of French, Mathematics, Physics, Chemistry, and Botany, sufficient to qualify them afterwards to take up special professional studies as teachers, engineers, superintendents of mines & manufactures, &c. The other party objected to this. They thought that a school so conducted would require recitations and discipline and thus be troublesome. They thought that it would tend to lower the standard of education by countenancing the idea that such a course is equal, as a preparation for professional work, to a full course embracing literature and philosophy. They therefore opposed the change and wished to have our school continue to be a professional school, giving instruction in special branches, and leaving each pupil free to make more or less complete preparation according to his opportunities, and to the wisdom with which he used them.

Hill had favored the latter group and, with Corporation support, they prevailed. The "said Professor" had favored the opposing plan, which was similar to that of Yale.

Hill felt strongly that anyone with "fair talents" not over twenty-four years old "*had better go thro' College* and then enter the Scientific School at Cambridge":

> If however he does not make up his mind to go thro' College, let him not go to schools like that at Troy or Yale, but let him prepare himself at a good academy or under private tuition with as much general study of *mathematics, Literature and Philosophy as he has time for, not forgetting French if he would be an Engineer, and German if he would study Chemistry*, and then let him come to Cambridge Sc. School. The atmosphere here at Cambridge and Boston is better for a student who would take the highest stand in his profession than it is at any place with which I am acquainted; and therefore better for any *student*, who really desires an education.

His opinion was "not at all shaken by the Professors [*sic*] opinion. . . . He doesn't *fully* assent to the doctrine of my inaugural address, and I do fully believe in it."

In a postscript Hill added that medical and law schools, designed specifically to prepare students for their chosen professions, offered no general instruction, now admitting that his Scientific School had not yet reached that desired state:

> So it seems to me that a school of Engineering, or of Chemistry, should not teach the French language, or the German, or simple Algebra, Trigonometry, &c. *We do teach these elementary things in our Scientific School at Cambridge,* as they do elsewhere, but we do not like to publish it, or ourselves to consider it as a part of our permanent system, it is a *temporary accommodation* of pupils. We hope that from year to year we may raise our standard and draw students here with higher qualifications to take higher rank in the school, as special students of Engineering &c.[15]

The professor who made the worrisome statement is not identified. Since Eliot had left Harvard by the time of this correspondence, it might well have been Asa Gray, who shared Eliot's view. Gray would later advise a friend to enroll his son in Harvard College rather than the Scientific School: "We have really—thanks to Agassiz and Peirce thwarting all good plans—no *Scientific School* at Cambridge. *They have one at Yale,* but here are separate schools: in one they teach Chemistry thoroughly, in one Engineering,—in another there are *lectures* on Zoology and Geology—of no use to a young beginner, and very little to an older hand." Gray saw "no cooperation—no combination for general and elementary Nat. History instruction; though there is a fine field open here, and students would pour in, if there was any system."[16]

Eliot would later speak of his efforts in the early 1860s to change the direction of the Lawrence Scientific School. He referred to his request at that time that the Overseers' Committee to visit the Lawrence Scientific School be enlarged and, as already noted, suggested that William Rogers be added. He had come to know Rogers through meetings of the Thursday Evening Club at which Rogers often spoke, recalling that his talks were always "clear, concise, persuasive, and attractive in the highest degree." He referred to a meeting of that committee in 1861–62 at which he presented his plan for reorganization:

> Professor Rogers listened to my statement carefully. I saw he was interested as I read it. He asked me for the paper, and read it carefully; and when the meeting adjourned he came to me and said, "That is a good scheme of yours for a general course in the Lawrence Scientific School, or anywhere else."[17]

Neither could have known then that an opportunity to work together would soon materialize.[18]

Early in January 1863 Eben Horsford resigned the Rumford, effective March 1, to devote his time entirely to his personal interests. Among them was the Rumford Chemical Works in Providence, Rhode Island, which he had established in 1856 for the manufacture of his invention of phosphatic yeast powder (known today as Rumford Baking Powder) and a derivative medicine and beverage marketed as Professor Horsford's Acid Phosphate.[19] His departure provided an opportunity for the Corporation to assess the relation of the Rumford Professorship to the Lawrence Scientific School and to consider whether or not it should in the future be linked with chemical instruction. Combined with the school's serious curriculum debate and Governor Andrew's attempt, at the behest of President Hill and Agassiz, to join the proposed School of the Institute of Technology with Harvard, it added yet another element to the developing Harvard–MIT rivalry.

In addition, the Rumford Professorship once again became a significant factor in the lives of the Rogers brothers. In 1847 it had been denied to Henry Darwin Rogers, whose disappointment then was probably tempered by the full-time commitment implied when the duties were combined with the responsibility for chemical instruction in the Lawrence Scientific School. But that arrangement was no longer in force, and now it would be William Barton Rogers who would aspire to this chair.

On what terms he was interested is not clear. Based on the information available, it seems that he hoped very much that the position would be offered to him and that he would have accepted it, a step that might be understandable only if the Rumford remained a part-time appointment. Even under such circumstances, it is difficult to see, given his precarious health, how he could also continue to fulfill his commitment to the Institute as its president and chairman of its Committee on Instruction. To leave entirely at this time could only incur the wrath of those who had sought his interest and support late in 1859 and would probably jeopardize the future of the entire institution.

In January 1863 Rogers had been president for less than a year, and the Institute had only recently begun operation as a Society of Arts. He was beginning to plead for at least a share of the funds to be derived from the Morrill Act, and in this connection he was fighting off the governor's attempt to fold into Harvard's proposal for the creation of a "great university" the School of the Institute for which no definite plan had yet been prepared, and which would not be seriously addressed for another year. And

Morrill Wyman

the $100,000 guarantee fund had not been secured. How many among the Institute's Government were aware of Rogers's aspirations for a Harvard post is not known, and it is possible that even the most ardent supporters among them did not appreciate fully the magnitude of the task that lay ahead. It is equally possible that not until Rogers sat down early in 1864 to write a more specific plan for the school would he fully understand the implications for the development of the Institute and the responsibility that had come with land-grant status.

Life and Letters contains no reference to his interest in the Rumford chair but includes several early 1863 letters to Henry, all with excisions. On January 20, several days after Horsford's resignation, William mentioned "a visit to Cambridge last week for the first time since the summer. . . . Wyman, with whom I dined, asked very kindly about you."[20] He must have learned at that time of the vacancy and mentioned his interest in it. A February 12 letter from Morrill Wyman implies that they had seen each other in the interim—possibly at a meeting of the Society of Arts or the American Academy:

> I had no opportunity when we last met of saying anything about the Rumford profp. As you are doubtless aware, the action of the Corporation has been stayed. As I understand it, there is question whether a new man shall be appointed, or whether in view of the finances of the Profp. Mr. Eliot shall combine the duties of the office with his present duties as director of the Laboratory.
>
> Should this last arrangement not be made, then I think there is but little doubt that a majority of the Cambridge people will support your claims though the gentleman from N. York has a few very earnest friends. The wish to have you here is stronger than I supposed.
>
> However there is no telling who is who until after the election, & no one can exactly foresee what influences may be brought to bear upon the Corporation.[21]

In closing he expressed the hope "that the wishes I expressed to you when we last talked of the subject may be fully realised."

As far as can be determined, there was never any official consideration of William Rogers, but the events of the next few months and the final decision with respect to the Rumford would nevertheless have a significant impact upon the future of the Institute of Technology.

The vacancy in the Rumford coincided with the approaching expiration of the five-year appointment of Eliot, who wanted very much to continue and hoped that the professorship and the responsibility for chemistry would once again be combined. While a committee of the Corporation was considering the situation, particularly its financial aspects, Agassiz and Peirce were busy promoting "the gentleman from New York" mentioned to Rogers by Wyman. Late in January Asa Gray, in a letter to President Hill, had expressed the opinion that if the chair were to be combined again with the chemical instruction in the Scientific School, it should go to Eliot. If it were to be separate, a physicist rather than a chemist should be appointed. With respect to the candidate recommended by Agassiz and Peirce, Gray had learned from private inquiries that no one in the country stood higher in chemistry and that he was "well posted in physics" and a man of integrity.[22]

This "gentleman from New York" was Wolcott Gibbs, a distinguished chemist and professor since 1849 at the Free Academy in New York, forerunner of the College of the City of New York. He was a graduate of Columbia, served briefly as an assistant to Professor Robert Hare at the Medical School of the University of Pennsylvania, and received a medical degree in 1845 from the College of Physicians and Surgeons in New York, which he had entered principally for the further study of chemistry. For additional advanced training he went to Germany and France, returning to America in 1848. Beginning in 1851 he was associated with Benjamin Silliman's *American Journal of Science*, particularly with respect to the fields of chemistry and physics.[23] His education, experience, and record of research were beyond reproach.

Peirce kept Alexander Dallas Bache, superintendent of the United States Coast Survey and a leading figure in scientific circles, informed of events at Harvard, reporting that, according to Hill, the Corporation was determined to appoint only those who would "overshadow" everyone else: "It is the shadowing which is darkness that is to be feared, not the overshadowing which is increase of light!" He reported also Hill's assurance that the appointment of Gibbs "*will take place*, before the summer is over."[24]

As the Corporation pondered the status of the Rumford, a difficulty arose with Eliot. In January 1863 President Hill informed Eliot that the decision on the Rumford would be delayed and made an informal proposal that he accept the professorship of chemistry in the Lawrence Scientific School at a salary of $1,500 with $900 additional to come from the receipts after all expenses, including his initial $1,500, had been paid. Asked for an answer by the following day, Eliot complied and said no.

He declined on several counts. Arrangements whereby a professor's salary was dependent upon student fees had been "practically disastrous" for the Scientific School, and the Corporation had voted in the fall of 1861 to stop the practice as soon as possible. Speaking as a teacher and a student of science, Eliot was disturbed by the specter of the "money relation between master and pupil." The system would "prolong indefinitely the poverty-stricken condition" of the school, for "not a cent would remain for the general expenses" or "adding to the present very meagre equipment." He thought it very unwise "to burden the Scientific School with a much heavier load than it ever carried before,—to draw the salary of a professor from a Department which till within eighteen months never met even its ordinary running expenses." He had been performing the duties in chemistry once assigned to the Rumford Professor for three terms and could not see why, with the post now resigned by Horsford, he could not continue to do so and receive the compensation that heretofore had gone to the incumbent.

That Hill was counting on the land-grant funds is easily inferred from Eliot's statement:

> You suggested yesterday, in explanation of the proposed delay in filling the Rumford Professorship, that additions to the corps of professors in the Scientific School might become possible through the action of the State as recommended by the Governor; if any such expectations should be realized, a new distribution of the work to be done in the School would be natural and proper, and the fact that the Rumford Professorship was filled would be no hindrance to such new arrangements. I confess that I do not understand why the hope of new resources should prompt the hoarding of those now possessed. The fund of that Professorship would not seem to need farther accumulation for its income already exceeds the full professor's salary.[25]

Eliot saw no difficulty for the professor in charge to deliver a course of lectures on technology, a requirement of the Rumford chair.

On February 27, 1863, he forced the issue, pointing out that since his term of appointment expired on that day, he would be unable to discharge his duties without some action by the Corporation. They asked him to stay on temporarily in charge of the laboratory until they could make permanent arrangements, implying that the matter would be solved within a few days. In April they asked him to stay until the end of the term. By May they were suggesting a further temporary appointment.

In a letter to the president and fellows Eliot declined, reviewed his own situation, and commented on the state of the Scientific School, based on his knowledge of the "history, plan, resources and needs of the School" and his "experience ... with the management of the practical details of the Departments of Chemistry and Engineering":

> The unwelcome conclusion has been forced upon me, that [it] is impossible to make the present income of these two departments meet the ordinary current expenses and the salaries of the two professors. The Corporation are aware that with the whole income of the Rumford Fund added to the present resources of the School, the annual expenditures for the thirteen years previous to 1861–62 so far outran the receipts that a very considerable debt accumulated, which though now nominally extinguished, has been really paid in great part out of the General Fund of the College. Not only did this debt accumulate, but the general condition of the School steadily deteriorated;—its building and its apparatus were suffered to fall into a condition of decay and disorder, which has been since but very imperfectly repaired. The condition of a large part of Lawrence Hall is simply disgraceful, and the equipment of both departments is very meagre, and the Engineering Department very dilapidated. Extraordinary expenses to the amount of $2500. to $3000. are urgently needed. If the School is to be permanently deprived of the Rumford Fund and is to receive no other fund in its stead, it will be impossible for any man to carry on the Departments of Engineering and Chemistry successfully, and make the receipts cover the expenses, even though the Professor of Chemistry should receive a salary much below the Academic standard. An examination of the accounts of the School and of its present condition cannot fail to satisfy the Corporation of the truth of this statement.[26]

In conclusion he raised very strong objections to recent attempts on the part of Harvard to raise money from his relatives to pay his salary for a few years. A second effort to secure a fund of $40,000 to endow a professorship permanently had so far produced no results. He respectfully pointed out that there really was no professorship of chemistry in the Lawrence Scientific School and he would "not wish to be a candidate for any office which would cease to exist as soon as a temporary provision for the salary of the incumbent should be exhausted."[27]

Pressure for the appointment of Gibbs had continued, and by the end of May 1863 the Corporation decided that the Rumford chair would be filled, the appointee to be responsible for chemistry in the Lawrence Scientific School. Wolcott Gibbs informed President Hill that he had no objection to taking charge of the department, regretting, however, that his election would result in the withdrawal of another candidate.[28]

Eliot would leave Harvard and go abroad. He would not soon forget this experience or the issues he raised; he would raise them again later, when he was offered a professorship at the Institute of Technology. Given his assessment of the state of the Lawrence Scientific School, a larger opportunity was open to the Institute than anyone had foreseen.

The appointment of Wolcott Gibbs to the Rumford was a major victory for Agassiz and Peirce, not only as Harvard faculty members, but also as members of a very small, informal, self-selected group of American scientists known as the Scientific Lazzaroni, a successor to the Florentine Academy, a similarly small Cambridge group including Peirce and Agassiz dating from the early 1850s. Alexander Dallas Bache, a Washington member of the Florentines, was "Chief" of the Lazzaroni, to which Gibbs also belonged. Asa Gray, William Rogers, Charles W. Eliot, and Matthew F. Maury have been described as their "opposition."[29]

Whether the Lazzaroni were of one mind, determined to control the development of American science, is a debatable point. They were, however, serious about the professionalization and promotion of science, and they were influential in the affairs of the American Association for the Advancement of Science, during the annual meetings of which they came together to wine and dine and discuss their common interests.[30] They did "electioneer" to secure faculty appointments for candidates of their choice, and Peirce and Agassiz made sure that Bache was fully cognizant of Harvard affairs. In informing him of their success with the Gibbs appointment, Peirce provided a complete account of the Gibbs-Eliot affair, stating his admiration for Eliot's administrative ability, but triumphant that "the Lazzaroni have carried the Corporation and Gibbs has the election to the Rumford Professorship."[31]

Yet another goal of Bache, Agassiz, and the other Lazzaroni was the creation of a national organization of scientists to provide advice to the government on scientific matters. In this they were successful, with the help of Senator Henry Wilson of Massachusetts. Joining Bache at his home in Washington on February 19, 1863, the senator, Agassiz, Peirce, and Benjamin Apthorp Gould prepared a draft of a bill for presentation to Congress working from plans drawn up by Bache and Admiral Charles Henry Davis, in charge of the Navy's Bureau of Investigation. On March 3 Congress passed an Act to Incorporate the National Academy of Sciences, and it was signed into law by President Lincoln on the same day. Empowered to prepare its own constitution and set its own rules, the academy's mission was briefly stated: "The Academy, shall, whenever called upon by any department of the Government, investigate, examine, experiment, and report upon any subject of science or art, the actual expense of such investigations, examinations, experiments, and reports to be paid from appropriations which may be made for the purpose, but the Academy shall receive no compensation whatever for any services to the Government of the United States."[32]

The scientific community was generally surprised by its incorporation, and not everyone was happy about the naming of its incorporators by the little band that had met quietly together on February 19. William Rogers was particularly disturbed. He was not afraid to say so even as he struggled not only to raise the $100,000 guarantee fund required by the Massachusetts legislature, but also to convince that body that at least a portion of the land-grant funds should be assigned to his institution. He had been at odds with Bache before over matters concerning the American Association for the Advancement of Science to the point where Bache complained to Peirce in 1854 that if "even a few 'leading men' (Rogers) stay away from the meetings the whole tone of things would at once alter."[33]

Rogers was ready to take Bache on again, and Agassiz as well, and he made sure that posterity would know why by preparing a detailed account of the new organization's first meeting, "Memoranda of the Meeting for Organising the National Academy of Sciences."[34] He began with "preliminary facts." He was unaware that an academy had been created and that he and his brother Robert were listed as corporators until James M. Gilliss of the Naval Observatory in Washington asked "'how I liked the new Academy' thinking of course that my Cambridge neighbors had acquainted me with the scheme which they were so active in getting up." Formal notification from Senator Wilson came later but without a copy of the congressional act or list of corporators. From "hearsay reports" Rogers concluded that "the Organisation seemed little more than an enlargement of the old clique," and at first he was disinclined to become involved. But a copy of the act borrowed from Benjamin Gould, who "seemed rather proud of the active part he had been taking," apparently convinced him that there was work to be done at the first meeting of the academy, scheduled to begin on April 22, 1863, at the University of New York.

Shortly before he left Boston Rogers heard that his name was not included on the original list of corporators "by those who cooked it up" but had been added at the insistence of Senator Wilson, who had himself been elected to membership in the Institute of Technology at a meeting of the Society of Arts on March 23, 1863. Rogers at first thought that his omission from the original list was a "misconception" but recorded that later events convinced him that it was undoubtedly true. Perhaps the first evidence to support the conclusion came on the evening of April 21, when he was snubbed by Bache, Agassiz, Peirce, Gould, and others in the lobby of the Brevoort House and not invited to join a dinner party that was to include Senator Wilson.

Rogers's overriding concern as he approached this meeting may have been the makeup of the list of corporators, which he felt contained "many little or not at all known as Contributors to Science" and omitted "others of established reputation for scientific work." But he also did not trust Bache, Agassiz, and Peirce, and as his knowledge of "these mysterious plans and proceedings" increased, he discovered other matters of great concern. Rogers came to the inaugural meeting prepared to do battle. First he raised the question of membership. When he was chided about the "rashness of men of Science who attempted to judge the Merits of those with whose department of study they were not familiar," and heard from Agassiz about the "danger of attempting too large a field and the necessity of concentrating the powers on special objects of investigation," he agreed to a certain extent with respect to the latter. But he "showed on the other hand that too exclusive devotion to specialty after the German fashion— was far less fruitful of high discovery and practical results than the more varied exercise of thought which had wrought in this country such variety of practical invention."

Appointed to the "Committee on Organisation" with Bache as chairman, Rogers sharpened his attack, successfully beating back an article that would provide life tenure for the top officers of the academy, an idea he thought "monstrous," not acceptable to scientific men anywhere, and certain to destroy the academy if it were allowed to stand. They settled on a six-year term, which he also thought too long. Later, in the full session, John S. Newberry joined him on this point, while their opponents, Rogers said, apparently "wished to see the President clothed with despotic power." Though Newberry and Rogers both stressed "the serious perils to the Academy which a six-year mismanagement would entail" and urged a shorter period, they were defeated "by a large majority." In committee Rogers also objected strongly to a provision allowing the president to exclude the Council from important decisions relating to academy activities, thus giving him "almost absolute control of all the scientific action of the Academy and centering in his hands the power of dispensing the prizes of scientific labour and reputation as he pleased."

Rogers looked forward to resumption of the general meeting as an opportunity to bring before the entire membership a number of important issues. When the committee's report on rules was read on the evening of April 22, several articles stimulated little discussion, but a grim reminder of the raging Civil War—a requirement for an oath of allegiance on the part of each member—"gave rise to much animated remark." Rogers seriously questioned its necessity. Though he was ready to take it himself, he felt that it "entirely excluded at any future time the admission of a person who may have [been] even slightly implicated in the rebellion." It looked like a "parade of loyalty" and "seemed not to comport with that entirely catholic spirit which should characterize an association having science for its object and standing aloof from all political action and opinions":

> I made no objection to the Oath but heartily endorsed it. Yet it seemed to me that it was practically unimportant to retain it, and that we would place ourselves on higher ground at home as well as abroad by omitting it. . . . But I had created an opportunity for loud declaration of loyalty and Bache, Gould, Barnard, Lesley and Gibbs made the most of it. One or two of these gentlemen are known to have halted between two opinions for a long time in the beginning of the rebellion. But their declamation was so blazing that I began to think that in spite of a lifetime spent in loyal labours for right and human liberty I might by some present be suspected of an alliance with the Copperheads, and therefore I made a short speech declaring not only my *loyalty* but my utter *abolitionism*.
>
> Yet I shall not be astonished to hear some of these days my doubts about the propriety of the Oath—adduced as evidence of a hesitating patriotism and that too by the man who watched the game with selfish cunning and did not declare for loyalty until he found it to be the stronger side.

On the following morning it was agreed that only a general description rather than a full text of the oath would be included in the rules, and the oath was administered to the members present on April 26, the final day of the meeting.

There were further disagreements, particularly on a proposal that every member be required, "unless excused for certain specified causes, *to furnish to the Academy every two years at least one memoir,*" a requirement Rogers considered would lead to "hasty work, giving us long memoirs enough perhaps, but loading our transactions with crudities and errors." In this his objection was sustained, and the provision was stricken.

In the end Bache was elected president; James Dwight Dana, vice president; Agassiz, foreign secretary; Wolcott Gibbs, home secretary; and Fairman Rogers, treasurer. Only the latter was not a member of the Lazzaroni. William Rogers was nominated for each of the four Council positions, "but although the vote for me was large—the banded strength of certain parties succeeded each time in keeping me out."

At the previous day's session Stephen Alexander, professor of astronomy at Princeton, had risen to speak about the academy's proposed organization, suggesting careful thought and urging that the rules adopted be printed to allow further study by the membership for action at a later meeting. Rogers, who encouraged him to speak out, "heartily seconded him" and felt grateful for his opening statement: "Stephen Alexander made the striking remark that while he did not assume it as a *supposable case* that such a body as this could come under clique govt., he thought that the Rules which had been made were as admirably adapted to secure such an end as if they had been specially contrived for the purpose."

On the last day Rogers returned to this point. Convinced that further time and a fuller meeting was of "vital importance," for "finally adopting a plan of Organisation, and certain that it was the purpose of those interested to have the present Code with its many almost intolerable features permanently forced upon the Society," he prepared a resolution that nothing be considered final until after a meeting in January 1864. An alternative resolution said to achieve the same end was proposed and passed, and he left New York believing that the academy would be "bound to consider at once any proposition for changing the code which I or others may see fit to offer at the meeting in question."[35]

Rogers thought he had succeeded in guaranteeing broader discussion of the issues relating to the governance of the academy and was disturbed to find, when he received a copy of the rules adopted in April, that the resolution passed to ensure a reconsideration and final vote on those rules had been ignored. He called Bache's attention to this omission in declining, because of the "pressure of engagements," an appointment to an academy committee to report on a hydrometer, commenting also that under the circumstances he "had not supposed that it would be thought expedient to enter upon the business of the Academy" until after the next meeting scheduled for December.[36] No response from Bache has been found, but he did write to Peirce: "What think you of W. B. Rogers addressing me as to an understanding (hah, hah, hah) that the President was to do nothing until next meeting, and that Caswell's minutes were incorrect!"[37]

Rogers was not alone in his misgivings about the National Academy. Locally, Asa Gray was also apprehensive about the direction the new organization might take under the leadership of Bache and his Lazzaroni friends, its effect upon scientific organizations already in place, and particularly the specter of government control of science. Though he stayed away from the organizational meeting and thus avoided the fray, his election as president of the American Academy of Arts and Sciences in May 1863 was perceived by Bache and Peirce as an affront to their efforts on the national scene. To make matters worse in their eyes, "that Villain," William B. Rogers, was at the same time elected corresponding secretary. "Splendid," said Bache, "and all because he isn't nobody in the National Academy."[38]

Rogers attended no further meetings of the academy in its early days, a time when the new organization was beset by many problems, and early in 1866 he informed a colleague that he presumed that his "membership had lapsed."[39] Academy records indicate that he was "removed from the roll of active members" in 1866 and "reelected in 1872." His brother Robert was also removed in 1866 and "returned to the roll in 1875."[40] William would be elected president in 1879, serving until his death in 1882, his term marked by a "sense of activity and purpose" during a time of "reconciliation and reassessment."[41] In his first annual report to the Congress he displayed a slightly broader interpretation of the academy's mission than his predecessor, adding to its mandate to "advance science" and to "investigate . . . and report on any subject of science or art" when asked to do so by the government:

> The object of the academy is to advance science, pure and applied, by original researches; to invite the attention and aid of the government to scientific inquiries of especial public importance, to be directed by the academy; and especially to investigate, examine, experiment, and report on any subject of science or art whenever called upon by any department of the government.[42]

The year 1863 was proving to be a critical time for the cause of science on the national scene and for scientific and technical education in Massachusetts. Despite early problems and crises, the National Academy would survive. On the local scene the situation at Harvard highlighted several familiar issues still of concern to contemporary institutions—teaching loads, policies with respect to outside consulting work on the part of faculty members, solid financial support for professorial salaries, and qualifications for faculty appointments. And above all rose the curriculum issue—could a student profitably pursue professional scientific and technical studies in combination with some general studies, or should he wait until after earning a general baccalaureate?

For William Rogers it was a busy, exhausting time leading to a summer of illness. With the Institute of Technology still two years away from the opening of its School of Industrial Science and no definite plan in hand, it had strong public support even if not financial support. The competition it might create for Harvard reinforced internal philosophical debates about the aims and organization of the curriculum of the Lawrence Scientific School, which continued to have its own financial woes. And events within Harvard, which left Charles Eliot free and open to other opportunities, set the stage for his imminent connection to the Institute of Technology.

Chapter 13

—◦✦◦—

*The Difficult Question
of Money*

T he question of finances was a paramount concern during the Institute's early
years and for many years to come.[1] By the spring of 1863, as the April 25
deadline for raising the guarantee fund approached, the need was urgent. Very
little progress had been made, and the total of $100,000 was still not in sight.

Nearly all of the Government members were actively engaged in wartime
activities, and William Rogers and M. D. Ross were in addition much involved with
the Natural History Society's plans. As the discussions about the Morrill Act were getting under way, however, serious attention was directed toward the Institute's difficult
question of money. Beyond the approaching deadline, Ross had quite rightly pointed
out that they could not expect aid from the land-grant fund if they had not proved that
they could survive and had the facilities to fulfill the act's requirements. In the background also was the desire of Governor Andrew to merge the school of the Institute
with Harvard as well as Rogers's hopes with respect to the Rumford Professorship.

The Institute's first Committee on Finance was chaired by M. D. Ross, who would
serve until 1865, when he transferred to the Committee on the Museum. There were
four additional members: Edward Atkinson, James Beebe, Edward Eldredge, and
Edward Tobey. When Atkinson transferred to the Committee on Instruction in 1863,
he was replaced by J. Wiley Edmands, a graduate of English High School, who had a
successful career in the textile field, first with the firm of A. A. Lawrence and later as
treasurer of the Pacific Mills. He had served a term in Congress from 1855 to 1857 and
was active in the Civil War, contributing both time and money to the cause. Over the

John Wiley Edmands

years he served as treasurer of the Massachusetts Charitable Eye and Ear Infirmary, vice president of the Provident Institution for Savings, and a director of the Massachusetts Hospital Life Insurance Company, as well as the Arkwright Mutual Fire Insurance Company.[2]

Edward H. Eldredge, a dry goods commission merchant with his own firm, had attended English High School before entering the business with his father. He had served as a member of the Boston Common Council and was an active member of the Union Club and the Horticultural Society. Eldredge died in the spring of 1865.[3] The final member, Edward S. Tobey, was also a merchant. Ill health had prevented his attending Harvard, and following a trip abroad he joined the firm of Phineas and Seth Sprague, shipping merchants, later becoming a partner. He retired in 1860. He was then president of the Boston Board of Trade, served on the U.S. Sanitary Commission during the war, was appointed postmaster of Boston in 1868 by President Ulysses S. Grant, and was reappointed by both Presidents Rutherford B. Hayes and Chester A. Arthur. He served also as a trustee of Dartmouth College. He had declined to run for mayor of Boston in 1860, causing the *Boston Advertiser* to complain that "good men" would not do so, citing his "mercantile integrity . . . business-like habits . . . enlarged, far-reaching views."[4]

Edward Silas Tobey

At a Government meeting on December 15, 1862, Ross joined with Tobey in urging a concerted effort to raise funds for current expenses and for the necessary buildings. Tobey in particular felt that, despite wartime demands, most business organizations were prospering and that the citizens appeared ready to contribute to good works. He also was convinced that "certain wealthy and munificent Americans now resident abroad, a proper representation being laid before them, would cheerfully contribute of their abundance." William Rogers alluded to John Amory Lowell's plan "to place at the disposal of the Government, for specific objects," the income of $50,000 of the Lowell fund. This, however, would provide $3,000 per year, as stated by Lowell in his letter of intent, solely for the support of the Lowell free evening classes for mechanics.[5]

Rogers's view of the problem of finances is curious, though it is important to remember that it was based on the Institute as described in the *Objects and Plan*, with the museum as its main feature. And his interest in the Rumford at Harvard appears to support the idea that he did not then expect the school, the final plan for which had not yet been prepared, to take center stage in the growth of the organization. Even so, while he acknowledged the need for money and stressed its importance, he does not appear to have foreseen how great an amount would be required if the organization were to succeed in all its branches:

> The President considered the subject a very important one; and at the present stage of the Institute's being, one of vital moment; inasmuch as it would be necessary to have the Halls, Workshops, &c. for a fair development of the Objects and Plans of the Institution. The amount requisite for these purposes was comparatively small bearing in mind the magnitude and importance of the enterprize. These pecuniary means will in large measure be needed only once for all; the *great capital* which will be constantly in demand, and which must be mainly relied on to sustain the various operations, that is the brain work, will be chiefly supplied gratuitously.[6]

It would be several months before legislative approval of an Institute share in the land-grant fund would be secured, a development inevitably leading to a major emphasis on the School of Industrial Science and an ever-increasing need for funds. The folly of Rogers's statement, however, would soon become apparent.

On the evening of December 17, 1862, the Institute met in its newly rented rooms at the Mercantile Building, the fifth meeting since its organization in May. Rogers presented a report to the members, mentioning the assurances that had been received of "large pecuniary aid" and expressing hope that the Finance Committee would be successful in securing the necessary funds, "for in the midst of the sad trials of which so many are called to partake, and in spite of the ever present cares and claims of the War, we have daily generous proofs that New-England, and especially Massachusetts, will continue to urge forward unrepressed the peaceful enterprises of Education and

Humanity; nor can we doubt that the great practical object of educating and ennobling Industry will command a hearty and helpful sympathy."[7]

Not until late February 1863, however, was the Finance Committee formally authorized to raise $150,000. Ross and Eldredge of the committee at once pledged $1,000 each. Rogers and R. C. Greenleaf, a member of the Museum Committee, each pledged $500.[8] In his annual report for that year, the secretary mentioned these donations, characterizing Rogers as "one who has already given, & still continues to give, unsparingly of his valuable time & intellectual resources."[9] An earlier gift of $1,000 from Henry Bromfield Rogers, plus the $3,000 transferred mortgage and $500 cash from the Townsend estate, were to be considered a part of this fund.[10] They were a long way from the $100,000 that would have to be produced by April 25.

A circular letter prepared by Rogers went out over the signatures of the Finance Committee early in March. It pointed to the Society of Arts, already in operation and well received, and the need for buildings with classrooms, lecture rooms, and laboratories, along with adequate exhibition space. Mentioning the assurances of "a liberal prospective endowment," it emphasized the immediate urgency of raising $100,000 by April 1

> to carry into effect its plan of practical instruction, and to place it in the front rank of the Institutions in this Country, devoted to industrial education, thereby supplying a want which all those engaged in the Manufacturing, Mechanical and other industrial Arts, have, for a long time, felt, and rendering it, alike, an honor to the Commonwealth, and an ornament to our City.[11]

This statement contains the first public mention of "Institutions in this Country, devoted to industrial education."

Rogers was optimistic, as usual, reporting to his brother Henry at the end of the month that the Institute was "growing in favour" and that "upwards of $20,000" had been subscribed. This time, however, he had better reason to be hopeful, for he added that a "very large sum, perhaps $100,000," might be forthcoming from an "old gentleman who has lately been very liberal to the Natural History Society."[12] The "old gentleman" was Dr. William Johnson Walker, who, as a benefactor of the Natural History Society, had been an obvious prospect to receive a copy of the Finance Committee's general appeal for funds. Rogers was at this time aware that Tobey and Beebe of the committee were meeting with Walker in Newport, Rhode Island, where he was then living.

Boston, March 7. 1863.

Dear Sir,

The Finance Committee of the Mass: Institute of Technology beg leave to present, briefly, the claims of that Institution for substantial assistance at the present time

A valuable tract of land, adjoining that occupied by the Bos: Soc: of Nat: History, has been granted, by the Commonwealth, to the Institute, on condition that a guarantee fund, of not less than one hundred thousand dollars, shall be provided, by the 1st of April next, for the general purposes of the Institution.

The association is already organized; its meetings, in a temporary hall, are well and zealously attended, and great interest is manifested, by those present, in the practical application of scientific principles shewn in the various mechanical and chemical inventions and combinations exhibited and explained. The establishment of an Institution of this kind, upon a permanent basis, requires large buildings with ample class rooms, lecture rooms and laboratories, and with sufficient space to deposit the various Models, Machinery, raw materials and manufactured products, offered for exhibition and examination

As assurances have been given of a liberal prospective endowment, equal at least to the income of one hundred thousand dollars, to sustain the active operations of the Institute, it will be seen that a present subscription of one hundred thousand dollars, for the benefit of the Institute, will not only secure to its use a tract of land, valued, at the present time, at not less than one hundred and fifty thousand dollars, and warrant the erection of a substantial and elegant building, but it will also put the Institute in possession of an income sufficient, at once, to carry into effect its plan of practical instruction, and to place it in the front rank of the Institutions in this Country, devoted to industrial education, thereby supplying a want which all those, engaged in the Manufacturing, Mechanical and other industrial Arts, have, for a long time, felt, and rendering it, alike, an honor to the Commonwealth, and an ornament to our City.

It is manifest that the subject could be easily elaborated and that its importance might justify a more extended exposition, but it is thought that a simple statement of facts, in relation to an Institution promising such great practical benefits, will be the strongest possible appeal to the liberality of the community.

M. D. Ross

Edward Atkinson

Ths M Bird

J S Tobey

C H Eldridge

Com. on Finance

A graduate of Harvard College in 1810 and the Harvard Medical School in 1813, William Walker had traveled abroad for training in France and England, returning to America in 1816 to begin a medical practice in which he achieved marked success. He was a consulting surgeon to the Massachusetts General Hospital and trained a number of young men for the profession, including Morrill Wyman, an executor of his estate, who in June 1863 would become a vice president of the Institute, succeeding John Chase. After a practice of some thirty years Walker retired, turning his efforts toward investments in manufacturing and railroad enterprises with a view to philanthropic support of education. In this, too, he was highly successful.

In 1860 he offered a gift to Harvard for the Medical School, but with several conditions, among them asking for changes in the curriculum and organization of the school aimed at needed improvements in medical education.

William Johnson Walker

He did not want any of his funds used for salaries, which he felt should be derived principally from student fees. Above all, he asked that the faculty be reconstituted and that new appointments, subject to his approval, be made. He assured the Harvard authorities that the latter condition stemmed not from personal feelings against the incumbents but rather from the need for competent faculty! But the Corporation did not wish to request the required resignations, and the offer was declined. Walker removed Harvard from his will.[13]

In his assessment of the quality of medical education in the United States in general and of that offered by the Harvard Medical School in particular, Walker was not off the mark. A brief historical account, citing the school's nominal connection with Harvard prior to 1869, contains an apt description:

> The Medical Faculty elected the Dean of the School, arranged the lectures and other exercises, collected the fees, paid expenses, and divided the surplus, if any there were, among themselves. . . . Medical students bought tickets to the courses of lectures, as they would for a series of concerts. They were supposed

to attend five or six lectures a day, and the same lectures were repeated year by year. To obtain a doctor's degree the student needed to pass only the majority of the formal examinations, and consequently might be profoundly ignorant of almost half of the subjects taught. In addition, he must present a certificate that he had studied medicine for at least three years with some regular practitioner, who might be a total stranger to all the Faculty. Further, the students to whom this deplorable system of instruction was applied were usually persons of scanty preliminary training. Very few were college graduates.[14]

William Walker has been described as a man of "imperious will and extreme independence"; at the same time a "fundamental kindliness made his professional career eminently successful." In 1861 he left his family and moved to Newport, where he would spend the rest of his days, during which he attempted to carry out his plans for the improvement of education. He deeded his house in Boston to the Natural History Society and gave Williams College funds for a natural history building. His total contributions to American education, including bequests, would amount to $1,250,000.[15]

Walker was also said to have been "of a singular and somewhat perverse disposition, of a hot and hasty temper, decided in his opinions, and often harsh in manner":

> Dr. Walker's enmities were as bitter as his friendships were devoted. His worst side seems to have been shown toward his fellow practitioners, his best toward young medical students, to whom he was always ready to give help and advice, and toward the poor, who benefited greatly by his charity. Shrewd in his judgments, keen in business, of a dry and pleasant wit, yet obstinate and sometimes overbearing, he was of a type of man common in New England, a type analogous to its unfriendly and yet beneficent climate.[16]

His appearance on the scene was "almost dramatic" and "almost providential," "practically unsolicited," and "not the result of impulse." But Rogers and the supporters of the Institute were nonetheless vastly relieved to learn early in April 1863 that he would provide a gift valued at "not less than sixty thousand dollars, and probably from ten to twelve thousand more."[17] It would be an outright gift of cash for the guarantee fund, and Tobey and Beebe deserve great credit for securing exactly what the Institute needed. Since their subscription effort had produced gifts and pledges totaling some $40,000, that fund was now assured. Tobey later attributed his role in this transaction to the fact that Walker had earlier been his family physician, and "when he saw my name as one of the Committee of Finance . . . he was induced to avail himself of my agency in bestowing his noble charity on this valuable institution":

The limited time had nearly expired when Dr. W. was then Providentially prompted to give the amount necessary to comply with the conditions imposed on the Institution by the State. It was my privilege to be connected with the very earliest efforts to establish the institution & its successful progress & development has been marked by the special guidance of Providence.[18]

It was a pivotal moment, and the Institute acted quickly. The Finance Committee joined with Rogers in informing Governor Andrew and in meeting with the Executive Council. All were "entirely satisfied" that the Institute had now met fully the conditions of the legislative act of 1861.[19] A council order dated April 10, 1863, formally authorized their taking possession of the land on the Back Bay.[20]

The members of the Government received the good news at a meeting on April 11, when Tobey reviewed their fund-raising efforts, announced that the donation would come from the proceeds of the sale of "certain property," and expressed gratitude for this "munificent gift." When Rogers asked "how far, if at all," the matter should be reported to the next meeting of the Institute, the decision was left to his discretion. Two days later he announced their good fortune, the news received by the members with "decided expressions of satisfaction."[21]

In closing his report, Tobey had stressed a very important point. If it were not for Walker, the Institute would indeed have been forced to seek yet another extension of time. And as he said, a refusal would have been "fatal to this valuable enterprise."[22] Even in the face of wartime conditions, such a request might well have been refused, the land denied, and the charter possibly forfeited, for their failure would have reflected unfavorably on an organization that had been unable to gain major financial support in a period of two years. Participation in the land-grant fund would have been impossible, and the forces—including Governor Andrew—that wished to join the proposed school of the Institute with Harvard would have had many an argument on their side.

At a special meeting of the Government on May 27, 1863, called at Tobey's request, he announced that "owing to recent business transactions," Dr. Walker now had a proposal to make, and he read the "trust" instrument related to the gift. Through this document Tobey had originally been empowered to give the Institute on Walker's behalf the proceeds of the sale of 600 shares of the Old Colony and Fall River Rail Road Company, provided the Institute had raised whatever balance might be needed to secure the guarantee fund. Walker now wished to retain these shares and offered $75,000 in cash, which was readily accepted.[23]

A document dated July 14, signed by President Rogers, the vice presidents, the Finance Committee, Webb, and fourteen members of the Institute, certified for Walker that the balance of the guarantee fund had been secured through other gifts and pledges. It was accompanied by a copy of the council order releasing the land.[24] The $75,000 was entered in the cash book on July 21.[25]

In the light of Harvard's experience, a rather ominous comment had concluded the Tobey-Beebe letter of April 10: "We may add, that it is probable that Dr. Walker may at an early day communicate directly to the Government of the Institute his views as to its future mode of carrying out its objects."[26] But encouraged by this timely gift, the Government immediately turned on April 11 to plans for the future, determined that "this Institution in its organization should be kept independent of all other Institutions," a belief in which Walker concurred. It is not, of course, surprising that he would hardly take kindly to an amalgamation with Harvard, which had spurned both his advice and his money. According to Tobey, Dr. Walker had "very decided views" on education, disapproving strongly of "one course of study and of one fixed mode of imparting information for all—irrespective of differences in mental capacity, intellectual tastes, and destination as to subsequent vocation." He preferred that young men, rather than distinguished professors eminent in their fields, should be engaged as teachers. And he wanted his money used to "effect the greatest good to the greatest number."[27]

Jacob Bigelow commented first that Walker's views were generally correct. But, certainly aware of Harvard's problem, he sounded a note of caution against seeking too much advice from him, thinking that "it would be best in this case to act upon the old maxim, 'Let well enough alone.'"[28] Appropriate resolutions of thanks were prepared, and Rogers, writing on behalf of the Government and the members of the Institute, expressed delight "in the most critical juncture of our affairs that so strong an arm was stretched out in support of that popular practical education which it has been my most earnest effort to promote." He promised that he and his colleagues would make a "faithful effort to make your benefaction productive of the greatest good to the greatest number by causing the Institute to dispense as widely as possible the blessings of sound practical and popular education":

> To teach exactly and thoroughly the fundamental principles of positive science, with their leading applications to the industrial arts, and to make this teaching as widely available as possible, are the cardinal ideas of our proposed School of Industrial Science. I need hardly add that in carrying them into effect the Institute will be glad to receive any suggestions with which you may please to favour them.[29]

Naturally they did attempt to keep Walker informed,[30] but they were wise in generally heeding Bigelow's advice not to place themselves in a position where they might find their own aims and the donor's ideas at variance, risking his displeasure and thereby cutting off the possibility of future gifts. Perhaps in their favor was Walker's failing health, leaving him with little appetite for confrontation and anxious to see his money settled where it could be useful. A year later, when the plan for the school was finally prepared, he acknowledged a copy:

> I have read the same with great pleasure and am neither able nor desirous of altering it in any point for the better. It meets my unqualified approbation. God speed the Institute.
>
> I should not wish the Plans [building plans] copied on my account. I am satisfied all is going on well. I can do but little mental labor.[31]

The Walker donation also prompted a decision to ask the legislature to repeal the requirement that the Institute make up any difference in the sale price of contiguous land sold by the state and the original appraisal, a provision that Rogers had always termed "ungracious." The suggestion was made by Tobey on the grounds that Walker had "made his noble gift untrammelled by conditions," and seconded by Beebe, who felt that Walker "would unquestionably be desirous of having the legislative restriction removed."

Jonathan Preston, who had been a member of the Board of Appraisers for the state on the value of the Back Bay lands, pointed out another incentive for the removal of this restriction. Linked to it was a further restriction preventing the sale of the contiguous land for at least two years. To free the Institute from its obligation would permit immediate sale should a favorable opportunity arise. Actually, the sale price of the lands had increased since 1861, and though the provision would thus be inoperative, the Institute viewed it as an objectionable feature. A repeal of the relevant sections of Chapter 183 of the Acts of 1861 was approved on April 29, 1863.[32]

The completion of the guarantee fund brought with it a spirit of optimism, prompting Rogers on April 11, 1863, to look to the future with renewed hope:

The President addressed the Government, contrasting the present glorious prospect of the Institute with that less flattering, indeed to some discouraging one which existed even but two months since. He considered that in consequence of the liberal donations made to the Institute, weightier responsibilities rested upon the Government, and that it had become still more incumbent upon both the Officers and Members of the Institution to strive to the utmost to form and sustain for it a character which should place it in the front rank of learned Associations of a similar kind.[33]

His reference here to "learned Associations" implies that he was still committed to the concept of the school as a satellite of the Society of Arts and the museum.

Though the Walker donation had enabled the Institute to secure its portion of Back Bay land, the difficult question of money was far from solved. Following a vote of thanks to the Finance Committee, Ross signified their willingness to continue their efforts at least until they had raised $150,000. He gave credit to every member of the committee and special thanks to Rogers "for his effective co-operation," stating also that "whatever misgivings may, at any time heretofore, have been entertained in regard to our great enterprize, there could no longer be any doubt of its success."[34]

Ross also mentioned on April 11 that a "proposition was being agitated among the manufacturing companies to contribute to our funds on certain conditions," which he did not specify, adding that the outcome was "uncertain."[35] A letter of April 7 from James B. Francis of the Committee on Instruction relates to this early idea of corporate support:

I find my ideas are still very crude on the subject we were discussing this morning, but I am satisfied that a brief statement is wanted of the material advantages the Institute will afford to the manufacturing interests. When the subject comes before a board of Directors of one of these Corporations, as a rule, they will feel bound to look at it simply as affecting the pecuniary interests of the Corporation. If they can see that these are to be promoted and that pretty directly, they will be more likely to see their way clear to appropriate part of the funds to aid the establishment of the Institute. On the other hand, if they do not see the strong probability of a pecuniary return, many will say at once, that they do not feel justified in appropriating the money of other people for such a purpose.

Some of the ideas which it appears to me should be touched upon in such a statement, are as follows.

The Rooms of the Institute are designed to be the center of information in all subjects relating to manufactures, and open to all parties connected with the same. A place where information on any particular subject may be looked for with confidence. All the Books & periodicals relating to the Industrial Interests will be found. Collections of raw materials, manufactures, machinery, patents &c. Instruction of persons who are engaged in or intend to devote themselves to any branch of manufacturing, by lectures and by special instruction in mechanics, drawing, design, chemistry, &c. General diffusion of knowledge relating to the arts in the community &c.[36]

There is no evidence that the idea was pursued further at that time.

The secretary's annual report for the year 1862-63 contained a general statement of the Institute's financial condition:

Land, valued at	$150,000
Subscriptions at 5/11/63	100,000 (includes Walker)
Prospective bequest	50,000 (Huntington)

Also expected:
Income of at least $50,000 from Lowell Institute [actually $3,000 per year]
Unknown amount from the Land-Grant Fund[37]

It should be noted that the Institute did not have title to the land, which was simply "reserved from sale forever" by the state, and the $100,000 subscription included pledges, most of which had not been paid by May 11.

The situation was, of course, vastly different from that of the preceding year, prompting Secretary Webb to look ahead with confidence:

The Government also have good reason for believing that that all-important & vitally essential materiél, without which pecuniary resources will be of little avail, but with the powerful aid of which, everything that the most reasonably sanguine can expect or desire may in time be attained, that *sine qua non* in such an enterprize, we mean brains, the Government feel well assured, can be commanded, both in quantity & quality adapted to the great work, & suited to the demands of the occasion.

Let the community but do its part, & the men of scientific attainments, & practical skill & ingenuity will do theirs: though weighed in the balance, they will not be found wanting.[38]

They had little reason to feel secure, however, and their financial situation would continue to be a matter of concern. Rogers was ill and not present at a Government meeting on November 24, 1863, when the subject was raised, Edward Eldredge of the Finance Committee pointing out that all of their funds had now been appropriated for the building. M. D. Ross felt that money would be forthcoming as soon as people knew what they needed it for, alluding to possible financial support for a School of Mathematics and a School of Mines. This led to yet another "interesting discussion in regard to developing the Institution":

> To what branches attention should first be directed?—what Schools of Instruction should be established?—how commenced and conducted? &c. &c.[39]

Unfortunately, the details were not recorded, but there is evidence of an increasing appreciation of the magnitude of their undertaking and a growing sense of the need to establish some priorities soon.

A committee had been appointed in June 1863 to explore the possibility of obtaining additional space and to "consider the purposes to which it should be applied," for it was clear that the building project on which they were about to embark would take some time to complete. They were ready by November to report the availability of two rooms adjacent to their current space in the Mercantile Building, "well suited among other purposes, for that of Class Instruction—the germ of our School of Industrial Science . . . and capable of being properly arranged and suitably fitted for the commencing organization of the Museum of Technology, or Conservatory of Arts." The premises would be available until January 1866 by which time they hoped their own building on the Back Bay would be finished. Since nearly everything they had was earmarked for construction and little available for current expenses, the rent would be paid by "a gentleman, who chose to have his name withheld."[40]

On January 14, 1864, a meeting of the Institute was informed that Walker had offered to contribute $20,000 toward the cost of the second building provided a matching sum could be raised, specifying that only the interest could be used. The offer was immediately accepted, with Rogers instructed to convey gratitude for "this new proof of the generous interest of our chief benefactor and patron in the objects of our Institution." Two weeks later the members of the Institute discussed the offer once more and referred the matter to the Government, along with "a request that early and efficient measures be taken promptly to fulfil said conditions and thus secure the dona-tion."[41] On February 10 the Government instructed the Finance Committee to "resort to such measures as may be deemed most judicious to obtain without delay" the req-uisite matching sum. By the end of the month they had decided to seek twenty dona-tions of $1,000 and announced that J. Wiley Edmands had already offered to be one of the twenty.[42]

That it took several weeks for constructive action on Walker's offer is but one early example of the cumbersome nature of the Institute's governance, with no formal mechanism in place, such as an executive committee, to take immediate steps to author-ize the Finance Committee to launch a second subscription. No effort was made to call a special meeting of the Government for this purpose, nor did there seem to be any realization that the lines of authority were unsuitable to a developing organization on a fragile financial footing.

Walker continued to press for the completion of this subscription: "When can we complete and collect the subscription for the second building? I wish to have it done."[43] By September he had increased his offer to $50,000, still with a matching pro-vision, and indicated that "efforts were being made again by *Cambridge* to reach him." Webb learned that Agassiz had approached Morrill Wyman about a possible visit with Walker but had not yet followed through. He called on Walker himself and reported to Rogers, who was abroad for several months during that summer, that the Institute had "nothing to fear if we manage rightly & act promptly":

> The Doctor . . . told me that after the proffered sum was secured, he should
> have something more for us; he could not say how much, but *something*.
>   On leaving, he pressed upon me the importance of immediate action, in
> which case we should secure the funds; otherwise we might lose all; he man-
> ifested great anxiety in this respect, being earnestly desirous of having his mind
> free from all care, perplexity & uneasiness, relative to this matter.[44]

Ross, fearful that Webb might rock the boat, also paid a visit to Walker and also reported to Rogers on the possibility of additional future gifts, though he had been unsuccessful in attempting to steer Walker toward more support for the school as opposed to the museum:

> What he wants is for us to raise funds enough to establish the several Schools
> of the School of Industrial Science and he will furnish funds to erect the
> museum building and he wants that building to be commenced next year. . . .

I endeavored to give him an opportunity to say that he would endow the School of Mathematics instead of putting the funds into the museum building but it was of no avail. He has got his mind fixed on having that building erected and so I thought best not to disturb him in his plans. . . . Dr. Walker hopes we will get the School of Mathematics under way this winter as he wants to see some of the departments producing fruit during his life time if possible.[45]

No formal agreement with respect to Walker's pledge of a matching grant has been found. Rogers assured him early in 1865 that the Finance Committee was hard at work, giving "promise of an early success":

I hear from Mr. Ross that the Finance Committee of which he is the efficient representative is earnestly engaged in trying to secure the subscription on which your further gift of $50,000 is conditioned & that they only need some additional time to be able to report to you entire success. I beg therefore to unite with Mr. Ross & the Committee in asking your indulgence of this unavoidable delay.[46]

It had not been an easy time to raise money. Ross informed Rogers that he was spending full time recruiting for the war, others were involved in related activities, and "extremely hot" weather had sent still other friends out of town. With the approach of fall, however, and the help of Edmands and James Little, he expected that a renewed effort would succeed.[47] They failed, unfortunately, to achieve the "entire success" for which they hoped in connection with their first offer of a matching grant and the first acknowledging the need for endowment, with only the interest to be used.

Walker lived to see only a preliminary session of the School of Industrial Science under way, for he died on April 2, 1865. A few days later, at the regular meeting of the Institute as a Society of Arts, the following resolutions were passed:

Resolved, that the late William J. Walker by his wise liberality towards the Institute of Technology, and kindred institutions of Education, has entitled himself to a lasting place among Public Benefactors.

Resolved, that the Institute will ever gratefully remember the services of the friend and patron whose timely munificence has so largely contributed to the initiation of its plans, and whose unabating interest in its progress has been a continued source of satisfaction and encouragement to its friends.[48]

His final will, dated October 23, 1863, stipulated that, after certain bequests to his family and others, the remainder of his estate was to be divided equally among the Boston Society of Natural History, the Institute of Technology, Amherst College, and Tufts College. The bequest to the Institute was "to be used and expended in the erection of any buildings necessary for the objects of the institution, and for giving instruction in the elementary branches of science connected therewith."[49] The document contained also an interesting message for his legatees:

> Finally I request the recipients of the above bequeathed property to realize that no inconsiderable portion thereof has been gathered as the fruits of a laborious vocation, exercised through anxious days and sleepless nights; that it is given to them, *in trust nevertheless*, to be expended so as to inure to the greatest advancement of sound education in the departments as above specified; and the public good. I request that its investment may be safely guarded; that its expenditure may be subject to the strictest economy; yet that it may be appropriated liberally where the objects aimed at justify an open hand, and cannot be afforded the cause of education and to the public good at less expense.[50]

Soon after Walker's death, Rogers was informed that the validity of the will would be contested by the family unless the institutions involved made over to them a share of the property for which they were residuary legatees. This matter required very delicate and careful attention, and a special committee of three was appointed—Chief Justice George Bigelow, William Rogers, and James Beebe—first to investigate and report and then with power to enter into any reasonable compromise with the executors and trustees of the estate.[51] Mrs. Walker presented specific claims relating to property arrangements included in earlier articles of separation between her and her husband, and there were claims also on the part of one of their daughters. An agreement was reached in the fall.[52]

M. D. Ross would move to the Committee on the Museum in 1865 and was succeeded as chairman of the Finance Committee by James Beebe. Edward Tobey remained, with two new members: J. Ingersoll Bowditch and William Endicott, Jr. When Endicott succeeded Dalton as treasurer of the Institute in 1866, he was replaced by John Murray Forbes.

Jonathan Ingersoll Bowditch was born in 1806 in Salem, the second son of Nathaniel Bowditch, whose mathematical bent he is said to have inherited. As a clerk for Ropes and Ward he served as supercargo on several voyages to the East Indies. From 1836 to 1864 he was president of the American Insurance Company in Boston and was a director of that firm at the time of his appointment to the Finance Committee. His directorships and trusteeships extended to numerous other enterprises, both industrial and educational, among them Harvard. He took a special interest in the Harvard Observatory, not surprisingly, as he had carried on the work of his father through several editions of the latter's famous work, *The New American Practical Navigator.* He was an overseer of the University from 1867 to 1873, served as a member of the Observatory's visiting committee, raised funds for it, and gave generously himself to the institution, which had granted him an honorary master of arts degree in 1849.

Jonathan Ingersoll Bowditch

In 1887, two years before his death, he would receive an honorary doctor of laws degree. A biographical memoir has praised his "exceptionally sound and safe judgment and superior executive capacity," as well as his many contributions as a "public benefactor."[53]

William Endicott had begun as an apprentice in his father's general store in Beverly and moved on to the firm of Hovey, Williams Company in Boston, dry goods importers. In 1851 he became a partner of the firm, by then involved in retailing and known as C. F. Hovey & Company. He was particularly noted for his financial acumen and was called upon for directorships or as an officer of banks and railroads, as well as service as trustee or treasurer for numerous charitable and philanthropic institutions. And he made major contributions during the Civil War through financial advice to the Union government and help in the recruitment of troops, supplies, and funds. A year after his appointment to the Finance Committee he became treasurer of the Institute, a post he would hold until 1872, when he

William Endicott

rejoined the committee. He would remain as a member of the Corporation until his death in 1914. One posthumous assessment remarked on his devotion during nearly fifty years of service and credited him with the Institute's survival:

> There is much reason to believe that, had it not been for his practical faith in the future of the school, it would have succumbed under successive financial shocks. During the years of struggle, from 1861 to about 1885, Mr. Endicott not only gave freely of his own money, not only, as treasurer, endorsed large notes of the Institute which the banks otherwise refused to receive, but more than once he saved the Institute from actual bankruptcy by securing personally, from his business friends and associates the money needed to keep it alive. By undertaking this most disagreeable and thankless kind of work he raised, by his own exertions, at least $600,000. . . . It may be said without exaggeration that at least a million and a half of the funds that came to Technology in the years when such funds were absolutely essential to its existence were the result of the personal exertions of Mr. Endicott.[54]

John Murray Forbes, born in 1813, would bring to the Finance Committee the business sense and experience that had made him a fortune in the China trade before he reached the age of twenty-five and, after he returned to America, a prominent figure in the financing and development of the railroads and their extension to the West. During the Civil War, he worked with Governor Andrew in mobilizing the state's efforts in defense of the Union and served as an adviser to the Navy Department. He was an organizer of the New England Loyal Publication Society, with which William Rogers was also involved. He is credited with a "clear head" and a love of exciting work, "best of all when it was devoted to some form of public utility through which he could fulfill his duty to his country and to his fellow men." His membership on the Government began with his appointment to the Finance Committee, and he would continue to serve on the board until 1892.[55] His brother, Robert Bennet Forbes, also a China trade merchant, was the first speaker at the first meeting of the Institute as a Society of Arts in December 1862.[56]

John Murray Forbes

Following an announcement in November 1865 that a portion of the Walker bequest would soon become available, J. Ingersoll Bowditch moved that it be set aside, invested, and held as an educational fund, the income to be used solely for current educational expenses. M. D. Ross raised a question about doing so, indicating that since more money would be required for the building, some of the Walker funds might be needed for this purpose. Bowditch would not be denied, however, stating that his motion had been offered precisely to "prevent any such use of the funds." Henry Bromfield Rogers seconded his motion. Edward Atkinson spoke in favor, along with Jacob Bigelow, who "expressed a hope that the Government would establish as a fundamental principle of action, *the keeping out of debt.*" William Rogers concurred. Ross persisted that in a discussion "lasting nearly unto midnight" Walker had "explicitly said that he wished his funds to be put in brick and mortar." But Rogers had a different recollection. His conversation with Walker not long before he died had left the impression that "his great desire then was for the suitable equipment of the school; it being rather to endow the school, than to erect buildings":

> The President also called attention to the fact that some of the most celebrated Schools abroad had no buildings specially erected for them, but accommodations were procured wherever they could be best obtained in the cities of their location. The aim there being to use the funds at command for fitting and furnishing the Schools, instead of for the erection of costly structures.[57]

After further remarks, a favorable vote was passed, "*nemine contradicente.*" Bowditch had prevailed.[58] Actually, Walker's will permitted use of the funds for both buildings and instructional purposes. A first installment of $100,261 was received early in December 1865.[59]

As recorded by Webb in 1864, Walker appeared to have plans not only for his own money, but also for that of others:

> The Dr. suggested whether his proposition could not be used to induce Mr. Huntington to give his $50,000 *now*, say on condition that an equal sum were raised towards establishing a School of Mines, or for some other good purpose

by him to be designated, & to induce Mr. Thayer to give $50,000 provided another $50,000 could be obtained for a School of Design, or for Instruction, &c. in those branches which will advance the manufacturing interest. He requested me to call (as I shall) & see Mr. Huntington & say, he does not know how *happy* he will become by giving his money whilst living, & that the sooner he does it, the happier he will be; and that this is not mere surmise with me, for I have tried the prescription & *it works well*.[60]

Walker's suggestion for Ralph Huntington did not bear fruit, however, until the summer of 1865. The arrangement, under which Huntington became the Institute's first life income donor, provided an immediate $30,000 to "complete the erection of the large Hall," a project already under way. It was agreed to on July 1 and formally confirmed by the Government in September:

In consideration thereof the said Institute hereby promises and agrees to and with said Huntington and his heirs, Executors, and Administrators, to pay him, during his lifetime, interest on said sum of Thirty Thousand Dollars, at the rate of six per centum, per annum, payable semi-annually. It being hereby further distinctly understood & mutually agreed that the principal of said sum is never to become payable: but at the decease of said Huntington said Thirty Thousand Dollars is to be regarded and acknowledged by said Institute as having been received in part payment of, and is to constitute by so much, an offset to any legacy or bequest which may become payable to said Institute according to the provisions contained in the last Will and Testament of said Huntington.[61]

Huntington died on May 31, 1866. In a resolution the Government acknowledged "his large contribution to the means of the Institute, and his warm sympathy in its success," ever to be gratefully remembered. A committee was appointed to confer with the executors of his estate. Early in January 1867 $17,000 was transferred to the Institute, representing $20,000 less a 6% U.S. legacy tax on a total of $50,000, since the $30,000 paid in the form of a life income fund in 1865 was considered to be an offset of an eventual bequest.[62]

Grateful though they were early in 1864 for Walker's offer of $20,000 on a matching basis, the Finance Committee had qualms about starting a second subscription since they had done nothing to recognize formally those who had contributed in the first round. A committee under the chairmanship of Edward Eldredge had been appointed in June 1863 to consider what recognition should be made, beyond the usual thanks, for donations received by the Institute. They had not yet reported. Now asked to do so immediately, they concluded "that it was unadvisable at the present time to recommend any further action than had already been taken relative to the Contributors."[63] Their request to be discharged was granted. Eldredge did, however, move, and the Government voted, that all who had contributed $100 or more be recommended to the Institute as candidates for membership. A week later twenty-eight benefactors were elected, among them James Savage, the father-in-law of William Rogers, and James Lawrence, the son of Abbott Lawrence, as well as three women: Mrs. Wm. Pratt, Mrs. M. F. Sayles, and Miss Wales.[64]

Shortly before Thomas Webb died in the summer of 1866, he informed Morrill Wyman that he was "quietly causing to have painted" a portrait of Walker. The Government was notified in October that the work was ready for delivery and that the artist, Henry C. Pratt, wished to be paid. A committee appointed to consider the matter, chaired by William Rogers, reported the same information in the spring of 1867. By June 3 Rogers announced that they had paid for it.[65] This problem may have stirred renewed concern about the proper recognition of major donors, for on June 3 they were prepared also to approve a permanent memorial not only for Walker, but also for Huntington and for James Hayward, from whose estate a bequest was received that year. The memorials for Walker and Hayward involved the naming of faculty chairs, that for Huntington the naming of a hall.

Although there had been general statements on finances from the beginning, the first formal report of the treasurer was presented by Charles Dalton in 1865 at the close of the Institute's third year of operation. Under way as a Society of Arts, still expecting to develop the museum, and a preliminary session of the school nearly completed, the Institute looked toward the opening of the regular sessions in the coming fall. In the light of these commitments, they were sadly lacking in funds. On May 22 they had $981.96 in cash—$140.17 in the hands of Secretary Webb and $841.79 in a checking account at the Revere Bank. In the fall of 1863 they had taken a note of the Pacific Mills, of which Edmands was treasurer, for $100,000, the funds to be on call with ten days' notice. By May 22, 1865, they had earned interest of $5,928.05 and withdrawn all but $14,000. Mortgage interest on a house at 32 Lowell Street from the Townsend estate would bring the return on investments to $6,558.05. Beyond this income and assessments and fees related to the Society of Arts and the preliminary session of the school, they had raised $119,350 since 1862, and they had already spent $102,122.68 on the building, far from completed and the most immediate financial drain. Their general expenses and costs related to the museum and the school totaled $8,836.81. This did not include compensation for those then teaching in the school's preliminary session, who would not be paid until late June and early July.[66]

The Finance Committee, therefore, was faced with a formidable task. John Runkle apparently felt that they needed a little prodding and told Rogers so:

> I told Mr. Ross that now is the time to raise funds, for we shall have a year or two or more, & they are not far distant, when it will not be so easy as now to do it. It would not do the Finance Committee any harm for you to push them a little now & then—for the fact is, they can not know as you do, the condition of an institution constantly *gasping for breath*. Ample means will secure the right men & all needful appliances & go far towards commanding success.[67]

By the end of the year a steady round of borrowing would begin, every loan endorsed by a member of the Finance Committee, or occasionally simply by a member of the Government.[68]

Chapter 14

The Building

On February 21, 1863, when the Institute government authorized an immediate effort to raise funds for the construction of a suitable building, the Committee on the Museum was asked to "consider and report a Plan for the Main or Central Building . . . with estimates of the cost."[1] At this time the chairman was Erastus B. Bigelow, and the members included Richard C. Greenleaf, Ralph Huntington, Frederic W. Lincoln, Jr., Jonathan Preston, Alexander H. Rice, and Stephen P. Ruggles. Bigelow is said to have requested that the chairmen of the remaining standing committees join with them for this task. In his mind, he was now chairman of *the* Building Committee of the Institute. Serious planning was in order, soon amid confusion, a condition that would persist until the first building was completed.[2]

With the distribution of the land-grant funds still in question, a final plan for the school not yet available, and the museum still looked upon as the central feature of the Institute, the Museum Committee was the logical center for the development of building plans. And Erastus Bigelow was particularly well qualified to lead this effort. He had designed and supervised the construction of several large structures, among them mills in Lowell and Lancaster, experience indicative of his "business talent, his constructive abilities, and clear far-reaching vision; . . . extensive, complex, various, and costly, as these works were, not even fifty dollars were lost from any change of plans."[3]

The Museum Committee minutes for February 21 reveal that a preliminary plan already existed, for members had been called together to consider the erection of a "separate building for a Laboratory." President Rogers, still hopeful that the

Committees of Arts would be an active force in the Society of Arts, was there to express concern that the "original design of having the laboratory in the basement" would provide neither adequate room nor lighting. A "well lighted, large and commodious" laboratory would be essential, he said, if the Institute were to develop in accord with the "expectations of its friends and advocates, the only present drawback being the want of funds to carry out the whole plan." At this time M. D. Ross displayed drawings for a separate structure "more in the way of suggestions and to call attention to the subject than as complete plans."[4]

These drawings can be traced directly to the participation of Rogers and Ross, as well as Jonathan Preston of the Museum Committee, in the plans for the Natural History Society. Rogers had been appointed to the society's Building Committee on April 17, 1861. Ross was also very much involved. As a member of the City of Boston's Commission on the Back Bay Lands, chaired by Preston, he was in a position to provide advice in relation to the preparation of the area for construction but appears also to have been consulted often on other aspects of the project.

A practicing "architect-builder," Preston had been invited, among others, to submit an exterior design for the society's building based on an existing ground plan. A façade designed by his son, William Gibbons Preston, then studying in Paris, was initially considered "too costly and too elaborate," but when difficulties arose over terms and projected costs for the preferred plan of Gridley J. F. Bryant and Arthur Gilman, the society turned to the Prestons in November 1861. A perspective view of the Preston design procured by Ross had been helpful. Among the reasons cited for their decision was its "unobjectionable style of roof," its "harmony with the building of the Institute of Technology to be erected on the same square," and the fact that "the same architect would thus be employed for all three structures" expected to be built on that square.[5] From this statement it would appear that some form of commitment to the Prestons for the Institute's building had been made by Rogers and Ross as early as 1861.[6]

Erastus Bigelow was not present on May 6, 1863, when the Government was informed of favorable legislative action with respect to the land-grant fund. They immediately appointed a Building Committee with "full powers to erect a building for the School of Industrial Science, after the Plans for said building have been accepted," an early sign that the promise of this money had begun in a subtle way to affect the development of the organization.

The new committee was chaired by Rogers and included Daniel Davies, Edward H. Eldredge, James L. Little, and M. D. Ross.[7] Davies was not a member of the Government, but he was an associate member of the Institute and a builder by profession. He was also a member of Boston's Commission on the Back Bay. A year later, when Rogers was abroad for several weeks, Stephen Ruggles, a member of the Committee on the Museum, would be added.[8] There is no record of discussion nor mention of the relation of this group to the Museum Committee or its enlarged version, and it is clear, as soon confirmed by Rogers, that no thought had been given to this potential problem.

The new Building Committee went to work at once. At their first meeting on May 7, with Thomas Webb serving as secretary, Rogers and Ross reported on the "early movements made to procure Plans and Models, as well as to obtain information that might be serviceable," acknowledging "important assistance rendered" by Jonathan Preston and his son, who had returned from Paris late in 1861. A subcommittee was appointed to "select and recommend" an architect. By May 11 the Prestons had presented their terms for performing the "duties pertaining to the Architectural and Superintendent's Departments for construction." The full committee voted to engage them and immediately authorized them to contract for the "necessary excavations, piles, and pile driving" and to prepare plans for "a building 150 feet by 90 to 95 feet."[9] There is no evidence that other architects were considered.

Word that the committee was pressing ahead and making final decisions soon reached Bigelow and led to ruffled feelings, in turn leading to concern on the part of Rogers that they might lose not only his "sympathy & help," but also the support of others. Among the latter would be Ralph Huntington of the Museum Committee, from whom they hoped to secure something beyond his 1862 commitment for a bequest. In a letter to Ross, Rogers claimed he thought Bigelow had been informed beforehand of the second committee and that those of the old group "were to go on at their leisure maturing the plan of a *museum* building. I regret however, that in our anxiety to push on the preparations for our central building for instruction we did not advert to the previous action of the Govt. as the course adopted does *seem* a little discourteous to the older committee, however *entirely* innocent we have been of any willingness to neglect their services or to disregard their feelings."[10] There are indications that attempts had been made to pacify Bigelow, but he seemed "disinclined to take part" at that time. Rogers now hoped that the government would add him, and "perhaps the Treasurer," to the new committee.[11] But this did not happen.

Bigelow convened his Museum Committee on May 26, 1863, to review the situation. Pointing out that the Government had increased its membership for the development of building plans "without understanding the duties" of the committee or "defining the duties" of the enlarged group, he proposed that they report on their own progress, ask to be relieved of the problem, and turn their plans and estimates over to the latest Building Committee. The members agreed.[12]

Boston May 7th 1863.

The First Meeting of the Building Committee of the Massachusetts Institute of Technology was held at the Office of the Institute in Mercantile Building, 16 Summer St. at 4 o'clock P.M. this Day.

Present all of the Members; viz. Messrs. Davies, Eldredge, Little, Rogers, and Ross.

The Committee was organized by the choice of Prof. Rogers, as permanent Chairman.

By request, the Secretary of the Institute consented to act as the Committee's Secretary.

The following are the Votes of the Government of the Institute, establishing a Building Committee, defining the powers thereof and designating the individuals constituting the same; viz.

Voted, that a Committee of five be appointed to act as a Building Committee, with full powers to erect a Building for the School of Industrial Science, after the Plans for said Building have been accepted by the Government.

Excerpt from minutes of the first meeting of the Building Committee, May 7, 1863

Bigelow had touched on an important problem. A deeper source of confusion than the appointment of seemingly parallel committees was a lack of substantive discussion and decision making with respect to the development of the Institute—a matter raised at intervals but never pursued to a conclusion, and increasingly important following the land-grant decision. Though a major crisis did not develop at this time, Bigelow's report on June 3, when the Government accepted his committee's recommendation, prompted another "long conversational discussion" among Rogers and several members on "suitable permanent accommodations for the Institute, the cost of erecting such, &c. &c." Everyone acknowledged that "at least one structure" must be erected as soon as possible, but there was "quite a difference of opinion" on whether they should wait until all the funds had been secured or begin immediately with the money on hand, "relying upon the community, in its well-known liberality, to furnish the residue, whenever, or prior to being needed"—a surprising optimism in view of their two-year struggle to raise the guarantee fund, only recently secured through the generosity of Dr. Walker. The record states that "no action was called for, and no vote was taken on the subject."[13] By this time, however, it was an academic question, for they were already launched on a project that would take longer than expected, cost more than they could afford, and in the process sorely strain the relationship between the architects and their client.

In view of the work they had already done, the choice of the Prestons was almost inevitable. Rogers and Ross had seen proposals from other architects in connection with the Natural History Society's building, the two groups had acted jointly to obtain the land from the state, and they did share the square that had been granted. Two harmonious structures would fulfill their promise to provide an attractive addition to the developing Back Bay.

Jonathan Preston was born in 1801, served an apprenticeship as a mason, became a masonry contractor, and is said to have "qualified" as an architect by 1830. He designed several structures in Boston, including the United States Hotel and the Boston Theatre, and was the contractor in 1849 for the Massachusetts Eye and Ear Infirmary designed by Edward Clarke Cabot. In 1850 he opened an office on Washington Street as "Architect and Builder." He was joined by William R. Emerson from 1857 to 1861, and thereafter by his own son William, on William's return from Europe. The elder Preston was then chairman of Boston's Commission on the Back Bay. In the late 1830s and early 1840s he served on Boston's Common Council and as an alderman, and was

Jonathan Preston

a member of the commission again in 1860 and 1861. In 1845 he was a state representative and in 1849–50 a member of the Senate.[14]

William Preston was born in 1842 and spent one year, 1859–60, at the Lawrence Scientific School before leaving for architectural study in a Paris atelier. He was only nineteen years old when the Natural History Society chose his design, his first commission in a career that would span nearly a half century.[15]

In the Building Committee's first report to the Government late in August 1863, Rogers, who was ill during part of the summer, acknowledged the "facts and suggestions, as well as the plans and drawings" they had received from the "Committee previously appointed to make a preliminary and more general investigation." And he announced the appointment of Jonathan and William Preston, "so usefully consulted" by the earlier committee. There had been no formal adoption of the idea of two separate buildings for the School of Industrial Science and the museum, he said, but they had proceeded on the assumption that this was "the general purpose contemplated." The space needed by the school and an "extensive drawing School," combined with the "large and constantly increasing accommodations demanded for even an incipient Museum," would require the larger of the two proposed buildings, serving both purposes in what he called a "temporarily twofold application." Since the museum would be transferred to the second building, designed specifically for its purposes, when it could be afforded, they had decided to conform the first to the requirements of the school. The decision could not have been otherwise, for the governor was not happy with the legislature's decision on the land-grant fund, and failure to show commitment to the school could well have resulted in a reopening of the question.

The committee had already secured detailed plans and drawings from the architects as well as proposals and estimates from "practical Mechanics prepared to contract for the work." Various options with total anticipated costs were presented, some covering only partial finishing of the interior and some with use of alternative building materials. A completely finished building, 150 x 100 feet, of brick and red sandstone with columns in front and a "cornice all around" would cost $150,624. No figure was presented for the cost of equipping or furnishing the building.

In requesting authorization to proceed, Rogers began by stating that it was beyond the duty of the committee to "refer to the considerations of a wise economy," which must of necessity influence the Government's decision on the "weighty question of expenditures" now before them. They did not "fear that any step will be taken which can by any chance involve the Institute in obligations which it cannot meet" and looked to the "liberality which has so generously smiled on our enterprise thus far." It was up to the Government, however, to decide how far they could count on "further aid for building purposes."

Rogers closed with a resolution calling for the adoption of the Preston plan and authorization to "proceed, so soon as the requisite funds shall be obtained, to contract for such parts of the Building as in their judgement will tend to forward its construction, to the best advantage." In the light of later developments, it is important to note that this wording resulted from a Building Committee discussion that forced a change from "proceed forthwith . . . to forward its speedy construction."[16]

Attendance at this meeting was very small, there being only twelve present, and Erastus Bigelow counseled careful thought and wider deliberation. He voiced his concern about the nature of the design "in all important features, little more than reproductions of the Natural History Building."[17] The plans were placed in the secretary's office so that Government members might study them at their leisure before the next meeting at which they hoped for better attendance.

When they reconvened on September 8, 1863, Rogers was absent and Jacob Bigelow presided. There was much discussion about the extent of the authority to be delegated to the committee. Erastus Bigelow thought it would be "proper" to place a limit on the amount they could spend and emphasized that they must not "lose sight of the cost of establishing the Institute after the *structure* shall have been erected." Ross, however, was optimistic, having "good reasons for supposing there would be a large accession to our pecuniary resources, but was not at liberty to speak more definitely at present." Finally, they authorized the Building Committee to proceed, making whatever modifications they deemed necessary, provided the "aggregate cost of the whole Building shall not exceed the estimate." Though the amount was not recorded, later references indicate that they had decided on a completely finished building for $150,624. When Morrill Wyman, then a vice president of the Institute, asked how much money would be left after the building was finished, Ross again "referred to the probable prospective means of the Institute."[18]

During that summer William Rogers had received through his brother Henry, then at the University of Glasgow, information on the buildings of the "Technology department at Edinburgh" and the School of Mines in London, as well as reports and catalogues of the South Kensington Museum.[19] He emphasized that the Institute's structure would be "designed mainly for the teaching department," a point to which he would return early in March 1864 as he neared completion of the final plan for the school:

> The building we are now erecting is not intended for a Museum, but for a school of Practical Science, in which, for a year or two, some space will be given to collections. Hence the arrangement of laboratories, lecture-rooms, drawing-schools, etc., is what most interests me now.[20]

Despite continued mention that a second building would one day house the museum, there were increasing signs of a change in direction for the Institute.

In November 1863, at Institute expense, young Preston left Boston for a tour of England and the Continent. Rogers would say that he did not expect much more from this journey than "useful hints and copies of external architecture and general interior division of space," and early in March 1864 mentioned the receipt of "several useful suggestions."[21] Only one letter from Preston has been found, a ten-page report from Paris dated March 26, 1864. He noted "some special *good* points" and also disadvantages in each of the schools he had visited but observed that the "objects" of the Institute were not "exactly within the scope" of any institution he had seen. Nevertheless, with the new building under way, he felt that a "few facts" might not be "amiss, . . . when every improvement adopted by others should certainly receive attention, before arriving at such a point in the construction as would render a change impossible or expensive."[22] This statement was not the kind of "useful hints" that Rogers expected, but it raised attention if not concern.

Preston praised the heating system, illumination, ventilation, and display arrangements of the Kensington Museum, citing also its "large and valuable library" for student use, something which "should not be overlooked in our Institute." He talked at length of a school he did not name at Châlons-sur-Marne in France [École des Arts et Métiers] for "*practical teaching . . . in mechanical pursuits*," describing in great detail the workshops and foundry, the curriculum and rigid schedule, and the discipline. He found the German schools "extremely primitive affairs" with respect to ventilation and heating and made special note of "uncomfortable" seats. He considered the lecture halls in Paris and England "much finer & more comfortably arranged," adding that the hall of the École [actually the Conservatoire] des Arts et Métiers in Paris merited "special notice." Of that he promised more later.

Preston returned again and again to the subject of ventilation:

And during the summer heats why might not a supply of *cooled* air be introduced into a lecture hall, in the same manner as in winter we supply that which is heated? This principle is, I think, carried into effect in some public halls in Europe, which I propose investigating before my return.

Our proposed hall is certainly one of sufficient importance to justify the adoption of all known improvements for the comfort of the audience.[23]

Though he would be asked to prepare a written statement of his "views and the results of his observation" on ventilation early in May 1864, the subject would not be seriously addressed for another year.[24]

The Building Committee would be continuously occupied with the problems of design and construction until their final report of March 2, 1867, by which time they had spent $254,830.71 and had thoroughly frightened more than one treasurer. Their minutes reveal that the project was approached one step at a time, with vitally important matters bearing on the whole dealt with in isolation on an *ad hoc* basis by various subcommittees as the need arose. Jonathan Preston is referred to throughout as the "Superintendent" and sometimes as the "Senior Architect," while his son is identified as the "Junior Architect."

The work continued slowly through the seventy-eight recorded meetings from May 7, 1863, through December 28, 1866. The committee did not meet between August 9, 1864, and February 4, 1865. Early in 1865 they appeared to be preoccupied with external ornamentation, "a matter of great moment, and one demanding extreme caution, both from the character of the building, and the probable expectations of the Public," according to Rogers. Edward Eldredge, also a member of the Finance Committee, was opposed to any "movement" on this matter until the building was finished and equipped. They did, however, obtain designs from several artists and paid an "award" to two selected with no commitment that they would be used. And they approved a list of "distinguished men of ancient and modern times identified with Science and the Arts" suggested by Rogers to be carved on the front and sides of the building.[25]

After the opening of a preliminary session of the school in February 1865, Rogers reported to the Government on an enrollment larger than expected. John Runkle predicted that when the regular session opened in the fall, the numbers could not be accommodated in the Mercantile Building on Summer Street and stressed the need for an accurate assessment of the completion date of the Boylston Street building. Jonathan Preston said that the part intended for the school would be ready by October. M. D. Ross, however, had longer-range concerns.

At the Society of Arts meeting on December 1, 1864, the first of the season, a report by Rogers on his recent visits to European institutions had prompted Ross to emphasize the "necessity of more space for the future development of this Institution" and the "importance of taking timely action for securing the addition needed."[26] From the beginning he had felt that the Natural History Society and the Institute should request more than one square, and now he urged that the Government apply as soon as possible for another grant of Back Bay land. Rogers, however, was doubtful about such a move, believing that they should "wait until the plans and purposes of the Institute are more fully developed so as to be surer of success, at least to avoid some of the difficulties encountered when the first application was made." If they were to do anything, he said, it should be merely to ask the legislature to withhold the "desired land" from public sale.

But Ross persisted. Their situation was different from the time when the project was "surrounded with doubt and uncertainty." "Now," he said, the "institute had become established," and he was confident that the legislature would respond favorably. As a member of the Finance Committee, Eldredge, apparently convinced that the state might impose a requirement for another guarantee fund, was not happy with the prospect of an enlarged fund-raising effort at a time when they did not have all the money necessary to finish the building and "suitably endow the Institute." But Ross did not "design to compromit the interests of the Institute," nor think that the legislature would place any "onerous conditions" if they approved a grant of land.

Following unrecorded discussion, Charles Dalton moved, Ralph Huntington seconded, and the Government voted that the procurement of a grant of another square of land be referred to the Building Committee to take whatever steps they deemed "expedient."[27] No further mention of this problem is contained in either the Building Committee or Government records, but on March 15, 1865, a petition was submitted to the legislature by President Rogers and Ross as chairman of the Finance Committee stating that the Institute would "early stand in need of large additional space" and asking that the "tract of land situated immediately west of that now in their possession and lying between Boylston and Newbury Sts" be "set aside for their use."[28] In the secretary's report to the members of the Institute presented on May 25, Webb indicated that the petition was withdrawn after the Commissioners on Public Lands agreed to reserve the requested land from sale for at least one year in consideration of the "wants of the Institute," and the "influence which the same may have upon the value of all the lands of the Commonwealth in the vicinity thereof."[29]

Government approval of an approach to the legislature was of no help in alleviating the immediate issues. Even if the building were completed by fall, an unrealistic assumption, it now appeared that it would not adequately serve their needs. But Rogers had an idea, and if the record is correct, he did not mention it at the Government meeting. On the next day he presented a possible solution to the Building Committee.

Rogers suggested that the problem be solved through the addition of a mansard roof, a form not at all compatible with William Preston's design for the building. Preston was asked to prepare for the next meeting a drawing showing the effect of such a change, a task he undoubtedly did not relish, and he did not do so, "through some misunderstanding." When he did produce a drawing, he presented also a model showing how the roof might be supported if the change were made, information that apparently generated no discussion on the part of the committee. The elder Preston was asked to prepare an estimate of the cost but was also slow to respond, finally reporting a figure of \$15,181, necessitating consultation with the Finance Committee.[30] Only James Beebe, chairman of that committee, joined them on April 13, 1865, but Edmands sent word that he was "adverse to putting a 'French roof' on the Building." Nevertheless, they voted to hire another architect, Carl Fehmer, to make sketches of a mansard roof, with Rogers and Davies in charge of the problem.[31] Though the Prestons were apparently as "adverse" to a French roof as Edmands, they could also not have been pleased with the entrance of another architect.

Carl Fehmer, twenty-seven years old, had come to Boston in 1852 from Germany and had spent several years as an apprentice in the architectural office of George Snell. At this time he appears to have been practicing in partnership with T. E. Coburn, though Coburn is not mentioned in connection with this French roof, a form with which Fehmer was familiar. In 1862 he had prepared a perspective view of a proposed Boston City Hall in the Second Empire style for Bryant & Gilman, a drawing that has been described as "sophisticated" and "almost photographic in its precision." It seems likely that he also prepared a drawing in 1864 for Gridley J. F. Bryant of two town houses on Beacon Street with a mansard roof, one of which was owned by Beebe. Fehmer would move on in 1867 to the office of William R. Emerson, practice on his own from 1874 to 1888, and from 1889 to 1908, with Samuel F. Page.[32] He would be responsible for a major Institute building completed in 1883 facing Boylston Street at the corner of Clarendon Street.

The Building Committee was not in total agreement on the wisdom of this change when Fehmer presented his design late in April 1865, and the matter was brought before the entire Government. Rogers stressed "the advantages in an economical point of view to be secured by *concentrating the whole activity* of the Institute for the first two or three years at least, in the *one building*." After much discussion, unrecorded, the change was approved because of the space to be gained and the "architectural effect" of Fehmer's design, and the Building Committee was authorized to proceed if a careful estimate of the cost did not exceed $25,000. Jonathan Preston was again slow in presenting a final estimate on the accepted design, but Fehmer was, nevertheless, asked to prepare working drawings.[33]

In mid-May, Rogers came to a special meeting of the Building Committee with news that Daniel Davies had examined the structure's upper walls and, as an experienced builder, reported that they would not support a mansard roof, an opinion corroborated by Fehmer. No one appears to have either recalled Preston's earlier model demonstrating how such a roof might be supported or realized at the time that he would not be presenting such a model if the existing walls could be expected to hold the roof up. Though the record does not show that he further emphasized this problem, it would seem that he had provided an opening for discussion.

The Building Committee actually considered altering the existing walls to accommodate the roof. Since cost estimates obtained exceeded the amount of their authorization, they decided against the expense. The problem of additional space remained, however, and they would settle for a proposal by the Prestons for a simpler solution—a smaller, setback addition at the roof level to cost no more than $6,000. The Government, when informed, concurred in both decisions. Had the Building Committee been properly informed of the wall thicknesses, Rogers said, they would never have entertained the idea of a heavier roof. "With whom rests the responsibility of the delay," he added, "the Government can best judge." Jonathan Preston was on hand to hear this accusation.[34]

Now the question of ventilating and heating the building was finally raised, and a Government appointment of a special committee to prepare plans is an indication of growing concern about the performance of the Building Committee. Rogers, Ruggles, and Runkle were appointed, along with J. Herbert Shedd, a civil engineer of the firm of Shedd & Edson and a member of the Institute though not a member of the Government.[35]

Shedd, who would be principally responsible for preparing the committee's report, correctly sensed a lack of communication with Jonathan Preston and advised getting Preston's intentions and a description of his plans on the record so that "the committee might be free from much future annoyance and trouble" and would not be "in danger of inferring from the plans and building, one thing, while Mr. Preston could say he meant another."[36] A few weeks later the Government's acceptance of the committee's report added $8,195 to the money needed. They were authorized to proceed.[37]

Late in November 1865, when Ross presented to the Building Committee a brief summary of the treasurer's accounts for the project, they decided that the Government should be informed.[38] On December 6 Charles Dalton, the treasurer, addressed a formal letter to Rogers as chairman of the Building Committee, stating that henceforth, to comply with the bylaws, the approval of the Finance Committee must "accompany any drafts you may make upon the Treasury."[39] By December 6 also, Ross was ready with an eleven-page account of their "doings." On the following day Rogers sent him a hurried note indicating that, despite his "anxiety about affairs here," he would be leaving by the night train for Philadelphia for an "important" visit, not to return until the following week. He would then wish to consult Ross's outline and requested specific information about costs for *"finishing plainly"* what was needed for the school "in order to shape such a brief report as seems to me most fitting & which I think the committee will approve."[40]

Dalton had been worried in May, when he had only $17,981.96 left, but alarmed when he heard the full financial report to the Government on December 19, 1865, at a time when the building was far from finished. In presenting a total cost to date of $182,012.49, Rogers attempted to explain the excess: underestimated costs, higher prices for materials and labor, changes and additions, overruns relating to the preparation of the land never presented to the Government for approval, and increasing costs of labor and material.[41]

Ross had been a bit more specific about the changes and additions by the committee, made, he said, "either upon their own judgment or with the advice and upon the suggestions of persons connected with the School of Industrial Science, or by the Committee on Ventilation." He believed that had the building been erected strictly on the basis of the original plans, the cost would probably have been closer to the estimate, but it would have been "deficient in many things not originally provided for." And he made the point that the committee was finding it "almost impossible to get at any reliable estimates" for finishing the structure in accord with the "wants of the Institute owing to the fact that in many details it is not known what is wanted . . . and cannot be very well known except as the work progress [*sic*] and the wants of the Institute are developed."[42]

The superintendent's accounts were in order, Rogers said, but the committee should have required regular financial reports. The worst, however, was yet to come. They now needed $86,000 to finish the interior "even in the simplest style." Urgently,

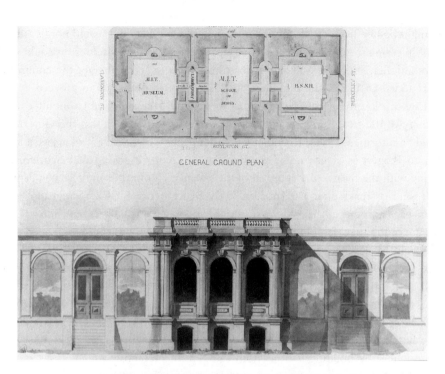

GENERAL GROUND PLAN

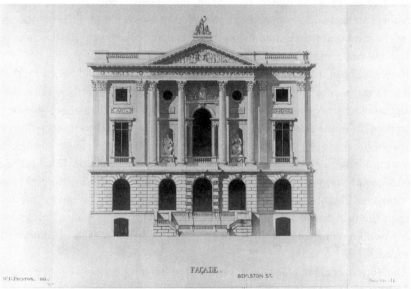

FAÇADE.   BOYLSTON ST.

A work in progress—architectural renderings by William Preston

MASS INSTITUTE of TECHNOLOGY.

W.G. Preston
Architect

Feb. 12th 1864

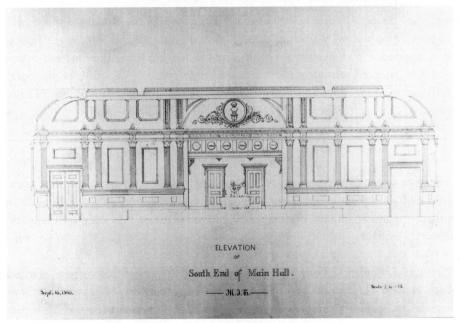

ELEVATION
of
South End of Main Hall.
—— M.I.T. ——

Sept. 10, 1864.

Scale 1 in = 1ft.

they needed about $13,548 for finishing enough to satisfy the needs of the school and the Society of Arts—classrooms and chemistry laboratories; windows finished and glazed; drainage, water, and seats for the classrooms. As they had concentrated on the "various details" of the project, some had relied on Preston's estimate that the cost would not vary more than 5 percent, and others on the "assured resources of the Institute for further means." Generally speaking, Rogers said, the committee felt that, "looking to the imposing proportions and generally solid character of the Building, and considering the peculiarly unfavorable conditions under which the work has been prosecuted," it could not have been done for less.

After a long discussion, the report was referred to the Finance Committee to consider how to discharge the liabilities incurred, how to get enough of the building completed and ready for use, and whether money could be saved by discharging the superintendent and appointing individuals to oversee various parts as needed—the latter a piecemeal approach akin to the methods that had caused some of the problems they now faced. The Building Committee narrowly escaped an immediate ban on all expenditures but were warned to incur none unless the situation was unavoidable. Ross cited finished work for which payment was due and pointed out that Preston had used his own funds for some of the expenses. Dalton announced that he had only about $4,000, except for some funds earmarked for educational purposes. The Finance Committee was authorized to borrow $10,000. And Erastus Bigelow was right when he said that "the error, if any, was committed at the onset of the Building movement."

The Committee on Warming, Ventilation and Drainage did not escape notice. Rogers responded with "general remarks," and when he, Ross, Preston, and others appeared to have different ideas about reasons for no evidence of action on the committee's part, Dalton moved that "their doings" also be investigated by the Finance Committee. Not a particularly happy session at the end of a busy year.[43]

The Finance Committee was empowered to add to their number for this serious investigation and asked Henry Bromfield Rogers, Edward Atkinson, and John Runkle to join them.[44] Early in January 1866 they sought expert advice from Edward Philbrick, a consulting engineer and a member of the Institute, asking Jonathan Preston to cooperate with him.

Edward S. Philbrick, born in Brookline in 1827, was graduated from Harvard College in 1846. He became a civil engineer and an acknowledged expert on railway bridge design, spending several years as a construction engineer for the Boston &

Worcester Railroad, and would later maintain an office as a consulting engineer. From 1860 to 1863 he had worked in a partnership with William R. Ware, listed as architects and sometimes as architects and civil engineers.[45] Ware was now the Institute's first professor of architecture, and though he appears to have had no particular connection with the Building Committee, he might have suggested that Philbrick be retained to review the situation.

It did not take Philbrick long to identify the source of the problem, and by late February 1866 his report was adopted by the Government. He recommended that they proceed to provide only for the "immediate wants of the School" through finishing the two lower stories and two rooms upstairs for the Drawing Department. The remainder of the building should be plastered. Contracts for the work, to be done in the "most economical manner" and the "plainest style consistent with good taste," should be secured immediately for completion by May 1, when the accounts should be settled. All other work would be suspended. To him the "future wants of the Institute" were "so far undeveloped" that it would be "nearly impossible" to finish the entire building in a manner to meet them "with any precision." And he cautioned that the "liberality of the community" should not be anticipated by "spending the money before it is contributed for such a purpose." He felt it would be "poor policy" to dismiss Jonathan Preston unless they could prove him to be "*unfit*," but saw no need of a superintendent once the authorized work was done. Later, when work resumed, "*one* man," he said, should be appointed to serve as full-time executive officer of the Building Committee and be required to report monthly on expenditures. The officer should not be compensated through a commission on the amount of those expenditures.[46]

As requested by the Building Committee, Philbrick was added to the membership and would become its secretary following the death of Thomas Webb in August 1866. Philbrick was already a member of the Government by virtue of his election in April of that year as chairman of the Committee on Tools and Instruments of the Society of Arts, serving from 1866 to 1869. Later he would serve as a regular member of the governing body from 1875 until his death in 1889.[47]

In May 1866 Dalton would resign as treasurer with expressions of gratitude from the Government for his "care and fidelity" in that post and his genuine interest in the Institute. He would continue to be a member of the Government, however, as a member of the Committee on the Museum. He was succeeded as treasurer by William Endicott. In those days the treasurer had no office at the Institute and received no compensation, but there is indication that he was reimbursed for payments to a clerk.[48]

M. D. Ross was assigned to see that the building was finished to the extent authorized. By August 1866, as they looked toward moving the school in time for the

No. 58.068

This Policy of Assurance Witnesseth,

THAT the PRESIDENT and DIRECTORS of the NATIONAL INSURANCE COMPANY, in BOSTON, do, by these Presents, cause

Massachusetts Institute of Technology, by W. Endicott Jr. ——

to be assured —— *Fifteen Thousand* —— Dollars, on

—— *Their stone & brick Building, now finishing, on Boylston and Newbury streets, Boston, with liberty for mechanics to work in and about the premises for three months from this date at noon. —— Liberty to have other insurance without notice till requested.* ——

Sept. 28th 1866. Liberty is given for mechanics to work in and about the above named premises for one month from 30th Sept. 1866, at noon, the assured paying therefor Fifteen Dollars additional. $15.

Sum Insured,
$15.000

against all loss or damage to the same by FIRE, originating in any cause, except Invasion, Foreign Enemies, Civil Commotions, Riots, or any military or usurped power whatsoever, for and during the term of —— *One year* —— commencing the risk the *thirtieth* —— day of *June* —— one thousand eight hundred and sixty- *six* at noon, and to continue until the —— *30th* —— day of *June* —— one thousand eight hundred and sixty- *seven* at noon, and no longer, unless the Policy should be renewed; provided that the said Company shall not be liable for more than the sum insured, in any case whatever.

And the assured hereby covenants and engages, that the representation given in the application for this Insurance, contains a just, full, and true exposition of all the facts and circumstances in regard to the condition, situation, value, and risk of the property insured, so far as the same are known to *them* and material to the risk; and that if any material fact or circumstance shall not have been fairly represented: or if *they* shall have made, or shall hereafter make, any other Insurance upon the said property, without the knowledge and consent of said Company: or if the said property should be removed without necessity to any other place: or if the situation or circumstances affecting the risk thereupon shall be so altered, or changed, by or with *their* advice, agency, or consent, as to increase the risk thereupon: or if the said property should be sold: or if this Policy should be assigned without the consent of the Company: or if the assured shall make any attempt to defraud the said Company: that, in every such case, the risk hereupon shall cease and determine, and the Policy be null and void — unless confirmed by a new agreement thereupon, written after a full knowledge of such facts or circumstances.

And the assured further covenants and agrees, that, in case of any loss or damage, the said Company shall have the right to enter upon and rebuild or repair the premises, or replace the property lost or damaged, with other of the same kind and equal goodness, within reasonable time after notice of the loss, or to pay for the same in sixty days after proof of the loss or damage thereon.

And it is further agreed, that, in case there should be any other Insurance made as aforesaid, on the property hereby assured, whether prior or subsequent, that the assured shall be entitled to recover, on this Policy, no greater proportion of the loss sustained than the sum hereby insured bears to the whole amount insured thereon. And whenever this Company shall pay any loss, the assured agrees to assign over all his rights to recover satisfaction therefor from any other person or persons, town or other corporation, or to prosecute therefor at the charge and for the account of the Company, if requested.

And in consideration of the sum of

Forty five Dollars

Premium,
$45.

received by the said Company, the said President and Directors do hereby bind the Capital Stock, and other common property thereof, to the assured *their* executors or administrators, for the payment of all sums that may become due under this Policy.

And the said Company further covenants and agrees, that, in case the assured should sell the property hereby assured, before the expiration of this Policy, on notification thereof, an equitable proportion of the premium received shall be returned, provided there be no loss: reserving three months' premium on the sum insured, which shall be retained by said Company in all cases of return premium, over and above the proportion which would be due up to the time of such notification.

And in case any Gunpowder or other article subject to legal restrictions, shall be kept by the assured in quantities greater than the law allows, or in a manner different from that prescribed by law: or if Camphene or Chemical Oils are used by the assured, unless said use, keeping, or storing, is especially provided for in this contract, this Policy is to be null and void.

And said Company reserve the right to cancel this Policy at any time, by giving to the assured or his agent, fourteen days' notice of their intention so to do.

And in case Steam Power is used in and about the property insured, and the boiler should burst: or any property insured is struck by Lightning, this Company is not to be liable unless Fire ensues, and then for the loss or damage by Fire only.

And in case any difference of opinion should arise between the parties hereto, the subject shall be referred to three disinterested men, one of whom to be chosen by each out of three to be named by the other party, and the third by the two so chosen.

N. B.—Bills of Exchange, Notes, Accounts, and Evidences or Securities of property of any kind, Books, Wearing Apparel, Plate, Furniture, Money, Jewels, Medals, Paintings, Sculpture, and other curiosities, are not to be insured, unless by special agreement.

IN WITNESS WHEREOF, the President of the said Insurance Company hath hereunto subscribed his name, and caused the same to be countersigned by their Secretary, at their Office in Boston, this *thirtieth* —— day of *June* —— one thousand eight hundred and sixty- *six.* ——

Geo. W. Kuhn   *A. McKean* President.
Secretary.

An asset worth protecting—MIT's first insurance policy, 1867 fall opening, he reported that more money would be required, and beyond that, the faculty had announced that even more space was needed to accommodate the school's increasing enrollment. Borrowing was the only recourse, and, contrary to Philbrick's advice, the entire building was finished with the exception of the large hall.[49]

On January 11, 1867, Philbrick presented a summary report of the Building Committee signed by Rogers, and on March 2 Rogers followed up with a final report. They had spent $254,830.71, exceeding their original authorization by $98,206, and were obliged to request an appropriation of $474.03 to pay outstanding bills already included in the total. This was not the end, however, for the same meeting appropriated nearly $17,000 for furnishings, heating, and ventilating beyond $5,000 previously allotted for furnishings.[50] They had been "pushed," Rogers said, "by the urgent wants of the School."[51]

The finished structure would contain chemical, mining, and metallurgical laboratories on the basement floor, and physical laboratories, lecture rooms, a room for the Society of Arts, and offices for the president and the secretary on the first floor. Lecture rooms, the drawing room and faculty studies were on the upper floors, along with an architectural museum. The two largest features were the hall on the second floor, creating also a "half story" on the floor above, and the "stairway hall . . . [a] great skylit atrium occupied by monumental stairs" of cast iron, and a "hazard of high order." Later building codes would force the addition of exterior fire escapes.[52]

William Rogers had earlier turned aside suggestions for a public cornerstone laying, and given his distaste for public displays of any kind, it is not surprising that there was no dedication ceremony when the building officially opened in the fall of 1866. Classes were already under way when he welcomed the members of the Institute, meeting as a Society of Arts, to "their new building" on November 15. This first session of the season was held in an approximately 50' x 28' room on the first floor set aside for the society's purposes, for the "large hall" of the original plan would remain unfinished until funds could be secured. At this meeting Rogers paid tribute to departed members, among them Ralph Huntington, who had died on May 31.[53] A Government resolution at that time had acknowledged his "large contribution to the means of the Institute, and his warm sympathy in its success," ever to be gratefully remembered.[54] He had become the Institute's first life income donor in 1865, with a payment of $30,000 of a $50,000 bequest contained in his will.

From the beginning M. D. Ross had looked upon Huntington as a good prospect for a large donation, and in return Huntington expected his name would somehow be attached to the Institute. When Huntington intimated that he was becoming increasingly interested in the institution and intended to give more than already included in his will, Ross was ready with a proposal. Before presenting it to the Building Committee, he sought Rogers's views. Sometime in 1864 he reported that Huntington initially thought his name would be on the outside of the building. When informed that "in that case, he would have to pay for the whole building," he was apparently willing to settle for "a handsome stone over the door or main entrance of the Large Lecture Hall and 'Huntington Hall' cut in the stone" and would "cheerfully pay" any extra cost involved.[55]

Rogers must have been against the idea, for a postscript to another Ross letter in 1864 stated: "About Mr. Huntington and the inscription on the Hall door nothing will be done at present. This will all come out right with patience."[56] Rogers clearly persisted in his opposition, for a year later, when Jonathan Preston referred to "Huntington Hall," Rogers announced that he did not favor attaching anyone's name to it.[57] Huntington, however, had specifically stated in his life income gift agreement that the $30,000 he was providing at that time was "for the purpose of enabling said Institute to complete the erection of the large Hall now in process of building."[58] During his early negotiations with Ross, he had stated that his daughter, Mrs. James, wanted his name over the entrance to the hall "to perpetuate her Father's name in connexion with this institution."

Finally, on June 3, 1867, a year after his death and a few months after the receipt of the remainder of his bequest, the Government voted to "mark in a permanent form its recognition of the liberal bequest of the late Ralph Huntington":

> Resolved: that the early assurances of pecuniary aid, and the more recent generous bequest of the late Ralph Huntington Esq., to the Institute of Technology, entitle his name to a permanent place among those of the founders and benefactors of the Institution,—and that, therefore, in consideration of his great service (and his understood expectations in this regard), the Government of the Institute hereby ordain that the great Hall of the Institute, on the second floor, fronting on Newbury St., be hereafter designated and known as "Huntington Hall."[59]

Huntington Hall was finally finished in the early 1870s and survived on Boylston Street after the Institute's move in 1916 to a new campus in Cambridge, for the Department of Architecture occupied the old building until 1938, when it, too, moved to Cambridge.[60]

Despite the checkered story of its construction, William Preston's building was an imposing structure on the edge of the developing Back Bay and would be named in honor of William Barton Rogers in 1883, a year after he died.[61] The school having assumed priority in the organization, every new building would be erected for academic purposes as the Institute became a major landholder in the area of which Copley Square is now the center. A separate structure for the museum, once taken for granted, would never be seriously considered, and in 1874 the second building would be a one-story drill hall and gymnasium with lunchroom facilities.[62]

The Society, the Museum, and the School

Chapter 15

The Society of Arts

A marked change took place in the concept of the Institute of Technology between its organization in 1862, based on the *Objects and Plan* of 1860, and the opening of the School of Industrial Science in 1865. In 1860 William Barton Rogers had looked for inspiration to British and Continental institutions whose aim was "the diffusion of practical knowledge." The models he cited were European museums or societies, some of which had been in operation for a century, to which schools or instructional programs were attached, and some of which were even then experiencing difficulties brought about by the changing times:

> In view of this recognized connection between industrial progress and an enlarged acquaintance with the objects and phenomena of nature and with physical laws, we find that the most enlightened communities of Europe have endeavored to provide for the practical co-operation of Education and the Arts, by the establishment of Museums, Societies, and Colleges of Technology. . . . The history of the Conservatoire des Arts and the École Centrale of Paris, and of the Kensington Museum, the School of Mines, the Museums of Economic Geology and Botany, and other like but less conspicuous institutions on the Continent and in Great Britain, has been such, both as regards the progress of the Arts and the diffusion of practical knowledge, as may well incite the friends of enlightened industry in this country to systematic efforts in the same direction.[1]

American societies were not mentioned at all, the most glaring omission being the Franklin Institute in Philadelphia, with which William Rogers and his three brothers had intimate connections and for which he and Henry had prepared a proposal for a School of Arts in 1837.

There are also no references to the European schools that had already influenced the development of Rensselaer or Sheffield at Yale, nor mention of any of them as models to be followed. To the contrary, every effort was made to assure the legislature and the public that the Institute did not intend to compete with existing educational institutions. It was clearly stated and often repeated that the contemplated school could not interfere "with the interests of the established schools of learning devoted to general literary and scientific education."[2] This was a political statement to a certain degree, designed to deflect the significant opposition that might come from Harvard, and yet there was a degree of truth in it. The museum, the society, and the various "schools" of design, mathematics, physics, chemistry, and geology that might be developed under the proposed arrangement were hardly a threat, except for the money they might attract, to these unnamed "established schools of learning."

The aim in 1860 appears to have been the creation in Boston of an organization comparable, for example, to the Royal Society of Arts and the Museum of Practical Geology in London and the Conservatoire des Arts et Métiers in Paris. All of these institutions were very much in the mind of Rogers and others when the *Objects and Plan* was prepared.

The Society for the Encouragement of Arts, Manufactures, and Commerce in London, the official title of the Royal Society of Arts, grew out of a suggestion in 1753 by William Shipley, described as a "portrait and landscape painter of no great merit," that a fund be established for the distribution of "premiums for the promoting of improvements in the liberal arts and sciences, manufactures, etc."[3] It was launched on an informal basis in March 1754 with seventeen members and organized in 1755. By 1759 its membership had reached nearly 1800, including a large representation from the peerage, who provided financial support, in addition to "statesmen, philosophers, philanthropists, painters, lawyers, divines, physicians, authors, dramatists, actors, musicians, bankers, soldiers, sailors, architects, historians, mechanicians, merchants." Women were welcome from the start.[4]

In several respects, parallels with the early organization of the Institute will be immediately apparent. The society had four vice presidents, a secretary, and a treasurer.

There were several standing committees, and business was transacted by the general membership. The society held "general meetings" and "ordinary meetings,"[5] as the Institute's Society of Arts would do, its general sessions being meetings of the Institute as a corporate body.

The Royal Society's chief function for many years was the encouragement of inventions beneficial to industry and commerce as well as agriculture through premiums or prizes, and its meetings were concerned with consideration of candidates for these awards. Much was done also to foster the development of the resources of colonial settlements, although these efforts were naturally discontinued for America after the Revolution. In the 1800s the society's emphasis began to change from that of "a purely premium-giving body into one whose main object became the dissemination of information about the industrial arts and sciences, and the publication of new discoveries and inventions of an industrial character."[6] Until 1829 only papers presented in connection with the premiums were accepted for presentation at the meetings. Thereafter, other papers were encouraged, these to be read at the ordinary meetings and later published, a practice received with much enthusiasm.[7]

From its early days, many of the communications presented to the society were published in pamphlet form. A regular series of *Transactions* was issued from 1783 to 1844 and sporadically until 1851, with an *Abstract of Proceedings* from 1845 until 1852, to be replaced by the *Journal of the Society of Arts* beginning in November 1852. The journal contained papers read at the ordinary meetings, notes of discussions, and information concerning society matters. In 1865 M. D. Ross presented seventy-five numbers of this journal to the Institute, which from the start had hoped to publish a similar *Journal of Industrial Science and Art*.[8]

There were other parallels, too. In 1845 the Royal Society's affairs were placed in the hands of a council—a body which Rogers included in a probable form of governance for the Institute. At that time the general business of the society was removed from the "ordinary meetings," with the main focus of the program centering on papers relating to new inventions and industrial developments, lectures on scientific and technical subjects, and their applications to industrial purposes.[9] A similar change in the orientation of its own Society of Arts would become necessary as the Institute of Technology developed.

Historical studies of the Institute have usually mentioned the tripartite nature of its early mission but have not emphasized how blurred the distinction was in the early days between the Society of Arts and the parent organization legally charged with responsibility for the entire institution. The root of the problem lies in the *Objects and Plan*. That document made clear that the Institute would consist of a "Society of Arts, a Museum or Conservatory of Arts, and a School of Industrial Science and Art."[10] But the discussion of organization was concentrated in Section I, entitled "Society of Arts of the Institute." Deeming it unnecessary to set forth any details on this point, the document stated that organizational matters would be "framed for the most part" with "a reference to the arrangements which similar societies elsewhere have found to be the simplest and most effective":

> Its general regulation would, as usual, devolve on a President, two or more Vice-Presidents, a Council, Secretary, and other necessary executive and financial officers, to be appointed in such form, and for such times, as might hereafter be deemed advisable. The effective operations of the Institute would, however, we think, mainly depend upon the Committees, Curators, and Professors appointed to the charge of its various departments.[11]

Fifteen standing committees, "of leading importance," were projected. Twelve, mainly covering various technical fields and called Committees of Arts, would "form in a large measure the working power of the Institute." The remaining three were for the museum, the school, and publications. Notably absent was an oversight standing committee on the Society of Arts itself.[12] An 1862 pamphlet containing a list of the officers and other members of the Government, an extract of the charter, and the bylaws included also an abbreviated statement of the "objects and plan" of the Institute. Here, too, the relationship of the Society to the Institute is not exactly clear, for the Institute would *organize a Museum of Technology* and *establish a School of Industrial Science*, but it would *act as a Society of Arts*.

Since the society was the only component of the Institute that could be activated in 1862, the failure to perceive a fundamental problem is understandable. Time may also have been an important factor, for a year had passed without formal acceptance of the charter, and the period for raising the $100,000 guarantee fund was running out. Trying to find the money and weighing the risks of asking for an extension of time undoubtedly took precedence over rigorous attention to the details of organization. That the Institute was expected to "act as a Society of Arts," however, reflects the example of the Royal Society of London, which Rogers had selected as one of his models. It is a reflection also of the way in which the Institute was originally expected to develop.

Circulation of the *Objects and Plan* in the fall of 1860 and the call to the January 11, 1861, meeting at which the Act of Association was signed resulted in the preliminary enrollment of an encouraging number of members and evidence of sufficient public support.[13] Some of the responses simply signified a willingness to join. Others added brief favorable comments. One serves as a reminder of the deepening political crisis facing the country and the possible relevance of the proposed institution in its aftermath:

> The "objects" aimed at appear to me very important, and more than ever so now that this political crisis is upon us: for N. England can better afford to keep the *moral* leadership of the country if by measures like the proposed she shall retain the *industrial* and *intellectual* leadership also. We must educate our artizans up to the point of independence: so that they can prosper *alone* if that be the price of our determination to protect the personal rights of every citizen or stranger upon our soil.
>
> Of the "plan" I cannot judge: but it looks elastic enough to give whatever is needed.[14]

When the *Account of the Proceedings Preliminary to the Organization of the Massachusetts Institute of Technology* was published in 1861, slightly over two hundred members had become "thus far associated," among them some of the most distinguished names in Boston.[15] In the months following, others signified their intention to join, and the secretary could report that the number of "Original or Foundation Members" was 246. By the end of the first year of operation, only 178 of these had paid dues, but another 17 would do so in the following year. Of the remainder, 8 had died and 43 had either moved out of Massachusetts, thereby becoming ineligible, were in the Union's service in the war, declined to follow up on their original intentions, or simply had not been heard from.[16]

With election and acceptance of new members in the first year, the membership reached 199, a large portion drawn from those who either lived in Boston or conducted business there. Roxbury, Dorchester, and Charlestown, now part of Boston, were listed separately with a total of 7, Cambridge with 11, and Lowell with 4. Only 20 of the more than 300 towns and cities of the state were represented, most with only one member.[17] While the Government nominated candidates for corresponding or honorary status, the Institute membership had the power of election. On April 13, 1863, 4 corresponding members were elected, all of whom later accepted.[18]

Nominees were not always consulted before nomination, undoubtedly because of the election process, and not all who were elected accepted membership. This fact plus deaths and resignations render the details of membership at any one time rather uncertain, but the total cumulative membership count reported by the secretary in his yearly reports is clear:

1862–63   199
1863–64   337
1864–65   377

The total in 1863–64 included 28 nominated by the Government in recognition of their financial contributions to the Institute.[19] Three were women, of whom Secretary Webb made special note in his second report:

> We would add, as a matter of just pride, that on our Roll will be found the names of several Ladies, who, by the liberal contributions they have made, evince the interest they take in our present efforts to increase and impart knowledge, and that they fully appreciate, and are ready generously to encourage by substantial gifts, a movement which, if judiciously conducted and amply sustained, must materially advance and improve every industrial class in the community, thereby adding to the sum of usefulness and happiness for the benefit and enjoyment of all.[20]

The Institute's membership consisted mainly of *"Manufacturers, Mechanics, Merchants, Artists, Educators, Men of Science, Clergymen, Lawyers & Physicians."* With respect to this list the secretary commented: "Many of the *Useful Arts* have as yet no representatives, and others have furnished a number by no means proportionate to their utility."[21] But while in 1860 and 1861 there had been a major effort to secure a substantial indication of support through solicitation of members, there was no concerted attempt, once the charter was secured and the Institute organized, to increase the membership, as indicated in the secretary's first annual report:

> There has been no direct effort made by the Institute or Government to procure additional Members; those who have taken the deepest interest in the enterprize deeming it wiser first to form a foundation which should ensure permanency. All ostentatious movements, indeed organized movements of any kind to acquire an accession of numbers, or to gain notoriety, have therefore been studiously avoided. Few, if any persons, have been admitted, excepting those who have first indicated a desire to join, and have manifested a taste for, or an interest in, the objects of the Institute.[22]

The Institute held four meetings in the spring of 1862,[23] and the Government met twice in April, once in July, and twice in September. The Government meeting on September 30 was important for its brief consideration of whether to proceed in light of the financial situation and wartime conditions. They did not meet again until December 5 and 15, when an *Order of Proceedings at the Ordinary Meetings* was approved.[24] The reading of minutes would be followed by the receipt of recommendations of candidates for membership and the election of members previously nominated. Next there would be "Correspondence and Reports relating to Practical Science and Art, including Reports of the Committees of Arts," the receipt and discussion of written communications, and oral communications with "exhibition of Specimens" and discussion. Finally, the business affairs of the Institute would be considered. No mention was made that for the technical presentations in these sessions the Institute would be functioning as a Society of Arts.[25]

On December 17, 1862, the members of the Institute gathered in the rooms on Summer Street for their "Fifth Meeting . . . the First Ordinary Meeting of the Season."[26] A review by Rogers of the "Progress and Prospects of the Institute" stressed the *"immediate usefulness* which now invited its earnest and zealous activity." He mentioned the "assurance it had received of large pecuniary aid, not however immediately available," and expressed confidence that the complete plan would succeed. He emphasized the importance of a "practical demonstration of the value of its purposes" and expected the Society of Arts to "at once commence a career of usefulness, substantial, and at a small expense":

> In its Meetings as a Society of Arts, twice in every month, the Institute will have in view, as its leading object, the promotion of the practical Arts and Sciences through the medium of written and oral Reports and Communications, and the exhibition of Models, Materials, Products, and other Objects relating to them, as well as through the explanations, discussions, and criticisms to which they may give rise. It will in a word aim to secure a free communication and interchange of valuable thoughts on all matters relating to the Industrial Sciences and Arts. It will desire to direct as well as to stimulate research and invention, and while marshalling in emulative effort, and co-operative labor the cultivators of the applied Sciences and Arts among us, will offer them an appropriate theatre for the exhibition of their researches, or their handiwork.[27]

Rogers urged the immediate organization of at least some of the Committees of Arts, and moved on to the remaining segments of the Institute, which he hoped soon to inaugurate:

> Let it not be supposed that in improving our opportunity of usefulness in the capacity of a Society of Arts, we are in any degree withdrawing our interest from the other and more important branches, the proposed School of Industrial Science, and the Museum of Practical Arts. These it is true can be carried into effect only in an imperfect and rudimental way without the extensive Buildings and arrangements which they require. Still even now a useful beginning can be made in both, and it should be our aim by such efforts as we can make in each of the Departments of our enterprize to give tangible evidence of its purposes and practical results.[28]

Though it was an address characteristically full of hope and optimism, the goals he emphasized would not be achieved as quickly as he appeared to promise, and significant problems would emerge along the way. Many months would pass before a plan for the school would be prepared and several more before a preliminary session could be inaugurated.

The program of December 17, 1862, then turned to the presentation of communications, becoming in essence a meeting of the Society of Arts: Robert Bennet Forbes on "Subaqueous Gunfiring" and the "Combination of Wood and Iron in Shipbuilding"; Edward S. Ritchie on "Improvements in Compasses for Boats and Ships"; Stephen P. Ruggles on "A New Form of Floats for Paddle Wheels"; and Cyrus M. Warren on a "Safety Heating Lamp for Laboratory Use." M. D. Ross "alluded to the importance of the culture of Flax," and Marshall P. Wilder added that a "thorough investigation of this subject" would be useful. The minutes for the next meeting record a warning by Mr. Warren that "Sulphid of Carbon takes fire at a lower temperature than that of the outside of his Safety Lamp, and he had found by trial that it could not be distilled over his lamp without risk of explosion"![29] Thus began the Institute's operations as a Society of Arts.

By November 1863, seven months after the favorable land-grant decision, George Emerson felt it was time to inform the public "specifically what is intended to be done in and by the several Departments." The standing committees, which then included the

Committees of Arts, were asked to prepare reports for their respective areas.[30] For the first time, it would appear, serious and detailed consideration of plans and goals was called for—a large order. Only John Runkle's Committee on Publication was able to respond on February 10, 1864, with a clear proposal, including a statement of their aims, the probable costs, and the potential value of a proposed journal. The report was tabled. At that time the committees on the Museum and Instruction presented brief oral comments but had no substantive document to offer.[31]

On March 17 Rogers, as chairman of the Committee on Instruction, could only say that they were still discussing the plan for the school and that "the subject, being a more comprehensive one than might at first thought appear, required careful consideration, and deliberate action."[32] This statement is a first indication that a change in the concept of the school as presented in the *Objects and Plan* might now be under consideration.

Erastus Bigelow, chairman of the Museum Committee, stated that their report had been deferred until the Committee on Instruction had formulated its plans. For his part, Runkle had not called up the tabled report of the Publication Committee for the same reason.[33] Throughout this period the lack of a general standing committee on the Society of Arts as the third component of the Institute and the blurred distinction between the Institute and the Society should have been abundantly clear. Yet this problem would not be recognized and addressed for several years.

Great importance was attached to the Committees of Arts as the "working power of the Institute." They were expected to conform to the "leading departments of the Museum" and attend to their "general interests":

> It would be the duty of these Committees, by correspondence or otherwise, to aim at increasing the treasures of the Museum, and to unite with the Curators in stated Reports on the condition and progress of the respective departments. They should, moreover, be charged with the consideration of all questions and interests relating to the several branches which may be brought to the notice of the Institute, and be empowered or required to report their conclusions and suggestions to the general meeting. It should also be their province to propose subjects for investigation in their respective departments, to recommend experiments and trials of processes and machinery, and to designate such inventions or improvements as may be deemed worthy of special commendation or honorary reward.[34]

ing been proved by satisfactory trials in actual
service, the Navy Department at Washington is
now substituting the Compass constructed by
Mr. Ritchie, for the old Compass in a number of
the National Vessels.

S. P. Ruggles on
"a new form of
floats for paddle
wheels."

　　　　　Mr. S. P. Ruggles exhibited a Boat furnished with a stern-wheel, the floats of which, instead of being straight as in the common paddle-
wheel, are formed of warped surfaces meeting at
an angle which points in the direction of the rotation.
　　　　　He stated that he had for some years
been accustomed to use a Boat of this form pro-
pelled by handpower acting through a crank,
and mounted with the ordinary straight float;
and for the past year had by this means compared
his new paddle-wheel with the former. His long
familiarity with the amount of effort required to
drive the Boat with the old wheel at a given speed,
has enabled him to make what he regards as a satisfactory comparison of the efficiency of the two forms
and has led him to conclude that his new float
possesses advantages which should commend it to
consideration.
　　　　　Although for convenience in experi-
menting, this new wheel is here used as a stern-
wheel, it is designed as a substitute for the ordinary side-wheel.
　　　　　1. The new float presents a much larger

The spirit of invention—excerpts from a summary of Stephen P. Ruggles's presentation on "a new form of floats for paddle wheels," December 17, 1862

S. P. Ruggles..
"a new form of
floats for paddle
wheels."

surface for action against the water than that which is commonly used, and in the opinion of the Inventor must, by a corresponding reaction, secure increased propelling power. The wedge shape in which the float moves through the water, will, it is true, reduce this effect, but from comparative experiments made with this and the ordinary floats on a wheel of the same diameter Mr. Ruggles was satisfied that the gain of power due to the increased surface was more than equivalent to the reduction arising from the angular shape.

2. Owing to the oblique position, and peculiar warped or spiral form of the float-boards they enter and emerge from the water in such attitudes as to separate the liquid without sensible jar or concussion, and neither lift nor depress the water in any appreciable degree, thereby avoiding the well-known evils attending the straight floats in ordinary use. The new form therefore secures the same result as the contrivances of Galloway and others for obtaining the feathering action, by shifting the position of the paddle-boards, as they revolve with the circumference of the wheel, while it has the advantage of greater simplicity, and is free from the liability to derangement which has thus far interfered with the practical use to any large extent of the wheels provided with movable float boards.

Twelve committees were originally proposed. The approved bylaws called for thirteen, a Committee on Agriculture and Rural Affairs having been added, perhaps with an eye to the pending land-grant legislation:

1. Mineral Materials, Mining, and the Manufacture of Iron, Copper, &c.
2. Organic Materials;—their Culture and Preparation
3. Tools and Instruments
4. Machinery and Motive Powers
5. Textile Manufactures
6. Manufactures of Wood, Leather, Paper, India-rubber, Gutta Percha, &c.
7. Pottery, Glass, Jewelry, and works in the Precious Metals
8. Chemical Products and Processes
9. Household Economy; including Warming, Illumination, Water-supply, Ventilation, and the Preparation and Preservation of Food
10. Engineering, Architecture, and Ship-building
11. Commerce, Marine Navigation, and Inland Transportation
12. Agriculture and Rural Affairs
13. Graphic and Fine Arts[35]

In May 1863 Joseph S. Fay expressed surprise that the bylaws had not included a Committee on Political Economy, "considering the value of this Science, and its more or less intimate relation to, or bearing upon, and controlling influence over, the subjects in charge of the several Standing Committees." He cited a similar deficiency in the newly organized National Academy of Sciences, and he trusted, vainly as it proved, that the Institute would respond to the need.[36]

There seemed to be nothing, however, that the officers of the Institute could do to inject life into the committees. Instead of an active "department of investigation and publication," the members of the Institute were for the most part content to attend the meetings, listen to presentations, participate to some extent in discussions, and enjoy an association which they found educational and of interest. Repeatedly in the early days the president and secretary exhorted the membership to organize themselves, but largely to no avail.

In November 1863 Secretary Webb informed the Government that the Committees of Arts should be "organized at an early day," none having done so to date:

They were designed to constitute an important feature of the Institute, and will, if rightly managed, furnish a never failing source of supply, whence to draw material for our Ordinary Meetings,—the spirit, interest, and value of which cannot otherwise be so well, nor so reliably and uniformly kept up.[37]

At a society meeting early in January 1864, President Rogers asked "every Member, who had not already done so, to notify the Secretary to which Committee he intends to attach himself."[38] This plea produced some small result, for by February 10, though unable to state their plan of operation, two of the committees had been formed—the Committee on Machinery and Motive Powers, with General Benjamin F. Edmands as chairman and William Watson as secretary, and the Committee on Household Economy, with the Honorable Otis Clapp as chairman and Frederic E. Stimpson as secretary. By this route Edmands and Clapp became members of the Government.[39]

At the annual meeting in May 1864, the secretary, reporting no further progress, called attention to the pertinent bylaw provision:

It will be observed that it is not left optional with the Members whether or not to join any Committee; it is obligatory upon every one to be enrolled in some Division, though each may decide to which, or how many, he will attach himself. . . . It is to be hoped *that* condition and requisition of the By-Law will be conformed with, so that by the opening of the next Winter Session, each and every Committee may be in readiness to coöperate with the others in advancing the designs of the Institute.[40]

In the same report he facetiously remarked that nothing had been heard from the Committee on Machinery and Motive Powers since its first meeting, "but from the nature of the business had in charge, it cannot remain inactive; it must keep moving." He also mentioned that one of its members, unidentified but presumably Stephen Ruggles, had long been interested in bringing together a collection of models illustrating the "Elements of Machinery."[41]

The Committee on Household Economy functioned for a time somewhat as initially planned. They held several meetings and appointed subcommittees on ventilation, drainage, and the preparation of food. They seem not to have taken any action with respect to a paper on "A New Evaporator for Hot Air Furnaces and Stoves" referred to them in February 1864 for examination, trial, and report.[42]

The committee did act, however, on a presentation in April 1864 by Jonathan Amory on a furnace, for which he had obtained a patent, with applications not only to locomotives and marine vessels but also to household heating apparatus.[43] The subject was referred to the committee, and their subsequent report would become the only pub-

lication to come out of these Committees of Arts. Entitled *Economy in Fuel*, it contained, in addition to Amory's paper, testimonials from various individuals and organizations, among them an 1853 statement from Eben Horsford reporting on experiments
by two students from the Departments of Engineering and Chemistry in the Lawrence
Scientific School which had affirmed the "decided superiority of the improved furnace." Later statements from marine engineers, a railroad engineer, and a dealer in furnaces and stoves were also included, along with a letter from Frederic Stimpson to Otis
Clapp. Dated May 11, 1864, the letter transmitted the following vote: "That the Chair
report to the Institute that this Committee are so well satisfied of the theory of Mr.
Jonathan Amory's method of effecting a saving of fuel, that they recommend a trial of
his application for warming dwellings and public buildings."[44] The matter seems to
have rested there.

In May 1863 Otis Clapp had presented a paper on drainage, with "special reference to the importance of a thorough system for the new portion of Boston, both in
a hygienic and a pecuniary point of view. He hoped, through the medium of the
Institute, to arouse a more general interest than at present exists in the community relative to so vitally essential a measure of Sanitary Reform."[45] After the Committee on
Household Economy was organized, its Drainage Subcommittee took up the subject
and prepared an "elaborate paper" on "Drainage and Utilization of Night Soil," presented as a report of the main committee at a society meeting in February 1865. It
stimulated a great deal of interest and comment and was taken up again in March,
when, in addition to discussion led by Clapp, Clemens Herschel, a civil engineer and
former student at Karlsruhe in Germany, presented remarks on the extensive work of
a commission on the improvement of the sewerage system of Berlin.[46] Clapp soon presented a resolution that a committee be appointed to raise the subject with the city
government and to recommend that they test the experiment, but the ensuing discussion resulted only in the referral of the matter to the Committee on Household
Economy for advice.[47] No further mention has been found, and it may be that uncertainty about the proper role of the Institute in such cases, an issue that would soon
become a matter of major concern, was beginning to take hold.

In spite of the failure of most of the Committees of Arts to organize, another was
added to the roster—a Committee on Ordnance, Fire-arms, and Military Equipment.[48]
The motive for the addition, bringing the total to fourteen, can be traced to the
Institute's success in securing the land-grant funds and the requirement that military
training be included in the curriculum. The subject probably also seemed fitting as a
topic for study against the background of the Civil War. No matter how compelling the
reasons may have been, however, it joined the ranks as another hope unfulfilled.

The concept of the Committees of Arts would encounter problems beyond an apparent lack of interest attributable partly to the fact that many members of the Institute simply did not possess the necessary background and experience to respond adequately to the intended mission as stated in the *Objects and Plan*. It is clear, too, that this mission had never been fully discussed or its implications carefully considered.

There were inherent difficulties in the charge to "propose subjects for investigation . . . recommend experiments and trials of processes and machinery" and issue "special commendations" for inventions "deemed worthy." The propriety of an institutional stand on matters of public import and the danger that the Institute might be used, through the Society of Arts, to advance the reputation and fortunes of those seeking to profit from inventions or other personal technical achievements would become a major subject for consideration by 1865. The use of the Institute's name in support of commercial developments was a particularly thorny issue for an organization pledged to foster the development of practical applications of science and technology.

Early in January 1863 William Edson had spoken to the Society of Arts on "A New Hygroscope, or Indicator of Atmospheric Moisture." Rogers commented on the paper and made suggestions for improvements of the instrument.[49] Two years later, in February 1865, Edson spoke again, this time on "A Hygrometrical Index." Rogers presided at this meeting, but no comments are attributed to him on the record.[50] Soon thereafter, Edson, having received many questions about the accuracy and utility of his index hygrometer, asked if the claims for the instrument could be examined and reported upon by a committee of the Institute.[51] His request was presented to the society, and on a motion by Runkle it was voted that the problem be referred to the Committee on Household Economy for investigation and report.

Immediately, however, John Cummings, later to become treasurer of the Institute, questioned its propriety. Might not inventors seek to "use the Institute as an advertising medium, and thereby open the way to many abuses?" Runkle, who must have discussed the matter previously with Edson, replied that to obviate this possibility "he had recommended that the Committee should simply state facts; and these it was not desirable to suppress, even were it practicable for the Institute to do so."

Rogers then entered the discussion:

It was entirely foreign from the purpose of the Institute or its Committees to advertise or recommend the inventions, improvements, &c. which might be laid before the Society of Arts; its legitimate purpose being to examine the principles involved, explain the constructions, processes, &c.; and point out such peculiarities as they may present.

In no case can the Institute as such, express a favorable, or unfavorable opinion.[52]

And he "presumed" that the committee would consider the matter "in the light of instructions." No correspondence or other reference has been found on the disposition of Edson's request.

In his 1865 annual report Secretary Webb enlarged on Rogers's earlier remarks:

The true position and action of the Institute . . . cannot be too strongly impressed upon the minds of its members, and . . . should be clearly understood by the community, and more especially by discoverers, inventors, and improvers. . . . Its true position is like unto that of an impartial judge, who hears the testimony on both sides, carefully weighs what has been adduced, pro and con, sums up the same, and without expressing an opinion, submits the case to others for a decision.[53]

Rogers's stated position, albeit a correct one with respect to the desired neutrality of the Institute, was not exactly compatible with the vision expressed in the *Objects and Plan*. Neither he nor Runkle appears to have recognized that in practice the examination, explanation, and identification of "peculiarities" along with a statement of facts could easily be construed as judgments on an invention. And the granting of "special commendation or honorary reward" would amount to an outright seal of approval.[54]

In January 1866 Edson would speak again to the society on "Moisture in the Atmosphere," exhibiting several forms of the hygrometer. There would be discussion and comment but no reference to possible committee consideration or action.[55] Within a few months Rogers learned from the manufacturer of Edson's hygrometer that Jacob Bigelow wished to have his opinion of the "merits of the instrument." He responded directly to Bigelow, including a two-page description of how it functioned:

This I cheerfully give, only regretting that our Institute examinations allow me no time for more than a very brief notice of Mr. Edson's improvements. I need hardly add that, from taste as well as a sense of duty to the Institute, I carefully abstain from *recommending the merchantable wares* of any inventions however valuable I may think them, & that in the present instance I speak only to you as a man of science, of the scientific value of the instrument.[56]

Saying that he felt Edson had "needlessly attached the new name of Hygrodeik" to the instrument, he stated that it was "an improvement on the well-known wet-bulb Hygrometer which for the last twenty-five or more years has been much used by meteorologists & other scientific discoverers."[57] Whether Bigelow had served in this instance as intermediary in a circumvention of Institute policy is a matter of speculation.

This is the first of two instances in which Rogers ventured to depart from his stated policy. Later in the year he was moved to make another recommendation. In April 1866 he had addressed the society on "The Shape of Railroad Trains," referring to experiments by C. and R. M. Copeland. R. Morris Copeland, an early member of the Institute, also spoke at that time on "The Proper Shape of Railroad Trains."[58] Rogers wrote to Copeland with a ringing endorsement:

> Having witnessed your experiments on the effects of atmospheric resistance with models of various shapes as exhibited last spring at a meeting of our Institute I have no hesitation in commending them to the careful consideration of scientific engineers & of all persons who are interested in R. Road transportation.[59]

The Committees of Arts continued to fall far short of expectations. In April 1866 the Government was notified that three more had organized: Tools and Instruments, with Edward Philbrick, chairman; Manufactures of Wood, Leather, Paper, India Rubber, Gutta-Percha, with John Cummings, chairman; and Chemical Products and Processes, chaired by Cyrus Warren. At this time these three became members of the Government.[60] But the Committee on Household Economy and the Committee on Machinery and Motive Powers appear to have met only once that year, to choose a chairman and secretary. In what would be his last annual report in May 1866, Thomas Webb had addressed the problem yet another time, reminding the members that these committees through their chairmen provided *"the connecting links between the Society of Arts, and the Government"* in line with the plan whereby they were to be "an important and prominent feature in the Institute's organization."[61]

In February 1867 the Committee on Chemical Products and Processes was asked to consider a "water furnace for burning pulverized fuel in the reduction of ores," a presentation on which had been made in January by Colonel J. J. Storer on behalf of himself and Dr. J. D. Whelpley, followed early in February by remarks from a Professor

Langley on the use of the furnace for the separation of copper from its ores. The committee was authorized to hold a public meeting on the subject if they wished and did so later that month with Langley as the speaker.[62] Cyrus Warren, who was appointed professor of organic chemistry in 1866, had been succeeded as chairman of this committee by John M. Ordway, an industrial chemist with the Bayside Alkali Works of South Boston and the Hughesdale Chemical Works of Johnston, Rhode Island. Ordway, who would in 1869 join the faculty of the Institute's school as professor of metallurgy and industrial chemistry, reported to the society early in April, explaining the process and stating the committee's opinion that it would seem to be "especially suitable for very poor ores" and that its "commercial value . . . can be arrived at only after long continued working on the manufacturing scale."[63]

Later in the year the committee would return to consideration of a related subject following a talk by Dr. Whelpley on a new process which could "effect a complete revolution in the working of metallic ores, especially the sulphides," this time with an indication that the committee would "probably report thereon to the Institute."[64] No record of a report has been found. Similarly, an earlier referral to the Committee on Machinery and Motive Powers of a hydrostatic scale seems never to have been mentioned again.[65]

A further assignment would come to the Committee on Chemical Products and Processes in February 1868: "to report what, if any, difference there is between the volatile hydrocarbons known in this market as gasolene, benzene, and naphtha; and wherein danger is to be apprehended in the use of these liquids for illuminating purposes."[66] In April Frederic Stimpson, then secretary of this committee, presented a report, demonstrated "the inflammability of these hydrocarbons, and the explosive character of their vapors when mixed with the proper amount of air," and announced a donation to the Institute of "various hydrocarbons" by the manufacturer.[67]

When the 1867–68 season began, nine of the projected Committees of Arts had still failed to organize. At the annual meeting in May 1867, Rogers reiterated what had become a perennial plea "for the supply of material for the Institute meetings, to stimulate and record the progress of mechanical science, and to give their co-operation and advice, through their Chairmen in the Government, in the management and direction of the Institute."[68] Webb's replacement as secretary, Samuel Kneeland, joined in this appeal in his annual report, citing the neglect of the bylaw requirement which applied to each member and the importance of the committees to the Government, the society's meetings, the mechanic and useful arts in general, and the "enlightenment of the public through the Journal of the Institute,"[69] the latter still only a hope. There is no indication that, aside from the activity of the Committee on Chemical Products and

Processes, either plea elicited any appreciable response. Nor did a similar attempt almost a year later.

There appeared to be little, if any, recognition on the part of Rogers and others that the failure of the committee concept might have been due to forces beyond the lassitude of the members. Actually, the concept belonged to another day and age and to a kind of institution quite different from that which the Institute was rapidly becoming, with its increasing emphasis on the school. Indeed, the school had assumed an energetic life of its own, responding to the needs of the times and looking to the future.

Rogers also did not seem to appreciate that the studies and recommendations he sought from these committees were not compatible with his resolve that the Institute remain aloof from testimonials or criticisms of inventions and new products and processes, from public positions that might compromise the Institute's integrity and involve it in controversy. When questions had been raised in 1865 about the propriety of such evaluations, he had warned that at no time should the "Institute, as such, express a favorable, or unfavorable opinion."[70] This restriction alone would have rendered any useful study meaningless and dampened interest in the committee structure, even if such interest could have been aroused at this late date.

Though more easily controlled, the selection of topics for presentation at the society's meetings required some caution and care in maintaining a spirit of disinterested discussion. Webb had addressed this problem in his annual report for 1866, reminding members and the community that the Institute was not to be held accountable for views and opinions expressed by speakers at the Society of Arts meetings. Though an invention or discovery might be referred to one of the Committees of Arts for "more minute and thorough examination, and a more detailed explanation," the Institute did not intend "to become enlisted for or against it":

> The Society of Arts should, at most occupy the position and exercise the functions of an impartial judge; hear the testimony on both sides; listen to the arguments pro and con; consider the subject in its bearings and dependencies; lay down and elucidate the law touching the case; sum up the evidence; illustrate where necessary, what under such and such combination of circumstances, in conformity with the laws governing like cases, must be the result. But here its duties cease; it is not to enter the jury-box, nor to assume to render a verdict in any case.[71]

A very fine line for the Institute to tread.

Yet another problem arose on March 7, 1867, when a statement appeared in the newspapers that "certain specimens of petrifaction, artificially produced, would be presented for examination" at that evening's meeting of the society. Rogers opened the meeting by setting the record straight:

> He hoped no persons were present in consequence of this wholly unauthorized announcement. As all papers presented to the Institute must be offered through the regularly appointed channels, and as other papers so presented would occupy the whole time of this meeting, the communication referred to could not be received at this time. It is essential to the interests of the Institute that it should not, even in appearance, be used as an advertising medium.[72]

Despite these difficulties, an impressive total of more than 350 presentations were included in the programs for the society's meetings between November 1862 and December 1870 (see Appendix 2). President Rogers, who was mainly responsible for arranging the programs, was also an active participant as a speaker and commentator. In addition to important papers by Jacob Bigelow and William Ware on educational matters, a wide range of subjects was covered, including apparatus, instrumentation, and machinery; problems of lighting and ventilation; bridge construction and railroad trains; telegraphy; minerals and their processing; improved steam boilers, a vital concern at that time; the artificial propagation of fish; and the manufacture of steel. A number of communications were of local interest—a case of spontaneous combustion at the Everett Mills in Lawrence; a ventilating fan invented by Stephen Ruggles, used in the Institute and soon to be installed in the State House; a talk on subaqueous tunnels, timely because of the "advantages derivable from a direct communication of some sort between Boston and East Boston"; a discussion of "Imperfect Ventilation," citing "a recent accident in a church in Newton, Massachusetts, by which 19 persons were made insensible, and more than 40 more or less sick"; the "Conveyance of Cochituate Water to East Boston and Chelsea," along with descriptions of devices to render the fountains on the Common "ornamental without too much expenditure of water"; and an experiment scheduled for the Common on "Gas-lighting in Street Lamps by Electricity."

Sixty-five people were in attendance on May 2, 1867, when Edward Pickering exhibited a machine of his own design, made by the janitor of the Institute, to "render visible the vibration of sound."[73] A year later Rogers would discuss Koenig's resonator, a piece of apparatus for similar purposes just received from Paris.[74] Professor Pickering made several appearances—in late 1866 speaking on the Washington aqueduct; in late 1867, an oscillating engine; in the winter of 1868 on the Boehm flute; that spring, a new form of rotary engine which had been invented by Nathanael G. Herreshoff, an Institute student; in December, a paper on the artificial production of ice.[75] Rogers commented on Herreshoff's invention:

> The President alluded to this specimen, as illustrating an important function of the Institute: viz: to develop and direct for practical purposes the mechanical talent of students of industrial science; and he thought the model exhibited was not only creditable to the pupil, but must be as gratifying to the Society of Arts as it was to the faculty of instruction in the Institute.[76]

From the fall of 1866, when records of attendance first appear, through the spring of 1868, the numbers generally ranged from 50 to 80. However, several programs, particularly in 1868, attracted 100 or more, with a high of 130. In his 1868 annual report, the secretary reported the election of 50 individuals, 37 of whom had taken up membership. Taking into account withdrawals and deaths, total membership was over 400, as it had also been for the two previous years:

1865–66	438
1866–67	469
1867–68	432

Nearly all members resided in "Boston or its vicinity, and do business in the city, embracing all the learned professions, scientific men, practical mechanics, merchants, manufacturers, and agriculturists."[77] An interesting addition had occurred in January 1867, when William Emerson Baker, originator of the old conservatory idea who severed connections with the Reservation Committee in May 1859, was elected to membership, having been recommended by M. D. Ross and Samuel Kneeland.[78]

There was still no aggressive effort to secure members, and had been none since the receipt of the Institute's charter. Rogers, always wary of any form of public display, had wished to proceed quietly without much fanfare. Webb's report for 1866 emphasized that it was not difficult for any who wished to join to "ascertain the steps necessary to be taken" for nomination, and such individuals, "unsolicited, but at the same time well recommended," would increase the "probability of accessions being of that character only, which it can be desirable to obtain."[79]

A Shift in Focus

As presiding officer, William Rogers brought the business of the Institute before the members and chaired the technical portion of the Society of Arts meetings. But he was also an active participant in the meetings, often commenting on presentations and suggesting lines of further investigation. During the first two years of the society's activities, the minutes record eighteen presentations of his own, on occasion more than one per meeting. Some consisted of demonstration experiments or the exhibition and explanation of apparatus. The frequency of his inclusion as a speaker very likely reflects the need to step in when others could not be found and undoubtedly reinforced his continuing pleas for the speedy organization of the Committees of Arts, which were originally expected to generate the programs for the Society's meetings. After the new season opened in December 1864, however, the problem appears to have eased, and though he continued his comments and suggestions, his statements were concerned almost entirely with the "progress and prospects" of the Institute and the development of the school.

Educational topics began to appear more regularly. In December 1863 William Watson read a paper on l'École Polytechnique of France, which he followed in January with a presentation on l'École des Ponts et Chaussées. Also at that meeting, a communication was presented by John S. Woodman of Dartmouth College, a corresponding member. Woodman addressed the society on "The Chandler Scientific School," of which he was in charge, presenting his views on how such schools should be conducted. The minutes contain no comments by Rogers on Watson's paper but do indicate that in regard to Woodman's he rose to point out "the difference between Establishments like the Chandler School, and the Institute of Technology, and showing however appropriate the judicious observations of Prof. Woodman were to the former, they were not in all respects applicable to the latter."[80] This response, though it seems slightly inhospitable, may be viewed in a different light by keeping in mind the original plan for the Institute, with the museum as its central feature. While this meeting took place several months after a share in the land-grant fund had been assured, no plan for the school had yet been prepared, and the ideas set forth in the *Objects and Plan* had not been altered. Making a distinction between the Institute of Technology and Chandler stems almost certainly from the original intent that the Institute's school would differ from and not attempt to compete with established educational institutions.

At the meeting on November 16, 1865, Rogers shared his enthusiasm about the opening of the first regular session of the school:

He [Rogers] spoke of the great success which had attended the opening and conducting of the Industrial School, which was no longer a matter of mere experiment, but was now firmly established on a sure foundation. The number of scholars have far exceeded the anticipations of its most sanguine advocates; the Corps of Teachers secured are well qualified for their positions, and the Pupils under their guidance and instruction have made commendable progress.[81]

Rogers reported also that "through the liberality of the Trustee of the Lowell Institute, Evening Courses of Instruction, under the supervision of this Institute are about being established, to which students of either sex will be admitted *free of charge.*"[82]

The program for the evening included an important paper—"The Limits of Education"—by Vice President Jacob Bigelow, who spoke directly to the basic philosophy of the school. Bigelow, an eloquent advocate of change in higher education, pointed out that the knowledge "appropriate to civilization which now exists in the world" had more than doubled in some instances and in others was more than ten times greater. It was no longer possible, he said, for any individual to "expect to grasp in the limits of a lifetime even an elementary knowledge of the many provinces of old learning, augmented as they are now by the vast annexations of modern discovery."[83] He attacked the study of Latin, Greek, and classical literature as a waste of time, except for the leisure classes for whom time was not precious:

They give pleasure, refinement to taste, breadth to thought, and power and copiousness to expression. Any one who in this busy world has not much else to do, may well turn over by night and by day the "exemplaria Graeca." But, if in a practical age and country, he is expected to get a useful education, a competent living, an enlarged power of serving others, or even of saving them from being burdened with his support, he can hardly afford to surrender four or five years of the most susceptible part of life to acquiring a minute familiarity with tongues which are daily becoming more obsolete, and each of which is obtained at the sacrifice of some more important science or some more desirable language. . . .

The admiration of the Old Romans for the Greek language and literature had its origin in the fact that in that age of limited civilization they found not much else of the kind to admire. They looked to Greece as the fountain of what had been achieved in art, philosophy, poetry and eloquence. Of consequence it was chosen as the great place of resort for educational objects, and Athens became the emporium of literary and philosophic instruction. But the Roman youth would never have been sent to Athens, had there been, as now, a railroad to take them to Paris, or a steamship to bring them to America. They would not have consumed their time in the groves of Academus, if they could have gained admittance to the École Polytechnique, or to the Royal Institution.[84]

Bigelow believed that "every individual is by nature comparatively qualified to succeed in one path of life, and comparatively disqualified to shine in another." It was necessary, therefore, to make an effort to determine an individual's natural abilities and interests at the outset. A good common school education should be obtained, followed by a "special or departmental course of studies" leading to "an appropriate sphere of usefulness. Collateral studies of different kinds may always be allowed, but they should be subordinate and subsidiary, and need not interfere with the great objects of his especial education."[85] Bigelow emphasized what the traditional college course could and could not accomplish:

A common college education now culminates in the student becoming what is called a master of arts. But this in a majority of instances means simply a master of nothing. It means that he has spent much time and some labor in besieging the many doors of the temple of knowledge, without effecting an entrance at any of them. . . . It may not be doubted that a few years devoted to the study of Greek will make a man a more elegant scholar, a more accomplished philologist, a more accurate and affluent writer, and, if all other things conspire, a more finished orator. But of themselves they will not make him what the world now demands, a better citizen, a more sagacious statesman, a more far-sighted economist, a more able financier, a more skilful engineer, manufacturer, merchant, or military commander. They will not make him a better mathematician, physicist, agriculturist, chemist, navigator, physician, lawyer, architect, painter, or musician. . . . It is common at the present day to say that the Greek language disciplines the mind, extends the compass and application of thought, and . . . trains the mind to a better comprehension of words, thoughts, and things. All this is no doubt true, and might have great weight as a governing motive in education, were it not that the same ends can be more cheaply obtained by the agency of other means. . . . It is easy to say that Laplace would have been a better mathematician, and Faraday a better chemist, if by chance they had been duly instructed in Greek. . . . At this day nobody believes that Watt would have made a better steam engine, or Stephenson a better locomotive, if they had been taught philosophy by Plato himself.[86]

Summarizing his own perspective on the mission of the school of the Institute, Bigelow observed:

> It is the province of the Institute of Technology, so largely and liberally sus-
> tained by the Legislature, by the munificence of individuals, and by the untir-
> ing labors of its distinguished president, to endeavor within its sphere to assist
> in providing for the educational wants of the most practical and progressive
> people that the world has seen. By its programme of instruction a separate path
> is provided for all who require to accomplish themselves in any one or more
> of the especial branches of useful knowledge.[87]

At the same time he acknowledged other efforts in "several of our larger universities, where the practical sciences and the modern languages are extensively taught."[88]

Yet another subject bearing directly upon the mission of the School was featured at the following meeting with a paper by William R. Ware, professor of architecture, outlining a course of architectural instruction. This, too, was enthusiastically received, the discussion which followed emphasizing "its bearings on the comfort, health, and prosperity of this city." John D. Philbrick expressed high praise:

> [He] deemed the Paper one of great interest and merit; highly creditable to
> the Author; and one that might be made exceedingly profitable to the
> Members of the Institute. He expressed a hope that the production would be
> put in such a form as to be accessible to the Public, that all so disposed might
> be benefited thereby.[89]

Entitled *An Outline of a Course of Architectural Instruction,* it was published by the Institute in 1866.[90]

Rogers seemed generally pleased with the society's development when he addressed the annual meeting in May 1868:

> It seems but proper that I should add a word of congratulation on the increas-
> ing value and success of these meetings. In no previous year have they been so
> largely attended, and in none have the communications presented and the con-
> sequent discussions been of greater interest, variety and importance. . . . this
> department of the Institute has continued to grow in popularity and useful-
> ness, until now we may venture to speak of it as an important instrumentality
> in promoting the practical sciences and arts in our community. We who have

marked the influence of these meetings from year to year and month to month have had ample occasion to recognize the benefits of a free interchange of ideas between those who are engaged in the theoretical studies and the practical applications of science, and have ourselves felt, as we have witnessed in others, the fruitful stimulation and guidance which those meetings have imparted and conferred. . . . it has been my aim to give to each contributor for the evening fair and ample opportunity for doing justice to his communication, whether in the form of an elaborate essay, a report, or an oral description and exhibition of mechanical or other inventions, and I am sure you have all listened as I have with pleasure and even pride to the clear and cogent expositions of many of those who without pretensions to literary skill have so modestly and yet vividly brought before us the results of their mechanical ingenuity.[91]

He voiced hopes for the publication of an annual "Proceedings," but he did not mention the Committees of Arts, nor did he refer to the museum. The major part of his address concerned the "other active department of the Institute"—the school, applauding the success it had so far achieved and the example it was setting for other institutions. The school was increasingly becoming the major focus, and when fundamental matters such as finances, buildings, and equipment were considered, their relation to the school was paramount.

A Shift in Governance

Of prime importance among a variety of issues in the early days was the governance of the Institute. Following the spirit of the *Objects and Plan*, a statement of intent rather than a carefully worked out organizational prospectus, the 1862 bylaws had established a framework that would not meet adequately the requirements of the Institute as it evolved and that indeed unknowingly did not correspond fully with the charter. That the exact relationship of the society, the museum, and the school had yet to be addressed is evident from the recurring discussions between 1862 and 1865 on how best to proceed, what should be emphasized, how to begin operations, what were their aims and goals, and, on one occasion at least, should they proceed at all.

In 1863 a minor adjustment had been made in the schedule for the ordinary meetings as a Society of Arts. It was approved by the Government and routinely accepted by the members of the Institute.[92] At a Government meeting late in February 1864,

Rogers appointed a committee to consider a revision of the bylaws: Erastus Bigelow, M. D. Ross, James Little, John Philbrick, and Charles Flint. Rogers was added by the Government. Their recommendations were approved soon thereafter, subject, in accordance with the rules, to acceptance by the members of the Institute, a meeting of which late in March would prove to be only the beginning of a major controversy.[93] Rogers's intention to read the proposed amendments at that time was deflected by Flint, who prevailed with a motion to dispense with the reading since the rules precluded an immediate vote. Rogers then promised that the revised version would be available for inspection in the office of the secretary.

With the reading of both versions in April 1864, when the changes came up for action, it became immediately clear that passage would not be easy. Although a motion to refer them for "examination" to a special committee of the Institute failed, a motion to consider them individually succeeded. A requirement that chairmen of the Committees of Arts be elected annually was approved, along with a change to election rather than appointment of the standing committees on Instruction, the Museum, Publication, and Finance. But an amendment to alter the nomination process for new members created a considerable stir. From the beginning "not less than two members" had been required for submission of a nomination. The amendment specified four, including two members of the Government. Francis Storer, soon to be a member of the school's faculty, asked for an explanation of the "object" of this change. Rogers simply replied, "the more securely to guard the interests of the Institute." When a motion to table failed, and an initial vote of 19 to 8 was announced by Rogers as sufficient for passage, the opposition objected, correctly citing a bylaw provision that three-quarters of the members present must be in favor. Forty-eight were there, and with a second vote of 27 ayes and 9 nays, "the President decided that the amendment was rejected."

The meeting would end with a difference of opinion on the Institute's rights with respect to amendments. Philbrick thought that the Institute could only accept or reject amendments initiated by and already accepted by the Government, but Jonathan Preston believed that even if the Institute could not originate an amendment, it had a "right . . . certainly to modify" a Government proposal. On this note all but the two articles accepted at the beginning were referred back to the Government—a rare defeat for Rogers.[94]

It is unclear why the Government sought to gain a measure of control over the nomination process. The lack of an aggressive campaign for members in 1862 is one sign of a desire to limit membership to those genuinely interested in the institution and willing to become active participants. But several factors may have played a role in the Government's decision to become involved in 1864. First, all of those who had indicated a desire to join prior to the spring of 1862 had not followed through and become active "Original Members" as allowed by the bylaws, and a fair number of those nominated and elected thereafter either did not respond immediately or declined. In spite of this erratic acceptance rate, however, membership numbers were increasing but appeared to be of no help with respect to the organization of the Committees of Arts to which Rogers still had a strong commitment. A Government voice in the nomination of members might help to solve both of these problems. And finally, if a more "comprehensive" plan for the school was about to emerge, some of the Institute membership, from which the Government was then drawn, must be properly qualified as potential candidates for the Standing Committee on Instruction.

That a perceived problem with the membership was the overriding concern is confirmed by Webb's second annual report in May 1864. Presumably to reassure the members, he pointed out first that the charter affirmed the eligibility of all citizens of the Commonwealth and that no one "regularly proposed and properly vouched for, would be refused admission." He moved on, however, to say what Rogers would have expressed more diplomatically had he gone beyond his terse reply to Storer:

> The bane of most Societies, indeed that which proves a serious obstacle to all progress, and finally deals the inevitable death-blow, is the indiscriminate admission of Members, regardless of all qualifications, and though the candidates be destitute of all inclination to acquire knowledge themselves, and of fitness or willingness to contribute towards the instruction and improvement of others.

Briefly tempering his remarks by allowing that the Institute had to date been "remarkably fortunate," Webb added that a continuation would require that each member "be at all times vigilant and circumspect":

> Whilst we should cheerfully greet with words of welcome every real laborer in our broad field, for the harvest is truly great, but the laborers are few in comparison, we should also resolutely set our faces against the wilfully ignorant, the persistently indolent, and the lifelessly unambitious.[95]

He continued by citing the need for "The Inventor and the Man of Science" to be brought together, for "the *brain* and the *muscle* . . . the intellectual and physical . . . by their combined efforts producing beneficial and useful results, often not otherwise attainable—never in so great perfection."[96]

With the bylaw revisions now back in the hands of the Government, Rogers added George Tuxbury and John Runkle to the committee at a meeting early in May 1864, when "much time was devoted to a consideration of the condition and true policy of the Institute, the dangers to which it is liable, and the most judicious course to avoid them," but no details of these deliberations were recorded. For this round they moved slowly, prompting M. D. Ross to ask in November whatever happened to the bylaws. That there was some disagreement within the committee is evident thereafter in several indications of readiness and delays. Finally approved by the spring of 1865, the amended bylaws were accepted by the Institute members on April 6.[97] Noteworthy among the revisions was a requirement that proposed bylaw changes in the future be accompanied by the signatures of a majority of the Government when submitted to the Institute for consideration.

The Committees of Arts were removed from the category of standing committees, their chairmen still to be members of the Government. The Society of Arts, not mentioned at all in the 1862 bylaws, appears briefly in Section I—"such Officers connected with the Society of Arts, the School . . . as it may hereafter be found expedient to appoint." No standing committee was established for the society, a flaw still not recognized.

A decided victory for the members of the Institute was the Government's retreat from its insistence on involvement in the nomination for membership, the procedure for which was not altered at all. The Government dared not risk another rejection of the entire proposal, and they wanted approval of a major change. Henceforth only Government members would comprise the Nominating Committee for officers and the standing committees, the president to be an *ex officio* member of each of the latter. And the Institute members would not elect these officers and committees, this duty now reserved for the Government, with a majority vote required for election. The Institute would, however, elect an Auditing Committee of three of their members, and the treasurer, in addition to the secretary, would be required to present to the Institute an annual report. Finally, amendment and repeal of the bylaws would require a vote of three-fourths of the members *voting* at any regular meeting of the Institute—a provision that would have helped Rogers in 1864—but a majority of the Government would be required to sign recommended changes presented in writing to the Institute for consideration.[98]

The governance again became a subject of concern in the fall of 1866 when, because of "certain discrepancies and deficiencies," Rogers appointed George Tuxbury and Alexander Rice to a committee under the chairmanship of Judge George Bigelow. Once again Rogers was immediately added.[99] At first glance his choice of an *ex officio* representative of the Commonwealth for this important task is somewhat surprising in light of his determination in 1863 to limit the state's representation on the Institute's Government. As chief justice of the Supreme Judicial Court, Bigelow had attended one meeting in the fall of 1863 and one in the spring of 1865. In the summer of 1866, however, when his advice was sought with respect to a proposal for scholarships, he was added to an existing committee, and he appears to have been responsible for the preparation of an indenture of trust in that connection, in the course of which he undoubtedly became familiar with the bylaws. It is possible, therefore, that he noted serious problems and suggested a careful review of the Institute's governance.[100] If so, he was an obvious choice as chairman.

The spring of 1867 brought renewed concern about the membership as a result of "several irregularities" related to admission and assessment fees, and a separate Government committee was appointed with full power to "revise the list of members and exempt . . . certain cases." The committee reported in June the elimination of "thirty-two original members and thirty-six associates by subsequent election" for "nonpayment or refusal of further payment." They had voted to remit fees for "Professors and Secretary of the Institute, Professors in Colleges, Clergymen, [and] Principals of High Schools and Academies," and had also seized the moment to return to the controversial matter of the nomination procedure, proposing the establishment of a "Committee on Elections" composed of Institute members to receive recommendations and submit for election by the Institute those deemed qualified. They did not specify whether the Government or the Institute would appoint this committee. Since the bylaws in force would require amendment, the proposal was referred to the bylaw committee.[101]

By mid-May 1868, with no word, at least on the record, from Judge Bigelow's committee, the Government called for "early attention" and a settlement of the matter before the opening of the next season of the Institute. Rogers's illness in the fall undoubtedly caused further delay, and they were not ready until mid-February 1869, when Judge Bigelow reported that a charter amendment would be necessary. Without legislative authority, the Massachusetts Institute of Technology, chartered in 1861 as a corporate body, had illegally transferred its "powers and privileges" to the "Government." The problem had begun with the 1862 bylaws and been compounded in 1865 when the members of the Institute were excluded from the nomination and election of officers. Bigelow prepared an act for submission to the legislature following Government and Institute approval,[102] and Chapter 97 of the Acts of 1869 was approved on March 20.[103]

This charter amendment legalized the "Government" then in place, which hence-forth would be known as the "Corporation," carefully specifying the continuance of the three Commonwealth *ex officio* members. It eliminated the body known as the "Members of the Institute," those on the rolls now "entitled to be members of the Society of Arts," forcing a reorganization of the society with the Committees of Arts under its jurisdiction. New bylaws for the Institute's Corporation would be in place by June 1870, and would finally include a Standing Committee on the Society of Arts. Separate bylaws for the society were approved by the Corporation on December 14, 1870, and adopted by the society on the following day.[104]

Rogers was tired at the end of the first school year and had looked forward to a sum-mer of "continuous rest," but learned on June 6, 1866, that Henry was gravely ill in Scotland. He sailed from New York on June 9, unaware that Henry had died on May 29, and did not return to Boston until the end of July, weary and "stunned by the loss" of his "favorite brother." The sudden death of Thomas Webb on August 2 brought fur-ther concerns and a delay in his departure for Sunny Hill. He was "thoroughly worn out" when he finally left Boston, and soon thereafter he developed "a slow fever which lasted many weeks and broke off all correspondence." Months later he would describe it as a "severe and prolonged illness."[105]

Webb's last entry in the Government Records for a meeting on June 27, 1866, was not signed. With a minor addition, these minutes were approved at the next meeting on August 22.[106] Vice President Wilder presided at both meetings, and Edward Philbrick, a member of the Government, acted as secretary *pro tempore* for the August 22 meeting. Webb's death was formally noted and a committee appointed to prepare resolutions, which were presented late in September.[107] Rogers had sent word that he relied "upon the discretion of his associates to act in his absence without delay" in selecting a replacement for Webb. M. D. Ross indicated that three applications had been received "probably from very eligible candidates," and a committee was appointed.[108]

On September 26 Ross reported for the committee that "conditional arrange-ments" had already been made with Samuel Kneeland, who had been "assorting papers and indexing records" for the past three weeks. Ross moved that the Government pro-ceed to an election. Twelve members were present. After discussion, Kneeland, with eight favorable votes out of nine cast, was elected secretary.[109] He would serve also as instructor of zoology and physiology from 1867 to 1869 and as professor from 1869 to the end of 1878. In addition, he was secretary of the faculty from 1871 to 1878, when he left the Institute.

Prior to the initial vote, Edward Atkinson, undoubtedly concerned about the state of Rogers's health and his ability to carry on, had urged the need for someone "either as Secretary, or by some other name," to act as "Executive Officer, to take charge of the finishing of the building and organizing the School." Immediately after the election, he was appointed chairman of a committee to consider the matter, along with the appointment of a janitor, a problem referred at once to the Building Committee. By mid-November another committee was appointed to "consider the establishment of the office of Engineer" to "take charge of the heating apparatus." Appointments as "Janitor" and "Engineer" were finally made, not without the appointment of still another committee, this time to settle the janitor's salary. The entire process would not be complete until the spring of 1867, underscoring the need for an executive officer, a position that was not created, nor is there further mention after September 26 of the Committee on an Executive Officer.[110]

Samuel Kneeland

Samuel Kneeland, born in Boston in 1821, was educated at Boston Latin School and Harvard. He was graduated from the College in 1840 and the Medical School in 1843, having studied also with several physicians, among them Oliver Wendell Holmes and Jacob Bigelow. After pursuing further medical studies in Paris, he opened a practice in Boston in 1845. With others he was a founder of the Boylston Medical School, which did not survive, and from 1851 to 1853 he was a demonstrator of anatomy at Harvard Medical. He traveled extensively, developed a keen interest in zoology, and eventually abandoned his practice. He was secretary of the Boston Society of Natural History for several years and through that connection became involved in the effort to secure land on the Back Bay for the society and the proposed conservatory, was secretary of the early committees, and prepared the first petition to the legislature. He served as a surgeon during the Civil War and was discharged early in 1866 with the rank of Brevet Lieutenant-Colonel of Volunteers.[111]

Rogers was sufficiently recovered to return to his duties early in October 1866, and presided in November at the Institute's first meeting of the season, welcoming the members to "their new building" on Boylston Street. At that time he paid "deserved tributes" to several members who had died during the summer, including Ralph Huntington, James Hayward, and Thomas Webb. He spoke in positive terms about the prospects of the school, with a registration of "about 130 students, a number not greatly exceeded by any of the old scientific schools of like character in Europe, and not surpassed in this country—a gratifying proof that the school meets a great and growing want of the community."[112] This is the first public statement in which he appears to acknowledge the existence in the United States of other "scientific schools," presumably "of like character."

As the year 1866–67 drew to a close, Rogers was formally thanked for a "very interesting and valuable series of meetings." He responded with thanks to the members for their interest and expressed his "gratification at the success of the Society of Arts, which he thought would continue to increase in value as a medium of communication between the scientific man and the practical mechanic and various industries and material productive interests of the State."[113] At the annual meeting on May 31, 1867, he credited the "early success" of the society with preparing "the way for the establishment of the second department of the Institute, the School of Industrial or Applied Science." Whether his reference to the "second department" indicates a displacement of the museum to third position in the objects of the Institute, or whether it signified simply the second of the three planned components to be inaugurated, is not clear.

Rogers made a special point of the society's impact upon the community:

This department of the plan, involving but little expense and requiring only a share of that intellectual activity and zeal which never fail in a community like this, commended itself even more promptly than was anticipated to the sympathy and coöperation of those who are interested in the industrial pursuits and the application of science to useful purposes. From year to year the meetings of the Society of Arts have been growing in importance. It is only necessary to look at the titles of the various communications received during the session now closing, and just read by the Secretary in his able resume of our meetings, to be impressed with the variety and solid nature of its labors, and to feel assured that this department of the Institute is already exerting an important influence in diffusing knowledge, awakening inquiry, and stimulating invention throughout the community. Ere long we foresee that this commodious hall will be insufficient for our meetings, and we shall gather in greatly increased numbers and with augmented activity in some larger room, perhaps in the great hall of the Institute.[114]

He also paid tribute to the "munificent benefactors of the Institute," and the "generous men and women now contributing or proposing to contribute to its funds," noting especially the "generous friend" who had also made it possible for "many deserving students standing in need of . . . assistance" to enroll in the school. And he noted also a "gentle lady" who had just given $2,000 for the purchase of "Philosophical Apparatus." In closing, he bid the members a "kind farewell," indicating that he would sail for Europe in a few days, hoping to return in the fall with "renewed health, and with valuable additions to the educational apparatus of the Institute."[115]

Rogers was bound for Europe as commissioner for Massachusetts to the Universal Exposition in Paris, for which Napoleon III had initiated the planning in 1863. In May 1866, following acceptance by President Andrew Johnson and Congress of an invitation for the United States to participate, the Massachusetts legislature passed a resolve authorizing Governor Alexander H. Bullock to appoint a commissioner. Rogers's appointment had apparently arrived while he was abroad following Henry's death, and his illness following his return prevented his entertaining the idea until much later. He at first declined because of the "state of his health and his duty to the Institute," but later agreed to accept. As assistants he chose Professors Charles Eliot and Francis Storer of the Institute's faculty.

On June 4, 1867, William and Emma Rogers sailed for Liverpool.[116] Before moving on to Paris they stopped in England, where he visited manufacturing establishments in Birmingham, and in London spent time at the Royal Society, the Museum of Practical Geology, and the British Museum.[117] He was busy every day at the Exposition and his brother Robert was along and helping him. The Exposition was far greater "in richness and extent" than he expected, but "too vast" and overwhelming: "The student who seeks to gather instruction from its collections in any one great department . . . could, I think profit more by a gathering of the really new and original or very superior products, undistracted by the crowd of things which, excellent in their way, are but repetitions of other previous exhibitions."[118] Institute faculty members William Watson and William Ware, and benefactor John Amory Lowell were all in Paris at some time during this period. In mid-August Rogers contracted pneumonia but was able to leave for home on September 21.[119]

The American exhibits in Paris provided, it has been said, "the first impressive proof to Europe of the advances in science and technology that had occurred in the midst of a civil war," and that "in many technological exhibits American contributions were recognized as more original and inventive." Prizes went to the Sanitary Corps for ambulances and pharmaceutical exhibits, to the McCormick reaper, Cyrus Field's Atlantic cable, the Sharp machine for making screws, Sellers planing machines, and the Corliss engine. The Howe sewing machine, the American Buttonhole Machine Company, and a telegraph printing machine capable of recording the greatest number of messages were among those recognized, along with carpets, textiles, shoes, washing machines, and Fairbanks scales.[120]

Following his return, Rogers presented his view of the Exposition at a meeting of the Society of Arts on November 7, 1867:

> The first impression on viewing the products of American industry at the Exposition was one of disappointment, but a more extended examination led the careful observer to the conviction that, though more might have been exhibited, the variety in the American department was sufficient to vindicate the character of our country for unsurpassed inventive faculty, displaying original thought and the productive idea in mechanism. This was admitted by qualified and impartial observers, whether English, French, or German, and it was candidly confessed that mechanical engineers must go to the American department for novelties and bold inventions in this branch of science; so that the feeling of disappointment was soon changed into one of approval and admiration. It was a grand display of the power of civilization and of the ability of the human intellect to control natural forces for human benefit, impressing one with a sense of the dignity and strength of industrious and thoughtful man.[121]

Rogers had opened the meeting with the usual congratulations on the flourishing condition of the Institute and a brief historical review. And he closed it with a tribute to John Andrew, who had died suddenly in October—"the wise, truthful, and warm hearted patriot—the earnest supporter of every thing pertaining to humanity and the education and progress of man" and a "benefactor and friend of the Institute":

He had more to do with its successful establishment than most of the members, except a few of the oldest ones, have any idea of; to him, while Governor, we are indebted for an early, firm, and zealous support; his commendation, and encouragement, and never-failing sympathy enabled the few early advocates of the Institute to pursue their difficult labor to a successful issue. . . . He was a member of the Committee on Instruction, and on the very day of the fatal blow was to have met with them on matters of importance to the Institute.[122]

Andrew had been appointed to the Committee on Instruction in May 1865, two years after he became an *ex officio* member of the Government by virtue of the charter amendment of 1863. Through his continuation on this committee following the completion of his term as governor of Massachusetts early in 1866, he became a regular member of the Institute's governing board. In his tribute, understandably, Rogers made no mention of Andrew's belief that Harvard's idea of a union of the school of the Institute with its own Lawrence Scientific School and Bussey Institution would have been the preferable decision with respect to the fund created through the Morrill Act.

Though the Committees of Arts never fulfilled expectations, the society would serve a useful purpose for many years. As time passed, however, its form would be adapted to changing circumstances brought about by the growth of formal technical education, as well as of professional scientific and engineering societies, and by increased public access to information about scientific and technical advances.

he first serious mention of a journal to be published by the Institute appeared in the *Objects and Plan* as a component of the Society of Arts. Though no definite assessment had been undertaken of the market for such a venture or of the time and money required to sustain it, William Rogers was characteristically optimistic about the projected *Journal of Industrial Science and Art* and the "warm welcome" it would receive. Its aims were threefold—to set forth the proceedings of the society, to report on the condition and progress of the museum and the school, and to furnish "a faithful record of the advance of the Arts and Practical Sciences at home and abroad":

> A journal devoted to these objects, judiciously and ably conducted, would, we are confident, prove an invaluable help in carrying forward the plans and promoting the success of the Institute; and would, at the same time, form one of the most powerful means for advancing the interests of the Industrial Arts and Practical Education throughout our country. Hitherto, in the United States, we have had no periodical occupying so large a field of the Applied Sciences as is here contemplated; and we cannot doubt that such a publication would be warmly welcomed by those who are professionally or otherwise interested in these pursuits.[1]

It was expected that the activities of the Society of Arts, the lectures it would present, and the studies made by its various Committees of Arts would provide a strong base for the new publication.

In the eighteenth and early nineteenth centuries a variety of scientific and technical periodicals appeared—many only briefly, some concerned with farming and agricultural interests, mechanics, science, and medicine. The *American Mineralogical Journal*, one of the first specialized scientific journals in the United States, was published between 1810 and 1814.[2] In New Haven Benjamin Silliman founded in 1818 the *American Journal of Science*. Considered the "greatest journal of general science" established during this period, "it was from the first influential in the development of American scientific thought. Well illustrated, and containing articles by the foremost American scientists, it occupied a high place from the first volume."[3] The *Boston Journal of Philosophy and the Arts*, a quarterly, appeared first in 1823. John Webster, John Ware, and Daniel Treadwell started this venture, which lasted only until 1826.[4] The *Mechanics' Magazine* in Boston appeared for a year, beginning in 1830. It was followed by the *Young Mechanic* in 1832, which became the *Boston Mechanic* and ceased publication in 1835. The *Mechanic-Apprentice* was another journal of one year's duration, 1845–46, but the *New England Mechanic* had far greater stamina, appearing from 1847 to 1865, when it moved to New Jersey. There, as the *New Jersey Mechanic*, and later simply *Mechanic*, it lasted until 1911.[5] There was also the very successful *Scientific American*, which began in 1845 and continues to be published to this day.[6]

After 1850 such publications became more specialized as various fields developed—railroads, iron and steel, telegraphy, manufacturing, among others, and the professionalization of science and engineering led to journals related to specific disciplines.

Who suggested that a journal be included among the activities of the proposed Institute is not known. Henry Darwin Rogers had been involved briefly in 1830–31, while on the faculty of Dickinson College, with the publication of the *Messenger of Useful Knowledge*, but it is hardly likely that the short-lived *Messenger* could have been the inspiration thirty years later. It is possible that the success of Silliman's journal made attractive the idea of a publication similar in nature but oriented toward industrial science. What seems most likely, however, is that Rogers looked to the Franklin Institute as a model.[7]

The founders of the Franklin Institute had hoped from the beginning to publish a useful journal. However, when the first issue appeared in January 1826 under the title of *The Franklin Journal, and American Mechanics' Magazine; Devoted to the Useful Arts, Internal Improvements, and General Science*, it was published only "under the patronage" of the institute and was edited by Thomas P. Jones, professor of mechanics there. Its aim:

> To supply the wants of the intelligent artisans and manufacturers of our country. Every number will contain a variety of processes in the mechanical and chymical arts; but it is intended also to insert articles of general interest . . . a great variety of matter interesting to the artisan, and to the man of general reading.[8]

It was designed to "diffuse knowledge, not to advance it" among the operative classes.[9]

In 1828 the institute assumed responsibility for the publication, and it became the *Journal of the Franklin Institute of the State of Pennsylvania; Devoted to the Mechanic Arts, Manufactures, General Science, and the Recording of American and Other Patented Inventions*, with a Committee on Publications overseeing its operations. Among its chairmen were Samuel V. Merrick, a founder of the institute; Isaac Hays, a physician; and Alexander Dallas Bache, then professor of natural philosophy and chemistry at the University of Pennsylvania. These three are credited with using "their control to make the Journal a serious scientific and technical publication," thereby creating "unquestionably the nation's outstanding technical periodical and, as a result of Alexander Dallas Bache's influence, at least the equal of any other American journal publishing in the physical sciences."[10] It was reorganized in 1836, and by 1861 was called the *Journal of the Franklin Institute of the State of Pennsylvania, for the Promotion of Mechanic Arts. Devoted to Mechanical and Physical Science, Civil Engineering, the Arts and Manufactures, and the Record of Patented Inventions*.

Here, then, was a clear model for a publication by the Institute of Technology in Boston. If the Society of Arts were to flourish and develop as expected, its activities would likely sustain a publication of this kind.

That these intentions were serious is evident from the provision for a Standing Committee on Publication in the bylaws of 1862. This first set of bylaws provided also that the members of this committee would automatically form part of the Institute's general Government, and spelled out their mandate: "The general direction of the printing

John Daniel Runkle

of the proceedings and other publications of the Institute, including the selection of papers and discussions which have been presented at the meetings."[11] The committee would remain in force until a bylaw revision effective in 1870 brought the governance of the Institute into line with reality, and the committee became a standing committee of the Society of Arts under a separate set of bylaws.

Because of his experience in the field of publications, John D. Runkle was an obvious choice for chairman of this committee, and his appointment was his first significant step toward a major role in the organization of the Institute. Born in 1822 and raised on a farm in the state of New York, he was educated in the district schools and briefly in a private school, and had studied advanced mathematics on his own. While working on a farm and teaching in a local school, he set about preparing himself for college. In 1847 he wrote for advice to Benjamin Peirce, who presumably suggested enrollment in the new Lawrence Scientific School at Harvard. He was graduated with the first class in 1851, awarded a bachelor of science degree and, in recognition of superior scholarship, an honorary master of arts.[12]

Prior to his graduation Runkle became an assistant for the *American Ephemeris and Nautical Almanac*. When Congress had appropriated funds for this publication in 1849, the office was established in Cambridge in order to be near to Harvard and particularly to Benjamin Peirce, "recognized as the leading mathematician of America," who was appointed consulting astronomer.[13]

In 1858, Runkle started a journal called the *Mathematical Monthly*. No such publication had existed in the United States since the demise in the early 1840s of the *Cambridge Miscellany of Mathematics, Physics, and Astronomy*. Edited by Benjamin Peirce and Joseph Lovering, also at Harvard, this quarterly lasted for only four issues.[14] Runkle had sought advice from prominent professors of mathematics before issuing a circular letter in connection with his proposed journal. William Rogers had received a copy and was later listed as a subscriber.

The journal was intended primarily for young students, with prizes offered for the solutions of published problems and essays on mathematical subjects.[15] It persevered, but with a diminishing subscription list, until 1861, when publication ceased. According to astronomer Simon Newcomb, an 1858 graduate of the Lawrence Scientific School and an assistant at the *Almanac* as well as the *Monthly*, "the time was not yet ripe for the growth of mathematical science among us, and any development that might have taken place in that direction was rudely stopped by the civil war."[16] Throughout this period Runkle had retained his association with the *Almanac* and would continue to maintain this connection for many years.

The members of the Committee on Publication, in addition to Runkle, were George B. Emerson, Charles L. Flint, John C. Hoadley, and Lorenzo Sabine.

A member of the Harvard class of 1849, Charles Flint had studied law and practiced at the New York Bar until 1853, when he became secretary of the Massachusetts Board of Agriculture. Flint held that position for more than twenty-five years, and his duties included editing the board's annual reports. He was also a founder and secretary of the Board of Trustees of the Massachusetts Agricultural College and would later serve briefly as interim president of the school.[17]

Charles Louis Flint

John Hoadley, born in 1818, had attended Utica Academy and worked on the enlargement of the Erie Canal. He became interested in mechanical engineering through his association with Erastus Bigelow, had been superintendent and general agent of the Lawrence Machine Shop, and was a successful inventor and manufacturer of portable engines. He was also a founder of the American Society of Mechanical Engineers. He is said to have been proficient in languages and the classics, and through his second wife he was a brother-in-law of Herman Melville. When he died in 1886, a resolution cited his contributions to the engineering profession and to the Institute, through gifts of apparatus and the time he devoted to its concerns, its faculty, students, and graduates.[18]

Lorenzo Sabine, secretary of the Boston Board of Trade for a decade beginning in 1857, was born in 1803, the son of a clergyman. Following the death of his father in 1818, he was apprenticed briefly to a publishing firm

John Chipman Hoadley

Lorenzo Sabine

Alexander Hamilton Rice

in Boston and in 1821 moved to Eastport, Maine, where he remained until the late 1840s. Essentially self-educated, with a keen interest in history, his career was particularly distinguished by its variety—clerk, frontier trader, builder and owner of fishing vessels, member of the Maine Legislature, and briefly editor of the *Eastport Sentinel*. In the late 1840s he returned to Massachusetts, served a brief term in Congress, and worked for the Treasury Department on problems of fisheries. Sabine was also a prolific author, contributing articles to the *North American Review* and noted particularly for *The American Loyalists*, published in 1847. A two-volume revised edition of the latter appeared in 1864, and that, in turn, was reissued in 1966. The introduction to the 1966 reprint edition describes Sabine as "one of the ignored scholars of the American past" and applauds his "objective appraisal of the American Loyalists." Bowdoin in 1846 and Harvard in 1848 awarded him honorary master of arts degrees.[19]

In 1865 Sabine was replaced on the committee by Alexander Hamilton Rice, a graduate of Union College in 1844 and already a member of the Institute Government through his membership on the Standing Committee on the Museum beginning in 1862. As a principal of his family's firm, the leading paper manufacturer of the day, later known as Rice, Kendall Company, his understanding of at least one facet of the business of journal publication was assured. He had already served two terms as mayor of Boston, in 1856 and 1857, at the start of the development of the Back Bay. He was a member of Congress from 1859 to 1867 and served three terms as governor from 1876 through 1878.[20]

On December 17, 1862, at the fifth meeting of the Institute, the first "Ordinary Meeting of the year 1862–63," William Rogers discussed progress and prospects. As he spoke of the aims and the value of the Society of Arts, he expressed the hope that its activities would "after a time, furnish also an appropriate medium of publication in the Journal which forms one of the features of the general plan."[21] Despite his optimistic tone, however, the future of the Institute was uncertain at best and would remain so through the discouraging months when the money for the guarantee fund continued to be elusive. But once the money was secured, plans could go forward, and by the fall of 1863 they could feel that they were really under way. At that time, George Emerson suggested that concrete planning should begin, and each standing committee was asked to prepare a report of its plans.[22]

No records have been found of the discussions of the Committee on Publication, nor any correspondence covering an exchange of views. That they were in consultation, however, is borne out by a letter from Emerson to Runkle early in January 1864 acknowledging his "very beautiful present" of three volumes of the *Mathematical Monthly* obviously sent to him as an example of what might be done:

> I have examined only enough to see the great beauty of the type & page, the neatness and good taste of the arrangement and the satisfactory appearance of the whole.
>
> I receive still more thankfully your expression of a willingness to devote to the Institute of Technology the talent and taste which have made this publication, to all appearances just what it should be. You have, what we should find it difficult to meet united in any other individual, experience & success in a similar labor, and that thorough knowledge of mathematics which will make all the difficulties in the applications of science comparatively easy to you.
>
> How proud we shall be, I venture confidently to hope, to see a volume equally faultless proclaim our sweep and to listen to the congratulations of the friends of art upon so auspicious a beginning.[23]

In his cover letter to Emerson, Runkle must have indicated that he would accept the editorship of the journal should the Government think it wise to proceed.

In February 1864, when the reports were finally called for, Runkle presented a very thorough consideration of the subject. It began with the premise that the Institute needed a periodical as a means of communicating with its members and with the public:

> Unless the Institute shall secure the active and permanent interest of its Members, it will gradually lose them; and unless it inform the Public of its

wants and aims and excite a desire for its success, it will look in vain for pupils for its Industrial School, specimens for its Museum, or funds to enable it to carry on the ends of its foundation.[24]

The committee had discussed alternative types of publication. The idea of a simple *Transactions* covering the Institute's meetings as a Society of Arts was dismissed, and citing the relevant passage from the *Objects and Plan* in support, the committee concluded: "We believe that this Institute can not possibly secure a more powerful means to aid in the accomplishment of *all* its ends, than by establishing and sustaining a Technological Journal of the very highest class."[25] The report covered matters of policy, editorial and business management, the need of a working library, and included a comprehensive consideration of probable costs and receipts.

The committee outlined two options should a decision be made to proceed. One would assume a small circulation of "five hundred, or at most one thousand," priced to "cover the least possible expense for which it can be issued." This would be "worth but little as an advertising medium." There were advantages, however, to a much larger circulation, say 20,000, with its manufacturing costs covered mainly through revenues from advertising to be secured through a "properly organized and energetically conducted" effort. This would enable the price to be set "so low as to bring it within the reach of all classes in the community which it is intended to benefit." As an example, the sale of 20,000 copies of a weekly edition at four cents each would bring in $41,600. The cost of manufacturing such an edition would be $27,144 per year. The remaining $14,456 could "cover the expenses of illustrations, editing, publishing, &c."[26]

The committee's confidence appeared to be unbounded—curiously so, it would seem, when the chairman's *Mathematical Monthly* had foundered so recently, not to mention the unsettled conditions of the war years:

This Institute has a much higher and an altogether nobler mission to accomplish in the establishment of a Journal than its mere pecuniary success; and, if by this instrumentality it can more surely and speedily accomplish any of its great aims, it has a duty in the matter which we sincerely believe it will not hesitate to perform.[27]

On the availability of material for publication, they were equally sure that an "abundant supply of matter will not be wanting," citing the records of the Patent Office "of our own and European countries" as "only an abridged History of Inventions" to form "no inconsiderable part of every issue."[28]

The committee presented a set of resolutions recommending that publication of the journal begin in the fall of 1864 under the supervision of a committee of three, and suggesting that a fund be raised to "meet any deficiency" which might be incurred.[29] Unrecorded discussion led to tabling for future consideration. An essential question had appeared quite early in the committee's report: "Is it practicable, both as regards matter for its pages and funds to meet the expenses, to begin the publication of such a Journal at the present time?"[30] And the tenor of the report had been favorable. It was Runkle, however, then actively working with Rogers on the plan for the school, who offered the motion to table.

To a question in March 1864 about the action to be taken with respect to the report, Runkle replied:

> He had not called it up, because at this time he deemed it all important to con-
> centrate thought and action upon the developing and putting in good work-
> ing condition the various Schools of Industrial Science. Until this object is
> accomplished, he considered it advisable to defer the publishing of a Journal;
> more especially, as a first class one (and none other should be countenanced)
> will require at the onset a considerable guarantee fund, and always a large and
> able Corps of Editors, to secure which ample means must be provided.
>
> Under present circumstances, he thought it might be better, perhaps, to
> issue, from time to time, a Bulletin containing a Program of the Schools, an
> account of the Proceedings of the Institute, &c.[31]

The hard realities of the Institute's precarious financial situation and the needs of the school required adjustments to the original plans.

The idea of a journal, however, did not go away. On May 30, 1864, on a motion by Vice President John Amory Lowell, the following votes were passed:

> *Voted* that it is expedient at an early day to establish a Journal, or other form
> of Publication under the direction of the Committee on Publication to be
> devoted to the advancement of the Practical Sciences and Arts, and in which
> the valuable materials already accumulated, or hereafter to be collected in the
> Records of the Society of Arts, and in the other Transactions of the Institute,
> may be regularly communicated to the Public—and as a step toward this end
>
> *Voted* further that the Committee on Publication, as soon as convenient, report
> to the Government the scale and plan of publication adapted to this object,
> and to the present condition of the Institute.[32]

There is no indication that Runkle objected to this. Perhaps the fact that the Committee on Instruction had finally reported a plan, albeit with much work to be done, gave some hope that the remaining goals of the Institute could soon be addressed. Runkle and his committee, however, were now enjoined to make a further report on the possibility of a publication more limited in scope than originally envisioned and with "the present condition of the Institute" in mind.

It did not take them long. On June 6, with William Rogers absent and Jacob Bigelow presiding, Runkle reported that they had considered the problem again, arrived at the same conclusions, and "had nothing further at this time to recommend." This forced consideration of the recommendations of the tabled original report. According to the secretary, "a long discussion ensued," not a word of which did he place on the record. The original resolutions were passed with two amendments, one giving full powers for appointments and contracts to the Standing Committee on Publication rather than the earlier suggested separate committee of three, and one, originating with Erastus Bigelow, speaking directly to the matter of expenditures:

> *Resolved*, that in the opinion of this Government, the publication of a Technological Journal of the highest character, will be a most efficient means for advancing the interests of this Institute; not more as a medium of communication for the Society of Arts, than as a most powerful aid in building up the Museum, and the School of Industrial Science and Art; and that the time has come to take the steps preparatory to the publication of such a Journal.
>
> *Resolved*, that the Committee on Publication have full powers to make all the appointments and contracts necessary to carry their Report into effect, provided that in so doing they shall not exceed the sum subscribed or contributed therefor.
>
> *Resolved*, that in the opinion of this Government, the first Number of the Journal should be issued next Fall; at the beginning of the Session of the Institute for 1864,—'65, and that the intervening time be vigorously devoted to the work of preparation.
>
> *Resolved*, that a fund be raised to meet any deficiency to which the Institute may become liable on account of the publication of the proposed Journal.[33]

No committee was appointed to raise the necessary funds, and the question of how publication could begin in the fall under these circumstances was either not broached or not recorded. Only Runkle and Flint of the committee were present at this meeting, attended by seven members of the Government, including Vice President Bigelow and Secretary Webb, a small showing.

The journal was not mentioned again until the secretary's report for the year 1864–65:

> Various impediments interfered . . . so that as yet nothing further has been accomplished.
>
> As the Government continues to entertain the opinion expressed in regard to the advantage and importance of a Journal, the earliest favorable opportunity for commencing its publication will undoubtedly be improved; and it may reasonably be anticipated that ere the return of another anniversary, this proposed organ of the Institute will be in successful operation.[34]

The Committee on Publication continued to bide its time.

Secretary Webb, in his annual report for 1865–66, would once again report no progress. He pointed out that no committee had ever been appointed to raise the necessary funds to cover whatever costs might exceed the receipts from the sale of the proposed publication: "The consequence was the matter here rested;—and here it still rests."[35] He added that the committee had felt that such a journal "would soon, if not from the onset, be self-sustaining and might easily be made, if deemed advisable, a paying enterprize," a curious attitude for an institution heavily in debt, "*pecuniarily* we mean—for in other respects there cannot be a question but that it would prove vastly profitable by bringing us into more close communication with kindred institutions, and by supplying us with the various Scientific and Arts' Journals in this Country and Europe."[36] Ever optimistic, he concluded by emphasizing that the committee hoped they would be able to test the accuracy of their predictions by an actual trial.

In May 1867 Secretary Kneeland reported that there was still no progress:

> The Committee on Publication have as yet not taken any active steps for the establishment of a Journal, as a means of communication between the Institute and other scientific bodies and the public. When funds accrue or can be spared for this purpose, the views of the Committee, as heretofore reported, will be carried out, to the great advantage of the Institute.[37]

The sanguine statements by both Webb and Kneeland provide further evidence of a lingering commitment to the early ideas of the *Objects and Plan*. Despite recognition that the proposed journal could not be initiated without additional funds raised specifically for that purpose, the Government had yet to face squarely the fact that some of their original intentions would have to be laid aside, not only because they could not afford them, but also because times were changing and it was the school that responded most closely to the needs of these times. True, it would be extremely difficult, only five years after taking up the charter, publicly to abandon any component—for which they had originally labored so long and so hard—and not only extremely difficult, but politically inexpedient. At the same time, it was incumbent upon the Government to make certain that they fulfilled the promise inherent in their struggle to secure part of the land-grant funds. It is significant that President Rogers made no mention of the journal in his annual report to the Institute for that year.[38]

In May 1868 a matter of a different sort was referred to the Publication Committee. At a Government meeting, William Rogers proposed that, in the interest of the Society of Arts and the school, a register of the Institute be published annually, containing a list of the members, extracts of the records, and a "condensed exposition of the condition and prospects of the Institute in its various branches." After consideration, the Publication Committee recommended that during that summer, under their direction, such a publication should be prepared by the secretary, to include the following:

> a condensed Report of the doings of the Institute for the year;

> the catalogue of the School, with an account of the courses of instruction, regular, special, and the free courses established by Mr. Lowell;

> a list of the members of the Society of Arts, with the By-Laws, and Reports of the Secretary and the Treasurer;

> such other information regarding the plan and operations of the Institute in its various departments, as the Committee may think expedient for the information of the community.

The probable cost of such a volume, $600, was appropriated at this time.[39]

The committee was also asked to consider "the expediency and the probable expense of publishing a larger volume, giving a history of the Institute from the beginning, with an account of its doings as a School of Industrial Science and a Society of Arts, to the present time." In turn, Runkle asked the Government to consider the wisdom, at "some future period, perhaps not far distant, of having a printer in the Institute building."[40]

At the annual meeting of the Institute on May 21, 1868, Rogers presented a review of progress during the year, referring particularly to the presentations at the meetings of the Society of Arts and the plans for publication:

> A survey of the contributions which have thus far been made at the meetings, as embodied in the Secretary's records, naturally suggests the desirableness of a serial or annual publication of the "Proceedings" in a permanent form. Steps have been taken by the Government to secure such a publication at an early day. This will include information on all important points connected with the organization of the Institute, the plan and condition of the school, and will in fact aim to present such details and general information in regard to the several departments of the Institute as the public may be interested to learn. A larger volume will also be prepared, embodying the history of the Institute from its inception to the present time, and including, in full or in copious extracts, the Proceedings of the Society of Arts from the beginning.[41]

Rogers's optimism did not bear fruit, however, and there is no indication that the Government's $600 appropriation was used as predicted. A catalogue of the school had, of course, been published annually since 1865, but its content was the sole responsibility of the faculty. Neither the catalogue nor the president's reports, which began to appear in 1872, fulfilled the original intent of the Committee on Publication. Separate bylaws for the Society of Arts, as required by the 1870 reorganization of the Institute's governance, would, however, provide for a Standing Committee on Publication with the following mandate: "The Committee on Publication shall select, from the papers and discussions presented to the meetings of the Society, such as they think calculated to advance the interests of the mechanic and other useful arts, and report the same, whenever they think proper, to the Council, for publication in a permanent form."[42] Abstracts of the proceedings would be contained in the annual report of the secretary of the Institute for a few years, and beginning in 1880 they appeared annually in a separate pamphlet. The goal of a scientific journal "of the highest character," however, was not pursued.

Carpentry (top left), Pottery (top right), Modeling (bottom left), and Glass Painting (bottom right)—sketches prepared by Paul Nefflen for mural in Huntington Hall (see p. 764).

Chapter 17

The Museum of Technology

The idea of a museum as a component of the Institute had its roots in the initial attempt to secure land on the Back Bay for a Conservatory of Art and Science. Though that effort provided a springboard for further action and though some of its spirit persisted as the project evolved, it differed markedly from the proposal set forth in the *Objects and Plan of an Institute of Technology* when it appeared late in 1860.

In his first memorial, which became House No. 13, January 1860, Rogers had refined and sharpened to some extent the original conservatory proposal. He also had before him the printed record of the meetings held on February 18 and March 11, 1859, neither of which he had attended and at both of which the example of European institutions had been cited. In February there had been particular mention of the "Museum of Practical Geology and the Kew Gardens—the one presenting the wonders of the mineral and the other of the vegetable world to public observation: such are not only attractive to strangers, but exceedingly useful to every citizen."[1]

The *Objects and Plan* presented a more clearly focused view than its predecessor documents and was the first statement in which segments of the original effort were eliminated. For example, the "Gallery of Fine Arts," along with the concept of separate structures for vaguely defined purposes, disappeared. Destined to survive were "Mechanics, Manufactures, Commerce, and Technology in general" and those portions of "Natural Sciences" essential to the progress of industry and commerce. The Natural History Society, an independent institution already in existence, had always intended to retain its own identity.

Though more definite, the *Objects and Plan* was not a carefully considered prospectus. Rogers himself termed it "a mere outline of a broad plan."[2] Prepared to garner support, public and legislative, it could not lightly ignore the considerable popular interest that had arisen for the conservatory idea. Indeed, the full title of the section devoted to the museum was "Museum of Industrial Art and Science, or Conservatory of Arts." By 1862, however, when the first bylaws of the Institute were adopted, it would be called the "Museum of Technology."[3] But beyond the wisdom of capitalizing on interest already aroused, many of the Institute's proponents believed that an industrial museum would respond constructively to a perceived need, have much to contribute to the effectiveness of the larger plan, and generate substantial public support for the entire effort. In their minds also was the concept of a museum as an effective medium of education.

As it appeared in the *Objects and Plan*, the museum was to be "the central feature of our proposed Institute of Technology"[4]—a significant statement representing an important intermediate step in the evolving plan. Over the years, as the school assumed the dominant place, historical statements have tended to overlook the first concept of the Institute—a museum at its center, as in the European institutions which provided inspiration and example, ample provision for popular lectures, and promise of future opportunities for more structured educational pursuits. Circumstances both within and without soon forced a shift in emphasis, but the idea of a museum would persist for some time.

In the *Objects and Plan* Rogers named several British and Continental institutions that might "well incite the friends of enlightened industry in this country to systematic efforts in the same direction." Among them were the Conservatoire des Arts et Métiers in Paris and the Museum of Economic Geology in London.[5] A brief consideration of these two possible models reveals many parallels with the proposed plan for the Institute in 1861. The more influential was undoubtedly the London example, for immediately after agreeing to accept the chairmanship of a committee to form a plan for a "Technological department," Rogers had sought the help of his brother Henry in obtaining information about several British institutions.

Because of his own professional interests in the field of geology, Henry Rogers had good reason to be familiar with the activities of the London institution known first as the Museum of Economic Geology and soon thereafter as the Museum of Practical Geology, then under the direction of Sir Roderick I. Murchison.[6] Henry had been a foreign member of the Geological Society of London since 1844, had been in Britain on several occasions, most recently in 1857, and had attended meetings of the British Association for the Advancement of Science. He had also been in touch recently with Darwin and others in relation to the controversy on evolution.

But beyond these professional ties there was an earlier link and a more personal association. During his 1832–33 sojourn in Britain, Henry had developed valuable contacts with British scientists then making significant contributions in the fields of chemistry and geology. One of these was Henry T. de la Beche (later Sir Henry), who became the first head of the museum, established in 1835 as a direct result of his geological survey of Great Britain. It was de la Beche who suggested that the collection be formed to illustrate "the applications of geology to the useful purposes of life," emphasizing that it should be "arranged with every reference to instruction." Geological specimens collected as the work progressed provided the nucleus of the ever-growing collection, further augmented by gifts from private sources, including models of mines and mining machinery. A laboratory was added "to promote a knowledge of the properties of soils, as well as to effect an examination of the various ores of metals, and of other mineral products of importance to the possessor of mineral property, the miner, the engineer, the architect, and of those interested in arts and manufactures generally."[7]

In 1839 a curator, who was also a chemist, was appointed, and in 1840 an Office of Mining Records was added. It appears that the laboratory accepted a small number of pupils in metallurgy and analytical chemistry. Public lectures in these fields plus mining and mineralogy and agricultural chemistry were also authorized by the government, but their inauguration was held in abeyance for lack of adequate facilities, which finally became available in 1851 with the completion of a new building on Jermyn Street.[8] The new building provided also the opportunity to establish, in association with the museum, a School of Mines, patterned after those already existing on the Continent. In 1838 private sources in Cornwall had opened a mining school on a small scale, but the effort was discontinued when local government support for a more ambitious undertaking was not forthcoming.[9] Now, however, British mining interests were pressing for adequate instruction related to mining.

His Royal Highness, the Prince Consort, presided at the opening of the new building in May 1851, the same month in which the Crystal Palace Exhibition in London was opened. On this occasion de la Beche referred briefly to the new venture, which expected to "receive pupils by regular courses of study,—to teach by means of lectures,—experimental researches in the laboratory,—and also by the aid of the Geological Survey in the field." The collections of the museum were also to be "gratuitously open to public view." Of their practical value de la Beche said:

they are alike scientific and practical. We feel that in this we are not likely to have erred in the opinion of those who believe, as we do, that the greater the amount of science, the greater will be the amount of its application. In addressing your Royal Highness on this subject, we know that we are addressing a Prince who feels a deep interest in it, and who justly appreciates its general bearing.[10]

In his response Prince Albert spoke directly to the point:

I rejoice in the proof thus afforded of the general and still increasing interest taken in scientific pursuits; while science herself, by the subdivision into the various and distinct fields of her study, aims daily more and more at the attainment of useful and practical results. In this view it is impossible to estimate too highly the advantages to be derived from an institution like this, intended to direct the researches of science and to apply their results to the development of the immense mineral riches granted by the bounty of Providence to our isles and their numerous colonial dependencies.[11]

When the proposed School of Mines and of Science Applied to the Arts, as it was called, opened in November 1851, de la Beche stressed that it would "not interfere with existing institutions" and explained its goals:

We propose to instruct by means of our collections, our laboratories, our mining record office, our lectures, and the Geological Survey;—thus teaching as well in the field as in this building, and so that the pupils can become practically acquainted with mining in our various mineral districts, be able to study geology, and those of its applications requiring it, on the ground itself, and so unite, in a manner not hitherto attempted, and yet in one for which our opportunities amply provide, a sound combination of science and practice; a combination also kept steadily in view in our laboratories, and in all branches of the instruction upon which it is now purposed to enter.[12]

He spoke also of the collections:

They are not intended to be mere assemblages of specimens, striking either for their brilliancy, colour, or form. In whatever department they may be found they are intended to be instructive with reference to the especial object proposed in that department, and to be employed in illustration of the teaching by lectures or other means adopted by those in charge of the different departments confided to them. The collections are arranged for this purpose, and so, also, that the general public, who have free admission to them during the first three days of the week, may readily understand them, by means of succinct treatises on each subject, to be had separately, and at small cost.[13]

He stressed the "usefulness and importance" of the laboratories for general chemistry and metallurgy, their relation to the School of Mines and of Science Applied to the Arts, and their contributions to public service.[14] And he announced plans for evening lectures for the benefit of the working man "to aid him and consequently the public for whom he labours."[15]

Pointing out the interdependence of the several branches of knowledge, de la Beche used geology as one example:

Geology is, nevertheless, one among them, requiring such direct aid from several sciences, as to stand out somewhat prominently, as is shown by the division of labour which has, of late, so much occupied the attention of its cultivators. Thus we have seen it requiring, and obtaining, the assistance of the mathematician, the astronomer, the physicist, the mechanician, the chemist, the mineralogist, the zoologist, and the botanist.

In applying such a branch of knowledge, it therefore, becomes important to view it as of a mixed kind requiring a corresponding system of instruction. … Hence the instruction proposed to be carried out at this institution is divided into various heads, so as to have reference not only to the miner and manufacturer, but also to the agriculturist, the architect, and the engineer, and so that the subjects taught should also be viewed in connexion with those arts to which they may be applicable.[16]

The professorships in the school covered chemistry, applied to the arts and agriculture; natural history, applied to geology and the arts; mechanical science as applied to mining; metallurgy and its special applications; geology and its practical applications; and mining and mineralogy. There were two classes of students: those taking a course of two years' duration, for which registration was small, and those—a greater number—who wished to attend on a part-time basis for selected lectures or subjects.[17]

The further development of the museum and the school is an extremely complicated story. By the time Rogers began to look closely at the organization, the Royal

College of Chemistry, founded in 1845 and conducted under private auspices, had been added (in 1853), and in 1857 the name of the school was changed to Government School of Mines. With later additions, it formed the basis in 1907 of a newly chartered Imperial College of Science and Technology.[18]

Echoes of de la Beche and the Museum of Practical Geology are discernible in the plans emerging for the Institute of Technology. Indeed, the final paragraph of his inaugural discourse in 1851 might well have formed the peroration of the *Objects and Plan*:

> Those whose duties or inclinations take them among our industrial population can scarcely fail to observe how much the term *practical* is becoming appreciated in its true sense. . . . It is the duty of all to assist in affording to those whose minds are alive to every application of knowledge the power to acquire that which they are desirous of applying, so that they may possess the means of analysing their practice successfully for general progress and the public good. The more real knowledge is diffused, the more will effective practice be increased. Science and practice are not antagonistic, they are mutual aids. The one advances with the other. Civilization advances science, viewed in all its strictness and height; and science, by its applications, advances civilization. Steadily bearing in mind these truths,—as we conceive them to be,—it will be our earnest endeavour at this institution to be useful, as far as our powers and abilities may permit, in promoting the progress of those for whom our teaching has especial reference; trusting, at the same time, to supply a national want, and, by so doing, assist in advancing the general good of our country.[19]

Rogers could not have been unaware of an 1854 article in the *American Journal of Science and Arts* by geologist Edward Forbes of the museum's school, which by then had been renamed the Metropolitan School of Science applied to Mining and the Arts. Entitled "On the Educational Uses of Museums," it was Forbes's Introductory Lecture, opening the courses for the year 1853. He began with a description of the school as "the only instance in Britain of an organized instructional institution arising out of a Museum, and being maintained in strict connection and relation with its origin." He stressed that "museums, of themselves alone, are powerless to educate. But they can instruct the educated, and excite a desire for knowledge in the ignorant." The lectures for the working men had been very successful—"they have crowded to our theatre and attended our courses with unmistakable earnestness and intelligence." The regular students who had entered in 1851 had satisfactorily completed their courses, and the entering class was larger than those of previous years. "Considering," he said, "how difficult it is in our country for any establishment on a new plan to make way, this evidence of progress may be taken as a fair subject for congratulation."[20]

Over the years the evening lectures attracted as many as six hundred, but up to 1859 the largest number of students completing the two-year course was eighteen.[21] If these statistics were available to Rogers, it is not surprising that he would estimate in the early days that the larger number of students at the Institute would be those enrolling only for part-time study.

About 1648 Descartes proposed the establishment of technical museums and schools in Paris, later cited as "one of the first definite proposals for what about a century and a half later became the *Conservatoire des arts et métiers* and the first *écoles des arts et métiers* in France."[22] Described as "the 'Solomon's House' of Francis Bacon and Descartes's museum of machines come true," the Conservatoire "combined a vast series of exhibitions of applied science with a great scientific and technical library, a group of distinguished teachers of science, and a number of laboratories for tests and research."[23]

Private collections and government accumulations of models and machinery formed the basis of the Conservatoire, founded in 1794, with the various collections brought together by 1799 in the buildings of the Priory of Saint-Martin-des-Champs, which the government had taken over. As early as 1796 a course of lectures in drawing applied to the industrial arts was offered, soon to be followed by the organization of a weaving school and regular elementary courses in geometry and statistics as well as drawing. The enrollment reached three hundred by 1810.[24] Beginning in 1819 public lectures in engineering were offered, and before 1850 General Morin, one of the professors, established "what seems certainly to have been the first teaching laboratory of engineering." Rogers made specific reference to Morin in the memorial he prepared in 1860 for presentation to the legislature by the petitioning committee chaired by Marshall Wilder.[25]

Despite a statement that "it would be premature at present to frame any very definite plan,"[26] Rogers did lay out in some detail in the *Objects and Plan* the museum's goals and objectives. Looked upon as an important vehicle of education, it was stressed as such in public statements and testimony before the legislature. Its emphasis would be on the practical:

Its several departments, therefore, should aim, in the first place, at forming a collection of objects of prominent importance, as illustrating the respective Arts, however common and familiar they might be; and at so arranging them as to exhibit their history as natural products, or devices of Art, their distinctive characters, and the successive changes wrought upon them by the application of science, or mechanical skill.[27]

Rogers emphasized further that in every part of the museum "the multitudinous gathering of materials" should not overshadow the "great purpose of *instruction*":

A mere miscellaneous collection of objects, however vast, has little power to instruct, or even to incite to inquiry. The practical teaching and the real suggestiveness of a Museum is almost wholly dependent on the clear and rational arrangement of its parts, and the leading ideas which rule in their classification.[28]

Whatever the final organization might be, there would be need for a paid curator for each of the five likely divisions, described at some length:

MINERAL MATERIALS, with the processes and products appertaining to them.

ORGANIC MATERIALS . . . the various crude products . . . in fact, the *whole history of each leading object, from its origin to its appropriation by the more advanced industrial processes.*

MANUFACTURING ARTS, the vast variety of fabrics and products . . . from foreign countries as well as from the manufactories at home.

IMPLEMENTS AND MACHINERY—the tools of the workers in woods, metals, stones, and other resisting materials; agricultural implements; weighing, measuring, and lifting apparatus; musical instruments; apparatus for philosophical experiments . . . different kinds of clock and watch work, and . . . endless forms of machinery employed in . . . applications of mechanical energy to industrial uses.

DOMESTIC AND GENERAL ARCHITECTURE, SHIP-BUILDING, INLAND TRANSPORT, and the various subjects of heating, illumination, water-supply, and ventilation . . . models and drawings of buildings . . . sailing and steam vessels . . . marine engines and propellers . . . locomotives, cars, and other vehicles . . . railway arrangements and electric telegraphs . . . the diversified mechanical and chemical contrivances employed in the supply and distribution of heat and light, water and air.[29]

There would be complex machinery "in actual *working operation*" and an "occasional *exhibition of new inventions*. . . . Rich sources of general and professional instruction" would abound, and great advancements would result through "large opportunities for comparison, and precious helps and incentives to improvement." There would also be a section on household economy: "Benefits of no small social importance might be anticipated from an ample illustration of the arrangements and inventions adapted to the economy of the household, and especially to the promotion of cleanliness, comfort, and health, in the workshops and in the homes of the poor."[30]

It is clear, even from the highly abbreviated statements above, that this was to be a very ambitious undertaking. But no thought had yet been given to fundamental questions that must be solved if the enterprise were to succeed. How and at what cost was this vast amount of material and machinery to be collected, housed, maintained, and kept current? Even more important at this juncture, how adequately did the organizational concept of the Institute, with the museum as its "central feature," respond to the rising need and demand for technical education? In London the Museum of Practical Geology and its school were already suffering a period of strain through an effort to broaden their mission by including the general field of science, a move strongly supported by Thomas H. Huxley, one of its distinguished professors.[31] Scientific and technical advances would have their own major impact on the way in which information would be transmitted to the general public, as well as on the design of formal instruction for those wishing to pursue technical fields professionally or for working people seeking specific instruction in the hope of improving their station in life.

Shortly after the Institute's plan was made public late in 1860, John Runkle included a notice in his *Mathematical Monthly*. He deemed the plan "well matured and eminently practical," but dared to ask, "Still, admitting all that its most enthusiastic friends claim for it, can the idea be carried into execution?"[32] He was optimistic, however, and believed it could be carried out, with "wise counsellors, and unyielding friends," already present on the committee, and "the most ample means," which they seemed certain would "not be wanting. . . . It only remains to be seen whether our State will add this last and crowning excellence to her unsurpassed educational system by granting the desired location, upon which private munificence will rear the Institution."[33] He was referring, of course, to the entire plan, but his question had particular relevance to the proposed museum.

Though the final paragraphs of the museum section of the *Objects and Plan* indicated some recognition of the magnitude of the task and the time it would take for complete fulfillment, Roger's tone conveyed his characteristic confidence:

> In framing its general plan, we have not hesitated to embrace the largest conceptions which the comprehensive nature of its objects and its prospective enlargement could suggest. We know, that, even under the happy auspices which seem to be gathering around our enterprise, the early development of the Museum must fall very far short of the imposing organization which our anticipations have traced; but it is the nature of such a plan to be susceptible of indefinite expansion. If we cannot begin with a long list of Departments and their attached Committees and Curators, we may group our first gatherings of Industrial Science and Art under larger and few subdivisions, and open our Museum with a smaller official staff, sure that its augmenting treasures will soon claim for it an organization far ampler and more complete. . . . We cannot doubt that it would acquire a practical value, even in its earlier stages, far beyond the measure of its extent,—a value as various and general as the interests and occupations illustrated by its collections; and commanding the hearty appreciation, not only of those immediately devoted to industrial pursuits, but of our intelligent fellow-citizens in every walk of life.[34]

In the 1861 hearings before the Committee on Education of the legislature, Rogers emphasized that "our own community, more than any other on the face of the globe, is dependent on a thorough cultivation of intelligence in connection with industry."[35] When he wrote the report of the legislature's Joint Standing Committee on Education recommending favorable action on the petition for the land, he cited the "example of England, France, and other states eminent for their progress in industry and applied science," and he urged "the great value to the public of each of the three departments of the institute." The museum, he said, "will offer a large treasure of knowledge for the instruction of the general public and for the guidance of all who are devoted to practical science and industrial pursuits." He predicted that "large numbers of teachers" would take advantage of the Institute's attractions and through them a "more thorough practical teaching in the common schools" would be achieved. And he further indicated that special lectures would be "arranged for the benefit of persons of this class."[36]

The *Objects and Plan* called for a Standing Committee on the Museum responsible for its "architectural arrangements, furniture, internal plans, and business concerns," for assigning space to the curators, and "advising with these officers in all important business details of their several subdivisions." In addition, the committee would "have general care of all the buildings and grounds of the Institute," and would be expected to act, together with the Committee on the School of Industrial Science, "in matters relating to the planning, furnishing, and allotment of lecture-rooms, and to the application of these or other parts of the building to lectures or other uses not designated in the regular operations of the Institute."[37] But the first bylaws of the Institute did not lay out the committee's duties in detail, simply providing that all members were to be members of the Government and would be responsible, under the direction of the Government as a whole, for the "internal economy, and business-concerns" of what was now entitled the "Museum of Technology."[38]

In reporting on the progress and prospects of the Institute at its meeting on December 17, 1862, Rogers stressed the importance of the Society of Arts and its Committees of Arts as the medium through which collections for the museum "might be greatly facilitated." He also pointed out that the current emphasis on the society in no way signified a lessening of determination with respect to the organization of both the school and the museum, which he termed "the other and more important branches," both requiring "extensive Buildings and arrangements." Though these were not yet available, or even in sight, he seemed confident that a small start could be made:

> It is therefore proposed at an early day, by the help of perhaps additional accommodations in this Building to make a beginning in some branches of the School of Industrial Science, and in the Collection of Objects suitable for the intended Museum.[39]

The "early day," however, would be a while in coming.

As chairman of the Committee on the Museum, Erastus Bigelow was a logical choice, given his wide manufacturing experience, his success as an inventor, and his knowledge not only of European technical developments in his own field, but also of museums abroad which they hoped to emulate and adapt to American conditions. Besides Bigelow as chairman, the committee appointed in 1862 included Richard C. Greenleaf, Ralph Huntington, Frederic W. Lincoln, Jonathan Preston, Alexander H.

Richard Cranch Greenleaf

James Lovell Little

Rice, and Stephen P. Ruggles. Joseph S. Fay and James L. Little were added in 1863.

Preston could be expected to be helpful in connection with the division of domestic and general architecture. Rice was a successful paper manufacturer, and it was essential to maintain the active interest of Ralph Huntington. Joseph Fay, an early member of the Institute, whose interest in the Back Bay plans undoubtedly stemmed from the expected participation of the Horticultural Society, had spent many years in the South as a merchant. Upon his return to Boston, he maintained a large estate at Woods Hole, pursuing his interests in horticulture and forestry, and was looked upon as a leader in the reforestation efforts of the state.[40]

Richard Greenleaf, another early member of the Institute, was a prominent dry goods merchant with the firm of C. F. Hovey and Company. A member also of the Natural History Society, his amateur interests in scientific matters included microscopy and meteorology, and he served the society as vice president.[41] Frederic Lincoln, a great grandson of Paul Revere, was by profession a nautical instrument maker and later general manager of the Boston Storage Warehouse. He had served as president of the Mechanics Library Association and also the Massachusetts Charitable Mechanics' Association, and he held honorary master's degrees from both Harvard and Dartmouth. He had been mayor of Boston from 1859 to 1860 and would serve again from 1863 to 1866. Ironically, he had worked unsuccessfully to preserve the Back Bay as open space, but he did succeed in obtaining federal government assistance for the preservation of Boston Harbor and in setting in motion plans for the improvement of the Public Garden. He was a member of the Committee of Twenty and appointed to the first Government, continuing until his death in 1893. Resolutions at that time cited his extensive committee service and his judgment and experience, a worthy example for future board members to follow.[42]

James Little, another highly successful dry goods merchant, had worked with a succession of companies, for some of which he had been foreign purchasing agent, before establishing a firm of his own, called Little, Alden and Company, later the James L. Little Company. This organization became the chief selling agent for the Pacific Mills in Lawrence, founded in 1853 with Abbott Lawrence as its first president. Little would eventually become treasurer of this firm. He had many philanthropic interests, the Institute of Technology prominent among them. He died in 1889, having given to it "the weight of his character and influence and contributing liberally to its funds." The Corporation resolutions paid special tribute: "It is hardly too much to say that at one period of its history, in a time of great depression, had it not been for the firmness and determination of Mr. Little and his active efforts, the institution could hardly have continued to exist."[43]

Stephen Preston Ruggles

All of these men were well versed in the needs of New England's industrial firms and committed to the educational orientation of the museum. But it was Stephen Ruggles who had a specific idea of the form in which the museum might begin operations. He was born in Windsor, Vermont, in 1808 and as a child demonstrated a distinct aptitude for invention. He was apprenticed to a printer at the age of fifteen. Between 1826 and 1832, in Boston and New York, he had produced a number of inventions for printing and engraving and in 1833 returned to Boston for a position with the Perkins Institution for the Blind, an association resulting in significant contributions to the printing of books and the making of maps for the blind. In 1838 he resigned to devote his energies full time to a variety of inventions, for which he received many awards.[44]

At an early meeting of the Government Erastus Bigelow spoke in support of securing suitable space for the museum as soon as possible, referring particularly to a proposal by Ruggles:

The highly important, and, as he believed, original idea of Mr. Ruggles, of forming a *Collection of Models, illustrating the Elements of Machinery and their simple combinations*; thus presenting as it were, a tangible Encyclopaedia to the student and seeker after practical knowledge, by the use of which he could obtain

1863.

A Meeting of the Committee on Museum of the Institute of Technology was held on Saturday Feby 21st at 7½ o'clock P.M., E. B. Bigelow Esq in the chair, to take into consideration the plan of erecting a seperate building for a Laboratory.

Mr. D. Ross chairman of Finance Committee exhibited drawing for such a building, more in the way of suggestions and to call attention to the subject than as complete plans

Prof W. B. Rogers advocated having a seperate building, particularly on account of light. The original design of having the labratory in the basement of the Institute building not affording, in his opinion, light or room enough. He further remarked that a well lighted, large and commodious building would be required for this department, if the Institute realised the hopes and expectations of its friends and advocates, the only present drawback being the want of funds to carry out the whole plan

Excerpt from Museum Committee minutes, February 21, 1863

a clearer and more definite idea, than by any other means, of those Laws & Principles by the legitimate application, and varied combining of which, so many wonderful results have been, and are yet to be, accomplished.[45]

President Rogers made a further point about the importance of a collection of this kind, describing it as "something more valuable even than an Encyclopaedia of Science, or the Lexicon of a Language, constituting as it actually would the very Alphabet of Mechanics."[46]

By the middle of 1863, following the legislative decision with respect to the land-grant funds, a subtle change in the priorities of the Institute began to appear, with more and more emphasis being placed on the school and, incidentally, the museum's relation to that which would soon replace it as the "central feature" of the Institute. In November M. D. Ross, reporting for a special committee on the need for additional space, indicated that an adjoining room could be secured in the Mercantile Building, "fronting on Summer and Hawley Streets, being well lighted from both, that is, from the South and West, and capable of being properly arranged and suitably fitted for the commencing organization of the Museum of Technology, or Conservatory of Arts."[47]

Members of the Museum Committee may have been consulting with one another informally that fall, but the next formal meeting did not occur until early December, when substantive matters were considered. Bigelow, stressing that the "great central object" of the museum should be "educational," urged that the members give their "undivided attention" to an immediate organization of its "various departments . . . especially those intended to embrace objects fitted to illustrate the course of instruction"; the "exhibitional part" should take a "secondary place." And he proposed that a "suitable person" be engaged to "take charge of the rooms, one who by his position, tastes and education would give a decided character to the work, who could open at once a foreign and home correspondence." He and Ruggles, who had presented some ideas of his own about the museum, were asked to confer with the Finance Committee on how best to "procure the means of carrying forward this great work."[48] Shortly thereafter they made plans to receive contributions "of models and machinery, or whatever might be offered for exhibition or permanent location," and Ruggles was asked to "procure a hot-air engine of sufficient power for driving such machinery as might be offered for the inspection of the public, with the necessary shafts and pulleys," and otherwise to put the museum's space in order.[49]

Bigelow's point about the supporting mission of the museum in relation to the school presaged the disappearance of the original concept from the organizational pattern of the Institute. The concept did not vanish immediately, but once is was decided that primary emphasis should be placed on collections complementary to the instructional program, the character of the museum assumed a more limited scope than envisioned in the early plans. This shift in outlook was emphasized again by Bigelow at a subsequent meeting of the Government, when he urged the importance of a "Collection of Models for Instruction purposes."[50]

The Committee on the Museum appears to have met only once in 1864. In February Bigelow announced that their report, as earlier called for by George Emerson, would soon be expected, covering a plan of operation and the funds needed to purchase the necessary models to be used in connection with the "educational branch of the Museum, which he considered the all important department." He and Ruggles were asked to draw up this report. Ruggles had already obtained a 2HP hot-air engine he had been asked to procure.

Raising funds for the "especial use of the Museum" was considered at this February meeting, with Bigelow commenting on "the great benefit manufacturers would receive from the Institute through its various departments, particularly in chemistry, designing, and machinery. He thought that if this could be presented understandingly to the directors of our manufactories, throughout New England, they would most willingly give material aid." James Little agreed and promised to use his personal influence to raise the subject with the boards of several mills of which he was a director. Though the committee decided that a circular should be drawn up and sent to all the New England manufacturers, along with their report to the Government, there is no evidence that this was done.[51] J. B. Francis and M. D. Ross had corresponded on the same subject in the spring of 1863, but that plan also seems not to have been carried out.[52]

In June 1864 the Committee on Instruction, having finally prepared its report, presented to the Government a tentative plan for the opening of the school. An important recommendation was "the purchase at an early day of an ample Suite of Models of Machines, & Construction, & of their Elements, and other Apparatus essential to the various branches of instruction." This recommendation was made in the belief that it would "have the earnest approval of the Comm. on the Museum, who will regard these Models & Apparatus as an appropriate & philosophical basis for a Museum intended to illustrate the applied Sciences & Arts." Bigelow vigorously supported the recommendation, and the Government authorized up to $1,000 for this purpose.[53]

The secretary's report for 1863–64 summed up the committee's activities:

The Museum Committee, for the want of suitable accommodations and necessary funds, has not, until recently, accomplished much; but the way having now been opened, and there being much energy among its members, we look forward to a brilliant career and highly useful results therefrom during the ensuing year.[54]

In the fall of 1864 Ross informed Rogers that William Walker was much interested in the museum and ready to provide funds for a building under certain circumstances:

The Doctor now proposes to give us $50,000 as soon as we raise a like sum and when that is done he intends to give us more. In fact, what he wants is for us to raise funds enough to establish the several schools of the School of Industrial Science and he will furnish funds to erect the Museum building and he wants that building to be commenced next year. He says that he has great confidence in our ultimate success and has no doubt if we once get the Museum building erected that the public spirit of our citizens is such that means will be freely offered to equip the Museum especially if the School and Society of Arts is in a prosperous condition. I think he is right about it.[55]

There are no recorded minutes for the Committee on the Museum from February 29, 1864, to February 9, 1865, at which time Bigelow stated that their report on "the wants of the Museum, was unnecessary, or was superseded" by the report of the Committee on Instruction.[56] Though Bigelow thought the time had not yet come to pursue contributions for the museum, given lack of proper space for working models, he raised again the question of appointing someone to take charge of what little they had. Stephen Ruggles was unanimously elected curator of the museum, with discretionary power to invite contributions on loan for exhibition or as permanent gifts.

In remarking on the future of the museum, Bigelow emphasized the large amount of money that would be required, citing the "rich endowment" of the Kensington Museum in England; expressed the hope that the "wealthy and liberal" of the community would provide financial support; and stressed the importance of raising funds designated especially for the museum's use. He briefly described their financial situation: "Not one dollar in our treasury that could be devoted to this object."[57] Ruggles cited their immediate needs:

The latest improvements in machinery of all kinds whether for motive power, stationary or locomotive, or for manufacturing purposes. The latest invented and best tools and impliments [*sic*] for all mechanical, mining or agricultural uses and so on through all the educational departments of the Museum, not filling the rooms with old and out of use inventions, but only such as would give the scholar the best idea of the latest and most approved methods of combining forces and helping the hand to perform its work.[58]

And Bigelow presented his view of the museum's ultimate organization:

1st. Educational, requiring suites of models and drawings of all the best machinery, plans for buildings, mining and engineering impliments [*sic*], specimens of minerals and metals.

2nd. Exhibitional. Working Models and new inventions of all kinds for the Society of Arts, open to discussion.

3d. Historical. Articles of curiosity, say old inventions, out of use impliments [*sic*] and articles generaly [*sic*] of past time, of no particular value except as showing the scholar and inventor the great stride that has been taken in all the arts of life.[59]

Though he agreed to remain as a member of the committee, Bigelow declined to serve as chairman for the year 1865–66. M. D. Ross, who became a member of the committee in that year, was elected in his place. Bigelow would resume the chairmanship in 1866. President Rogers, even when not so listed, was understood to be an *ex officio* member of all the standing committees.[60]

The secretary's third annual report on May 25, 1865, stated that the Museum Committee had "been by no means idle, but cannot be so actively engaged as is desirable, until it has the control of suitable apartments and conveniences."[61] The concerns of the Government during this period were increasingly directed to the building on the Back Bay, much behind schedule, to serious financial difficulties, and to the development of the school, the concept of which had undergone considerable change in the three years between the publication of the *Objects and Plan* and the appearance of the *Scope and Plan*.

This shift foretold a change also in the future role of the museum, public perception of which at this time was still rooted in the original conservatory proposal. Some of the early gifts for the museum, most of which were to be held by their donors until suitable arrangements were available for their display, were very much in the mode of William Emerson Baker's 1859 appeal for "relics of historical value, . . . family relics," and "coins, minerals and curiosities of the animal and Vegetable kingdom."[62] Among the early donations were a collection of spears and mechanical impliments from New-

Holland and elsewhere; specimens of material and samples of cloth and of various ores; a pair of shoes representative of those worn by the natives of Calcutta in 1849; and a collection of varieties of steel pen manufacture.

Records of the Committee on the Museum are sparse for the years 1865–68. There were no recorded meetings between June 1865 and October 1866, when two attempts to achieve a quorum failed.[63]

In his annual report of May 1866, Secretary Webb characterized the year, as far as the museum was concerned, as one of little accomplishment for lack of suitable accommodations to "develop the plans long cherished by some of its number,"[64] this phrase implying that the committee membership was not unanimous in its view of the role of the museum in the Institute. Webb himself appears to have been among those not yet ready to abandon the old conservatory idea:

> Once fully carried out, and energetically sustained, as we know, and liberally supported and encouraged as we believe they will be, the third grand division of the Institute, the *Conservatory of Arts*, will be elevated to the position & assume the importance contemplated by the originators of the enterprize, and thus be enabled to furnish some auxiliaries for imparting valuable practical information, and facilitating the diffusion of useful knowledge.
>
> The *Curator's services*, even in this almost ante-embryotic state of the Department, have in various ways proved of material advantage; and with the prospect of a suitable Hall in the new Building we have reason to anticipate, during the approaching year, beholding in the Museum, rich fruits from the labors of himself and coadjutors.[65]

When the Government learned in September 1866 that the scientific library and geological collections and illustrations of the late Henry Darwin Rogers would be presented to the Institute by his widow, the matter was referred to the Museum Committee.[66] Though two meetings, on October 4 and 5, failed to produce the necessary quorum, this was a significant gift requiring immediate attention, and appropriate resolutions for Government action were prepared at once:

> Resolved: that the Massachusetts Institute of Technology hereby expresses its appreciation of the great value of the donation by Mrs. Henry D. Rogers to

its Museum and Library of which it may be considered the foundation gift.

Resolved: that the sincere thanks of the Institute be tendered to Mrs. Rogers for this generous and valuable gift and for her selection of the Institute, in whose plans and success her lamented husband took so deep an interest, as the recipient of his scientific treasures.

Resolved: that with the approbation of the Government the Museum Committee assign a distinct place for this gift, to perpetuate the name and memory of the deceased, whose life long labors in the field of science entitle him to the grateful remembrance of every lover of knowledge.[67]

In 1867 the annual report of Secretary Kneeland, Webb's successor, cited the gift of the Rogers collection and a few miscellaneous items, among them a donation from Dr. William R. Lawrence of a section of oak from the U.S. frigate *Constitution*, given to his father, Amos Lawrence, in 1847 when the vessel was in the dry dock at Charlestown. On the whole, however, there had been "little progress . . . all the energies of the Institute having been directed to the equipment of the School."[68] Kneeland made a direct appeal to the members:

Now that the Institute has a fine building, nearly complete, with ample room, it is hoped that additions of books and specimens, relating to all departments of applied science, models, raw materials, &c., will be given. Almost every one has some book or specimen, which he could well spare, that would add to the educational apparatus of the Institute, and thus do tenfold the good that it would do in his own house.[69]

During 1867–68, the Committee on the Museum held two quorumless meetings for which no records were kept. Finally, on January 17, 1868, with a sufficient number in attendance, they organized for the year, Erastus Bigelow continuing as chairman and Richard Greenleaf as secretary.[70] Stephen Ruggles presented a paper containing an ambitious, costly plan for the organization of the museum in which the collections would be "strictly of an educational character, leaving entirely out of the question any and every thing that is merely of a curious or amusing character." He suggested a better name for the museum, perhaps "Tangible Cyclopedia," and outlined what it should contain. There should be "working models of all the elementary principles of machinery and all simple combinations," important, he said, both for the public and the inventor. He called for a "complete set of philosophical apparatus in perfect working order and made on a large scale." Such a display would be too large for the lecture room, but in the museum it "could be daily seen and operated by the students and the public." He called also for a complete set of astronomical apparatus, "perhaps a grand orrery or a planetarium," and a large globe. "All the productions (natural) of the earth should be shown," he said, "and many of them in an advanced state of manufacture."

Despite questions already raised in the Society of Arts about the wisdom of endorsing products and inventions, Ruggles suggested that models of the "first machinery ever made to produce certain results" be exhibited and that a "medal or diploma" might be awarded "without prejudice to the Institution," not "so much for the machine" but in recognition of "the opening of a new field for inventions." A catalogue of "every thing that has been in operation or suggested up to the present time" should be maintained in the Institute's library and brought to the attention of the public. And he ventured to hope that some individuals might assume responsibility for the support of certain sections of the museum.

In the discussion which followed, Ross quoted William Walker's statement that the "Museum should be a great sifter or winnowing machine, throwing out all superfluous things like chaff." Erastus Bigelow, however, described his "close observations" during a recent trip abroad of "what was being done there in advancing the cause of education in the department of mechanics, particularly where his examinations would bring aid to the work in which the committee were now earnestly engaged." Ruggles proposed that a summary of his plan be circulated to inventors and manufacturers of machinery and apparatus with an appeal for donations of their latest inventions and models, but there is no indication that his suggestion was pursued. There is also no indication of any action on the part of a subcommittee appointed to "take in charge the organization of the Museum in accordance with the plan drawn up by Mr. Ruggles."[71] More than a year would pass before the main committee would meet again.[72]

In May 1868 the secretary's annual report did not mention the Committee on the Museum or the proposed museum itself but did urge those with books or models "of use to the School" to consider making a donation. William Rogers, at the annual meeting of the Institute, also said nothing about the museum, though he spoke at some length about the Society of Arts and especially about the school, with its "enlarged facilities and means of scientific instruction," including apparatus and his brother's geological collections:

> I may allude to the very valuable collection of apparatus relating to sound and light, and other branches of experimental Physics, which have been added to our cabinet, and to the various and extensive suite of apparatus lately transferred from the Lowell Institute, which, through the kindness of Mr. John A.

Lowell, we are enabled to make use of in the instruction of our classes. Nor should I omit to add that the large suite of rocks and fossils, together with the maps, diagrams and geological illustrations and the scientific library of my deceased brother Prof. Henry D. Rogers, have been so far arranged as to be available for use, and as you have no doubt seen in the adjoining room, have already been largely employed in our geological teachings.[73]

Evidence was growing that neither the museum as foreseen in the *Objects and Plan* nor Ruggles's museum of the elements of machinery would adequately support the needs of the school. Both were firmly rooted in the conservatory idea. Their basic aims were different, particularly in view of the school's emphasis on laboratory instruction providing a hands-on experience. Above all, there was hardly enough money to furnish and equip the school. A sign of changing priorities had already become evident in the fall of 1867 when the Government voted that a portion of the space set aside for the museum in the new building be assigned instead to the school for the growing collections of apparatus and instruments used by the classes.[74]

Early in 1869, Erastus Bigelow, still committee chairman, would present to the Government a report of the Committee on the Museum, pointing out that no real progress had been made on its original plan or the Ruggles proposal. Lacking any clear direction on whether the committee's mandate included oversight of the needs of the various departments of the school, they had nevertheless ventured to consider the requirements of the school and could report a deficiency in "apparatus and models for instruction." In his plea for an appropriation for a European collection available for purchase which the faculty was anxious to have, Bigelow emphasized that the collection was "designed to aid the professional teacher," whereas that of the Ruggles plan was "intended for the more general use of aiding inventors and constructors in their works of practical construction."[75] Though he did not elaborate, he would in this way identify a conflict for the Institute of Technology, with the school rapidly overtaking the museum as the "central feature" of the organization.

Chapter 18

The School of Industrial Science

T he year 1863 marks a subtle but significant turning point in the history of the Institute. Though discussions continued on how best to develop the institution, the details were not recorded, and there is no evidence of a formal Government decision on the relative emphasis to be placed on the three entities included in the charter. On this point, however, the decision had essentially been made for them, for the development of the school was required by the April 27, 1863, legislative Act which brought land-grant status. In the light of that achievement as well as the Institute's success in rejecting amalgamation with Harvard, it was imperative that the public be assured that every effort would be made to open the school at the earliest opportunity. On June 30 the Government appointed a committee to explore the possibility of obtaining additional space in the Mercantile Building, "to consider the purposes to which it should be applied, estimate the probable expense of fitting and furnishing the same for use and report thereon to the Government as early as practicable."[1]

During this period William Rogers was far from well. Except for a few visits to Boston and a brief trip to Vermont, he spent most of the summer at Lunenburg. Late in September he informed his brother Henry that he had "only partially put on the harness" of his "customary duties" and intended to "keep in mind the importance of working moderately." A "good deal" of "work and care" lay ahead. He was responsible for organizing the programs for the Institute's ordinary meetings and for preparing some course offerings for a "preliminary trial" of the school during the fall.[2] By mid-November, however, he concluded that he could not work:

The protracted, though slight illness, which I suffered before removing to the city, operating on a system a good deal reduced by the cares and anxieties of the past year or two, brought me down to the point at which I have always been liable to much nervous perturbation, and I expect for some time yet to pay the penalty of my forgetfulness of this constitutional peculiarity. I feel that I am slowly recruiting, but I am compelled to abstain from all business or study, and may be under the necessity of a continuance of this abstinence for some month or two longer. You must not be anxious about me, as I am doing well and have only to observe patience and prudence, which I shall certainly do, to reinstate myself.[3]

And he left Boston for a recuperative trip to Philadelphia.

Rogers was not present, therefore, at a Government meeting late in November 1863 when M. D. Ross reported that two halls in the Mercantile Building could be rented for $1,000 a year—one suitable for "Class Instruction—the germ of our School of Industrial Science" and the other for "commencing organization of the Museum of Technology, or Conservatory of Arts." The space would be available for approximately two years, at the end of which the Institute's own building should be ready. An anonymous gentleman had offered to pay the rent. The arrangement was approved.

An estimate that it might cost $5,000 to fit the rooms for use led to another interesting discussion—"to what branches attention should first be directed?—what Schools of Instruction should be established?—how commenced and conducted? &c., &c." This, in turn, led to George Emerson's suggestion that each standing committee prepare a report of its plans and objectives. Emerson proposed further that "some suitably qualified person" be sent abroad to "examine the various Institutions having a greater or less similarity" to the Institute. The reference to "less similar" institutions may have indicated a belief that the present concept of the Institute—particularly the school—must change to meet the requirements of the Land-Grant Act. If Rogers could be persuaded to go, "it would decidedly advance the best interests of the Institute, and also prove the means of reinvigorating his system." Joseph Fay concurred and, confident that a subscription could be raised to pay Rogers's expenses, proposed that they send him off to Europe for the winter. When Secretary Webb cautioned against "hurrying Prof. R. out of the country," not knowing if "it was prudent for him, or he even was desirous of going," M. D. Ross was asked to secure his views.[4]

Writing from Philadelphia, Rogers was pleased that additional rooms were available and grateful for the anonymous "liberal friend who has made this step so easy." He appreciated the Government's concern for his health, their proposed remedy, and their generosity in offering to pay the expenses of a trip abroad. But he did not wish to go at this time and would not accept money at any time: "I have made it a principle from the very incipiency of our enterprise to give all the service in my power to this cause so dear to me as a pure offering of zeal and affection, and I am resolved on no occasion and for no consideration to depart from this purpose." His "medical friends" confirmed his own opinion that a European trip would not be helpful now, but might be "serviceable" in the spring if he was not completely recovered:

> Meanwhile I am steadily, although slowly, recruiting my strength and overcoming the nervous irregularities from which I have been suffering, so that I may look confidently for such a measure of strength during the coming winter as will enable me to share in the business of the Institute, at first only partially, but I trust as the season progresses, nearly to the extent which my interest and zeal would prompt me. . . . It pains me not a little that I am not able at once to open one of the courses of instruction to which I have been looking forward with such pleasant anticipation. But I shall be strong enough for this— I earnestly hope—in the progress of the season.[5]

A further reference to his health appears in a December 20 letter to his father-in-law, James Savage: "I am expecting even more rapid improvement on our return to the comforts of Temple Place, but I cannot flatter myself that I shall be in fair working condition for some months to come."[6] Rogers had already given a friend in England a different reason—the Civil War—for not traveling abroad:

> I cannot think of leaving my country even for a short absence until this great treason has been entirely defeated and subdued. Doubtless in a year or two this consummation, so devoutly prayed for by the friends of human progress, will have been reached; and then, with many a grateful memory and happy anticipation, I and my friends will seek to renew the quiet delights of a visit to the fatherland.[7]

But there was another, unstated reason why he should not go. The Committee on Instruction had not yet prepared a report on the school, which had arrived at this juncture with no definite plan. Problems of organization, courses to be offered, and faculty and equipment requirements had not yet been addressed.

Governor Andrew's annual message in January 1863, based on information supplied by Rogers, had indicated that the Institute, though still without its guarantee fund and planning to ask for a reasonable extension of time, was preparing to make a beginning in some branches of the School of Industrial Science. Earlier in the same address, however, the governor had reported on the Congressional Land-Grant Act and set forth the proposal, in words supplied to him by President Hill and Professor Agassiz of Harvard, for the creation of a great university at Harvard that would include the "means and instrumentalities" of the Institute of Technology. In January 1864 Andrew said again that the Institute was preparing to begin courses of practical instruction and the organization of its industrial museum.[8] There was still no plan for the school, however, and it would be another full year before a preliminary session could be opened.

Edward Parsons Atkinson

In 1864 the Committee on Instruction, including William Rogers as chairman, consisted of nine members: Edward Atkinson, James B. Francis, Augustus A. Hayes, John D. Philbrick, Henry Bromfield Rogers, Thomas Sherwin, Nathaniel Thayer, and George W. Tuxbury.

Edward Atkinson would become one of the most influential members of the Institute's Government, serving until his resignation in 1890. Born in Brookline in 1827 and apprenticed to a Boston commission house at the age of fifteen, he rose to become treasurer of several cotton mills and an acknowledged expert in the financial aspects of cotton textile manufacturing. In 1878 he became president of the Boston Manufacturers Mutual Fire Insurance Company, founded in 1850, the first such company in Massachusetts. A man of many interests, he has been credited with "an innate predilection toward engineering science" and an "unqualified admiration of the professional engineer."[9] He has been described also as "a diligent statistician, gifted public speaker, economist, financier, and industrious and prolific writer."[10] He was in addition deeply interested in dietetics and developed the Aladdin Oven, designed for slow, temperature-controlled cooking with low fuel costs.

Atkinson gave credit to his fellow member, James Francis, chief engineer of the Locks and Canals Company of Lowell, for developing the "most complete system of protecting a great range of hazardous factories from loss by fire." Francis, born in England in 1815, had at the age of fourteen assisted the engineer on a harbor project in South Wales. After emigrating to America in 1833, he worked under William Gibbs McNeill and George W. Whistler on the New York, Providence, and Boston Railroad. A year later he accompanied Whistler to Lowell, where he would remain for the rest of his life. In the beginning he was concerned with locomotive design for the Proprietors of Locks and Canals, and in 1837 he succeeded Whistler as chief engineer. By the mid-1840s the company had turned its attention from locomotives to water power, with Francis as their agent and engineer, responsible for the construction of canals and guard dams. A large gate installed in 1850, initially viewed by some as Francis's folly, saved the city two years later from the highest freshet ever experienced above the dam on the Merrimack River. To the Committee on Instruction he brought experience as the foremost hydraulic engineer of his day, with a clear understanding of the need for sound training in mathematics and applied mechanics, a lack he had early remedied for himself through concentrated study on his own. Francis was widely sought as a consultant and received honorary master of arts degrees from both Harvard and Dartmouth. He was a strong and loyal supporter of the Institute until his death in 1892.[11]

Augustus Hayes, whom Rogers had recommended to Governor Andrew as an alternative choice for gas inspector in 1861, was an early member of the Institute and was appointed to the committee in 1862. A native of Vermont and a graduate of Norwich Academy, he had also studied chemistry with Professor James F. Dana at Dartmouth, from which he would later, in 1846, receive an honorary M.D. degree. He taught briefly at New Hampshire Medical College before moving to Boston in 1828. There he became a consulting industrial chemist, recognized both in the United States and abroad, and served for a time as state assayer of Massachusetts. Though his service on the committee, and hence the Government, ended in 1865, he continued to be a member of the Institute.[12]

John Philbrick, superintendent of the Boston Schools, had graduated from Dartmouth in 1842 and, as a teacher in Boston, he began a long career in the field of education. In 1848 he organized the city's first grammar

John Dudley Philbrick

Henry Bromfield Rogers

school, the Quincy School. Four years later he was called to Connecticut to organize a state normal school, of which he became principal, and was soon given additional responsibilities as superintendent of the common schools. He returned to Boston in 1857 as superintendent, charged with the reorganization of the city's school system. A member of the State Board of Education for ten years and active in educational circles at the national level, he was an early Institute supporter, serving as a Government member until his death in 1886.[13]

Henry Bromfield Rogers, sometimes erroneously identified as William's brother, was an 1822 graduate of Harvard and a wealthy lawyer. When he died in the spring of 1887, he was one of the few remaining members of the first Government. A resolution at that time expressed special gratitude for his "constant" contributions to the Institute's treasury and revealed that he was the "unknown donor" of a substantial fund at a critical moment: "In the early days of difficulty and danger he contributed perhaps more than any other, by his wise counsel and large pecuniary contributions, to uphold the hands of our first President in his difficult task, and through all the subsequent years, whether of success or of discouragement, he has never wavered in his belief in the usefulness of the Institute, or in his best efforts to make it a success."[14] The resolution cited also, among many other philanthropic interests, his work for the National Sanitary Commission during the Civil War, his nearly half-century of service as a trustee of the Massachusetts General Hospital, for many of those years either as president or chairman, and his generosity to the Museum of Fine Arts, on whose board he served as a representative of the Institute.

Thomas Sherwin, the headmaster of Boston English High School, brought a varied background of experience to this committee. Born in 1799, he was twenty-two when he entered Harvard College, having served an apprenticeship with a clothier and taught in a district school. Following graduation in 1825 he taught at Lexington Academy for a year before returning to Harvard as a tutor in mathematics. He briefly considered taking up the law and then in 1827 turned to engineering, working for Loammi Baldwin in Charlestown and with James Hayward on an early survey for the Boston and Providence Railroad. But he soon returned to teaching and in 1829 was appointed submaster of English High. In 1837 he became the third headmaster, the first having been George Emerson. Sherwin was active in educational circles and is credit-

Thomas Sherwin

ed with enhancing the reputation of the school, which became a model for others. When he died suddenly in 1869, a Government resolution expressed appreciation for his help in the founding and organization of the Institute and his "faithful and judicious performance" as a member of the Committee on Instruction. The Institute had lost a "thorough" and "liberal-minded educator," an "accomplished scholar," and an eminent "guide and instructor of youth." A memorial scholarship fund was established at the Institute in 1871 for graduates of English High School.[15]

Nathaniel Thayer was a highly successful financier and the senior member of the firm of John E. Thayer & Brother, concerned primarily with the capital development of large manufacturing companies and railroads and the predecessor firm of Kidder, Peabody and Company. He gave generously throughout his lifetime to charitable and philanthropic causes, and was a large benefactor of Harvard. A special patron of Louis Agassiz and a trustee of the Museum of Comparative Zoology, he contributed to a fund for the purchase of Agassiz's collection for the museum and financed his 1865–66 Brazilian exploring expedition, often referred to as the Thayer Expedition. He would be an overseer of Harvard from 1866 to 1868 and a fellow of the Harvard Corporation from 1868 to 1875, in the latter capacity said to have been "the dominant factor in the financial management of the College." He became a member of the Institute's Government in 1863 and served until his death in 1883. In 1869–70 he was one of the four vice presidents. A resolution in 1883 cited his "repeated and large donations to the Institute" and praised his "practical wisdom," "clear, cool judgment," and his integrity. Thayer was well aware of the need for superior technical education if the nation were to develop its resources and prosper economically. His fortune had been accumulated largely in a business directly related to developments in transportation and manufacturing enterprises, all heavily dependent on technical and scientific progress. And as the son-in-law of

Nathaniel Thayer

George William Tuxbury

Stephen Van Rensselaer, founder of the Rensselaer Polytechnic Institute, he certainly knew much about that institution in Troy and was perhaps anxious to see a similar effort succeed in Boston.[16]

The final member was George Tuxbury, a lawyer who handled the affairs of Ralph Huntington, and a member of the Boston School Committee. A graduate of Phillips Exeter Academy and Dartmouth College, he had taught briefly at Ipswich Academy before turning to the law. After passing the Suffolk Bar in 1848, he served as counsel to several corporations and was active also in the administration of estates. He had been a member of the Boston Common Council in 1857 and 1858, having previously served on the School Committee from 1855 to 1857. He returned to the School Committee in 1860, serving until 1865.[17]

Despite the lack of a formal Government decision on how the organization should proceed, the response to George Emerson's call for substantive reports from the standing committees indicates that priorities were changing. The Museum Committee decided that its collections should support the Institute's instructional program, and the Committee on Publication, which presented a careful, detailed report, felt that its plans should be set aside until decisions could be reached about the school.[18]

Rogers was unable to address himself seriously to the task until early 1864. His goal was to give concrete expression to what he had earlier identified in a letter to Dr. William Walker as the "cardinal ideas of our proposed School of Industrial Science": "To teach *exactly & thoroughly* the fundamental principles of positive science with their leading applications to the industrial arts & to make this teaching as widely available as possible."[19] In mid-January, with his health improving, he had been able to give his "attention" to the meetings of the Institute, which he found "quite pleasant," and also to those of the American Academy of Arts and Sciences. He informed his brother Henry that he had received catalogues, pamphlets, and other material from the Kensington Museum and the School of Mines in London.

The kind of institution to which Rogers still looked as models is important. Though he intended to avoid "all serious study and all matters of care," he revealed to his brother Henry that plans for the school were under way with the help of John Runkle and William Watson, a University Lecturer at Harvard and a recently elected member of the Institute:

> With the aid of Professor Runkle and Dr. Watson, a graduate of the Ponts et Chaussées, I am framing a course of applied mathematics for our Institute, reaching from the very elements up to the fullest demands of the scientific engineer. The same thing I shall do in applied physics, chemistry, etc., so as to present—
>
> First. A general course for the benefit of those who have no disposition or opportunity for college studies, including mechanics, merchants, etc.
>
> Second. Special Courses, consisting of extensions of the former in the direction of Civil Engineering, Mechanical Engineering, Mining Engineering, Manufacturing, Chemistry, etc. Tell me what you think of so extensive a plan.[20]

Rogers's reference to "so extensive a plan" may be an early sign that a change in the concept of the school was under consideration. Since the formal record of the Committee on Instruction does not begin until October 29, 1866, a year after the regular sessions of the school were inaugurated, it appears that the committee members were not active participants in the earliest stages of the planning.[21]

This is the point at which John Runkle began to assume a major role in planning for the school. With Rogers's apparent decision to focus first on the "School of Mathematics" as included in the *Objects and Plan*, it was natural that he should turn to Runkle for assistance. And the involvement of William Watson, whose Harvard appointment covered the academic year 1863–64,[22] very likely came through Runkle.

Born in Nantucket on January 19, 1834, Watson was graduated from the Lawrence Scientific School with the degree of bachelor of science, *summa cum laude*, in 1857 and a second bachelor's degree in 1858, also *summa cum laude*, on the basis of continued work in mathematics, a subject in which he served as tutor. In 1859 he went to Europe for advanced study at the Friedrich-Schiller-Universität at Jena, from which he received his doctor of philosophy degree in 1862. He then enrolled for courses at the École des Ponts et Chaussées.[23] While abroad he made a study of technical education in other institutions as well, reporting on them for Runkle's *Mathematical Monthly*. His articles on L'École Polytechnique and L'École des Ponts et Chaussées appeared in 1861.

William Watson

These papers were read before the Society of Arts late in December 1863 and January 1864, respectively. Their presentation at that time may have been more than coincidental. The minutes indicate that similar talks were planned for future programs, but one by Watson on "The Technical University at Zurich" was not presented until 1870.[24]

Two biographical notices of Watson—one by Charles R. Cross of the class of 1870, and the other by Tenney L. Davis of the class of 1913, both long-time members of the faculty—refer to his participation in the planning of the Institute's school:

He made an extended examination of European technical schools his knowledge of which proved highly serviceable in connection with the laying out of the engineering courses in the Massachusetts Institute of Technology then in process of organization.[25]

While he was in Europe, during the years 1860 to 1863, he collected information on technical instruction which in 1864 was used as a basis in planning the organization of the Massachusetts Institute of Technology.[26]

A more precise allusion was made in 1902 by Harry W. Tyler of the class of 1884, professor of mathematics and secretary of the faculty: "Prof. Watson . . . stated that he believed his own experience in Paris at the École Centrale and the École des Ponts et Chaussées had an important bearing on the change of Prof. Roger's [*sic*] plans from the rather popular character represented by the Objects and Plans [*sic*], to the more advanced work embodied in the Scope and Plan as subsequently carried out."[27]

Whatever advice Runkle and Watson were providing was offered against the background of the recent curricular debates at the Lawrence Scientific School, with which Rogers, as a member of its visiting committee, was familiar. And Watson's firsthand experience with institutions abroad was useful. But the terms of the Morrill Act of 1862, intended to support a higher level of education than would be possible through satellite "schools" attached to a museum, must have been the most influential factor in the developing plans. And Governor Andrew's annual message of 1864 contained perhaps an additional incentive for a major departure from the outline presented in 1860.

In a section entitled "Military Academy," he discussed a report of a commission created by the legislature in 1863 to "inquire into the expediency of establishing an academy for the instruction of young men in mathematics, civil, military, and practical engineering, and other studies in connection with infantry, artillery and cavalry drill and tactics, and to report a design for such an institution." The commission had been asked also to present a complete plan for the organization of this military academy and to investigate "whether the Commonwealth has any, and what, property available" for its endowment.

Edward Everett was chairman of this commission, which had visited West Point and the Naval Academy at Newport and had looked into the military schools of France and England. The commission's extensive report of January 5, 1864, recommended that a first-class institution be established and that it be supported by the state's School Fund. It presented a complete plan covering buildings, governance and organization, courses of instruction and professorships, admissions requirements, and regulations. In addition to military tactics, the curriculum would include military and civil engineering, natural and experimental philosophy, mathematics, ethics and English studies, chemistry, mineralogy and geology, as well as drawing and French. Governor Andrew was strongly in favor, believing its establishment to be "wise and expedient . . . we cannot safely neglect it . . . we ought not to delay it." He felt it would not only elevate the "public schools, but also the scientific professions—the higher industrial pursuits," and he looked forward to the "education of numbers of young men . . . in those branches of learning which fit them for mechanicians, engineers, experts in chemistry, physics, and various applications of science to the arts."[28]

In January 1865 Governor Andrew asked the legislature to consider the establishment of a military academy, as well as the inclusion of elementary military instruction in the public schools, but he did not mention the subject in his special message or his valedictory address in January 1866, when he was succeeded by Alexander H. Bullock. The end of Andrew's term as governor also brought to a close his ex-officio membership on the Institute's Government, but he had been elected to the Committee on Instruction at the annual meeting in May 1865, and would continue on that committee, thus becoming a regular member of the Government, until he died in October 1867.[29]

On February 10, 1864, Rogers informed the Government that "several members of the Committee . . . had been busily occupied with the duties incumbent upon them, but their labors had not yet assumed that definite shape prerequisite to the rendering of a satisfactory Report."[30] This is the point at which the committee members made a concerted effort, undoubtedly because of the Institute's shift in focus.

On February 27 Rogers presented a brief outline and assured the Government that a document would soon be ready: "The subject being a very comprehensive one, embracing a large field of operation, and also a very important one as regards the reputation of the Institute and the best interests of the community, requires careful consideration, and deliberate action both on the part of the Committee, and of the Government."[31] On March 17 he said essentially the same thing, referring to the plan, still under consideration, as a "more comprehensive one, than might at first thought appear." He hoped that "the Institute might be able to procure a complete set of Models, and Implements for Instruction, so as to commence the contemplated Schools, next Fall, well equipped." He understood that the Committee on the Museum had "abstained from reporting, in order to cooperate with the Committee on Instruction."[32]

Finally, on May 30, 1864, a special meeting of the Government was called to hear the committee's report. It was formally adopted with a request for an indication as soon as practicable on the extent to which it might be implemented in the coming fall. The plan was presented to the Institute at its annual meeting on the same evening.[33] When published, it would be called the *Scope and Plan of the School of Industrial Science of the Massachusetts Institute of Technology*. As Rogers had said, it was a "very comprehensive plan . . . embracing a large field of operation." Its scope, indeed, was much wider than that projected in the *Objects and Plan*.

This report of the Committee on Instruction opened with a brief statement of the aims of the proposed school:

> It is the design of this School to afford to the public at large opportunities of instruction in the leading principles of science, as applied to the arts; and, at the same time, to provide for systematic students of the applied sciences the means of a continuous and thorough training in the studies and practice appertaining to these subjects.[34]

It called for two divisions: the "First Department, the General or Popular Course," and the Second Department, for "Special and Professional Instruction."

The "General or Popular Course" would consist principally of five series in a "Programme of General Lectures" related to mathematics, physics and mechanics, chemistry and its applications, geology and mining, and botany and zoology.[35] No examinations would be required for admission, which was open to both men and women seeking "such useful knowledge as they can acquire without methodical study and in hours not occupied by business." Prospective students were expected to include primarily "persons engaged in mechanical, manufacturing, and mercantile pursuits," as well as "teachers and students in the Normal and other schools," and "others whose taste and leisure lead them to avail themselves of such instruction."[36] A "fully equipped Drawing-school" would offer "systematic exercises in elementary and free-hand drawing" and instruction in "artistic design and modelling, as applied to manufactures, architecture, and decoration." This instruction would be free through an expected connection with the Lowell Institute Drawing-school, the first reference to such a possibility.[37] Finally, the Committee on Instruction hoped to provide special courses covering the "more extended and technical treatment of branches of industrial knowledge," such as textile and paper manufacture and printing and engraving. And "perhaps, at an early day," these offerings might develop into a "distinct and extended course, under the head of Special Technology." Here the specimens and models from the proposed industrial museum "would find their most useful medium of interpretation."[38]

This portion of the report could not have been difficult to prepare, for it stemmed directly from the *Objects and Plan*. But the Second Department, encompassing Special and Professional Instruction—in essence the necessary response to designation as a land-grant institution—required greater time and thought.

Here there would be two classes of students—those seeking a full course of scientific studies to fit them for the professions of mechanical, civil, or mining engineering, building and architecture, or practical chemistry; and those interested in training only in "one or more branches of applied science: . . . descriptive geometry applied to construction, perspective, &c; chemical analysis; machinery and motive powers; general physics and chemistry, with manipulations; geology and mining; navigation and nautical astronomy; metallurgy of iron, copper, &c."[39]

Five professional four-year courses were included in the full curriculum, described in some detail:

1. Mechanical Construction and Engineering
2. Civil and Topographical Engineering
3. Building and Architecture
4. Practical and Technical Chemistry
5. Practical Geology and Mining

Regular students would follow a common set of studies for the first two years, with some differentiation in the third, and "more complete separation" in the fourth. Military tactics would be mandatory for all regular students.[40] Those applying for the first year must be at least sixteen years old and by "examination or otherwise" show evidence of preparation in elementary mathematics and "other subjects taught in the common schools." Special students would be allowed to enroll for subjects beyond the first year with satisfactory evidence of adequate preparation.[41]

"Methods and Apparatus of Instruction" were discussed in some detail: lectures and expositions rather than the traditional method of textbook recitations; regular oral and written examinations; practice in physical and chemical manipulations; laboratory training; drawing and construction of plans; practical exercises in surveying; and "visits and excursions" to shops, mills, chemical works, engineering constructions, and buildings "as a means of initiating students into the actual details of the professions for which they are preparing."[42] Great importance was attached to the four laboratories projected: Physics and Mechanics; General Chemical Analysis and Manipulation; Metallurgy and Mining; and Industrial Chemistry. And the plan looked beyond the central role they would play in the regular courses to service to the Committees of Arts and possible "original researches":

> While intended primarily for the instruction of the students, these laboratories will be used for the prosecution of experiments and investigations on subjects referred to them by the Committee of the Museum or the several Committees of Arts, including the examination and testing of new machines and processes, and the conducting of original researches in the different departments of applied science; and in these critical studies and experiments the advanced students may, when expedient, be permitted to assist.[43]

No plan had been devised for the supervision of experiments that might be proposed by the Committees of Arts, only two of which had recently been organized, nor did Rogers appear to recognize at this time that dissemination of the results of such investigations could be in direct conflict with his determined stance that the Institute must maintain its neutrality. But the possibility of original research and the involvement of advanced students in the process pointed to a direction in which the Institute would go as it developed over the years.

Diplomas and certificates would serve as "a reward to the student for his diligence and attainments," but, equally important, they would represent "an assurance to the public of his knowledge and skill in the particular department of applied science to which it relates."[44] The Institute charter did not, however, include degree-granting powers. In 1861 a school not expected to compete with "established institutions" had no need of them. The *Scope and Plan* appreciably altered the character of the school, but in 1864 Rogers felt that the "First Department, the General or Popular Course," would be the larger of the two proposed divisions. Nevertheless, the proposal did talk of "degrees or diplomas," even mentioning the availability of a bachelor of science for the completion of a general scientific course which could be designed for students desiring to become teachers. For those following the professional courses, the "degree" would be simply that of mechanical engineer, civil and topographical engineer, builder and architect, industrial chemist, and geologist and mining engineer.[45] But not until a class was ready for graduation in 1868 did the Institute seek and receive from the state permission to grant such degrees. Chapter 247 of the Acts of 1868, "An Act in Addition to an Act Incorporating the Massachusetts Institute of Technology," was approved on May 25 of that year.[46]

The Committee on Instruction, asked on May 30, 1864, to report on the proposed organization of the school and when it might feasibly be inaugurated, now had further work to do. Rogers, however, was sailing for Europe on June 8 for the trip he had declined to take in 1863. He expected to be "on the ground to direct matters" by November 1, when he hoped that some courses could be offered. Two letters to his brother Henry in the spring tell something of his health and plans and serve also as a reminder of the Civil War:

> Although I am slowly mending in health I could hardly hope to recover my ability for work even in moderate degree, without the relaxation of such a visit as we have in view. . . . The annoyance of the perverse public sentiment in England and the high rate of exchange at this time would make us postpone the trip, but for the consideration of my health and the desirableness of some inquiries among the Technical Institutions.[47] '

He wanted to determine "(1) the best means of collecting a large suite of models of elements of machinery, of bridges, roofs, arches and other works of civil construction and architecture, to be used as aids in our School of Practical Science, and (2) to examine the recent and best arrangements for working-laboratories and lecture-rooms." He hoped also to take along a "fund for the purchase of mechanical and other models, of which there is a great manufactory at Darmstadt." In the meantime, he said, "I shall have as much as I can do (at half-stroke) to get matters arranged for our departure."[48]

Rogers was at Sunny Hill in Lunenburg on June 5 when he sent a hasty letter to M. D. Ross. The report requested by the Government was not ready, and he could not attend its meeting on the following day. Normally, he said, the Committee on Instruction should have an opportunity to review, amend if they wished, and accept a report before presentation to the Government. Nevertheless, he would outline briefly what he intended to submit for the committee's approval and suggested that in his absence John Philbrick represent them, leaving to the judgment of the Government "whether it be desirable to take immediate action upon it."

Rogers felt that the interests of the Institute would be "materially promoted" by the organization in the fall or early winter of such parts of the school as would be practicable in their rooms in Summer Street and, if necessary, with an occasional use of the building's large lecture hall. He suggested opening evening lectures in experimental and industrial physics, experimental and industrial chemistry, geology and mining, and practical mathematics. And he also thought they should open the regular courses of instruction for the first year, and "if called for," the second year of the professional department, as well as special studies for those years "according to the preparation & wants of the Pupils"—a very ambitious suggestion. In addition, he asked for an appropriation for models and apparatus, confident that the Committee on the Museum would concur in this request.[49]

After discussion, the Government referred his "views and wishes" to the Committee on Instruction with full power and authorization to open "the Popular and the Systematic Professional Courses so far as they may find it practicable or expedient to do so, during the coming Season." And they appropriated £1,000 for the purchase of models, photographic illustrations, and apparatus.[50]

Rogers had promised to send a copy of the *Scope and Plan* to Dr. Walker and suggested that a "good large no." of copies be ordered. He was not sure, however, whether they should be distributed immediately or closer to the opening of the school.[51] The Government authorized publication. An edition of fifteen hundred was printed, the secretary's annual report in 1865 noting that it had been "extensively circulated at home and abroad."[52]

At this time also, despite Rogers's earlier refusal to accept funds to defray his expenses, the Government voted, since his trip "in part at least" would benefit the Institute, to give him £250 "in consideration of the valuable services rendered by Professor Rogers to the Institute, and the continued interest manifested by him in its prosperity."[53] Informed immediately by Webb of the Government actions, Rogers responded before he left on June 8 with gratitude for the appropriation for equipment, but declined the "personal appropriation so kindly & generously offered—[it] would only swerve me from my long cherished purpose."

This argument lasted until after he returned in the fall of 1864. He would reaffirm his stand to M. D. Ross in mid-June, and late in September, when Charles Dalton transmitted a letter of credit for £250 payable in London, it was promptly returned.[54] The matter would be on the agenda for a Government meeting on November 4, when an early October letter to Ross was entered into the record. Vowing "not to speak of it further," Rogers had said in part:

> You will, I know, understand my feelings in doing this, as you know perhaps better than any other my desire to preserve my connexion with the Institute wholly unmixed with pecuniary considerations. I need not say to you that like your own, my devotion to its interests is "a labour of love"; and since my own resources are quite sufficient for my wants, I prefer greatly to continue the good work of organizing our Institute as an earnest volunteer whose example may, perchance, inspire others to give their energies to the noble enterprise.[55]

Finally, citing the president's attitude as "evidence of the deep interest by him taken in the prosperity of the Institute" and his "noble devotion" to its cause, the Government, following the suggestion of Jacob Bigelow, accepted the returned draft as a Rogers donation.[56]

Rogers did not sail for Europe with money in hand for models and apparatus. Early in August Ross informed him that the delay in releasing the funds was caused by the "enormous rise in gold and exchange." With an added burden of a 15 percent tariff imposed by Congress on the import of items in which they were interested, it was evident that they could not purchase as much as they wished at this time.[57] Webb reminded Rogers that the Government's appropriation should not be considered "peremptory" but "discretionary." Both believed that he was in a position to "make selections" for later purchase, Webb particularly pointing out that there was no reason to hurry

> as our Schools are yet in an embryotic state, & no one here has the ability or disposition to impart vitality thereto, months must elapse before any number

of Models will be absolutely required; & before they are, there is some reason for believing that, the Money Market will be in a more healthy state.[58]

Webb reminded him also that Stephen Ruggles of the Museum Committee believed that a "very large proportion" of the models required could "be as well made here as abroad; and so far as the Institute is concerned more cheaply. . . . He evidently desires, so far as practicable, that there should be built up an *American* Institution, & Europeanize only in so far as we cannot, or cannot so well, Americanize."[59]

Given the current situation, Webb believed that they could "well afford to await the result" of giving Ruggles "an opportunity to prove the correctness of his positions, or disabuse himself of the notions which he entertains." Though his immediate concern was American-made models, Ruggles may have "entertained" a broader "notion"—that American institutions should be indigenous to this country, also a firm belief of Charles W. Eliot, who would soon become a member of the Institute's first faculty.[60]

While there was general agreement that purchases should not be made until "fair rates" prevailed, Rogers did request and receive in September £170 for some items he was anxious to procure while in Paris.[61] Throughout the summer Ross had attempted to keep him informed of matters at home, including the war, which, as he said early in August, had "gone badly in many respects." Everyone was "gloomy" about Grant's defeat at Petersburg, "about equal to the Bull Run disaster," but he sensed a "deep seated determination amongst the people now to carry on the war to a successful termination *cost what it may.*" Ross had been engaged "almost constantly" in the recruitment of troops, particularly among European "emigrants coming here for the sole purpose of enlisting in the Federal cause." He had just enlisted 380 Germans, 150 of whom would join the Second Massachusetts Regiment. More were on the way, he said, and he would be "absorbed in this kind of business all summer." Yet he did have news of the Institute and its prospects and was "longing" for a report on Rogers's impressions of the institutions he had visited:

I daily meet with our friends and am constantly seeing and hearing of the growth of encouraging Elements and I have never been so well satisfied as I am at this time that our long cherished hopes will at no distant day be more than realized. The Institute has become a fixture in the minds of our best citizens, its friends are daily multiplying, and its opposers have all disappeared. . . . The Building is progressing very well, the 2d floor is now being laid on, and begins to make quite a show on the Back Bay to the surprise of croakers who in the beginning had no faith in us. Mr. Runkle is in Vermont with his family [and] will not be here again until September. He writes me about the Institute and is anxious to be at work in the autumn. Watson & Ruggles are wide awake.[62]

Both Ross and Webb repeatedly urged Rogers to get enough rest and, if necessary, to prolong the trip in favor of a less hurried schedule. It would be better, Webb said, to return with "health restored and strength renewed" than to risk "mental exhaustion and physical prostration."[63] Ross believed they could not do "very much in the way of class teaching" until the building on Boylston Street was ready. He did hope that "something" might be started during the winter—not too much, however, for "nearly all the hard labor" would inevitably fall on Rogers:

> We cannot afford to wear you out so fast as such hard labour would result in. We are all feeling bright because we hear of your improved health and are unanimous in our feeling that hereafter you must be relieved from much of the mere drudgery of the Institute labour to which you have been subjected heretofore.[64]

Ross continued to keep him informed. By the fall President Lincoln appeared to be the favorite in the forthcoming election, General Grant was "whipping the Rebels," the price of gold was declining, government stocks were "better appreciated," and "things are looking better in this country." Ross reported, too, on the continuing interest and plans of Dr. Walker and was concerned that the sometimes impolitic Dr. Webb had recently been in touch with the latter, though he had not yet done any harm. Walker was ready to provide $50,000 if the Institute could raise an equal amount, and Ross was prepared to see if he could do so. In general, he was *"greatly encouraged."*[65]

Rogers may have been overseas, but he was preoccupied nonetheless with the war and the considerable British sentiment in favor of the South. He was quick to perceive that this was a topic "carefully avoided by our entertainers." He was appreciative, however, of the "high and honourable ground" taken by some British newspapers and critical of "all the rest . . . either perverse or profligate in their devotion to the South."[66] He was particularly grateful to friends such as Sir Charles Lyell and his wife for being "true to the cause of Liberty and the Union," with "almost daily occasion to fight for us in their quiet, persuasive way."[67] He was "astounded" at the "ignorance of the so-called upper classes here in regard to the institutions as well as the geography of the United States. . . . But this would be unimportant, or at least quite tolerable, were it not coupled with the prejudice and false sympathies which, partly through fear of republican predominance, and more through the activity of Southern maligners and Northern copperheads, have acquired such astonishing ascendancy in the British mind."[68]

Rogers's stay had begun in Scotland with his brother Henry, who had been Regius Professor of Natural History at the University of Glasgow since 1857. In Edinburgh he visited the School of Art and Archer's Museum, the plan and arrangement of which he would later say he liked "even better than that at South Kensington for purposes of practical instruction."[69] Both there and in England he and his wife, Emma, were warmly greeted and entertained, and the surviving letters contain many references to important people with whom he met—Sir John Maxwell, Thomas Huxley, and Charles Francis Adams, then America's minister to Britain, among others.

Rogers described his London visits to museums and laboratories as "pleasant observation" and mentioned plans to attend the meeting of the British Association in Bath in September. He made a special visit to Kensington's School of Design and collected "Reports, Catalogues, Programmes, Examination Papers, &c. of the Science & Art Dept.," purchasing "copies of drawings, illustrating the methods pursued in Kensington's Schools." And he talked with the registrar of the University of London.[70] In Paris he attended a meeting of the Académie des Sciences and was "daily occupied with visits to schools and museums," with special mention of the Conservatoire des Arts et Métiers and reference to "other institutions especially in my line":

> But unluckily here, as in England, all the professors are taking holiday in the country. As far as laboratories and lecture-rooms are concerned I believe we have little to learn either in England or Paris.[71]

From France he went to Germany, but no letters from there survive.

As the trip progressed, Rogers felt that his health was improving. He shunned "crowds and ill-ventilated places" and watched for signs of weariness, limiting his activities to what seemed most important, thus heeding the advice of Henry, who cautioned against "over-fatigue of body and mind":

> Remember you have undertaken a work of majestic dimensions, demanding much time, and careful, slow elaboration, a work which, from its very nature, no mortal can mature rapidly. . . . Plan your Technological Museum and College well, begin them on the sound principles you have so admirably set

forth . . . open up some of the channels for the future reception of ideas and specimens, and all judicious promoters of your Institution will tell you that for one season, or year, you have done amply enough.[72]

Rogers returned to America early in November 1864 and promptly reported to the Government that his observations abroad had strengthened his view of the "vastness and importance" of their efforts. He was convinced also of the "superior condition" of the "middling classes" in this country when compared with those abroad, and the "infinitely greater opportunities and advantages available here." He assured the members of his "renewed health and strength" and "determination to labor for the benefit of the Institute—to promote its growth, and enlarge the sphere of its usefulness."[73]

On December 1 he reported to the members of the Institute and exhibited some of the models he had purchased at the end of his trip. A *Boston Journal* article fully covered his presentation, described as "highly instructive" and "interspersed with eloquent thoughts springing from the topics treated." He had concluded that the United States could profit by the example of the museums he had visited but believed that "our educational system is in many particulars abreast of the Old World schools, and in the elementary principles decidedly in advance of them":

> Looking to scientific education and methods of instruction, there is such vitality, quickness of observation and ready, flexible application belonging to our countrymen, that we have already embraced some of the most important ideas introduced in Europe. What is wanted is for American students to give time enough to secure thoroughness in the study of applied sciences. The students at the Central School of Arts and Sciences in Paris are required to pass three or four years in the study of a very large range of sciences, including mathematics, chemistry, geology, mineralogy, drawing, engineering, building, and indeed all the branches of industry to which science is applied, thus laying a broad foundation of scientific study, and building upon it practical education.[74]

This account is particularly noteworthy for its reference to "Carlsruhe" in Germany as the preferred model for the Institute:

> The Polytechnic Institute at Carlsruhe, which is regarded as the model school of Germany and perhaps of Europe, is nearer what it is intended the Massachusetts Institute of Technology shall be than any other foreign institution. It has an extensive museum of models of all conceivable mechanical

combination, chiefly of metal, which are the objects of constant study by the pupils. Another extensive collection of models represents structures, as roofs, arches and everything else that concerns engineers or architects. Another collection represents forms used in mining,—the mines themselves as well as implements,—and so all through the practical arts. There are also series of laboratories adapted to the different branches of chemistry. Every part of the establishment is designed for use, and not for show. On the basement floor is a series of workshops, where the students are given practical instruction.[75]

In conclusion, Rogers announced that some classes would be offered during the coming winter and that prior to January 1, 1865, friends of the Institute would have an "opportunity" to aid in securing a $50,000 contribution which had been offered on a matching basis. Dr. Walker's name was not mentioned in this connection, but a fragmentary file copy of a January 1 letter from Rogers—most likely, from internal evidence, to Walker—indicates that copies of the *Scope and Plan* were already in the hands of individuals abroad: "Some eminent scientific friends including one of the directors of the Conservatoire des Arts et Métiers, & the ablest mathematical engineer of G. Britain expressed a very high appreciation of the scheme as set forth in the pamphlet."[76]

Though the museum still appeared to be an important part of the overall plan of the Institute, the opening of the school had become an increasingly urgent matter, with several members of the Government anxious to see the instruction program under way. Late in November 1864 Ross had inquired about the progress of the Committee on Instruction. Rogers repeated remarks made on earlier occasions and moved on to an account of the models and other items he had purchased abroad. Finally, he stated that "some of the Mathematical Classes might be advantageously commenced early in the approaching year." And the Government, referring to their June 6 action calling for the opening of the Popular and Systematic Professional Courses, "authorized the Committee to act accordingly."[77]

When Ross had informed Rogers of the additional gift offered by Dr. Walker, he reported that Walker was anxious to see the results of his philanthropy before he died. Walker wanted the museum building to be erected during the coming year and hoped also that the classes would be opened. Ross had failed, however, to divert the doctor's attention from the museum building to the "School for Mathematics," a term reminiscent of the *Objects and Plan*.[78] Now Ross offered to provide $1,000 himself as a guarantee fund to enable its establishment "at an early day," prompting Erastus Bigelow to ask if the "proposed School was to be confined to Mathematics." Rogers said no. Bigelow then asked what "means were on hand for School purposes." The answer was none, and Bigelow pointed out the urgency of increasing their funds for this purpose, stating that "in no other way could the best interests of the Institute be subserved at this time than by raising at least Ten Thousand Dollars to develop the Schools of Instruction."[79]

In January 1865 Runkle worked closely with Rogers and played an important role in laying out the courses and determining how many professors would be needed. They would recognize that the failure of the Lawrence Scientific School to adopt Charles Eliot's proposed curricular revision had opened an opportunity for the Institute to move boldly to fulfill its obligation as a land-grant institution. On January 15 Runkle expressed confidence in the *Scope and Plan*:

> I have analyzed it with the greatest care, carrying in imagination students through each of the courses from year to year, & I find it to my mind, perfect in all its parts. I am sure that in this country, (& I doubt if in any other, even in France, where the largest experience & study have been devoted to the subject), no institution has ever been based upon so comprehensive & perfect a plan; & I trust that the Government of the Inst. will not rest satisfied until they have secured every facility for its complete execution.

Moving on to specifics, he remarked on what they might look for in recruiting faculty:

> But the Professorships was the point to which I wished to refer. I have first considered the purely scientific courses, or the foundation on which the professional courses are to be built.
> These fundamental or scientific courses are gone over mainly in the first and second years, & the applications made in *these years* are primarily, if not mainly, to illustrate and expound these courses—& the Professors having charge of them should therefore necessarily be entirely familiar with all the applications, as part of the apparatus, so to speak, of their instruction.[80]

In mid-January Rogers informed the members of the Institute that applications had already been received for a preliminary session that would "facilitate the progress of all who are desirous of entering on the regular exercises of the School." Early in February he indicated that the number of students expected to register would be small but that "this practical exemplification of our Plan and method of work would secure us ample number of students, when the regular courses are opened."[81]

A circular letter dated January 24, 1865, in an edition of 750, had been distributed with copies of the *Scope and Plan*. It urged recipients to "encourage your young friends, to avail themselves of this preliminary organization," in which the following subjects would be offered: "Elementary Mathematics, with Practice in the Use of the Chain, Level, &c.; Elementary Physics; Elementary Chemistry, with Manipulations; Drawing; the French Language." No costs or entrance conditions were specified, this information being available at the rooms of the Institute, where the session would commence "about the middle of February." Promising that the "various departments" would be "permanently organized, and put in operation" in the fall, the letter outlined briefly the aim of the school:

> The studies and exercises of the School are so organized as to provide a complete course of instruction and training, suited to the various practical professions of the Mechanician, the Civil Engineer, the Builder and Architect, the Mining Engineer, and the Practical Chemist; and, at the same time, to meet the more limited aims of such as desire to secure a scientific preparation for special industrial pursuits,—such as the Direction of Mills, Machine Shops, Railroads, Mines, Chemical Works, Glass, Pottery, and Paper Manufactures, and of Dyeing, Print, and Gas Works; and for the practice of Navigation and Surveying, of Telegraphy, Photography, and Electrotyping, and the various other Arts having their foundation in the exact sciences.
>
> The Courses of Instruction, while thus providing for the scientific study of the Constructive and Manufacturing Arts, offer a variety of general as well as special studies, which may be advantageously followed by students preparing for commercial occupations; and they present to such as are desirous of becoming teachers of science in our schools and other institutions the opportunity of equipping themselves for this profession, by practice in manipulations, as well as by an ample course of scientific studies.[82]

By early February the opening date of February 20, 1865, was publicly announced.[83]

A Voluminous Enterprise

Chapter 19

The School Opens

he preliminary session of the school opened on February 20, 1865, with 15 students in attendance.[1] William Rogers entered in his diary:

Organized the School! Fifteen students entered. May not this prove a memorable day![2]

In a brief address at the opening session he explained the methods of instruction, the rules the students would be expected to follow, and the "value and dignity of the practical professions for which they aimed to prepare themselves." Within a few days, as chairman of the Committee on Instruction, he could report to the Government that the enrollment was greater than expected and "quite as large as can be conveniently accommodated. . . . From the somewhat extensive correspondence which had occurred respecting the school, with individuals residing in various sections of the Commonwealth, and elsewhere, he was satisfied a wide-spread interest was awakened in regard to it."[3]

At the Government meeting on February 27, 1865, John Runkle reported on the "wants of the School." He accurately estimated that when the regular sessions opened in the fall, the total enrollment would be about 75, a number that could not be accommodated in their present space. He was particularly anxious to know, therefore, whether the building on Boylston Street would be finished in time. Jonathan Preston believed that whatever was needed for the activities of the school would be ready.[4] The projection would miss the mark, however, and the Institute soon faced its first major problem of space.

It became immediately apparent in the fall of 1865 that more classroom space was needed, and Rogers could report to the Government late in October that he had been able to rent the first and second floors of the Congregational Library building on Chauncey Street. He and the chairmen of the Finance and Museum Committees were authorized to secure whatever additional temporary space might be necessary.[5]

By December the Government was much concerned, the record stating that "classrooms and other accommodations were quite insufficient" for their present needs. A particular problem was lack of space for instruction in chemical analysis, a subject in which many of the students were particularly interested. Though space in the basement of the building on Boylston Street had been promised for early November, the rooms were "still far from complete." There was a rising fear that should the delay last much longer, the school's reputation would be "liable to grave injury" for it could not fulfill "its engagements to its Pupils and the Public."[6] A move of the regular classes to the new building would not, however, be possible until the fall of 1866. In the fall of 1865 an arrangement between the Institute and the Lowell Institute had been finalized for a series of Free Evening Courses, among them one in chemistry, and on February 16, 1866, through this course taught by Professor Storer, the Institute "after repeated delays and disappointments . . . had the satisfaction of first opening the doors of its new Building for one of the legitimate purposes to which the structure" would be dedicated.[7]

The first regular session of the school of the Institute opened on October 2, 1865, on Summer Street, with the date for completion of the new building in the Back Bay very much in question. The opening had been advertised in the local papers early in September, those wishing to enroll asked to present themselves for conferences with members of the faculty on or after the twentieth of the month:

Mass. Institute of Technology, SCHOOL OF INDUSTRIAL SCIENCE.

The regular course of this Institution will be opened on MONDAY, Oct 2, and be continued without interruption through a period of eight months. Applicants for admission into the first year's course should be familiar with the subjects usually taught in our English schools, including expertness in the leading rules and processes of Arithmetic and a ready use of the pen. They should, moreover, be familiar with the elementary operations of Algebra, and have a clear knowledge of the earlier theorems of plane Geometry. There will be no formal or extended examination, and no classification of candidates prior to admission into the FIRST year's course, but all such students will be required to pursue their studies in common, until the *first stated examination* (in November), after which they will be classified into an upper and a lower section, according to the preparation and aptitude shown by them in this and in their daily examinations.[8]

Rogers and others had been much encouraged by the response to the preliminary session in the spring and subsequent inquiries from prospective students and parents. M. D. Ross had said in August that he was "almost daily meeting with persons who want to send students to our school."[9]

No catalogue was available for the opening, nor would there be one until the recently elected faculty could lay out the various courses and attend to the myriad details of organizing a school very different from any institution in the Boston area. It was not yet clear how many students would seek admission, particularly for the full program, how prepared they would be to succeed, and which of the courses would be most popular. Every faculty member, however, was fully involved in the deliberations covering admissions, fees, discipline, examinations, the details of the instructional program, and the exact wording of the catalogue. By this careful process of proposal, discussion, review, revision, further discussion, and final acceptance, decisions about policies, curriculum content, and the arrangement of studies were ready by mid-November for presentation to the Committee on Instruction, along with a copy of the proposed catalogue, the final preparation of which had been assigned to Rogers, Runkle, and William Atkinson.

Approved on November 14 by the committee, the catalogue was presented to the Government on the same day for final approval and permission to publish. John Philbrick "testified to the great labor bestowed upon it, and the diligence and care exercised in its preparation by the Faculty." This statement is borne out by the records for that fall—a total of sixteen meetings between their first on September 25 and December 4, some in the evening and some on Saturdays. In addition, various *ad hoc* committees worked on specific problems relating to the curriculum and the organization of the school. The Government authorized publication.[10]

The faculty, however, had some second thoughts and on November 17 were discussing not only revisions to introductory statements, but also a change in the title page. When published, the cover and title page would refer simply to the "School of the Massachusetts Institute of Technology" rather than the "School of Industrial Science" so prominent in the *Scope and Plan*. A year later the faculty would vote first to strike "School of the" from the title page but then decide to retain it.[11] The catalogue for that academic year (1866–67), however, not published until 1867, contains both versions, the cover retaining the phrase and the title page eliminating it. In the next issue the phrase was gone.[12]

On November 14, 1865, the Government had approved a faculty request for a significant change in Rogers's title as head of the school—from "Principal" to "President," and henceforth he would be president of the Massachusetts Institute of Technology and president of the school and of its faculty. Coupled with the close attention to the details of the title page, this request seems to reflect a movement to elevate the character of the school and to place it on a collegiate level in the minds of the public as well as the legislature that had granted participation in the state's land-grant fund. Whatever the reason, it would appear also that the distinction between the Massachusetts Institute of Technology and its school was beginning to blur.[13]

Finally ready in December 1865, the first catalogue contained a list of the members of the Government, the "Officers of Instruction," and the names of enrolled students, together with the "Programme of the Course of Instruction" and other information about the school.[14] By January 20, 1866, 2,533 copies had been distributed, including those sold at cost to the students through the janitor. The cost for printing was $391.95.[15]

The *First Annual Catalogue* is a significant document in the history of the Institute, not only because of what it contains and how it is presented, but also because of what it does not contain. It was based on the *Scope and Plan*, some parts of which were adopted verbatim and some sections revised. Both the organizational pattern and the objects of the school received meticulous faculty scrutiny, with "full discussion and considerable amendment." In a few short weeks their diligent work removed, as far as the school was concerned, the last vestiges of the old Conservatory proposal that had carried over into the *Objects and Plan* to some extent and in a lesser way to the *Scope and Plan*, in which Rogers had endeavored to lay out for the Committee on Instruction how the school might be "most usefully organized and conducted."[16] To the latter report, which had not attempted to set forth the complete details of the proposed curriculum, the faculty applied its own experience and educational views.

The *Scope and Plan* had called for two distinct "departments": the "General or Popular Course," comprising evening instruction open to both sexes and designed for individuals otherwise occupied during the day and the "Second Department," offering a "full course of scientific studies and practical exercises" in preparation for professional work, and training for those seeking instruction only in "some one or more of the branches of applied science."[17] In contrast, the final version of the catalogue's opening statement eliminated the plan for two distinct divisions and set out the following objects of the school:

> *First*, To provide a full course of scientific studies and practical exercises for students seeking to qualify themselves for the professions of the Mechanical Engineer, Civil Engineer, Practical Chemist, Engineer of Mines, and Builder and Architect.

> *Second*, To furnish such a general education, founded upon the Mathematical, Physical, and Natural Sciences, English and other Modern Languages, and Mental and Political Science, as shall form a fitting preparation for any of the departments of active life; and—

> *Third*, To provide courses of Evening Instruction in the main branches of knowledge above referred to, for persons of either sex who are prevented, by occupation or other causes, from devoting themselves to scientific study during the day, but who desire to avail themselves of systematic evening lessons or lectures.[18]

Through the elimination of the concept of two separate "departments" and the incorporation of evening instruction as the third object of the school, the faculty created a unified image for the academic program and brought the institution one step closer to substantial professional technical and scientific education. In the process they introduced an element of "general education," and, in a notable change, limited the possibility of "special instruction" in particular branches of applied science to subjects offered in the evening—a goal not to be reached easily.

The availability of part-time study in the "Second Department—Special and Professional Instruction" had been emphasized in the report of the Committee on Instruction, known as the *Scope and Plan* when published and distributed. And it seems unlikely that the new school could have abandoned the idea at the outset even if it wished to do so, not to mention the financial considerations for an institution sorely in need of income, with nearly all of its funds committed to the construction of a building destined to cost far more than anticipated. Part-time study for qualified individuals would still be possible, therefore, but mention of it was relegated to a later section covering "conditions of admission: . . . To make the opportunities of instruction as widely accessible as possible, students will be allowed to enter special divisions of either of the courses,—as, for example, the classes of mathematics, of mechanical construction, of chemistry, of physics, or of mining and metallurgy,—on giving satisfactory evidence that they are prepared to pursue such special studies with advantage."[19]

John Henck, professor of civil and topographical engineering, felt that the opportunity should be more prominently displayed and urged that a sentence with respect to special students be added. It was likely at his behest that the following brief statement appeared after the introductory listing of the six regular courses: "Special students will be admitted to partial courses in any of the departments of the School."[20] This did not appear in succeeding issues of the catalogue, but the statement under "Conditions of Admission" remained. By 1871–72 the term "special students" was replaced by "persons not candidates for a degree," but the former designation returned in 1878–79. In 1872–73 proof of preparation for these students would come from successful passage of the regular entrance examinations, omitting those not relevant to the subjects they wished to take. In the following year the entry made clear that admission to drawing classes required no examination.[21] Thus, special students were indeed accepted, although their numbers would in later years become a matter of considerable debate.

In this respect and in other matters of educational policy, the influence of Charles W. Eliot is evident, as his biographer has pointed out:

> None of the first Faculty of the Institute were able to forget that they were engaged in an experiment. Their meetings were lively, for questions of method and policy kept coming up. Eliot would not have avoided such questions if he could. He had been thinking about them since he began to teach in the [Harvard] College. They had been his constant subjects of inquiry abroad.[22]

Later, in 1869, when Eliot presented his views on scientific and technical education in two important *Atlantic Monthly* articles, he spoke to the problem of partial courses and special students, whom he placed in two categories. There were "men of age and acquirements" seeking "special training in some professional subject, some one application of science to the arts." To accommodate their needs was "one of the most useful functions of the technical schools." There were also "young men of imperfect preliminary training, whose parents think, or who themselves think, that they can best become chemists by studying nothing but chemistry, or engineers by only attending to the mathematics and their applications, or architects by ignoring all knowledge but that

of architectural design." He called this a "very crude" notion that "deceives many unin-
structed parents and inexperienced young men." Such students, "out of step," he said,
"injure their school, both by interfering with the order and discipline of the school
while they are students, and by failing in after life, and so bringing unjust discredit upon
scientific education."

Also harmful to the technical school, Eliot suggested, were "students who take a
part of the regular course simply because they are incompetent or too lazy to do the
whole." The majority of those admitted by the scientific schools had come from "that
excellent and numerous class of young men who have more taste and capacity for science than for language and literature and who have followed their natural bent in making choice of a school and a profession." But these schools, he said, had often "been the
refuge of shirks and stragglers from the better organized and stricter colleges":

> This evil is a temporary one, incident to what has been the experimental con-
> dition of education through science. It will correct itself, when the new sys-
> tem of education is as well organized as the old, and when the community
> understands the legitimate inlets and outlets of the new schools,—how to get
> into them, and what they lead to.[23]

While acknowledging that the scientific schools had indeed provided a service to
the country by training "a certain number of specialists" to "very useful functions," and
that "genius, or even an unusual vigor of mind and will" can often overcome "an inadequate or mistaken training in youth," Eliot spoke out strongly for the merits of a regular course of study. "At present," he said, "it is the wise effort of the faculties of all the
leading polytechnic or scientific schools to carry as many of their pupils as possible
through the 'regular' course of study; in other words, they recommend their pupils to
lay, during three or four years between seventeen and twenty-two, a broad and strong
foundation for the strictly professional studies, of which a part are pursued in the
school, and a part during the apprenticeship which should follow their school life."[24]

Ironically, it was Professors Eliot and Storer who were asked at the first faculty
meeting, September 25, 1865, to "consider and report on the subject of fees for partial
or special courses of study in their department." On the following day their recommendation of $125 for the current year was accepted.[25]

In the *First Annual Catalogue* the "Evening Courses of Instruction," open to both
sexes, were fully described, to begin each year in November and continue for five
months. An added note, however, indicated that for the current year they had been
"unavoidably delayed." This delay was related to a decision by John Amory Lowell as

FIRST

ANNUAL CATALOGUE

OF THE

OFFICERS AND STUDENTS,

AND

Programme of the Course of Instruction,

OF THE

SCHOOL OF THE MASSACHUSETTS INSTITUTE
OF TECHNOLOGY,

1865-6.

BOSTON:

PRINTED BY JOHN WILSON AND SONS.

1865.

Trustee of the Lowell Institute to support a similar series starting in December, free of tuition, and taught by members of the school's faculty. The Lowell Courses of Evening Instruction were fully described and in effect supplanted the original plans of the Institute of Technology in this regard.[26]

Though concessions were made with respect to part-time study, it is clear that in the first catalogue the faculty established the regular four-year professional program as the emphasis of the Institute's school. In 1867 they voted to discontinue a separate listing in the catalogue for special students. Henceforth their names, with an appropriate figure for the year of the subjects they were taking, would be mingled with the regular students of the relevant years. Special students were thus less prominently displayed in the annual catalogues. The faculty's position would be further reinforced by the opening statement for the issue of 1868–69:

> The Massachusetts Institute of Technology provides a four years' course of scientific and literary studies and practical exercises, embracing pure and applied mathematics, the physical and natural sciences with their applications, drawing, the English language, mental and political science, French, and German. The course is so selected and arranged as to offer a liberal and practical education in preparation for active pursuits, as well as a thorough training for the professions of the Civil and Mechanical Engineer, Chemist, Metallurgist, Engineer of Mines, Architect, and Teacher of Science.[27]

In the earliest proposals, the kind of student the Institute expected to attract was not very clear. The suggestion of a "polytechnic college," in addition to the more popular means of instruction through the museum and the lectures of the Society of Arts, had at best been rather vague. The *Objects and Plan* looked toward "systematic training in the applied sciences" for "persons destined for any of the industrial pursuits" and part-time study for those interested in particular subjects, a goal also maintained in the *Scope and Plan*. In the latter, however, certain conditions of admission were mentioned briefly, setting a minimum age of sixteen for the first year and seventeen for the second, with evidence of training in elementary mathematics. Other subject requirements were to be specified later.[28]

The September 1865 advertisement in the local papers was more specific. For admission to the first year, familiarity with "subjects usually taught in our English schools . . . expertness in the leading rules and processes of Arithmetic . . . elementary operations of Algebra," and a "clear knowledge of the earlier theorems of plane Geometry" were required. And a "ready use of the pen" was important. In November the student's "preparation and aptitude" would be assessed through an evaluation of daily performance and the results of the *"first stated examination."* Each student would then be classified accordingly.

Those wishing to enter the second-year course were expected to show evidence of ability in mathematics through Plane Trigonometry and the elements of Physics and Chemistry, as well as Drawing and the translation of French into English. Students who could not be fitted neatly into one or the other year would be placed at their proper level in individual subjects following the first examination, and even thereafter, they might be advanced or returned to a lower level as the term progressed. Those interested only in certain subjects would be required to show evidence of adequate preparation.[29]

For first-year applicants, the 1865 catalogue called for evidence of competence, "by examination or otherwise," in "arithmetic, algebra, geometry, English grammar, geography, and the rudiments of French," the latter not mentioned after 1865. Special emphasis was placed on the ability to "write a rapid and legible hand, as the examinations and other exercises of the School will be in great part conducted in writing." Preparation at "the best High Schools and Academies" would generally be considered "suitable." Second-year applicants, along with those who might later seek entrance to the third and fourth years, would be required to show as much evidence of preparation as required of a regular student to advance to the next year.[30]

How did the Institute's practice compare with other institutions? At Rensselaer the minimum age for admission was sixteen, though most entrants were eighteen. Applicants were expected to be "well prepared in geography, English composition, arithmetic, including the metric system; plane geometry, and algebra to equations of the second degree."[31]

At Yale's Sheffield Scientific School applicants for the regular courses leading to the degree of bachelor of philosophy after three years of study were to meet the minimum age requirement of sixteen and present "satisfactory testimonials of good character." They would be examined in arithmetic, algebra, geometry, plane trigonometry, elements of natural philosophy, English grammar, geography, and the history of the United States. For the mathematics and science subjects, the books on which the examinations would be based were specified. Acknowledging the inadequate preparation of some students, a warning added that "the examination for admission is strict and full. As the studies just named are not pursued in the school, and are essential to successful progress, no one can be received as a scholar who is not well acquainted with these branches." Latin was also mentioned, recommended as a help in the study of the sciences and

modern languages, the catalogue indicating that it would probably soon be a requirement for admission. Those seeking advanced standing were required to pass both the
entrance examinations and examinations covering material for the years preceding the
one in which they wished to be enrolled. Special students were those "who have
already made a considerable degree of proficiency in some department of science, and
are now pursuing certain special studies under the personal direction of some of the
professors." All students—regular, advanced, and special—were required to show evidence of good character.[32]

At Harvard's Lawrence Scientific School, eighteen was the official minimum age
for entrance, a requirement that Eliot would refer to as "elastic." There were no general entrance examinations, the catalogue calling for a "good common English education" and the ability to "pursue to advantage" whatever studies one might choose to
follow. Also necessary was "satisfactory evidence of good moral character." Students
were admitted by the individual department, which consisted of one professor, and
both chemistry and engineering appear to have attempted to establish some standards
beyond the general statement of a "good common English education." Chemistry,
though not requiring an examination, indicated that "the more thorough the previous
acquaintance of the Student with Mathematics, Mechanics, Physics, and General
Chemistry, the better." And engineering examined candidates for the department in
algebra, geometry, and plane and analytical trigonometry.[33]

A hallmark of the Institute's school in the early years was the vast amount of adjustments, fine tuning, and changes as the faculty endeavored to refine the program in light
of daily experience in the classroom. In 1866 French was eliminated as a requirement
for admission, and the "otherwise" alternative to an entrance examination disappeared
from the catalogue. Formal entrance examinations were inaugurated covering arithmetic, algebra as far as equations of the second degree, plane geometry, English grammar, and geography. Admission to years above the first depended on satisfactory
performance not only in the regular entrance examinations, but also in examinations
on the studies of the prior years, a practice, as already noted, in effect at Sheffield.[34]

By 1868 the "Classical Schools" were added as suitable sources of preparation, and
while Latin was not an admission requirement, a knowledge of the language was
"strongly recommended to young men who propose to enter this School";[35] in the
same year Sheffield announced that henceforth Latin would be among the entrance
examinations.[36] By 1868 also it became obvious that, with increasing numbers of applicants, the matter of admissions would require a more systematic procedure beyond a
letter of intent or a personal visit to the school. Accordingly, an application form for
admission, prepared by a committee chaired by Professor William Ware, was adopted.[37]

꒰ꜟꜟ꒱

Entries in the Day Book indicate that for the first regular session, 1865–66, both first- and second-year students paid $100 and that students taking partial courses paid varying amounts.[38] When the first catalogue was published late in 1865, however, the fee, as set by the Committee on Instruction, was $100 for the first year's course; $125 for the second; and $150 each for the third and fourth. No fee was anticipated for the use of laboratory apparatus, which was expected to be maintained in "good order." Special student fees varied depending on the subjects taken and the length of time spent at the school, action with respect to these being the prerogative of the faculty. Midway through the year fees were set on an individual basis for students taking a variety of subjects.[39]

A comparison with the fees of the Lawrence Scientific School underscores the very different nature of the two schools. For chemistry, at Lawrence the student paid $50 per term plus $50 for apparatus and supplies. Students in engineering, however, paid $75 per term, supplying their own drawing materials and textbooks. Three hours a week in mineralogy, offered in the second term, cost $5. For other departments the fee was "agreed upon with the instructor." A student from one department could take a course in another for $5, attend "Academical Lectures" without charge, but pay $5 for a "modern foreign language" in the university. Those accepted for shorter periods of time would pay proportionately less. Not only students in the other professional schools, but also the public, could attend lectures in the Scientific School for $5.[40]

By the fall of 1866, a committee of Rogers, Storer, and Runkle recommended a schedule of fees for special students in chemistry. Their proposal of $30 for one month to $150 for a year, adopted by the faculty, reveals the extent to which they were prepared to accept students who wanted only a limited amount of instruction. How these students were to be accommodated in relation to the regular classes is not clear, and the range of periods from one or two months up through five or six months to a year would tend to support Eliot's concern with respect to the problems caused by part-time students.[41]

Late in 1867 the Committee on Instruction voted to increase the first-year fee to $125 and to raise the second year to the $150 that the third- and fourth-year students were already paying. And in 1869 the regular fee for every year was set at $150. Students taking a partial course for an entire year would pay "in general, the full fee." By 1872 the tuition was raised to $200 per year, $50 higher than the Lawrence Scientific School. It would remain at that figure until the year 1902–3, rising then to $250.[42]

The 1866–67 catalogue, not published until 1867, is the first containing notice that each year every student, regular or special, must, within ten days of enrollment, file a $200 bond secured by two bondsmen, one a citizen of Massachusetts and both "satisfactory to the Secretary of the Institute." There is no record of discussion or correspondence on this requirement. Most likely the Institute was following an established practice at Harvard, where the filing of a similar bond was a requirement for admission. The Institute, however, offered an alternative—a $200 deposit at the beginning of each year from which tuition would be deducted. Those presenting bonds paid half the annual fee at the beginning and the remainder in the middle of the academic year, at the end of which a final accounting would be made.[43]

The key to the return of the bond or the balance of a deposit was behavior. William Rogers had endured enough rebellion on the campus of the University of Virginia to be clear on exactly what was expected of the student body. The *First Annual Catalogue*, under the heading of "Discipline," called simply for compliance with the school's regulations and "decorous" behavior, with a reminder that "conduct inconsistent with the good order of the School will be followed by the dismissal of the offender." "Punctual attendance" would be required, and parents would be notified of absences. The catalogue stated further that "beyond the limits of the Institution, the student is in no way under the control of the Faculty."[44]

The *Second Annual Catalogue*, however, would set the pattern with respect to discipline for the remainder of the nineteenth century:

> While within the limits of the Institute, students are expected to behave with decorum, to obey the regulations of the School, and to pay a due respect to its officers; they are specially required to avoid all running, loud talking, or other noise in the entries of the building. Every student will be held responsible for the furniture which he uses, and the cost of repairing any damage thereto will be charged to him. In case of injury to the building, or to any of the furniture, apparatus or other property of the Institute, the damage will be charged to the student or students known to be immediately concerned; but, if the persons who caused the damage are unknown, the cost of repairing the same will be assessed equally upon all the students of the School. Conduct inconsistent with the good order of the School, if repeated after admonition, will be followed by the dismissal of the offender.[45]

Tardiness—entering a class more than five minutes after the appointed hour—and absences would be reported on a weekly basis to parents of students "not of age." All regular students were expected to "devote themselves to the work of the School" from 9 to 5 daily, except for the "interval for dinner" between 1:30 and 3 and Saturday afternoon. A "study-room," in which "perfect order and quiet will be preserved," was available for times not scheduled for lectures, laboratory work, or the drawing-room.[46]

There is evidence that from the beginning some members of the Government and other interested persons quietly helped worthy students by supplying funds to the treasurer to cover tuition. When a plan for the establishment of "free scholarships" was put forward in 1866, however, individual student need for financial assistance does not appear to have been the prime concern. Rather, these proposed scholarships were a by-product of the dire need for funds and the search for ways to attract money.

The financial plight of the Institute when the school opened was serious and of great concern to several members of the Government. With the cost of the building on Boylston Street already far in excess of the original estimates, some comprehension dawned concerning the magnitude of the funds necessary to equip, staff, and operate an educational institution of this kind. In their enthusiasm, members of the Government—with one or two exceptions, particularly Erastus Bigelow—had tended to overlook from the start the financial requirements of their project and to turn aside an occasional word of caution about the expenses they were about to incur. Nor had they fully appreciated the financial implications of the change in the concept of the school. As costs mounted and borrowing became their only option, a measure of disagreement arose on how to deal with the ever-increasing debt burden. In November 1865 the Government had wisely decided to preserve the funds from the Walker estate as endowment, the income to be used in support of the educational expenses of the school.[47] This was an essential step, but it did not solve the fundamental problem.

The gravity of the Institute's financial condition had become abundantly clear with the completion of the Finance Committee's investigation into the construction of the building. The committee had been joined in that task by three other members of the Government, Edward Atkinson among them. When late in February 1866 Atkinson reported on their behalf, he indicated that they had initiated an attempt to raise $150,000, one-third to equip the school and the remainder for completing the building, liquidating the debt, and current expenses.[48]

Despite some progress, an immediate need for cash called for a special Government meeting on March 5 at which the treasurer was authorized to borrow $50,000. A brief discussion on the amount of money that might be required for the establishment of a named professorship brought no formal decision but the appointment of a committee to consider the matter. Atkinson believed they should concentrate on achieving the $150,000 and issued a strong warning: "Indeed he believed should this movement fail, we might as well cease all further endeavors, and abandon the Institute, as at best, in that event, it must sink down to the level of a second or third rate establishment."[49]

This was the second time since the charter had been granted that a serious question was raised about the Institute's prospects. In 1862 Erastus Bigelow, as chairman of a committee to find suitable rooms for the new organization, had initiated discussion about the wisdom of continuing. Now, in 1866, as on that earlier occasion, Rogers took an optimistic view, appearing not to be as deeply concerned about the situation as some of his fellow Government members:

> Whilst assenting to the great importance of succeeding in this trial to obtain funds, [he] was not willing to admit it to be of such vital moment that the Institute could not flourish without it.
>
> He remarked, there have already been connected with the School nearly one hundred Pupils, and it is not unreasonable to anticipate that there will be at least two hundred in attendance at the commencement of the next year's Course of Instruction.
>
> Therefore, unless the School is crippled, by its Corps of Instructors being reduced in numbers, or by its pecuniary means now relied upon being diverted to other purposes, it must succeed provided it be furnished with suitable accommodations, whether the entire Building is at present completed or not.[50]

In mid-April, Rogers and Atkinson were at odds again. Rogers reported that $35,000 had been pledged, but progress was slow because of the "state of the times" and competing fund-raising efforts. J. Ingersoll Bowditch of the Finance Committee suggested finding ten people who might give $300 for five years, enabling the Government to take $50,000 from the Walker fund for general purposes, an idea that Henry Bromfield Rogers promptly discouraged. Atkinson worried that the $150,000 would never be raised, in which case they would lose the $5,000 contributions given with the understanding that the target would be achieved. William Rogers did not agree—individuals he knew had "subscribed unconditionally." He even questioned whether they ever looked upon the $150,000 as an immediate rather than a long-term goal. At this point they needed $20,000 more for the building. John Philbrick moved that the existing committee be augmented by ten to "solicit subscriptions for the school."[51]

Late in May 1866, against this background, Atkinson suggested that gifts to the Institute might be more easily obtained if the donor could receive in return the right to name a pupil to attend the regular four-year course free of charge. The Government appointed a committee to consider the amount that might be required to entitle the donor to do so. Joining Atkinson on this committee were John M. Forbes, John Cummings, M. D. Ross, and Rogers.[52] Within a few days the illness and death of his brother took Rogers to Scotland. He was not on hand late in June, therefore, when Atkinson was ready with a report, signed also by Cummings and Ross, on a plan for "free scholarships."

Under this plan, contributions of $5,000 each would be sought toward a goal of $200,000 and a limit of forty such scholarships to provide a "firm foundation" for the "regular courses of instruction," at the same time "promoting a close union between the Institute and the various High Schools of Massachusetts." The Government accepted the report and appears to have approved the basic plan. In return for each $5,000 donation, the donor would be granted the "perpetual right to nominate, and keep in the School of the Institute, one pupil," and if he so desired could delegate this right of nomination to a "school or any other association." The Government adopted three of four suggested votes, rejecting one which would have allowed $10,000 of the Walker Fund to be set aside as a source of additions to contributions by donors who could not quite offer the required sum. Since the funds were to be placed in a trust, the report was returned to the committee for the preparation of a necessary indenture and, it seems, some unidentified "alterations." In response to a committee request, their membership was increased by two with the addition of John Amory Lowell and George T. Bigelow. Bigelow was then an *ex officio* member of the Government as chief justice of the Supreme Judicial Court and later, when his term on the bench ended, a regular member.[53]

Rogers returned at the end of July 1866, faced immediately the death of Thomas Webb, and then retreated to Lunenburg, exhausted and ill. He did not resume his duties until the fall, when he presided over an October meeting at which Judge Bigelow presented an indenture for Government approval. There was still some uneasiness, however. William Endicott, then treasurer, believed that they should complete their current subscription for the building before embarking on another fund-raising effort, but Charles

Dalton, his predecessor, emphasized the prime importance of raising for the school money which "could not be diverted from the purpose for which it was given." He prevailed, and on November 15 the Government authorized Judge Bigelow, Rogers, and Atkinson to seek immediate approval of the members of the Institute.

That evening the members took no action beyond requesting that the plan be printed for their consideration. They approved it on December 6, 1866.[54] The indenture was finally signed on December 31 by William Rogers as president and Samuel Kneeland as secretary, representing the Institute, the party of the first part, and the three trustees of the "Income Fund of the Massachusetts Institute of Technology": James M. Beebe, chairman of the Finance Committee; William Endicott, the treasurer; and "J. Ingersoll Bowditch, Esq., of West Roxbury, in the County of Norfolk, and Commonwealth of Massachusetts."[55] Beebe and Endicott fulfilled a requirement that the trustees must include the Institute's Finance Committee chairman and treasurer. The indenture specified that the third trustee must be a "citizen of the Commonwealth." Should he die, resign, become disabled, or leave the Commonwealth, his successor would be appointed by the Institute Government, a stricture that would apply forever. Each person leaving the board would be required to "execute all needful instruments to convey to and vest in his successor all his rights, title and interest in the trust, estate, and premises."[56]

No explanation has been found for what would appear to have been an effort to ensure outside representation on this board through the "citizen trustee." It may have been inserted by Judge Bigelow as a reminder that some of the operating income of the Institute was derived from the Commonwealth by way of the fund established through the Morrill Land-Grant Act. Nor is there any supporting evidence to explain J. Ingersoll Bowditch's appointment as the "citizen." He was very much a part of the Institute as a member of its Government and its Finance Committee. However, in view of Rogers's success in 1863 in limiting to three *ex officio* members the representation of the Commonwealth on the Institute's Government, it is not likely that he would now have wished to open the door to outside representation with respect to this new Income Fund. Also, the indenture did not specify that a member of the Institute's Government would be ineligible to serve as the "citizen"— possibly one of the "unidentified alterations" the committee had been asked to make in June. Thus might the way have been paved for the appointment of "Mr. Bowditch of West Roxbury," who may well have been chosen not only because he was a member of the Finance Committee, but also for his reputation, sound financial sense, and recognized ability "to elicit gifts even from those whose sympathies are not easily moved."[57]

According to the indenture, the trustees were to "receive all such moneys and property as shall be contributed, whether by subscription, donation, legacies, or otherwise," create the "Income Fund of the Massachusetts Institute of Technology," and invest and manage it "according to their best judgment." They were barred from investing in any land or buildings to be used by the Institute. The fund's income would be turned over to the Institute for the support of the school, and an annual financial report to the Government was required.

The right to a free scholarship, the number limited to forty, would not become effective unless the donor of $5,000, or property worth that amount, "at the time of making such contribution," signified a wish to take advantage of this option. The student thus nominated would be "entitled to attend all the regular courses of instruction . . . without charge for tuition, so long as he shall conform to all the regulations of the School and the Institute; provided that no pupil shall be received or retained, if, in the judgment of the Officers of Instruction of the Institute, his intellectual qualifications, moral character, or conduct, render him unsuitable." The donor's right could be transferred, along with the power of nominating a pupil, to "any person, persons or association, by an instrument in writing . . . giving notice thereof to the Trustees, or by his or her last will." Anyone gaining the right to nominate a pupil in this manner would also be able to transfer the privilege in the same way. The power of nomination would pass to the "Officers of Instruction of the Institute" should a donor die without making a transfer of the right to a scholarship in his will. The so-called "founders" would be allowed to attach a name, approved by the trustees, to the scholarships established through their donations, and the trustees could attach names to those where the donors had not taken advantage of this privilege.

Both the report of the Committee on Free Scholarships and the indenture were included in a pamphlet published in 1867 for "general information." How widely it was distributed is not known. It was obviously intended as a promotional piece, and in at least one instance William Rogers made use of it.[58]

In the fall of 1867 Rogers took advantage of an opportunity to suggest that one of the individuals quietly providing funds for needy students might wish to consider participation in the "Free Scholarships" plan through an increase in her contribution. One paragraph appears to confirm that the Government felt they had little to lose through the admission of as many as forty students free of tuition, provided the return on the investment exceeded the fee:

> The Scholarships authorized by the Govt. of the Institute as described in the accompanying pamphlet are fixed at 5000 to be placed in the hands of the

trustees named in the document. The donor has the right to nominate for the place. The sum is more than enough to cover by its interest the school expenses of a student, but the plan was framed in the belief that many friends of the Institute would be willing to aid its finances in this way who would not be disposed to give that amount outright to the Institute.[59]

In the spring of 1871 the "free scholarship" plan was mentioned in connection with a memorial to Thomas Sherwin, a Government and Committee on Instruction member who had died in 1869. It was intended to aid a worthy graduate of the English High School of which Sherwin had been headmaster, the candidate to be chosen by the trustees of the Institute in cooperation with the current headmaster of the school. There was one condition, however. The $5,000 must be maintained in a discrete fund, and "while never anticipating any such contingency," the committee wanted to ensure that "should the Institute ever be discontinued, the fund shall revert to the benefit of the English High School." This was not an idle speculation, for a second Harvard attempt to annex the Institute's school had been a concern for more than a year. Though the agenda for the April 12 meeting at which the scholarship was discussed contained also an agenda item confirming a final rejection of Harvard's proposal at least for that round, the Committee on the Sherwin Memorial Fund was wise to look to the future, for the problem would arise again late in the nineteenth century. That same day the Corporation (formerly the Government) voted to accept "the trust, *substantially in accordance* with the 'Indenture of Trust' adopted in 1866," but Rogers and Atkinson were appointed to "suggest certain modifications" to the committee from English High. The funds were actually received late in May. By June 14 authorization to sign the instrument of transfer was granted. The indenture is entered in the record as approved and confirmed at the next Corporation meeting on October 11, 1871.[60]

Evening Instruction and the Lowell Free Courses

In keeping with the opening statement of the first catalogue in which the evening courses of instruction were presented as the "third object" of the school, the section on these courses appeared at the end. Though their inauguration had been "unavoidably delayed," henceforth they would be announced in October of each year, begin in November, and run for five months. "This department of the School," the first catalogue read, "is intended for the benefit of persons of either sex who are prevented by occupation or other causes from availing themselves of scientific instruction during the day, but are desirous of pursuing such studies in a systematic way by the aid of evening lessons and lectures."[61] The subjects offered would "more or less" vary from year to year, including "in their entire scope, instruction in mathematics, mechanics, physics, chemistry, geology, natural history, navigation and nautical astronomy, architecture, engineering, philology, and literature."[62] A maximum fee of $5 would be charged for "a course of not more than twenty lessons or lectures," though provision might be made for "gratuitous instruction" for some courses. Those enrolled were expected to conform to the following conditions: "As it is the object of this branch of the school to provide substantial teaching, rather than merely popular illustration of the subjects, it is expected that all persons attending these courses will come with a serious purpose of improvement, and that they will cheerfully comply with such rules in regard to attendance and to order in the class or lecture-room as may be prescribed."[63]

For 1866–67, when the catalogue was not issued until early 1867, the department was entitled "Afternoon and Evening Courses of Instruction." Both mechanics and philology were dropped from the proposed offerings, and literature became "the English and other modern languages and literature." The fee was mentioned but not specified. By 1868, when the catalogue began to be issued in more timely fashion, the "afternoon" was dropped.[64] The issue for 1869–70 is the last containing a separate entry for this "department."[65]

Throughout these years the catalogues had also included a separate section on "Lowell Courses of Evening Instruction," the first of which had opened on December 5, 1865. Not until the issue for 1870–71, however, were the original intentions for evening instruction publicly linked with the classes supported by the Lowell Institute.[66] The change was inevitable. Given the Institute's precarious financial situation, its limited facilities, the growth of the regular school, and the responsibilities of a small faculty, a parallel set of evening classes was neither feasible nor sensible.

In the spring of 1862, when John Amory Lowell had obliged William Rogers by providing a letter of intent to be used as evidence of progress in raising the required guarantee fund, he referred to his long desire to establish under the aegis of the Lowell Institute, of which he was sole trustee, a "school for the instruction of mechanics in the sciences connected with their trades." He stated, further, that if the new institution were to "become successfully established," he would open "this school on their premises, and devote to this object a sum not less than $3,000 a year."[67]

There the matter would rest until late October 1865, when Lowell, also a vice president of the Institute of Technology, informed Rogers that he now proposed to "institute evening courses of instruction to be opened gratuitously to the public under such regulations as may be deemed advisable." The proposed association, he implied, might not be permanent:

> It has occurred to me that these courses might with advantage be delivered, in the first instance, under the supervision of the Massachusetts Institute of Technology and by their professors, the programme of course to be acceptable to me.
>
> I shall devote to this purpose $3,000 a year to be divided among the teachers in proportion to the time devoted by each.
>
> If such an arrangement would be acceptable to the Government, I shall be happy to confer with you on the subject.[68]

John Amory Lowell

Through a reference to "the amount appropriated by Mr. J. A. Lowell, Trustee of Lowell Institute (Subject to withdrawal at his pleasure), income of which is payable to the Institute for educational purposes," the Treasurer's Statement for 1866 confirmed that Lowell would make an annual payment to support these courses and also that the arrangement was not irrevocable.[69]

Lowell probably approached Harvard first, although when is not clear. He had been a fellow of the Harvard Corporation since 1837 and could easily have explored the possibility in an informal way. Perhaps he had done so as early as 1846, when Henry Darwin Rogers—then a candidate for the Rumford Professorship—was lecturing for the Lowell Institute and had, with the help of his brother, presented to Lowell a proposal for the establishment of a polytechnic school in Boston. Or perhaps Lowell had approached Harvard just prior to his commitment to William Rogers in 1862.[70]

In any event, Rogers and Lowell conferred in the fall of 1865, and the plan, to be put into effect immediately, was presented to the Government on November 14. M. D. Ross expressed some doubt that a sufficient number of applicants would respond to such a late announcement, but Rogers stated that "the intention of having evening courses of instruction this Winter was quite extensively known." A rather large number of applications was expected, probably even too many to be accommodated. Many were apparently already in hand. With this assurance, the Government voted to accept with gratitude "this liberal and timely contribution to its Department of evening instruction" and authorized the president and the chairman of the Finance Committee to "arrange with Mr. Lowell the details necessary for carrying his liberal purpose into effect."[71]

The courses were announced in the papers on November 22, and the December publication date for the 1865–66 catalogue permitted the inclusion of information about these Lowell offerings. The classes were to be open to both men and women "free of charge." Eighteen was the minimum age. No student would be allowed to take more than four lectures a week. A maximum enrollment of 40 students in mathematics and 100 in English and French was set, with provision for drawing by lot should applications exceed these limits. Application was to be made in writing with information about current or prospective occupations and "preliminary training" for courses requiring preparation.[72]

By December 19 the Government was informed that the classes had begun auspiciously and that the demand had indeed far exceeded the number that could be accepted. John Runkle was giving a course of eighteen lectures on Mathematics twice a week with 40 students, to be followed by William Watson on Descriptive Geometry, with Applications to the Arts. For these two classes more than 70 "Engineers, Architects, and those engaged in various Mechanical pursuits" had enrolled. The large hall in the Mercantile Building could accommodate the 100 who enrolled for William Atkinson's lecture once a week on English Language and its Literature. About half were women school teachers, and the men, "Clerks." Language instructor Ferdinand Bôcher also had 100 for French Readings, mostly teachers or those preparing to teach. Both the English and French classes had attracted 250 applications. Since the building on Boylston Street was not ready, it was necessary to postpone Frank Storer's Chemistry of the Non-Metallic Elements, scheduled to meet twice a week, followed by Charles Eliot's Chemistry of Metals with three sessions weekly. To Storer fell the honor on February 16, 1866, of being the first to offer instruction in the new building. Thomas Webb said that many of the students enrolled could not have enjoyed the advantages of such instruction without the "liberal provision" of the Lowell Free Courses.[73]

On December 19, 1865, Runkle called the Government's attention to the large number of excess applications for mathematics, mentioning that several gentlemen were ready to contribute the means to offer a second course. If an additional course were to be approved, he offered to teach it until another instructor could be engaged. The matter was referred to the Committee on Instruction, but no action appears to have been taken.[74] With no formal records available for the Committee on Instruction for this period and very few agenda notes in the Rogers papers, whether the committee ever discussed the matter cannot be ascertained. In any event, it seems unlikely that a competing section of mathematics independent of the Lowell courses would have been established. Because interest had far exceeded the published maximum of 40, no set quota was specified in future catalogue issues, the number to be accepted by the faculty simply stated as "limited." The first payment of $3,000 per year in support of this instruction was not received until January 1867, so it is reasonable to assume that compensation for 1865–66 was paid directly by the Lowell Institute to those involved.[75]

Lowell's intentions had broadened to some extent since the early 1860s, especially through the inclusion of both English and French alongside instruction for "mechanics in the sciences connected with their trades." Applicants for admission reflected a more diverse segment of the population, which in turn pointed to a shift in the character of the school of the Institute of Technology. And from a purely practical point of view, the courses inevitably reflected the disciplines of the professors available to teach them.

Subject to Lowell's approval, the president and the faculty annually laid out the subjects offered, which from the outset responded to a definite need and were very popular. By the year 1868–69 some 500 individuals were taking part in the program. There was an afternoon class twice a week, on Wednesday and Saturday, for thirty lessons in Qualitative Chemical Analysis taught by Eliot and Storer. And meeting twice a week for eighteen lessons were four sets of evening classes: Mining and the Mineral Regions and Deposits of the United States, with methods of working, etc., taught by Professor Alfred P. Rockwell; English History and Literature, by Professor William Atkinson; Comparative Physiology and the Laws of Life, by Dr. Kneeland; and French, by Professor Bôcher, with "elementary knowledge of the language" required.[76] The subjects varied slightly from year to year, and over the years the number of offerings increased in what came to be thought of as "a primary venture in adult education."[77]

The Lowell Institute's connection with the Institute of Technology would be extended still further. In the summer of 1866 John Amory Lowell asked M. D. Ross if the Lowell Institute might use some of Technology's rooms and if so, what the rent might be. Ross suggested the possibility of using the space rent-free but "appropriating certain funds to certain branches of instruction, in cooperation with the Institute of Technology." In reporting this conversation to the Government, he added that the idea, favorably received by Lowell, had been presented to Rogers, who was too ill to consider it.[78] This may indicate early consideration by Lowell of establishing courses of free instruction in industrial design, a plan that did not come to fruition until the early 1870s. What soon became known as the Lowell School of Practical Design, but called in its early stages the "Lowell Course of Industrial Art," was approved by the Government on September 11, 1872, with Lowell to provide the funds for the salary of the head of this school. The instruction would cover "the art of making patterns for Prints, Delaines, Silks, Paper-Hangings, Carpets, Oil-Cloths, etc." An important part of the Government vote stated that "no distinction of sex shall be made in the admission of pupils to the Lowell School of Industrial Art."[79] Eight students were enrolled when the course opened on October 7, 1872.[80]

Women and the Institute of Technology

The admission of women as special students in regular classes of the shool was considered early in 1867, with requests for the privilege coming from some who had taken the Lowell course in chemical manipulation and who hoped to pursue further studies. Two members of the Government received letters of inquiry.

Miss Augusta R. Curtis wrote to Edward Atkinson, a member of the Committee on Instruction:

> The time of the "Lowell" class in Chemical Manipulation is drawing to a close, and some of the ladies of the class, who are very much interested in the subject, wish to go on with it.
>
> Will it be possible for them and me to join any class now formed in the Institute so to continue our studies? If so, what would be the conditions as to terms and time? We hear that there is to be a meeting of the Board of Instruction this week. Could you bring this matter before them.[81]

Atkinson forwarded the letter to Rogers, asking if there could be "any objection to ladies entering as special students except possibly want of room in the laboratory."[82] Nathaniel Thayer heard from Anita E. Tyng and Rebecca K. Shepard in a similar vein, confirming an interview with him on behalf of "four ladies, regular attendants of the present Lowell class in Chemical manipulations."[83]

These requests were seriously considered at a Committee on Instruction meeting on February 2, 1867, which Atkinson but not Thayer attended. Fragmentary agenda notes reveal that Rogers came prepared to offer a suggestion: Might they be able to accept women for laboratory instruction "if 10 or 12 would unite at 50 dolls each for the season?" Perhaps they could in this way, without cost to the Institute, hire an instructor who could also be available to help out "at other times in the Laboratory."[84]

Although the final decision was negative, the idea was not completely rejected: "It was agreed that the admission of female students was not consistent with the present condition of the school and organization of the classes; but that, at the beginning of the next year arrangements might perhaps be made by which this class of pupils could avail themselves of the privileges of the Institute."[85] Rogers was authorized to send the following message to Thayer:

> Please say to them that the Faculty and the Committee of Instruction appreciate the earnestness with which they & their associate lady pupils in the Laboratory are disposed to pursue their scientific studies & would gladly afford them such opportunities of systematic instruction as are compatible with the objects & plan of the Institute, but that we could not comply with their present request without seriously embarrassing[86] the organisation of the Laboratory and other Departments of the School as connected with the regular courses now in progress.
>
> The plan of evening (including afternoon) instruction, forming a department distinct from the so-called regular courses of the School, has been incorporated into the general organisation of the Institute for the purpose of enabling lady-students, as well as gentlemen, to have the benefit of systematic scientific instruction under the conditions best suited to their convenience & advantage, & to the interests of the school at large.
>
> This Department of the Institute, embracing the Lowell free instruction as a part, will it is hoped be so organized in another year as to meet the wants of the ladies whom your correspondents represent, & I need hardly add that the Faculty & Committee will gladly welcome them to the classes thus organized.[87]

It would have been difficult, in any event, to add a few women who had completed thirty lessons in chemical manipulation to the classes in the second term of the academic year. They would have been out of step with the regular students, whose first-term instruction had been designed as part of an extensive four-year course in chemistry. And given the Institute's financial situation, it would have been equally difficult to arrange for a special section, though Rogers had at first entertained the possibility should a sufficient number of women be interested.

In August 1867 a further application was received by William Atkinson, then secretary of the faculty, who wrote to Rogers:

> Application has come from one young woman—a rather remarkable teacher—who desires to avail herself of the instruction of the Institute. I was

sorry to have to reply that nothing was open to her save the Lowell courses. There is a large and increasing class of young women who are seeking for something more systematic in the way of a higher education. If we continue a special technical school ours will not be the place for them—but if we should expand into a modern university—and I am confident there is room for one— by taking the bold step of opening our doors freely to both sexes I believe we should distance all competitors. It is a step sure to be taken somewhere.[88]

Since Atkinson did not specify chemistry as the subject in which the young lady was interested, it is probable that she had other interests. As far as chemistry was concerned, however, the admission of women was not forgotten, for in November 1867 the Government confirmed the following vote of the Committee on Instruction: "that the President and Prof. Storer ascertain the practicability of affording to women the opportunity of systematic laboratory study, and that, if this can be done without cost to the Institute, the Committee will approve of their admission."[89]

This was a difficult time for the Institute on several counts. The school was operating with a minimum of faculty. The Institute's finances were precarious, its mode of instruction demanding a high order of expenditure for equipment, apparatus, and laboratory supplies, and some faculty members were spending their own money for materials needed for their classrooms. They were already running out of space in a building that had cost far more than anticipated. And their president was in poor health. It is not surprising, therefore, that no immediate action was taken in 1867 on the admission of women for systematic laboratory study.

Besides, the school's professional curriculum would have been of little interest to women seeking admittance to higher education at the time. Chemistry, however, and particularly laboratory work in chemistry, was the subject that would open the door. In 1870 Ellen H. Swallow, a Vassar College graduate, seeking only instruction in laboratory practice, would be accepted as a special student in the chemical laboratory. In 1873 she would be the first woman to receive an Institute degree.[90] There would not be another until 1881, and in that year there were two.[91]

Mrs. Margaret Stinson, the first female employee of the Institute, was thirty-two years old and a widow with four children when she was hired in February 1865 to take charge of the chemical supply room. She was on hand for the preliminary session of the school and would remain for forty-six years, finally retiring in 1911.[92] Before she

Margaret Dayton Stinson

died in April 1912, she talked to Ellen Swallow Richards about how she met President Rogers and first came to work at the Institute:

> I first knew him through Prof. J—. They were friends. Prof. Rogers asked him one day if there were any ladies in the public library that he could recommend to go there and take this position. He remembered about me. He was a member of the church where I attended. But he didn't know where to find me. He spoke to Dr. Bowditch and he knew just where I was. . . . I knew him from a child. . . . They wrote to me and I went to Temple Place and engaged with Prof. Rogers at that time. . . Dr. Bowditch said all he could for me.[93]

The identity of Mrs. Stinson's two references—Professor J— and Dr. Bowditch—remains uncertain, but Dr. Bowditch was probably either J. Ingersoll Bowditch, a member of the Government, or Henry Ingersoll Bowditch, the eminent physician and abolitionist who at the time was Jackson Professor of Clinical Medicine at Harvard Medical School.

Not only did Mrs. Stinson care for all the chemical apparatus, she also filled the role of nurse when accidents happened in the laboratory: "a good many patched up faces and hands" came under her charge and care. This maternal style, coupled with her efficiency as a technician, may have kept her from experiencing the kind of hostility—or at least pranksterism—that a woman employee or student likely would have been subjected to at this essentially all-male bastion:

> [The students] said that if they were going to have a woman there they would make it hot for her; she wouldn't stay long. They looked down upon us. Well I did what I could for them, but they never made it hot for me. They were very good to me. . . . [Prof. Rogers] said a woman in a place like that would get along much better if they used a little diplomacy with [the students]. . . . I never had a disrespectful word said to me. . . . Not one unkind word; never one word that I could feel a bit hurt about. . . . They didn't want any woman around in those days.

Mrs. Stinson understood that hers was a special case, and that an influx of women almost certainly would not have been tolerated at the time.

Loyal almost to a fault, she worked from 9:30 to 5 every weekday for forty-six years. Even during her one and only time away—owing to a bout with pneumonia—she continued to carry out her responsibilities as best she could and to worry about what might or might not get done in her absence:

Never missed any time only those three weeks, and in that time I did my work. I was delirious a greater part of the time. I didn't forget one thing; did all my work. One thing I remember most strongly. One of the boys invariably forgot to hang his bag and coat up. I was going out and saw the bag, and I said to myself that the first thing Monday morning I will hang up the bag. I had to wait for a car twenty-five minutes. As I stood there waiting I could feel a chill and when I got home I could not lift my arms to take off my coat. During the sickness I was delirious and kept talking about hanging that coat and bag up.

Following Mrs. Stinson, Miss Charlotte A. Thayer would become the second female employee, formal approval for her appointment recorded by the Committee on Instruction on November 15, 1866. On October 1 the faculty had voted unanimously to ask the committee "for the appointment of a lady assistant librarian to take charge of the library and the study-room and keep order therein." Rogers was absent from the meeting, and it would take a further vote on October 20 "respectfully" requesting that he "take such informal action as may seem to him best in order to secure the *immediate* employment of a lady in the study-room" before Miss Thayer would be appointed. But no funds having been appropriated for this purpose, Rogers and William Atkinson, then librarian, paid her wages out of pocket until June 1867, when the Government voted to provide $100 and reimburse them.[94] Miss Thayer would be followed in 1870 by Miss Augusta R. Curtis, who had earlier inquired about admission to the regular chemistry classes. Appointed assistant librarian, she, too, was in charge of the reading room but would also be an assistant to William Atkinson in the examination of written exercises.[95]

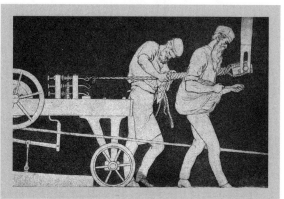

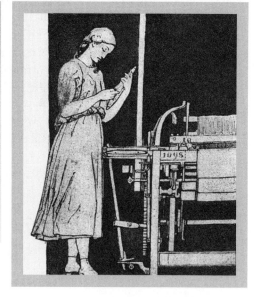

Mining (top left), Ropewalk (top right), Chemistry (bottom left), and Weaving (bottom right)—sketches prepared by Paul Nefflen for mural in Huntington Hall (see p. 764). Mining was called "a masterpiece, well composed and vigorously drawn . . . thoroughly American, appropriate to its setting, purpose, and subject." Chemistry depicts the manufacture of sulphuric acid. Weaving was conceived in recognition of "forgotten New England mill girls." (See note on Bourne, p. 761.)

$$\mathscr{C}hapter\ 2\ 0$$

$$\mathscr{T}he\ \mathscr{F}irst\ \mathscr{F}aculty$$

Instructors for the preliminary session beginning in February 1865 were assembled by tapping the services of Institute insiders and of informal contacts on the outside. William Rogers, in charge, would also teach physics. John Runkle and William Watson had helped to lay out the plans for the regular program; Runkle would teach mathematics, and Watson would take charge of civil construction. Francis Storer, engaged for chemistry, was a member of the Institute and a former assistant to Josiah Cooke of Harvard, whom both Rogers and Runkle knew well. Storer was a consulting chemist with a laboratory of his own in Boston. He was connected also with the Boston Gas Light Company, and no doubt Rogers, while gas inspector for the Commonwealth, had frequent occasion to be in touch with him. Ferdinand Bôcher was then an instructor in modern languages at Harvard, a logical place for Rogers to look for a teacher of French. Finally, it is likely that for free-hand drawing the services of W. T. Carlton, a teacher at the Lowell Drawing-school, were secured through the offices of John Amory Lowell. Carlton's connection with the Institute ceased with the end of the preliminary session.[1]

Rogers never accepted compensation for his teaching, and the others were not paid until after the preliminary session was over. In June Runkle, Watson, and Storer received $500 each, and Bôcher, $350. Early in July Carlton was paid $250.[2] Student fees were collected by Secretary Webb and for this session amounted to $1,105, entered in the cash book on May 23, 1866, identified as an entry from "Dr. Webb's accts. current on file."[3] He also collected the admission fees and annual assessments of the members of the Institute and kept his own accounts, using these funds for current expenses and later settling with the treasurer.

As they prepared for the preliminary session of the school, Rogers and Runkle were already looking toward a fall 1865 opening of the regular program. Runkle wrote to Rogers in January, listing fourteen professorships, more than they had originally discussed; expressing uncertainty as to whether all should be ranked as full professors; and indicating which should be in charge of the several planned laboratories. He outlined the various elements of the mathematical subjects, including their theoretical and practical applications, which should be covered in the early years, for the "Prof of a professional course will not interrupt his course to instruct in the elements of any of the above subjects." He concluded that it might be best to appoint for many of these positions young men who would "take them on small salaries":

> They would thus grow up under your eye & direction, & would probably make better men than older ones who should come in with long settled methods & habits of instruction.
>
> Taking all things into account I am not sure but this is the very best course the Institute could adopt—because the plan consults present economy & future efficiency.[4]

As Rogers and Runkle worked together at Lunenburg during the summer of 1865, it was clear that nearly all who had taught in the preliminary session, "having given proof of skill and capacity," would be offered appointments.[5] There may have been some consultation with the members of the Committee on Instruction at this time, but with both men active in the Boston scientific community, and Rogers with many contacts on the national scene, they were easily able to identify those who might fit best into the plans for the new institution. There had been a few expressions of interest from outside sources, and others would be received once the school opened. The members of the first faculty fell conveniently into place, however, with virtually no mention of alternative candidates.

On September 15, 1865, at a special meeting of the Government, Rogers presented a report on the "management of the School of Industrial Science, the organization of the Faculty, &c.," which laid out the duties and areas of responsibility of the faculty and the Committee on Instruction and their relation to the Institute's Government. The professors and a presiding officer to be called the "Principal" would be elected by the Government upon the recommendation of the Committee on Instruction, which could also recommend the removal of such individuals after due investigation, a majority vote of the Government required. The principal would preside at faculty meetings and "act generally as the executive head of the School." Assistant professors and "other subordinate Teachers" could be appointed by the committee upon the recommendation of the faculty, but only full professors would be "entitled to a seat in that body." In practice in the early days, however, a seat was sometimes granted to someone of lower rank if that person was the only representative of a particular discipline. Conversely, it appears that occasionally a full professor in a subject already represented by another would not be granted a faculty seat.

With Government approval, the Committee on Instruction would "designate the Chairs to be established," set the salaries, regulate tuition fees, and after consultation with the faculty, set fees for partial courses and prescribe the rules for student conduct and penalties for violation. The report made very clear that, again with oversight of the committee and the Government, the "details of organization of the several Departments of the School, and the conduct of its Instruction and Government shall be entrusted to the Faculty of the School." The faculty would be responsible also for the scheduling of classes and the conduct of examinations, and they would "prescribe the age and degree of preparation requisite for admission to the School." They would elect a secretary "from the Corps of Instructors." In addition to the normal duties related to notices and minutes of meetings, the secretary would assist the principal with correspondence and the preparation of publications relating to the school. He would keep the "Matriculation Book" and the tuition accounts, forwarding the latter to the "Secretary of the Institute for Collection."[6]

The Government adopted Rogers's report, established eleven recommended professorships, and confirmed the following nominations:

William B. Rogers	Principal
John D. Runkle	Mathematics and Analytical Mechanics
Frank H. Storer	General and Industrial Chemistry
Charles W. Eliot	Analytical Chemistry and Metallurgy
William B. Rogers	Physics
William B. Rogers	Geology
William Watson	Mechanical Engineering and Graphical Works
John B. Henck	Civil and Topographical Engineering
James D. Hague	Mining Engineering
William R. Ware	Architecture
William P. Atkinson	The English Language and Literature
Ferdinand Bôcher	Modern Languages[7]

Thus a faculty of ten, with one serving not only as principal, but also as the holder of two chairs, was in place. Of these, Rogers, nearly sixty-one, was the oldest, and Hague, twenty-nine, the youngest. Henck was fifty; Atkinson, forty-five; and Runkle, forty-three. The rest were in their early thirties. Most were Harvard-educated: Runkle, Storer, Watson, and Ware held bachelor of science degrees from the Lawrence Scientific School. Ware also had earned a bachelor of arts degree from Harvard College, as had Eliot, Henck, and Atkinson. Hague had attended the Lawrence Scientific School, and Bôcher resigned as an instructor at Harvard in order to accept the language professorship.

Though the Lawrence Scientific School had fallen short of meeting the needs for broader availability of technical education in support of a growing industrial demand, it had produced, together with Harvard College, nearly all of the faculty of the new school. Even Rogers, through his appointment to the visiting committee for the Lawrence Scientific School, had a Harvard connection.

William Parsons Atkinson

William Parsons Atkinson, born in Boston in 1820, earned his bachelor of arts degree from Harvard in 1838 and a master of arts in course in 1841.[8] A teacher all his life, he served briefly as principal of the Brookline High School, succeeding one who had been dismissed and soon resigning himself following public censure of his performance by the Brookline School Committee. In a published statement addressed to parents, he expressed an unwillingness "to leave a post where I have labored very hard, without saying a word in my defence against what I consider a very hasty condemnation." He emphasized the deplorable condition of the school when he took over, despite what he considered to be good effort on the part of his predecessor, pointing out its lack of organization, the varied and inadequate preparation of the pupils and their consequent "habits of idleness" and moral short-comings, the lack of proper textbooks, and the diffuse attempt to combine "a Primary, Grammar, Latin, and English High School in one."[9] That his ideas about the organization and conduct of public high schools came to be appreciated is evident in his later membership on the school committees of Brookline and Cambridge and his advice to the Boston School Board as it considered in 1869 a reorganization of the city's high schools.[10]

Following his Brookline experience Atkinson appears to have devoted himself chiefly in Cambridge to the preparation of boys for admission to college. He was an elder brother of Edward Atkinson, a member of the Institute Government, but his early documented contacts with William Rogers stemmed from his interest in referring prospective students to the new School of Industrial Science. Educated himself in the classical tradition, he was nevertheless quick to recognize both the growing need and the value of technical training, a perception emphasized at the time of his death in 1890 by his colleagues on the Institute faculty:

> He was one of the first among professional teachers to appreciate the essential truth and large importance of the radical educational ideas underlying the scheme of instruction at the newly established School of Technology, a point especially worthy of note in view of the fact that his own training, his especial professional interests, and all his associations would naturally have led him to cling to the older system of a purely classical training. But he clearly saw the importance of the new methods of education of which the Institute was the leading exponent; and so was led, almost at the very outset, to ally himself to an institution unpopular among his associates, and unappreciated except by a very small circle of his friends.[11]

Atkinson's espousal of the cause of technical education had preceded the opening of the Institute's school, however, as revealed by an exchange of letters in 1862 with Charles W. Eliot concerning Eliot's proposal for the reorganization of the Lawrence Scientific School. Atkinson commented on this plan, saying in part:

> My experience as a schoolmaster long ago convinced me that the opportunity to pursue some such course of study as you have marked out was very much needed by a large class of young men who either now get no good education, or are sent to College for want of any other alternative, and who find themselves quite out of place there. . . . It is very strange that the intensely practical New Englanders should be so scantily provided with the means of preparation for scientific pursuits and for practical life. I take it for granted that the theory that one and the same training is equally good for all minds and as a preparation for all the occupations of life is pretty generally exploded;—yet, practically, a drill—better or worse—in Latin and Greek is all that is to be had in the shape of higher education.[12]

Atkinson had sent several boys to Rogers for the Institute's preliminary session, and as early as February 1865, in a letter concerning a prospective student, he may have hinted at an interest in a teaching position: "I wish you could add to your course exercises in English grammar and analysis and *Logic*."[13] During the summer Rogers spoke to him about lectures on English literature, which he was "quite prepared to do," having given similar lectures at the Salem Normal School. M. D. Ross had also mentioned the possibility of the position of secretary of the Institute—then held by Webb, whom Rogers could not "see the way clear" to replace. Ross urged some appointment for Atkinson, however, offered to help defray the expenses, and proposed that Atkinson might be helpful in the organization of the museum, the committee for which Ross was chairman in 1865–66.[14]

Chosen secretary of the faculty at their first meeting, Atkinson was assigned to further duties as librarian, without salary, when the faculty recommended the establishment of this post in the fall of 1866. In 1868, when asked to give the instruction in History and Political Economy as well, he resigned as faculty secretary. Beginning in 1871 he was professor of English and history, serving until 1889, when he retired and was appointed professor of English and history, emeritus, a title not automatic upon retirement in early days but granted only by vote of the Government.[15] He died soon thereafter, on March 10, 1890.

Ferdinand Bôcher, Professor of Modern Languages, was born in New York City in 1832 but grew up in France. Returning to the United States as a young man, he settled in St. Louis, teaching French for a time at Washington University before a period of travel and study in Europe from 1859 to 1861. In 1861 he was appointed instructor in modern languages at Harvard and is said in addition to have taught French at the Boston Latin School and the Cambridge High School. He was also a university lecturer at Harvard from 1864 to 1866 and again in 1869 and 1870.

There is little information available about Bôcher in the records of the Institute, but he comes to life in a history of Harvard in which he is described as a "thoughtful, rather elegant young man of twenty-nine

Ferdinand Bôcher

or thirty" when he was appointed instructor in French in 1861. "With a cane and a French accent—unusual, to be sure, in looks, but with little suggestion of his subsequent short-legged rotundity. Already his were the magnificent eyes and the impressive bass voice." He was a "book-lover, a reader, insatiably curious" and an "adroit practical linguist," fluent in several languages. He was not particularly interested in "authorship" but did publish an "adaptation" of a much-needed French grammar and a "College Series" of French plays and other writings:

> A mind richly stored, a fascinating manner, a contagious enthusiasm, coupled with geniality and humor, made him an alluring guide to letters. And allure he did, drawing not only the studious but the habitually idle into acquaintance and familiarity with good authors.[16]

He would leave the Institute for a Harvard appointment as professor of modern languages effective January 1, 1871, and remained there until his death in 1902.[17]

Committed as he was to the cause of scientific and technical education, Charles William Eliot, Professor of Analytical Chemistry and Metallurgy, was a significant appointment to the first faculty. Though his tenure would be brief, his education and experience at Harvard were invaluable for the new institution.

Leaving Harvard in 1863, Eliot and his family went to Europe, where he planned to make a firsthand study of educational practices. In France he visited the Conservatoire des Arts et Métiers, l'École Centrale, the Sorbonne, the Jardin des Plantes, and the secondary schools. In Germany he observed many facets of education and spent some time in the laboratory of Hermann Kolbe at the University of Marburg in Hesse. In the spring of 1865, when he was in Italy, he was offered the superintendency of the Merrimack Company mills in Lowell. The offer promised far more than the salary of a professor, but he declined in favor of pursuing an academic career. His biographer, Henry James, son of William James, the philosopher, and nephew of Henry James, the novelist, observed that Eliot "did like teaching, and his head was now full of what should be done for education in America."[18]

In his travels, Eliot observed that the "famous universities of Europe" had been founded by "Princes or privileged classes" and that the polytechnic schools he had visited were "supported in the main by Government." He added, "Now this is not our way of managing these matters of education, and we have not yet found any equivalent, but republican, method of producing the like results. Science, whether pure or applied, is not yet naturalized in the United States":

> The Puritans thought they must have trained ministers for the Church and they supported Harvard College—when the American people are convinced that they require more competent chemists, engineers, artists, architects than they now have, they will somehow establish the institutions to train them. In the meantime, freedom and the American spirit of enterprise will do much for us, as in the past.[19]

From Italy Eliot traveled to Austria, with plans to visit Germany and France again and come home by way of England. He was in Austria when a letter arrived from William Rogers offering a professorship of chemistry. Rogers was aware that Eliot had declined the offer from the Merrimack Company and applauded his determination to "hold to his scientific pursuits." In the ensuing exchange of letters, the questions raised by Eliot had roots in his Harvard experience and show that he had a firm grasp of issues of governance and organization, was fully aware of the need for clear lines of authority and adequate funds, and was anxious to assess the Institute's prospects of success.

Rogers had written "in haste" on June 6, 1865, mentioning those who had been teaching in the preliminary session, adding that some of the students who had attended would be ready for second-year studies in the fall. And he reported that the Institute was "awaiting the final adjustment" of a bequest from William Walker, expected to be used in support of the school:

> My great anxiety now is to make up a good faculty of instruction, and I want you to be one of the number. What say you to taking charge of the Laboratory, with such other Chemical matters as you & Storer might arrange between you? We shall need at the beginning two Chemical Profs., one having General Chemistry, including lectures on some of the Chemical Arts, & the other Laboratory instruction in its various branches, including metallurgy—but the details might in many cases be interchanged, if found expedient & agreeable.[20]

Though the Government had not acted on the matter of salary, Rogers felt "safe in promising" $2,000 for the first year, seemed confident of an increase the following year, and hoped to make the professorships "sufficiently remunerative to place the Profs. at ease in regard to income." He asked for an early reply:

There is much work to be done,—and you can greatly aid in doing it. . . . I wish you were here to see as I do the proofs of the hold we have already secured on the public confidence & the basis on which I build such assurance of success.[21]

Rogers's letter arrived in Vienna on June 20. Eliot, who appears on an 1861 list of members of the Institute, had left home several months before Rogers completed the 1864 *Scope and Plan* and had many important questions. He replied on the same day "without that time for consideration which your proposal demands," but believing that "an instantaneous, categorical answer" was not expected. He welcomed the opportunity for "an interchange of letters," since his long absence had resulted in "ignorance of much in the history and present state of the Institute," which he needed to know to reach a decision:

I never remember to have seen the "Constitution" or fundamental "Charter" of the Institute, nor do I know who its Trustees or Government are. Secondly, you speak of a new building as nearly ready—is this a School building or a Museum building? Is there a laboratory appertaining to this building, or is the laboratory yet to be created? Are any collections, or apparatus or other tools for instruction already provided, or are those still to be obtained? In whose hands will be the practical arrangement of the course of studies? In the hands of the Faculty, or of the higher Govt. of the Institution? Has any particular policy in regard to the course of studies or the discipline of the School been decided upon, or is all to be developed hereafter as experience may show the way? Thirdly, to what class of men does the Institution look for that money support which it will need. Will the State give further help? You perceive at once the drift of these questions. You invite me to join in a new & difficult enterprise—I should like to understand, as well as I can at this distance, the condition of the work already done, the leverage we could bring to bear & the prospect of success. That the School is new & its success something to be conquered, does not make it any less attractive to me. Nothing has struck me more in Europe than the great & prompt success which all the well organized Polytechnic Schools have had—Paris, Carlsruhe, Stuttgart, Zurich, Vienna, all illustrate the wonderfully rapid growth & wide usefulness of these technical Schools. Looking at these Schools I have often felt how useful would be the work in which you have been engaged these several years in Boston, provided only that the community gave you an adequate support. What

Governments do in Europe, individuals must do with us—and ours is infinitely the best way in the long run.[22]

The salary for the first year, he said, would be satisfactory: "One does not expect to make money in Science." The opportunity to work with Storer would be a "very strong inducement," the idea "delightful," for they were old friends. He apologized for his "elementary questions" and expressed appreciation "of the honor you have done me in making this proposition."[23]

Also on June 20 Eliot wrote to John Amory Lowell with questions on three critical points:

1. Has the Institute of Technology won to any extent the confidence and respect of the community? I remember that in its infancy it was evil spoken of.
2. Has it any permanent fund whose principal is applicable to salaries?
3. Are its proposed objects and methods, as you understand them, so different from those of the Scientific School in the University at Cambridge, that no injurious competition could arise?[24]

Lowell responded on July 7. He believed that the Institute could be of "great service and command the respect of the community." He mentioned the financial drain caused by the building and did not know how much would be received through the Walker bequest. On the whole he was cautiously optimistic:

I see no reason why they should injure the Scientific School, being designed for a class of students who rarely find their way to Cambridge. So far as rivalship is concerned, the stimulus may be advantageous.

I think you may safely try the experiment without engaging yourself at present for more than a year.[25]

Rogers answered Eliot on July 17, pleading that "it is out of my power by a written statement of what has been done or is proposed by the Institute to make you fully acquainted with its position and prospects, and that from the nature of the case some of your queries must remain almost unanswered." He explained the terms of the charter and the Institute's organization and bylaws, indicating that he understood Storer had sent Eliot some pamphlets and a printed list of the Government, from which he would learn "something of its general tone and character." The building should "afford sufficient space for all the operations of the school for many coming years." Rogers expected, too optimistically, that it would be ready for classes by October 1865, with "two and perhaps three rooms" finished for "chemical purposes, including, at least in outline, a regular working laboratory," adding that the "provision as yet of the apparatus and materials of instruction is inconsiderable." He was confident, however, that satisfactory equipment for the chemical and other departments would be available in time for the opening. The Committee on Instruction had taken no action on the "practical arrangement of the course of studies," and he could only speak from his "own convictions." He expected, however, that such matters would be left to the professors, "subject to such control of the faculty of instruction as may be needed to secure coöperation and prevent interference":

> Long experience has taught me the importance of giving to each professor a wide latitude in the choice and use of his plans and means of instruction, making him, in fact, within reasonable limits, the sovereign in his department, but at the same time holding him of course responsible for its successful administration.
>
> The object of the school being to afford instruction to all who are prepared to benefit by its teachings, whether in a continuous curriculum of studies or in some particular division of them, its policy in the admission of students and in the individual distribution of studies will be one of pliancy rather than rigidity, helping the development of a special talent, as well as the general capacity of the pupils; at the same time stimulating and enforcing industry, and maintaining good order by stated oral and written examinations.[26]

Rogers enclosed a list of those to whom they might "look for sympathy and pecuniary help." As for state aid beyond participation in the land-grant fund, the Institute had made "no calculations, nor should we desire it if accompanied by legislative control and political management."[27]

Eliot accepted the offer on July 31 from Paris, acknowledging that "no written statement of the position and prospects of the Institute can be perfectly adequate and satisfactory," but grateful for the information just received. Along with letters from Storer and "other kind friends," he had everything needed for an "intelligent decision":

> It will be my desire and aim to carry out to the best of my ability your own views and those of the Faculty in regard to the organisation and development of the School.

And now, My Dear Sir, let me say that I look forward with great pleasure to coming home to a definite and useful occupation in my own profession, and that I am very sincerely obliged to you for the opportunity thus afforded me—an opportunity all the more satisfactory because I feel very sure that the Institution which is growing up under your guidance will achieve a prompt success and become an honor to the State & the City.[28]

Eliot's old friends at home had all urged his acceptance, particularly Asa Gray, Jeffries Wyman, and Ephraim W. Gurney in addition to Lowell—"four of the wisest men who had watched his work in his old position." A letter from Wyman, Hersey Professor of Anatomy, took pleasure in reporting a change under discussion in the Scientific School:

There should be introduced collateral studies of about the same amount and kinds as were laid down in your program which was so summarily rejected. What will amuse you still more is that the proposal came from Prof. Agassiz himself, apparently in utter forgetfulness of his former defiant attitude.[29]

Wyman also told Eliot that the Institute in his hands could become "an educational power which is needed to meet a real want." Gurney, then an assistant professor of Latin, shared this view and did not see why the Institute's direction, after Rogers passed from the stage, would not be as desirable as almost any educational post—except the presidency of Harvard, "in which I am determined to live to see you!"[30]

The idea that Eliot might succeed Rogers, along with the notion that he would "take to power" in the Institute "as a duck takes to water," became local gossip, which troubled Storer, who informed Eliot about it. But this talk apparently troubled neither Eliot nor Rogers:

It is clear that Rogers was not disturbed by what Storer reported. He knew all about Eliot's unsuccessful attempt to reform the Scientific School. Indeed, the program had seemed to him to be an excellent one, and its author had pleased him accordingly. Eliot's views had been quite of a piece with those which Rogers had been urging upon Boston's attention for several years, and they accorded with his policies for the new Institute. He and Professor Runkle, his nearest counsellor, knew their man and knew they wanted him.[31]

The most unusual member of the first faculty earned this distinction because he never took up his duties—James Duncan Hague. Having been duly elected, however, he was over the years carried on the Institute's records as Professor of Mining Engineering from 1865 to 1868, and dutifully recorded as absent at every faculty meeting from September 1865 through the end of the academic year 1867–68, at which time his connection with the Institute *in absentia* was severed.[32] His phantom status notwithstanding, the story of his appointment and later withdrawal provides an interesting glimpse of the way in which Rogers worked to secure what he felt would be a superior faculty.

Hague, the son of a Baptist minister, was born in Boston in 1836, attended private schools, and in 1854 enrolled in the Lawrence Scientific School at Harvard, where he spent one year. From 1855 to 1858 he was abroad, studying at the University of Göttingen and at the Royal School of Mines in Freiberg. In succeeding years he was a chemist on a South Seas expedition and served for a time during the Civil War in the United States Navy. From 1863 to 1866 he was superintendent of the Albany & Boston Copper Mine in the region of Lake Superior and was involved in the Calumet and Hecla copper mines in Michigan.[33]

Rogers appears not to have known Hague personally. On August 2, 1865, he turned for advice to Professor George J. Brush, then professor of metallurgy and mineralogy at Yale's Sheffield Scientific School and later its dean.[34] Brush responded promptly with a glowing recommendation:

> Hague is a very superior man and my advice would be to secure him if possible. Few men in the country are equal to him in ability and fewer still have had his opportunities for theoretical training and practical experience in Mining.[35]

But he doubted his availability, believing that Hague would be unwilling to leave his position at the Albany & Boston Mine "until he has realized all that he has promised the company."

Rogers asked Hague's father about his son's "probable future plans & predilections," indicating that he did not know what other candidates might be considered but *believed* he could receive an appointment "should he only express a desire to have it & be prepared at an early day to enter heartily upon the work of the department." Reverend Hague, though sure that his son—to whom he forwarded Rogers's letter— would "welcome the proposal," was unable to say whether an "insurmountable obstacle" might prevent his acceptance.[36] The Committee on Instruction recommended

Hague's appointment, and he was confirmed along with the others on September 15. Willing or not, he was officially a member of the faculty. In October Rogers informed the Government that Hague had not yet decided to accept the position, adding that his indecision did not really matter, since the classes were not far enough advanced to require his subjects, and it would be some time before the Department of Mining Engineering would go into active operation.[37]

Hague was listed in the first catalogue of 1865–66 through the 1867–68 issue. By 1867, however, the question of his continued connection with the Institute became important. In the catalogue for that year a footnote explained what appeared to be a temporary substitution—the instruction in mining engineering would be given by Alfred P. Rockwell, professor of mining engineering at Yale's Sheffield Scientific School.[38]

Some years earlier the Lawrence Scientific School had had difficulty in finding an engineering professor, and by 1865 the supply of trained civil engineers and teachers in that field had not increased in proportion to the need. The Institute was fortunate, however, that John Benjamin Henck, a successful engineer in Boston, was willing to consider the task of organizing and taking responsibility for the instruction in civil engineering as Professor of Civil and Topographical Engineering.

John Benjamin Henck

Henck was born in Philadelphia in 1815 of German parents, one of eight children. His father's death in 1831 brought family responsibilities and scant time for formal schooling. He studied independently, however, was admitted to Harvard, and was graduated at the top of his class in 1840 with a bachelor of arts degree, later receiving a master of arts, presumably in course. He had supported himself by tutoring and upon graduation became principal of the Hopkins Classical School in Cambridge. He was professor of Latin and German at the University of Maryland from 1841 to 1843 and at the Germantown Academy in Philadelphia from 1843 to 1848.

Seeking a more financially rewarding career, he returned to the Boston area, entering the firm of Felton & Parker, civil engineers, in Charlestown. Soon he formed a partnership with William S. Whitwell for general engineering work. Whitwell left the firm in 1859 to become treasurer of the Boston & Roxbury Mill Corporation, and Henck then carried on alone, accepting apprentices interested in the profession. By that time Henck's experience included field assignments on the Fitchburg Railroad for Felton & Parker, work on the first street railways of Boston with Whitwell, and most important, beginning in 1855, the development of the Back Bay lands from planning to construction work, an association that continued until 1881.

This project was a massive, complicated undertaking that provided ample evidence of his skill and knowledge as an engineer. And it also brought him into close contact with the supporters of the Institute.[39] He was thus known to the founders, particularly to William Rogers and M. D. Ross, the latter a member, with Jonathan Preston and James Francis, of the Commission on the Back Bay appointed by the city of Boston. At Harvard Henck had been a favorite pupil of Benjamin Peirce, who would undoubtedly recommend him highly and probably had earlier suggested him to Runkle as a contributor to the *Mathematical Monthly*.[40] He had served also as one of three judges for essays submitted to the *Monthly* for cash prizes and publication.[41]

Henck was a logical choice for the school's first engineering professor. Though his formal teaching experience had been in other fields, he had accepted apprentices in his company, and his active engagement in the profession fitted very well with Rogers's idea of a practical approach to scientific and technical education. He had, in addition, taken an early interest in the Institute, his response to the distribution of the *Objects and Plan* in the fall of 1860 indicating that he would do what little he could "in carrying out so excellent a design, especially since I feel satisfied that the control of it has fallen into the best possible hands." His name appeared on the 1861 list of those "thus far associated."[42]

Before January 15, 1865, Runkle had talked with Henck as one "especially qualified" to fill the place of civil engineering, but had informed Rogers that Henck "does not see how he could take it without breaking in too much upon his own professional work."[43] Rogers told Eliot in June that he hoped to have Henck "take charge of Engineering."[44] There must have been many discussions as Henck tried to reconcile the needs of his professional work with the probable demands of setting up a curriculum for a new institution and assuming the associated teaching duties. In the end he decided in the affirmative and continued to maintain his firm, concentrating chiefly on the work related to the Back Bay lands. As with all the original faculty—except, of course, Hague—Henck was an active participant in the supervision of the school, and he was ready when the faculty began to consider his proposed program for civil and topographical engineering.[45] He would serve from 1865 to his retirement in 1881.

Francis (Frank) Humphreys Storer, Professor of
General and Industrial Chemistry, was born in 1832,
the son of Dr. David Humphreys Storer, professor of
obstetrics and medical jurisprudence at Harvard from
1854 to 1868 and dean of the Medical School from
1855 to 1864.[46] His father was, in addition, a distinguished naturalist, with special interests in fishes and
reptiles, and an avid collector of coins and shells.
Charles Eliot later pointed to the "atmosphere of scientific research and publication" in which Storer grew
up as a contributing factor to his "strong tendency to
scientific studies," leading him to follow a route different from that "ordinarily prescribed for the sons of
successful professional men in Boston." [47]

Francis Humphreys Storer

Storer enrolled in the Lawrence Scientific School
in 1850. Following one year of study, he served for two
years as assistant to Josiah P. Cooke, then Erving
Professor of Chemistry and Mineralogy. During this period he also taught a private
class in chemical analysis at the Harvard Medical School.[48] In 1853 he joined the
United States North Pacific Exploring Expedition as chemist and after his return
received a bachelor of science, *summa cum laude*, from the scientific school in 1855.[49]
He left immediately for Europe and spent two years studying with Robert W. Bunsen
at Heidelberg, Theodor Richter in Freiberg, Julius Stöckhardt in Tharand, and Émile
Kopp in Paris.[50]

In 1857 Storer set up a laboratory in Boston "as an analytical and consulting
chemist for all manufacturing, pharmaceutical and commercial purposes," carrying on
"with great industry and success" until 1865.[51] He also served as chemist for the Boston
Gas Light Company, daily testing the gas furnished to consumers and conducting "miscellaneous scientific researches upon the composition and illuminating power of coal
and gas."[52] This connection would have placed him in frequent contact with William
Rogers, who was then the state's gas inspector.

Storer showed an early interest in the proposed Institute of Technology and, like
Henck and Eliot, was among those listed as members in 1861.[53] The educational plans
had special appeal: "President Rogers's plans for creating a strong School of Technology
in Boston commended themselves very much to Storer's judgment; and he was also
eager to attempt to teach chemistry by the laboratory method, a method strongly
favored by Professor Rogers in all the sciences."[54] Storer taught in the preliminary ses-

sion and was influential in helping to convince his friend Eliot, whose sister he would later marry, to join the faculty. Together they made distinguished contributions to the Institute in the teaching of chemistry by the laboratory method, and they collaborated on textbooks which were widely used for over fifty years. He remained with the Institute only until 1870.

William Robert Ware, Professor of Architecture, was born in Cambridge in 1832, the son of the Reverend Dr. Henry Ware, Jr., a Unitarian minister then professor of pulpit eloquence and pastoral care at the Harvard Divinity School. He was also the nephew of Dr. John Ware, adjunct professor and later Hersey Professor of the Theory and Practice of Physic at the Harvard Medical School, who had, from 1823 to 1826, been associated with Dr. John W. Webster and Daniel Treadwell in the publication of the *Boston Journal of Philosophy and the Arts.*

William Ware was educated first at Phillips Exeter Academy and then at Harvard, where he earned a bachelor of arts degree in 1852. He worked as a private tutor in New York until 1854, when he enrolled in the civil engineering course at the Lawrence Scientific School. He received a bachelor of science degree in 1856. Following graduation he studied in the architectural office of Edward Clarke Cabot and his brother, J. Elliott Cabot.[55] One of the original members of the Institute, Edward Clarke Cabot had been appointed in January 1861 to the Committee of Twenty.[56] He is listed among the incorporators, therefore, but he never served as a member of the Government. His presence on the Committee of Twenty is interesting, for he had no connection with any previous committees relating to the efforts to obtain land on the Back Bay. In the *Objects and Plan,* however, the projected museum was expected to include a Department of Domestic and General Architecture, an area in which Cabot could be expected to be helpful.

William Robert Ware

Ware remained with the Cabots until 1859, when he went to New York to study with Richard Morris Hunt, a noted architect and the first American trained at the École des Beaux-Arts in Paris. Though the instructional program at the École included formal lectures, its most important component was practical design work carried out in separate ateliers under the supervision of professional architects. Ware served a kind of apprenticeship with Hunt, who much later, in 1887, set up in his own office a form of atelier, though naturally without ties to an established architectural school, there being none. This offered a far more structured environment than the apprenticeship system then in force, and Hunt was looked upon by 1876 as "the father of high and successful architectural education in this country." It has also been said that his "most important direct influence on architectural education in the United States came through his pupil William R. Ware."[57]

Ware returned to Boston in 1860 and joined with Edward Philbrick in a partnership, listed as architects or sometimes as architects and civil engineers, until 1863.[58] He then established a firm of his own, a venture in which he was soon joined by Henry Van Brunt, a Harvard graduate and also a pupil of Hunt. Together they followed Hunt's example in accepting students in their firm: "Following, in general, the same course that had been followed with us, we endeavoured, so far as other avocations allowed, to add some practical information to this purely theoretical course, and achieved a very satisfactory success, perfectly answering our own immediate purpose, of obtaining a valuable company of auxiliaries, and we accumulated a capital portfolio of drawings made by them during their pupilage, which was quite a show among our friends."[59] To the success of this effort he attributed the "attention of the managers of the Massachusetts Institute of Technology," which "led to their inviting my co-operation in the Architectural Department of their School, and to the organization of that department."[60]

There are no records to indicate whether others were considered. It is reasonable to believe that Edward Clarke Cabot would have been consulted, and it is possible, in addition, that William Watson, who had helped to some extent in the planning of the curriculum, might have put forward Ware's name; Watson and Ware had been students at the same time for at least a year at the Lawrence Scientific School. The possibility of attracting any of the "accomplished senior architects or master builders of Boston" was remote, and Ware fared well by comparison with them anyway. His "background indeed looked good," though he lacked "exposure to contemporary European architecture" and had only "limited experience in the business and design aspects of architectural practice." He could offer, however, his "determined efforts at teaching in the midst of establishing his professional practice" and a "mind disciplined enough to think through the requirements of a systematic architectural education."[61]

Ware was a person of large acquaintance with a busy social calendar. Visits early in 1865 to William Rogers's home, as well as a March gathering at the home of Henry

Bromfield Rogers, were very likely social but could also have offered an opportunity to raise informally the subject of architectural education. Ware visited the Institute in January, probably for a meeting of the Society of Arts, was elected to membership in the Institute in February, and attended a meeting of the society in March. In March also his partner, Henry Van Brunt, became a member.[62]

Ware's earliest formal communication with the Institute was a letter addressed not to William Rogers but to John Runkle in April 1865: "You have once or twice made the suggestion that the Institute of Technology is likely presently to take up the problem of Architectural education, and that you hope to avail of the experience Mr. Van Brunt and I have had of late with our pupils in the solution of it." He continued with a discussion of the necessary elements of an instructional program, saw an opportunity for significant contributions to architectural education, and expressed an interest in becoming involved should the Institute decide to offer such a program, since "the work would be one in many respects congenial to my tastes and so far as I thought myself qualified to engage in it I should be glad to do so."[63] He spoke also of his "long deferred hope" for the "advantages of a tour of study and observation in Europe," and suggested that an absence of "one or two years" abroad might further the Institute's aims and "would jump with my own inclinations. I should not consider myself competent to take any great part either in the organisation of the school or its administration without the aid of a special preparation."

Ware met with Rogers in late July or early August. A letter to his sister on August 2 was confined chiefly to the death of James Savage, Jr., Rogers's brother-in-law, who had been wounded in the Battle of Cedar Mountain. He did not mention an Institute appointment, probably because a condition he had placed on its acceptance—the opportunity to spend some time abroad and the provision of funds to equip his department—had not been resolved.[64]

By September 25, 1865, when the faculty first met, however, Ware was referring to his "Technology appointment," with an indication that the arrangements had been satisfactorily concluded:

Today I have had a very satisfactory afternoon, a general powwow of the newly appointed functionaries, and excellent talks tete-a-tete with Mr. Runkle, Eliot, Mr. Henck (sentimental) and Mr. Rogers. So far as I can see my work will be very light for a couple of years, chiefly getting somebody to look after the drawing, and seeing that that and indeed all branches are conducted with a due regard to the interest of the Architectural students. By keeping the run of what is doing in Mathematics, Physics & Chemistry, I can make sure that everything is brought into these courses which the Architectural neophyte requires. I hope that this will enable me to spend a large part of these two years abroad, though it is a question whether I had better go at once or bye & bye after things are a little more under way. This question . . . is likely to be settled however by the state of my affairs in my office.[65]

The "affairs" in his office referred to commissions to design Memorial Hall at Harvard and the First Church in Boston.

Ware would become an active member of the faculty, with some of their meetings held in his architectural office in the Studio Building on Tremont Street. He soon became very much involved in matters of general import to the school while at the same time preparing a preliminary outline of the proposed architectural course, a paper based on his letter to Runkle and read before a regular meeting of the Society of Arts in December.[66]

All of the Institute's early years were difficult financially. The costs of the building were rising and far exceeding original estimates, the laboratories needed equipment and instructional apparatus, and various general expenses had to be met. In short, the Institute was a precarious venture. Those who had taught in the preliminary session had not been paid until the term was over, and it is unlikely that without the experience of several months of operation, anyone could really know exactly how much would be available for faculty salaries. A badly deteriorating financial situation had led to extensive borrowing. Even so, it is somewhat surprising that the Government did not consider the salaries for the year 1865–66 until the spring of 1866.

Rogers accepted no compensation as president of the Institute, professor, or head of the school. Written communications with respect to initial salary have been found only for Eliot and Hague. The figure of $2,000, which Rogers had felt "safe" in mentioning to Eliot, he presented to Hague as a figure "not to be exceeded" but an amount that he "supposed" would soon "advance beyond that limit."[67] On April 12, 1866, however, the Government approved a Committee on Instruction recommendation of $1,500 each for Eliot, Runkle, Storer, and Watson for the year which had begun on the first Monday of October 1865 and ended on the first Monday of October 1866, with $500 additional for teaching in the evening courses to come from funds provided by the Lowell Institute. Atkinson and Bôcher were to receive $1,000, with $500 extra for evening teaching, and the salaries of Ware and Henck were set at $1,200.[68]

Records

Of the Faculty of the School of the Massachusetts Institute of Technology.

Monday Sep 25, 1865

The first meeting of the faculty was held at the rooms of the Institute in Summer St at 3 P. M: all the members being present except Prof. Hague. Prof. Atkinson was appointed Secretary.

Election Secretary

Prof Runkle read a programme of the course of mathematical study, Prof. Watson a programme of study in descriptive geometry and Prof. Bôcher one in the study of modern languages and the subject of the arrangement and order of studies was discussed at length.

Programmes Courses.

The professors of Chemistry were requested to consider and report on the subject of fees for partial or special courses of study in their department

p.3.
Fees for Special in Chemistry

After some informal discussion of other subjects connected with the School

Adjourned to Tuesday 26th at 3 P.m.

Tuesday Sep 26 1865

The Faculty met according to adjournment; absent Professors Hague and Ware

Professors Henck Storer and Atkinson

Minutes of the first faculty meeting, September 25, 1865

Ware had been given $500 on account in March, and Eliot, a similar amount early in April.[69] Following Government approval, Runkle received $500 on April 20. On May 1 Watson and Storer were paid $750, and Bôcher and Atkinson $500. Henck's first payment of $600 came on May 7. With some variation in payment dates for succeeding installments, all reached their total basic salary for 1865–66 on October 8, 1866, except for Ware, whose final payment was recorded on December 10. These payments were charged to the Walker Educational Fund.[70]

The paymaster was William Atkinson, secretary of the faculty, who, in accordance with a Government vote, was to prepare the payroll "under the direction of the President" and "draw on the Treasurer for the amount of the Salaries of the Professors as they from time to time become due."[71] Such an assignment was not without precedent; Professor George J. Brush at Sheffield performed a similar duty, though his responsibilities for the management of that school went far beyond compiler of payrolls and dispenser of funds. But the "inconvenience and unnecessary complication" of this arrangement for the Institute soon became apparent, and in 1868 the treasurer assumed responsibility for paying the instruction staff, quarterly or monthly, on the basis of a "payroll approved by the President."[72]

Committee on Instruction recommendations for the ensuing year were also considered by the Government in April 1866. In a preliminary estimate of income and expenses Rogers had contemplated professorial salaries of $2,500, a figure reduced by the committee to $2,000, to be paid in quarterly installments to each professor whose department was "completely organized and in full operation." The gross amount paid would include the compensation for evening instruction. The record indicates that "Salaries were fixed as recommended," but they were apparently not firm until the second term of the academic year 1866–67, when the committee formally adopted the arrangement for each member of the initial faculty except Ware, whose compensation remained at $1,200, since his department was not yet in full operation.[73]

As the school grew, additional appointments would become necessary, and not every new professor was compensated at the level of the original appointees. One chair was established with the understanding that no salary would be involved. Assistant teachers received $300 to $500, in some instances paid by the faculty members they were employed to help. Eliot, on leave in 1867–68, was expected to furnish the funds for the substitute he would provide.

On November 23, 1867, the time lag in appropriations for salaries was rectified, and the Government agreed with the Committee on Instruction that the Lowell Fund should no longer be applied to basic salaries, thus restoring the payment of an additional $500 to those called upon to teach an evening course. The basic salary for the initial members of the faculty would be $2,000, except for Henck and Ware.[74]

Henck had indicated that the work involved in his department, including extra hours in field practice, was consuming so much of his time that it would be impossible for him to do justice to his responsibilities if he did not give up a major part of his professional work, which had already suffered from the press of Institute duties. He was willing to devote himself wholly to the Institute even at "pecuniary sacrifice," but he needed some assurance of additional compensation "sufficient for the maintenance of his family." The committee agreed to Rogers's proposal that $500 be added to his salary to make it commensurate with those employed in the evening courses, and the Government concurred.[75]

When Ware left in 1866 to observe architectural education abroad, his request for full salary was denied. His compensation remained at $1,200, and he was required to furnish an assistant to handle the drawing instruction in his absence.[76]

From the beginning the faculty salaries were lower than Rogers had hoped. That he was not himself in need of funds and never accepted payment for his efforts on behalf of the Institute did not lessen his desire that the faculty be fully compensated for their work. There was no thought of direct payment of fees to the professors by the students. As a former faculty member at two leading institutions, Rogers had experienced such a system firsthand and knew how unpredictable a professor's income could be and how prone to inequities. He had also seen how easily an institution could be deprived of funds necessary for general expenses and improvements if no cap were placed on the amount that faculty members might retain from student fee payments.

Missing also from Rogers's salary plans was any statement about the limits of what a professor might be asked to do. Generally, however, each was expected to organize his department, of which in the beginning he was the sole member, and the subjects to be taught; plan for needed equipment and apparatus; obtain faculty approval of his proposed program in the context of the overall curriculum; and set to work. He was also expected to participate actively in general faculty responsibilities for the conduct of the school.

As the "difficult question of money" became ever more difficult, the Government resolved to make a concerted effort for a substantial increase in funds. In the spring of 1866 M. D. Ross raised the question of named professorships and called for an early decision with respect to the amount necessary to establish a chair, believing that "whilst soliciting subscriptions, gentlemen might be found, who would prefer adopting this course to aid the Institute."[77] Until a determination could be made, Rogers felt it would be reasonable to assume that $25,000 would be the "minimum price," though the income from that amount would have to be supplemented from other sources to pay the salary of a professor. The Government soon accepted a Committee on Instruction recommendation:

> *Voted*, that the sum necessary to endow a Professorship shall be not less than Twenty Five Thousand Dollars: and whenever the Government shall receive such a sum from one or more persons, or a perpetual annual income equivalent thereto, the Committee on Instruction shall be authorized to name some Professorship after said person or persons, provided they deem it for the interest of the Institute so to do.[78]

It was further voted that such funds be kept separate and never be used for any other purpose.

Almost from the beginning a recurring worry had been proper recognition for those who had made significant financial contributions, but the Government had done nothing beyond rewarding them with life memberships. The issue was raised again following the receipt early in 1867 of Ralph Huntington's bequest, and on June 3 the Government accepted a committee recommendation that the "great hall" of the Institute be named in his honor. Having done so, they could hardly ignore the contributions and bequest of William Walker and an important bequest in 1866 from James Hayward.

Named professorships provided the solution. In this manner the first such chairs in the Institute's school were established by the Government to recognize in "permanent form" the benefactions of these two individuals. This was done without reference to the 1866 decision on the endowment of professorships, setting a precedent that would be followed for most of the nineteenth-century named chairs.[79]

The Walker Professorship of Mathematics and Analytical Mechanics was created to honor Dr. Walker, then the Institute's greatest benefactor, to mark his "munificence" and "in consideration of his known love for mathematical science."[80] Runkle became the first holder of this chair, a designation he would retain during his years as second president of the Institute and until his death in 1902.

The Hayward Professorship of Civil and Topographical Engineering honored James Hayward, a distinguished railroad pioneer, who had signified his intention of becoming a member of the Institute in 1860.[81] Born on a Concord farm in 1786, he was twenty-nine years old before he was able to afford the liberal education he so much wanted. Entering Harvard, he was graduated with a bachelor of arts degree in 1819 and enrolled in the Divinity School. For six years, beginning in 1820, he was a tutor in mathematics and in 1826 was promoted to College Professor of Mathematics and Natural Philosophy. In 1827, however, he decided to follow the profession of civil engineer and joined the State Board of Internal Improvements. In succeeding years he was employed on surveys for railroad lines in Massachusetts and other states and superintended the construction of the Boston and Maine Railroad, serving as its president in the mid-1850s. Through membership on the Board of Harbor Commissioners he worked for the preservation of Boston Harbor. His publications include many reports covering his work on railroad surveys and an 1829 textbook, *Elements of Geometry upon the Inductive Method.* He died on July 27, 1866, leaving $20,000 to the Institute.[82] A United States legacy tax of 6 percent reduced the amount received to $18,800.[83]

Though Hayward's bequest was small compared with the total received from Walker, it was, nevertheless, not a negligible sum for the time. Roughly equal to a bequest to Harvard, to which he had double ties as an alumnus and former faculty member, it signified his genuine interest in the Institute, belief in the importance of its educational mission, and appreciation for its urgent need for funds. The arrival of this money in 1866 could not have been more opportune, and a professorship was created despite the fact that it did not meet the requirement of "not less than $25,000." In fulfillment of the Government vote, John Henck became the Hayward Professor in 1867, a post he held until his resignation in 1881.[84]

The first contribution to be designated for a particular professorship by the donor, and in accord with the specification of the Government's 1866 vote, came from Nathaniel Thayer, then a member of the Committee on Instruction. While abroad for the Paris Exposition in the summer of 1867, Rogers received the good news that Thayer "had put his name down for $25,000 . . . and wishes it to be a foundation for the Professorship of Physics." The full amount was received in January 1868.[85]

In his annual oral report to the Institute in May 1868, Rogers announced that the previous summer had seen both the achievement of a $50,000 subscription effort and a "crowning gift" that had "swelled the amount to seventy-five thousand dollars"— Thayer's donation, the "latest of his generous contributions." The name of the donor was already "prefixed to the Professorship of Physics" held by Rogers.[86]

Also established before 1870 was the William Powell Mason Professorship of Geology. Born in 1791, Mason was graduated from Harvard College in 1811 and studied law with Charles Jackson, who would soon become a member of the Supreme Judicial Court. Following admission to the bar, Mason was appointed reporter for the First Circuit Court of the United States, and his published case reports over the years were praised as a "veritable store house of legal information." He served several terms in the legislature and was active in the Boston Social Law Library as treasurer and secretary. His considerable wealth derived chiefly from real estate interests inherited from his father, Jonathan Mason, one of the Mount Vernon Proprietors responsible for the development of the Beacon Hill area of Boston.[87]

When William Mason died in 1867, his will included a bequest to the Institute of $20,000 for the support of a professorship, the field to be chosen jointly by his son and President Rogers. This gift may have been influenced by Mason's brother-in-law, Henry Bromfield Rogers, although Mason certainly was familiar with the Institute and William Rogers through negotiations for space in the Mercantile Building, which he apparently owned. On April 1, 1868, the Government gratefully accepted this bequest, which equaled that of Hayward and was also subject to the 6 percent United States legacy tax, and voted "to set it apart as a permanent fund under the title of the 'William P. Mason legacy,' the income of which shall be applied exclusively toward the support of the Professorship of (blank) in the School of the Institute."[88] A few days later Mason's son wrote to William Rogers informing him of the transfer of the money, minus the legacy tax: "Yours of the 10th inst. is rec'd & I have this morning paid $18,800 to Mr. Endicott to be devoted to the support of the Professorship of Geology."[89] Mason's note is very clear that they had already agreed on the bequest supporting the chair of geology.

In his oral report to the Institute for 1868 Rogers also mentioned Mason's "noble legacy ... for the support of another of its chairs.... I need scarcely say that such benefactions are precious not only from their intrinsic value, but as marking the interest which our labors have inspired, and will I trust continue to command among the promoters of education and science in our community."[90] But why did he not mention the decision that the bequest support the geology professorship?

There are several possible reasons. First, there is no record that the Government had been told of the decision reached by Mason and Rogers, though the treasurer had been informed by Mason when he transferred the money, and the cash book entry on April 11, 1868, supports this statement. Secondly, even if there were tacit acknowledgment by Government members that geology was the Mason designation, Rogers, who still held the Thayer Professorship of Physics, had not been formally named, and it would have been uncharacteristic of him to make a public statement under these circumstances. There was, too, the problem of one member of the faculty holding two endowed chairs, an important consideration despite the fact that Rogers accepted no compensation. Finally, there were changes on the horizon about which he was not prepared to speak publicly. His health had been poor, and he undoubtedly had already decided to withdraw soon from the Thayer Professorship. He knew also that he needed help with geology and hoped to get it from the professor of mining, but the future status of the absent Professor Hague was questionable. Soon Rogers would be corresponding with Alfred P. Rockwell, Hague's substitute, about a more permanent arrangement, with duties in geology specified. That this would be a final solution to the problem, however, was not evident. The relevant four-year course for those interested in geology—and they were few—was at that time combined with that of mining. Possibly the chairs in those fields would also be combined. It was much safer at this moment, then, not to identify the chair to which Mason's bequest would be devoted.

Rogers could not foresee that another change lay ahead, leading to unsettled times. Illness would force him to request an extended leave of absence. During this period he would continue to be listed as the professor of geology with no indication that he was not active and no substitute indicated. Indeed, he continued to be so listed beyond the point where he thought he had made clear that he had definitely resigned. This situation lingered until the appointment in 1871 of T. Sterry Hunt. But why the Mason name was not attached to the chair then is a mystery, for with Hunt's appointment, it became necessary for the first time since the opening of the school to pay the professor of geology. In 1883 the Corporation cleared beyond a doubt with William Mason's son that he and Rogers had agreed on geology for the professorship, but the Mason name was never publicly attached to it.[91]

Endowed or not, the faculty that Rogers assembled had excellent credentials and gave full measure of their time and energies to the school, often spending their own money for necessities when Institute funds were not available, and taking a personal interest in the success of the endeavor. As a group they were in effect officers of admission, overseers of discipline, guardians of the building, schedulers of classes, proctors of the drawing rooms, supervisors of the drill, watchdogs for absences, monitors of academic performance—all this plus the lecturing, laboratory supervision, and examining duties related to their classes and the subjects which they had themselves designed. They dealt minutely with every detail of the catalogue and the curriculum, and revised and adapted their plans as experience dictated. As a group and in committees they were concerned with every aspect of the school, including additions to the instructional staff, and with every detail of its operations not the prerogative of the janitor. They met frequently, in the daytime and in the evening, and by April 1867 had settled on Saturday morning as their regular time to come together, with additional meetings to be called when necessary. The Institute, in short, absorbed almost their every waking moment.

Physics and Astronomy (top) and Printing (bottom)—sketches prepared by Paul Nefflen for mural in Huntington Hall (see p. 764).

The First Students

*A*mong the young men who showed up on the first day of the preliminary session of the school, February 20, 1865, three—Walter Tuckerman, Henry O. Preble, and Louis Higginson—arrived with a testimonial from their teacher, William Atkinson. Atkinson, a specialist in preparing young men for college and soon to join the Institute faculty as professor of the English language and literature, laid out the overall preparation and aptitude of his charges, trying at the same time to individualize his comments so that the strengths and weaknesses of each would be apparent:

I send you the boys I mentioned to you on Saturday. French has not quite determined to come and wishes to see what it is. I shall advise his father to send him. The others are ready to join.

Tuckerman and Higginson have a good knowledge of Elementary Algebra, have been over Davies' Elementary plane Geometry and have some knowledge of plane trigonometry. Preble has a little knowledge of algebra and plane geometry. He has been an invalid and but little at school. French knows Algebra and plane geometry pretty well but nothing of trigonometry. They are all lads of fair average ability, not more. They are all excellent fellows interested and in earnest in what they undertake.

I was just preparing to put them carefully through a thorough review of their Algebra and a careful study of Davies' Legendre[1]—but I tell them they can get so much more from you than I can furnish that they had better by all means join your class.

Young Tuckerman has read with me a large portion of Gânot's Physics[2] in French, and he has some knowledge of German.[3]

No one by the name of French enrolled for the first session, but Atkinson was probably referring here to either of the brothers William M. R. or Daniel C. French, who were both soon to attend classes at the Institute. William came as a "special student" in 1866–67, Daniel as a "partial student" in 1867–68. Special or partial status was reserved for those pursuing selected subjects rather than a full course. Both brothers, as it turned out, were more inclined to the arts than to science or engineering: Daniel went on to become a prominent sculptor, perhaps best known for his rendering of Abraham Lincoln for the Lincoln Memorial in Washington, D.C.; William started out intending to become a civil engineer, but moved into landscape architecture and ultimately into art education as director of the Art Institute of Chicago. Daniel later observed that the most important thing he learned at the Institute was how to draw accurately.[4]

News of the school spread quickly. Paid advertisements appeared in several local and regional papers; just over three weeks after the opening, for example, Institute secretary Thomas Webb paid two dollars for a notice in the *Bridgewater Banner*.[5] In response to such publicity, as well as to encouragement from friends, family, and teachers, some prospective students made inquiries on their own. A few—particularly those interested in engineering careers—considered transferring from the Lawrence Scientific School at Harvard, attracted by the prospect of a more practical, professionally oriented education than Harvard could provide. One Harvard student, Charles Barney, wrote to Rogers in February 1865:

> I would like to gain some information of the Mass. Inst. Tech. I have completed my first year at the Lawrence Scientific School, during which time I have finished Descriptive and Analytical Geometry and the Calculus. I have also some knowledge of Geology & Chemistry. Now I would like to know how far along in the course I can get at the commencement of the next term. . . . I wish to fit myself for a Mining Engineer as soon as possible. If everything proves satisfactory, I shall come myself and bring 2 or 3 of my classmates with me.[6]

In a postscript, Barney asked which mechanics textbook would be used in class. James Parker, one of Barney's classmates also considering a transfer, wrote two days later about fees and requirements for admission.[7] Neither, in the end, enrolled at the Institute. Another prospective student asked Rogers for an opinion as to whether "the School offers advantages as good as or better than those of any other Scientific School in the Country."[8]

Parents also sought information, without always grasping the level of education required or the goals underlying the Institute's curriculum. F. P. Appleton, for example, suspected that the Institute would make a fitting way for his son to brush up on a couple of subjects for admission to Harvard. "I write to ask whether any pupil can join now," Appleton inquired of Rogers in late March 1865. "My son has been studying with a view to entering the Scientific School at Cambridge, & as his teacher has given up his School, I am anxious that he should enter the Institute classes in Chemistry & French, as soon as possible."[9] Frederick S. Cabot's inquiry was more open-ended: "Will you have the kindness to let me know what the qualifications will be for admission to the School connected with your institution? I wish to enter my eldest boy if he can be ready for the regular course."[10] Rogers wrote to Cabot outlining the requirements for admission to the first year: "The student will be expected to be expert in Arithmetic . . . to have mastered the primary operations of Algebra including the solution of simple equations and to have a good knowledge of the elements of plane Geometry." There were no other prerequisites, but Rogers advised that some knowledge of physics, drawing, and French would "lighten the labors" of the first year.[11] Appleton's son, Nathaniel Walker Appleton, joined the Institute's preliminary session in midstream, a month or so late, while Cabot's son Lincoln enrolled for the first full session beginning in the fall of 1865. Both fathers were industrial magnates—Appleton of the Lowell Bleachery and Dye Works, Cabot of the Boston Steel and Iron Company—and apparently ambitious for their sons to pursue careers in science and industry. "I wish my son," wrote another parent, "to secure the best possible practical education which shall fit him for charge of manufactures, or general business."[12]

By the end of the preliminary session, 28 students were enrolled:

Appleton, Nathaniel Walker	Lowell
Bailey, Abraham	Charlestown
Bowers, Harry Clay	Philadelphia, Pa.
Cutler, Elisha Pomeroy, Jr.	Charlestown
Eastwood, Sam	Framingham
Forbes, Eli	Clinton

Gorham, Arthur	Jamaica Plain
Hall, Albert Francis	Charlestown
Higginson, Louis	Cambridge
Jackson, William	Brighton
Kreissmann, Charles	Boston
Lee, Charles Tennant	Charlestown
Peterson, Andrew C.	Roxbury
Preble, Henry Oxnard	Cambridge
Richards, Robert H.	Boston
Ross, Waldo Ogden	Boston
Russell, Andrew Howland	Plymouth
Sanford, Oliver Nason	Dorchester
Sherman, F. C.	Brookline
Stevens, Eben Sutton	Webster
Stone, Joseph	Charlestown
Thom, George Henry	Bedford
Thorndike, George Francis	Boston
Tilden, Bryant Parrott	Boston
Tolman, James Pike	Roxbury
Tryon, William	Boston
Tuckerman, Walter	New York, N.Y.
Willey, Walter Tolman	Boston[13]

The geographic distribution of students by place of origin was fairly narrow—most came from the Boston area—but a few came from townships as far away as Plymouth, and two came from out of state.

One member of the group, Eben Stevens, recalled that first semester nearly half a century later:

> About February 15, 1865, there appeared in the Herald a small advertisement announcing that the School of the Institute would open February 20 at 16 Summer Street in the Mercantile Library Building where three long narrow rooms had been rented.
>
> Here assembled fifteen young men as the class of '68. They were a "picked-up lot" in that there was no preparatory school for such an institution of learning in those days and little or no examination as the writer recalls. The faculty consisted of ten gentlemen with Rogers as professor of physics; a most

remarkable man, who left his impress upon everyone with whom he came in contact, whether business men who furnished the sinews of war or students who revered him beyond words to express.

Rogers was genial, attractive, with a pleasant smile upon his strong face never to be forgotten, especially that prominent nose. A scientist of broad culture with such command of exceptional English that students were forced to obtain "Jenkins' Vest Pocket Lexicon," by the aid of which we were enabled to elaborate the professor's meanings. Of course we watched such a mind for some flaw which was never discovered except that he always spelled balance with two l's.

We put the work of the first year into four months.[14]

By the time Stevens wrote this piece, his memories had faded into anecdotal generalities, but they do give a flavor of student life at the fledgling Institute.

Assessing the first semester on its completion posed a challenge because of the novelty of the enterprise and the need to balance student encouragement with vigilance on academic standards. The faculty opted mostly for encouragement, however, as of the original 28 students, only 3—Arthur Gorham, Louis Higginson, and F. C. Sherman—did not register for the following session. Higginson's grammar school teacher, William Atkinson, had asked Rogers for frank advice on his former charge:

> My excellent neighbour Mr. Stephen Higginson is in some perplexity as to the disposal of his son Louis, one of the three young men I sent in to you. His question is whether to undergo the expense of keeping him at the school another year, with the prospect of making him an engineer, or to put him next fall into a counting-room. He has *eight* sons—*five* have been in service in the war—and having so many claims upon him, he does not want to push the education of this one without good evidence that it wd be best for him to do so. If he clearly has talent, and could turn a scientific education to really good account, Mr. H. does not wish the expense to stand in the way. If on the other hand the young man wd be as likely or more likely to succeed in business than in a profession, his father thinks that next autumn will be the time for him to begin.[15]

Atkinson thought of Higginson as "an excellent and amiable young man, of fair abilities, but with no special aptitude for scientific study, and a little lacking in the energy that wd be needful for a successful career as an engineer." While Rogers concurred in this assessment—"our young friend . . . has sufficient capacity but is perhaps lacking in the zeal & energy required for the studies & the active labours of an Engineer"—he deliberately did not offer a judgment on the advisability of Higginson's continuing at the Institute, even suggesting that scientific talent takes time to blossom.[16] Higginson's father decided, in any event, not to send him back.

Atkinson also wondered about the progress of another of his former students, Walter Tuckerman. Tuckerman's father, Lucius Tuckerman, a friend of Atkinson's, was unhappy with his son's performance: "Mr. T. is a driving business man," Atkinson wrote to Rogers, "making a great deal of money under the high-pressure New York system, and is a little impatient if everything does not move as fast as he does."[17] Atkinson hoped that Rogers would find a way to put Tuckerman's mind at ease. Rogers's response does not survive, but he apparently succeeded as young Tuckerman registered again in the fall of 1865 and remained at the Institute for two more academic years. His record was inconsistent and not entirely compatible with the Institute's emphasis on the practical—fine work in languages and English, deficient in mathematics, sometimes irregular in attendance[18]—and he left in the spring of 1867 before earning a degree. He transferred to the Lawrence Scientific School, however, and earned a bachelor of science degree there in 1870.[19]

Rogers kept a number of parents informed about their sons' work, particularly where progress did not live up to expectations or to the Institute's standards. At the conclusion of the preliminary session, for example, he wrote to E. P. Cutler of Charlestown about the performance of his son, Elisha Pomeroy Cutler, Jr. It was a summary statement, yet composed in such a way that both father and son could glean essential advice on how to proceed without feeling discouraged:

[Your son] has probably informed you of his standing at the two preceding examtns. The final examtn was comprehensive of *the whole course* & therefore a severer trial than the others.

In Chemistry & Physics your son has found less difficulty than in his mathematical studies. Should you desire his Continuance in the Institute as a regular student, he ought to enter the 1st years Course in Mathematics—

His attention to his duties & his amiable deportment have the regard of all his teachers.[20]

Rogers's concerns were apparently well-founded, as young Cutler returned for the fall 1865 semester but continued to struggle academically. Near the end of the semester, he was one of five students advised to move back to first-year studies rather than continue in the second year.

Rogers was determined that the Institute's mission would reach beyond the privileged classes dominating institutions like Harvard. From the beginning, the Institute had been thought of as a place where people from across the social spectrum—rich and poor, tradesmen and mechanics, educated and uneducated—could find an outlet for their talents and interests and an opportunity for educational and professional development, particularly in pursuits related to science and technology. Indeed, the whole venture was conceived partly as a means of redirecting focus away from traditional gentlemanly modes—the liberal arts approach—toward a more specialized, professional style, with practical goals that would appeal as much, if not more, to the working classes as to moneyed aristocrats. The earliest mission statements emphasized "systematic training in the applied sciences, which can alone give to the industrial classes a sure mastery over the materials and processes with which they are concerned," and this pattern of populist rhetoric persisted through the 1860s.[21]

As it turned out, however, the first class was populated by a higher proportion of the well-to-do and the well-connected than probably had been anticipated. While there had never been any intention to exclude such people—and there may even have been a late-day recognition that the Institute would need them and their families, sooner rather than later, for political influence and financial support—Rogers went to some pains to ensure that the breadth of the Institute's target population was not forgotten. In 1866, for example, he talked and corresponded with an officer of a charitable institution concerned with educating disadvantaged youth in technical trades:

> You may recollect we had a moment's conversation concerning sending a few young men to the Institute of Technology, on behalf of the Mechanic Association. Will you please communicate to me on what terms one to four pupils could be admitted, & when such admission would be desirable. Knowing these points, I would like to submit the matter to our School Committee.[22]

The "Mechanic Association" referred to here was undoubtedly the Massachusetts Charitable Mechanics' Association, founded in 1795 by Paul Revere. Its primary objective was to aid unfortunate mechanics and those dependent on them, but it also loaned money to young mechanics and assisted in establishing schools and libraries for the use of apprentices. Whether or not the Institute recruited many "mechanics" and "apprentices" to its student body in the early years, it is clear that there was some enthusiasm for the effort.

Because of the quality of the Institute's faculty and the novelty of its mission, pressure quickly built to serve students in medicine and other constituencies with science- and technology-related interests. Rogers was open on this to a point, but stood firmly against the idea of generating professional courses outside of engineering. Writing to Horatio Storer, brother of Frank Storer, in the spring of 1867, he offered a word of caution:

> I write a hurried line . . . to guard against any misconception which might arise either in your mind or that of Dr. Miner from my ready assent to the proposed interview on Friday afternoon.
>
> In agreeing to meet you to learn about the purpose of hearing what you may have to propose as to the admission of Medical Students to the Cheml. Instructions of the Institute I was influenced simply by feelings of friendship & Courtesy, but I wish to be distinctly understood as in no wise either directly or by implication participating in the plan of a new Medical School. I am, as you are aware, not in a position to judge either of the need for such a school or of its probable success if undertaken. Whatever enterprises may be originated elsewhere, my first consideration must be the safety & growth of the Institute & in this view I would say that while our institution may perhaps admit as special students persons who are studying Medicine at any of the Medical Schools, it cannot safely enter into any arrangement making its Cheml. Dept. ancillary to a particular Medical School.[23]

Storer, professor of obstetrics and medical jurisprudence at the Berkshire Medical College in Pittsfield, Massachusetts, had been investigating new opportunities because his college was closing permanently. Part of Rogers's concern here had to do with the need to avoid perceived competition with existing institutions such as the Harvard Medical School: a phrase elided from the draft of this letter, for example, refers to the need to avoid doing "any thing to invite the hostility of a part of the Community." But it was a choice based on more than mere political expediency; Rogers fully subscribed to his own statement as a matter of principle and institutional philosophy, that the Institute should focus its educational programs on budding engineers.

Even as the Institute's educational mission remained well defined and increasingly focused, there were efforts to broaden its reach beyond Boston and the New England area. By 1867, in fact, it was clear that the Institute would not be a provincial center for long, that it was heading for national stature as a school of technology and innovation. Rogers corresponded with one newspaper in Cincinnati, Ohio, for example, about the wording and placement of an advertisement. The editors wrote to him:

> We will insert the enclosed advertisement in the Presbyter. One Time $1.00 One Mo. $3.00 Three Mo. $7.00 And in the Christian Herald, & Journal & Messenger for the same price. Our papers have a large and very valuable patronage from institutions of Learning of every description all over the United States. And as we get advertisements from the same persons year after year we naturally suppose that they must derive some benefit from their insertion.[24]

The advertisement read, in part:

> Massachusetts Institute of Technology.—A scientific school for the Professional Education of Mechanical, Civil, and Mining Engineers, Practical Chemists, Builders, and Architects, and for the general education of young men for business life. Instruction given in Mathematics and the Physical Sciences, Modern Languages and English Studies. Students received in special studies.

It concluded with contact information and a schedule of entrance examinations. While Rogers was notoriously conservative about such advertising, which he considered generally too crude for a respectable academic establishment (newspapers at the time were filled with advertisements for unscrupulous "diploma mills" of all kinds), he balanced this caution against the need to inform potential students in places where word of the Institute might otherwise be slow to arrive. The nation's hinterlands, as it turned out, would be important in a number of ways besides student recruitment: westward migration and the burgeoning railroad industry, in particular, became primary sources of professional opportunity for the Institute's earliest graduates.

Among the students in the first full session, 1865–66, was Nelson W. Conant, of Louisville, Kentucky. While it is perhaps unfair to characterize him, strictly speaking, as a migrant from the hinterlands—since he had attended high school in the Boston area—by the time he wrote of his interest in the Institute, he was again residing in Louisville and the return journey would have been arduous:

> Having decided to enter a Scientific Institution in order to continue my education, I take the liberty to address you for information concerning the School of Industrial Science, which I hear is to be opened in Boston next October.
>
> I attended the schools of the Messrs Allen, at West Newton, Mass. last year and studied with the intention of entering the Institute at Troy N.Y. but my parents prefer that I should attend school in or near Boston, if possible.
>
> I would therefore be obliged to you for a circular and any other information concerning the School.[25]

Thus, the Institute was already competing for applicants with Rensselaer Polytechnic, in spite of Rogers's ongoing efforts not to draw too much attention to this potential trend. And, as there was no comparable institution west of the Appalachians, talented young Midwesterners like Conant had little choice but to look east to Lawrence (Harvard), Sheffield (Yale), Rensselaer, and—the newest addition to this specialized group—the Massachusetts Institute of Technology.

The Institute's geographic reach, in fact, broadened quite rapidly in its first five years. By the second year, students were coming from as far away as Arkansas and California, and the first foreign students had arrived (Ernest A. Harris, from Truro, Nova Scotia, and W. A. Kimball, from Canada); the first student from outside North America—Enrique Ruiz, from Peru—arrived in the fourth year.

Number of Students from Outside Massachusetts, 1865–70

1865–66	5
1866–67	22
1867–68	21
1868–69	33
1869–70	43

The Institute's professional focus, compared to most colleges, drew the attention of older students—some of whom had attended an undergraduate program, were already in the work force, and sought specialized coursework as a means of advancement in their careers:

I am nearly twenty-three (23) years of age, left college (Amherst) during the 2nd term of Junior Year to enter the Army, in which I have been serving for nearly three years. I have studied almost all the branches set forth in your catalogue as pertaining to the 1st & 2nd years, still, as you may suppose, a very active military life of nearly three years has not tended to keep them fresh in my mind.

At my age I cannot afford to spend four years in study. My desire is to study "Geology & Mining Engineering," as a profession.[26]

Rogers encouraged this prospective applicant, outlining the preparation required for entry and suggesting that he probably qualified as a third-year student, but nothing came of the inquiry.[27] Among the 63 students listed in the first manuscript register, however, 11 were 20 years of age or older—and one was 31 years old. A broader spread of ages was represented than would have been the case at a liberal arts college, for example.

Age of Students on Entry, 1865–66[28]

Age	No. of Students
15	2
16	15
17	11
18	16
19	8
20	2
21	2
22	1
23	1
24	2
25	1
26	1
31	1

One of the few surviving accounts by a student who attended the first full session, 1865–66, was written by Ernest W. Bowditch, probably around 1910. The Institute remained important to him long after his student days (1865–1869); he served as a Corporation member (1911–1918), which explains, in part, the interest he took in

No.	NAME, (in full.)	Date of Birth. YEAR. MONTH. DAY.	Age.	Place of Birth.	Name of Parent or Guardian.
1865-6.					
1	Henry Kirk White	1844 Oct. 8	21	Templeton.	Abner White
2	Charles Augustus Smith	1846 Oct. 1st	19	St. Louis Mo.	Charles R. Smith
3	James Taylor Fox	1843 Oct 24	22	Providence R.S.	James A. Fox
4	Bryant Parrott Tilden	1846 June 6	19	Sault St. Marie Mich	J. R. Tilden
5	Josiah Lewis Chapin	1847 Aug. 18	18	Tiverton R.I.	W. C. Chapin
6	Edward Pike Chapin	1849 Aug 19	16	Tiverton R.I.	W C Chapin
7	Lincoln Cabot	1849 Oct 18	16	Hingham	F. S. Cabot
8	Charles Chadbourne Gilman	1848 July 28	17	Chelsea	C. Gilman
9	Nelson Whitney Conant	1848 Feb 11	17	Louisville Ky	N. W. Conant
10	Theodore Eames Wardwell	1847 Apl. 4	18	Andover Mass	W. H. Wardwell
11	Edward S. Safford	1847 Sept. 6	18	Boston	Geo. W. Safford
12	Frank H. Perkins	1847 May 7	18	"	Saml. S. Perkins
13	Robert Hallowell Richards	1844 Aug 26	21	Gardiner Me	Mrs F Richards
14	Charles Kreissmann	1849 Mard 19	16	Boston	Aug. Kreissmann
15	George Francis Thorndike	1846 Sept 26	19	Boston	John H. Thorndike
16	Henry Oxnard Preble	1847 Jan. 4	18	Portland, Me	Geo. Henry Preble
17	Oliver Ngson Sanford	1847 Sept 21	18	Boston	Oliver S. Sanford
18	Ben Lincoln Cushing	1849 Sept 5	16	Boston	Levi L. Cushing Jr
19	Walter Tuckerman	1849 Mard 29	16	New York City	Lucius Tuckerman
20	W. E. Bowditch	1850 Apr. 10	15	Brookline	Wm J. Bowditch
21	G W Preston	1848 Jan 8	17	Boston	Jas. W. Preston
22	Eli Forbes	1849 Feb 3	16	Lowell	Franklin Forbes
23	Frank H. Allen	1845 Oct 7	20	Boston	Benj F. Allen
24	Stuart M. Buck	1842 Oct 24	23	Boston	David Buck
25	Oben Sutton Stevens	1846 Dec. 11	18	Webster	Hy H. Stevens.
26	Charles Tennant Lee	1849 Feb. 23.	16	Boston	James Lee Jr.
27	James Pike Tolman	1847 Nov. 7	18	Boston	James Tolman
28	John Peck junr.	1847 Sept. 6	18	New York	John Peck
29	Ernest O. Saltmarsh	1849 Dec 15	16	Windsor Vt	Seth Saltmarsh
30	Walter L. Bouvé	1849 Oct 28	16	Boston	Thomas T. Bouvé

Excerpt from the first register, fall 1865

Residence of Parent or Guardian.	School.				REMARKS.
Chelsea Mass.	Appleton Academy				✓
Cambridgeport	Brown High School Newburyport M.				✓
Boston	Private.				✓
Boston	Chauncy Hall				✓
Lawrence Mass	Oliver High School				✓
Lawrence Mass	Oliver High School				✓
Brookline	P. Pierce grammar				✓
Chelsea Mass	West Newton E.&C.S.				✓
Louisville Ky	West Newton E.&C.S.				✓
Roxbury Mass	Dearborn Grammar				✓
Boston	English High School				✓
"	" " "				✓
18 Boylston Pl. Boston	Phillips Exeter Academy				✓
14 Hudson St. Bost	Private Teacher				✓
29 Edinboro' St. Boston	P. School Farmington, Me.				✓
Mt. Auburn St. Camb.	W. P. Atkinson's.				✓
Dorchester Mass.	Dwight School.				✓
N. Cambridge Mass	Camb. H. School.				✓
New York N.Y.	W. P. Atkinson				✓
Brookline Mass.	Brookline High School.				✓
Boston	Private School Cambridge				✓
Clinton Mass.	Grammar School Clinton				✓
Somerville	Somerville High School.				✓
Boston	Williams College				✓
Webster Mass	Highland School Worcester				✓
Charlestown Mass.	Charlestown High School				✓
Roxbury Mass.	Roxbury High School				✓
New York	L. P. Jenks N.Y.				✓
Hubbardston Mass	Lawrence Acad.y Groton				✓
Boston	Phillips School				✓

reliving memories of the school half a century later. Although written late in life, Bowditch's narrative evokes personalities, places, and events in sharp detail. It begins with his very first visit to the Institute:

> In the spring of 1865 I went to the Secretary's office of the Institute, at that time located in the old Mercantile Building on Summer Street, opposite C. F. Hovey & Company, where I met Professors Rogers and Runkle. The rules of the school as then established provided that, in addition to passing certain examinations applicants would be at least sixteen years old—a wise proviso but abrogated at once in my favor by Professor Rogers, who I judge wanted me, perhaps for the name but probably to swell the numbers of the incoming class, which was the first regular class to go through the school, though there was at that time a class ('68) that was perhaps three or four months ahead of us.
>
> He argued that I was already in my sixteenth year, and allowing me to enter in the autumn of 1865 would in fact not be stretching the by-laws greatly. It was found, too, that the training received in the second year of the Brookline High School would fit me to pass the entrance examination for the first year class in Technology. I have no recollection of passing any entrance examination, though there must have been one, as I recollect Professor Bocher talked with me regarding my knowledge of French, and accepted the two years' work at Brookline under Miss Abby Bartlett as sufficient.[29]

The account proceeds with recollections of the first instructors, cited by the nicknames awarded them by students; some nicknames appear to have been affectionately applied, others with more hostile intent, but generally they reflected a candid assessment of the pedagogical or personal skills of each instructor:

> There were not many professors at the school at that time—Rogers, Runkle, (John S.), Ware, (Billy Bobby), Storer, (Frank), Eliot, (Hog), Bocher, (Musher), Watson, (Squirty), Kneeland, the latter acting also as Secretary. . . . Of all the Professors—and every one was much in earnest—Storer was far and away the best *teacher*. He was cross, irritable and, if you please, at times unreasonable; but his explanations were always entirely to the point, clear and concise. Not afraid to say he did not know, always ready to help, never too tired to assist anyone who asked advice; he hated a sham or dishonesty of any description, and would not tolerate a lazy boy. . . . This view of his powers as a teacher is shared by many of the former Technology boys who studied under him. Eliot was not

popular; he was an indifferent lecturer, and when, years after, he left to become the head of Harvard College, there were many who felt that it was a change for the better for all concerned.

Professor Rogers, of course, by his personality many times held the school together, and very likely kept peace in the faculty. A great student, with a tremendous capacity for solid work, he yet had a keen sense of humor, and undoubtedly at times saw things going on that he purposely did not see, and where opportunity offered was a good deal of a boy himself. What he taught was physics, and though much of it proved dry and uninteresting to many of us, still his interest was very inspiring and lasting.

Bowditch perhaps felt free to take a swipe at Charles W. Eliot, in particular, because of the ongoing rivalry between Harvard and the Institute, generated by geographic proximity, clashing rather than complementary perspectives on education, and periodic "hostile takeover" efforts on the part of Harvard.

He was equally sharp in describing the atmosphere, layout, and everyday life for students, all in the context of contemporary Boston before it became a bustling hub:

> Some of the lecture and study rooms were in Mercantile Building on Summer Street; some in Judge Jackson's old dwelling house in Chauncy Street, and the balance (laboratories) were in what is now Rogers Building on Boylston Street. . . . Going to school in three different buildings, so to speak, one of which was fully a mile from the others, had its disadvantages. The time occupied in going from one to another was considerable, and though this was arranged so that exercises at the Rogers Building were usually in the afternoon, it was a long tramp from Chauncy Street and a cold one as well, as there were no structures on Boylston Street below Arlington Street Church except the Natural History Building, and a plank sidewalk only a portion of the way, west of the Public Garden.
>
> The few street cars available were drawn by horses, and ran from the Paddock Elms on Tremont Street along the Common to Boylston, through the latter to Clarendon, thence to Marlborough, where they terminated. I seem to remember that they ran every fifteen minutes. . . .
>
> Most of us from out of town brought our dinners with us, in little tin cases, and we were allowed to eat it in one of the lecture rooms, or, better, in one of the corridors. With me this lasted till the third or fourth year, when I was allowed to go with others to a boarding house on Berkeley Street, near

Tremont, kept by a Mrs. Page, where we luxuriated in hot dinners at $1.50 or $2.00 per week.

When exercises were in Rogers Building in the forenoon, it was my custom to come from Brookline by train, getting off at what was then known as the Providence Railroad Crossing (Huntington Avenue Station), and go more or less directly across lots to the Institute building. At that time, the intervening space was all either vacant land or water, and no sidewalks of any description.

Returning in the evening it was customary to go down Columbus Avenue from Berkeley Street and take a train on the other side of the Providence R.R. Crossing, near what is now Trinity Place Station. There was neither station nor platform for shelter, and sometimes if the train was late, possibly raining or snowing, it was a bad, draughty place to wait, but was all there was.

Some of the boys of the class (there were thirty of us) were even more handicapped. One came every day from Fitchburg, another from Foxboro, while two of them from Maine boarded at Mrs. Page's on Berkeley Street, rooming together in what was intended to be the back entry of the house and was mostly doors and windows—a sort of a general passage-way during daylight hours.[30]

The day's work was from nine A.M. to five P.M., with two hours off in the middle of the day. After five was the only time, practically, that remained for study, and if a boy lived out of town it meant rather late hours, or early ones next morning. Practically, the work and surroundings were all new, and perhaps therefore the more interesting. To see thirty or forty boys of my own age, every one of whom appeared anxious to learn everything in sight, was of itself inspiring. Besides this, it was impossible that all of the studies and the laboratory practice could fail to be interesting. . . .

During the four years' course we had very many good times among the boys; some of them a trifle irregular, perhaps, but on the whole not very bad, and none of them really vicious.

Opposite the school on Boylston Street, between Berkeley and Clarendon, was vacant land, on which we were in the habit of playing ball, particularly what was at that time called football. On the corner of St. James Avenue and Berkeley Street was the Academy of Notre Dame, where quite a lot of girls went to school. The grounds around the Academy (a large yard, really) were surrounded by a somewhat high, close board fence. It was surprising how frequently the football was kicked over the fence, and how necessary it was for a number of boys to go after it—particularly if it happened to be recess time for the young ladies, and the displeasure of the nuns in charge only added to the pleasure.

Bowditch's reference to "good times . . . some of them a trifle irregular" undercuts an earlier observation that this was a more mature group than the typical undergraduate class of the day. But even though a fifth of the students in the Institute's first class were over 20 years old, the remainder were in fact teenagers ranging in age from 15 to 19. It is hardly surprising, then, that discipline was sometimes a problem. Student pranks, usually benign if irritating, occasionally assumed more serious risks and consequences, particularly when scientific curiosity was involved.

Benjamin T. Prescott, Jr., for example, found himself in trouble more than once for misbehavior in the laboratory—the first time in January 1868, when the faculty voted "that the case of Prescott who endangered the laboratory by inexcusable carelessness in handling chemicals which did not belong to him be referred to the President and Sec'y with full powers"; and a month later, when they voted that "the case of Stevens and Prescott charged with breach of order in the Laboratory be referred to the President and Prof. Storer."[31] Prescott tried to head off the consequences for this second serious breach with a letter of apology to Rogers two days before the faculty meeting:

> I take this opportunity to express my shame and sorrow for what occured [sic] in the Laboratory the other day.
>
> I in an ungarded [sic] moment was carried away by my temper for which I most sincerely beg pardon.
>
> Hopeing [sic] to still remain in the Institute I am willing to be put on trial for good behavior the rest of the term.[32]

He had been in academic difficulty as well, his father having been warned in December 1867 that his son was "not making proper progress in his studies."[33] Prescott was probably not a good match for the Institute anyway; he was registered one year in an eclectic mix of courses at the 1st, 2nd, and 3rd year levels, with little obvious plan or goal.

Such serious infractions, fortunately, were the exception rather than the rule, and most students were serious, hardworking, and motivated—even when they encountered academic difficulties along the way. Channing Whitaker, who went on to become a professor of mechanical engineering at the Institute, did not start out as auspiciously as his later career might suggest. He struggled, for example, in languages. While he had entered with advanced standing as a second-year year student in 1866,

Channing Whitaker

he was warned at the end of the third year (his second) that he would only be allowed to enter the final year in the fall of 1868 "on condition of making up his German, omitted on account of weak eyes."[34] Rogers took a special interest in the matter, perhaps sensing Whitaker's deep potential, and offered advice on extra language work. Whitaker thanked him in a letter written from Lowell, Massachusetts, where he had found summer work, in 1868:

Kind Sir,

I can hardly tell you how much pleasure the receipt of your very kind and unexpected letter has given me.

I hope I do not need to assure you that I have felt deeply the interest which you had previously taken in me and the assistance which you have rendered me, yet I did not at all anticipate that you would think of me during the summer months and offer me such substantial aid.

I feel that I should be very ungrateful not to do the best that I can to get some knowledge of German during the remainder of the vacation. . . .

. . . Hoping that you will be sufficiently mindful of your health to rest a little from your duties during this *hot* weather . . .[35]

Whitaker was genuinely amazed that this very busy man, who was also in poor health at the time, would take a particular interest in one student's academic problems.

Later that summer, he sent an update on his progress:

I hope you will not think that I have forgotten all about my German because you have not heard from me. . . .

. . . Since my return from Salem I have been under her [Miss Dana's] tuition. I recite two evenings in a week. She gives me from as early in the evening as I can get to her house, until half past nine. Her terms are one dollar per lesson. I shall be able to have before she goes away nine lessons.[36]

Whitaker was anxious to repay Rogers's generosity with conscientious effort. But his difficulty with languages went beyond "weak eyes"; he also experienced trouble with

French, which he was allowed to drop in the fall of 1868, and failed German again in the spring of 1869. He managed, nonetheless, to pass a makeup later that summer which allowed him to graduate on time with his 1869 classmates, the second group to receive diplomas.[37]

Whitaker was among the more enthusiastic and diligent of that early student cohort. He kept abreast of the evolving careers of those who had graduated before—and was particularly excited, as were a number of his peers, about prospects for adventure and professional advancement in the opening up of the American West:

> I presume you may know that Mr. [Charles A.] Smith and also Mr. [Bryant P.] Tilden[38] start today for the Pacific Railroad, their offer to them being such that Mr. Smith thought best to leave Mr. Francis although his pay had been increased and he [was] placed in the permanent force. He is to have One Hundred Dollars per month, his expenses all paid.[39]

It was clear to him that students with applicable knowledge of the kind acquired at the Institute would be in ever-increasing demand among employers in the newest, most progressive industries.

Whitaker took such pride in the Institute that, as a student, he became an unofficial recruiter on its behalf, in the days before an alumni association had even been thought of and long before any program was in place to recruit students in a systematic way. He started by talking up the Institute at his place of summer employment—the Lowell Machine Shop—and encouraging young technicians there to think of the Institute as an ideal start toward advancement in the technical professions. Near the beginning of the 1868–69 academic year, he reported to Rogers:

> I will be very greatly obliged to you if you will let me know whether you will be in town about the middle of this week, and whether you will be sufficiently at liberty to allow me to call on you with a young friend, a draughtsman at the Machine Shop, who would like very much to be a student at the Institute. I will write you more fully about him tonight.

After a hard day's work, he continued:

> There are two other young men here whom Mr. Hildreth is urging to take the same course so soon as they shall be prepared to enter.
> I think you would like Mr. Mansfield, should he go to the Institute for he is orderly and modest as well as capable.

> The chief difficulty with him seems to be, and indeed the reason why he did not himself move in the matter is that he has so small a stock of funds on hand that he has not felt as if he would be justified in doing so.
>
> Mr. Hildreth has known, however, ever since I introduced Mr. Smith to him last summer, that a few students who were competent have been employed as instructors or assistants with the younger classes, and has suggested that it may be possible he may be able to meet the expense of his tuition in that way.[40]

The kind of candidates Whitaker was recommending would have appealed to Rogers, if for no other reason than that they were of the mechanic or industrial class, a group somewhat underrepresented at the Institute. Also intriguing here is Whitaker's reference to a type of early work-study program—an experiment in peer tutoring—through which needy students could help defray the cost of their education. Whitaker appears to have been in need of financial assistance himself, as he held such a tutorship during his student days.

In any event, Mansfield's supervisor in the Lowell Machine Shop followed up a week later with a positive recommendation, and Albert Mansfield was admitted to the first-year class in the fall of 1868. He attended the Institute for just one year and earned no degree, but, like many other special students before and after him, probably came away with a higher level of technical competence in his chosen field.

Mansfield may have been unable to continue for financial reasons, which was certainly the case with a number of students at the time. Rogers often went out of his way to encourage such students to take the long view and make whatever sacrifices might be necessary to finish their educations. Charles True, of Yarmouth, Maine, was one student in this position. A solid student never in any academic or disciplinary difficulty, he attended the Institute for two years (1866 to 1868), having entered with advanced standing. As he anticipated completing his final year (1868–69), however, undisclosed "circumstances" arose that required him to find immediate employment. He wrote to Rogers from his home in Maine:

> If you deem me worthy such a favor, I should be very glad to receive a recommendation or certificate of commendation from you.
>
> I am still looking for employment and, unless I find a reasonable prospect of work here, shall soon go West.
>
> With the most pleasant recollections of you and of the Institute . . .[41]

Judging from True's subsequent letter, near the start of the fall 1868 semester, Rogers offered some form of assistance that he hoped would persuade True to return. But circumstances still did not permit:

> I am happy to acknowledge the receipt of your letter of the 5th inst. and the kindness that prompted you to write it.
>
> I thank you heartily for the interest you take in me, and for your kind offers: and only regret that I cannot profit by them. I should like very much to be with you again but circumstances oblige me to forego my own desires.[42]

Rogers must have been disappointed by the loss of such a conscientious, respectful pupil, who signed himself "Your humble but appreciating servant."

Because the educational side of the Institute had become its main focus, supplanting the museum and other planned ventures, Rogers and his colleagues concentrated full energy on the progress of their students. Even in the throes of serious illness, in 1869, Rogers was kept abreast of how things were going by John Runkle, who was in charge in his absence. Runkle would write to Emma Rogers, whose practice was to convey only the essentials to her husband; he was too ill to read for himself at the time. One report from Runkle to Mrs. Rogers reads:

> You can hardly realize the sense of relief I feel this afternoon. This morning the last faculty meeting of the session was held, and all the work of the past year together with the admission examinations are settled. There were six applicants for graduation, and four of them passed: viz, Whitaker, Edmands, Nichols and Carson. Baker & Tebbetts not. In the case of Tebbetts I think the result was just, but most unjust in the case of Baker. That hateful prejudice which gave us so much trouble at the last graduation, this time carried the day—and if the President were here I should decidedly advise him to carry the matter before the Gov. and get Baker his degree.
>
> There were 33 applicants for the new class, 30 of whom passed. This is quite as many as I expected, from the fact that this examination is some six weeks before the close of the High Schools; and teachers wish to send their boys as well prepared as possible.[43]

Runkle closed with a request to meet with Rogers as early as possible, probably to address the issues surrounding the unnamed "hateful prejudice" against Baker. The matter was resolved and William H. Baker did end up in the degree list for 1869. While Emma Rogers was deeply protective of her husband on his sick bed, she was also aware that some issues were too important to keep from him, particularly one, as here, that could affect a student's welfare and prospects.

Rogers, in fact, was almost universally adored by the students for his support, solicitude, and spirit of fairness. They worried when his health took a turn for the worse in the late 1860s. Runkle, for example, conveyed the following offer to Mrs. Rogers from one concerned student in the summer of 1869:

> One of our students, Herreshoff, of Bristol whose brother makes the famous yachts wants to call at New Port and take the President on a short cruise. I told him that I would notify you of his wish, & as soon as the President is able I would write him. This brother is *blind*, & yet is one of the best of designers and workmen.[44]

Nathanael G. Herreshoff, from Bristol, Rhode Island, attended the Institute as a special student for three years, 1866 to 1869, and went on to become a prominent marine engineer, naval architect, and shipbuilder, in partnership with his blind brother, John B. Herreshoff, in the Herreshoff Manufacturing Company. Nathanael was recognized later as the leading designer of yachts in the United States, and also designed the U.S. Navy's first seagoing torpedo-boat.[45]

Still very ill, Rogers continued to preoccupy himself with students—recruiting new ones, reinstating lapsed ones, and reaching out to new constituencies. He wrote to acting president Runkle from Philadelphia in 1870, remarking on the Institute's bright prospects:

> I am expecting soon to see young Fox (late of the Inst.) who with his friends I learn is very sorry to have been compelled to give up his studies there. I believe that ere long we may look for a consid: number of pupils from Phila. & the State, as our scheme of education is becoming known, & is well adapted to a Community so much devoted to various industrial arts. . . .
>
> The Institute already has taken the first place among the Scientific Schools of the U.S. and if *untrammeled* will evidently continue to grow in reputation & numbers. Those who know our History know that the success is due to the opportunity we have had under the inspiration of modern ideas.[46]

Fox was probably James Taylor Fox, who entered as a second-year student in the first full session, 1865–66, but could not maintain the level of attainment required and was moved back to the first year following the mid-semester exams, fall 1865; in the second semester, spring 1866, he became a special student "in such studies as he is competent to pursue except German and Geology, with the understanding that he attend the exercises regularly."[47] He appears not to have reentered the Institute, in spite of Rogers's best efforts to encourage him to do so. Because of its deep industrial base, however, Pennsylvania, as Rogers anticipated, became both a fruitful source of students seeking to enter technical fields and a favored site for summer field trips, thesis projects, and independent study.

As few firsthand accounts of the earliest days at the Institute survive, it is worth quoting here from one other to supplement the above narrative by Bowditch. William E. Hoyt (graduate of 1868) reminisced on his student days in a speech to the Technology Club of Rochester more than forty years later. He spent only two years at MIT, 1866 to 1868, having come in with advanced standing—as a third-year student—after a year in college when he grew "dissatisfied with a strictly classical collegiate course."[48] It is no coincidence that the accounts by Bowditch and Hoyt were prepared around the same time (1910), since by then people were starting to think about the Institute's half-century landmark, which could have been celebrated in 1911 (50 years after the granting of the charter) or 1915 (50 years after the opening of the school)—1911 was the date chosen.

The Institute's general layout and atmosphere remained vivid in Hoyt's mind, despite the caveat in his opening sentence:

> I recall, not very clearly now, a September morning in 1866 when I found myself duly installed as a student, soon after the first new building on the Back Bay had been dedicated.
>
> We were a mere handful of students then, and the recitation-rooms seemed big and empty as we went by the doors,—always standing open, even during lectures and recitations.
>
> I wish I could show you now a picture of the Institute just as it was then, and of the surroundings. The massive Rogers building stood out, sharply defined, against the sky, for there was nothing beyond it to the south save a broad expanse of water from Columbus Avenue on the east to Beacon Street

on the west. The embankment for Clarendon Street had been made, and out beyond there was no land to be seen, between that and the highlands of Brookline in the distance, save a slender line of roughly built little railroad over which a tiny locomotive ran slowly backward and forward, dragging strings of miniature gravel cars behind. The puffing of this little engine and the grinding of the car wheels on the gravel-strewn rails broke the dead silence of that desert region which the Back Bay Corporation was creating by making land out of water, so that Boston might grow and expand into a city of befitting size.[49]

Hoyt's memories of the faculty were both sharp and positive:

Professor Osborne . . . taught us spherical trigonometry and kindred subjects. He was the cleverest demonstrator in the lecture-room I ever listened to. Every word he uttered was right to the point, and with his explanations all difficult things became simple. He chose his text-books with great care, and had few of them. If we came to him with a problem after his lecture, he seemed to take it as a favor, and he was pleased to show us how to work out hard things in mathematics.

Then there was our French teacher, Ferdinand Bôcher, who taught us German also, a great, good-natured man overflowing with kindness. He had excellent taste in selecting reading matter for his classes, and he contrived to fill us all with enthusiasm over our work. If I remember rightly, he taught in those days at Harvard also, giving the Institute only a portion of his time. Then on certain days Professor Bôcher had French readings down town in Boston, to which the Institute students were invited, and it was a rare privilege to attend these very fashionable gatherings of Boston's Four Hundred.

William P. Atkinson was our professor of English, and we profited by his instructions. He was a kindly man, and did in his measure good work which was helpful and sane.

Of the instructions in architecture I knew but little, save that the department was in competent hands. Professor William R. Ware was a man of high artistic attainments, and the many beautiful buildings he designed in and about Boston were monuments of his skill. He had the love and respect of all his pupils.[50]

And, of course, there was the focal figure—the Institute's founder and guiding force:

> Professor Rogers . . . was a man of commanding presence and of striking personality, genial always, but with dignity in his manner.
>
> It was a delight to hear his lectures. He had a wonderful clearness of expression combined with grace of utterance, and the attention of his listeners was fixed by his opening words, and held throughout his discourse to the very end. Even now, after more than forty years have gone by, I can recall the very words he used in some of his talks to us. . . .
>
> He seemed to me a man of indomitable will and of tremendous enthusiasm, who gave inspiration to all about him.
>
> His ideas of education differed widely from those of many others, and he wanted the Institute to be founded on a new plan and to be conducted in a new spirit different from that of most existing institutions of that grade. He pleaded for pliancy rather than rigidity in the modelling of the courses and the conduct of studies. He wished to have a division of courses, if required in some cases, rather than a continuous curriculum, so as to help the development of special talent as well as the general capacity of the pupils.[51]

The First Graduates, 1868

Ellery Cushing Appleton	Mining Engineering
Nelson Whitney Conant	Mining Engineering
Frank Russell Firth	Civil and Topographical Engineering
Eli Forbes	Science and Literature
Charles Chadbourne Gilman	Mining Engineering
Charles Ezra Greene	Civil and Topographical Engineering
Albert Francis Hall	Mechanical Engineering
William Edwin Hoyt	Civil and Topographical Engineering
Robert Hallowell Richards	Mining Engineering
Walter Herbert Sears	Civil and Topographical Engineering
Charles Augustus Smith	Civil and Topographical Engineering
Joseph Stone	Civil and Topographical Engineering
Bryant Parrott Tilden	Mining Engineering
James Pike Tolman	Mining Engineering

Walter Herbert Sears, ca. 1868—the only known surviving image of a member of the class of 1868 during their student days

The graduates of 1868 were an eclectic group in some ways, but patterns emerge in the evolution of their post-Institute careers. The clearest of these is enthusiasm for westward migration—a trend that had begun earlier in the century with the Louisiana Purchase, the War of 1812, the Battle of the Alamo, the Gold Rush of 1849, and the Missouri Compromise, but that assumed fresh momentum with the growth of the railroad industry as a spur to western settlement. The earliest graduates, steeped as they were in engineering skills, found ample opportunity for employment on the railroad. Of the 14 graduates in 1868, 8 spent at least part of their careers with railroads. Once out west, they worked in technical fields integral to the development of new communities: water and sewage systems, mining, surveying, and public utilities. They were employed in both the public and private sectors, sometimes both simultaneously. Those who ended up as teachers and academics often had their start in industry, manufacturing, or public service—and generally maintained these contacts as private consultants in tandem with their university appointments. Indeed, most of the Institute's earliest graduates appear to have thrown themselves into the excitement, enthusiasm, and adventure typical of the "pioneer spirit," even when confronted by the hardships of frontier life.

Four members of this class deserve special mention because of later relations with the Institute. Albert Hall, who had been an assistant in mechanical and plan drawing while a fourth-year student, was appointed instructor in 1868 and remained through 1871. William Hoyt was instructor in civil engineering from 1870 to 1877, a period during which he appears to have been active also as a consulting engineer. Robert H. Richards was appointed an assistant in general chemistry in 1868. In 1869 he was promoted to instructor in assaying and qualitative analysis and in 1870, to assistant professor of analytical chemistry. He became a full professor of mineralogy and assaying, in charge of the Mining and Metallurgical Laboratory, in 1871. At that time he was given a seat on the faculty and would serve until he retired in 1914. He was the last surviving member of the class of 1868 when he died in 1945 in his 101st year. Finally, James P. Tolman, for many years president of the Samson Cordage Works, was an active member of the Institute's Corporation from 1882 until his death in 1915. He had served as president of the Alumni Association from 1881 to 1883.

Golden reunion, 1909—members of the classes of 1868 and 1869.
In front seated (l-r), William Jackson, Joseph Stone, Joseph Revere; at rear (l-r), unidentified, Ernest Bowditch, Robert
Richards, Charles Fillebrown, Eben Stevens. Only two of these "survivors" (Stone and Richards) were graduates of
the Institute; the rest had come and gone without degrees, yet retained their ties with MIT over the years.

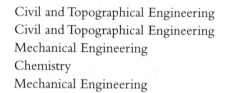

The Second Graduates, 1869

William Herbert Baker	Civil and Topographical Engineering
Howard Adams Carson	Civil and Topographical Engineering
John Rayner Edmands	Mechanical Engineering
William Ripley Nichols	Chemistry
Channing Whitaker	Mechanical Engineering

The Third Graduates, 1870

Edward K. Clark	Mechanical Engineering
Charles Robert Cross	Science and Literature
Russell Hurd Curtis	Civil Engineering
Charles William Hinman	Mining Engineering
Sampson Douglas Mason	Civil Engineering
Nathan Frederick Merrill	Chemistry
Theodore Francis Tillinghast	Civil Engineering
Edmund Kimball Turner	Civil Engineering
Daniel Wheelock Willard	Mechanical Engineering
Lawrence Francis Joseph Wrinkle	Mining Engineering

Russell Hurd Curtis

Edmund Kimball Turner

Sampson Douglas Mason

Charles William Hinman

Charles Robert Cross

Edward K. Clark

Daniel Wheelock Willard

Theodore Francis Tillinghast

Lawrence Francis Joseph Wrinkle

William Ripley Nichols

The graduates of 1869 and 1870 reflected several of the career patterns established by their predecessors in the class of 1868: enthusiasm for westward migration; innovative work in technical fields, especially railways, surveying, mining, construction, and water works; and teaching in scientific and technical disciplines. Among those who spread out across the country were Baker, Mason, Curtis, Willard, and Wrinkle. Most who remained in the New England area—Carson, Edmands, Clark, Tillinghast, and Turner—entered technical fields, sometimes more than one over the course of their careers. Four became long-term educators—Nichols, Whitaker, Cross, and Merrill. Nichols, Whitaker, and Cross were faculty members at MIT, Merrill at the University of Vermont. Even when their academic work was grounded more in pure than applied sciences, they often pursued intellectual cross-fertilization and practical relationships with industry, commerce, manufacturing, and government—a trend that would become an important part of the Institute's emerging educational and research mission.

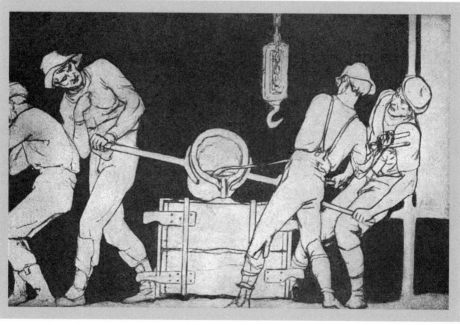

Glass Blowing (top) and Iron Casting (bottom)—sketches prepared by Paul Nefflen for mural in Huntington Hall (see p. 764).

The Early Curriculum
and Methods of Teaching

$\mathscr{C}hapter\ 22$

$\mathscr{T}he\ \mathscr{F}irst\ \mathscr{S}ix\ \mathscr{C}ourses$

T he first formal meeting of the faculty elected on September 15, 1865, was held on September 25 with the opening of the school just one week away. Nine of its members, including William Barton Rogers, were there. The tenth, James Hague, professor of mining engineering, had not taken up his duties and would never do so.[1] For the next two months, only preliminary classroom lectures and recitations would be held, pending an evaluation through examination of the preparedness of the students and final decisions on the proposed curriculum.

Within the context of the rough outline presented in the *Scope and Plan*, each professor was responsible for the design of the program for his department, of which he was the sole representative, and most were ready to report at the first meeting. As the placement of subjects within the curriculum and the arrangement of course schedules were carefully considered, changes and adjustments were called for. Even Rogers's proposals for physics were recommitted for this purpose. Though proof sheets for the catalogue appeared to be ready for final consideration by October 21, their availability brought forth only the appointment of *ad hoc* committees for their revision.[2]

The *Scope and Plan* had promised a "schedule of studies" covering all of the first two years and parts of the third and fourth for a "general scientific course" for prospective teachers, indicating that a "BACHELOR OF SCIENCE will be conferred." Late in October Rogers, Charles Eliot, and William Atkinson were asked to "prepare a course of study for the degree of S.B." Their "programme of study for the degree in Science and Literature" was adopted soon thereafter, without mention of a baccalaureate, undoubtedly because the Institute had no authority to grant one.[3]

As finally designated in the *First Annual Catalogue*, the six courses were:

Mechanical Engineering
Civil and Topographical Engineering
Practical Chemistry
Geology and Mining
Building and Architecture
General Science and Literature

The "general" course became simply "Science and Literature" in succeeding issues.[4]

A major challenge for the faculty had been to assess the stated objects of the school and to design a four-year academic program combining basic scientific and technical subjects with professional studies, emphasizing laboratory and field work, and including an element of "general culture," the latter not mentioned in the *Scope and Plan*. The common curriculum for the first two years represents their view of the level and character of the basic preparation necessary for professional studies in the later years:

FIRST YEAR
Mathematics—Algebra, Plane Trigonometry, Solid Geometry, Spherical
    Trigonometry
Mechanical Drawing
Free-Hand Drawing
Elementary Mechanics—General Doctrine of Motions and Forces, Mechanics of
    Solids, Mechanics of Liquids and Gases, Phenomena and Laws of Sound
Chemistry—two courses in the Elements of Inorganic Chemistry: the
    Chemistry of the Non-metallic Elements and the Chemistry of the
    Metals, both with laboratory instruction in Chemical Manipulations
English Language and Literature—English composition, the history and structure
    of the English language, and critical study of standard English writers
Modern Languages—French

SECOND YEAR
Mathematics—Plain [*sic*] Co-ordinate Geometry, Analytic Geometry of Three
    Dimensions, Differential Calculus, Integral Calculus

Navigation and Nautical Astronomy

Surveying

Descriptive Geometry and its Applications

Mechanical Drawing

Free-hand Drawing

Experimental Physics—Phenomena and Laws of Heat, Light, Magnetism, and
    Electricity

Chemistry—Qualitative Analysis with laboratory practice

English—General and Comparative Grammar, the history and structure of the
    English language, reading of English standard writers, and continuation of
    English Composition

Modern Languages—French continued, German begun[5]

Atkinson and Eliot prepared separate drafts of an introductory statement relating to the studies of the third and fourth years, with Eliot's version adopted and included in the first catalogue:

> Up to the end of the second year, the studies are the same for all regular students; each thus obtaining such an acquaintance with the whole field of practical science as is needed for the further pursuit of the studies of the School, in any of its departments; but, at the beginning of the third year, the system becomes so far elective, that each student may select one of the courses of study prescribed for the attainment of a degree.[6]

This statement did not appear in subsequent catalogues. Eliot's description of the professional curriculum as "so far elective" in allowing each student to select one of the prescribed courses illustrates the limited application of the elective principle at the school of the Institute, and serves as a reminder of the difference between the freedom to choose one of several prescribed programs in specific fields and the freedom to choose particular subjects from a wider range of offerings. With this distinction in mind, Eliot's description also belies statements over the years that Rogers had established a "system of free electives" as a founding principle of the new institution. In this connection some have referred to Rogers's experience at the College of William and Mary and the University of Virginia as the source of such a plan.[7]

    Yet even in those institutions the application of the elective principle was limited. The College of William and Mary is generally credited with priority in establishing the principle, a policy described in 1780 by its president, James Madison, in a letter to the Reverend Ezra Stiles, president of Yale College:

> The Doors of ye University are open to all, nor is even a knowledge of ye ant.
> Languages a previous Requisite for Entrance. The Students have ye Liberty of
> attending whom they please, and in what order they please or all ye diffr.
> Lectures in a term if they think proper. The time of taking Degrees was for-
> merly ye same as in Cambridge, but now depends upon ye candidate. He has
> a certain course pointed out for his first Degree, and also for ye rest. When
> Master of Either, ye Degree is conferred.[8]

If a student wanted a formal degree, therefore, he had specific requirements to meet in
an essentially rigid curriculum.

In 1824 the Board of Visitors of the University of Virginia voted to allow every
student to attend the "schools of his choice, and no other than he chooses."[9] Yet here,
too, the example set earlier by William and Mary was followed.[10] Rogers had discussed
the elective principle in his 1844 report for the Committee of Schools and Colleges of
the Virginia House of Delegates. He spoke of "the privilege allowed to students of
selecting such studies as have a more immediate reference to the pursuits in which they
design afterwards to engage" and cited the example of William and Mary, where "liberal methods of instruction found a home long before they were adopted by the
thronged and applauded colleges of New England."[11] The election of studies, he said,
"originating in a wise regard to the practical wants of society, has been found well
adapted to the genius of our country, and at the same time eminently favourable to that
thoroughness of knowledge which in a just plan of education is even more important
than variety of attainment." This system allowed a student to select a particular field in
which to concentrate without having "to spend his resources and his time in the
acquirement of branches which are but slightly related to the objects he has in view."[12]

Rogers pointed out, however, that "custom has established a particular order of
studies to which, with some modifications, the great majority conform. Besides, all are
aware that, although a separate diploma is conferred in each department, nothing short
of a full and thorough course in all the academic schools can prepare the student for
the highest honours to which he may aspire." He added that the "advantages of such
an election of studies. . . have been substantially recognized of late by the adoption at
Harvard, and we believe other prominent institutions abroad, of a similar feature, to
replace the Procrustes system hitherto in general use":

> But we may be allowed to add that, while engrafting upon their old established
> methods this liberal improvement, they have allowed much *latitude* of election
> even to *their candidates for the higher honours*, and, thus departing from the stern

requisitions of our university, have held out inducements to the student to choose his studies rather in accordance with his fancy or love of ease, than with the claims of a rigorous mental discipline and a more profound and thorough scholarship.[13]

Pressure for student election of studies and the role of the elective principle in collegiate reform were for some years mainly the concern of the traditional colleges and universities as they attempted to respond to lack of student motivation and enrollment, as well as to utilitarian trends, the growing interest in scientific and technical subjects, and a generally increasing demand for modern languages. But for an institution devoted principally to scientific and technical education, there would be little room for freedom in working toward a degree even for those following a general course.

When the regular sessions of the school of the Institute of Technology opened in the fall of 1865, those who had attended the preliminary session were ranked through examination either as first- or second-year students. Given satisfactory performance, the latter were deemed ready in the fall of 1866 to proceed to the professional curriculum of the third and fourth years, only an outline of which had appeared in the first catalogue.[14]

The second catalogue, for 1866–67 but not published until 1867, was more specific. There would still be certain general studies common to all in these final two years: logic, rhetoric, and the history of English literature in the third year and lectures on history, political economy, and the science of government, as well as on mental and moral philosophy, in the fourth; and continuation of modern languages in both years. Physics was continued for all in the third, and the content of mathematics and drawing varied with the major course selected. Physics and mathematics did not appear in any of the fourth-year programs. The remaining subjects fell within the appropriate professional field. All students were required to take military instruction. The third- and fourth-year programs for Mechanical Engineering and Practical Chemistry are representative of the professional studies at that time.[15]

THIRD YEAR
I.—Course in Mechanical Engineering.
1. Differential and Integral Calculus; Analytic Mechanics.
2. Applied Mechanics; comprehending—
     Strength of Materials used in construction; Estimation of the Resistances

of Friction and Rigidity; Pure and Applied Cinematics; Dynamics of Solids, and the Application to the Theory of Machines; Hydrostatics and Hydrodynamics; Thermodynamics; Hydrostatics and Hydrodynamics; Thermodynamics; Estimation of the Useful Effect of Machines; Principles of Mechanism.

3. Descriptive Geometry applied to Masonry, Carpentry, and Machinery.

4. Drawing of Machinery.

5. Physics continued.

6. Logic, Rhetoric, and the History of English Literature.

7. Extended study of French and German, for the first of which Spanish may be substituted.

III.—Course in Practical Chemistry.

1. Chemical Analysis, quantitative,—embracing the Analysis and Commercial Testing of Ores, Metals, Alloys, and Mineral Materials; Soda-ash, Bleaching-salt, Saltpetre, Paints, Drugs, and Manures; Drinking and Mineral Waters.

2. Lectures on Industrial Chemistry: on the Manufacture of Glass, Pottery, Soda-ash, Acids, Soap, Gas, etc.; on the Arts of Dyeing, Calico-Printing, Tanning, Brewing, Distilling, etc.

3. Descriptive and Determinative Mineralogy.

4. Lectures on Structural and Systematic Geology.

5. Drawing,—of Apparatus, and of Machinery and Plans for Chemical, Dyeing, and Print works.

6. Physics continued.

7. Logic, Rhetoric, and the History of English Literature.

8. Extended study of French and German, for the first of which Spanish may be substituted.

FOURTH YEAR

I.—Course in Mechanical Engineering.

1. Construction of Machines and Study of Motors.
    Calculation of the Strength and Proportions of the Parts of a Machine.
    Hand Machinery; as, Cranes, Derricks, Pumps, Turn-tables; Water-Pressure Engines.
    Power and Strength of Boilers.
    Steam Engines,—Stationary, Locomotive, Marine; Air and Gas Engines.

Construction and Arrangement of Machinery in Mills for Grinding, for Textile Manufactures, etc.

2. Lectures on Combustion and Fuel; and on Warming, Ventilating, and Lighting.
3. Lectures on the Chemistry and Geology of the Materials used in Construction.
4. Descriptive Geometry applied to Masonry, Carpentry, and Machinery.
5. Drawing of Machines, Working Plans and Projects of Machinery, Mills, &c.
6. Lectures on History, Political Economy, and the Science of Government.
7. Lectures on Mental and Moral Philosophy.
8. Instruction in Zoölogy, Physiology, and Botany.
9. Extended study of French and German, for the first of which Italian may be substituted.

III.—Course in Practical Chemistry.
1. Quantitative Analysis continued; Organic Analysis.
2. Preparation of Chemical Products, and Special Researches.
3. Lectures on Combustion and Fuel.
4. Lectures on Warming, Ventilating, and Lighting.
5. Drawing as in Third Year.
6. Lectures on History, Political Economy, and the Science of Government.
7. Lectures on Mental and Moral Philosophy.
8. Instruction in Zoölogy, Physiology, and Botany.
9. Extended study of French and German, for the first of which Italian may be substituted.

The inclusion of modern languages—French and German—from the very beginning came about as a practical necessity, for textbooks and reference material in a number of prime areas of study were accessible only in one or the other of those two languages, with German perhaps the more important. It was considered essential, therefore, that every student should learn, through a thorough and systematic training, to read fluently and accurately a foreign scientific work. The first catalogue emphasized that these languages "will not be cultivated as *accomplishments* . . . the first aim will be to enable the student to read such works as may have a bearing upon the studies pursued in the School,—so that, in the latter years of the course, French and German textbooks may be used in any department, as well as English ones."[16] French would be started in the first year with emphasis on reading and translation into English and continue into the second year, when German would be started.[17] In 1866 German, with "special attention to grammar," was moved to the first year and French to the second. The two would continue into the third and fourth years, with German a requirement and a substitution of Spanish and Italian for French in the third and fourth years respectively. By 1870 both French and German were required in the first and second years, continuing into the third and fourth with the above substitution for French offered.[18]

The content and design of the early professional curricula reflect the influence of European practice and experience, particularly in the French and German polytechnic schools and "schools of application." In the fall of 1863 George Emerson's suggestion that Rogers might profitably undertake a visit to various European "Institutions having a greater or less similarity" to the Institute followed by a few months the receipt of land-grant status and preceded by several months the presentation to the Government of the *Scope and Plan*.[19] As an educator of considerable reputation, Emerson appears to have recognized that the terms of the Morrill Act would undoubtedly alter the nature of the Institute and its proposed school. That America was lagging behind Europe in the matter of technical education had been a major argument in support of the establishment of the Institute of Technology. It is significant, therefore, that Emerson proposed visits to a broad spectrum of institutions, not limited to those in Britain and on the Continent whose pattern was more closely allied to the original plan of the Institute whereby the school's instructional program would be oriented toward individual disciplines functioning as satellites of a museum.

By the time Rogers made the trip in the summer of 1864, the *Scope and Plan* had been completed, laying the foundations for an educational effort already much different in character from that originally envisaged. Though the transformation was not yet complete, it was becoming less "popular" and more "professional." With this end in view, Rogers had set about informing himself on the character and methods of some of the most prominent schools of Europe. When in December 1864, fresh from this first-hand survey, he had presented an account of his recent observations to the Society of Arts, he identified Karlsruhe as the institution closest to his perception of the Institute's current goals: "The Polytechnic Institute at Carlsruhe [*sic*], which is regarded as the model school of Germany and perhaps of Europe, is nearer what it is intended the Massachusetts Institute of Technology shall be than any other foreign institution."[20]

At Karlsruhe all students intending to enter one of the technical schools—or departments—had first to complete a two-year basic preparatory curriculum in the so-called Mathematical School. The requirements of the first year included Differential and Integral Calculus, Plane and Spherical Trigonometry, Plane Analytical Geometry, Descriptive Geometry; Elements of Mechanics; Experimental Physics; German Literature, French Language; Freehand Drawing and Modelling. The second year required Differential and Integral Calculus, Analytical Geometry of Space, Analytical Mechanics, Descriptive Geometry; Technical Drawing, Practical Geometry; Higher Physics with laboratory exercises, General Chemistry, Mineralogy and Geology; German Literature, French Language, English Language; Freehand Drawing and Modelling. Following successful completion of this two-year foundation, the student was free to elect any one of a number of professional courses—General Engineering, Building and Architecture, Forestry, Chemistry, and Mechanical Engineering—varying in length from two to four years.

The nature and scope of these advanced technical courses can be seen in the curriculum of General Engineering as given in the Karlsruhe catalogue for the year 1864–65. The curriculum was intended to encompass all branches of engineering technology, with the exception of fortification, and to prepare graduates for a wide variety of industrial fields.

FIRST YEAR

Integration of Partial Differential Equations, Methods of Least Squares, Advanced Geodesy, Applied Mechanics; Chemical Technology; Road and Dike Construction I, Science of Machinery I, Machine Construction; Architectural Technique, Drawing and Sketching of Architectural Objects, Stone Construction, Wood Construction, Landscape Drawing; Political Economy, English Language, German Literature, Recent History

SECOND YEAR

Road and Dike Construction II, Railroad Construction, Exercises in Construction; Science of Machinery II, Mechanical Technology; Advanced Architecture, Drawing and Sketching of Architectural Objects; Select Chapters of Mathematical Physics; Popular Law Instruction, National Economy of Trade and Commerce; German Literature, Recent History

All students were required to devote available time to practical work. Each year excursions were made with an instructor to examine buildings under construction and industrial plants in operation. Another half year was possible for students with special objectives or interests.[21]

There were also institutions in the United States, however, to which the enlarged mission of the Institute's school was closely allied and whose existence and example must be acknowledged. The curricula of three—Rensselaer, Sheffield at Yale, and the Lawrence Scientific School at Harvard—deserve closer attention for comparative purposes.

William Rogers's failure to mention Rensselaer Polytechnic Institute as a model or a kindred institution in any of the discussions leading to the founding of the Institute of Technology stems almost certainly from the original concept of the Institute, leading to his repeated early statements that it would not compete with established institutions offering scientific and technical education. In 1849 B. Franklin Greene had reorganized the curriculum and methods of teaching at Rensselaer to conform with French and German practices. Certainly Rogers was aware of this, for the revision was well under way when he visited Rensselaer in 1851 at the time of the annual meeting in Albany of the American Association for the Advancement of Science, during which one day's sessions were held at the campus. He paid tribute on that occasion to Stephen Van Rensselaer and the institution he had founded: "He has left a legacy—the richest that man can transmit; the results of his liberality in establishing this institution, one more meritorious than which the country could not boast, were seen in the progress of science." Rogers also acknowledged the work of Amos Eaton, its first leader, whom he knew: "the true teacher of philosophy, [who] has sent out some of the most distinguished on the roll of scientific men."[22]

A further connection to Rensselaer was Nathaniel Thayer, a member of the Institute's Committee on Instruction, whose wife was the daughter of Stephen Van Rensselaer. And John Runkle was also surely familiar with the institution, for he came from upstate New York and had taught in the area before enrolling in the Lawrence Scientific School. That the work of Franklin Greene was not ignored is suggested by the fact that annual registers of Rensselaer containing course outlines for the years 1860 and 1863 through 1867 are listed in the catalogue of the MIT Libraries. It is possible that this material was at hand when Rogers and others began to lay out the course of study for the new school.

In 1865 Rensselaer was offering four major courses—Civil Engineering, Mechanical Engineering, Topographical Engineering, and Natural Science, with the expectation that Mining Engineering would soon be added, the latter to be both "*Comprehensive and Practical*" and intended for graduates of the Natural Science course who wished to specialize in this field.[23] In 1835 a charter amendment had officially recognized the engineering course, which until then had been included under the heading of general science, enabling legislation becoming effective on May 9 of that year: "The said board of trustees shall have the power to establish a department of mathematical arts, for the purpose of giving instruction in engineering and technology, as a branch of said institute."[24] The bachelor of arts, the only degree awarded up until that time, was eliminated, replaced by a bachelor of natural science and the degree of civil engineer.[25] With Greene's reorganization of the curriculum in 1849–50, Natural Science became a two-year course, leading to a bachelor of science, and Civil Engineering, a three-year course for the degree of civil engineer.[26] Thereafter, the preponderance of graduates earned the latter degree, with a small number obtaining degrees in Mining Engineering and Topographical Engineering.[27]

In 1865 the degree program at Yale's Sheffield Scientific School, leading to a bachelor of philosophy, covered three three-term years, with a common curriculum in the first year, the years designated as freshman, junior, and senior. Seven courses were offered: Chemistry, Civil Engineering, Mechanics, Mining and Metallurgy, Agriculture, Natural History and Geology, and a Select Course in Literature and Science. Mechanics was described as "Industrial Mechanics, or Mechanical Engineering." Graduates in Civil Engineering could continue with a "Higher Course, designed to give a special training, preparatory to professional practice" and receive the degree of civil engineer. At that time a similar advanced course was foreseen for graduates in Mining and Metallurgy. There was a chemical laboratory, as well as surveying and field engineering, along with visits to machine shops and industrial plants, reflecting many similarities with the course outlines for the Institute's school.

Sheffield's physics was taught by textbook and lectures, as it would be at MIT until a laboratory was established in 1869. Though instruction was "given chiefly by recitations and by inciting the student to engage in the thorough investigation of such topics as are brought before him," courses of lectures were given annually "for awakening the interest of the scholars in their various studies, for bringing out the latest results of scientific inquiry, and for introducing practical and experimental illustrations."[28] In contrast, the Institute's school would attempt to include the practical and the "latest results of scientific inquiry" in the regular subjects.

At Sheffield "meritorious students, after a thorough examination" could receive, in addition to the regular diploma, a certificate testifying to proficiency in a particular subject, this certificate to be "considered as the personal recommendation of the professors who sign it."[29] For an unspecified "higher course of study," students holding a bachelor's degree in Philosophy, Science, or Arts either from Yale or some other institution could obtain a doctor of philosophy degree. Demonstration of "some proficiency" in Latin and Greek was required for admission to this program.[30]

Sheffield offered more limited opportunities for part-time students than the school of the Institute. In addition to those enrolling for the bachelor's or graduate degrees, it accepted "special students, who have already made a considerable degree of proficiency in some department of science, and are now pursuing certain special studies under the personal direction of some of the professors."[31] Citing the "incomplete preparation of many" of the applicants, "full and strict" entrance examinations were required for degree candidates, and Latin was cited as "facilitating the study of the sciences and of the modern languages," with an indication that it might soon be required for admission. By 1869 those seeking admission for the regular three-year program leading to a Bachelor of Philosophy degree would find Latin on the list of entrance examinations: "In Latin, an acquaintance with six books of Virgil, or with an equivalent amount in some other author, and a familiarity with the Grammar, (or so much of it as given in Allen's 'Manual Latin Grammar') will henceforward be required."[32]

The school of the Institute of Technology, in its description of the studies in English language and literature, made clear in its first catalogue that a knowledge of Latin was not required for admission, adding that the "course of instruction in English will be adapted to the wants of those who have not, as well as of those who have, studied it." It pointed out, however, the "great importance of some knowledge of the language as an element in a thorough study of English, as well as of French and the languages of Southern Europe," and recommended the acquisition, "whenever possible, [of] such a knowledge of Latin as will enable [students], at least, to read easy Latin prose." Latin never became a requirement for admission, but references to the language continued to appear in the catalogue through the mid-1930s.[33]

While the similarities in the programs of Rensselaer and Sheffield and those of the Institute's school are notable, the differences with the plan of the Lawrence Scientific School are even more significant. Politically, it had been expedient for Rogers to assure the legislature that the Back Bay land the Institute was seeking would not create an organization that would trespass on the province of an existing local institution. This was certainly true of the Institute as conceived in the *Objects and Plan*. By the fall of 1865, however, much had changed. The school had become a first priority, and the curriculum laid out in its first catalogue was not only a genuine attempt to respond to the needs of the times, but also, if successful, a threat to the enrollment of the Lawrence Scientific School.

Early in 1869 the *Atlantic Monthly* published a piece entitled "The New Education: Its Organization," in which Charles Eliot presented his views on the future course of higher education in the United States. At the time, in addition to his professorship at the Institute, he was a member of Harvard's Board of Overseers and would soon be nominated to succeed President Thomas Hill, who had resigned in the fall of 1868.

The piece appeared in two installments. In the first, drawing on his earlier experience as acting dean of the Scientific School, Eliot presented a firsthand assessment of its character and shortcomings:

> The Lawrence Scientific School at Cambridge is, and always has been, what the Yale school also was at first,—a group of independent professorships, each with its own treasury and its own methods of instruction. The several departments are so distinct that the student in one department has no necessary connection with any other. Each student is, as it were, the private pupil of some one of the professors, and the other professors are no more to him than if they did not exist. . . . There is no common discipline and no general course of co-ordinated studies which all candidates for any degree must pass through. A young man who has studied nothing but chemistry, or nothing but engineering, and who is densely ignorant of everything else, may obtain the sole degree given by the school,—that of Bachelor of Science. There appears never to have been any examination for admission, except that some knowledge of algebra, geometry, and trigonometry has been required, before a student could join the department of engineering. It has been the practice to receive students into the chemical laboratory without requiring any previous knowledge of chemistry, or indeed of anything else. . . . This system, or, rather, lack of system, might do for really advanced students in science, for men in years and acquired habits of study,—in fact, the school has been of great service to a score or two of such men,—but it is singularly ill adapted to the wants of the average American boy of eighteen. The range of study is inconceivably narrow; and it is quite possible for a young man to become a Bachelor of Science without a sound knowledge of any language, not even his own, and without any knowledge at all of philosophy, history, political science, or of any natural or physical science, except the single one to which he has devoted two or three years at the most.[34]

This article was in press when the Harvard College Catalogue for 1868–69 became available, and Eliot was able to add a footnote stating that "there are changes for the better in the Scientific School; but they are not of a fundamental character."[35]

Wolcott Gibbs, then Rumford Professor and dean of the Scientific School, took exception to several of Eliot's statements and sent a letter dated February 19, 1869, to the editor of the *Atlantic Monthly*. The editor held it until Eliot's second installment appeared (March) and then published it in the April issue. Gibbs closed his response with a pointed reference to the Institute of Technology:

> Perhaps a single statement as to the results of the system adopted at the Lawrence Scientific School will prove the best answer to hostile criticism. Since the foundation of the school, fifty-eight persons, who have for a longer or shorter time pursued their studies in it, have obtained professorships in colleges, or held professorships while students. To this number must be added fifteen assistants virtually, though not nominally, professors. Finally, of the thirteen professors in the Massachusetts Institute of Technology, in the interest of which the paper on the New Education appears to have been written, nine are graduates of the Lawrence Scientific School.[36]

There were only seven Lawrence Scientific School graduates on the Institute faculty in 1868–69. Gibbs undoubtedly included John Trowbridge, then an instructor, and Eliot, who was a graduate of Harvard College. Together, Lawrence Scientific School and Harvard College graduates did indeed account for a large proportion of the Institute's earliest faculty. It does not necessarily follow, however, as Gibbs implied, that the Lawrence Scientific School's system provided an adequate response to the rising demands for scientific and technical education.

In the beginning, diplomas—but no degrees—were granted by the Scientific School. Starting in 1851 the degree of bachelor of science was offered following a minimum of one year's attendance and the successful completion of an examination on the studies of the student's department. Yale's Sheffield had followed in 1852 with a bachelor of philosophy. According to one account, the "two old foundations" in this way "kept the B.A. degree inviolate and protected it from dilution"; the science programs had lower admissions standards and shorter terms of study, and in "both institutions the scientific students were considered second-class citizens"—Yale, for example, segregating the Sheffield students from the regular academic students at chapel.[37]

Eliot indicated that normally students took from eighteen to thirty months to satisfy the degree requirements. During this time distinguished performance would be rewarded by a *summa cum laude*, with *cum laude* and *magna cum laude* added after 1869. By 1871, two years after he became president of Harvard, a prescribed course of three or four years was required for the bachelor's degree.[38]

The Institute's *Scope and Plan* had contained no mention of subjects today classified as "humanities," other than two modern languages—French and German—and Runkle's suggestions for professorships in January 1865 did not include any "liberal" or "general" subjects. It is not clear when the decision was made to broaden the scope of the curriculum through the inclusion of such studies as English, history, and political economy, but it may have been under the influence of William Atkinson that they were added as an essential part of the academic program.

The choice of Atkinson as the first professor of the English language and literature was fortunate for the school and its future. He understood the rising importance of science and the objectives of the school, but he was also committed to the goal of a fairly balanced education. He would serve for many years as the sole instructor of rhetoric and composition, literature, history, and political economy. The time available for such studies was very limited. Atkinson recognized and understood this, and he shaped his style of teaching accordingly. In his lectures he presented broad sketches and views of history and literature, rather than minute discussions of technical points. He endeavored, first, to excite the interest of his students, and then to teach them how to read, think, and judge for themselves. By 1868 he was giving instruction in history and political economy as well as English, and his title changed in 1871 to professor of English and history. He was librarian as well and taught some of the Lowell free evening classes. To him also fell the oversight of the sixth course, Science and Literature.

The Science and Literature course as it appeared in the first catalogue was intended to prepare the student "for any of the departments of active life." Following the common curriculum of the first two years, and including in the third and fourth years all of the "general studies" of the professional courses, Science and Literature would in the last two years contain "selections" from the following: "Analytical Mechanics and Astronomy; Specialties of the Professional Courses; Physics (continued); Analytical and Higher Chemistry; Geology (continued); Zoology, Botany, and Paleontology; Physiology and Comparative Anatomy. In making the selection, regard will be had, in each case, to the best scientific training of the student, to his special aptitudes for science, and to his future aims in life."[39]

A similar course had been in existence at Yale's Sheffield School since 1860. Designed for those who "wished a general knowledge of science, without specializing in any particular field," this "Select Course in Science and Literature" was made up of "a selection from the other courses of study, and also such special instruction as will tend to furnish a good degree of intellectual training and prepare the scholar for higher studies or for the active duties of life." Students following this option would "have access to the lectures of President Woolsey and other instructors" of Yale College.[40]

The final two years, following the completion of the common curriculum of the first year, included:

JUNIOR YEAR: Mechanics, Agricultural Chemistry, Astronomy, Physical Geography, Zoology, Botany, Mineralogy, Drawing—Free Hand and Architectural, History, Literature, German, and French

SENIOR YEAR: French or German, Botany and Zoölogy, Geology, Meteorology, Human Anatomy and Physiology, Astronomy, History and Political Philosophy, International Law, Political Economy, Ethics, and Metaphysics

Some of the subjects consisted of both lectures and recitations; others, only lectures. Astronomy would include "practical problems; Botany, the preparation of a Herbarium; and Zoölogy, excursions as well as lectures in the third term of the Junior Year." The language classes in the Senior Year included lectures on Language and Linguistic Ethnology and required "compositions." There was a thesis requirement in the final year and a "graduating examination" for the degree.[41]

Sheffield's course may well have been used as a model for the Institute's Science and Literature program. There are obvious similarities, even to the inclusion of zoölogy, botany, paleontology, and physiology and comparative anatomy, these subjects not represented on the Institute faculty at the time. But the Institute did not possess similar resources for the "academical" subjects available to Sheffield through Yale College, so the course never attracted many students. Whether such a general course should be continued, and if so, in what form, would be a recurring problem for the Institute in the years ahead.

As the faculty prepared the catalogue in the fall of 1865, working out the content of the subjects of the major courses, it gave attention naturally to the requirements for graduation. In light of the concept of the school in 1861, the Institute would have had no grounds for requesting that degree-granting powers be included in its charter. It is very clear, however, that the school opened in 1865 was a far more ambitious undertaking, and the early catalogues contained repeated references to "degrees or diplomas" for those satisfactorily completing the required subjects of the regular four-year programs. Yet there are no records of discussion about requesting the necessary powers at that time. The faculty was, of course, focused on the emerging curriculum, and there was no prospect of a graduating class in the immediate future.

But there may have been another, more important, reason. Rogers was well aware that when Connecticut chose Sheffield to receive the funds derived from the Land-Grant Act, a Board of Visitors was appointed, consisting of the governor, the lieutenant governor, the three senior senators of the legislature, and the secretary of the State Board of Education. They were required to visit the school twice a year and report to the General Assembly annually on the "practical working of the institution."[42] And Rogers had not forgotten that in 1863 the Joint Committee of the Massachusetts Legislature had recommended, in connection with the land-grant funds, a similar board of "overseers, or visitors . . . with all necessary powers for the better aid, preservation, and government" of the Institute. He was against the "merely political influence" implied in such a plan and succeeded in having it removed from the enabling legislation, in return for which he accepted as *ex officio* members of the Government the governor, the chief justice of the Supreme Judicial Court, and the secretary of the State Board of Education.[43] It is possible that his political instincts told him that, unless absolutely necessary, he should stay away from the legislature in the fall of 1865.

The Institute's graduation requirements included satisfactory performance on "graduating examinations" at the end of the final year, both oral and written, covering "the whole course of studies and exercises prescribed . . . including the elementary and general, no less than the advanced and special subjects." The examinations also entailed the preparation of "drawings and projects," the carrying out of laboratory exercises, and the demonstration of a good working knowledge of French and German.[44] There was also a thesis requirement: "a dissertation on some subject included in the course of study, . . . an original report upon some machine or work of engineering, or some mine or mineral survey, or scientific investigation, which shall be approved by the Faculty."[45]

That the fourth-year students in 1867–68 had serious concerns about the examinations is clear from a December 1867 petition to the faculty raising questions that had never been addressed. Would the students be required to take the usual annual examinations at the end of that academic year in addition to the graduating examinations? Would the degree decisions be based "exclusively" on the results of the latter examinations, "or, in a measure, be it greater or less," on their standing in the course? Would the professional degree depend only on their grades in the professional studies? Or would "proficiency be required in all the various branches pursued in the four year course"? Though they did not mention the added burden of the thesis requirement, the students pointed out how little time would be available for preparation for the comprehensive examinations in view of the demands of their current studies. The petition, signed by sixteen students, including its author, Charles E. Greene, urged that the faculty give "early consideration to the above matters."[46]

On December 21, 1867, the faculty voted that the annual examinations of the fourth-year class, "for this class," be made part of their degree examinations. The concession to "this class" may indicate that the faculty was taking into consideration the conditions under which the students had labored. Most had attended the preliminary session in 1865, several months before a faculty had been elected and a curriculum put in place, a curriculum that was really a work in progress. And at least half of their first full year, 1865–66, was spent in the Summer Street quarters, far from adequate, and other rented rooms downtown.

A further vote referred the "memorial of the fourth-year's class . . . to the President with full powers." Rogers was, of course, on hand as chairman, for he is not listed as absent for this meeting,[47] but no written response has been found. Early in May 1868, however, the faculty voted to close the laboratories and eliminate the regular exercises of the school during the last two weeks of the term, a move possibly recommended by Rogers. The students may have raised the thesis issue as the end of the term neared, for no time had been allotted in the course schedules for thesis preparation. And the closing of the laboratories would have been yet another obstacle for those needing access to complete their thesis work.

In any event, in mid-May the faculty set the first Monday in September as the due date for the theses of those passing the graduating examinations, a practice that would remain in place for several years. Diplomas for the earliest graduates, from 1868 through 1873, were not granted, therefore, until the end of the calendar year or early in the following year. In November 1873 the faculty voted that thesis preparation be incorporated in the "exercises" of the student's department in the final term, and degrees were awarded at the end of the fourth academic year thereafter.

The "degrees," or diplomas, were to be granted in the six "divisions" of the School—Mechanical Engineering, Civil and Topographical Engineering, Practical Chemistry, Geology and Mining Engineering, Building and Architecture, and General Science and Literature. Certificates in special subjects would be awarded to partial students who "on examination, are found to have attained the required proficiency in them."[48] The first catalogue emphasized the exact significance of these diplomas and certificates: "As the diploma or certificate is intended to be not only a reward to the student for his diligence and attainments, but an assurance to the public of his knowledge and skill in the particular department of science to which it relates, it will be conferred on such students only as by their examinations and other exercises give proof that they possess the prescribed qualifications; but all persons who fulfil this requirement shall be entitled to the testimonials of the Institute, without regard to the length of time they may have spent in the School."[49]

Early in January 1867, President Rogers and Professor Runkle were appointed by the faculty to prepare a suitable certificate for students completing a partial course of study. Their suggestion was soon adopted, and on January 12 the awarding of the first Certificate of Proficiency was confirmed for Samuel Eastwood of Framingham, listed in the first catalogue as a second-year student who had attended the preliminary session. His certificate was to be signed by Professors Bôcher, Henck, Runkle, and Watson.[50] In the spring of 1869, a form of certificate of attendance was adopted, presumably for students who may have attended faithfully but did not wish to submit to the necessary examination. The faculty strengthened the requirements for the Certificate of Proficiency in 1875, voting that henceforth an acceptable thesis must be completed. There is no formal record of the number of certificates awarded. The faculty minutes, however, mention fewer than twenty between 1867 and 1883.[51]

In 1868, shortly before the graduating examinations of the fourth-year class, the lack of degree-granting powers was finally acknowledged. On the advice of Judge George T. Bigelow and J. Ingersoll Bowditch, members of the Government, Rogers entrusted his petition to the Honorable Richard H. Dana, Jr., a member of the House of Representatives in 1867–68, his covering note for the petition on April 29 saying in part:

> The examinations of our fourth year class will begin next Saturday & continue past the middle of May.

Some twelve or more of the candidates will pass the ordeal & will do credit to the Degrees to which they aspire.

I feel it to be but just to them & to the thorough Course of Studies which the Institute is laboring to establish, that we should have granted us the usual formal authority for conferring the appropriate degrees.[52]

The petition cited the increasing enrollment of the school and the "extensive accommodations & appliances of instruction in the various studies & exercises," pointed out that the original Act of Incorporation did not include "formal authorization" for conferring degrees, and asked for passage of an act granting such authority "to award degrees or diplomas appropriate to the several courses of study set forth in the programmes of instruction, & on such conditions and according to such tests of proficiency as shall best promote the interests of sound education in the Commonwealth."[53]

By mid-May the petition had passed through several stages and was approved on May 25. Chapter 247 of the Acts of 1868 contains the following addition to the 1861 Act of Incorporation:

> The Massachusetts Institute of Technology is hereby authorized and empowered to award and confer degrees appropriate to the several courses of study pursued in said institution, on such conditions as are usually prescribed in universities and colleges in the United States, and according to such tests of proficiency, as shall best promote the interests of sound education in this Commonwealth.[54]

Several months would elapse before the Government considered the form of the degree and the wording of the diploma. There was no hurry, as the theses required for graduation would not be submitted until the fall. The wording Rogers had proposed for the professional degree in the *Scope and Plan* had been similar to that of Sheffield's "Civil Engineer," but with the addition of the sixth course—Science and Literature— the titles would have to be slightly altered.

Because of Rogers's illness and leave of absence, it was Runkle who, as president pro tem, in December 1868 presented to the Government for confirmation the names of the degree candidates and a proposed form for the diploma, which he said had received the "careful consideration" of President Rogers. The form of the degree, approved by the Committee on Instruction and the Government, appeared in the catalogue for 1868–69 as "Graduate of the Massachusetts Institute of Technology in the

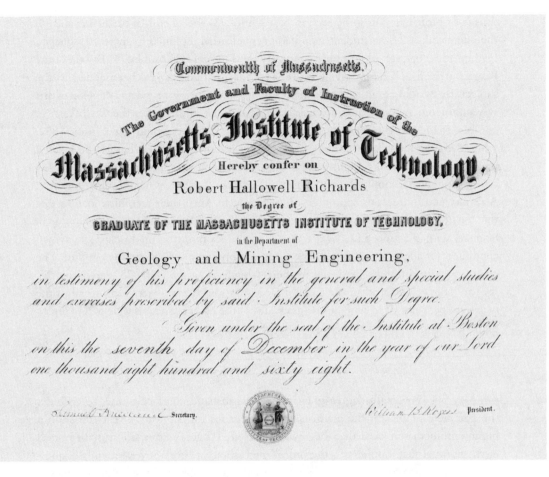

Department of _____." The diplomas would be signed by the president and the secretary of the Institute.[55]

    Rogers may have chosen "Graduate" for the degree title to reinforce his earlier statement that the school of the Institute would not compete with existing institutions, or perhaps to distinguish it from the bachelor of science awarded by the Lawrence Scientific School on the basis of a shorter period of study more limited in scope. More likely, however, he looked to the system in place at the University of Virginia during his tenure there. In 1831 the Board of Visitors had confirmed the following system of degrees: "(1) the graduate,—the student who had proved his mastery of an entire school, like mathematics, or a branch of a school, like chemistry; (2) the winner of a certificate of proficiency in some section of a school; (3) the doctor of medicine; and (4) the master of arts,—the student who had been awarded diplomas in ancient languages, mathematics, natural philosophy, chemistry, and moral philosophy."[56] By the time Rogers arrived in Charlottesville in 1835, modern languages had been added to the subjects that could count toward a master of arts, and during his stay a bachelor of arts was authorized. A bachelor of science was not authorized until after the Civil War.[57]

No change in the form of the degree at the Institute would occur until 1872, when then President John Runkle brought two important matters before the faculty: the addition to the curriculum of graduate studies and the degrees to be awarded— both postgraduate, should the curriculum be extended in this way, and undergraduate. A faculty committee was appointed immediately. In April their recommendation that the "first degree be Bachelor of Science, with the title S.B., and the second, Doctor of Science, with the title S.D.," was referred to the Committee on Instruction, which appointed yet another committee. The Corporation granted final approval in June. The change appeared for the first time in the catalogue issue for 1872–73. Early in 1873, for the "sake of uniformity," the Corporation approved the retroactive conferral of the degree of bachelor of science on the graduates of the early classes, offering a new diploma to any who might wish to have it.[58]

On May 30, 1868, with degree-granting powers in hand, the faculty met to consider the complete reports of the graduating examinations for the fourth-year class, and it became immediately clear that they had a problem. Rogers's expectations with respect to the number that would "pass the ordeal" had fallen far short. Several members questioned in a "protracted discussion," not recorded, the "propriety" of granting degrees to these students. Finally, however, they voted 8 to 1 to accept all the final examinations as "satisfactory," and to issue no marks for them. Rogers was to "notify each deficient student of the character of his deficiencies and of the reasons which governed the action of the Faculty in not allowing them of sufficient weight to deprive him of his degree."

Who cast the dissenting vote raises an interesting question. It could not have been Charles Eliot, for he was on leave in Europe during the 1867–68 academic year. And it could not have been Rogers, who had so recently advised the legislature that "twelve or more" would succeed. Indeed, he had apparently drafted a statement for the papers announcing that the final examinations had ended on May 30 and the Institute was closed for vacation. "This session will be memorable," he said, "as the first in which examinations for degrees were held," adding that fourteen had "passed the long ordeal . . . with success." A further statement that "though the examinations were searching, the students had generally acquitted themselves satisfactorily" is firmly crossed out on the draft.[59]

There were no individual student records in the early days—simply lists of the numerical grades for the semi-annual and annual examinations. The "4th Year Annual Examination 1868" record encompassed, as promised, the "graduating examinations," for it contains the results of fifteen or sixteen separate tests for each student, with no mention of military drill. It also lists the degree awarded following the later receipt and acceptance of the required thesis.[60]

What influenced the faculty's final vote to consider the results of the examinations "satisfactory" and to issue no marks? First of all, Rogers's expectations were on record with the legislature, and the public consequences of an apparent failure on the part of the Institute's first class could be considerable. It should be noted, however, that aside from the dismal marks, there were some 80s, 90s, and even 100s. But the faculty must also have recognized that during the previous three years none of the candidates for graduation had habitually come up for poor performance in the regular examinations or classroom work. The faculty probably realized that more attention should have been paid to concerns expressed earlier by students about the examination process.

Now changes would be made. The 1868–69 catalogue eliminated a special paragraph on "Graduating Examinations," which had heretofore called for the preparation of "drawings and projects" and "laboratory manipulations" in addition to the written tests. It did, however, require satisfactory grades in examinations on the studies of the student's department—"the elementary and general, no less than the advanced and special subjects." By 1870–71 the degree examinations were limited to the "studies and exercises" of the third and fourth years of the student's department. A statement in 1873 required the students to pass all subjects previously taken and a "final, or degree examination" in the subjects relating to one's course. By 1893 the wording had changed to passing grades in all the prescribed studies during the four years and "final examinations, if required," on subjects relating to one's course. Robert H. Richards, a member of the first class, would later refer to the experience of 1868 as "indicative of how the faculty groped to find the way to make a Massachusetts Institute of Technology."[61]

	German	French	Calculus	Mechanics	Eng'g 2 & 3 yr	Eng'g 4 yr	Desc Astron	Theor Astron	Physics	Geology	Engine Chem	Genl Chem
Appleton	80	100	64	45	49	48	72		60	77	42	69
Conant	55	70	53	63	48	57	67		69	85	70	80
Fitch	90	100	95	94	74	77	80	45	95		70	81
Forbes	85	65	79	82	55	75	65		82	80	57	77
Garrison	95											
Gilman	70	75	59	39	51	59	33		55	80	44	48
Greene	100	100	83	97	86	78	45	35	81		65	69
Hall	70	70	75	82	84		51		69		21	27
Hoyt	90	95	54	75	57	69	57	60	66		29	44
Kinsman					64	62						
Richards	50	50	53	39	35	29	71		53	74	69	83
Searl	85	100	55	52	47	61	75	20	79		42	57
Smith	95	90	90	82	74	90	95	63	83		54	65
Stone	65	60	41	73	52	64	50	42	62		66	60
Tilden	90	100	53	77	45	61	84		71	90	64	85
Tolman	85	100	76	68	69	67	63		67	88	38	45
Av. of 1st half	92	99+	80	84	72	74	78	63	80	87	66	77

Drawk Anal	Apaying	Desc Geometry	Stereotomy	Mechanism	Motor Power	Mechan Engine	Machine Machinery	Ananal Chemistry	Graduate in
40	89	50		61	39				Mining Eng ✓
61	70	65		50	31				Mining Eng
68	64	96	80	93	78				Civil Eng / Mining Eng }
96		53		58			60	54	Sc & Lip
48	69	57		37	50				Mining Eng
		89	74	95	90				Civil Eng
		95	56	89		88	90		
		58	50	50	50				Civil Eng
96	85	58		39	20				Mining Eng
		66	58	56	50				Civil Eng
		66	73	83	85				Civil Eng
		53	53	45	53				Civil Eng
77	86	52		56	64				Mining Eng
45	79	57		51	52				Mining Eng
84	84	76	76	76	71	88	75	54	

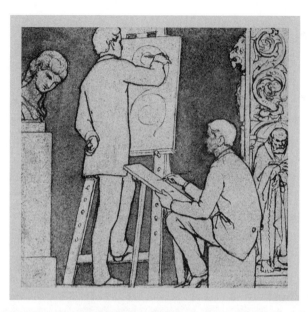

Freehand Drawing (top) and Mechanical Drawing (bottom)—sketches prepared by Paul Nefflen for mural in Huntington Hall (see p. 764)

*T*he course called Building and Architecture would prove to be a pioneering contribution to the cause of architectural education in the United States, and for this reason its inclusion in the curriculum of the school deserves special attention. The *Objects and Plan* had dealt only sketchily with the "School of Industrial Science and Art," and no "school" of architecture was projected at that time, though a "School of Design" was mentioned, "looking chiefly to industrial uses" and offering "practical training in the appropriate branches of drawing and design" necessary not only for "the pursuits of the engineer, architect, and machinist," but also for the "manufacturing arts."[1] In the *Scope and Plan* of 1864, however, a course of Building and Architecture was included in the "Second Department" for "Special and Professional Instruction." The first two years of this four-year program, leading to a degree as "builder and architect," would follow the common curriculum for the several courses planned. The third-year studies would be the same as those for Mechanical and Civil Engineering. The final year would include an extended treatment of structures; warming, ventilation, lighting, and the distribution of water and gas; and lectures on building or practical architecture, on architecture as a fine art, and on architectural drawing.[2] The proposed course moved closer to a full-fledged program in architecture, but it is doubtful that a professional architect would have considered it sufficient to the needs of the profession. What the profession did require was a complete academic program, and an opportunity to develop one was soon recognized by the supporters of the Institute of Technology.

Efforts at Harvard had not worked out. When Benjamin Peirce presented his "Plan of a School of Practical and Theoretical Science" to President Everett in February 1846, he envisioned that such a school would appeal to "Civil Engineers, Surveyors, and Architects," among others. He suggested that a course in "Design" be included, to be taught by a "drawing master under the direction of the Rumford and Perkins Professors." "Drawing from models and nature" and "architectural drawing—plans—elevations—sections—profiles" were to be included. In his initial letter about the establishment of a "school for the purpose of teaching the practical sciences," Abbott Lawrence also mentioned architecture and drawing as "studies to be pursued." Neither proposed a full architectural program. President Everett pursued the matter of architecture, however, proposing Edward Clarke Cabot as professor. Later, deferring partly to Lawrence's wishes, the Corporation voted to limit the program to "Physical and exact Science" and decided definitely against the inclusion of architecture. Everett was much disappointed, believed that Cabot was eminently suited to the task, and felt that the affair had been "awkwardly managed by us in Cambridge." He blamed himself for having "greatly overrated" his own influence with the Corporation.[3]

Writing to John Runkle in April 1865, near the end of the Institute's preliminary session, William Ware heartily approved of the inclusion of architecture in the curriculum:

Next to a School of Mining a school of Architecture seems to me just the thing for you to take up. It is eminently adapted to the wants of the community and to the resources of the School. There is not now in the country any adequate instruction in Construction and in Design none whatever, while the demand for skilled draughtsmen and competent architects is rapidly increasing in every part of the country. To meet this want would require a comparatively slight extension of your programme, the requisite teaching in physics, chemistry, mathematics, descriptive geometry, mechanical and freehand drawing and the elements of design being already as I understand in contemplation, and it would from the moment of its establishment afford a practical end which these could subserve and give to each of these studies the definite direction and immediate purpose which is essential to their successful pursuit. Perhaps no one branch of study would serve to organize so many others.[4]

Ware emphasized the need for an "architectural department in the museum" for models and casts, drawings, and photographs. Citing the lack of an adequate collection of architectural books in the United States, he called also for a "comprehensive library."

Ware described an "eminently practical" program, "consonant to the general scope of the Institute," that he believed would "do more than any other possible agency to raise the character of our architecture." It would be designed for special part-time students, with certificates granted at "different stages of progress" to draftsmen, those at the highest level to be ranked as "assistants or as clerks of works." He also suggested that, "recognizing at the start the highest possible ultimate attainment," the Institute might consider going beyond this basic training by offering a full-fledged professional program, "graduate architects complete, and issue diplomas accordingly." He warned, however, that this would not be easy:

> I think I have said enough to show you how important and necessary and at the same time how difficult and delicate a task the Institute is undertaking when it attempts to establish an Architectural School. The only way in which it can be done well is to start right, and to start right it is necessary to have a thoroughly elaborated and well digested scheme to start with. . . . in the absolute absence of experience and precedent in this country and the existence on the other side of the water of examples so exactly to your purpose as the [British and French] institutions I have named, not to mention the German and Italian schools, . . . the first thing to be done is to use every available means of studying them so as to perfect your own methods by the light of their experience.[5]

During the fall of 1865 Ware drew on this letter in preparing a paper on architectural instruction, portions of which he read to an American Institute of Architects meeting in New York. The full paper, when presented to the Society of Arts in December, was well received and, at the suggestion of John Philbrick, was printed for private distribution as *An Outline for a Course of Architectural Instruction.* A prefatory note, dated February 1, 1866, carries the address of Ware's office—36, Studio Building, Boston. And a later letter to Runkle indicates that Ware had borne the expense of its printing.[6]

The paper was intended to make better known to the public and the profession the Institute's plans for an architectural program in the hope of gaining their "favor and support." And it sought also the "friendly advice and suggestion of the whole body of builders, architects, and artists, upon whose countenance and co-operation it must ultimately rely for its success—a criticism of which, from the novelty of its undertaking, it stands in particular need." "Approbation and disapprobation" would be "equally welcome."[7]

In this paper Ware presented his view of the current state of the architectural profession:

> In the hands of mechanics, many of whom are first-rate; of contractors and superintendents, who are mechanics with a talent for affairs, and many of whom take the name of architects; of architects proper, few of whom have an adequate training in the higher branches of their calling, while they are, of course, vastly inferior to the others in a knowledge of the lower branches; and lastly of architects' assistants and draughtsmen. It is upon these last that the whole system turns; and in any community the character of the work done depends, in a great degree, upon their attainments and qualifications.[8]

And he saw a unique opportunity for the Institute to offer instruction very much in accord with its goals and not available anywhere else in the United States:

> While almost every other one of the important branches of applied science has multiplied seminaries in every part of the country, the art of building, upon which more money is spent, and more money misspent, than upon any other, is handed down from generation to generation by personal tradition alone. In former times, the system of apprenticeship served a certain purpose in preventing this work, which especially needs to be done with deliberation, learning, and reason in design, from coming under the sway of haste, ignorance, or caprice. But the system of apprenticeship has disappeared, as being unsuited to the temper of the time; and no other sufficient means of education has yet taken its place.[9]

He emphasized the "useful art," or "Building proper"

> peculiarly open to the good offices of the Institute. . . . The trouble is technological; there is a want of system and method, and of means for a general collection, and general diffusion of their results. It seems possible to find in this School the means both of collecting and of disseminating this knowledge. . . .
>
> If the School were organized to impart this discipline and this information, and the work were well and sufficiently done, its pupils would be welcomed in every part of the country, and its beneficial influence would be felt on the profession wherever they penetrated.[10]

In short, its benefits would be three-fold:

> To the student of architecture, and to the builder's or architect's assistant or draughtsman, it proposes to open an opportunity for systematic study. . . .

> To the architect and to the builder, it promises a superior class of assistants and coadjutors; relieving them, meanwhile, of a good deal of the labor and responsibility of training their young men themselves. . . .

> To the community at large, it promises the advantage of having some influence at work to introduce uniform and improved methods in the most important of the useful arts.[11]

But Ware also stressed that the "School cannot, if it would, avoid the consideration" of architecture's relation to fine art, or "Architecture proper, into which building naturally grows":

> It remains, then, for us to consider how we had best take up this instruction in Architecture proper, so as to inculcate sound and serviceable ideas in regard to architectural composition and design. There may be good building without it; but there can be no good architecture unless it is taught and taught well. . . . The thing to be taught is the theory and practice of architectural design; and this is to be learned by studying its history, which everywhere illustrates its principles, and its principles, everywhere illustrated by its history.[12]

He described the methods of instruction of the École des Beaux Arts in Paris, with the practical work carried out in various *ateliers* of local architects, in contrast to Kensington in London, where both instruction and practical work were concentrated in the school. As for the Institute, he said:

> Whatever scheme of instruction may ultimately be adopted, it will be the aim of the School to exhibit to its pupils the field of knowledge in all its extent and variety, and teach them to explore it for themselves; to give them such varied and strenuous exercise as shall lead them truly to know their own powers; and to train them into thorough workmen.[13]

Flexibility was particularly important. "Every student," Ware said, "must determine for himself how much study he needs, or can afford." Draftsmen and assistants working in architectural offices could "keep their names in the School, attend such partial courses as their leisure might permit, or needs require; presenting themselves for examination when they were ready." Ware would also extend to the regular students, following a "more condensed and continuous course," the privilege of "staying as long as their means or ambition might permit, passing all the examinations and carrying off all the distinctions they could. Whatever may be the case in the other departments of the School, the architectural course will probably have no fixed limits of time; each student's position being determined, not by time spent, but by progress made."[14] He reiterated the need for "extensive apparatus," a "well-selected library," and proper collections, including "first-rate architectural drawings," important also for the museum and "as useful to the profession as to the School, and a source of instruction and pleasure to amateurs and to the public."[15] And he called attention to the contributions that architectural studies might make in a liberal education:

> Not the collections alone, but the whole Course, has an interest for the public at large, and for amateurs, as affording a singularly attractive means of obtaining a general education. A Course of General Culture, founded not upon a classical and literary, but upon a scientific basis, has already found a place in the School. The architectural studies here sketched out afford a truly liberal variation of this course. . . . it would be hard to find a study now, in the modern re-action against an exclusively literary training, better adapted to the wants of those who wish to try experiments in education.[16]

Ware's plea for critical comments elicited a response from his old friend Charles D. Gambrill, then practicing architecture in New York. Gambrill was a Harvard graduate and had been a student with Ware at both the Lawrence Scientific School and Richard Morris Hunt's studio in New York. He viewed the plan as "admirable" but refrained from commenting on its details, considering himself not "sufficiently conversant with the practical ways of imparting information":

> All the architects here are delighted with your project. . . .
>
> To me it seems perfect—and if you were in New York or I in Boston I would put myself under your tuition. One man expressed the fear to me that so much science would drown the artist—an absurdity I could easily refute by pointing to the author of the outline . . . not to mention Leonardo da Vinci and masters of his time and stamp. . . .
>
> All success and glory to your great undertaking, and my sincere congratulations to the school which has secured your services.[17]

Ware's *Outline* supplied the basis for an innovative curriculum that he would design for the Institute's architectural course. It has been called an "exhaustively argued demonstration of educational theory," speaking also to the "current concerns and expectations of practicing architects."[18]

There is a possible connection between Ware's ideas and those of David Boswell Reid, who in 1856–57 had presented a series of six lectures on "Ventilation and Acoustics" before the Lowell Institute.[19] Reid was a graduate in medicine of the University of Edinburgh and taught chemistry there for a time. Chiefly, however, his teaching was done through private instruction in both theoretical and applied chemistry, with laboratory experiments performed by the students. His curriculum also included lectures on the importance of proper sanitation and ventilation of buildings in the prevention of disease. Together with his interest in illumination and acoustics, these concerns led to the development of relevant systems and ultimately to suggestions for architectural study. He came to the United States in 1855, where his public lectures were followed by a brief period on the faculty of the University of Wisconsin. He died in April 1863, shortly after his appointment as an inspector of military hospitals.[20]

Reid's interest in the training of architects is evident in his article entitled "A College of Architecture," published in Henry Barnard's *American Journal of Education* in December 1856:

> But what has society done for the education of the architect, who exercises so important an influence on us in the design and construction of our dwellings and public buildings? . . . It is true, that at the most distinguished institutions for education in physical science, instruction is given in natural philosophy, chemistry, mineralogy, geology, drawing, and other subjects that may form, along with an apprenticeship to an architect engaged in the practice of his profession, a sure basis of high professional attainments. But it is considered that these are neither sufficiently numerous and accessible to meet the present wants of society, nor so special in the direction and course of studies as to give the student of architecture parallel advantages with those the student of medicine enjoys. A professorship of architecture is required for the full elucidation of this subject.[21]

"To keep pace with the progress of the day," he said, "as extended a course of study as is given in any department of learning for other professional pursuits" would be needed. The "wants of the times, the progress of science," and new resources and appliances available for building and construction demanded that architectural study be "placed on a more systematic footing."[22]

Just out of the Lawrence Scientific School and working in the office of J. Elliott and Edward Clarke Cabot, Ware may have attended Reid's 1856–57 Lowell Institute lecture series, undoubtedly of timely interest to local architects. And it seems unlikely that the piece in the *American Journal of Education* could have escaped the attention of those, like Ware, who were becoming increasingly concerned about the problems of their profession and the preparation for it. As he became intensely interested in architectural education following his experience at Hunt's studio and through his own venture with Henry Van Brunt in accepting pupils in their firm, Ware may well have surveyed the limited literature on the subject.

There are parallels between Ware's letter to Runkle and Reid's piece. Like Reid, Ware emphasized the information that should be gathered and made available for dissemination, greater demands upon the profession brought about by increased building construction, and the advantages of flexibility in any architectural curriculum. And he would echo Reid's belief that scientific and technical institutions were well positioned for the addition of architectural study. Over the years Ware may have developed his own philosophy of architectural education, and his *Outline* is a more extensive piece than that of Reid. Since both were addressing the same problem, some similarities would be difficult to avoid. In any event, it was Ware's prospectus that came to be recognized as the first truly definitive American proposal for architectural study.

By late April 1866, Ware was ready to lay out for Rogers and the Committee on Instruction the means by which he intended to make his "theoretical scheme a practicable working system." His first priority would be a "thorough study of the corresponding institutions on the other side of the water":

> It would be, as I have said, "but a poor illustration of our own methods of procedure, if we attempted single-handed to work out the great variety of questions that must come up, while an almost identical problem is in course of solution in half-a-dozen cities of Europe. The field is new, and we shall doubtless fall into new and original errors. We can, at least, save ourselves from the old ones."[23]

A year abroad, he said, was essential before he opened the architectural course. A proper collection of models, drawings, photographs, and casts, along with other necessary equipment, could be assembled at the same time and information obtained would facilitate later orders. He would consult with practicing architects about their perceptions of the instruction needed and the methods by which it might best be achieved, and he would see at firsthand what European schools were doing.

All of this brought him to the question of money and interim arrangements for instruction in drawing, for which he was responsible. He asked for a leave of absence for the academic year 1866–67 and requested funds for the purchase of materials abroad. He could see no harm in delaying the instruction in his course and felt that the plan would "add to the éclat of the Department and of the School," demonstrating to the public that "we are in earnest in undertaking to afford the best things." He pointed out that students in the other courses would not start their professional subjects until the fall of 1867. Even if he were at the Institute, he said, the instruction in mechanical and free-hand drawing and all the graphical work, as well as "superintendence of the Drawing rooms," would of necessity be delegated to a "subordinate officer of the school," whom he would presumably nominate, and thus his "absence would not be felt in any way."[24]

In late May 1866, having received no response, Ware wrote again. He understood that salary payments were dependent on the commencement of instruction in the various departments, but believed he was entitled to an exception because the "novelty of the undertaking" required much "difficult and responsible" preparatory work:

> The Department must be hard at work for a long time before instruction can be begun, and I do not suppose it was the intention of the Committee who reported the resolution in question, that this labor should go unrewarded. It is this work which I propose to pursue in great part abroad, where alone indeed a great part of it can be performed, and where I can have the freedom from other cares indispensable to its performance.[25]

Admitting that he hoped to achieve some "private ends" during his absence, he stated that he could not afford the "extra expense which the proper serving of the School would entail." Though most of the items he sought could be ordered after his return, "friends of the Institute" had indicated that donations from their private collections depended on evidence that a "nucleus" had been established. And for this he needed two or three thousand dollars for immediate purchases while abroad.[26]

During that spring the Government was preoccupied with the problems of the new building and mounting debt. Rogers was away from early June to late July, having been summoned to Scotland because of the illness and death of his brother Henry. Added to these circumstances was the slow machinery of the Institute's governance.

A special meeting of the Committee on Instruction on June 13, 1866, called for a formal consideration of Ware's application lacked a quorum, and could take no action beyond asking Secretary Webb to inform him of their "views and opinions." There is no mention of the fund for purchases in the record of a Government meeting late in June when Webb placed the salary question before them. The Government referred it back to the committee with power, for it seemed unlikely that they could raise a quorum at that time of year for confirmation of the committee's decision. It would be October 29, several weeks after Ware's departure, before the committee, again without a quorum, denied his request for full salary while on leave but agreed to a payment of $1,200 for the year, he to be responsible for furnishing an assistant to take charge of the instruction in freehand drawing. This action was ratified at their next meeting in mid-November.[27]

Ware's leave is not mentioned in the catalogues for the relevant period, nor is there a listing for William Pitt Preble Longfellow, whom he hired and paid to teach drawing. The faculty moved more expeditiously than the Government, for they had approved Ware's nomination of Longfellow in July.[28] Longfellow, a nephew of Henry Wadsworth Longfellow, had been graduated from Harvard in 1855 and from the Lawrence Scientific School in 1859, following which he joined the office of Edward Clarke Cabot. He substituted for Ware for only one year prior to spending 1867–68 in study abroad. He would later serve, in 1881–82, as adjunct professor of architectural design at the Institute.[29]

Rogers's estimate of expenses for the academic year 1866–67 contained a $3,000 item for purchases abroad by Ware, obviously fulfilling a commitment made at the time of his appointment.[30] It was not approved, however, and according to Ware, the problem was solved in 1866 through a "scheme" suggested by Rogers. Ware was to raise the money, to be spent as he wished for items in support of the teaching program, from Milton friends with the understanding that in return a scholarship would be established at the Institute for a Milton High School graduate. This scheme would form the basis of a bitter controversy between Ware and the Institute extending for some twenty years. By then he had left to establish a Department of Architecture at Columbia University, and Rogers, who he said was "responsible for the whole undertaking," had died before a final settlement could be achieved late in December 1885. A Milton High School student was appointed early in 1886 to the "perpetual free Scholarship" that had just been established.[31]

Ware left for Europe in August 1866, traveling first through England and on to Edinburgh for a longer stay. He then spent several weeks in London, where he began in earnest his observation of professional education in architecture and the collection of items for his department. He was invited to take part in the Ordinary General Meeting of the Royal Institute of British Architects in January 1867. Speaking "On the Condition of Architecture and of Architectural Education in the United States," he also explained the purpose of his visit—to "collect the materials . . . which must form our educational apparatus, . . . to perfect our plans by the study of European Schools of Art, and to chasten our judgments and correct our aims by the counsel of men whose insight or experience fits them to be our counsellors." He presented a copy of his *Outline* and expressed gratitude for "valuable suggestions and sagacious counsel already received."[32] He made valuable contacts in London, visiting architectural offices and various institutions, among them the South Kensington School of Design, the Royal Academy, and the classes of the Architectural Association. By attending lectures at University College and King's College he obtained a firsthand view of a formal architectural program in operation.[33]

Moving on to the Continent in mid-February 1867, he visited France, Italy, and Germany, returned briefly to London, and at the end of June settled in Paris, where he would remain until late October. He located an apartment in the Latin Quarter with Robert S. Peabody, who had worked in his office. They were joined by Charles F. McKim and Francis W. Chandler, all three young men in Paris for study at the École des Beaux-Arts. Chandler, who had been a student and draftsman in Ware's office, would later recall their pleasure in his company as he reported in the evening on visits to the École, its associated ateliers, and the École Centrale d'Architecture, as well as the additions he had secured for his collections. It appears that Ware also studied rendering at the end of his trip in one of the Paris drawing schools.[34]

Early in 1867 his "suggestion" for an increase in compensation was denied—understandably, given the large debt incurred for the building on Boylston Street. In responding to a "kind" letter from William Rogers, he stated confidentially that he had wanted to "disabuse" the Government of any notion that they had initially acted "very handsomely when there is no sufficient ground for such an opinion." And he wanted them to "understand that they were rather under an obligation" to him for "charges they might reasonably be expected to bear." He enclosed a report showing that he had spent more time than "expected to their service, and of course have sacrificed more of my funds. Of this I do not complain. Having undertaken the thing I am willing to put it through at what it costs."[35] He also asked Rogers about the likelihood of an extension of his leave for another year to provide more time abroad and time also to work up his program. The

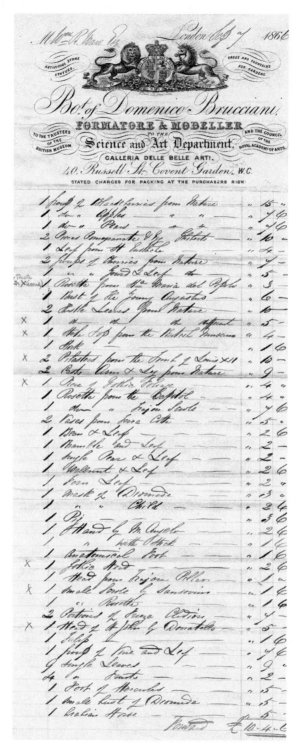

Bill of sale, 1866—items purchased in London by William Ware in furtherance of his mission to "collect the materials . . . which must form our educational apparatus"

Committee on Instruction did grant permission to delay the architectural course until
October 1868, but specified that Ware return in time to take charge of the mechanical
and freehand drawing in the second term of the academic year 1867–68.[36]

In the summer of 1867, while Rogers, Charles Eliot, and Frank Storer were all in
Paris for the Exposition, Rogers kept in touch with Runkle, reporting late in July on
a variety of matters and mentioning a "merry" dinner party of eleven which included
Ware and Malcolm Forbes, just returned from a trip to Switzerland. William Watson
was also in Paris during the summer, though not present on that occasion.[37] There were
undoubtedly other times as well when the talk would turn to matters concerning the
Institute and its prospects.

By September Rogers, still in Paris, was having second thoughts about the wisdom of Ware's not being on hand for the opening of the fall session and was sure that
the Committee on Instruction would be "disappointed (and even dissatisfied)."
Longfellow was leaving for Europe, and Eliot had asked for a leave because of his wife's
illness. On the grounds that the subject should be "satisfactorily provided for," and considering the "counsel and help" that Ware could provide in the general work of the
Institute, Rogers asked him to reconsider.[38] This Ware agreed to do, emphasizing that
it had been planned from the beginning that another should take over the drawing, an
assignment he had been willing to assume at the start because he wanted it begun correctly and he wanted to get to know the students. But now he felt it essential that a
capable teacher, adequately paid, be found.[39]

A week later, having decided against returning for the fall opening, Ware promised
Rogers that he would be in Boston as near to December 1 as he could and provided
him with a statement for the Committee on Instruction—a "somewhat modified and
much abridged" version of an earlier draft they had discussed. Ware's proposal, which
had also been discussed with Watson, suggested that Watson's instruction in "geometri-
cal and mechanical drawing" be offered in the first half of the year, and his own free-
hand drawing in the second. He indicated that he was searching for a drawing teacher
and reminded the committee of the difficulty of the task he had accepted.[40]

⁂

Ware's *Outline* had not attempted to set forth a detailed curriculum, nor had he worked
out a complete plan for the first catalogue. The section on Building and Architecture
in the first catalogue stressed the importance of the common first two years as a foundation for the professional work to follow. It did add, however, that special students
would be admitted and that "practising draughtsmen" were encouraged to take advan-

tage of the opportunity.[41] Though the next two catalogues were more specific about the final two years, a precise program awaited Ware's return from Europe.

Following his arrival in December 1867, he was busy with his drawing classes, active on general faculty matters, and was asked to study the problems of heating and ventilation which had beset the new building from the start. At the same time he was involved with Henry Van Brunt on their work for Harvard's Memorial Hall. By late summer 1868, however, he had organized his architectural museum and laid out his "programme." On August 21 the Government authorized its publication and distribution as a supplement to the *Third Annual Catalogue* for 1867–68. A prefatory note stated that after a "proper study of the European Schools of Architecture" and the "collection of the necessary material of instruction," and having received "every encouragement, both here and abroad," a "more particular statement" of the courses that would be offered in the fall could now be presented to the "public and to the architectural profession." Also at the August 21 meeting Ware's salary was confirmed at $1,200, and Rogers was authorized to assure him that an appropriation would be made for the expenses of the department.

Ware divided the course into three components covering two years, "so arranged that they can be pursued simultaneously by the same student." Combined, they represented the final two years of the regular four-year program:

1st. — A course of Composition and Design
2nd. — A course of Construction and Professional Practice
3rd. — A selection from the Scientific and Literary studies pursued by students in the other departments of the School during their third and fourth years.

Special students would be allowed to enroll for partial courses, choosing "studies as they may prefer, or as their previous training may permit them to follow," including subjects among those required for regular students in the four-year program. Only students who could demonstrate ability "by examination or otherwise" would be accepted, and satisfactory performance would lead to a certificate of attainment in specific studies, attesting to "qualifications as an Architectural Draughtsman or Assistant." A diploma as evidence of proficiency to practice one's "profession as Architect" could be obtained by satisfying the requirements of the four-year course and the presentation of "Original Designs, upon a prescribed subject."

The constraints of the regular program, Ware said, did not allow sufficient time for attaining the optimum level of competency in design. Therefore, he advised regular students to take the "different courses successively, instead of all at once, extending their studies over a greater length of time, and devoting a chief part of their time and attention, throughout, to those exercises in original design to which, indeed, all the rest of their labor is properly subservient." The diploma would be granted whenever they were "qualified to receive it." Ware urged similar flexibility for the "practising draughtsmen and assistants" working in architectural offices. He advised students to obtain places in architectural offices during the summer vacation to "accomplish themselves in matters which it is not the purpose of the school to take in hand." In outlining the course of instruction, he added a fourth and fifth component—"Exercises in Drawing and Exercises in original design."[42] Also described was the architectural museum, which would be accessible not only to the students but to the public as well, and "especially to the architectural profession."[43]

The 1868–69 Institute catalogue set out the intentions of the program:

> To give to its students the instruction and discipline that cannot be obtained in architects' offices, rather than to cover the whole ground of architectural study. The course is, however, practical as well as theoretical, and, besides the scientific study of construction and materials, pursued in connection with the Department of Engineering, it comprises the study of building processes, and of professional practice and procedure, as well as that of composition and design, and of the history of art.[44]

Degree requirements in accord with Ware's plan were stated, along with a caution that skill in executing original designs must be developed through additional study, and the extension of studies beyond the usual four years was suggested.

In the fall of 1868 Ware's class in design did not begin until November. Anxious to attract students and believing that earlier statements should be supplemented, he placed an advertisement in the papers of October 31 and November 2. In the absence of Rogers, confined to his home since his stroke in mid-October, Ware asked Samuel Kneeland to sign the notice as secretary of the Institute. Since Rogers's diary indicated that he "seemed to be getting better," he probably either saw or was told about the first of these notices. He did not approve and likely informed Kneeland, who in turn told Ware that an immediate explanation would be in order.

Ware began a letter to Rogers on November 2 with the news that he had invited John Philbrick and Samuel Lothrop of the Committee on Instruction to attend his first design class to "see what we are doing and proposing to do." He had also invited a few prospective students. He then mentioned the advertisements signed by Kneeland, who was "at hand," adding that without "authority for advertising," he had paid for them himself, with "special funds, of course." He should have "perhaps" consulted with Rogers first and "only later," and "even now indeed only faintly," had he remembered that it was Rogers rather than the secretary who should sign. He apologized for this "irregularity" caused by his "haste."[45]

Rogers set the record straight that same day. He began by asking that his "frankness" be excused, "knowing that I have but one object—the interest of the whole School:"

> It is a rule of obvious propriety that no advertisement relating either to a Departt. of the School or to the whole School should be published without the formal sanction of the Faculty or at least of the Prest. who represents that body to the public.
>
> A recognition of the equality of the different Departs. of the School in such things is vitally important. What one department does to-day others may equally claim to do tomorrow, & it is easy to imagine the confusion & dissatisfaction which would arise if each prof were at liberty to advertise his department when & as he pleased.
>
> We cannot in such matters afford to be in "haste."[46]

He was careful, as always, to emphasize the role of the faculty as a whole, alongside his own authority as president.

In the fall of 1869 Ware reviewed for Runkle, then president pro tem of the Institute, the activities of the previous year and was especially proud of his architectural museum, considering it an asset not only for the department but for the Institute as a whole. "Between four and five hundred ladies and gentlemen" had visited the rooms by special invitation, not to mention "casual visitors" and the many who had come when the building was open to the public. The members of the Boston Society of Architects had been among the first special visitors.

Figures vary, but for the year 1868–69 Ware reported four "students of the School," who were special students, and ten "outsiders," who appear not to have been registered but who paid a fee of $25 for each subject taken. He acknowledged both "successes and failures," to be expected in a new venture, and was pleased by the favorable student reaction. He was confident that those enrolling for 1869–70 would constitute a "capital class both in numbers and in quality, as good in both respects as I could have wished or expected at this stage of our work." Increased numbers meant more work, and he had hired Francis W. Chandler, then working with Ware and Van Brunt, as his "personal assistant." This was a "personal arrangement" looked upon by both as "experimental," and though Ware did not want him or any other person he might engage to be formally "recognized as an assistant" in the department, Chandler was listed with the "Officers of Instruction" in the catalogues for 1869–70 and 1870–71.[47] Other commitments prevented him from remaining beyond the spring of 1871. In the fall of 1871 he was appointed Assistant Supervising Architect of the United States Treasury Department, serving until 1874, when he returned to Boston to work in partnership with Edward Clarke Cabot.[48]

Chandler's reminiscences of Ware following Ware's death in 1915 provide a glimpse of these early days:

> When I returned to America in 1869 the new department was in a very flourishing condition. Its success was already assured, but it had laid an incredible amount of work on Professor Ware's shoulders. He was giving the lectures on architectural history, and on practice. He was carrying alone the classes in design—perspective and some architectural descriptive geometry were subjects in which he was greatly interested, and which must come under his instruction or not be given at all.
>
> At that time the poverty of the Institute demanded such strict economy that every instructor was forced to carry a burden that would make the member of a labor union wince. But in addition to all this, Professor Ware had a new department to form for which there was no precedent, and for which the curriculum of the Institute was unprepared.[49]

Ware's experience with Chandler convinced him that he had found the solution to instruction in design, and Chandler's departure in 1871 left a void very difficult to fill. Qualified replacements were scarce, and even those were otherwise occupied and not available. Ware was forced, therefore, to look abroad and to await the end of the Franco-Prussian War to explore the possibility of obtaining a suitable candidate trained at the École des Beaux Arts.[50] He recruited Eugene Létang, trained at the École and the atelier of Emile Vaudremer. With Létang's arrival began the influence of the École on the Department of Architecture. At the time he was the "only native French, École-trained architect teaching design" in the United States.[51] Ware referred to this appointment as a "somewhat adventurous step, which from the circumstances of the case I was obliged to take almost upon my sole responsibility."[52] The appointment was confirmed by the Corporation on January 3, 1872.[53]

Ware felt that the task of building a department had "proved more arduous than it seemed at first, and constantly grows more and more difficult as we enter upon its higher paths." He could see not only the "dangers we have escaped," but also the "difficulties of the road before us." Yet he looked to the future with confidence:

> The best work, of course, that a school can do is to discover and develop first-rate talent and to turn it towards the work for which it is best fit, and it is the aim and ultimate hope of this Department to attract the attention of young men of superior capacity, so to arrange its methods of instruction as to stimulate their best efforts. . . . It is as yet too soon to say what measure of success may be reached in this regard. . . . There is already reason to believe that we are not behind other nations in the quality of our raw material. The quality of our products will depend on the perfection of our educational processes.[54]

Chapter 2 4

Methods of Teaching

T he rise of technical and scientific education in America had been largely influenced by European practice and experience, and from Europe, too, came new ideas on methods of teaching. The traditional approach was an assignment of reading in textbooks, followed by questions from the professor and recitations by the students, amounting to little more than quotations from a prescribed text. It was principally an exercise in memory, with the professor functioning as a drill master rather than as a teacher. Increasingly it was recognized that this old and established system failed to inspire independent thinking and failed also to promote the close, human interchange between teacher and student essential for the development of character and understanding. At the University of Virginia, Thomas Jefferson, following the example of William Small at William and Mary, introduced a new plan of instruction. He was convinced that teaching by lectures instead of by textbook, followed by oral questioning and written examinations, "would stimulate independent thought on the part of the student, create a desire for original investigation, and discourage mere memorizing." This imposed a greater burden on the teacher in the preparation of his subject and required greater talent in imparting knowledge.[1]

In his years at Virginia William Rogers was imbued with the spirit of this approach to teaching and learning, whereby teacher and student work together, and learning is acquired not only by reading but also by doing. As the Swiss psychologist Piaget expressed it, "Knowledge is derived from action." That these ideas were fundamental to the earliest educational philosophy of the Institute is apparent from a statement in the 1868–69 catalogue:

Instruction is given by lectures and recitations, and by practical exercises in the field, the laboratories, and the drawing rooms. The progress of each student is tested by frequent oral examinations. Text-books are used in many, but not in all departments. A high value is set upon the educational effect of laboratory practice, drawing, and field-work.[2]

The *Objects and Plan* of 1861, in its description of the proposed "School of Chemistry," had pointed out that while the "general doctrines and laws of chemical re-actions" could be "taught by the demonstrations of the lecture-room," the "study of the practical and industrial branches of the subject. . . . could not be prosecuted in a manner to be practically available without personal training in analysis and experiment, and would therefore demand the facilities of an ample and well-appointed *Laboratory*. This we should hope to see early connected with the School of Industrial Science, and so equipped with the implements of practical chemistry as not only to provide for the ordinary exercises in analysis, but for the examination of soils, manures, and organic products, and for the illustration and study of the leading processes in dyeing, tanning, metallurgy, and the numerous other arts in which chemical re-actions are concerned."[3] And in 1863 Rogers's suggestion of a separate laboratory building appeared in a plan showing a structure containing separate laboratories for the students and the professor and a balance room.

By 1864, with plans under way for a much more ambitious undertaking, the *Scope and Plan* for the school called for two departments—one, a general or popular course of lectures mainly in the evening; and the second, a complete academic program of "special and professional instruction." The complete program was designed to give the student a "prolonged and thorough training" providing a "ready command over the problems with which, as a mechanician, engineer, builder, practical chemist, or scientific miner he may be called upon to deal." Beyond lectures and oral and written examinations, its "methods and Apparatus of Instruction" would include "Practice in Physical and Chemical Manipulations, Laboratory Training in Chemical Analyses, Metallurgy, and Industrial Chemistry; Drawing and the Construction of Special Plans and Projects of Machines and Works of Engineering and Architecture; Practical Exercises in Surveying, Levelling, Geodesy, and Nautical Astronomy; and Excursions for the Inspection of Machines, Motors, Processes of Manufacture, Buildings, Works of Engineering, Geological Sections, Quarries and Mines."[4] Four laboratories were to be established: Physics and Mechanics, General Chemical Analysis and Manipulation, Metallurgy and Mining, and Industrial Chemistry. These were to be used not only in teaching but also for experiments and investigations initiated by the Committee on the Museum and the various committees of the Society of Arts, "including the examination and testing of new machines and processes, and the conducting of original researches in the different departments of applied science." Advanced students might "when expedient" be allowed to "assist," presumably the professor in charge of the laboratory, in these "critical studies and experiments."[5]

For chemistry, laboratory facilities were essential and would take precedence at the outset. With only two rooms available for the school at the temporary quarters on Summer Street, one served for lectures and the other was a small chemical laboratory for which limited means could provide only a modest amount of equipment. Of necessity, therefore, student laboratory work was postponed until the building on Boylston Street was ready. In April 1865 Rogers wrote to his friend George J. Brush, professor of mineralogy in the School of Applied Chemistry at the Sheffield School at Yale, for advice about the costs of fitting up a proper chemical laboratory. Brush replied that, in addition to associated building costs, about $6,000 would be required for fixtures and equipment, including furnaces and sandbaths, and the necessary installation.[6]

Though their tenure on the Institute faculty would be rather brief, Francis Storer, professor of general and industrial chemistry, and Charles Eliot, professor of analytical chemistry and metallurgy, were wise choices for Rogers, both for the design of the chemical courses and the planning and equipping of the chemical laboratories. Each had served as an assistant to Josiah P. Cooke, Erving Professor of Chemistry and Mineralogy at Harvard, who had established a laboratory for undergraduates in 1858. Storer had studied for two years in Germany and France and had been operating a laboratory as a consulting chemist since his return. Eliot had restored the chemical laboratory at the Lawrence Scientific School to a firm footing prior to his departure from Harvard, and could bring to bear his general observations of technical education abroad and his experience for a brief period in the chemical laboratory at Marburg.[7]

Eliot prepared an "Estimate of Cost of Fittings and Apparatus for the Chemical Laboratories" totaling $10,000, furniture and gas and water fixtures not included. Of this total, $2,700 represented "first stock" of chemicals and glassware. The estimate is undated, but probably was prepared some time in the fall of 1865. A separate sheet entitled "Chemical Department" appears to be an account of funds committed in the amount of $2,705, $1,000 of which was for "foreign goods *ordered*," with an indication that $2,000 in outstanding bills remained for fixtures and apparatus *already used*. Not counting the excluded items, some $15,000 would be required.[8] Though minuscule by today's standards, the total cost was considerable for an institution with severe funding problems.

A statement from the 1868–69 catalogue describes the method of instruction adopted in chemistry:

> In the first year, instruction is given in Inorganic General Chemistry by a weekly exercise which combines a recitation and an illustrated lecture, and by a weekly lesson in the laboratory, where every student is provided with a desk and the necessary apparatus, and is required to perform, under the supervision of the professors, a large number of experiments selected to illustrate the laws of chemical action and the properties of all the important chemical elements. In the second year, a systematic course of instruction in Qualitative Analysis is given, by laboratory practice and oral and written examinations. Every student works in the laboratory twice a week during the greater part of the year. Towards the close of the year instruction is given in the Elements of Organic Chemistry. Manuals, specially prepared for the purpose, are used in aid of the laboratory instruction given to the classes of the first and second year. In the third and fourth years the principal subjects of study are Quantitative Analysis, Assaying, Mineralogy, the Use of the Blowpipe, Metallurgy, and Industrial Chemistry. Competent students are encouraged to undertake special researches, and are assisted in bringing them to useful results.[9]

The words "useful results" reflect a view and purpose that was ever present in the minds of the founders and early faculty. The first catalogue had expressed this objective even more clearly: "Special attention will always be given to the description of those substances and processes which are of importance in common life or in the useful arts"[10]—a far cry from the philosophy of the classical college.

No textbook on the conduct of laboratory experimentation had as yet been published. In response to this need, Eliot and Storer published in 1867 *A Manual of Inorganic Chemistry, Arranged to Facilitate the Experimental Demonstration of the Facts and Principles of Science*, followed two years later by *A Compendious Manual of Qualitative Chemical Analysis*. These works appeared in a number of revised editions and were for many years standard texts in the teaching of college chemistry.[11]

Of the four projected laboratories, that for physics has attracted the most attention over the years, and many have hailed it as the first in the United States. Though such a claim is questionable, there is no doubt about Rogers's conviction that a direct encounter by the student with the laws of nature through laboratory experience was as essential to the teaching of physics as in the teaching of chemistry, and he listed it first among the four planned laboratories for the Institute's school.

Despite a statement in the first catalogue that students "by small classes at a time" would carry out experiments, the limited equipment and space then available could not have allowed much more than the usual method of illustrated lectures and demonstrations.[12] The same issue did, however, describe the "variety of mechanical and physical processes and experiments" that would be included in laboratory instruction once the proposed Laboratory of Physics and Mechanics had been established:

> Thus he [the student] may learn practically the methods of estimating motors and machines by the dynamometer, of experimenting on the flow of water and air and other gases, and of testing the strength of the materials used in construction. He may become familiar with the adjustments and applications of the microscope; be trained in observing with the barometer, thermometer, and hygrometer; and, in a room fitted up for photometry, may learn the mode of measuring the light produced by gas and other sources of illumination, and the value of different kinds of burners, lamps, and their appendages.[13]

No effort was made, however, when the new building opened in the fall of 1866 to establish such a facility. The Institute was in debt, and Rogers was faced with both financial worries and a multitude of administrative and professorial duties. The catalogues for the following two years stated simply that "at an early day" a "Laboratory for Physical Manipulations" would be established.[14]

Though Rogers had concluded in 1865 that he would need help with his teaching duties, no action was taken until late 1866, when Edward Pickering was appointed "Assistant Instructor in Physics." Only twenty years of age and an 1865 *summa cum laude* graduate of the Lawrence Scientific School, he was a brilliant addition to the instructional staff. He was already associated with the Institute through his appointment in the spring to the Committee on Chemical Products and Processes of the Society of Arts, one of the few committees that ever

Edward Charles Pickering

reached the point of organization. At that time a classmate at the Scientific School had sent a note of congratulations on this "well deserved" honor and took the opportunity to comment on the Institute's school:

> The Technological Institute is beginning to make itself heard. Will not its school interfere with the "Scientific"? I am sure I hope it will not unless it be to imbue it with a spirit of generous rivalry. I think competition will be very beneficial to both schools. I of course swear by the "Scientific" and always mean to. I have had a good many discussions on its merits as compared with the Troy "Polytechnic" with gentlemen here. If my arguments were not strong enough to convince them, they at least must have seen that I could not appreciate the force of theirs.[15]

Pickering took up his appointment in February 1867, and within a few days was substituting as lecturer for Rogers. Rapidly he began to assume all major responsibilities for the teaching of physics. Soon Rogers proposed that he be made assistant professor in view of the increased amount of work expected with the arrival of a new class in October, and the Government agreed.[16] With his promotion in August 1868 to the Thayer Professorship of Physics, replacing Rogers, Pickering's salary was raised to $1,700, an increase of $200.[17] The move proved to be timely in view of Rogers's sudden illness in the fall and eventual resignation in 1870.

John Trowbridge, another 1865 *summa cum laude* graduate of the Lawrence Scientific School, was appointed in 1868 to the dual role of instructor in physics and superintendent of drawing, thus joining his classmate as a member of the Institute's instructing staff. In 1869 he was promoted to assistant professor of physics, without a seat on the faculty, retaining his duties in drawing. The following year he was called to Harvard as assistant professor of physics, "brought into the Department as a new force" by then President Charles Eliot. He would have a long and distinguished career there, would press for adequate research facilities for physics, and would later serve, from 1888 to 1910, as director of Harvard's Jefferson Physical Laboratory.[18]

Pickering was completely in accord with Rogers on the need for a laboratory approach to the teaching of physics, viewing as remarkable the fact that chemistry had outpaced physics in this respect: "While Physics is almost as much an experimental science as Chemistry, it is yet taught even in our best schools by text books or lectures, illustrated by such experiments as the teacher has the skill or inclination to give; nor is there a laboratory in the country in which instruction is given in physical research."[19] By 1868 he had set aside a room for advanced students "where they carried on physical investigations, as is done by many physicists, with their special students."[20] The catalogue for 1868–69 stated that the "various branches of the subject are treated both mathematically and physically," and cited a course of "Physical Manipulation and Research" in the third and fourth years. Though there was no mention of the establishment of a physical laboratory, it is clear that Pickering was developing a plan for one for regular students and beginning to assemble some of the necessary apparatus. A "friend of the Institute" had made possible the purchase of an "extensive collection of acoustic apparatus, including sets of organ pipes, forks, resonators, a large Seebeck's sirene, phonautograph and other instruments" for sound experiments. And the Lowell Institute had loaned much of its apparatus useful for "pneumatics and electricity" experiments.

In the spring of 1869, when Rogers was on leave in Philadelphia, Pickering mentioned his plan in a letter to Mrs. Rogers.[21] Shortly thereafter Runkle was also in touch with her:

> I am more & more impressed with the great treasure we have in him [Pickering]. He has drawn up, in quite full detail, a Plan for the Physical Laboratory, which I will send you before long. I have had it put into type in order the better to submit it to the consideration of a few persons for judgment and advice. Pickering is very anxious to be ready by Oct. next to instruct the 3rd year's class by laboratory work, & if our experience of one year shall be favorable, as I feel it must be, we can then gradually enlarge our facilities & take in the lower classes. I am convinced that in time we shall revolutionize the instruction in Physics just as has been done in Chemistry. I find that [the] Cornell Univ. Catalogue stated that a Physical Laboratory is in early contemplation; and I also learned that Gibbs intends to open one in Cambridge. Now you know that this idea belongs to our dear President, and was one of the prominent features of his plan of the School of the Inst.; & I can not endure the idea of some other school first putting the idea into execution.
>
> I know if he were here, he would encourage Pickering as I am doing. We are now designing the tables & finding what apparatus we still need.[22]

In May the plan was approved by the Government and permission given to proceed provided that no additional funds would be necessary for the current year.[23]

In Newport by June, Rogers was apparently still considered too ill to be told even good news about the school, but Runkle sent word again through Mrs. Rogers explaining that he had refrained from writing, knowing that "this was one of the things which should not be brought to Mr. Rogers' attention":

I have had two motives in taking the step now. First, other Institutions are moving in the matter, & heard privately that Prof. Gibbs [at Harvard] intends to attempt something of the kind soon; and second, Pickering had become deeply interested in it, and it would, in my opinion, have been unwise, to have discouraged him, when the success of the Laboratory depends so much upon him.

The idea belongs to the President, & we ought to be the first to put it into execution.[24]

Returning from an August meeting of the American Association for the Advancement of Science in Salem, Runkle wrote again, this time directly to Rogers, with the news that the "sailing at Cornell is not so smooth after all":

Many of the departments, & among them that of Physics is in a lamentable condition—Instead of a Physical Laboratory, they have not even settled upon the course in Physics, & are very destitute of apparatus. Quite a large number of members visited us, & were much impressed by what they saw. We have every reason to be gratified with our success & standing among the Institutions of the country.[25]

Pickering had set to work immediately following Government approval, and in November 1869 Runkle was able to report to the Society of Arts that the Physical Laboratory was successfully under way, thirty students already at work, and "anticipated objections of breakage, and too great consumption of time" had proved to be more theoretical than practical.[26] At the end of the academic year, Pickering could say in a report that "the scale on which this laboratory has been tried, is such as to render its success no longer a matter of conjecture." Sixty students, including special students, had performed hundreds of exercises and experiments, acquiring thereby "a far more practical knowledge of physics than by devoting the same time to lectures" and "as extended a knowledge of practical physics as is needed for everyday life."[27]

But the purpose of the laboratory was broader than simply to impart a body of useful knowledge:

Its first object is to enable the regular students of the Institute, after attending a course of lectures on Physics, to verify its laws and measure its constants, also to learn to use the more important pieces of apparatus. Secondly, to instruct special students in the use of particular instruments, or branches of physics, as the spectroscope, microscope, photometry, electrical measurements, etc.

Thirdly, to prepare teachers of this science. And fourthly, to afford facilities to physicists to carry on investigations at the Institute.[28]

As an example of the more advanced work Pickering cited a paper by Charles R. Cross published in the *Journal of the Franklin Institute* in June 1870. Cross, then a fourth-year student in the Science and Literature Course, was also listed that year as an assistant in German, and after receiving his degree became an instructor in physics. His paper, dated May 3, 1870, entitled "On the Focal Length of Microscopic Objectives," was identified as a contribution from the Physical Laboratory of the Massachusetts Institute of Technology and carried with it a footnote by Professor Pickering:

> During the past year, we have fitted up rooms in which our regular students ver-ify many of the laws and measure the principal constants of physics, while more advanced pupils carry on original investigations. In developing the first part of this plan, many unexpected results have been arrived at, and, thinking that they may be of value elsewhere, I hope to make them the subject of a future paper. I think the accompanying article by Mr. Cross will show, that although we can-not always expect to have students with his skill and perseverance, yet that such a laboratory ought to furnish many additions to physical science.[29]

In his report, Pickering also emphasized the facilities available to individuals who wished simply to conduct "investigations of a high order," citing adequate space for large-scale experiments and the availability of assistance from advanced students. It was "scarcely necessary," he said, "to point out the advantages of the laboratory system of teaching physics, since the tendency of all technical education is now in this direction."[30]

Ample space had been provided on the first floor for a physics lecture room and two laboratory and apparatus rooms, but sufficient funds were lacking. Pickering had devised a system whereby a different experiment, illustrative of physical principles and methods of research and with the required apparatus and instruction, was set up at indi-vidual tables, each with gas and water fixtures, so that students could progress from one to another, eventually completing all of the required exercises through efficient use of limited apparatus and time. The instructor would move steadily about the room, at each table helping the student with his problems and observing his skill and progress. Pickering designed and constructed much of the apparatus with the aid of his students and a few local workmen.

With the trial period an unqualified success, Pickering had moved immediately in the spring session of 1870 to make the laboratory available to members of the second-year class. He decided also to extend the scope of the laboratory work to assigned experimental investigations, followed by an opportunity for those who wished to pursue more advanced work to carry out original research and to publish their results. He had encouraged this from the start, and hoped that the laboratory would serve not only for teaching purposes but also as a research facility. A number of papers were published during the Pickering era on original work accomplished with the aid of his students. Particularly important for those who might wish to enter the teaching profession was the opportunity for special instruction in building apparatus and in supervising others who might do so, as well as for lecturing to student audiences and at meetings of the Society of Arts.

Pickering's plan attracted much attention, and though he made no grandiose claims, other institutions looked to his effort as an example to be followed. The matter of priority, however, in the initiation of laboratory instruction in physics deserves special comment, best approached through Rogers's own statements on two separate occasions.

Early in 1870, not long after Pickering set the plan in motion, Rogers praised his efforts in a communication to the Government:

> It gives me pleasure to refer to the ability with which Prof. Pickering has carried out my views of a Laboratory of Physical Instruction. This is, I believe, the *first* laboratory of the kind ever established, and, as it furnishes practical training not hitherto attempted in any systematic way, will give the students of the Institute peculiar advantages in their studies, and in future researches in this very important branch of Science.
>
> Already the chemical laboratories of the Institute under the guidance of Prof. Storer and his colleagues have won a high reputation throughout the country for the excellence of their equipment and the thoroughness of their teaching, and we may anticipate that these examples of practical instruction will exert a beneficial influence on the methods of scientific training far beyond the circle of our own operations.[31]

Later, in 1872, expressing thanks for the naming of the Physical Laboratory in his honor, Rogers appeared to have little doubt that the idea was an innovative step without precedent:

Laboratories of Chemistry and of Metallurgy have long formed a part of the instrumentalities for instruction in scientific institutions in this country and in Europe; but many years ago, while engaged in the teaching of Physical Science, I was impressed with the great need of a similar practical means of instruction in connection with the Department of Physics. The introduction, therefore, of this appliance as a part of the system of our School was a cherished purpose in drawing up the "Scope and Plan" of the Institute of Technology.

I may perhaps be allowed to add that when, in preparing this pamphlet in the spring of 1864, I included a Physical Laboratory as among the practical means of instruction to be established in our School, and stated in brief some of the leading objects of such a laboratory, I indulged the belief that I was initiating a very important improvement in the methods of scientific training, for which hitherto no provision had been made either abroad or at home.

The extent to which this idea of a physical laboratory has been followed out in other institutions, and the number of instances in which our own Laboratory, so admirably organized and directed by Professor Pickering has been consulted by them as an example, show very clearly how prompt and general has been the recognition of the value of this step in educational progress.

Our Institute may thus, I think, in this as well as in other features of its organization, claim the credit of having made an advance in practical scientific education.[32]

But Rogers's statement in the *Scope and Plan* about the proposed Laboratory of Physics and Mechanics was brief and made no claim to primacy either in America or abroad. His later claim was accepted by many contemporary scientists and historians and perpetuated over the years through quotation and citation by succeeding generations and even by Institute publications.[33] Pickering, however, was somewhat more modest. For him the innovation lay in the size of the classes and his plan of instruction. In a brief article published in January 1871, he wrote:

It is well known that chemistry can be taught far better by a laboratory in which the student performs the various experiments, than by any system of lectures. Now, although for many years physicists have been in the habit of instructing their special students and assistants in this way, yet it is only recently that the same plan has been tried with large classes in physics. One of the first institutions to attempt this method, in America at least, was the Massachusetts Institute of Technology in Boston; and as I find many colleges here establishing physical laboratories, I trust that our experience may prove of some interest.[34]

Actually, Rensselaer Polytechnic under Amos Eaton in 1824 was the first educational institution in the United States to emphasize a laboratory method of instruction. The professors gave lectures and conducted examinations, but each student carried out experiments of his own design followed by lectures to his classmates explaining procedures and discussing results. Eaton was convinced that hands-on experience gained from laboratory work was essential to the proper training of students as teachers and, more broadly, for "the application of science to the common purposes of life."[35] Similarly, Rogers's proposal had been a natural extension of his belief in laboratory experience as a key to understanding all branches of science. Starting from Rogers's premise, Pickering created a plan for the teaching of physics to large classes through direct laboratory experience as well as through textbooks and lectures.

Among the few surviving contemporary accounts of the curriculum and teaching methods, the most extensive was left by Albert F. Hall—actually a series of documents, rather than a single, discrete account. A conscientious student, Hall kept meticulous notes in his classes. His algebra and physics notebooks (dated February 1865 and March 3–6, 1865, respectively) illustrate the content and level of coursework in the Institute's preliminary session.[36] Hall's algebra notebook starts out with basic definitions of numbers ("groups or collections of things which may be counted") and the relation between arithmetic and algebra ("In Arithmetic numbers are represented by figures; but in algebra numbers are also represented *by letters*"), and proceeds quickly—within a month—to relatively complex topics such as the use of brackets, propositions, and proofs.

Science subjects in the early years appear to have been taught primarily with a view to their utility in practical lines of work. In fact, the first-year course had no "physics" per se, but rather, "elementary mechanics," which covered basic principles such as motions and forces; mechanics of solids, liquids, and gases; and laws of sound.[37] Hall's physics notebook (March 1865) starts out with references to "quiescent preassure [*sic*]," "dynamometer," "measures of moving forces," "laws of motion," and other topics that a budding engineer would have found useful in his professional training. The experimental examples used—often railroad analogies—reflected this emphasis:

If we attach as a link in a chain connecting the Locomotive with the cars the dynamometer [*sic*] the graduations will show the force exerted by the Locomotive in pulling the cars. When the Locomotive has compressed the spring with all its force then the forces are said to be in equilibrium. The friction of the axles of the cars and the tendency of the spring to resume its proper position length, is just counter-balanced by the force of the Locomotive.[38]

This paragraph was annotated by Rogers, the physics professor, who followed a common pedagogical method of the time: gathering, reviewing, and correcting student notes. In this case, he felt that Hall had misunderstood the concept conveyed in the last sentence ("The friction of the axles . . . of the Locomotive"), and rephrased it thus: "The aggregate of the friction at the axles of the cars & on the rails and the resistance of the air is just counter-balanced by the force of the Locomotive, & the Spring shows the [?] of this balanced force." This, in fact, was the only annotation by Rogers in the entire notebook, suggesting that he was especially conscious to demand precision of his students where theoretical concepts met "real-life" events.

The start of another of Hall's notebooks (first entry dated December 28, 1863) predates his admission to the Institute, but continues afterwards at least through the end of his first semester there.[39] It begins with a series of mathematical calculations, including the application of square roots, triangles, circles, and cube roots; there are also page references to an unidentified textbook. An entry dated April 7, 1865, outlines experiments that Hall conducted with fellow student Walter Tuckerman in the first "chemical manipulations" class at the Institute:

> Made Hydrogen by passing steam over heated *copper turnings* in an iron tube.
> . . . Made Binoxide of manganese, by pouring nitric acid on copper turnings.
> Extinguishes burning sulphur, and charcoal. . . . Detected arsenic in some green paper.

Hall was a meticulous note-taker who left an extensive record of both *how* the faculty was teaching and *what* the students were learning. In an essay composed in October 1866 for Professor Atkinson's class in "logic, rhetoric, and the history of English literature," in response to Professor Atkinson's assignment that students write about their summer vacations, Hall described a trip he had taken to Pennsylvania the previous summer. Among the places visited, he wrote, was a "Quaker church," which Professor Atkinson corrected to "meeting-house" (Atkinson's annotations, written in red, appear as elisions, insertions, or marginalia throughout the essay). Most striking, however, is Hall's description of his visit to a coal mine:

> On finishing my business at Philadelphia I started home by the way of the Lehigh valley. I left by the North Penn. R.R. at 5 o'clock P.M. and arrived at Mauch Chunk at 10 P.M. This is the great mining region of the Lehigh Navigation Co. I presented my introduction to the engineer in charge, and was very cordially received, and directions were given me in relation to going over the mines. The next morning at 7:25 I started in the coach for mount Pisgah. There we took the cars up the inclined plane of this mountain, the ascent being 2322 ft long and 662 ft high. We were drawn up this plane by a stationary engine of 240 horse power. Arriving at the summit we waited about five minutes to look around us upon the beautiful scenes. It was magnificent: we were about 1200 feet above the village which lay below on the plains, surrounded by hills on every side. We started again down another plane moved by gravity alone, and rode this for 7 miles until we reached mount Jefferson. There we were drawn up another inclined plane 2070 ft long 462 ft high. We again proceeded on our way moved by gravity as before until we came to Panther Creek plane No. 1. up which we were drawn. This plane is 1800 feet long and 250 ft high. Arriving at the summit we went on our course and our next stopping place was "Coal Dale," where we visited the breaker, and saw them break up the coal ready for market. After looking at the machinery etc., we again started and went on until we came to Panther Creek plane No. 2. which is 2400 ft long 375 ft high, arriving at the top of this plane, up which we moved as though we were shot from a gun, we proceeded on to "Summit Hill," the headquarters of the company. Here I took dinner, after which I was driven in a buggy by the engineer in charge to mine no. 1. I went down the slope leading to the mine, which is 450 feet, by an elevator. Upon reaching the bottom, I went to the face of the mine, which is about a quarter of a mile distant from the slope. I mined a piece of coal of course as all visitors do, to bring home as a keepsake. After examining the machinery connected with the mine, I started again for "Summit Hill" where I took the cars for Mauch Chunk 9 miles distant, where we arrived in 25 minutes, all safe and sound, having been *25* miles on inclined planes. At 4:30 P.M. I took the cars for N.Y. All along the route I saw the great Iron smelting furnaces which looked like volcanos, at night.

The aesthetic side of the excursion—a dramatic vista from the mountain-top—is buried amidst technical issues that were of more immediate interest to the author, along with close observation (backed by precise quantities and measurements) of distances, planes, energy, momentum, and mining processes. An English teacher elsewhere might well have suggested that such a catalogue was not a very imaginative approach to the assignment, but here it reflected exactly the kind of expository "clearness and precision"—empirical data, facts, practical information, writing as *useful* skill—that the Institute was reaching for as it started training students for focused occupations in engineering.

The "field trip," in fact, was fundamental to the Institute's core mission, symbolizing, in its emphasis on practical, hands-on experience, what made an Institute education special compared to that offered by other institutions of higher learning. The faculty was well attuned to this emphasis. Typical correspondence between Runkle and Rogers, for example, waxed enthusiastic whenever such prospects materialized: "Our Mechanical Engineers," Runkle wrote to Rogers in 1869, "are spending their summer in the Machine Shop of the Navy Yard, by the kind permission of Com.[?] Rogers. A splendid opportunity!"[40]

The first catalogue had emphasized "visits and excursions for observation and practice" as a core part of the curriculum:

In aid of the practical studies of the School, and as a means of initiating students into the actual details of the professions for which they are preparing, they will be required from time to time, in the progress of the course, assisted by one or more of their teachers, to make visits of inspection to machine-shops, engines, mills, furnaces, and chemical works, and to important buildings and engineering constructions which are within convenient reach.

With a like view, and under the same direction, they will be expected to spend a part of the vacations of the second and third years in excursions for observation and practice, extending sometimes to distant points, and so arranged as to afford to each class the experience and training most likely to be useful to them in their future pursuits.

Thus, in consonance with their special studies, they will severally employ themselves in the details of road, railway, and topographical surveys, barometric measurement, triangulation, and geodetic astronomy; in taking notes and making drawings of such processes, machinery, works of engineering, and buildings, as are instructive or remarkable; and in making themselves practically familiar with the working details of laboratories, print-works, furnaces, forges, rolling-mills, and founderies [*sic*]; with the methods of geological exploration, the tracing of veins and beds, the sinking of shafts, the conduct of open and underground operations, the mechanical arrangements for raising the product to the surface and preparing it for use; and, in general, with all the processes and constructions appertaining to the practice of industrial metallurgy and the working of quarries and mines.[41]

The point about "excursions . . . to distant points" was omitted in subsequent years, possibly because the faculty felt it was unreasonable. Many students were obliged, after all, to find summer work to support themselves, contribute to family finances, or save for next year's tuition and expenses. By 1869–70, the catalogue listed dozens of specific industrial establishments recently visited by students; while most of these were in Massachusetts, a few were in Rhode Island as well—still, technically, "within convenient reach."[42] Nevertheless, students sometimes followed Albert Hall's lead and ventured further afield: Professor Henck, for example, took a group on a month-long excursion in the summer of 1872, with stops in Philadelphia, Pittsburgh, Cincinnati, Louisville, St. Louis, Kansas City, Fort Wallace, Denver, Colorado Springs, Pueblo, Colorado City, among other places, to study bridge construction, oil works, and other industrial operations.[43]

Sometimes there was a tension between the Institute's simultaneous goals—one for focus ("provide a full course of studies and practical exercises for students seeking to qualify themselves for the professions"), the other for breadth ("furnish such a general education . . . as shall form a fitting preparation for any of the departments of active life")—and there was ongoing debate in the early years about which should take precedence. This debate spilled over into the classroom, too, probably by design. A favorite assignment in Atkinson's English class was to write about how the curriculum should evolve and where the emphases ought to lie. This was more than a rhetorical exercise, as the opinions expressed by Atkinson's students sometimes came up for discussion by the faculty—an unusually democratic approach, perhaps, but a wise one considering that the Institute was in the earliest stages of curricular experimentation.

Albert Hall's essay on this topic, written for English class in March–April 1867, went through more than one draft (two drafts survive); Professor Atkinson clearly felt that "revision" was an excellent way to hone one's argument. The stated theme was: "The manner in which education should be conducted." Hall argued that an Institute education should focus on specialized professional training. General education subjects like English and languages, he said, were helpful in a way, but should not be forced on students who might wish to give undivided attention to their engineering specialty (Hall was in the mechanical engineering program).

This utilitarian emphasis, a familiar one at the Institute in subsequent years, started out with a sense that general education was a luxury for the leisure classes (at Harvard, for example) and that people who had to make a living could not afford much of it. Hall, for one, did not share Rogers's vision of the mutual dependency between technical and humanistic studies:

> I believe that the studies should be arranged in our Institute, that a student who desires to study for a particular profession and desires to give his time to that and nothing else he may do so. Again, if he desires it, he may pursue other studies. I believe that studies not immediately connected with the desired object should be elective, and that a student who pursues such studies should not be compelled to pass an examination in them unless he wishes to obtain a certificate of merit in those departments.

He also argued that examinations are not, in general, a good way to test a student's abilities, and that class work should be afforded at least equal value. In conclusion, he stated his hope that "this matter will be considered before the first class graduates from the Institute."

Hall buttressed his argument in the final draft with references to Jacob Bigelow's critique of classical education as it existed at Harvard and other liberal arts colleges,[44] peppering his essay with aphorisms culled from Bigelow: for example, "Every individual is by nature comparatively qualified to shine in one path of life, and comparatively disqualified to shine in another." Professor Atkinson almost certainly directed Hall to Bigelow's essay; he was open-minded enough not only to entertain student perspectives with which he disagreed, but also to help students enhance the credibility of their perspectives through reference to authorities who could hardly have been described as friendly to his own area of interest, the liberal arts.

In general, students expected and found a "technocentric" emphasis at the Institute. The arts subjects were of lesser concern, except insofar as they might affect a student's performance in science or engineering, the burden always being on the arts to prove their "usefulness." While students' academic deficiencies were recorded for both arts and science subjects, performance in the arts was considered less of a challenge, easier to improve on, and not as integral to the curriculum—even though it continued, both theoretically and rhetorically (at least in Rogers's mind), to be sustained as essential: "It is intended to secure to every student, whatever his special course of study, a liberal mental development and culture."[45]

Architecture was one area of instruction where art met science in the 1860s, if not as coequals then as close partners. The first two years, the preprofessional curriculum common to full-time students, included "mechanical drawing" and "free-hand drawing," the latter more creatively and less geometrically based than the former. Two out of six and seven components, respectively, of the professional curriculum for architecture in the third and fourth years—"Architectural Design" and "Drawing"—had a strong artistic emphasis, dealing with topics such as ornamentation, composition, design, landscape, the human figure, sketching, and "drawing from memory." The remainder dealt with technical issues: building materials and processes, applied mechanics ("stress, stability, strength, and stiffness"), applications of geometry to masonry and carpentry, contracts and specifications, engineering (structures in wood, stone, and iron—along with foundations, walls, arches, domes, beams, trusses, girders, and roofs), heat, light, ventilation, and acoustics.[46]

The balance is reflected in two surviving artifacts from the period. Abraham Hun Berry, a special student in architecture, 1869 to 1871, took notes in two different notebooks, one for each academic year: "Lectures on Architecture—by Wm E Ware [*sic*]— Prof. of Archtre. Mass. Inst. Techy—Season of 1869 & 1870"; and "Lectures on Architecture by Wm. R. Ware, Prof of Archtre. Mass. Inst. Techy—Season of 1870 & 1871."[47] Berry wrote in pencil in class, and later (possibly the same day) added marginalia in ink—usually brief subject headings as an aid, presumably, to reviewing the notes. There are numerous sketches throughout.

The first notebook includes jottings on construction, specifications for drawing, contractor's responsibilities, and other technical details. Types of wood are listed, with brief remarks on useful qualities to keep in mind: "Red cedar as good as white pine if planed," "Pine knots get loose and fall out," "Maple—Hard and compact, twists badly, & full of birdseyes," "Blk. Walnut—Brown coarse, brittle, tough to split, Changes color on being oiled light color if waxed," "Beech—hard as maple fine uniform grain not much used ex for planes & Carpenter's tools," and "Hard pine—Hard or southern pine heavy, strong, close, true—good for bare upper floors—valuable for trusses principals— for floors better than anything else." On December 22, 1869, Professor Ware assigned the class its first problem, a design for a small dwelling—"Each cottage shall comprise Kitchen, Sitt room & 2 or 3 B.R. also entry and staircase scullery open fireplace in S.R. may have a piazza Sketch & as far as possible to be brought in Dec. 29." One week (over the Christmas holiday, no less) hardly seems like enough time to complete such an assignment, but Berry threw himself avidly into it—his sketches were a bit rough in the execution, but painstakingly thought out.

Early in the new year, January 1870, the class turned its attention to fine-detail work such as wood moldings; the emphasis appears to have been on geometrics (horizontal orientation, etc.), but Berry's sketches started to show more creative flair. By April the class was working in iron, a medium with its own advantages and drawbacks. As Berry observed: "Iron work—Characteristics—Strength enables it to be used smaller than wood or stone . . . it is used 'stingily' or for open work where stone & wood can not be used with effect—Its maleability [*sic*] is characteristic & renders it very useful for different purposes as plates & bars & from them twisted & warped or curved work." His sketches here became quite imaginative, interspersed, of course, with specifications for welding, riveting, and strapping. The class also learned to use the sparest possible writing style: "Specifications—how written—Copied not composed—Write sentences on one line if possible—Make margins in specifications for notes to include or divide heads or different parts of building—Begin with important word not 'the' or 'a'—Much easier for everybody—Make short lines as possible—First-line short generally."

Berry's second notebook begins in November 1870 with the topic of design, and here the technical and the artistic come together quite closely. Professor Ware, moreover, brought in history, sociology, and geography as key elements in understanding architecture as both art and engineering: "Roofs—Darwinian Theory applicable to architecture . . . French roofs are propagated on Darwinian theory whether of imitation of foreign taste or cheapness on brick or stone bdgs or Convenience—an upright being more convenient than a sloping roof." Berry may not have caught Ware's full drift here, but the attempt at social-historical analysis is significant. Also important is the emphasis on esthetics:

> Architecture is to produce a beautiful work—Constructional features are beauties in themselves as also materials . . . 2 things to do—1st to meet the case in hand 2nd To make work as dectve art to satisfy the eye the moral intellectual aesthetic sense—Moral sense, boldness not badness admired in a bold bad man so in archtre. . . . Good sense is also necessary as not to put a buttress where there is nothing to hold up or a window where no light is needed— Eng. Archt. have adopted dogma not to construct decoration but to decorate construction and have argued the point wisely but only too well and have carried numerous archts with them—Archt does not decorate construction nor construct decoration but carries the whole work together & the archt taking the materials as he finds them uses them together to make beautiful objects.

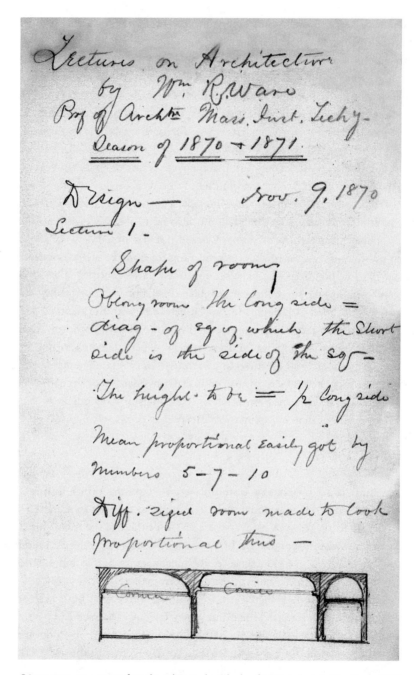

Science meets art—excerpt from the architectural notebooks of MIT student A. Hun Berry, 1870

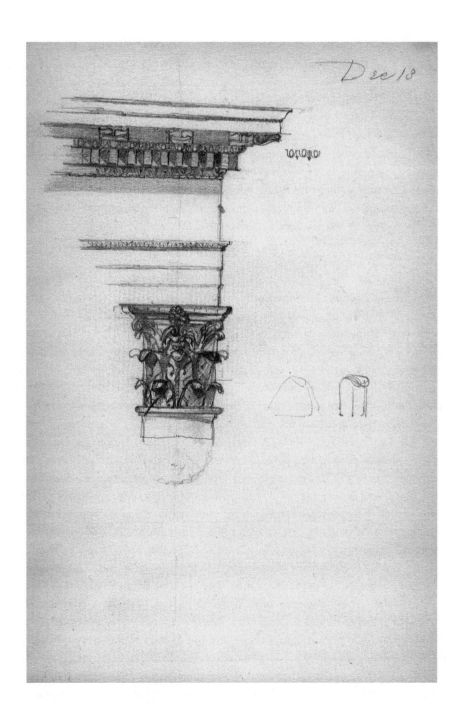

Berry's sketches became more lovingly detailed as time passed, now with three-dimensional renderings of square, oblong, polygonal, circular structures, and of a roof with cornice supported by a Corinthian-style column. While some of the "problems" assigned by Ware continued to be basic and structural ("Construct a fence & gate of iron with two stone posts"), others were quite elaborate: "Problem for Monday—Chapel attached to Church of Renaissance for the honor safety & spiritual welfare of the soul of His Imperial Majesty—With the usual appendages of R.C. Church—Plan Section & Elevation." By the time Berry left the Institute in the spring of 1871, his creative and engineering talents had blossomed; how (or if) he put them to use is unclear, but we do know that he continued to jot and sketch in this second notebook at the Massachusetts Normal Art School in 1875, where he also took classes with Professor Ware.

"Natural history," a subject later thought of as "hard" science (if not as hard as physics, chemistry, and mathematics), was prescribed for "general studies" in the 1860s, along with modern languages, history, political economy, philosophy, and English. Contemporary approaches in natural history tended toward the taxonomic and descriptive, rather than the quantitative and analytical; the subject provided students with a basic introduction to zoology and physiology, and occasionally to botany (botany was mentioned until 1868, but not thereafter). Samuel Kneeland doubled as secretary of the Institute Government and "instructor in zoology and physiology" ("professor of zoology and physiology" starting in 1869). A physician by profession, he was also an avid naturalist and collector who had prepared an edition of Charles H. Smith's *Natural History of the Human Species* (1851), served as one of the editors of *The Annual of Scientific Discovery* (1866–1871), and in later years journeyed on collecting expeditions to Brazil, the Lake Superior copper region, Iceland, and the Hawaiian and Philippine islands.

The surviving class notes of one of Kneeland's students, Walter Sears (among the first group of graduates in 1868), suggest that the subject was taught in a rather cursory fashion, even for the standards of the time.[48] Beginning on February 20, 1868, Sears wrote in pencil in a small notebook entitled "Notes on Natural History from Lectures by Sec. Kneeland." These notes are quite rough, with lists of brief, disconnected facts about various vertebrates and invertebrates interspersed with hastily drawn sketches. Kneeland's emphasis appears to have been on curious details about the animal kingdom: "Lady bug useful—eat plant lice," Sears wrote on March 26, and later: "Poisonous and nonPoisonous rattler not for giving warning—rattlesnake not so fatal as supposed—get drunk after the bite suck the wound—moccasin snake the same—rattles no indication of age Cobra of Indies more dangerous—very fond of music ... Used to be Crocodiles in Europe but none now—venerated as a god in Egypt." Much of this information was clearly apocryphal, but the emphasis on *usefulness* (whether or not any of it was, in fact, very useful) nonetheless reflected the Institute's pedagogical focus.

Engineering subjects, as expected, were taught with more rigor than either natural history or English. In the spring of 1867, Rogers recruited a substitute—Alfred P. Rockwell, from the Sheffield Scientific School at Yale— to teach mining for a year in place of the perennially absent James Hague. When Rockwell asked about the students' level of preparation for advanced work in mining engineering, Rogers replied at some length, evidently delighted to have found someone who understood the importance of high standards:

Alfred Perkins Rockwell

> In your very acceptable letter recd some weeks ago, you make inquiry as to the stage of preparation which will have been reached by the Class in Mining Engineering of which you will have in part the charge next Autumn at our Institute. In Mathematics they have gone through a good course in the Calculus & Analytical Mechanics; they have studied portions of Applied Mechanics and have worked up the Studies of the 1st and 2nd year in Surveying & Construction. They have given much time to Laboratory work including blow-pipe exercises & furnace assaying & have begun their Course in Geology & not quite completed that in Physics. They are somewhat proficient in Descriptive Geometry, & Mathematics & Mechl. drawing. The Prof. of Mod. Languages tells me that they could readily make use of Burat as a Text Book for your Course if you should so desire.[49]

Rockwell worked out so well, in fact, that at the end of his substitute year he was persuaded to leave Yale and return to the Institute as a member of the permanent faculty, serving as professor of mining engineering until 1873.

At the beginning of the 1869–70 academic year, Rockwell attached an interesting postscript in a letter to his wife "Kate" [Katharine], remarking on the evolution of the Institute's student body as well as on one key aspect of its curriculum:

> The Institute is in a very promising condition. The entering class numbers about 100 the largest yet received and among them are several college graduates—In general an older and better class of students.—They tell me we shall number about 200, that is about 30 more than last year. This gives us more money. Then arrangements have been made with the Coast Survey very advantageous to us making this school in a certain way as a preparatory one for young men who want to get on the Survey as assistants. Also the Mechanical Engineering students are to have access during the summer vacation at the workshops of the Navy Yard to pursue a practical course without pay.[50]

Some faculty members, thus, were as convinced as Albert Hall that the best model for an engineering education was one where applications of knowledge and practical experience were paramount.

While it was neither a professional program nor a "general study," experimental physics was taught in the second and third years (following elementary mechanics in the first year) as part of the coursework required in all the engineering disciplines. A sound grasp of the principles of physics was understood to be essential for an engineer. With this in mind, the physics faculty—Rogers himself, soon supported by Edward Pickering—focused their instruction on phenomena and laws of sound, heat, and light. Pickering left a record of lecture notes, outlines, and examination papers revealing something about how physics was taught in the 1860s.[51]

The second-year class, for example, received the following test on November 25, 1867:

1. Give the laws of transverse elasticity.
2. What is meant by work, vis viva, horse power? Give an example.
3. What power can be exerted by a hydrostatic press by 10 lbs applied as in figure?
4. Describe the hydrostatic paradox. What principle does it illustrate?
5. Find the total pressure on a cube 1' [?] submerged to a depth of 1'.
6. What is the condit. of equilib of floating bodies?
7. What is meant by metacentre? How is the stability of a floating body influenced by its position?
8. How is the Hydrostatic Balance used in deter. the spec. grav of bodies?

One notable aspect of Pickering's teaching style was the effort that he made to encourage students to think of science broadly rather than in a compartmentalized way. In a lecture entitled "Classification of Science," given on October 8, 1867, he ranged across a wide spectrum:

Science, that is all human knowledge divided Mental & Physical. Sciences of Mind, as Logic Sci. of Reasoning Physical those relating to mater. objects
Physical Science—
Natural History
Zoology
Botany
Mineralogy
Anatomy
Veget. & animal
Natural Philosophy
Mechan. Philosophy
Chemistry
Geology
Physiology
Veget and animal
Regard bodies as quiescent or changing
Every change is effect and its cause is called a force
Natural History, quiescent as they exist
Natural Philosophy, as changing, cause and effect, and laws of alteration
Closely united cannot study one without other, yet princip aim of every science is either to study the properties of bodies or their effects on each other
Zoology. Science of living being. Zool. describes ands classif. animal but has little to do with the reasons why some breathe with lungs and others with gills, or why some live on land and others in the water.
Botany or Science of Plants also
Mineralogy Science of Minerals
Anatomy. Construction of Anim. or Veget. Organism.
Natural Philosophy
These sciences quite diff. object.
Mechan. Philos. Included what is commonly called Nat. Philos. or Physics. Study of the *changes* bodies undergo without alter. of material substance of which they are composed. Copper

PHYSICS.

LECTURES

delivered at the

MASS. INSTITUTE OF TECHNOLOGY.

—by—

ASST. PROF. PICKERING.

October — February

VOL.I.

1867.

First pages of physics notebook kept by second-year student Charles Cross, who went on to teach at MIT from 1870 to 1917.

MOLECULAR
FORCES.

LECTURE I.
ELASTICITY.
Delivered October 14, 1867.
– # –

The first effect of any force acting upon a body, is to alter its form. Thus if I press on this table, the first effect of the pressure is to compress the molecules of the wood, and they yield, but if I continue the pressure there comes a point beyond which I cannot compress them by the greatest exertion of any strength – If now I remove my hand a reaction takes place, the disturbed molecules retaking their former position, – This force which resists the further change by pressure and which causes the molecules when disturbed to retake their primitive position upon the removal of the disturbing force, is elasticity.

If we represent the disturbing force by D, the force of recovery by R, $\frac{R}{D} = e$, will be what is called the coefficient of elasticity, i.e., the ratio of the force of restoration to the force of disturbance.

Chemist. on the other hand, changes accompanied by alteration of material.
Import. distinct. Ice, water, steam . . .
In Mech. Phil. and Chem. deal not with classif. of bodies or [drug?] or even
their properties as much as with laws of the changes they undergo.
Geology deals compos. and arrange. of earth crust. . . .
Physiology phenom. of living bodies and studies nutrition, growth circul.
blood
All sciences closely connected. Astronomy, Mineralogy, Chemis. Geol.
although properly part of Mech. Philos. Geologist needs knowledge of
almost every other branch in above table.

It is remarkable that Pickering would try to cover all of this in a single lecture, but his
interdisciplinary perspective is important, especially in light of the highly focused goals
of the Institute curriculum.

According to the Land-Grant Act of 1862 a recipient college was required to include
the teaching of military tactics in its curriculum, with the responsibility for ensuring
the proper fulfillment of the requirement left to the individual states, which would also
control and administer the funds derived from the provisions of this legislation. The act
itself was unclear about the nature of the prescribed instruction, and the interpretation
varied from state to state, with a number of land-grant institutions giving little attention to the quality and amount of training to be offered. At the other extreme, President
Andrew D. White of Cornell took the matter of military training very seriously and
organized the new university along the lines of a military school, a pattern gradually
altered and abandoned by 1875.[52]

In awarding a share of the income of the land-grant fund to the Institute of
Technology in 1863, the Commonwealth of Massachusetts made very clear, through
an act in addition to the charter, that "instruction in military tactics" must be provided. But how this instruction was to be organized and presented was left unde-
fined. As in the federal legislation, there was no statement specifying whether or not
every student was obligated to take the military drill which had become a legal
"object" of the Institute under the charter amendment.[53] There can be no doubt,
however, that the Morrill Act of 1862 called for military instruction in the land-grant
colleges, a proviso not included in the 1859 version of the legislation vetoed by
President Buchanan. This shift in language and intent is probably attributable to the

"Instruction in military tactics," mandated by the terms of MIT's land-grant status—seated (l-r), William Henry '70 (lieutenant), S. Mathews Cary (lieutenant), Channing Whitaker '69 (major), Henry Preble '70 (quartermaster), Ernest Bowditch '69 (captain), George Hardy '70 (captain); standing (l-r), Theodore Tillinghast '70 (lieutenant), Edmund Turner '70 (lieutenant), Edward Clark '70 (sergeant major), William Bannard '70 (adjutant).

North's poor showing in the early days of the Civil War against Southern troops, many of whom had received some form of military instruction in military schools or colleges where provision for military training dated back to the early nineteenth century.[54]

The responsibility for compliance lay with the states, and Massachusetts made certain through the Institute's charter amendment that the letter of the law would be obeyed. Rogers had made clear in his organizational plan for the faculty that they would be responsible for and in complete control of the curriculum. And it was they who voted early in 1866 that it was "expedient to commence the military drill of the students immediately," making it compulsory for all regular students.[55] The first catalogue, issued in December 1865, contained the following statement: "The regular students of the School will be taught the use of small-arms, and the simpler parts of tactics; and, for this purpose, will be organized into one or more companies, to meet on stated days for military instruction and exercise."[56]

The responsibility for securing an instructor rested with the Institute, and Rogers arranged with Hobart Moore, an officer in the militia and drill master at volunteer camps in the Boston area during the war, for instruction in military tactics on Saturdays for $75. Moore apparently continued under this ad hoc arrangement until his formal appointment as instructor in military tactics in 1868, when his name appeared in the catalogue for the first time.[57] In that year the catalogue description of the subject was altered:

> In conformity with the requirements of the Act of Congress of July 2, 1862, and of the Act of the General Court of Massachusetts in furtherance thereof, the Institute provides instruction in military tactics. All students are required to attend a weekly exercise in military tactics, unless specially excused. For these exercises the School is organized as a battalion of two companies. Arms and equipment are lent to the School by the State. The matter of attendance at drill is under the control of the Secretary of the Faculty; but excuses of general application can only be granted by the Faculty.[58]

Moore would remain until 1872 and return in 1883, serving until 1892. During this period he was listed in the catalogue as General Hobart Moore. He was never a member of the faculty.[59]

From the start there was indecision on the part of the faculty with respect to the status of drill as a requirement. On February 16, 1867, they voted that drill be compulsory only for the first- and second-year classes, but immediately reconsidered and retained the requirement for all regular students, with fines for absence to be equal to those assessed by the state militia for similar failures to appear. The requirement was made more stringent when a short time later, on March 2, they voted that *all* students be required to take drill unless specially excused by the faculty, a significant vote very likely influenced by Rogers.[60]

Since the federal government did nothing to meet the need for military supplies and equipment, Rogers had sent a memorial to the legislature in January seeking arms and reporting that the "regular students of the Institute are now organised as a battalion and are statedly drilled & exercised under the direction of an experienced instructor."[61] For the faculty to eliminate military instruction for all but the first two years at that time could have proved exceedingly embarrassing; conversely, the vote to extend the requirement to include every student, regular or special, was evidence not only of Rogers's keen political instincts, but also that the Institute was anxious to comply with the requirements of the law.

The memorial stated that "the old musket thus far used by the Corps has been found in many respects ill-adapted" to the thorough training which the Institute hoped to provide. "In view of these facts," Rogers added, "& especially of the consideration that the Military Instruction of the Institute has been established by Legislative enactment, the undersigned would respectfully ask your honorable body to pass an act authorizing the proper officer to provide for the use of the Military Organisation of the Institute as many of the improved Springfield Muskets & accoutrements as may be needed for the instruction of the corps in military tactics."[62]

On March 2, 1867, a resolve of the legislature to issue arms to the Institute was approved by Governor Alexander H. Bullock: "*Resolved*, that his excellency the governor be authorized to issue to the president and faculty of the Massachusetts Institute of Technology, such arms for the use of that institution as in his judgment may be so issued without detriment to the militia service: *provided* the said president and faculty shall be held personally responsible for the same."[63] Within a few days the requested arms arrived.

Questions on the proper rules and conduct of military instruction were discussed and debated at length. How much time must a student devote to military requirements, and during what years? Under what circumstances and by whom might he be exempted from military drill? The faculty received a petition from seventy-two students asking for an extra hour of drill each week. At the same time, others were cited for disorderly conduct during drill or for refusal to comply with regulations. Excuses were granted to some for physical disability or the "special character of their course," and others for "previous military service" or their status as "assistant instructors." By the fall

Benjamin Franklin Edmands

of 1869, the third- and fourth-year students were exempted from drill,[64] but problems and questions persisted. Finally, in 1871, the faculty appointed Professor Alfred P. Rockwell, no doubt because of his service in the Civil War, "to draw up a plan to be submitted to the Government for the improvement of the Military Drill, the report to include the consideration of the feasibility of the appointment of an Army officer to superintend the military instruction in accordance with the provisions of the law of Congress."[65]

The military program was controversial enough among those who opposed its compulsory status at the Institute, but even more so among those who considered it an integral part of the curriculum. Benjamin F. Edmands wrote to Rogers in the fall of 1868 complaining about unfairness in the treatment of his son, John Rayner Edmands:

I regret to be under the necessity, on behalf of my son, of protesting most earnestly against the injustice which has been done to him in the appointment of Officers for the Battalion of the Institution.

I do it on two grounds: *first*: because the appointment cannot be justified on any ground except one calculated to disgrace or degrade him in the minds of his companions; and *secondly*: because the manner in which his offered rank was decided upon will not bear that military test for which the Institute should have credit on such a matter; for, if military tactics and discipline are to be taught therein, the teaching should be joined with correct economy in organization. . . .

. . . I have satisfied myself that his claims are founded upon correct principles and views; and I think the highest military authority connected with your Institution will rank him as second to but one pupil in knowledge of military *tactics*, and I know personally that his knowledge of military economy is by no means inferior. . . .

. . . I believe the military branch of education is one of great importance, perhaps second to none of those taught in the Institution, and that it should be managed with care. Especially should it be guarded with vigilance that it may not become unpopular by neglecting military merit, and thus discourage pupils not only in this branch of study and practice, but also in their efforts in other branches, and in their love for the Institute.

I respectfully ask,—that the Faculty will investigate this matter before the nominees enter upon any discharge of their duties of military office: and further—an early acknowledgment of this communication, with some intimation whether this latter request will be acceded to.[66]

Rogers sought an immediate meeting with Edmands,[67] and while it is unclear how the matter was resolved, Edmands was someone to be reckoned with. A wealthy dry-goods merchant in Boston, he had been a supporter of the Institute from the beginning and a charter Government member; he was also a prominent military man, a retired major general of the Massachusetts militia with considerable expertise in that area. How strongly he felt about the issue is perhaps suggested by his phrasing—"your Institution" rather than "our Institution"—and, in fact, he only remained one more year as a member of the Government.

The thesis was the final hurdle to the diploma. Some students, like Ernest Bowditch and Andrew Russell, failed to submit one, and, as a result, even though they had completed all other requirements, were not awarded diplomas. Others submitted late and did not receive diplomas with their class, resulting in confusion at times as to class affiliation—Albert Hall, for example, submitted late and was listed sometimes (mostly) as class of 1868, occasionally as class of 1870; Charles Greene's diploma, on the other hand, was not approved until January 1870, yet his affiliation with the class of 1868 remained constant.

The regulations stated that each student "must prepare a dissertation on some subject included in the courses of study, or submit an original report upon some machine or work of engineering, or some mine or mineral survey, or scientific investigation, which shall be approved by the Faculty." Theses were to be presented at the time of the final examinations in the fourth year, and, "where expedient, their authors will be called upon to explain and defend them."[68] In reality, the requirement was less burdensome than it sounded: theses were accepted months after the final examinations (students often used the summer and fall after their final examinations to complete them); the faculty rarely called on students to defend them; and the terms "dissertation" and "original," implying depth and length, were applied rather loosely (most theses, in fact, were superficial, brief, and somewhat formulaic or derivative). Generally there was just one reader for each thesis; that reader would then present his opinion (usually favorable) in pro forma style at a faculty meeting, and the thesis would be accepted.[69] In 1869, the faculty modified the guidelines slightly—"Voted that the graduating theses must be placed in the hands of the Secretary of the Inst. on or before Sept. 1; that each candidate must select a subject which belongs to that department in which he seeks his degree, and which has been approved by the head of that department"[70]—but the wording suggested a more liberal, if not more flexible, outlook than implied in the original. In practice, too, theses appear to have been accepted well after the September deadline.

Of the first 27 theses (1868–1870), 18 survive. None survives from mechanical engineering or science and literature (the earliest in mechanical engineering dates from 1884); 10 survive from civil and topographical engineering, 2 from chemistry, and 6 from geology and mining engineering.

Surviving Graduation Theses, 1868–1870

Civil and topographical engineering

> *1868*
> Frank R. Firth
> Engineering notes upon Mississippi and Missouri River bridges
>
> Charles E. Greene
> Bangor and Piscataquis Railroad
>
> William E. Hoyt
> Pile foundations
>
> Walter H. Sears
> The Brooklyn Water Works
>
> Charles A. Smith
> Upon a kind of truss of built beam
>
> Joseph Stone
> The Hoosac Tunnel
>
> *1869*
> Howard A. Carson
> The Canal Railroad Bridge across the Westfield River

1870
Russell H. Curtis
Review of the Britannia Bridge

Sampson D. Mason
Design for an iron girder bridge

Edmund K. Turner
Wrought iron girder bridge for a double track, narrow gauge railway

Chemistry

1869
William R. Nichols
Contributions to the history of the compounds of oxalic acid

1870
Nathan F. Merrill
Fermentation: a few points of different theories briefly discussed

Geology and mining engineering

1868
Nelson W. Conant
Review of the smelting works of the Revere Copper Company

Charles C. Gilman
Opening up and working of an anthracite coal mine

Robert H. Richards
Description of the Calumet Mine

Bryant P. Tilden
Description of a geological section in Addison Co., Vermont

James P. Tolman
Geology of the Snake Mountain Region

1870
Charles W. Hinman
A new volumetric assay for lead ores

Fermentation:—

A few Points of different Theories briefly discussed.

Although aware of the fact that this entire subject was still a matter of the liveliest controversy, I indulged a hope that by taking a sort of general survey of the whole field which has been occupied by so many of the most eminent chemists and physiologists of the day, one might derive some advantage in the way of forming correct conclusions, even over those who have made extensive original experimentation, and have built theories upon the exclusive grounds within the limit of their own research.

In making a review of the various chains of evidence which have been presented in support of as many different theories, one cannot fail to become apprized of the fact, that altogether too exclusive study has been given to that particular form of fermentation generally known as the alcoholic or vinous modification, and until the subject has been studied in a more general sense, it is easy to perceive the difficulty with which any

The final hurdle—excerpts from graduating theses in chemistry (Nathan Merrill, above) and geology and mining engineering (Charles Gilman, opposite)

Opening up and working of an Anthracite Coal
Mine.

In selecting a subject for my thesis, I have decided
to adopt the foregoing for several reasons, the principal
of which is, having spent some time at a coal mine,
think I shall be able to write more intelligently on
this subject than on one in which my whole knowledge
is purely theoretical.

I have taken a general case in order
to show the different methods employed in working
mines, where the pitch is very steep and also where it
is very slight. I take a single vein of considerable thick-
ness for these reasons; the veins as yet worked in the
Anthracite region of Penn. are quite thick, a single
vein is considered, because the majority of the mines
are opened only on one, and indeed working two or more
veins does not differ materially from working a single
one. In this thesis I shall consider the vein to have a run
East and West, with a North and South crop, which
has been traced and proved for the entire Basin.
I shall suppose the distance from the East and West
extremities of the Basin to be two and a half miles;

The geology and mining engineering theses share several features of the theses in civil and topographical engineering—concern with practical applications, technical problems, economic and social impact—along with a departure now and then into the broader, theoretical kind of approach found in the chemistry theses. The sample is too small and time-restrictive to reveal much about educational emphases and professional trends in any of the disciplines, but it does give a flavor of how students handled the final hurdle to the diploma.

The essential need for a thorough hands-on experience on the part of every student in the Massachusetts Institute of Technology was central to Rogers's educational philosophy, inherited from his father and deepened throughout his years at the College of William and Mary and the University of Virginia. A lecturer might carry out physical demonstrations to hold the attention of his audience and to illustrate a point, but the student in the laboratory must prepare an experiment, observe its reactions, analyze its results, and draw his own conclusions. This approach to learning was active rather than passive, and, in Rogers's view, the key to understanding nature's laws. The early Institute faculty shared his outlook. For the students it was a new kind of learning experience, as Robert Richards (class of 1868) later recalled:

> The method of teaching was completely new to all of us. We found ourselves bidding goodbye to the old learn-by-heart method, and beginning to study by observing the facts and laws of nature. We learned from experiment and experience what might be expected to happen if a given set of forces started to act. In short, our feet were set at last in the way of real knowledge. We learned, perhaps falteringly at the outset, the four steps that mark the only route into true science: how to observe, how to record, how to collate, and how to conclude. The effect on the classes was totally different from anything that I had seen in any school before.[71]

Again, those recurring themes: theory and practice, knowledge and observation, *mind and hand.*

$\mathcal{E}pilogue$

n October 24, 1868, the faculty meeting had been "suddenly terminated by the illness of the President."[1] *Life and Letters* contains Rogers's own account of the event and the days which followed, as recorded in his diary, now lost:

"Faculty Meeting at ten, all present but Ware. I felt as well as usual, though as the meeting proceeded the heat disturbed my head strangely. About twelve, slight faintness with giddiness, and all at once I perceived that my articulation was oddly obstructed on the left side of my mouth, and I soon found that I was struck with a slight hemiplegia. The meeting was broken up, and I was conveyed by dear Runkle and Atkinson and Storer in a carriage to my house. Dr. Putnam was called. . . . At 2 P. M. was assisted, slightly, upstairs, and in two or three minutes all the paralytic feeling vanished."

The next day he writes: "Had a comfortable night, dined and took tea downstairs. Some fulness of head, caused, perhaps, by conversation with friends in parlour."

On the 26th: "Tolerable sleep. This morning weak and a little dizzy. At desk, and evening walked in Common."

27th: "An uncommonly good night. Ate with relish. Head still in tottering equilibrium, easily disturbed. What a bore to be ever conscious that you have a stomach and a brain!"

28th: "Only tolerable night. Interview with Professor Runkle. Gave him memorandum of the Lowell courses and directions about the examinations of the theses. Went at 8 P. M. with E. and little Mary to 90 Boylston Street, Mrs. Homans's, to witness the great torchlight procession. Very superb and curiously picturesque from the shining mantles of many of the corps, made of rubber cloth, red and steel-colored. One and a quarter hours in passing our window. I did not suffer."[2]

On October 31 Rogers was able to write to John Amory Lowell, sending him in a very clear hand the list of the Lowell free courses proposed for 1868–69. He did not mention his attack, though Lowell, as a member of the Government and vice president of the Institute, would certainly have been informed. He did express regret, however, that he would be unable to present a course of lectures at the Lowell Institute that year.[3]

Rogers was unable to preside at the opening meeting of the Society of Arts on November 5:

"Wrote to Dr. [Erastus] Bigelow, asking him to preside at meeting of Society of Arts to-night. What a struggle it costs me to be absent from this first meeting! But I hope yet to have strength to resume these duties."

November 6: "Wakeful until 1 A. M. Took valerian. Had a better night. Think I am getting better. Let me but have patience and give my brain rest for a little while longer, and all will go right."

November 7: "A decidedly better night. Wrote Runkle, asking for judgment of faculty on the theses. 'And the string of his tongue was loosed and he spake plain.' This day shows decided improvement."[4]

At this point his diary entries became "briefer and rarer":

November 17: "Cannot apply thoughts continuously, dare not read. E. has read to me most of Mr. Parkman's 'Jesuits in North America.' A graceful, animated narrative. . . . The best day yet."

November 20: "Learn from Storer that M. P. W. presided last night at Society of Arts. How much more fitting to have had Runkle."

November 21: "Visit for an hour from my good friend Runkle. I bore this visit well, thanks to his calmness and my improved strength. . . . I am much better to-day than since my attack."

November 22: "Not so good a night. Visit from Copeland at lunch. I became excited in talking after lunch and felt the ill effects—giddiness . . . throughout the rest of the day."[5]

By late November, recognizing that he would not be able to perform all the duties required of the president of the Institute and the school, Rogers requested a leave of absence to spend the winter in Philadelphia with his brother Robert:

December 3: "A comfortable night. Sent letter to Dr. Bigelow for action of government which meets to-day at 1 P. M., also form of diploma and the theses. Government granted my wish of one year, if needed, and that Runkle should perform my duties as President of the Institute meanwhile. Also Rockwell confirmed (as Professor of Mining)—and Richards appointed at $400 (as assistant)."

December 8: "Had a short interview with my good friend Runkle. Left for Philadelphia, via Bristol (R. I.) and Sound. Violent head wind. Heavy thumps of the sea."

December 9: "Left New York by 12:30 cars. Reached W. Philadelphia a little past 4."[6]

The Government record for the meeting of December 3, 1868, contains the following note of Rogers's request: "In the absence of any direct communication to the Government from the President, Dr. Bigelow read portions of a letter to him from Mrs. Rogers, expressing a wish that Prof. Runkle act as President pro tempore during the time which his failing health compelled him to take rest from his labors connected with the Institute."[7] The letter was indeed in the hand of Mrs. Rogers, but the very clear signature was that of the president himself.[8]

The Government voted "that while we sincerely regret that our President must leave us for a time in order that he may regain his health and strength sacrificed in part in our service, we grant to him the leave of absence for one year which, in accordance with our forms, must be entered upon our records—hoping and trusting that he may return to us again, to give to us the service which he has so long rendered, and that we, his friends and associates, may once more co-operate with him in the work we have undertaken together."[9] In transmitting to Mrs. Rogers the Government votes of December 3, Samuel Kneeland added a personal word:

Everything is going smoothly here, but we miss the cordial greeting and genial smile of the President. I hope he is getting stronger and better. . . . I think we all love him here, and miss him as so many children miss their father, and long for the time when he shall come back to his Institute family.[10]

Rogers's condition deteriorated, however, and "for many long months" he could take only a "few steps in his room," could not read or be read to, or "do any mental work whatever."[11] His departure could not have happened at a more pivotal moment for the Institute, and for the School of Industrial Science in particular. The Society of Arts was functioning well, at least as far as its meetings were concerned, but the museum had yet to be organized and the school was just beginning its fourth year of operation.

The Government was much concerned, but in retrospect, no one could have been surprised. Rogers's health had been precarious on a number of earlier occasions. His frequent illnesses in fact preceded by many years his association with the effort to form an Institute of Technology, but in working on behalf of this endeavor he ended up taxing an already limited store of energy. In the summer of 1868 he complained that he was "too much exhausted by the almost unremitted work of two years."[12] In September, Kneeland wrote to say that he hoped a stay at Long Branch would bring back his "health and strength," urging him to "pick up all the strength you need."[13] It was, therefore, only a partially recovered Rogers who collapsed on the morning of October 24, 1868.

At the December 3, 1868, meeting of the Government, Runkle was at first approved acting president. However, because of doubts whether under the bylaws an acting president could legally perform certain functions relating to contracts or the receipt and expenditure of money, the vote was changed to appoint him president *pro tempore*, the term Rogers himself had suggested, "to take the place and perform all the duties of the President till the next Annual Meeting." Runkle thanked them for "this proof of the confidence reposed in him, and pledged himself to do all in his power to perform the new duties which by this vote devolved upon him, in concurrence and with the assistance of the Government."[14]

Thus began the period in which Runkle would preside over the Institute—first as president pro tem, and following the resignation of Rogers in 1870, as its second president. When Runkle resigned in 1878, Rogers would again serve as president, 1878–1881; he died—fittingly, some would say—while delivering an address to the graduating class in Huntington Hall on May 30, 1882. Under Rogers, Runkle, and other dedicated educators, the establishment of the Institute's school and the emergence of its curricula had been important steps in responding to the country's needs, as business and industry became increasingly reliant on a steady supply of trained minds and hands. The decades ahead would be a time of further growth and change, of challenges and opportunities, and of ongoing efforts to shape the "special and well selected path of study"[15] for which MIT became best known.

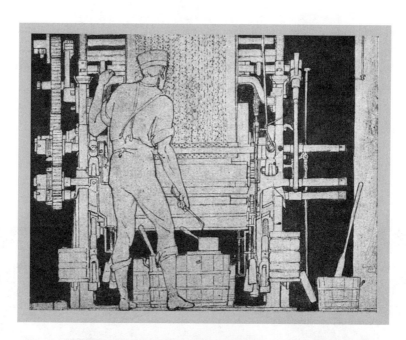

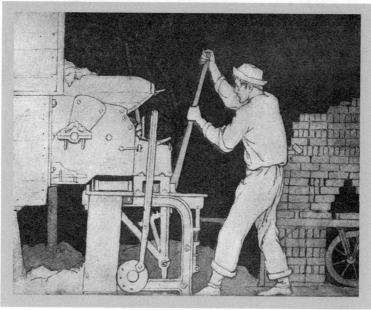

Textile Printing (top) and Brick Making (bottom)—sketches prepared by Paul Nefflen for mural in Huntington Hall. Previous page: Navigation. (See p. 764.)

Appendix 1

Committees and Officers
of the Institute
1860–1870

Committee of Associated Institutions, May 1860

William B. Rogers, Chairman

James M. Beebe

Erastus B. Bigelow

Amos Binney

Samuel Cabot, Jr.

Charles H. Dalton

George B. Emerson

Charles L. Flint

Samuel H. Gookin

Samuel Kneeland

Alfred Ordway

John D. Philbrick

George W. Pratt

Alexander H. Rice

Matthias D. Ross

Benjamin S. Rotch

Edward S. Tobey

R. C. Waterston

Marshall P. Wilder

*Committee of Twenty, 1861
William B. Rogers, Chairman
Thomas Aspinwall
James M. Beebe
Erastus B. Bigelow
Edward C. Cabot
John Chase
Charles H. Dalton
James A. Dupee
Charles L. Flint
James B. Francis
Samuel H. Gookin
John C. Hoadley
Frederic W. Lincoln, Jr.
John D. Philbrick
Thomas Rice
John Parmalee Robinson
Matthias D. Ross
John D. Runkle
Francis Humphreys Storer
Edward S. Tobey
Marshall P. Wilder

*Rogers's election as Chairman of the Committee of Twenty brought the total to twenty-one, but the committee title was not altered.

Committee on Publication, 1862–1870
John D. Runkle, Chairman
George B. Emerson
Charles L. Flint
John C. Hoadley
Alexander H. Rice (appointed 1865)
Lorenzo Sabine (1862–1865)

Committee on the Museum, 1862–1870
Erastus B. Bigelow, Chairman, 1862–1865, 1866–1870
Matthias Denman Ross, Chairman, 1865–1866
John Cummings, Jr. (appointed 1867)
Charles H. Dalton (appointed 1866)
Joseph S. Fay (appointed 1863)

Richard C. Greenleaf
Ralph Huntington (died May 31, 1866)
Frederic W. Lincoln, Jr.
James L. Little (appointed 1863)
Jonathan Preston
Alexander H. Rice
Stephen P. Ruggles

Committee on Instruction, 1862–1870
William B. Rogers, Chairman
John A. Andrew (appointed 1865, died 1867)
Edward P. Atkinson (appointed 1863)
James B. Francis
Augustus A. Hayes
Samuel K. Lothrop (appointed 1866)
John A. Lowell (1862–1863 only)
John D. Philbrick
Henry Bromfield Rogers
Thomas Sherwin (appointed 1863)
Nathaniel Thayer (appointed 1863)
George W. Tuxbury

Committee on Finance, 1862–1870
Matthias Denman Ross, Chairman, 1862–1865
James M. Beebe, Chairman, 1865–1870
Edward P. Atkinson (1862–1863 only)
J. Ingersoll Bowditch (appointed 1865)
J. Wiley Edmands (appointed 1863)
Edward H. Eldredge (died April 26, 1865)
William Endicott, Jr. (1865–1866 only)
John Murray Forbes (appointed 1866)
Edward S. Tobey

Officers of the Institute, 1862–1870

President
William B. Rogers   1862–1870 (on leave 1868–1870)
John Daniel Runkle   President Pro Tem, 1868–1870

Vice President

Jacob Bigelow	1862–1870
John Chase	1862–1863
John Amory Lowell	1862–1870
Marshall Pinckney Wilder	1862–1870
Nathaniel Thayer	1869–1870
Morrill Wyman	1863–1869

Treasurer

Charles H. Dalton	1862–1866
William Endicott, Jr.	1866–1872

Secretary

Thomas H. Webb	1862–1866
Samuel Kneeland	1866–1878

Appendix 2

———

Society of Arts Communications
1862 – 1870

December 17, 1862   Robert Bennet Forbes
Subaqueous Gunfiring

Robert Bennet Forbes
The Combination of Wood and Iron in Shipbuilding

Edward S. Ritchie
Improvements in Compasses for Boats and Ships

Stephen P. Ruggles
A New Form of Floats for Paddle Wheels

Cyrus M. Warren
A Safety Heating Lamp for Laboratory Use

January 14, 1863   Cyrus M. Warren
A Safety Heating Lamp for Laboratory Use (continued)

Edward S. Ritchie
The Motions of a Liquid in a Filled Vessel

William Edson
A New Hygroscope, or Indicator of Atmospheric Moisture

William B. Rogers
The Measurement of Illuminating Gas

Matthias Denman Ross
The Importance of the Agricultural and Rural Affairs Division of the Institute

January 28, 1863
O. P. Drake
An Automatic Apparatus for Impregnating Air with Illuminating Vapors

Augustus A. Hayes
An Automatic Apparatus for Impregnating Air with Illuminating Vapors

Matthias Denman Ross
The Enriquita Mine in California

February 9, 1863
Edward S. Ritchie
His Liquid Compass

William B. Rogers
The Methods of Testing the Purity of Illuminating Gas, illustrated by a number of experiments and demonstration of his new absorption apparatus

Robert Bennet Forbes
New Life Preservers

February 23, 1863
Edward Atkinson
Cotton Culture and Manufacture

William B. Rogers
The Topography and Geology of the Cotton Region

William B. Rogers
Photometric Apparatus for Testing Illuminating Power of Gas

March 9, 1863
William B. Rogers
The Geology of the Iron Deposits of the United States

Robert Bennet Forbes
The Combination of Wood and Iron in Shipbuilding

March 23, 1863
James Eaton
Improvements in Mule-Spinning

George W. Fuller
A Submarine Lamp

Luther Robinson
A New Method of Ventilation

April 13, 1863	John Ridgway *A New Revolving Battery and a discussion of recoil*
	John Ridgway *A New Revolving Field Piece*
	John M. Batchelder *Paper from Corn Husks*
	Alexander H. Rice *Sources of Materials for Paper*
April 27, 1863	John M. Batchelder *The Power Required to Drive the New Spindle of James Eaton*
	Benjamin F. Edmands and James Hamblett, Jr. *A New Electro-Magnetic Watch-Clock*
	William B. Rogers *The Progress of Electro-Magnetism*
	Thomas E. Sherwin *The Erratic Course of Cannon Balls*
May 11, 1863	Augustus A. Hayes *Native Antimony from Lower Canada*
	William B. Rogers *Lighting Gas by the Electric Spark*
	F. E. Stimpson *A New Mechanical Lamp*
	William B. Rogers *The Manufacture of Gas*
	Augustus A. Hayes *The Manufacture of Gas*
May 25, 1863	Eben N. Horsford *A New Safe*
	Otis Clapp *Drainage*
June 8, 1863	Erastus B. Bigelow *Wire Woven Cloth*

Benjamin F. Edmands
*An Improved Electro-Magnetic Telegraph Apparatus
Manufactured by Edmands & Hamblett*

Charles Stodder
American Microscopes

Richard C. Greenleaf
Test Plates

December 10, 1863   Stephen P. Ruggles
A New Printing Press for the Blind

Benjamin F. Edmands and James Hamblett, Jr.
A New Apparatus to Measure the Rise and Fall of Gas or the Tides

Thomas Gaffield
The Action of Sunlight on Glass

December 24, 1863   William Watson
The École Polytechnique of France

John S. Woodman
The Chandler Scientific School

William B. Rogers
Salt Formations

January 14, 1864   Stephen M. Allen
Flax Culture and Manufacture

David C. Perrin
The Manufacture of Palm Leaf Articles by Machinery

Edward S. Ritchie
The Concussion from Heavy Ordnance

January 28, 1864   William Watson
The National School of Roads and Bridges at Paris [École Nationale des Ponts et Chaussées]

J. Edson
Self-Adjusting Street Sweeper

William B. Rogers
The Industrial Uses of Manganese

February 11, 1864　　　Stephen M. Allen
Substitutes for Cotton and Wool

Justin Jones
A New Evaporator for Hot Air Furnaces and Stoves

February 25, 1864　　　William B. Rogers
Mr. Ruggles's New Mode of Coupling

Robert M. Copeland
A Model in Plaster of His Plan for Laying Out the Central Park of New York

William B. Rogers
An Apparatus for Determining the Amount of Sulphur in Coal Gas

William B. Rogers
The Albert Coal Mine

March 10, 1864　　　S. H. Roper
His Improved Calorie Engine

William B. Rogers
The Coal Bearing Rocks, with comments on the importance of a School of Mines in the Institute

Henry D'Aligny
Remarks on Importance of Training Mining Engineers

March 24, 1864　　　Robert Bennet Forbes
The Combination of Wood and Iron in Shipbuilding

T. H. W. Moseley
Iron for Bridges

Henry D'Aligny
The Mining Districts of Lake Superior

William B. Rogers
Slate Cutting Machine of J. Edson

William B. Rogers
True Stratification

April 14, 1864　　　Jonathan Amory
New Patent Furnace for Economizing Fuel

Appendix 2

Dr. Brown
Unbranned Wheat

H. W. Williams
An Instrument for Determining the Focal Power of the Eye

April 28, 1864   Jonathan Amory
Further Explanation of his Furnace

Robert Bennet Forbes
The Disintegration of Cast Iron Under Water

L. Trouvelot
American Silk

William B. Rogers
Water Glass

May 12, 1864   Edward S. Ritchie
Deviation Indicator

Thomas Gaffield
Siemens's Patent Regenerative Gas Furnace

May 26, 1864   Gilman Joslin
A Heat Regulator

William Wickersham
Nail Cutting Machine

December 1, 1864   Robert Nelson
A New Method of Raising Water by the Combustion of any Volatilizable Hydro-Carbon

Robert Nelson
A New Steel Cylindrical Projectile

William B. Rogers
Technological Institutions in Europe

William B. Rogers
A New Process for Manufacturing Steel

December 15, 1864   John W. Griffith
Marine Architecture

John W. Griffith
Iron Ships

630

January 5, 1865   H. F. Bond
                         A New Kerosene Lamp Trimmer

                         B. Jay Jeffries
                         The Opthalmoscope

                         Col. J. J. Storer
                         A New Machine for Crushing Ores

                         Moses G. Farmer
                         An Apparatus for Producing Electrical Light

January 19, 1865   Moses G. Farmer
                         The Origin and Measure of Electromotive Force

                         J. W. Osborne
                         Improvements in Photo-Lithography

February 2, 1865   B. F. Nutting
                         Map of Boston and Vicinity (as though taken in vicinity of Harvard and 2000 feet up)

                         Edward S. Ritchie
                         Deviation of the Compass Caused by Iron in Construction of Vessels

                         George W. Fuller
                         An Improved Method of Raising Sunken Vessels

                         Otis Clapp
                         Report of Committee on Household Economy on Drainage and Utilization of Night Soil

February 16, 1865   Edward S. Ritchie
                         A New Form of Azimuth Compass

                         William Edson
                         A Hygrometrical Index

                         William Wickersham
                         A Machine for Weaving Hats

                         S. R. Calthrop
                         A New Form for Railroad Trains

March 2, 1865   Thomas Hill
                         An Instrument for Projecting on a Chart the Moon's Apparent Place in the Sky

Jacob Bigelow
A Model for Soldiers' Monument at Mt. Auburn

April 6, 1865   Robert Carsley
A Machine for Turning Spherical Bodies

M. V. Cummings
An Automatic Railroad Switch

William P. Atkinson
On the Neglect of Science as an Element in the English Higher Education

April 20, 1865   James B. Francis
On the Lowell System Against Fires

S. R. Calthrop
The Proper Form of Railroad Trains (for increased speed)

May 4, 1865   J. Herbert Shedd
The Ventilating and Heating of Buildings

J. W. Osborne
*On Instruments for Making and Recording Observations at Sea on the
Motion of a Vessel, with Reference to Seasickness*

William Falls
*Improvements in Fire Arms—the Magazine Breech-loading Pistol and a
Single Loader Invented by H. F. Wheeler*

William Wickersham
*An Improvement in the Sewing Machine, by Which Independent Stitches
May be Made*

May 18, 1865   Thomas P. Ritchie
An Electrical Apparatus for Exploding Torpedoes

William P. Atkinson
The Public School System of England

November 16, 1865   Jacob Bigelow
On the Limits of Education

Edward P. Bond
Paper and Cloth Manufactured from Corn Fibre

December 21, 1865   William R. Ware
Architectural Instruction

January 4, 1866   John M. Batchelder
                   A Rotary Dynamometer

                   W. E. Hawkins
                   His Miniature Steam Engine

                   William Edson
                   Moisture in the Atmosphere

                   Marshall P. Wilder
                   Influence of Moisture and Heat on Fruits and Vegetables

January 18, 1866   William B. Rogers
                   Value and Importance of the Microscope

                   Richard C. Greenleaf
                   Modifications and Uses of the Microscope

                   William B. Rogers
                   The Recording Dynamometer of S. P. Ruggles

                   Burt G. Wilder
                   Silk-Making Spider of South Carolina

                   Charles H. Wing
                   *Magnesium Lamps Now in Use in Boston, New York, Philadelphia and
                   other Theatres*

February 1, 1866   Professor [?] Cooke
                   A New Method of Producing Rotary Motion in Machinery

                   William B. Rogers
                   Artificial Leather

                   S. R. Calthrop
                   A New Cooking Stove

                   Burt G. Wilder
                   The Silk Spider

                   Charles Stodder
                   The Use of Vulcanized Rubber in the Stands of Microscopes

                   Charles Stodder
                   The Camera Lucida

                   Charles Stodder
                   The Use of the Microscope in Determining Adulterations in Food

February 15, 1866	Horace McMurtrie *Lansdel's Steam Siphon*
	Samuel Kneeland *Red River Bridge, Louisiana*
	William B. Rogers *The Coal Cutting Machine—or Iron Man*
	Henry Weld Fuller *The Anthracite Region of Pennsylvania*
March 1, 1866	H. W. Williams *The Way in Which the Eye Accommodates Itself to Vision of Near Objects*
	N. C. Keep *The Use of Aluminium in Dentistry as a Base for Artificial Teeth*
March 15, 1866	Clemens Herschel *Bridge Architecture*
	General Samuel Hunt *A Cotton Picker*
	James Hamblett, Jr. *New Telegraphic Instruments*
	J. M. Batchelder *A Case of Spontaneous Combustion at the Everett Mills, Lawrence*
April 5, 1866	J. M. Batchelder *A Pressure Tide Meter and Sounding Apparatus*
	William Wickersham *Experiments with Edson's Hygrometer*
	F. Braun *Laying Submarine Cables*
April 19, 1866	R. M. Copeland *The Proper Shape of Railroad Trains*
	William B. Rogers *Amsden's Hydrostatic Scale Proposed as Substitute for Canal Weigh Locks*
May 3, 1866	William Wickersham *An Improved Cotton Gin*

Thomas H. Leavitt
A Machine for Condensing and Preparing Peat Fuel

N. M. Lowe
A Universal Pulley

N. M. Lowe
A Spring-Making Machine for Piano-forte Action Invented by Benjamin R. Harwood

May 17, 1866   Charles H. Wing
The Magnesium Light

R. M. Copeland and S. R. Calthrop
Experiments on Atmospheric Resistance to Railway Trains

[?] Johnson
Felting Process

[?] Bradford
An Automatic Machine for Leathering Tacks

Burt G. Wilder
A Reel for Drawing Out Spider's Silk

November 15, 1866   Edward Atkinson
An Account of a Trip to the Coal and Iron Regions of Pennsylvania

William B. Rogers
Coal Region of Pennsylvania and English Coke

[?] Barry
The Pantascope. A European invention for photographic purposes

December 6, 1866   Thomas E. Sherwin
A Mirage

Edward Atkinson
Apparatus for Detaching Boats from Davits

Edward C. Pickering
The Washington Aqueduct

Charles Stodder
New Illuminator for Opaque Objects and a Small Telescope Made by Mr. Tolles

December 20, 1866	Rufus S. Sanborn *Steam Fireproof Safe*
	E. H. Derby *Minerals of Nova Scotia*
	William B. Rogers *R. B. Tolles's Telescope*
	William B. Rogers *Ascent of Steep Grades on Railroads by a Central Rail*
January 3, 1867	Colonel J. J. Storer *Whelpley and Storer's Water Furnace*
	D. J. Browne *Wine and Brandy from Native Grapes*
	Marshall P. Wilder *Grape Culture and Wine Product of the United States*
	H. R. Storer *Ventilating Apparatus*
February 7, 1867	Thomas Boyd *Solar Ventilator*
	John W. Langley *Separation of Copper from Its Ores*
February 21, 1867	Thomas Gaffield *Coloration of Glass by Sunlight*
	A. L. Fleury *Two New Chemical Processes: Iodine from Sea Water and Hydrate of Silica from Decomposition of the Sulphide of Silicium*
March 7, 1867	F. E. Stimpson *Economical Use of Gas*
	Thomas Doane *Hoosac-Tunnel Drills*
March 21, 1867	Edward Atkinson *Oyston Patent Nozzle*

E. S. Ritchie
Modified Holz Electrical Machine

Peter Lear
Conical Ventilator

Marshall P. Wilder
Permanent Labels for Fruit Trees

Edward Atkinson
Payment of the Debt of the United States

April 4, 1867
John M. Ordway
Reactions in the Whelpley-Storer Water Furnace

Charles Stodder
New Microscope and Eye Piece by Mr. Tolles

N. M. Lowe
Ventilators

[?] Hovey
Fire Extinguisher

April 18, 1867
Peter Lear
Horizontal Paddle Wheel

Joseph A. Miller
Engineer Improved Steam Boilers

May 2, 1867
F. E. Stimpson
Gas Meters

[?] Ehrhardt
New Blasting Power

Edward C. Pickering
Machine to Render Visible the Vibrations of Sound

May 16, 1867
James W. Hicks
Improved Steam Boiler

Thomas Doane
Hoosac Drilling Machines and Explosives for Blasting

[?] Gates
Horizontal Machine Drills

	Clemens Herschel *Subaqueous Tunnels*
November 7, 1867	E. S. Ritchie *Rotary Air Pump*
	John W. Langley *Machine for Extraction of Tannin from Barks*
November 21, 1867	John Ridgway *Revolving Battery*
	Stephen P. Ruggles *Ventilating Fan*
	Stephen P. Ruggles *Grooves in Wood Produced by Passage of Grain Over It*
December 5, 1867	J. D. Whelpley *New Copper Process*
	Charles Stodder *Nobert's Test and Mr. Tolles's Lenses*
	William B. Rogers *New Forms of the Hydraulic Press as Exhibited at Paris Exhibition*
December 19, 1867	Colonel [?] Lee *Burglar-Proof Vaults*
	J. D. Whelpley *New Iron Process*
	H. S. Noyes *Petroleum Stove*
	F. E. Stimpson *D. F. Hartford's Double Stringed Drill*
	Edward C. Pickering *Oscillating Engine*
	William B. Rogers *Jumping Flames*
January 2, 1868	E. S. Ritchie *Wave Motion Apparatus Devised by Professor Lyman of Yale*

	R. K. Huntoon
	Huntoon Governor for Steam and Water Power and Harcot Governor
January 16, 1868	Moses G. Farmer
	Thermal Electricity, Thermal Battery and Gas Lighting by Electricity
	James Hamblett, Jr.
	Telegraphic Registering Instruments, Magneto-Electric Clock, and Magnetic Vane
February 6, 1868	[?] Wilcox
	Wilcox Portable Engine
	[?] Brackett
	New Form of Cotton Gin
	A. P. Garratt
	Medical Battery
	William B. Rogers
	Foucault's Improved Electric Regulator
February 20, 1868	Edward C. Pickering
	Boehm Flute
	Theodore Lyman
	Artificial Propagation of Fish
	William Wickersham
	Wax Thread Sewing Machines
	C. L. Ridgway
	Water Gauge and Lever Corkscrew
	Speaker unnamed
	Kindling Apparatus
	N. M. Lowe
	Thermometer for House Use
March 5, 1868	Horace McMurtrie
	Wright's Variable Cut-Off Steam Engine
	B. W. Williams
	Wood Wall Hangings
	Thomas Gaffield
	Action of Sunlight on Glass

Charles Stodder
Large Kaleidoscope

March 19, 1868

Clemens Herschel
Subaqueous Tunnels

Josiah L. Lombard
Relation of Heat to Mental Work

E. S. Ritchie
Perforation of Glass by the Electric Spark

[?] Addy
Welding of Iron by Heat from Friction

April 16, 1868

F. E. Stimpson
Report on Volatile Hydrocarbons

James D. Whelpley
Use of Pulverized Fuel

H. F. Shaw
Differential Motion Machinery

[?] Liscom
Lever Bridge

April 30, 1868

N. M. Lowe
Imperfect Ventilation

F. E. Stimpson
Defective Construction of Stoves and Furnaces

William B. Rogers
Permeability of Red Hot Iron to Gases

John M. Little
New Way of Cracking Glass

John Johnson
Equalizing Steam Heating Apparatus

N. M. Lowe
French Annular Diamond Drill

William B. Rogers
Koenig's Resonator

May 7, 1868	W. W. Whitwell *Conveyance of Cochituate Water to East Boston and Chelsea*
	W. W. Whitwell *Fountain Jets on the Common*
	W. W. Whitwell *The Reservoir at Brookline*
	C. P. Sykes *Process for Carburetting Street Gas*
	William B. Rogers *Bowditch's Method of Increasing Illuminating Power of Gas*
	Edward C. Pickering *New Form of Rotary Engine*
	N. M. Lowe *Hygrodeik*
	Samuel Kneeland *Model Made by U. S. Colored Soldier in Mobile from Found Materials*
May 21, 1868	[?] Bean *Gas-lighting in Street Lamps by Electricity*
	Paul B. Du Chailler *Arts and Manufactures of Equatorial African Natives*
	H. J. Smith *New Condenser and Fulminate*
November 5, 1868	Charles L. Spencer *Method of Converting Reciprocating into Rotary Motion*
	Francis L. King *Machine for Dressing Stone*
November 19, 1868	Norman Niard *The Explosion of Steam Boilers, Their Cause and Prevention*
	L. B. Sawyer *Iron Observatory*
December 3, 1868	William Wickersham *The Mineral Regions of Pennsylvania and New Jersey—Blasting by Electricity and the Annular Diamond Drill*

Edward C. Pickering
Artificial Production of Ice

John D. Runkle
Lunar Volcanoes

December 17, 1868   J. D. Whelpley
Manufacture of Steel—Bessemer Process and Whelpley and Storer Process

Josiah Tisdale
Peat Machine

Thomas H. Leavitt
Peat as Fuel

January 7, 1869   Stephen P. Ruggles
Museum of Elements of Machinery

William Wickersham
Breakage in Telegraph Cables

I. Pitman
Ventilation

Thomas Boyd
Ventilating Cap

Thomas Boyd
Solar Ventilator

January 21, 1869   Hon. Elisha Dyer
Earth Closet

Dr. Sim
Process for the Preservation of Meats

[?] White
Portable Music Stand

February 4, 1869   J. D. Whelpley
New Form of Steam Engine

Henry Kelley
Ventilator

Edward C. Pickering
Magnesium Lantern

	H. P. Langley *Machine for Testing Chains*
February 18, 1869	Col. T. W. Clarke *New Form of Steam Engine*
	Hon. N. E. Atwood *Patent Harpoon*
	William Wickersham *Automatic Railroad Chair*
March 4, 1869	Nathanael G. Herreshoff *Herreshoff's Rotary Engine*
	Marshall P. Wilder *South Carolina Lime Beds*
	Thomas Gaffield *Siemens' Furnace*
	Elisha Stone *Safety Elevator*
March 18, 1869	F. E. Stimpson *New Gas Stove*
	Henry B. Leach *Water Meter*
	George A. Osborne *Astronomy and Navigation*
	Clemens Herschel *Heliography, or Sun Engraving*
April 1, 1869	John A. Coleman *Harrison Boiler*
	Jesse A. Locke *Process of Fine Casting*
	[?] Gardner *Mining on the Pacific Coast*
April 15, 1869	Horace McMurtrie *American Boiler*

F. P. Canfield
Self Sustaining Elevator

John D. Runkle
Universal Calendar of Mr. Chandler of Hadley

Edward C. Pickering
Uses of the Spectroscope

April 29, 1869

F. E. Stimpson
Circulation

Jonathan Amory
Perfect Combustion and Amory Furnace

H. P. Langley
Economical Boiler and Inspection of Boilers

William Wickersham
Need for an Experimental Laboratory

James B. Francis
Evaporation Test

John A. Coleman
The Value of a Boiler and a Safe Boiler

May 6, 1869

H. P. Langley
Boiler Circulation

Edward S. Ritchie
Experiments on Light

A. P. Garratt
Hygienic Ice Chest

N. M. Lowe
New Car Coupling

Speaker unidentified
Randall Grate Bar Model

Richard Lavery
Mercurial Steam Boiler

May 20, 1869

Thomas Adams
Theory of the Slide Value

Speaker unidentified
Samson Scale

Gerard Sickles
Water Meter

May 27, 1869   N. M. Lowe
Electricity in the Female

November 4, 1869   William Watson
New Process in Lithography

William Watson
Old French Map of Siege of Boston

Edward C. Pickering
Oldham's Universal Joint

H. P. Langley
Machine for Testing Metals

November 20, 1869   H. P. Langley
Miniature Steam Engine

Charles R. Cross
Method of Measuring the Focal Length of Objectives

William Watson
Experiments on Torsion of Iron

John M. Ordway
Bessemer's High Pressure Furnace

George W. Bond
Fifteen Specimens of Wood

F. E. Stimpson
Explosion of Gas at Cincinnati, Ohio

December 2, 1869   Speaker unidentified
Hall Treadle Attachment

William Watson
Flannel from Pine Leaves

John Trowbridge
Constitution of the Sun

December 16, 1869   Thomas Gaffield
Photography Without a Camera

Thomas Gaffield
Photography from Nature

Joseph B. Stearns
New Kind of Crab Engine

[?] Leclerc
Metallic Thermometer

January 6, 1870   Edward C. Pickering
New Spectroscope Lately Presented to Physical Laboratory

F. E. Stimpson
Portable Photometer

F. E. Stimpson
Loss of Light through Shades of Ground Glass

William Watson
Models for Instruction in Descriptive Geometry, etc.

January 20, 1870   [?] Clark
Knitting Machine

Alfred P. Rockwell
Hydraulic Mining in California

February 3, 1870   J. C. Blasdel
Elastic Sponge

John M. Ordway
Chinese Method of Tin Mining

February 17, 1870   A. C. Hamlin
Gems of North America

March 3, 1870   S. C. Maine
Ventilation

Nathaniel Shaler
Ventilation for Hospitals

March 17, 1870   A. C. Martin
Ventilation by a Draught Chimney

April 7, 1870	Horace McMurtrie *Low Water Detector*
	S. H. Roper *Steam Velocipede*
	Chauncy Smith *Artificial Stone*
April 21, 1870	William Watson *Technical University of Zurich*
	William Watson *Water Pressure Engine*
	William Watson *Speaking Machine*
May 5, 1870	H. P. Langley *Friction of the Hydraulic Press*
	Edward C. Pickering *Photometry*
	Edward C. Pickering *Gas Measurements*
	Francis L. Capen *Astronomic Meteorology*
May 19, 1870	Orrin L. Brown *Machine for Setting Type*
	W. Nichols *Quinn's Compound Mercurial Steam Gauge*
	Charles E. Avery *Tripoli from Massachusetts*
	Mr. Leighton *Wooden Boxes*
November 17, 1870	F. E. Stimpson *Economy of Gas Burners*
December 1, 1870	R. M. Copeland *Utilization of Sewage*

December 15, 1870   H. P. Langley
                      Iron for Cannon

                      H. P. Langley
                      Rodman Gun

                      F. E. Stimpson
                      Savery Engine

                      Charles Houghton
                      Automatic Steam Pump

Notes

Publications listed under Select Sources (pp.745–760) are identified in the notes by author and title only; publications not listed there appear with full citations. Only the most frequently cited archival and manuscript collections appear under Select Sources. Unless otherwise noted, archives and manuscripts are in the Institute Archives and Special Collections, MIT Libraries.

Abbreviations

AAAS	American Association for the Advancement of Science
AAcadAS	American Academy of Arts and Sciences
ACAB	Appletons' *Cyclopaedia of American Biography*
ANB	*American National Biography*
APS	American Philosophical Society
BA	Boston Athenaeum
BPL	Boston Public Library
BSNH	Boston Society of Natural History
CWE	Charles William Eliot
DAB	*Dictionary of American Biography*
DNB	*Dictionary of National Biography*
DSB	*Dictionary of Scientific Biography*
ECP	Edward Charles Pickering
ER	Emma Rogers

GPO	Government Printing Office
HDR	Henry Darwin Rogers
HLHU	Houghton Library, Harvard University
HUA	Harvard University Archives
JAL	John Amory Lowell
JAS	Julius Adams Stratton
JBR	James Blythe Rogers
JDR	John Daniel Runkle
LSS	Lawrence Scientific School
MDR	Matthias Denman Ross
MHS	Massachusetts Historical Society
MIT Archives	Institute Archives and Special Collections, MIT Libraries
NAS	National Academy of Sciences
NCAB	*National Cyclopaedia of American Biography*
PKR	Patrick Kerr Rogers
RER	Robert Empie Rogers
THW	Thomas Hopkins Webb
TR	*Technology Review*
UVaA	University of Virginia Archives
WBR	William Barton Rogers
WPA	William Parsons Atkinson
WRW	William Robert Ware

Prologue

1. The Institute charter and the grant of land for its use as well as the grant of land for the Boston Society of Natural History are combined in one document. *An Act to Incorporate the Massachusetts Institute of Technology, and to Grant Aid to Said Institution and to the Boston Society of Natural History,* Approved April 10, 1861, Acts of 1861, Chapter 183, *Acts and Resolves of the General Court relating to the Massachusetts Institute of Technology* (Cambridge, 1931), 1–4.
2. Ibid., 1. "Arts" in this context referred to the industrial arts. The Back Bay lands involved contained approximately 100 acres, covering an area 1,485 feet wide and 2,800 feet long. This area was laid out in streets crossing at right angles. In 1861 the boundaries were as follows: east, Public Garden; north, Beacon Street, with Roxbury Mill-Corporation property beyond; south, Boylston Street and land owned by the Boston Water-power Company; west, privately owned lands. Marlborough and Newbury Streets and Commonwealth Avenue were parallel to and between Beacon and Boylston. Arlington, Berkeley, and Clarendon Streets existed at that time. The square granted to the Boston Society of Natural History and the Massachusetts Institute of Technology was bounded by Berkeley, Newbury, Clarendon, and Boylston Streets. M. D. Ross, *Estimate of the Financial Effect of the Proposed Reservation of Back-Bay Lands* (Boston, 1861), 7–8.
3. *Objects and Plan of an Institute of Technology* (hereafter cited as *Objects and Plan*), 6–7.
4. Ibid., 13, 14.
5. Ibid., 21–22.

Chapter One EUROPEAN ORIGINS

1. See Melvin Kranzberg and Carroll W. Pursell, Jr., eds., *Technology in Western Civilization*, vol. 1, pt. 1.
2. Francis Bacon, *Novum Organum*, vol. 8 of *The Works of Francis Bacon*, ed. James Spedding, Robert Leslie Ellis, and Douglas Denon Heath (Cambridge: Riverside Press, 1863), Aphorism III, 67–68.
3. Ibid., Aphorism LXXXI, 113.
4. Ibid., Aphorism LXXX, 112.
5. William E. Wickenden, *A Comparative Study of Engineering Education in the United States and Europe*, 9.
6. Frederick B. Artz, *The Development of Technical Education in France, 1500–1850*, 47–48, 82.
7. John Hubbel Weiss, *The Making of Technological Man*, 12–13.
8. Artz, 82–84, 86; Wickenden, 9–11.
9. The École des Mines, founded in 1783, followed the example of the Freiburg Bergakademie in Germany, founded in 1765. Weiss, 12.
10. Artz, 151–165; Wickenden, 12–14.
11. Artz, 11–12.

12. Ibid., 143.

13. Charles R. Day, *Education for the Industrial World*, 19.

14. Artz, 143–150; Day, 18–21; Wickenden, 14–15; *Grand Dictionnaire Encyclopédique Larousse* (1982), s.v. "Morin, Arthur."

15. A. Wolf, *A History of Science, Technology, and Philosophy in the Eighteenth Century*, 2d ed., rev. D. McKie, 42.

16. Part of the Rogers Book Collection in the MIT Libraries, undoubtedly procured by William Barton Rogers while in Paris in 1864, is A. Morin's *Conservatoire Impérial des Arts et Métiers, Catalogue des Collections*, 4th ed. (Paris, 1864).

17. Weiss, 16–18. The scientists were Jean–Baptiste Dumas, Théodore Olivier, and Eugène Péclet; the engineer, Philippe Benoit.

18. Artz, 250.

19. Day, 12.

20. Weiss, 224–225.

21. Artz, 247–253; Day, 13–18; Wickenden, 16–18. Weiss, *The Making of Technological Man*, is a detailed study of the first twenty years of the École Centrale.

22. Franz Schnabel, "Die Anfänge des technischen Hochschulwesens," in *Festschrift anlässich des 100 jährigen Bestehens der Technischen Hochschule Fridericiana zu Karlsruhe*, 1–44; Wickenden, 43–50.

23. Reasons for the early British lead are summed up by Melvin Kranzberg, "Prerequisites for Industrialization," in Kranzberg and Pursell, 1:217–230. For an interesting assessment of provincial science and industry in eighteenth–century England, see also Robert E. Schofield, *The Lunar Society of Birmingham*.

24. James Muir, *John Anderson, Pioneer of Technical Education and the College He Founded*, 1, 3, 7–8, 29–40.

25. Ibid., 86–88.

26. Ibid., 88–89, quoted extract from will.

27. Ibid., 98–99, 101.

28. Ibid., 108; C. DeLisle Burns, *A Short History of Birkbeck College*, 18–19.

29. A. Humboldt Sexton, *The First Technical College*, 2.

30. C. G. Wood, Librarian, The Andersonian Library, University of Strathclyde, Glasgow, to JAS, May 5, 1977.

31. Jeremy Bentham, *Chrestomathia: Being a Collection of Papers, Explanatory of the Design of an Institution, Proposed To Be Set on Foot under the Name of the Chrestomathic Day School, or Chrestomathic School, for the Extension of the New System of Instruction to the Higher Branches of Learning, for the Use of the Middling and Higher Ranks in Life*, vol. 8 of *The Works of Jeremy Bentham*, title page, 1–191.

32. Ibid., tables 1 through 5; M. P. Mack, *Jeremy Bentham*, 111–112.

33. Thomas Kelly, *George Birkbeck, Pioneer of Adult Education*, 69.

34. Bruce Sinclair, *Philadelphia's Philosopher Mechanics, a History of the Franklin Institute 1824–1865*, 15–19.

35. Kelly, 79–81; *DNB*, s.v. "Birkbeck, George."

36. Burns, 27.

37. Ibid., 33.

38. Kelly, 89. Professor Millington later emigrated to America and in 1836 succeeded William Barton Rogers as professor of natural philosophy and chemistry at the College of William and Mary.

39. Burns, 47–48.

40. *The London Mechanics' Register*, vol. 2, 3d ed. (London, 1827). The preface is dated October 21, 1825, and the issues contained in the volume all bear a date of 1825.

41. Charles Alpheus Bennett, *History of Manual and Industrial Education up to 1870*, 306, 308.

42. Burns, 78, 156; *International Handbook of Universities*, 13th ed. (1993), s.v. "University of London."

43. Kelly, 88, from Rules and Orders of the Institution.

44. Sir Eric Ashby, *Technology and the Academics*, 50.

45. Wickenden, 35–36.

46. Eugene S. Ferguson, "Expositions of Technology, 1851–1900," in Kranzberg and Pursell, 1:706–726.

47. C. W. F. Everitt, *James Clerk Maxwell*, 34, 57; *DAB*.

Chapter Two MIGRATION OF A HERITAGE

1. Henry Steele Commager, *The Empire of Reason*, xi.

2. Victor S. Clark, *History of Manufactures in the United States*, vol. 1, 1607–1860, 22; Edwin J. Perkins, *The Economy of Colonial America*, 17.

3. Perkins, 22–23.

4. E. Neal Hartley, *Ironworks on the Saugus*, 3, 8.

5. Ibid., 8, 9, 102, 126.

6. Ibid., 138.

7. Perkins, chap. 2, "Foreign Trade," 17–38; Clark, 30.

8. Clark, 33; chaps. 3 & 4.

9. Ibid., 67–68.

10. See, for example, Carl Bridenbaugh, *Cities in Revolt, Urban Life in America, 1743–1776*; Brooke Hindle, *The Pursuit of Science in Revolutionary America, 1735–1789*; Brooke Hindle, ed., *Early American Science*; and Raymond Phineas Stearns, *Science in the British Colonies of America*.

11. Stearns, 678–680.

12. Carl Bridenbaugh, *Early Americans*, 155–158. In this chapter, "Philosophy Put to Use: Voluntary Associations for Propagating the Enlightenment in Philadelphia, 1727–1776," Bridenbaugh points out that Franklin had "appropriated almost without change" the "Rules of a Society, which met once a week for their Improvement of useful Knowledge and for the promoting of Truth and Christian Charity," as described in John Locke's (1632–1704) *A*

Collection of Several Pieces. And he adds, "This, it appears, is how the magic, motivating phrase 'promoting useful knowledge' was incorporated into the Philadelphia vocabulary."

13. Ibid., 160. Similar suggestions had earlier been made: in 1728 that "a Virtuoso Society" be founded and in 1737 that a branch of the Royal Society be organized, both in Boston.

14. *APS Year Book 1986* (Philadelphia, 1987), 286.

15. Some references to this society eliminate the word "Propagating."

16. Edwin G. Conklin, "A Brief History of the American Philosophical Society," *APS Year Book 1975*, 39–43. In the beginning the society looked to Franklin's proposal of 1743 as the date of its origin. In 1840, however, the president of the society, Peter Stephen Du Ponceau, recommended 1727, the founding date of Franklin's Junto, as the proper date, a suggestion rejected by a committee reporting a year later. The question having been raised once again, a committee in 1914, after extensive deliberations and not unanimous in their conclusion, favored the 1727 date. This was henceforth used by the society, which held a two-hundredth anniversary celebration in April 1927. The decision was later deemed in error, and on April 24, 1948, the society voted "to recognize the date of Franklin's Proposal (May 14, 1743) as the date of origin of the American Philosophical Society and to restore this date on the official seal and stationery, as it stood for one hundred and forty-five years before it was changed." Even with this change to the later date the society could feel secure in its position as "the oldest learned society in America," with a comfortable thirty-seven years between 1743 and the 1780 founding in Boston of the American Academy of Arts and Sciences. See *APS Year Book 1950* (Philadelphia, 1951), 11 n. 2, Francis X. Dercum, "The Origin and Activities of the American Philosophical Society. . . ," *The Record of the Celebration of the Two Hundredth Anniversary of the Founding of the American Philosophical Society Held at Philadelphia for Promoting Useful Knowledge, April 27 to April 30, 1927, Proceedings, APS* 66 (1927): 19–30; Carl Van Doren, "The Beginnings of the American Philosophical Society," *Proceedings, APS* 87 (1944): 277–289.

17. Quoted in Lyman H. Butterfield, "Benjamin Rush as a Promoter of Useful Knowledge," *Proceedings, APS* 92 (March 1948): 28.

18. *APS Year Book 1975* (Philadelphia, 1976), 64.

19. See Hindle, *Pursuit of Science*; George H. Daniels, *Science in American Society, A Social History.*

20. Clark, chap. 10, 215–232.

21. Dumas Malone, *Jefferson the President, Second Term 1805–1809*, 109–110, 477–479.

22. Ibid., 420–422.

23. Ibid., 481.

24. Ibid., chap. 26, "The Lesser Evil: The Embargo," 469–490.

25. Ibid., 649. For a full account see chapters 22 through 26 and 31 through 35. See also Samuel Eliot Morison, Henry Steele Commager, and William E. Leuchtenburg, *A Concise History of the American Republic*, 156–159.

26. Malone, *Jefferson the President*, 628.

27. Ibid., 629.

28. Thomas Jefferson, *Notes on the State of Virginia*, edited with an Introduction and Notes by William Peden, 165; Malone, *Jefferson the President*, 24.
29. Merrill D. Peterson, *Thomas Jefferson and the New Nation*, 458–460.
30. Harold C. Syrett and Jacob E. Cooke, eds., Introductory Note to "Report on the Subject of Manufactures," in *The Papers of Alexander Hamilton*, 10:5. The editors cite a June 23, 1791, letter from Jefferson to David Humphreys. Hamilton's final version of the report, December 5, 1791, 230–340.
31. Dumas Malone, *The Sage of Monticello*, 146–147.
32. Ibid., 147.
33. Harry L. Coles, *The War of 1812*, 268–269; John W. Oliver, *History of American Technology*, chap. 10, "An Age of Auspicious Beginnings—1789–1816," 125–143.

Chapter Three   THE RISE OF TECHNICAL EDUCATION IN AMERICA

1. Bennett, 326, 340.
2. Ibid., 327.
3. *DAB*, s.v. "Van Rensselaer, Stephen."
4. Persifor Frazer, "The Franklin Institute," *Journal of the Franklin Institute* 165 (April 1908): 246–247.
5. *First Annual Report of the Proceedings of the Franklin Institute* (Philadelphia, 1825), 7; reprinted with Introduction by Henry B. Allen in *Journal of the Franklin Institute* 247 (April 1949): 289–402.
6. Sinclair, 109.
7. Ibid., 65.
8. Ibid.; "Proposed Polytechnic and Scientific College, in Philadelphia," *The Franklin Journal, and American Mechanics' Magazine* 1 (March 1826): 189–191.
9. For an extended discussion of the opposition to Browne's plan both within and outside the Franklin Institute, see Sinclair, 65–69, 122–124.
10. Ibid., 124.
11. Walter R. Johnson, "On the Combination of a Practical with a Liberal Course of Education," *The Franklin Journal, and American Mechanics' Magazine* 6 (July 1828): 55–57; (August 1828): 108–113; (September 1828): 166–169; (October 1828): 275–278; (November 1828): 353–355; (December 1828): 367–369. Johnson was later active as a scientific consultant and in 1845 was appointed, with John B. Jervis, to investigate possible sources of water for Boston. *Report of the Commissioners appointed by authority of the City Council to examine the sources from which a supply of pure water may be obtained for the City of Boston* (Boston: J. H. Eastburn, 1845).
12. Sinclair, 127–128.
13. John H. B. Latrobe, *Picture of Baltimore*, 196.
14. Stephen E. Ambrose, *Duty, Honor, Country, a History of West Point*, 22.
15. Ibid., 38–61.

16. Ibid., 67.

17. Ibid., 57–61.

18. Ibid., 64–65.

19. Ernest R. Dupuy, *Sylvanus Thayer: Father of Technology in the United States*, 3–7; Ambrose, chap. 5, "Thayer's Curriculum and Faculty," 87–105.

20. For Thayer's contributions to West Point, see also Ambrose, chap. 4, "Sylvanus Thayer," 62–86.

21. James Lunsford Morrison, Jr., *The United States Military Academy, 1833–1866: Years of Progress and Turmoil*, 147, 166.

22. Ibid., 174–176.

23. Ibid., 195, 176.

24. William A. Ellis, *Norwich University, 1819–1911*, 1:6–7. Chapters 1 through 4 of this volume deal especially with the early period.

25. Ibid., 60.

26. Ibid., 8, 63–64.

27. Ibid., 64–66.

28. Ibid., 66–69.

29. Ibid., 72.

30. Ibid., 12–13.

31. Ibid., 75–76.

32. *DAB*, s.v. "Gardiner, Robert Hallowell."

33. Bennett, 348–349. Hale left Gardiner in 1827 and went to Dartmouth as professor of chemistry. In 1828 he was ordained an Episcopal minister, a step not welcomed by the Congregational clergy among the trustees, and his appointment was terminated in 1835. From 1836 to 1858 he was president of Geneva College in New York, later known as Hobart College. *DAB*, s.v. "Hale, Benjamin."

34. Bennett, 349.

35. Ibid., 349–350; see also James Gregory McGivern, *First Hundred Years of Engineering Education in the United States (1807–1907)*, 46–48.

36. Ethel M. McAllister, *Amos Eaton, Scientist and Educator*, 364–367. This Ph.D. dissertation contains a very complete account of the life and works of Amos Eaton. Palmer C. Ricketts, *History of the Rensselaer Polytechnic Institute, 1824–1894*, chap. 1, "The Foundation of the School," 1–11. Ricketts does not emphasize, as does McAllister, Eaton's pivotal role in the founding.

37. McAllister, chaps. 7 & 8, 159–211.

38. Letter, Amos Eaton to Stephen Van Rensselaer, McAllister, 366–367.

39. Ibid., 367–371. McAllister states, 367–368, "That this letter was composed by Amos Eaton there can be no doubt, for Eaton, from the beginning until the end of Stephen Van Rensselaer's relations with the school, was Van Rensselaer's 'ghost writer.'"

40. Ricketts, 77–79.

41. Samuel Reznock, *Education for a Technological Society, A Sesquicentennial History of Rensselaer Polytechnic Institute*, 39.

42. Ricketts, 84.

43. Ibid., 93.

44. Wickenden, 63.

45. Charles R. Mann, *A Study in Engineering Education*, 12.

46. Ricketts, 99–101.

47. *Extracts from the Report of Director B. Franklin Greene Upon the Reorganization of the Institute, Printed in 1855*, Rensselaer Polytechnic Institute Engineering and Science Series no. 32 (Troy, N.Y., January 1931), 3. In 1949, when Rensselaer celebrated its 125th Anniversary, a facsimile reprint from Greene's report was published under the title *The True Idea of a Polytechnic Institute* (Troy, N.Y., 1949).

48. Over the years many have erroneously believed that MIT was the first institution of its kind in the country. In 1930, soon after the inauguration of Karl T. Compton as president, questions about a New Haven Railroad dining car menu card, identifying MIT in this way, culminated in an exchange of letters between Compton and Palmer C. Ricketts, president of Rensselaer Institute. Though Compton could not determine the source of the statement, he indicated that the unwitting cause might have been his recent inaugural address, in which he had referred to MIT as the "founder of a sturdy and illustrious family" of technical institutions both in the United States and abroad. Regretting the error, he promised to "take every opportunity to correct this statement." Ricketts graciously responded that he had once failed to give proper credit to the Gardiner Lyceum. MIT Office of the President, Records, 1930–1959 (AC 4), box 206; Compton's Inaugural Address, *TR* 32 (July 1930): 438.

49. McGivern, 82.

50. *Scientific American* 8, no. 37 (May 28, 1853): 293.

51. *Historical Record of the Polytechnic College of the State of Pennsylvania*, 1st ed., 1853–1890 (Philadelphia: Alumni Association, n.d.).

52. Advertisement, *National Almanac and Annual Record for the Year 1863* (Philadelphia: George W. Childs, 1863), n.p.

53. Ibid.

54. McGivern, 86.

55. Advertisement, *Scientific American* 10 (August 25, 1855): 399; n.s. 7, no. 13 (September 27, 1862): 198.

56. Samuel Eliot Morison, *Harvard College in the Seventeenth Century,* 1:208.

57. Galen W. Ewing, *Early Teaching of Science at the College of William and Mary in Virginia*, 5; Samuel Eliot Morison, *Three Centuries of Harvard*, 79.

58. Stanley M. Guralnick, *Science and the Ante-Bellum American College*, 13–14.

59. *Vital Facts, A Chronology of the College of William and Mary*, 12. Ewing, *Early Teaching of Science*, 26, refers to this course as "surveying."

60. Philip Alexander Bruce, *History of the University of Virginia, 1819–1919*, 2:126. The "School" is included here under "Minor Courses of Instruction."

61. Guralnick, chap. 2, 18–46.

62. *DAB*, s.v. "Wayland, Francis."

63. Francis Wayland, *Report to the Corporation of Brown University, on Changes in the System of Collegiate Education, Read March 28, 1850* (Providence: George H. Whitney, 1850), 12–13, 16, 17–18.

64. Ibid., 12, 20.

65. Frederick Rudolph, *The American College and University*, 237–240.

66. Excerpts from these two papers are included in Richard Hofstadter and Wilson Smith, eds., *American Higher Education, A Documentary History* 1:334–375; 2:478–487.

67. Since the establishment of the Lawrence Scientific School at Harvard has particular significance for the story of the founding and development of the Massachusetts Institute of Technology, it will be discussed in a separate chapter.

68. Dixon Ryan Fox, *Union College, An Unfinished History*, 14; *DAB*, s.v. "Nott, Eliphalet."

69. Mortimer F. Sayre, "Squire Whipple and Union College," 6.

70. Sayre, 6; Guralnick, 37–38.

71. Andrew Van Vranken Raymond, *Union University* 1:156; Guralnick, 38.

72. Raymond, 1:216–220; *DAB*, s.v. "Gillespie, William Mitchell." Several letters from Gillespie to President Everett in 1846 and 1847 reveal his interest in a position at Harvard—either the Rumford Professorship or a professorship of engineering.

73. George P. Fisher, *Life of Benjamin Silliman, M.D., LL.D.* 1:96. This two-volume work is drawn chiefly from Silliman's manuscript reminiscences, diaries, and correspondence. A copy in the Rogers Book Collection in the MIT Libraries was inscribed to William B. Rogers in 1866 by Silliman's son Benjamin. The elder Silliman died in 1864.

74. Ibid., 92.

75. Ibid., 195–196.

76. Russell H. Chittenden, *History of the Sheffield Scientific School of Yale University* 1:27–30.

77. Ibid., 37–38, 42–46; Arthur W. Wright, *Biographical Memoir of Benjamin Silliman, 1816–1885* (Washington: NAS, June 1911); later published also in NAS *Biographical Memoirs* 7, 1913, 115–141.

78. Chittenden, 1:41–42.

79. Ibid., 47–48.

80. Ibid., 48–50.

81. Ibid., 50.

82. Ibid., 51.

83. Ibid., 51–54.

84. Louis I. Kuslan, "The Rise of the Yale School of Applied Chemistry (1845–1856)," in *Benjamin Silliman and his Circle: Studies on the Influence of Benjamin Silliman on Science in America*, 146–149. This chapter and a preceding piece on the School of Applied Chemistry include details not presented in Chittenden's history.

85. Chittenden, 1:58–59, 61.

86. Ibid., 56–57.

87. Ibid., 56–61.
88. Ibid., 54–56.
89. Kuslan, 175–176. The appointment was approved by the Yale Corporation on July 26, 1853, but Silliman did not return to New Haven until 1854.
90. Chittenden, 1:62–63.
91. Ibid., 65–74, 213.
92. Ibid., 75–77; Rudolph, 232.
93. Chittenden, 1:91–99, 112–113, 171, 196.
94. Ibid., 122, 166–167.
95. WPA to WBR, August 27, 1871, WBR Papers (MC 1), folder 66.
96. *ACAB*, s.v. "Chandler, Abiel"; George Gary Bush, *History of Education in New Hampshire*, no. 22 in U.S. Bureau of Education, Circular of Information, no. 3 (Washington: GPO, 1898), 163.
97. Leon B. Richardson, *History of Dartmouth College,* 1:422–423.
98. Ibid., 423–424.
99. Ibid., 425–427.
100. Richardson, 2:531–532. The problems continued, and in 1892 a trustee committee recommended the establishment of a Chandler Scientific Course as a branch of the college, with higher admission requirements, the transfer of Chandler's faculty to that of Dartmouth, and central control of the entire institution. The school's board of visitors, which had resisted previous attempts of this nature, agreed, and the school was abandoned, effective in 1893. Curriculum revisions in succeeding years resulted eventually in the disappearance of the Chandler name.
101. Edwin Connery Lathem, ed., *The Beginnings of The Thayer School of Engineering at Dartmouth College.* This volume is a selection of Thayer correspondence between 1867 and 1871 relating to the founding of the school. Facsimile of General Thayer's Original Instrument of Gift, July 4, 1867, 19–23. In Thayer's initial letters of intent he referred to a School of Architecture and Civil Engineering, but Architecture was later dropped from the title. See William Phelps Kimball, *The First Hundred Years of The Thayer School of Engineering at Dartmouth College*, 7.
102. *Thayer School of Engineering, Dartmouth College Bulletin* (August 1987), 5, 145.
103. Wilfred B. Shaw and Frank E. Robbins, "The Early History of the University of Michigan," in *The University of Michigan, An Encyclopedic Survey*, vol. 1, ed. Wilfred B. Shaw, 26–32.
104. A. Franklin Shull, "Achievements in Science," in *Centennial Celebration of the College of Literature, Science, and the Arts of the University of Michigan, 1841–1941*, 50; Harlan Hatcher, *"The University of Michigan," 140 Years from Michigan Wilderness to a World Center of Learning! 1817–1957*, 9.
105. Jesse S. Reeves, "Historical Development of the College," in *Centennial Celebration of the College*, 7; Shaw and Robbins, 35; Arthur D. Moore, "The College of Engineering," in *The University of Michigan, An Encyclopedic Survey*, vol. 3, ed. Walter A. Donnelly, 1161.
106. Elizabeth S. Adams, "The Administration of Henry Philip Tappan," in *The University of Michigan, An Encyclopedic Survey*, 1:39.

107. Moore, 1161–1162.

108. Ibid., 1161–1170. Professor Greene, a graduate of Harvard College in 1862, had resigned an Army commission in 1866 to enter the School of the Massachusetts Institute of Technology as a third-year student, in accordance with its admissions policy for college graduates, and graduated as a civil engineer with the Institute's first class in 1868. In the summer of 1881 he would seriously consider and eventually decline an offer of a professorship at the Institute, deciding in favor of Ann Arbor, where he remained until his death in 1903. WBR Papers, folders 115–117, several letters in 1881, beginning in May, some addressed to John D. Runkle, Greene's final decision dated July 2, 1881, to Rogers.

109. Rudolph, 232–233; S. Edward Warren, *Notes on Polytechnic or Scientific Schools, in the United States; Their Nature, Position, Aims and Wants.*

Chapter Four A FAMILY AFFAIR

1. For general biographical information on William Barton Rogers, see *In Memory of William Barton Rogers, L.L.D., Late President of the Society [of Arts]*; Josiah P. Cooke, "Notice of William Barton Rogers: Founder of the Massachusetts Institute of Technology"; Francis Amasa Walker, "Biographical Memoir of Wm. Barton Rogers"; Walker, "Sketch of Prof. William B. Rogers," *Popular Science Monthly* 9 (September 1876): 606–611; "Prof. W. B. Rogers," *Nature* 26 (June 22, 1882): 182–183; and "Centennial Commemoration of William Barton Rogers, 1804–1904"; also, entries in *ANB* (1999), *DAB* (1928–1936), *DSB* (1970–1976), and *NCAB*, vol. 7 (1892).

   For Henry Darwin Rogers, see John W. Gregory, *Henry Darwin Rogers . . . An Address to the Glasgow University Geological Society, 20th January 1916*; and Patsy Gerstner, *Henry Darwin Rogers, 1808–1866: American Geologist*; also, entries in *ANB* (1999), *DAB* (1928–1936), *DSB* (1970–1976), and *NCAB*, vol. 1 (1891) & vol. 7 (1892).

   For James Blythe Rogers, see Joseph Carson, *A Memoir of the Life and Character of James B. Rogers, M.D.: Professor of Chemistry in the University of Pennsylvania*; and Edgar F. Smith, *James Blythe Rogers, 1802–1852, Chemist.*

   For Robert Empie Rogers, see James W. Holland, *A Eulogy on the Life and Character of Prof. Robt. E. Rodgers [Rogers], M.D.: Introductory to the Course of 1885–86 at Jefferson Medical College: Delivered September 30th, 1885*; Edgar F. Smith, "Biographical Memoir of Robert Empie Rogers, 1813–1884"; and Chalmers L. Gemmill and Mary Jeanne Jones, "Robert Empie Rogers, M.D., L.L.D., 1842–1852."

   For the brothers as a group, see William S. W. Ruschenberger, *A Sketch of the Life of Robert E. Rogers, M.D., L.L.D., with Biographical Notices of His Fathers and Brothers*; William H. Ruffin, "The Brothers Rogers," [1895]; and Hugh Miller Spencer, *The Life of John William Mallet, B.A., Ph.D., LL.D., Hon. M.D., F.R.S.; and the Four Distinguished Sons of Patrick Kerr (1776–1828) and Hannah Blythe (ca. 1775–1820) Rogers.*

2. Patrick Kerr Rogers, "An Investigation of the Properties of the Liriodendron tulipifera, or Poplar-tree," copy preserved on microfilm in the Bernard Becker Medical Library, Early American Medical Imprints, 1668–1820, no. 1617.

3. "Lyceum," Philadelphia, March 12, 1811, WBR Papers, folder 1.

4. Patrick's fourth son, Robert Empie Rogers, adopted his middle name as a young man out of respect for Adam Empie, president of the College of William and Mary (1827–1836).

5. John Augustine Smith, president, College of William and Mary, 1814–1826.

6. WBR to JBR, December 22, 1819, *Life and Letters of William Barton Rogers* (hereafter cited as *Life and Letters)*, 1:17.

7. Probably Elisha DeButts (1773–1831).

8. JBR to WBR, 9 November 1821, *Life and Letters* 1:20–21.

9. Patrick Kerr Rogers, *An Introduction to the Mathematical Principles of Natural Philosophy, Adapted to the Use of Beginners; and Arranged More Particularly for the Convenience of the Junior Students of William & Mary College, Virginia.*

10. PKR to Thomas Jefferson, ca. 1823, *Life and Letters* 1:26. William's proofs published in Patrick's text: for Prop. 14, "If perpendiculars drawn from the same point to the directions of the elementary forces be inversely as those forces, that point will be in the direction of the resultants" (19); Prop. 35, "In similar motions compared with each other, the acquired velocities are as the spaces described in equal times from the beginning" (34–35); Prop. 68, "If several bodies are situated in the same right line, their common centre of inertia will so divide it, that the sum of the products of the masses and distances on one side = the sum of the similar products on the other side" (59–60); Prop. 93, "The distance of the centre of gravity of a triangle, from the centre of gravity of the base is to its distance from the vertex, as 1 to 2" (96).

11. Possibly Bryan Robinson, who in 1739 published his colleague Richard Helsham's *A Course of Lectures in Natural Philosophy*, one of the earliest texts to lay out the ideas of Bacon, Descartes, Boyle, Newton, and other scientists in a simple, straightforward way for university students; the text went into several editions, and portions were reprinted for use in university courses well into the nineteenth century.

12. French mathematicians Etienne Bézout (1739–1783) and Pierre-Simon Laplace (1749–1827).

13. PKR to Thomas Jefferson, March 14, 1824, *Life and Letters,* 1:30–31. First and second excision by Emma Rogers.

14. Ibid., 30. Also in 1824, coincidentally, a translation of Bézout's text was published for the use of students at Harvard College: *First Principles of the Differential and Integral Calculus: Or the Doctrine of Fluxions, Intended as an Introduction to the Physico-Mathematical Sciences* (Cambridge, Mass.: Hilliard & Metcalf, 1824).

15. PKR to WBR, October 17, 1825, *Life and Letters,* 1:32. The editorial notation "[teaching]" inserted by Emma Rogers.

16. WBR to PKR, November 3, 1826, ibid., 35.

17. Ibid., 35–36.

18. John E. Semmes, *John H. B. Latrobe and His Times, 1803–1891*, 413, 415.

19. *Life and Letters* 1:36–37.

20. WBR to PKR, January 25, 1827, ibid., 37–38.

21. Ibid., 39.

22. HDR to PKR, April 13, 1827, ibid., 42–43.

23. WBR to PKR, December 27, 1827, ibid., 46–47.

24. WBR to PKR, February 19, 1828, ibid., 48.

25. WBR to the Governors of the Maryland Institute, April 13, 1828, ibid., 49–50.

26. *Baltimore Commercial and Daily Advertiser*, April 21, 1828.

27. HDR to PKR, May 3, 1828, *Life and Letters,* 1:50.

28. *Baltimore Commercial and Daily Advertiser*, May 13, 1828.

29. WBR to PKR, May 12, 1828, *Life and Letters,* 1:51.

30. HDR to WBR, October 3, 1828, ibid., 60–61.

31. *Life and Letters,* 1:58.

32. WBR to HDR, December 6, 1828, ibid., 69.

33. Ewing, *Early Teaching of Science at the College of William and Mary in Virginia,* 24–25.

34. WBR to James Rogers, November 28, 1830, WBR Papers, folder 70. James Rogers, a brother of Patrick Rogers, is mentioned in *Life and Letters,* vol. 1, on pages 51, 65, 174, and 195. He is described as a Philadelphia merchant, "a gentleman of courtly and most agreeable manners." Emma Rogers says that the uncle played an important part in family affairs after the death of Patrick. At the end of his life, Uncle James lived with William for some years.

35. WBR to HDR, February 26, 1830, *Life and Letters* 1:85.

36. RER to WBR, November 15, 1833, ibid., 109.

37. HDR to James Rogers, July 27, 1834, Adams Collection. See also WBR to HDR, November 30, 1834, *Life and Letters,* 1: 112–113; WBR to J. C. Cabell, December 31, 1834, University of Virginia Archives.

38. *Geology of the Virginias, by the Late William B. Rogers, L.L.D.: A Reprint of Annual Reports and Other Papers on the Geology of the Virginias,* 754–756.

39. See "William Barton Rogers, First State Geologist of Virginia (1835–1841)"; Joseph K. Roberts, "William Barton Rogers and His Contribution to the Geology of Virginia"; Richard C. Sheridan, "William Barton Rogers and the Virginia Geological Survey, 1835–1842"; and Arthur Bevan, "William Barton Rogers, Pioneer American Scientist." Bevan, who was State Geologist of Virginia at the time he wrote the paper, focused almost entirely on Rogers's work in geology, despite the broader scope implied by his title. Russell Smith, Sketches of Albemarle County Scenes, 1844, Accession #9939, 9939a, University of Virginia Library, are drawings of the Rivanna River, Southwest Mountains, and Blue Ridge Mountains commissioned by Rogers as illustrations for his geological reports.

    For the Pennsylvania survey led by Henry Darwin Rogers, see Henry D. Rogers, *The Geology of Pennsylvania: A Government Survey: with a General View of the Geology of the United States, Essays on Coal-Formation and Its Fossils, and a Description of the Coal-Fields of North America and Great Britain.*

40. University of Virginia, Minutes, Rector and Visitors, vol. III, 1837–1855, 345. Information about the University of Virginia during Rogers's time there may be found in Dumas Malone, *Jefferson the Virginian*; Hofstadter and Smith, *American Higher Education, A Documentary History,* vol. 1; Herbert B. Adams, *Thomas Jefferson and the University of Virginia*; Bruce, *History of the*

University of Virginia, 1819–1919; and Roy J. Honeywell, *The Educational Work of Thomas Jefferson.*

41. Draft notes by WBR, "For the Establishment of a School of Arts. Memorial of the Franklin Institute of the State of Pennsylvania, for the Promotion of the Mechanic Arts, to the Legislature of Pennsylvania," n.d. [1837], WBR Papers, folder 14b.

42. Quoted in Bruce, 2:166.

43. Started as the Association of American Geologists; the term "Naturalists" was added in 1842. The role of the Rogers brothers in the early history of the American Association for the Advancement of Science is outlined in Sally Gregory Kohlstedt, Michael M. Sokal, and Bruce V. Lewenstein, *The Establishment of Science in America: 150 Years of the American Association for the Advancement of Science* (New Brunswick, N.J.: Rutgers University Press, 1999).

44. John L. Hayes, June 4, 1882, quoted in *Life and Letters,* 1:209–212.

45. Ibid., 233–234.

46. WBR to RER, September 11, 1841, ibid., 191–192.

47. HDR to WBR, April 30, 1843, ibid., 223.

48. Advertisement in the *Boston Daily Advertiser,* 1843, quoted in *Life and Letters,* 1:230.

49. HDR to WBR, March 8, 1846, ibid., 257–258.

50. WBR to HDR, March 13, 1846, ibid., 259.

51. WBR to HDR, March 21, 1846, ibid., 263.

52. WBR to HDR, March 13, 1846, ibid., 259–262; "A Plan for a Polytechnic School in Boston," ibid., 420–427.

53. "A Plan for a Polytechnic School in Boston," ibid., 426–427.

54. WBR to HDR, October 20, 1847, ibid., 277.

55. WBR to HDR, May 10, 1848, ibid., 286–287.

56. HDR to WBR, April 18, 1850, ibid., 313.

57. *Elements of Chemistry: Including the History of the Imponderables and the Inorganic Chemistry of the Late Edward Turner* (Philadelphia: Thomas, Cowperthwait & Co., 1846), 7th ed.; includes outlines of organic chemistry by William Gregory, with notes and additions by James B. Rogers and Robert E. Rogers.

Chapter Five HARVARD

1. *The Autobiography of Nathaniel Southgate Shaler,* 117; A. Hunter Dupree, *Asa Gray,* 149.

2. Morison, *Three Centuries of Harvard,* 29–31, 58; I. Bernard Cohen, *Some Early Tools of American Science,* 49.

3. Morison, *Three Centuries of Harvard,* 79–81.

4. Ibid., 92–93.

5. Cohen, 124–125.

6. I. Bernard Cohen, "Harvard and the Scientific Spirit," *Harvard Alumni Bulletin,* February 7, 1948, 393–398.

7. See Sanborn C. Brown, *Benjamin Thompson, Count Rumford*, from which this brief account is chiefly drawn.

8. Ibid., 11. Morison, *Three Centuries of Harvard* (93) states that Winthrop imparted "the first impulse to at least one greater American scientist than himself—Benjamin Thompson (Count Rumford), who described him as 'an excellent and happy teacher.'"

9. Brown, 174.

10. Ibid., 207–210. Brown believes that Rumford had told King he would not accept and, therefore, the letter of September 8 was "for the record." President Adams's letter of approval is reproduced in Charles Francis Adams, *The Works of John Adams* 8:660–661. King and Rumford letters are contained in George E. Ellis, *The Life of Count Rumford*, 351–358. Ellis dedicated this work to Jacob Bigelow as the first Rumford Professor, and, referring to MIT, the dedication contains the following statement: "Your published lectures, The Elements of Technology, have recently had the title which you assigned to them adopted by an Institution of highest promise with us in its field and objects. This Institution, also, you most happily inaugurated."

11. Brown, 208.

12. Morris Berman, *Social Change and Scientific Organization, The Royal Institution, 1799–1844*, 14 n. 52.

13. Brown, 225–227.

14. Ibid., 306.

15. This account of Jacob Bigelow is partly drawn from a memoir prepared for the Massachusetts Historical Society—George E. Ellis, *Memoir of Jacob Bigelow, M.D., LL.D.*. The memoir includes excerpts from an unfinished autobiographical account in which Bigelow states that he was simply a lecturer on materia medica at the time of his appointment to the Rumford chair. *The Historical Register of Harvard University, 1636–1936*, however, lists him as Professor of Materia Medica and Lecturer at the Medical School beginning in 1815.

16. "Jacob Bigelow," *Proceedings, AAcadAS* 14 (1878–1879): 333–342. This volume does not cite Holmes as the author, but he is mentioned in this connection by George E. Ellis, *Memoir*, 7.

17. Chester E. Stellhorn, M.D., "Jacob Bigelow, M.D., LL.D.," *New England Journal of Medicine* 213 (August 29, 1935): 406.

18. A copy in the Rare Book Collection of the MIT Libraries contains the bookplate of Henry D. Rogers, but it had originally belonged to his brother, James Blythe Rogers, whose signature appears on the title page.

19. Jacob Bigelow, *Elements of Technology*, iv, v.

20. Ibid., 1–2.

21. Shortly before the publication of *Elements of Technology*, Zachariah Allen of Rhode Island published *The Science of Mechanics, As Applied to the Present Improvements in the Useful Arts in Europe and the United States of America* (Providence, 1829). Allen, a graduate of Brown University, where he studied medicine, mechanics, chemistry, and physics, later studied law and passed the bar but turned to the textile business and became a successful wool and cotton manufacturer. He traveled extensively abroad, studying and observing textile manufacturing methods, and

his book also contains a comparative account of British and American practices: "Adapted as a Manual for Mechanics and Manufacturers" is its descriptive subtitle. It has been praised as a "significant book in the history of American engineering" and the first domestic work intended for "practical mechanics and manufacturers." Gary Kulik, Roger Parks, and Theodore Z. Penn, eds., *The New England Mill Village, 1790–1860* (Cambridge: MIT Press, 1982), 103.

However, Eugene S. Ferguson in his *Bibliography of the History of Technology* (62) categorizes the Allen and Bigelow books as "Handbooks or Compendia of Technology," characterizing Bigelow's as a "pretty thin potion" as compared to Oliver Evans's *The Young Millwright and Miller's Guide* (Philadelphia, 1795, 1st edition, being revised over the years with a 15th and final edition in 1860). Allen's he cites as "one of several books on the borderline between handbook and dictionary" but calls attention to the informative comparison of American and British manufacturing, and he credits Bigelow with acknowledging his indebtedness to a variety of sources.

22. Bigelow, *The Useful Arts*, iv–v.

23. Augustus Lowell, *Commemorative Address, June 3, 1890* (Cambridge, Mass.: John Wilson & Son, 1890), 3.

24. Henry G. Liddell and Robert Scott, *A Greek Lexicon*, rev. ed., Sir Henry S. Jones (Oxford: Clarendon Press, 1940; first published in 1843, many editions over the years); *The Oxford English Dictionary* (Oxford: Clarendon Press, 1961). An extensive essay on the history of the word "technic" is J. E. Heyde, "Zur Geschichte des Wortes 'Technik,'" *Humanismus und Technik* 9, no. 1 (December 19, 1963): 25–43.

25. *Glossographia: Or, a Dictionary Interpreting the Hard Words*, 4th ed. (London: Thomas Blount, 1674); E. Coles, *An English Dictionary* (London, 1685).

26. Edward Cocker, *Cocker's English Dictionary* (London: John Hawkins, 1704); John Kersey, *Dictionarium Anglo-Brittanicum*, 1708, a Scolar Press Facsimile (Menston, England: Scolar Press Limited, 1969); N. Bailey, *Dictionarium Britannicum, Or a More Compleat Universal Etymological English Dictionary Than Any Extant* (London, 1730; a first edition published in 1721).

27. *Grundsätze der deutschen Landwirtschaft*, 1769; *Anleitung zur Technologie*, 1772, 1777, and a number of other editions; *Entwurf der Allgemeine Technologie* (Göttingen, 1806). See also Wilhelm Franz Exner, Johann Beckmann, *Begrunder der technologischen Wissenschaft* (Vienna, 1878).

28. *Works of Jeremy Bentham,* 8:148.

29. Noah Webster, *A Compendious Dictionary of the English Language*, a facsimile of the first (1806) edition (Crown Publishers, 1970).

30. Noah Webster, *An American Dictionary of the English Language* (New York: S. Converse, 1828).

31. The following account is chiefly drawn from Morrill Wyman, M.D., "Memoir of Daniel Treadwell," in Centennial Vol. 11 of *Memoirs, AAcadAS*.

32. Ibid., 383.

33. Ibid., 488. Later, in 1871, Treadwell made a contribution to the American Academy for the preparation of an index of the works of Count Rumford.

34. Ibid., 441; MIT Corporation Records (AC 278), February 11, 1874. The current location of Treadwell's cannon is unknown.

35. *Bulletin of the Bussey Institution*, vol. 1, 1874–1876 (Cambridge, Mass.: John Wilson & Son), 2.

36. Ibid., 2–3.

37. Ibid., 4; William Morton Wheeler, "The Bussey Institution," in *The Development of Harvard University, 1869–1929*, ed. Samuel Eliot Morison, 508–509.

38. John M. Bullard, *The Rotches*, 409–410, 412; *Endowment Funds of Harvard University, June 30, 1947* (Cambridge, 1948), 299–300; Benjamin Lincoln Robinson, "Botany," in Morison, *Development of Harvard University*, 357–358.

39. Benjamin Peirce to Josiah Quincy, August 15, 1838, College Papers 9, HUA.

40. Henry Greenleaf Pearson, *Son of New England, James Jackson Storrow, 1864–1926*, 277. A brief account of the life of Charles Storer Storrow, the grandfather of James Jackson Storrow, is contained in the Appendix, 275–281.

41. Baldwin's father, Loammi, Sr., had obviously foreseen a technical career for his son, for as early as 1799 he had written to Count Rumford inquiring about the possibilities of an apprenticeship abroad with a mathematical and optical instrument maker for young Loammi, whose genius, he said, "inclines him strongly to cultivate the arts."

42. George L. Vose (Hayward Professor of Civil and Topographical Engineering in the Massachusetts Institute of Technology), *A Sketch of the Life and Works of Loammi Baldwin*, 26.

43. This brief account of Baldwin has been drawn both from Vose and from Frederick K. Abbott, *The Role of the Civil Engineer in Internal Improvements, The Contributions of the Two Loammi Baldwins, Father and Son, 1776–1838*. It should be noted that Abbott incorrectly cites James Storrow rather than Charles as "Baldwin's former student . . . who ten years later was one of the moving spirits behind the foundation of the scientific school in Harvard College," 218.

44. Vose, 13. The Baldwin Collection is now part of the Rare Book Collection of the MIT Libraries. Begun by the elder Baldwin, the collection at one time numbered some 4,000 volumes, half of which were later destroyed in a fire. The remainder, encompassing the natural and physical sciences, engineering, manufactures, and agriculture, plus architecture and building, was presented in 1899 by Loammi's niece to Woburn's town library with a provision allowing the books to be transferred to the Massachusetts Institute of Technology at the town's discretion. The transfer occurred in 1914. A Chester Harding portrait of the younger Baldwin came later to the Institute and now hangs in the MIT Museum.

45. Vose, 21–22.

46. College Records 8, August 16, 1838, HUA. The committee included President Josiah Quincy, Judge Joseph Story, and Judge Lemuel Shaw.

47. Peirce to Quincy, July 8, 1839, College Papers, 2d ser., 9, HUA.

48. College Records 8, July 9, 1839, HUA.

49. Ibid., April 25, 1840.

50. Noah Webster's *American Dictionary of the English Language* defines "literature" as "Learning; acquainted with letters or books. *Literature* comprehends a knowledge of the ancient languages, denominated classical, history, grammar, rhetoric, logic, geography, &c. as well as of the sciences. A knowledge of the world and good breeding give luster to *literature*."

51. College Records 8, December 27, 1845; Report of the Committee on the Scientific Department of the College, January 3, 1846, College Papers, 2d ser., 13, HUA.

52. Edmund Quincy, *Life of Josiah Quincy of Massachusetts*, 480–481.

53. Paul Revere Frothingham, *Edward Everett, Orator and Statesman*, 9–24.

54. Morison, *Three Centuries of Harvard*, 224–227, 234.

55. Frothingham, 115.

56. Ibid., 270.

57. College Records 8, January 3, 1846; February 5, 1846, HUA.

58. Morison, *Three Centuries of Harvard*, 276.

59. Ibid., 277.

60. Ibid., 280–281.

61. Edward Everett, *Orations and Speeches on Various Occasions*, 2d ed. (Boston: Charles C. Little & James Brown, 1850), 2:496–497.

62. Ibid. 1:616–617.

63. For President Everett and the Honourable, the Fellows of the Corporation of Harvard University, February 27, 1846, College Papers, 2d ser., 13, HUA.

64. Ibid.

Chapter Six THE LAWRENCE SCIENTIFIC SCHOOL AT HARVARD

1. Edward Everett Diary, February 5, 1846, MHS.

2. Robert Cantwell, *Nathaniel Hawthorne: The American Years*, 305–306; James R. Mellow, *Nathaniel Hawthorne in His Times*, 585. Among Hillard's publications are his five-volume edition of the poetical works of Edmund Spenser, a translation of Guizot's *Character and Influence of Washington*, a biography of George Ticknor, and, perhaps his best known work, *Six Months in Italy*.

3. Robert Chambers, *Vestiges of the Natural History of Creation* (London: J. Churchill, 1844; New York: Wiley & Putnam, 1845). Four editions within seven months attest to its popularity.

4. Owsei Temkin, "The Idea of Descent in Post-Romantic German Biology: 1848–1858," in *Forerunners of Darwin: 1745–1859*, ed. Bentley Glass, Owsei Temkin, and William L. Strauss, Jr. (Baltimore: Johns Hopkins Press, 1959), 345. See also Peter J. Bowler, *Evolution, the History of an Idea* (Berkeley & Los Angeles: University of California Press, 1984), 134–141.

5. Dupree, 145–146.

6. Whether Henry Rogers knew Robert Chambers at this time is not clear, though he could have met him during his stay in England in 1831–32. In 1857, however, in a letter from Edinburgh to his nephew William, the elder son of James Blythe Rogers, he mentioned a "most refreshing trip of a week through the Highlands with Mr. Robert Chambers." HDR to WBR II, August 6, 1857, WBR II Papers (MC 3), folder 7. This nephew has sometimes been referred to erroneously as William Barton Rogers, Jr.

7. Asa Gray to John Torrey, January 26, 1846, Torrey Correspondence, Torrey Herbarium, New York Botanical Garden. A mid-January letter from Gray to Joseph Henry, then at Princeton,

reveals that he had placed his name before a member of the Corporation as a worthy candidate for the Rumford, believing that he might be persuaded to come "for a consideration." At the end of the month Henry informed his brother of an "intimation from Harvard College that if I will accept the office I can be elected to the chair of Technology . . . something of a compliment since in Massachusetts they do not often consider much merit to exist beyond the Hudson." Though "some things" about the position seemed attractive, the salary was not one of them. In any case, Henry was reluctant to leave Princeton and had not given the idea "very serious thought." See *The Papers of Joseph Henry*, vol. 6, ed. Mark Rothenberg, 368–370, 371–372.

8. Dupree, 149.
9. *The Papers of Joseph Henry*, vol. 2, ed. Nathan Reingold, 290–291 n. 13. This note describes groups such as "the club" as "a stage in the development of the community of professional scientists."
10. Benjamin Peirce to Alexander Dallas Bache, January 29, 1846, Benjamin Peirce Papers, HLHU.
11. Some biographical notices of Morrill Wyman indicate that he had worked briefly in 1833, prior to attending medical school, as an assistant engineer on the construction of the Boston & Worcester Railroad. He maintained a medical practice in Cambridge and was interested in the "scientific aspects of medicine," ventilation, and surgical instrumentation. He would serve as a Harvard overseer from 1875 to 1887. Wyman's association with the Institute of Technology (vice president, 1863–1869) is not mentioned in *ACAB*, *NCAB*, and *DAB*. The latter does not mention his 1833 work on the Boston & Worcester Railroad.
12. Peirce to Bache, January 29, 1846, Peirce Papers, HLHU.
13. Bache to Peirce, February 2, 1846, Letters to the Treasurer 10, HUA.
14. In addition to those cited in the text, the collection includes letters from Franklin Bache, professor of chemistry, Jefferson Medical College, Philadelphia; J. W. Bailey, professor of chemistry and mineralogy at West Point; Clement C. Biddle, lawyer and economist, of Philadelphia; George B. Emerson, prominent Bostonian, naturalist, and educator; Horace Gray, brother of Francis Calley Gray; Edward Hitchcock, geologist and president of Amherst College; Matthew F. Maury of the Observatory in Washington; William McIlvaine of Philadelphia; William Gibbs McNeill, civil engineer, forwarded by F. F. Marbury, a New York lawyer; Samuel G. Morton, president of the Academy of Natural Sciences in Philadelphia; Daniel B. Smith, president of Haverford College; and Henry Vethake, professor of mathematics at the University of Pennsylvania. Ibid.
15. George Hillard to Benjamin Curtis, undated but probably early February 1846, as he enclosed a letter from William B. Rogers dated January 27. Ibid.
16. Ibid.
17. Ibid.
18. Ibid.
19. WBR to Hillard, January 27, 1846, ibid. Enclosed with undated letter, Hillard to Curtis.
20. WBR to J. W. Bailey, February 10, 1846. This letter from the Bailey papers at West Point was called to our attention (November 19, 1971) by Professor John B. Rae, formerly of MIT, then chairman of the Department of Humanities and Social Sciences at Harvey Mudd College.

21. WBR to James Hall, May 28, 1838. For a copy of this letter we are indebted to William Brokaw Rogers, Senior Scientist, Petrology, New York State Museum and Science Service (not related to William Barton Rogers).

22. *DAB*, s.v. "Horsford, Eben N."; Samuel Rezneck, "The European Education of an American Chemist and Its Influence in 19th-Century America: Eben Norton Horsford," *Technology and Culture* 11, no. 3 (July 1970): 368–369.

23. John Webster to Samuel Eliot, February 18, 1846, Letters to the Treasurer 10, HUA.

24. Webster to Everett, February 25, 1846, ibid.

25. Everett to Samuel Eliot, February 27, 1846, College Letters, Edward Everett 1, HUA.

26. HDR to WBR, March 8, 1846, *Life and Letters,* 1:256–257 (excisions by Emma Rogers).

27. JBR to WBR and RER, March 12, 1846, WBR Papers, folder 24.

28. WBR to HDR, March 13, 1846, *Life and Letters,* 1:259. A portion of this letter in WBR Papers, folder 24.

29. College Papers, 2d ser., 13, March 28, 1846, HUA.

30. WBR to HDR, July 17, 1846, *Life and Letters,* 1:266–267.

31. Eben Horsford to Everett, March 26, 1846, College Papers, 2d ser., 13, HUA. A similar letter of the same date was addressed to the Corporation; Everett to Horsford, May 13, 1846, College Letters, Edward Everett 1, HUA.

32. E.g., Hall to Webster, April 2, 1846, College Papers, 2d ser., 13, HUA.

33. Webster to Everett, May 15, 1846, College Papers, 2d ser., 13, HUA.

34. Everett Diary, July 27, 1846, MHS.

35. Joseph Lovering to Corporation, September 26, 1846, College Papers, 2d ser., 14, HUA.

36. Peirce to Everett, September 28, 1846, ibid.

37. Corporation Papers, November 28, 1846; and College Records 8, same date, HUA; Everett to Liebig, November 28, 1846, Everett Letters, MHS.

38. Everett Diary, January 6, 7, & 11, 1847, MHS.

39. JBR to HDR, January 27, 1847, WBR Papers, folder 26; Everett Diary, January 27, 1847, MHS.

40. JBR to HDR, February 6, 1847, WBR Papers, folder 26; Report of the Committee on the Scientific School, January 30, 1847, College Papers, 2d ser., 14, HUA; Corporation Papers, February 13, 1847, HUA; Everett Diary, February 18, 1847, MHS.

41. Everett Diary, January 12, 1847, MHS. In June Everett sent a letter to Henry Rogers relating to a book review for the *North American Review*. He made no reference to the Rumford chair or the Scientific School. Everett to H. D. Rodgers [*sic*], June 3, 1847, Everett Letters, MHS.

42. Gray to Torrey, February 20, 1847, Torrey Correspondence, Torrey Herbarium, New York Botanical Garden.

43. Dupree, 248. Mention of the "distinguished" Rogers family usually refers to the four brothers, of whom James was the eldest. He had died in 1852, however, and William was the eldest of the three survivors.

44. Scientific School of the University at Cambridge, January 30, 1847, College Papers, 2d ser., 14.

45. Everett Diary, January 29, 1848, MHS.

46. James Walker to Everett, January 20, 1847, College Papers, 2d ser., 14, HUA.

47. Corporation Papers, February 27, 1847, and College Records 8, March 13, 1847, HUA.

48. Everett to Jared Sparks, May 13, 1847, College Letters, Edward Everett 1, HUA.

49. Sparks to Everett, May 15, 1847, College Papers, 2d ser., 14, HUA. In 1849 Sparks would succeed Everett as president and serve until 1853.

50. Everett Diary, May 29, 1847, MHS.

51. Everett to Dr. Holland, July 30, 1847, Everett Letters, MHS.

52. Everett to Horsford, February 19, 1847, College Letters, Edward Everett 1, HUA.

53. College Records 8, March 27 & April 24, 1847, HUA.

54. Corporation Papers, June 7, 1847, HUA. The meeting was attended by Shaw, Walker, Curtis, and Eliot. Lowell was not there, nor Everett, absent because of a dinner engagement in Medford, according to his diary. Everett did send a letter to Eliot expressing his pleasure in "Mr. Lawrence's liberality." College Letters, Edward Everett 1.

55. Everett to Abbott Lawrence, June 8, 1847, College Letters, Edward Everett 1, HUA.

56. Everett Diary, June 9, 1847, MHS.

57. *DAB*, s.v. "Lawrence, Abbott"; Hamilton Andrews Hill, *Memoir of Abbott Lawrence* (Boston, 1883).

58. See Pearson, *Son of New England*, 279; "Mr. Charles S. Storrow and the Lawrence Scientific School," letter by John R. Freeman, *Engineering News* (September 1, 1892), 207; Freeman's letter was prompted by "The Lawrence Scientific School," *Engineering News* (May 5, 1892), 459–461, no. 8 in an extended series, "The Engineering Schools of the United States."

59. Pearson, *Son of New England*, 277.

60. Ibid., 277–279.

61. Lawrence to Samuel Eliot, June 7, 1847, College Papers, 2d ser., 15, HUA. It is interesting to note Lawrence's reference to the concepts of mind and hand, later to be a hallmark of the Massachusetts Institute of Technology.

62. Lawrence to Samuel Eliot, June 7, 1847.

63. Everett Diary, June 12 & 14, 1847, MHS.

64. Everett to Samuel Eliot, June 23, 1847, College Letters, Edward Everett 1, HUA.

65. Samuel Eliot to Everett, July 8, 1847, College Papers, 2d ser., 15, HUA; Everett Diary, July 17, 1847, MHS.

66. Lawrence to Samuel Eliot; Lawrence to the President and Fellows of Harvard College, both July 19, 1847, College Papers, 2d ser., 15, HUA.

67. Everett Diary, August 16, 1847, MHS.

68. Everett to Lawrence, August 19, 1847, College Letters, Edward Everett 1, HUA.

69. College Papers, 2d ser., 15, August 25, 1847, HUA; Everett Diary, August 25, 1847, MHS. Lawrence's name survived until 1906, when the Lawrence Scientific School was superseded by a newly established Graduate School of Applied Science. Several years later, in 1913, with funds donated for the support of the Scientific School by his sons Abbott and James, gradu-

ates of Harvard College in 1849 and 1850 respectively, the Corporation established in their honor an Abbott and James Lawrence Professorship of Chemistry and a similar Professorship in Engineering. Hector James Hughes, "Engineering and Other Applied Sciences in the Harvard Engineering School and its Predecessors, 1847–1929," in Morison, *Development of Harvard University*, 428; *Historical Register of Harvard University*, 59.

70. Corporation Papers, August 21, 1847, HUA; *List of Students of the Lawrence Scientific School, 1847–1898* (Cambridge, 1899), [3].

71. Everett to Holland, June 15, 1847, Everett Letters, MHS.

72. *Life and Letters,* 1:272.

73. College Records 9, September 25, 1847, HUA.

74. Everett to William Gillespie, November 20 & 22, 1846, College Letters, Edward Everett 1; Everett Diary, November 26, 1846, MHS; Eliphalet Nott to Everett, December 4, 1846, College Papers, 2d ser., 14; Gillespie to Everett, February 8, 1847, Corporation Papers; Everett to Gillespie, February 10, 1847, College Letters, Edward Everett 1; Gillespie to Everett, June 11, 1847, Corporation Papers; Alonzo Potter to Lawrence, June 13, 1847, Letters to the Treasurer 10; Alexander H. Everett, Jr., for Edward Everett, to Gillespie, June 15, 1847, College Letters, Edward Everett 1; Gillespie to Everett, August 13, 1847, Letters to the Treasurer 10; all HUA except as noted.

75. Everett to Holland, June 15, 1847, Everett Letters, MHS; Freeman letter, *Engineering News*, 207.

76. Clark A. Elliott, *Biographical Dictionary of American Scientists: The Seventeenth through the Nineteenth Centuries*, s.v., "Courtenay, Edward H."

77. Samuel Eliot to Everett, August 10, 1847, Corporation Papers, HUA; Everett Diary, August 16, 1847, MHS; Edward Courtenay to Samuel Eliot, August 28, 1847, Letters to the Treasurer 10, HUA. Henry Rogers knew in late June that Courtenay had been approached, felt that he would be well qualified, but correctly assumed that the salary would make it difficult for him to accept. The editors of *Life and Letters,* (1:272–273) considered that "the man naturally sought for to fill it [the engineering professorship], and regarded as 'well qualified,' was a university professor of Mathematics, who had had no other engineering experience than that of a West Point graduate." The editors err with respect to Courtenay's experience, however, which included several engineering projects, among them Fort Adams in Rhode Island and Fort Independence in Boston, along with a period at the Brooklyn Dry Dock as chief engineer, and a year with the New York & Erie Railroad. See *NCAB* 5, 519–520, s.v. "Courteney [*sic*], Edward H."

78. Letters to the Treasurer 10, October 23, 1847, HUA; College Records 9, September 21, 1848, HUA.

79. Samuel Eliot to Everett, January 21, 1848, College Papers, 2d ser., 15; Everett to Peirce, January 31, 1848, and Everett to Charles Beck, College Letters, Edward Everett 2; Cornelius C. Felton, January 31, 1848, College Letters, Edward Everett 2; LSS Faculty Records, February 8, 1848; all HUA; Everett Diary, January 29, 1848, MHS.

80. Everett to Sir Charles Lyell, February 11, 1848, Everett Letters, MHS.

81. Everett Diary, November 11, 1847, MHS.

82. Hillard to HDR, December 29, 1847, loose letter among volumes of Journals of George S. Hillard, MHS.

83. Everett to Samuel Eliot, December 11, 1847, College Letters, Edward Everett 1, HUA.

84. Everett Diary, March 31, 1848, MHS.

85. Ibid., May 12, 1848; August 28, 1848.

86. February 26, 1848, College Records 9, HUA.

87. Everett Diary, October 9 & 13, 1848, MHS; Everett to Louis Agassiz, October 12 & 20, 1848, College Letters, Edward Everett 2, HUA.

88. Everett to Dr. Walker, presumably James Walker of the Corporation, July 1, 1848, Everett Letters, MHS.

89. Faculty to Everett, January 12, 1849; Everett to Faculty, January 15, 1849, Edward Everett Correspondence, MHS.

90. Agassiz to Lawrence, July 15, 1849, College Papers, 2d ser., 17, HUA.

91. Ibid.

92. Lawrence to Samuel Eliot, September 20, 1849, College Papers, 2d ser., 17, HUA.

93. Ibid.

94. Sparks to Henry Eustis, October 2, 1849, College Letters, Jared Sparks 3; College Records 9, September 29, 1849; College Papers, 2d ser., 17, October 6, 1849, HUA; *DAB*, s.v. "Eustis, Henry L."

95. For an account of the Webster-Parkman affair, see Morison, *Three Centuries of Harvard*, 282–286.

96. JBR to HDR, January 19, 1850, WBR Papers, folder 30; College Papers, 2d ser., 18, January 16, 1851.

97. Morison, *Three Centuries of Harvard*, 293. A discussion of the events of this period, 286–293.

98. House no. 164, April 1850, 2, 3; College Papers, 2d ser., 17, HUA.

99. Ibid., 4.

100. Emerson to Samuel Eliot, February 27, 1846, on Rogers, and Webster to Samuel Eliot, February 18, 1846, on Horsford, Letters to the Treasurer 10; Eliphalet Nott, December 4, 1846, on Gillespie, College Papers, 2d ser., 14, HUA.

101. House no. 164, 9.

102. Ibid., 12–14.

103. Morison, *Three Centuries of Harvard*, 289.

104. Ibid., 286.

105. Samuel Eliot to Sparks, April 6, 1849, College Papers, 2d ser., 16, HUA.

106. Morison, *Three Centuries of Harvard*, 280. For a discussion of his teaching methods, see James David Teller, "The Manner and Method of Agassiz' Teaching," in *Louis Agassiz, Scientist and Teacher*, chap. 4.

107. H. J. Hughes, "Engineering," 416.

108. William Dallam Armes, ed., *The Autobiography of Joseph LeConte*, 141.

109. Runkle's acknowledgment of honorary master of arts degree, December 27, 1851, College Papers, 2d ser., HUA. The two other recipients of bachelor's degrees in 1851 were David A. Wells, A.B., Williams, 1847, and LeConte's cousin, William Louis Jones, A.B., University of Georgia, 1845, and M.D., College of Physicians and Surgeons, New York, 1848.

110. H. J. Hughes, "Engineering," 417–418.

111. E. N. Horsford, Report to the Committee of Conference on the part of the President and Fellows of Harvard College, April 26, 1854, College Papers, 2d ser., 21, HUA.

112. Agassiz to Walker, September 28, 1854, College Papers, 2d ser., 21, HUA. The official name of the Jardin des Plantes is Musée National d'Histoire Naturelle.

113. Sparks to President Walker, February 12, 1855, College Papers, 2d ser., 22, HUA.

114. Visiting Committee Report to President Walker, March 3, 1855, College Papers, 2d ser., 22, and another, April 26, 1856, 2d ser., 23.

115. H. J. Hughes, "Engineering," 418.

116. HDR to WBR, February 27, 1848, Rogers Family Papers, 1811–1904 (MC 2), folder 19.

Chapter Seven PRE-HISTORIC ANNALS OF THE INSTITUTE

1. Hamilton Andrews Hill, "Memoir of the Hon. Marshall P. Wilder, Ph.D., LL.D." (Boston, 1888), 10. Reprinted from the *New England Historical and Genealogical Register*, July 1888.

2. The personal information about Baker is drawn largely from Leslie G. Crumbaker, *The Baker Estate or Ridge Hill Farms of Needham*. This piece is not historically correct with respect to the founding of MIT.

3. Hill, 10–11.

4. Ibid., 11.

5. Building Committee Minutes, BSNH, Museum of Science Archives, pages mostly unnumbered. The early part of these "minutes" is in the nature of a narrative report and some entries also appear to be summaries rather than ordinary minutes.

6. *Address of His Excellency Nathaniel P. Banks to the Two Branches of the Legislature of Massachusetts*, January 7, 1859, Senate no. 1 (Boston, 1859), 30–31.

7. Ibid., 25.

8. Ibid., 26.

9. George B. Emerson, *Education in Massachusetts: Early Legislation and History* (Boston: John Wilson & Son, 1869), 32.

10. Ibid., 32–33 (excision by Emerson).

11. Ibid., 33. The funds used had come from two sources: the United States, representing payment for disbursements relating to military services rendered by Massachusetts in the War of 1812; and the sale of state lands in Maine as a result of the 1820 act which effected the separation of Maine from Massachusetts, legislation which provided that state lands in Maine would be equally divided between the two states. See Louis C. Hatch, "Separation of Maine,

1784–1820," 548–580, in *Commonwealth History of Massachusetts*, ed. Albert B. Hart (New York: States History Co., 1929), 3:577. In 1854 the fund reached $1.5 million through the addition of state shares in the Western Railroad Corporation.

12. Ibid., 33–34.

13. Ibid., 34.

14. *Address of His Excellency Nathaniel P. Banks*, 31–33.

15. One biographer of Agassiz agrees on this point: "Early in January, 1859 . . . an ex officio member of the Board of Overseers, Governor Nathan [*sic*] Banks, took the first step in securing public support for the new institution. His annual address to the legislature of Massachusetts contained a strong recommendation for state financial support for the Harvard museum, an appeal that testified to the cumulative effect of years of public pleading on Agassiz's part." Edward Lurie, *Louis Agassiz, a Life in Science*, 228–229. For Agassiz and the Museum of Comparative Zoology, see chapter 6, 212–251, from which this account is largely drawn, except where otherwise noted.

16. *Address of His Excellency Nathaniel P. Banks*, 7.

17. *Memorial to the Legislature of Massachusetts*, in relation to a Conservatory of Art and Science, March 9, 1859, House no. 260.

18. *Proceedings at a Banquet Given by His Friends to the Honorable Marshall Pinckney Wilder* (Cambridge, Mass.: University Press, 1883), 69. The occasion was Wilder's eighty-fifth birthday. On February 7, 1884, Wilder presented to the Massachusetts Institute of Technology an inscribed copy from "its sincere friend."

19. *Proceedings, BSNH* 7 (January 19 & February 2, 1859): 23, 26; Building Committee Minutes, BSNH.

20. *Proceedings, BSNH* 7 (February 2 & 16, 1859): 28, 30.

21. James M. Barnard had been a member of the first committee. He devoted most of his life to public service and charitable activities, but he was a student of Agassiz and for a period of several years enrolled in the Lawrence Scientific School from 1854, when he was thirty-five years old, until 1860. Biographical notice, *Proceedings, AAcadAS* 39 (1904): 838; *List of Students of the Lawrence Scientific School, 1847–1898* (Cambridge, 1899), 128.

    Dr. Cabot's son, Godfrey Lowell Cabot, would be a member of the class of 1881 at the Massachusetts Institute of Technology and serve on the Corporation from 1930 to 1935 and again from 1936 to 1962. In 1949 in a letter to Dr. Karl T. Compton, he noted that he had been introduced to William Barton Rogers as a young boy and that he had been "impressed by his very scholarly features." He was under the impression that Rogers had come to discuss plans for the Institute, but it is more likely that the two were discussing the plans of the Natural History Society, since Samuel Cabot was concerned only with the society's participation in the petition for the Back Bay land. G. L. Cabot to Compton, January 14, 1949, MIT Office of the President, Records, 1930–1959, box 43, folder 14. Thomas D. Cabot, Godfrey's son, became a Corporation member in 1946 and Thomas's son, Louis Wellington Cabot, was elected in 1963.

22. *Life and Letters,* 2:3–9.

23. Printed record of the meeting, [February 18, 1859], WBR Papers, folder 33.

24. Ibid. All or part of this account also appeared in the *Boston Daily Advertiser,* the *Daily Evening Traveller,* and the *Conservatory Journal.*

25. John Philbrick alluded to a "grand plan" of such a school formed by Dr. Henry Barnard, chancellor of the University of Wisconsin. A history of the university contains no reference to plans for a polytechnic institute at that time, though there was legislative pressure in 1858 for a reorganization of the institution and a more practical and utilitarian curriculum, a reorganization that proved to be more nominal than substantive. In January 1859 Barnard had accepted the position of chancellor. But his tenure there was brief, and his resignation, submitted in the summer of 1860, was accepted in January 1861. He had "never assumed active management of the University, and only a few transitory changes can be traced to his administration, none of fundamental importance." His failure there has been attributed to "his bad health, his unwillingness to give up his multifarious activities, and the desperate financial condition of the University." Merle Curti and Vernon Carstensen, *The University of Wisconsin, 1848–1925* 1:113, 168, 169. The history contains a passing reference to a museum of practical science but no further information.

26. Walter Muir Whitehill, *A Topographical History of Boston,* 2d ed., 156, 269 n. 22.

27. To the Honorable Senate and House of Representatives, in General Court Assembled, February 25, 1859, WBR Papers, folder 33.

28. *Transactions of the Massachusetts Horticultural Society* (1859): 149. The remaining members were Josiah Stickney, Samuel Walker, C. M. Hovey, and W. C. Strong.

29. This committee would later be referred to as the Reservation Committee and eventually as the Committee of Associated Institutions.

30. As reproduced in the printed record of the second meeting relating to the proposed Conservatory of Art and Science held on March 11, 1859, WBR Papers, folder 33.

31. *Boston Daily Journal, Daily Evening Traveller,* March 10; *Boston Daily Advertiser,* March 11, 1859.

32. Printed record, meeting of March 11, 1959.

33. Ibid.; accounts also appeared in the *Boston Courier* on March 14, and in the *Conservatory Journal* on April 9, 1859.

34. Ibid.

35. *Daily Evening Traveller,* March 18, 1859; also in the *Advertiser,* same date.

36. *Boston Journal,* March 15, 1859.

37. MIT History, Charter folder, MIT Museum.

38. *Boston Traveller,* March 23, 1859.

39. *Boston Transcript,* March 18, 1859.

40. Ibid., March 22, 1859.

41. *Boston Journal,* March 31, 1859.

42. *Boston Transcript,* April 5, 1859.

43. *Acts and Resolves of the General Court, 1859,* Chapter 154, Massachusetts State Library.

44. *Conservatory of Art and Science*, House no. 260, March 30, 1859, 2, 3.
45. Ibid., 3.
46. Ibid., 5–6.
47. Ibid., 7–8.
48. Ibid., 8.
49. *Boston Traveller*, March 28, 29, 31, & April 8, 1859.
50. *Boston Journal*, May 9, 1859.
51. *Boston Transcript*, April 12, 1859. No continuous record of such meetings has been found.
52. *Conservatory of Art and Science* (containing Joint Special Committee Report, March 30, 1859, House no. 260; Memorial to the Legislature, minus March 9, 1859, date and names of petitioning committee; and added comments, undated, with names of reconstituted committee), 11–12. Though the complete pamphlet contains no date, events of that spring relating to Baker indicate that it was probably issued sometime after May 4.
53. *Conservatory Journal* 1, no. 1 (April 9, 1859), MHS. *TR* 4 (April 1902): 138–169, contains an article entitled "The Conservatory Journal," with excerpts.
54. *Conservatory Journal* 1, no. 2 (April 23, 1859).
55. *Boston Journal*, April 26, 1859.
56. Building Committee Minutes, BSNH.
57. As reproduced in *TR* 4, 162–163; also appeared in *Boston Advertiser, Journal, Traveller,* and *Transcript*, May 7, 1859. A printed version of the special notice is in the WBR Papers, folder 33. It may have received wider distribution than the available records indicate. In a letter to Marshall Wilder dated May 30, 1859, Baker asked if the "Committee endorsed the sending of their peculiar Special notice—in circular form to various prominent gentlemen and Scientific Societies in the State." Baker to Wilder, May 30, 1859, WBR Papers, folder 33.
58. *Boston Journal*, May 7, 1859.
59. Ibid.; also in *Transcript* and *Traveller* and *TR* 4, 162–163.
60. *Conservatory Journal* 1, nos. 3 & 4 (May 7, 1859).
61. Ibid.
62. *Boston Daily Journal*, May 9, 1859.
63. *Conservatory Journal* 5. Two identical copies at the Massachusetts Historical Society bear different dates—May 14 and May 21, 1859.

Years later, in 1902, MIT received from the estate of John D. Philbrick documents relating to Baker's Conservatory of Art, Science, and Historical Relics, and an extensive article was prepared for the *Technology Review*. James Phinney Munroe, a graduate of the Institute in 1882 and editor of the *Review* from 1889 to 1908, ascribed the ultimate failure of Baker's efforts to "the opposition of those who believed Baker's methods unwise and the insufficiency of support from those who thought them wise. It is not for a later generation to pass judgment upon this enterprise. Most of the great objects for which it stood ... have been accomplished in far greater measure and perfection than he could have possibly foreseen. It is no more than just to believe that this *Conservatory Journal*, in its short and checkered life, contributed its part toward building up that public opinion without the support of which an enterprise of such magnitude as this can never be established." (Record of the meetings of the Publication Committee, Association of Class Secretaries, 1900–1907, January 13, 1902 [AC 41], box 1.) Munroe opened his article by claiming priority for the *Conservatory Journal* as the first of an "honorable line of Institute periodicals," rather than the *Spectrum*, a student publication in 1873–74. But the weight of the evidence points otherwise, for Baker's large scheme and his publication could claim at best only a tenuous connection with the real effort to found an Institute of Technology. After seven issues, two combined into one paper, the *Conservatory Journal*, with a final printing of June 18, 1859, disappeared.

Munroe would have a long connection with the Institute. Following graduation in 1882 he became an assistant to President Francis Amasa Walker and two years later, secretary of the faculty. In 1889 he left to join his father in business but at the same time became managing editor of the *Technology Review*, serving until 1908. In 1909 he was elected a life member of the Corporation. Harry W. Tyler, Class of 1884, "James P. Munroe, '82 (1862–1929)," *TR* 31 (March 1929): 273–274.

64. Whitehill, 156.
65. Baker to Wilder, May 30, 1859.
66. Much later, Baker acquired a considerable amount of property in the Needham-Wellesley area and embarked upon a large project known as the Ridge Hill Farms—described as a "great Educational Amusement Park, Formal Gardens and Art Exhibit" and an "amazing combination of wealth, and second-hand odds and ends; of imported works of art, and displays of picks, shovels and old wheel hubs; of extensive live animal exhibits, and a dead bear buried with great ceremony in a solid-copper casket." Crumbaker, iii.
67. Resolution on the death of M. D. Ross, presented by Professor John D. Runkle, Corporation Records 4, December 14, 1892. Biographical information obtained from *John Hamilton Ross, 1860–1931*, a privately printed volume loaned by Thorvald S. Ross, Jr., a grand-nephew of M. D. Ross.
68. John M. Ordway to William B. Allbright (Class of 1878), January 17, 1882, enclosed in E. P. Collier (Class of 1878) to Isaac Litchfield (Class of 1885), March 15, 1917. Litchfield was editor of *Technology Review* from 1908 to 1917. MIT Office of the President, Records, 1897–1930 (AC 13). A partial and not completely accurate copy of the Ordway letter is in the records of the MIT Office of the President, Records, 1930–1959, box 145, folder 4.
69. *Life and Letters,* 2:3.
70. WBR to HDR, February 8, 1859, ibid., 4.
71. WBR to HDR, February 14, 1859, ibid., 4–5. The "cruciform structure" refers to the building proposed by Baker.
72. WBR to HDR, February 22, 1859, ibid., 5.
73. WBR to HDR, April 4, 1859, ibid., 8–9.
74. Building Committee Minutes, BSNH; WBR to HDR, November 1, 1859, *Life and Letters,* 2:15; WBR to HDR, January 2, 1860, ibid., 19.

75. Board of Visitors Minutes, June 30, 1859, University of Virginia Archives. No correspondence has been found, either in the MIT Archives or at the University of Virginia, related to William B. Rogers and this chair.

76. Bruce, 3:52. Bruce does not mention that Rogers was nominated.

77. HDR to WBR, July 15, 1859, *Life and Letters,* 2:10–11 (excision by Emma Rogers).

78. S.B., 1854, Lawrence Scientific School; later Assistant Professor of Zoology, 1860–1865.

79. Agassiz to Walker, June 9, 1859, College Papers, 2d ser., 26, HUA.

80. Kneeland to WBR, October 8, 1878; Kneeland to the Corporation, November 13, 1878, WBR Papers, folders 83 & 85.

81. Kneeland to Holman, December 28, 1885, Silas W. Holman Papers (MC 46), box 1, History of MIT folder.

Chapter Eight AN AUXILIARY TO THE CAUSE OF EDUCATION

1. November 2, 1859, Building Committee Minutes, BSNH. This states that one of the squares would be sought for the "proposed Institute of Technology," undoubtedly an anachronism, which tends to confirm that portions of these "minutes" were prepared later as summary accounts.

2. WBR to HDR, November 1, 1859, *Life and Letters,* 2:15.

3. WBR to HDR, January 2, 1860, ibid., 19. On January 9 the *Transcript* reported that this memorial had been submitted to the legislature by Marshall Wilder.

4. House no. 13, January 1860, WBR Papers, folder 182. A copy in a collection of documents collected by Charles R. Cross also bears a notation attributing authorship to Rogers. The *Boston Advertiser,* January 28, 1860, published House no. 13 under the heading "A Polytechnic School," though the latter was mentioned only briefly in the memorial. House no. 13 is also reproduced in *Life and Letters,* 2:403–418.

5. House no. 13, 14.

6. Waterston to WBR, February 22, 1860, WBR Papers, folder 35.

7. Building Committee Minutes, BSNH, entry dated November 2; The Reverend Andrew P. Peabody, "The Unitarians in Boston," in *The Memorial History of Boston,* ed. Justin Winsor 3:480; Charles K. Dillaway, "Education, Past and Present," in Winsor, 4:268.

8. Biographical notice, *Proceedings, AAcadAS* 15 (1879–1880): 378. Information about Bigelow is also drawn from *DAB* and *NCAB*; John S. Ewing and Nancy P. Norton, *Broadlooms and Business Men,* 15–20, 61–65; and *Biographical Encyclopaedia of Massachusetts of the Nineteenth Century* (New York: Metropolitan Publishing & Engraving Co., 1879), 114–123. In a 1912 reference to the development of the Institute, President Richard C. Maclaurin would refer to "the days when it was founded by the practical efforts of Bigelow, Beebe, and other public-spirited merchants of fifty years ago." Maclaurin to Jerome Jones, May 2, 1912, MIT Office of the President, Records, 1897–1930, folder 103.

9. Erastus B. Bigelow, *Remarks on the Depressed Condition of Manufactures in Massachusetts,* 28.

10. Corporation Records 3, December 10, 1879.

11. House no. 13, January 1860.

12. Ibid., 3–5.

13. Ibid., 6.

14. Ibid., 7.

15. Ibid., 7–8.

16. Ibid., 2, 9–10.

17. Ibid., 11–12.

18. Ibid., 2, 12–13.

19. Ibid., 12.

20. Ibid., 2, 13–14.

21. *Transactions of the Massachusetts Horticultural Society* 4, Annual Meeting (January 1860): 122.

22. *Boston Advertiser,* January 16 & February 21, 1860.

23. Hand copies and copy, newspaper clipping, n.d., WBR Papers, folder 35; reproduced in *Life and Letters,* 2: app. A, 419–423. The State Teachers' Association does not appear here but is included with the others in *An Account of the Proceedings Preliminary to the Organization of the Massachusetts Institute of Technology; with a List of the Members Thus Far Associated, and An Appendix, Containing Petitions and Resolutions in Aid of the Objects of the Committee of Associated Institutions of Science and Art* [*sic*] (Boston, 1861), 15–23 (hereafter cited as *Account of the Proceedings*).

24. WBR to HDR, January 17, 1860, *Life and Letters,* 2:19.

25. WBR to HDR, January 30, 1860, ibid., 19–20.

26. Address by William B. Rogers before a Legislative Educational Meeting, February 16, 1860. A clipping from the *Boston Journal* in the Rogers Papers contains an extensive account of Rogers's address, and though labeled February 16, 1860, it obviously appeared after the occasion. WBR Papers, folder 238.

27. House no. 119, Report of the Joint Standing Committee on Education, February 23, 1860, 1–2.

28. Ibid., 2.

29. Ibid., 2–3; *Eighth Annual Report of the Commissioners on the Back Bay*, Public Document no. 12, October 14, 1859, 11, 9; *Ninth Annual Report of the Commissioners*, Public Document no. 18, October 15, 1860, with supplement, December 1, 1860, 2. The supplementary report covered sales since the issuance of the annual report and indicated that an initial distribution would be made in August 1861 to Agassiz's Museum of Comparative Zoology and other institutions included in Chapter 154 of the *Acts and Resolves* of 1859. If no further sales were completed by that date, Agassiz's share would amount to $20,000.

30. Accompanying *Resolve*, House no. 119, 4–5.

31. *Boston Traveller*, March 16; *Boston Advertiser*, March 17, 1860.

32. Senate no. 186, April 1859. *Boston Transcript* reported on February 27, 1860, that hearings would be held on the following Friday.

33. George Snelling, *Proposed Modification of the Plan of Building on the Back Bay Territory*, v–vi.

34. *Boston Advertiser*, March 23, 1860.

35. *Boston Advertiser*, March 23, 24, & 26; *Boston Transcript*, March 22, 23, 28, & April 2; *Boston Traveller*, April 4, 1860.

36. WBR to HDR, March 30, 1860, *Life and Letters,* 2:29.

37. *Boston Advertiser*, March 23, 1860.

38. *Boston Transcript*, March 23, 1860.

39. Building Committee Minutes, BSNH, entry of November 2, 1860, reviewing the events of that year.

40. *Boston Traveller*, May 12, 1860.

41. *Boston Transcript*, May 30, 1860; WBR to HDR, May 29, 1860, *Life and Letters,* 2:34.

42. Kneeland to WBR, January 30, 1861, *Life and Letters,* 2:36.

43. *DAB*, s.v. "Emerson, George B."; Biographical notice, *Proceedings, AAcadAS* 16 (1880–1881): 427–429; Corporation Records 3, May 18, 1881.

44. [MIT], "Incorporators," comp. Charles F. Read (Class of 1874), MIT Archives.

45. William Endicott, "Charles Henry Dalton," *TR* 10 (April 1908): 149–152.

46. *Account of the Proceedings*, 3.

47. WBR to HDR, May 29, 1860, *Life and Letters,* 2:34.

48. Charles Darwin, *On the Origin of Species by Means of Natural Selection, or The Preservation of Favoured Races in the Struggle for Life* (London: J. Murray, 1859); *Proceedings, BSNH* (February 15, 1860): 231–235; (March 7, 1860): 241–245; (March 21, 1860): 246–252; (April 4, 1860): 271–275. See Lurie, chapter 7; Dupree, chapter 15.

49. WBR to HDR, April 3, 1860, typed copy, WBR Papers, folder 35.

50. Edward J. Pfeifer, "United States," in *The Comparative Reception of Darwinism*, ed. Thomas F. Glick, 178. This piece includes a detailed account of the debates. See also David N. Livingstone, *Nathaniel Southgate Shaler and the Culture of American Science*, 24–25.

51. Excerpts from WBR to HDR, February 21, 1860, typed copy, WBR Papers, folder 35; a partial version of this letter appears in *Life and Letters,* 2:22–23.

52. Extract from a letter of WBR to his brother Henry, June 12, 1860, copy in the hand of Emma Rogers, WBR Papers, folder 35.

53. Livingstone, 105, 116–117.

54. Rogers Family Papers, folder 34.

55. "Bibliography of William Barton Rogers," in Robert R. Shrock, *Geology at M.I.T. 1865–1965: A History of the First Hundred Years of Geology at Massachusetts Institute of Technology* 1:199–201. Shrock lists 31 papers by Rogers published between 1859 and 1861.

56. WBR to HDR, March 30, 1860, *Life and Letters,* 2:30 (excisions by Emma Rogers).

57. Jules Marcou, *Life, Letters and Works of Louis Agassiz* 2:109.

58. Livingstone, 117.

Chapter Nine FACTS OF THE FOUNDING

1. See *Proceedings, AAAS* 14 (Cambridge, Mass., 1861), Physiology section, "Some Experiments and Inferences in Regards to Binocular Vision," 187–192; "On Our Inability from the Retinal Impression Alone to Determine Which Retina is Impressed," 192–198. Rogers was requested to present a report at the next meeting on the "Present State of the Theory of Binocular Vision." He presented three additional papers, listed among those for which titles were published, 225–227: in the Mathematics and Physics section, "On the Actinism of the Electric Discharge in Vacuum Tubes"; in Natural History, "Jottings on the Geology of the Eastern Part of Maine, Etc.," and "On the Recent Discovery, by Mr. Norman Eastop, of Fossils in the Conglomerate of Taunton River."

2. WBR to HDR, September 24, 1860, *Life and Letters,* 2:41.

3. Augustus Lowell, *Commemorative Address*, 3. Graduation Exercises, twenty–five years after the opening of the Institute's school, Huntington Hall, Rogers Building, June 3, 1890.

4. Corporation Records 3, February 12, 1879.

5. Printed call to meeting, October 1, 1860, WBR Papers, folder 35. The committee list omitted George Pratt, possibly an oversight, since he appeared in the 1860 and 1861 editions of the committee's report (*Objects and Plan*), and he attended the committee meetings for which there are a few records in late 1860 and early 1861. Charles Dalton was included, presumably having been added to the main committee when he joined the subcommittee.

6. E. B. Bigelow to WBR, August 30, September 24, & October 6, 1860; MDR to WBR, October 8, 1860. One might wonder whether it was *Erastus* rather than *Jacob* Bigelow who suggested the name for the Institute, but again, there is no manuscript evidence to shed light on this point. In his August letter he refers to the "polytechnic." WBR Papers, folder 35.

7. *Boston Advertiser*, October 6, 1860; the *Traveller* of October 8 also reported on this meeting, with Rogers identified once more as coming from Cambridge.

8. *Boston Advertiser*, October 6, 1860.

9. E. B. Bigelow to WBR, October 6, 1860, WBR Papers, folder 35.

10. MDR to WBR, October 8, 1860, ibid. There are occasional references in the WBR Papers to an executive committee without indication of its membership. The term probably refers to the subcommittee "to mature a plan for a Polytechnic Institution"—Rogers, Erastus Bigelow, Beebe, Ross, and Dalton.

11. WBR to HDR, October 30, 1860, *Life and Letters,* 2:44.

12. *Account of the Proceedings*, 4. The title page of this document uses the singular "Art" in the designation of the Committee of Associated Institutions of Science and Arts.

13. Printed circular letter, November 1860, WBR Papers, folder 36; drafts of *Objects and Plan*, ibid., folder 36A.

14. *Objects and Plan*, 5.

15. Ibid., 6.

16. Ibid.

17. Ibid., 7.

18. Ibid., 7–13.

19. Ibid., 13, 14.

20. Ibid., 19–20. Both for the museum and the school, "art" refers to the industrial arts.

21. Ibid., 20–21.

22. Ibid., 21–22.

23. Ibid., 22–26.

24. Ibid., 27.

25. Ibid.

26. Ibid., 27, 28.

27. Ibid., 28–29.

28. "Names to which Circular & Pamphlet have been sent," prepared by W. B. Rogers; "Schedule of persons to whom pamphlets should be sent say during the month of December," M. D. Ross, WBR Papers, folder 36. The latter bears a date of December 1860 in another hand (similar to the handwriting of Silas Holman) and with a finer pencil. It is more likely, especially in view of Ross's heading, that it was prepared earlier. The 1861 edition of the *Objects and Plan* contained no changes other than a slightly different order of the committee list.

29. Several letters in WBR Papers, folder 36.

30. Sherwin to WBR, December 10, 1860, ibid.

31. "Boston English High School was founded for the purpose of furnishing young men, not intended for college, with the means of obtaining such an education as should fit them for commercial, mechanical, and scientific pursuits. The course of study embraces the French, German, and Spanish languages, physics, mathematics,—pure and applied,—mental and moral science, rhetoric, and history. For youths not destined for the learned professions, the training imparted here is, probably, quite equal to that afforded by any of our colleges; and,—the tuition being free to residents of the city,—it is emphatically the people's college." "Thomas Sherwin," *Biographical Encyclopaedia of Massachusetts*, 223.

32. Building Committee Minutes, BSNH; *Objects and Claims of the Boston Society of Natural History* (Boston: John Wilson & Son, January 1, 1861). The Rogers papers contain a few draft pages, introductory in nature, of this document, but he later gave credit for its preparation to Amos Binney.

33. *Boston Transcript*, December 1, 1860; *Daily Evening Traveller*, December 18, 1860.

34. The account of the December 31, 1860, meeting is drawn from four pages of handwritten minutes by Samuel Kneeland as secretary of the Committee of Associated Institutions, labeled, in another hand, "Records of Meetings held in 1860–61." These records cover only three meetings: December 31, 1860, January 8, and April 20, 1861, the latter adjourned for lack of attendance.

35. *Boston Journal*, January 4, 1861.

36. *Address of His Excellency John A. Andrew*, January 5, 1861, Senate no. 2 (Boston, 1861), 17–18; *Boston Advertiser*, January 7, 1861, and *Boston Transcript*, January 5, 1861.

37. Senate no. 2, 19.

38. Petition of the Boston Society of Natural History, January 1, 1861, Massachusetts State Archives.

39. *Transactions of the Massachusetts Horticultural Society*, Annual Meeting, 1861, 84.

40. *Daily Evening Traveller*, January 8, 1861.

41. Petition of the Massachusetts Horticultural Society, January 14, 1861, Massachusetts State Archives.

42. Printed circular letter, January 7, 1861, WBR Papers, folder 37. Some 100 signed responses are included in this folder. Also published in *Account of the Proceedings*, 6.

43. *Boston Daily Evening Transcript*, January 10, 1861.

44. M. D. Ross, "Schedule of persons to whom pamphlets should be sent," WBR Papers, folder 36.

45. WBR, undated notes, certainly for meeting of January 11, 1861, WBR Papers, folder 38.

46. A *Boston Transcript* article, January 12, 1861, as quoted in *Life and Letters,* 2:62–63.

47. Ibid., 63.

48. Act of Association of an Institute of Technology, January 11, 1861, WBR Papers, folder 39.

49. *Account of the Proceedings*, 7.

50. Ibid.

51. Ibid., 8. Some biographical information derived from "Incorporators"; some occupations from List of Members, 1862, in *Eighth Annual Report*, Boston Board of Trade, 1862. M. D. Ross list, undated, but with some individuals numbered, almost certainly prepared in anticipation of the January 11, 1861, meeting. Labeled in another hand "Memoranda re Objects & Plan 1860–61," WBR Papers, folder 38.

52. To the Honorable Senate & House of Representatives of the Commonwealth of Massachusetts in General Court assembled. Document undated, but bears notation "Presented by Mr. Davis of Greenfield, January 14, 1861," Massachusetts State Archives.

53. *Account of the Proceedings*, 15–16; also presented by Mr. Davis of Greenfield on January 14, 1861, according to copy in Massachusetts State Archives. *Life and Letters,* 2:57–58. Footnote on 57 labels this incorrectly as House Document no. 13, 1861; that document related to the incorporation of a utility company.

54. *Boston Transcript* and *Boston Advertiser*, January 17, 1861.

55. *Boston Advertiser*, January 18, 1861; *Daily Evening Traveller*, January 17, 1861.

56. *Boston Daily Advertiser,* January 19, 1861.

57. Ross, *Estimate of the Financial Effect of the Proposed Reservation of Back-Bay Lands*, prepared for the Committee of Associated Institutions of Science and Art [*sic*].

58. WBR Papers, folder 38. The original manuscript of the testimonial also contains the signature of J. D. Runkle, which did not appear in the printed version.

59. December 1, 1860, Supplement to *Ninth Annual Report of the Commissioners on the Back Bay*, Public Document no. 18.

60. Petition of the Massachusetts Horticultural Society, January 14, 1861; accounts of Emerson, Breck, and Strong testimony drawn from *Boston Daily Journal*, January 24, 1861.

61. *Boston Daily Journal,* January 24, 1861.

62. MDR to WBR, January 31, 1861, WBR Papers, folder 38.

63. Felton had been a member of the Board of Education going back at least to 1858. Joseph White had succeeded George Boutwell as secretary, the latter having become a regular member of the board.

64. WBR list of advocates and opponents in the House, advocates out of the Legislature, and Great enemies, n.d., WBR Papers, folder 38; WBR to HDR, February 5, 1861, *Life and Letters,* 2:67–68.

65. *Boston Traveller,* February 6, 1861.

66. MDR to Andrew, February 8, 1861, John A. Andrew Papers, MHS.

67. MDR to WBR, February 13, 1861, WBR Papers, folder 38.

68. Fourth Hearing of the Committee of Associated Institutions before the Committee on Education, *Boston Journal,* February 16, 1861, clipping in WBR Papers, folder 238.

69. Ibid.

70. Ibid.

71. Ibid.

72. WBR to HDR, February 18, 1861, *Life and Letters,* 2:69; *Boston Transcript* and *Boston Journal,* February 13, 1861, WBR Papers, folder 38.

73. A bill introduced by Joseph H. Ramsey of Schoharie, N.Y., Senator from District 14, *New York State Senate Journal,* 1861. A memorandum by Harry W. Tyler in 1902, when he was preparing an article in tribute to John Runkle, contains an interesting statement by William Watson, a member of the first faculty of the School of Industrial Science, to the effect that "Prof. Runkle secured through his brother the introduction of a bill for the establishment of an Institute of Technology in New York and that this finally turned the scale with the legislature of Massachusetts." If true, an interesting bit of political maneuvering. The Runkle papers do not shed any light on this, but he did have a brother in New York. Memorandum of Conference with Prof. William Watson, June 11, 1902, Harry Walter Tyler Papers, 1887–1939 (MC 91).

74. MDR to WBR, February 12, 1861, WBR Papers, folder 38.

75. *DAB,* s.v. "Cooper, Peter."

76. Edward C. Mack, *Peter Cooper, Citizen of New York,* 253; Allan Nevins, *Abram S. Hewitt, With Some Account of Peter Cooper,* 175–176.

77. Second Annual Report of the Trustees of the Cooper Union for the Advancement of Science and Art, January 1861, 40–41.

78. Nevins, 176.

79. *Scientific American,* n.s. 1, no. 20 (November 12, 1859): 328; n.s. 2, no. 2 (January 7, 1860), 26.

80. *Boston Transcript,* March 22, 1861, folder 38. Second Annual Report of the Trustees of the Cooper Union, 32–33, with quotation from *Objects and Plan,* 33–40.

81. Agassiz to Andrew, March 2, 1861, Andrew Papers, MHS.

82. Agassiz to Andrew, March 27, 1861, ibid.

83. WBR to Andrew, March 2, 1861, WBR Papers, folder 38; also in *Life and Letters,* 2:74.

84. Andrew to WBR, March 9, 1861, WBR Papers, folder 38; also in *Life and Letters,* 2:75, where the abbreviated words of the original are spelled out.

85. WBR, draft of Legislative Committee report, n.d., WBR Papers, folder 38; Rogers's final version, Massachusetts State Archives. An MIT Archives copy of the printed version contains a handwritten notation by Rogers: "Written by W.B.R. for the Comm:." Portions of this appear as Appendix B, *Life and Letters,* 2:424–429.

86. House no. 171, March 19, 1861, 1–8.

87. Ibid., 7–8.

88. Ibid., 2.

89. Ibid., 5. This paragraph appears in the State Archives copy.

90. Building Committee Minutes, BSNH.

91. House no. 171, 8.

92. *Account of the Proceedings.*

93. WBR to HDR, February 18, 1861, *Life and Letters,* 2:70.

94. Editorial entitled "Institute of Technology," *Boston Journal,* March 2, 1861, WBR Papers, folder 241.

95. WBR to HDR, March 19, 1861, *Life and Letters,* 2:73.

96. *Boston Transcript,* March 23, 1861.

97. *Boston Daily Advertiser,* March 23, 1861.

98. *Boston Advertiser,* March 23 & 25, 1861.

99. E.g., copy of John R. Rollins of Lawrence to Colonel Thomas A. Parsons of the Legislature, March 28, 1861, and draft or file copy, WBR to Honorable Alex. H. Bullock, April 7, 1861, WBR Papers, folder 38.

100. *Boston Advertiser,* April 2, 1861; also in the *Journal* and *Transcript.*

101. WBR to HDR, April 2, 1861, *Life and Letters,* 2:75–76.

102. *Boston Advertiser,* April 9, 1861.

103. *Acts and Resolves of the General Court relating to the Massachusetts Institute of Technology* (Cambridge, 1931), Acts of 1861, Chapter 183, April 10, 1861, 1–4; Acts of 1863, Chapter 226, 6 (hereafter cited as *Acts and Resolves,* 1931).

104. Building Committee Minutes, BSNH. 114. WBR to HDR, April 16 & May 7, 1861, *Life and Letters,* 2:80, 85–86.

105. WBR to HDR, April 16 & May 7, 1861, *Life and Letters,* 2:80, 85–86.

Chapter Ten PERSISTENT PERSEVERANCE

1. *Boston Evening Transcript,* May 1, 1861, WBR Papers, folder 255. The clipping in the Rogers papers contains the initials "W.B.R." in his usual fashion.

2. WBR to HDR, October 13, 1862, *Life and Letters,* 2:134.

3. Edith Ellen Ware, *Political Opinion in Massachusetts during Civil War and Reconstruction,* 123.

4. WBR to HDR, March 31, 1863, *Life and Letters,* 2:156.

5. Ware, 122–123; Frank Freidel, ed., *Union Pamphlets of the Civil War, 1861–1865* 1:12–13; Sarah Forbes Hughes, ed., *Letters and Recollections of John Murray Forbes* 1:324–329; George Winston Smith, "Broadsides for Freedom: Civil War Propaganda in New England," *New England Quarterly* 21 (1948): 291–312; Henry Greenleaf Pearson, *An American Railroad Builder, John Murray Forbes*, 135–137.

6. Undated clipping, with internal references to August, 1863, WBR Papers, folder 238. The committee list also contains the names of several others associated with MIT.

7. Notice of the final meeting for the organization of the Protective War Claim Association, October 23, 1862, ibid., folder 43. Edward Atkinson was also a member of this group. Undated clipping, "Educational Commission for Freedmen," ibid., folder 236.

8. WBR to HDR, August 22, 1862, *Life and Letters*, 2:130–131.

9. WBR to HDR, September 5, 1862, ibid., 132, 136. William Rogers appears to have written a poem, "To the Memory of James," a copy of which is contained in the James Savage, Sr., Papers, folder 1858–1906, at the Massachusetts Historical Society. It is unsigned but is almost certainly in the hand of Rogers. In 1890 Henry Lee Higginson gave Harvard thirty-one acres of land for an athletic center, where the stadium was later built, to be named Soldiers Field, with a stone as a monument to six Harvard friends who had died in the Civil War, among them James Savage, Jr. Morison, *Three Centuries of Harvard*, 411; Bliss Perry, *Life and Letters of Henry Lee Higginson*, 330–337.

10. E.g., D. C. Gilman to WBR, August 27, 1862, WBR Papers, folder 43.

11. Shrock, 1:200–201; *Proceedings, AAcadAS* 5 (1860–1862): 73, 382; 6 (1862–1865): 128, 141–142.

12. WBR to Andrew, June 20, 1861, WBR Papers, folder 41.

13. "Augustus Allen Hayes," *Proceedings, AAcadAS* 18 (1882–1883), 422–427; "Incorporators," 25; WBR to HDR, June 25, 1861, *Life and Letters*, 2:91–92.

14. WBR to Rollins, May 9, 1861; copy of Rollins to Colonel Thomas A. Parsons, March 28, 1861, WBR Papers, folder 38; WBR to Andrew, June 20, 1861, WBR Papers, folder 41.

15. WBR to Andrew, June 20, 1861 (also in *Life and Letters*, 2:90–91); WBR to Rollins, June 23, 1861 (copy in Emma Rogers's hand); WBR to Hayes, June 24, 1861, WBR Papers, folder 41.

16. WBR to HDR, June 25, 1861, *Life and Letters*, 2:91–92; printed circular letter, September 10, 1861, WBR Papers, folder 41.

17. WBR to Rollins, June 23, 1861, WBR Papers, folder 41.

18. WBR to HDR, September 1, 1861, and January 7, 1862, *Life and Letters*, 2:95, 106; H. K. Smith, 60.

19. See, for example, Sally Gregory Kohlstedt, "From Learned Society to Public Museum: The Boston Society of Natural History," in *The Organization of Knowledge in Modern America, 1860–1920*, ed. Alexandra Oleson and John Voss, 391.

20. WBR to HDR, April 2, 1861, *Life and Letters*, 2:76.

21. WBR to HDR, January 7, 1862, ibid., 106.

22. MDR to WBR, June 10, 1861, WBR Papers, folder 41.

23. MDR to WBR, June 20, 1861, ibid.
24. WBR to MDR, June 21, 1861, file copy, ibid.
25. Ibid.
26. WBR memorandum, April 4, 1862, ibid., folder 43.
27. Huntington to WBR, April 7, 1862, typed copy, Huntington biographical file, MIT Museum.
28. MIT Building Committee Minutes (ASC 11), November 20, 1865.
29. MDR to WBR, June 10 & June 20, 1861; WBR to MDR, June 21, 1861.
30. Building Committee Minutes, BSNH, meetings early 1862. Noted in minutes for February 1, 1862.
31. Receipt, Bouvé to WBR, March 20, 1862; typed excerpt, WBR to HDR, March 18, 1862, WBR Papers, folder 43. There has been in the past an erroneous impression that William's brother, Henry Darwin Rogers, was active in the founding of the Institute and served as a member of its Government. It was rather Henry Bromfield Rogers, a Boston lawyer, and his name will be used in full whenever it occurs. His last name, of course, causes additional problems with respect to William, whose full name will also be necessary unless the context makes it clear that he is the one involved. The potential for similar confusion exists with respect to Jacob and Erastus Bigelow and becomes worse with the advent of George T. Bigelow as a member of the Government.
32. WBR to HDR, February 5, 1861, *Life and Letters,* 2:68.
33. WBR to J. A. Lowell, March 29, 1862, file copy, WBR Papers, folder 43; also in *Life and Letters,* 2:110–111. In the final paragraph of this letter Rogers states that unsolicited money had already been donated for the Institute in the amount of "several thousand dollars." It seems likely that he was referring to an indication from William Minot, an executor of an estate, that help might be forthcoming from that source. A January 7, 1862, letter from Minot to Rogers suggests that Minot may have been responding to an appeal from Rogers for a personal contribution, and he promised to call on Rogers after reviewing the estate's situation. Minot to WBR, January 7, 1862, WBR Papers, folder 43.
34. J. A. Lowell to WBR, April 2, 1862, *Life and Letters,* 2:111–112.
35. WBR to J. A. Lowell, March 29, 1862, file copy, WBR Papers, folder 43. In *Life and Letters,* 2:110–111, the word "annoyance" is eliminated.
36. File copy of WBR notice, April 4, 1862, contains a notation that 250 copies were ordered for delivery to M. D. Ross at the office of the Back Bay Commissioners. No copy of the printed version has been found, and the records do not show who or how many attended the meeting. File copy of separate notice to Committee of Twenty, April 4, 1862. WBR to J. A. Lowell, March 29, 1862. All in WBR Papers, folder 43.
37. First meeting of the Massachusetts Institute of Technology, April 8, 1862, Society of Arts Records 1; first meeting of the Government, April 8, 1862, Government Records 1. A record of the latter is in WBR Papers, folder 43, in the hand of Runkle. After Thomas Webb was elected secretary of the Institute in July, he copied the minutes of meetings prior to his election into the permanent volume. By virtue of the Institute's organization, some records of the

Institute proper and the Society of Arts are thus intermixed in the early days so that both must
be consulted. Several handwritten copies of April 9, 1862, acceptance of charter, in WBR
Papers, folder 43.

38. *Acts and Resolves*, 1931, 1.

39. Massachusetts Institute of Technology. *Officers. Extracts from Act of Incorporation. Objects and Plan*
    (abbreviated statement only). *By-Laws*. (Boston, 1862), 7 (hereafter cited as *Officers; Extracts;
    Objects and Plan; By-Laws*). Full text of bylaws also in Society of Arts Records 1, April 8, 1862.

40. Ibid., 9–10.

41. Ibid., 7, 9–11. The original version did not include an Auditing Committee, but the omission
    was corrected in time for the printed version. "Mem's relating to Institute, with agenda for
    meetings of Government, April 22, Annual Meeting of the Institute, May 6, and a regular
    meeting of the Institute on May 20, 1862," WBR Papers, folder 43.

42. Ibid., 8.

43. Ibid., 11–12.

44. Ibid., 12.

45. Society of Arts Records 1, April 8, 1862.

46. *Account of the Proceedings*, 10; "Incorporators."

47. Society of Arts Records 1, April 8, 1862.

48. Ibid.; Rogers incorrectly identified the "venerable lady" as "Sarah P. Townsend." Elsewhere in
    Institute records she appears as "Mary." Minot to WBR, January 7, 1862, WBR Papers, folder
    43; MIT Office of the Treasurer, Cash Book no. 1, 1862–1872 (ASC 6), 1. In 1861 Harvard
    had received a bequest of Miss Mary P. Townsend—$20,000, the income for the "benefit of
    Indigent Scholars," and $5,000 for the Divinity School. *Endowment Funds of Harvard University*,
    159, 214.

49. Society of Arts Records 1, April 8, 1862. Several copies, including a draft of the petition for
    extension of time, April 9, 1862, WBR Papers, folder 43.

50. Draft of "Statement for Mr. B. of the Legislature," April 11, 1862, WBR Papers, folder 43.

51. Acts of 1862, Chapter 142, approved April 25, 1862, *Acts and Resolves*, 1931, 4.

52. Society of Arts Records 1, May 6, 1862; Government Records 1, July 15, 1862.

53. *Officers; Extracts; Objects and Plan; By-Laws*, 1. The name of E. H. Eldredge is here misspelled.

54. [MIT], "Members of the Corporation Deceased," vol. 1, comp. Charles F. Read (Class of
    1874), MIT Archives; Samuel A. Johnson, *The Battle Cry of Freedom*, 13–14. The brief account
    of the Emigrant Aid Company and Webb's association with it is largely drawn from this
    work.

55. Johnson, 288.

56. Ibid., preface, unnumbered page.

57. Ibid., 13, 36. Twenty editions of this pamphlet were later issued.

58. Society of Arts Records 1, May 6 & 20, 1862.

59. WBR to Everett, May 13, 1862, draft or file copy, WBR Papers, folder 43; Society of Arts
    Records 1, May 20, 1862.

60. Government Records 1, September 23, 1862. The matter of space in the Boston Public Library was later fully reported to the Institute. The texts of an undated WBR letter to the city council and the response of the library trustees of August 5, 1862, are entered in Society of Arts Records 1, December 17, 1862.

61. Government Records 1, September 30, 1862.

62. Ibid.

63. Ibid.

64. First Annual Report of the Secretary, May 11, 1863, presented at Adjourned Annual Meeting, June 17, 1863; Society of Arts Records 1, 142–143.

65. Society of Arts Records 1, December 17, 1862.

66. Government Records 1, December 5, 1862.

67. Ibid.

68. Ibid.

69. Everett to Samuel Eliot, June 23, 1847, College Letters, Edward Everett 1, HUA; also Everett Letters, reel 27, MHS.

*C*hapter Eleven THE LAND-GRANT ACT OF 1862

1. Government Records 1, December 5 & 15, 1862.

2. *Land-Grant Fact Book*, Centennial Edition, 28; Hofstadter and Smith, 568.

3. *Land-Grant Fact Book*, 28–29.

4. Ibid., 17–18.

5. Ibid., 18.

6. Ibid, 25, 27. This *Land-Grant Fact Book* contains a detailed discussion of the bill and its problems in the House and Senate. Also Leonard P. Curry, *Blueprint for Modern America*, 108–115.

7. *Land-Grant Fact Book*, 4–5. Mary Turner Carriel, *The Life of Jonathan Baldwin Turner*. Carriel dates the first public announcement of this plan as May 13, 1850, but an editor's note (69) indicates that she may have erred and that it very likely occurred on November 18, 1851. The latter date is used in Burt E. Powell, *The Movement for Industrial Education and the Establishment of the University, 1840–1870*, vol. 1 of *Semi-Centennial History of the University of Illinois*, 133. Chapters 1 through 6 relate to this period. The *Land-Grant Fact Book* cites both dates. References appear also to differ on whether the Illinois resolutions were submitted to Congress in 1853 or 1854. Henry's introduction to Carriel book, ix–x.

8. William Belmont Parker, *The Life and Public Service of Justin Smith Morrill*, 273.

9. Earle D. Ross in *Democracy's College*, 51–54, presents a balanced view of the controversy, giving credit to Morrill as familiar with the general pressures for improvement in agricultural education and full credit for initiating the legislation and seeing it through.

10. In 1917, the Carnegie Foundation for the Advancement of Teaching issued a report on federal aid for vocational education. In his introduction to this report, Henry S. Pritchett, the president of the foundation, a post which he had assumed after serving from 1900 to 1907 as

the fifth president of the Massachusetts Institute of Technology, disparaged the way in which this legislation came about. "Congress had before it no clear, well-considered educational project. Senator Morrill himself knew very little of education. His wish was 'to do something for the farmer.' . . . Perhaps no circumstance of the original Morrill legislation was more remarkable than the entire absence of any educational conception as to what sort of colleges were to be created." (Introduction by Henry S. Pritchett in I. L. Kandel, *Federal Aid for Vocational Education*, Carnegie Foundation for the Advancement of Teaching, Bulletin no. 10 [New York, 1917], v, vi.) While Pritchett's criticism of the lack of any substantive educational plan in the legislation may on some counts be well taken, his comment on Morrill's lack of knowledge about education seems unfair, and he seems to have looked narrowly at the act in his emphasis on the farmer and agricultural education.

11. Daniel Coit Gilman, "Our National Schools of Science," *North American Review* (October 1867): 498–499.

12. Ibid., 506.

13. Ibid., 499.

14. Ibid., 507–508.

15. Fabian Franklin, *The Life of Daniel Coit Gilman*, 73.

16. Parker, 268–269, part of a Morrill 1874 memorandum. Wilder's military title stems from the days when he was colonel of the Twelfth Regiment of New Hampshire.

17. Gilman had left Yale for the presidency of the University of California in 1872 and in 1875 was appointed the first president of the new Johns Hopkins University in Baltimore, a post he still held in 1897. Francis Amasa Walker, the third president of the Institute, died suddenly in January of that year, and Professor James Mason Crafts was appointed to assume the office temporarily. The presidency was discussed at a special meeting of the Executive Committee on July 16. There is no detailed record of the discussion, but Gilman's biographer reveals that the offer of the presidency came in a letter of July 16 from Augustus Lowell, the "Senior Member" of the Institute's Executive Committee. Gilman responded promptly, expressing surprise and gratification but pointing out that he was sixty-six years old and "strongly bound" to Johns Hopkins. He agreed to consider it, however, and urged that the offer never be made public. Six days later Lowell wrote again, and on July 24 Gilman declined. He is not mentioned in the records of the Corporation or the Executive Committee, and no correspondence has been found other than that published in the Gilman biography. Crafts was appointed president on October 20, 1897. Augustus Lowell to Gilman, July 16, 1897; Gilman to Lowell, July 20, 1897; Lowell to Gilman, July 22, 1897; Gilman to Lowell, July 24, 1897; all in Franklin, 300–302. Executive Committee Records 3 & 4, July 16, September 7, & October 19; Corporation Records 4, January 27 & October 20, 1897.

18. Marshall P. Wilder, *History and Progress of the Massachusetts State Board of Agriculture for the First Quarter of a Century, with a Report on Fruits,* Annual Meeting, February 5, 1878 (Boston: Rand, Avery & Co., 1878), 4.

19. Ibid., 5.

20. Marshall P. Wilder, *Address before the First Graduating Class of the Massachusetts Agricultural College*, July 19, 1871, 17.

21. *Twelfth Annual Report of the Secretary of the Massachusetts Board of Agriculture* (Boston, 1865), 246. Statements by Charles Flint and Governor Andrew at a public meeting of the board in Greenfield on the establishment of an agricultural college and the Morrill Act (44–54) and a section of Flint's report entitled "The Agricultural College" (246–248) give further details and mention the Bussey Institution.

22. Morison, *Three Centuries of Harvard*, 304–305.

23. Ibid., 304.

24. Hugh Hawkins, *Between Harvard and America: The Educational Leadership of Charles W. Eliot*, 318 n. 57.

25. Agassiz to Andrew, December 16, 1862, Andrew Papers, MHS.

26. Ibid.

27. Agassiz to Andrew, December 17, 1862, ibid.

28. Private letter, Agassiz to Andrew, December 22, 1862, ibid.

29. Ibid.

30. Andrew to WBR, December 22, 1862, WBR Papers, folder 43; *Life and Letters,* 2:141. There are slight differences between original and printed version in *Life and Letters.*

31. *Life and Letters,* 2:141.

32. Andrew to WBR, December 30, 1862, slight difference between original and printed version in *Life and Letters,* 2:142. As it appears in *Life and Letters,* Rogers's response of December 30 contains no reference to the Land-Grant Act or discussion of the governor's proposal. There is, however, an excision at the end. WBR to Andrew, December 30, 1862, and postscript, January 1, 1863, *Life and Letters,* 2:143–145. A surviving partial draft, difficult to read, contains no reference to the governor's proposal, nor does a further draft with date of January 2. WBR Papers, folders 43 & 45.

33. Hill to Andrew, December 24, 1862, College Letters 6, HUA; also in Andrew Papers, MHS.

34. Agassiz to Andrew, December 25, 1862, Andrew Papers, MHS.

35. Agassiz to Andrew, January 4, 1863, ibid.

36. *Address of His Excellency John A. Andrew,* January 9, 1863, Senate no. 1 (Boston, 1863), 43–65.

37. Ibid., 52–53; Andrew quotes Hitchcock's report (House no. 13, 1851); *DAB,* s.v. "Hitchcock, Edward."

38. Ibid., 54.

39. Ibid., 56–57.

40. Ibid., 58, 64.

41. Ibid., 64–65.

42. Ibid., 65–66.

43. Peirce to Bache, early January 1863; January 25, 1863; n.d., but spring, 1863, Peirce Papers, HLHU.

44. Bache to Peirce, February 9, 1863, Peirce Papers, HLHU. Bache was not a graduate of Harvard but of West Point and must have used the term "Alma Mater" as it related to Peirce, or possibly in the more literal sense of "fostering mother."
45. Agassiz to Andrew, February 5, 1863, Andrew Papers, MHS.
46. Henry Greenleaf Pearson, *The Life of John A. Andrew* 2:235–236. Pearson had a long association with MIT, beginning in 1893 as instructor in English. He was head of the Department of English and History for many years, retiring in 1938.
47. Ibid.
48. "President Eliot and M.I.T.," *TR* 22 (1920): 430–431.
49. WBR to HDR, January 20, 1863, *Life and Letters,* 2:147–148.
50. WBR to HDR, February 10, 1863, ibid., 149.
51. Report of the Finance Committee, February 21, 1863, Government Records 1, 40.
52. WBR to HDR, March 17, 1863, *Life and Letters,* 2:153.
53. WBR to HDR, March 31, 1863, ibid., 157.
54. Senate no. 108, March 26, 1863, 4. The report contains a typographical or arithmetical error in stating that 360,000 acres at $1.25 per acre would yield $456,000.
55. *Land-Grant Fact Book*, 31.
56. Senate no. 108, 8. "Mens et Manus" had not yet been adopted as the motto of the Institute but may have been under consideration by Rogers.
57. Ibid. The Hon. Stephen Fairbanks, Harrison Loring of Lowell, and Franklin Forbes of Clinton were also on this committee.
58. Senate no. 108, 10.
59. Draft resolutions, WBR Papers, folder 45; WBR to HDR, March 17, 1863, *Life and Letters,* 2:153.
60. Senate no. 108, 13–14.
61. Abbott Lawrence to Samuel Eliot, June 7, 1847, College Papers, 2d ser., 15, HUA. The words would be used later, in 1894 and in a different context, by MIT president Francis Amasa Walker in a section on "Gymnastics and Athletics" in his report for that year: "The students in general understand perfectly well that this is a place for men to work, and not for boys to play; and they organize their athletic teams and carry on their contests in a very sensible and practical spirit." *Annual Report of the President and Treasurer*, Massachusetts Institute of Technology, December 12, 1894 (Cambridge, 1894), 49.
62. Senate no. 108, 16.
63. Ibid., 46, dated March 30, 1863.
64. Ibid., 30, 31–33, 42–43.
65. Ibid., 35–40.
66. Ibid., 20–21.
67. Unfinished copy of letter to unidentified individual, March 21, 1863, WBR Papers, folder 45.
68. Senate no. 108, 43.
69. *Acts and Resolves*, 1931, 5.

70. Copy of order signed by Oliver Warner, secretary of the commonwealth, April 10, 1863, WBR Papers, folder 45.
71. WBR to Dr. William J. Walker, May 4, 1863, *Life and Letters,* 2:163–164; draft copy in WBR Papers, folder 46a. In this letter Rogers referred to receiving "*three-tenths* of the proceeds" of the congressional grant of land rather than the "one-third" normally mentioned. There are other occasional references to this amount. One-tenth of the total having been set aside for land for the agricultural college, nine-tenths remained for investment. Three-tenths of this remainder is obviously equivalent to one-third of the invested fund.
72. Government Records 1, May 6 & June 30, 1863.
73. Ibid., March 17, 1864.
74. Ibid., April 4, 1864.
75. File copies, THW to Professor Alexis Caswell, Brown University, April 7, 1864; THW to the state secretaries of Connecticut, New Hampshire, New York, and Pennsylvania, April 11, 1864; and THW to the state secretary of Vermont, April 16, 1864, Massachusetts Institute of Technology Letters (ASC 22), 17–19.
76. Letter, Henry F. French to J. Herbert Shedd, Esq., May 6, 1864, entered into Government Records 1 as part of the minutes of May 9, 1864, meeting.
77. Andrew to Ross, May 7, 1864, ibid.
78. Government Records 1, May 9, 1864.
79. Second Annual Report of the Secretary, May 30, 1864, Society of Arts Records 1, 255.
80. Third Annual Report of the Secretary, May 25, 1865, Society of Arts Records 2, 128.
81. Government Records 2, January 25, & March 2, 1867.
82. E. D. Ross, 84.
83. *Land-Grant Fact Book,* 31. Carl Becker, *Cornell University: Founders & the Founding* (116) gives a lower figure of $594,000 for the initial sale proceeds.
84. Becker, 81–89, 92–93, 115–118. For a detailed account of Cornell and the Morrill Land-Grant Act, see also Morris Bishop, *A History of Cornell,* 71–73, 183–188. In late 1863, while the New York discussions were going on, President Amos Brown of the People's College in New York sent a pamphlet on the institution to President Hill of Harvard. Hill's response reiterated the arguments put forward by him and Agassiz earlier on the need for a great university (College Letters 6, January 2, 1864, HUA), which was the last thing that Brown either intended or was prepared to work toward.
85. E.g., Hill to Hon. A. W. Dodge, February 9, 1864, and to John Hastings, Esq., March 31, 1864. Hill's ideas were also communicated in February 19, 1864, to Hon. G. Volney Dorsey, treasurer of the state of Ohio, College Letters 6, HUA.
86. *Address of His Excellency John A. Andrew,* January 6, 1865, Senate no. 1 (Boston, 1865), 56–57.
87. Ibid., 59–61; copy of Rogers's report to Andrew, December 27, 1864, WBR Papers, folder 48. Rogers dated this December 27, a correct date. Emma Rogers later placed a date of October 27 on the manuscript.

88. MIT Office of the Treasurer, Cash Book no. 1, 1862–1872; Ledger no. 1, 1862–1882 (ASC 5), 68–69, account identified as Agricultural Fund; Treasurer's statements, 1865–1883 (AC 63); Treasurer's reports, 1865–1883 (AC 80).

89. *Survey of Land-Grant Colleges and Universities,* 1:16.

90. A second Land-Grant Act, also proposed by Morrill, would become law in 1890, providing each state with an annual appropriation of federal funds derived from public land sales, starting with $15,000 in 1890, with yearly increases for ten years to reach a permanent level of $25,000. At that time MIT's right to a share would be seriously questioned, strong opposition coming from the Massachusetts Agricultural College. Kandel, 30; *Federal Laws and Rulings Relating to Morrill and Supplementary Morrill Funds for Land-Grant Colleges and Universities,* 7–8.

Chapter Twelve HARVARD AGAIN

1. Agassiz to Andrew, December 16, 1862, Andrew Papers, MHS.

2. Everett to Horsford, February 19, 1847, College Letters, Edward Everett 1; College Records 8, April 24, 1847; LSS Faculty Records, 1848–1871, February 8, 1848, HUA.

3. Horsford to the Committee of Conference on the Part of the President and Fellows of Harvard College, April 26, 1854, a 14-page report, College Papers, 2d ser., 21; Report of Committee on Expenses of the Chemical Department, June 23, 1861, ibid., 28; September 27, 1861, ibid., also in LSS Faculty Records; LSS Faculty Records, November 5, 1861; all HUA.

4. Henry James, *Charles W. Eliot* 1:36–66; letter to his mother, March 16, 1854, 60.

5. Ibid., 67, 69; College Records 10, January 26, 1861, HUA.

6. LSS Faculty Records, 1848–1871, November 5 & December 17, 1861, HUA.

7. James, 1:95–96.

8. College Records 10, December 28, 1861, HUA; *Historical Register of Harvard University, 1636–1936* (Cambridge: Harvard University, 1937), 4.

9. LSS Faculty Records, September 30, 1862, HUA. Lurie's *Louis Agassiz* (326–327) confuses the 1861 and 1862 efforts at curricular reform and implies that Eliot was acting dean in 1861.

10. LSS Faculty Records, October 7, November 4 & 11, 1862; C. W. Eliot to Hill, November 4 & 15, 1862, College Papers 29, HUA.

11. LSS Faculty Records, November 18, 1862, HUA.

12. C. W. Eliot to President and Fellows of the Corporation, November 24, 1862, College Papers 29, HUA.

13. LSS Faculty Records, December 2, 1862, HUA.

14. Hill to M. G. Grove, Esq., November 20, 1863, College Letters 6, HUA.

15. Hill to Putnam, November 24, 1863, ibid.

16. Quoted in Dupree, 315–316.

17. "President Eliot and M.I.T.," *TR* 22 (1920): 430–431.

18. The Rogers papers contain no reference to William Rogers's participation in the 1862 meeting of the visiting committee for the Lawrence Scientific School, and *Life and Letters* does not

mention it either. A partial letter from Henry Rogers printed in *Life and Letters* does contain a passing reference to William's nomination for that committee in 1864. One might easily assume that this was his first formal connection with the committee, but the Harvard president's reports covering the years 1861–62 through 1865–66 indicate that he was a regular member for that entire period. The reports reveal, too, that several others associated with MIT were members of this committee, some going back beyond 1862—among them Jacob and Erastus Bigelow. Earlier committee lists include the name of Henry Darwin Rogers, his association also not mentioned in the Rogers papers or *Life and Letters*. It is difficult to say whether William was an active member after the year 1862, and there were reasons why he might wish not to be, but it is clear that he was in a position to know the general situation at the Scientific School and to be aware of Eliot's efforts to effect a change. HDR to WBR, April 1, 1864, *Life and Letters*, 2:191; *Annual Reports of the President and Treasurer of Harvard College*, 1852–53 through 1854–55 and 1860–61 through 1865–66.

19. College Papers, 2d ser., 30, January 15, 1863, HUA; College Records 10 also notes Horsford's resignation under date of January 24; Charles T. Jackson, "Memoir of Eben N. Horsford," *Proceedings, AAcadAS* 28 (1892–1893): 340–346. Reznick in "The European Education of an American Chemist" (384) states that Horsford's partner in the firm was George F. Wilson, a "former textile manufacturer interested in chemical problems."

20. WBR to HDR, January 20, 1863, *Life and Letters*, 2:147 (excision by Emma Rogers).

21. Wyman to WBR, February 12, 1863, WBR Papers, folder 45.

22. Gray to Hill, January 30, 1863, College Papers, 2d ser., 30, HUA.

23. F. J. Clarke, "Wolcott Gibbs," *Biographical Memoirs* 7, NAS (Washington, D.C.), 3–7.

24. Peirce to Bache, several letters in 1863, Peirce Papers, HLHU.

25. C. W. Eliot to Hill, January 31, 1863, College Papers, 2d ser., 30, HUA.

26. C. W. Eliot to Hill, February 27, 1863; Eliot to the President and Fellows, May 19, 1863, ibid.

27. C. W. Eliot to the President and Fellows, May 19, 1863.

28. Gibbs to Hill, June 5, 1863, College Papers, 2d ser., 30, HUA.

29. Lurie, 182–184. The remaining members were James Dwight Dana, Silliman Professor of Natural History at Yale; John Fries Frazer, professor of chemistry and physics at the University of Pennsylvania; Benjamin Apthorp Gould, an astronomer associated with the Coast Survey in Cambridge; and Joseph Henry, secretary of the Smithsonian Institution. Cornelius C. Felton, Agassiz's brother-in-law and president of Harvard from 1860 until his death in 1862, was a classical scholar and had been the only nonscientist in the group. Some accounts of their activities consider Admiral Charles Henry Davis, in charge of the Navy's Bureau of Navigation, as one of the group beginning in 1863, having been a "member in good standing of the 'Cambridge clique'" in earlier years. James Hall and Henry Wilson have been cited as "Friends of the Lazzaroni." See Lillian B. Miller, Frederick Voss, and Jeannette M. Hussey, *The Lazzaroni: Science and Scientists in Mid-Nineteenth-Century America*, v–vii, 44.

30. Mark Beach, "Was There a Scientific Lazzaroni?" in George H. Daniels, ed., *Nineteenth-Century American Science: A Reappraisal*, 118–119.

31. Peirce to Bache, June 24, 1863, Peirce Papers, HLHU.

32. Rexmond C. Cochrane, *The National Academy of Sciences: The First Hundred Years, 1863–1963,* 52–58, 596.

33. Bache to Peirce, May 5, 1854, Peirce Papers, HLHU.

34. "Memoranda of the Meeting for Organising the National Academy of Sciences," undated but presumably shortly after the meeting held April 22–25, 1863, WBR Papers, folder 45. Senator Wilson's notification to WBR was dated March 5, 1863, ibid; also *Life and Letters,* 2:150.

35. "Memoranda," passim; folder 45 also contains a 19-page typed transcription deciphering WBR's sometimes difficult handwriting.

36. Bache to WBR, May 25, 1863; WBR to Bache, May 31, 1863, WBR Papers, folder 46a.

37. Bache to Peirce, June 8, 1863, Peirce Papers, HLHU.

38. Dupree, 318–320; Bache to Peirce, June 8, 1863, Peirce Papers, HLHU.

39. WBR to James Hall, January 30, 1866, file copy, WBR Papers, folder 54.

40. Cochrane, 625.

41. Ibid., 137, 138.

42. *Annual Report of the National Academy of Sciences* (Washington, D.C., 1880), 5. This change is specially noted by Cochrane, 136.

Chapter Thirteen THE DIFFICULT QUESTION OF MONEY

1. Some have believed that the Institute did not lack for funds in the early days; e.g., Hawkins, *Between Harvard and America* (39), in connection with the land-grant funds, cites "Cornell and M.I.T., where they were linked to large private philanthropy." Also Howard S. Miller, *Dollars for Research* (82) in connection with the Lawrence Scientific School, "after 1862, outside competition from the richly endowed Massachusetts Institute of Technology" (Seattle: University of Washington Press, 1970).

2. "Members of the Corporation Deceased."

3. Ibid.

4. "Incorporators"; Foster W. Russell, *Mt. Auburn Biographies, a Biographical Listing of Distinguished Persons Interred in Mount Auburn Cemetery, 1831–1952* (Cambridge, Mass.: Proprietors of the Cemetery of Mount Auburn, 1953), 165; *Boston Advertiser,* December 3, 1860.

5. Government Records 1, December 15, 1862.

6. Ibid.

7. Society of Arts Records 1, December 17, 1862.

8. Government Records 1, February 21, 1863.

9. First Annual Report of the Secretary, Society of Arts Records 1, 118.

10. Government Records 1, February 21, 1863.

11. Finance Committee circular, March 7, 1863, WBR Papers, folder 45. This folder also contains drafts of this statement in the hand of WBR.

12. WBR to HDR, March 31, 1863, *Life and Letters,* 2:156–157.

13. *DAB*, s.v. "Walker, William Johnson," sketch prepared by Amos A. Lawrence. Cornelius Felton to Dr. Walker, December 30, 1860, College Letters 5, HUA. Lawrence cites this incident as the source of Walker's disenchantment with Harvard.

14. Frederick C. Shattuck, M.D., and J. Lewis Bremer, M.D., "The Medical School," chap. 35 in Morison, *Development of Harvard University*, 556–557.

15. *DAB.*

16. "William Johnson Walker," *TR* 1 (October 1899): 421–423.

17. Tobey and Beebe to WBR, April 10, 1863, mentioning a document dated April 2 related to this gift, WBR Papers, folder 45.

18. Account of Walker given by E. S. Tobey, presented to MIT on June 10, 1917, by Tobey's grandson, Edward T. Stuart of Philadelphia. Edward S. Tobey Papers (MSC 82).

19. WBR and Finance Committee to His Excellency John A. Andrew, Governor, and the Honorable Council of the Commonwealth of Massachusetts, April 10, 1863, copied into Government Records 1, April 11, 1863; Finance Committee Report presented by Tobey, ibid., 43–46.

20. Copy of council order, April 10, 1863, WBR Papers, folder 45.

21. Government Records 1, April 11, 1863; Society of Arts Records, April 13, 1863.

22. Remarks of Edward Tobey, April 11, 1863, Government Records 1.

23. Government Records 1, May 27, 1863. Tobey had actually been authorized to sell within 60 days 1,000 shares of the stock but give the Institute the proceeds of only 600. The shares had increased in value in the interim, and both Beebe and Tobey assured the Government that Dr. Walker's decision to retain them stemmed not from "pecuniary motives," but "other reasons." The "trust" instrument read by Tobey was copied into the record of that date by Secretary Webb, who also made a paper copy to put with the "valuable documents" of the Institute. He labeled the latter "Copy of an Instrument of Gift from Dr. Wm. J. Walker to the Mass. Institute of Technology, dated April 2d, 1863." The paper copy is missing several words ("by legal vote of the Officers of said Institution") on the second page. The *Technology Review* article cited above reproduces the document "in part" but does not indicate where an excision of more than a page occurs, thus giving the impression that the "instrument" was addressed directly to the Institute. It was, however, an authorization for Tobey to carry out Walker's instructions. Tobey presumably retained it for his own files.

24. Signed, sealed, and witnessed statement certifying completion of guarantee fund, July 14, 1863, with appended certification of Walker gift, July 16, 1863; also copy of April 10, 1863, order issued by the secretary of the Commonwealth, June 12, 1863, with certification of its authenticity by Thomas H. Webb, secretary of the Institute, July 8, 1863, WBR Papers, folder 45. These copies were prepared to satisfy Walker's requirement for proof that the Institute had raised the balance of the guarantee fund and that the state had agreed to release the land.

25. Cash Book no. 1, July 21, 1863.

26. Tobey and Beebe to WBR, April 10, 1863, WBR Papers, folder 45.

27. Government Records 1, April 11, 1863.

28. Ibid.

29. WBR to Walker, April 14, 1863, WBR Papers, folder 45; also in *Life and Letters,* 2:159.

30. For example, WBR to Walker, May 4, 1863, WBR Papers, folder 46a.

31. Walker to THW, July 2, 1864, copy contained in THW to WBR, July 19, 1864, ibid., folder 47. This copy differs from the version contained in *Life and Letters,* 2:197–198, in which the second quoted paragraph is eliminated without indication of an excision.

32. Government Records 1, April 11, 1863; Acts of 1863, Chapter 226, approved April 29, 1863, *Acts and Resolves*, 1931, 6.

33. Government Records 1, April 11, 1863.

34. Ibid.

35. Ibid.

36. Francis to MDR, April 7, 1863, WBR Papers, folder 45.

37. First Annual Report of the Secretary as presented at the Annual Meeting held on June 17, 1863 (adjourned from May 11), Society of Arts Records 1, 141. The secretary referred to a detailed Treasurer's Report, which does not survive.

38. Ibid., 144.

39. Government Records 1, November 24, 1863.

40. Ibid., June 30, 1863 (committee consisted of Erastus Bigelow, Dalton, Ross, Ruggles, William Rogers, and Preston); November 24, 1863. The "gentleman" may have been Henry Bromfield Rogers.

41. Society of Arts Records 1, January 14 & 28, 1864. The offer came through a December 23, 1863, letter to Thomas T. Bouvé, a prominent member of the Natural History Society and also a member of the Institute. He would later serve on the Institute's Corporation, 1872–1896.

42. Government Records 1, February 10 & 27, 1864.

43. Postscript, Walker to THW, July 2, 1864.

44. THW to WBR, September 13, 1864, WBR Papers, folder 48.

45. MDR to WBR, October 4, 1864, ibid.

46. WBR to Walker, file copy, January 1, 1865, ibid., folder 50.

47. MDR to WBR, September 9 & October 4, 1864, ibid., folder 48.

48. Society of Arts Records 2, April 6, 1865, 48–49.

49. *DAB*; compared copy of will of William J. Walker, Walker folder, Document File, MIT Treasurer's Office.

50. Compared copy of Walker will.

51. Government Records 1, April 15 & 18, 1865; Society of Arts Records 2, April 20, 1865.

52. A. J. Wheeler to WBR, September 9, 1865, with enclosure, WBR Papers, folder 52; Government Records 1, October 23, 1865; Walker folder, Document File, MIT Treasurer's Office.

53. Biographical Memoir, *Proceedings, AAcadAS* 24 (1888–1889): 435–437.

54. James P. Munroe (Class of 1882), "William Endicott," *TR* 18 (January 1915): 21.

55. *DAB*, s.v. "Forbes, John Murray"; Pearson, *An American Railroad Builder*, 11.

56. Society of Arts Records 1, December 17, 1862.

57. Government Records 1, November 14, 1865.
58. Ibid.
59. Walker folder, Document File, MIT Treasurer's Office; *Report of the Treasurer for the Year Ended June 30, 1994*, MIT, 143, 289. Over the years the Institute received nearly $272,000, from the first gift in 1863 through funds received in 1916 and 1917 from final remainder interests in the estate. The William J. Walker fund still exists, the income used for general purposes.

    It would be years before the additional building on Boylston Street, in which Walker had expressed a special interest, could be afforded. It was completed in 1883. Ironically, it would not be named for him though it would bear the name of Walker. In the fall of 1891 the Executive Committee, believing that then President Francis Amasa Walker's name should be "associated with the Institute in some appropriate manner," voted to call it simply the "Walker Building," following the precedent set earlier in the naming of the first building as simply the "Rogers Building." Over the years the omission of Walker's first name has led some to believe incorrectly that it was named for William Walker. There is no record that his name was considered in the discussion leading to the naming of this building. Executive Committee Records 2, November 3, 1891; Corporation Records 4, December 9, 1891. In a sense this was the "second" of the two major buildings originally foreseen at the time of the founding, but the actual second structure on the square of land was the drill hall and gymnasium, with lunch room facilities, built in 1874.

60. THW to WBR, September 13, 1864, WBR Papers, folder 48.
61. Government Records 1, September 15, 1865.
62. Government Records 2, June 5, 1866 (the committee included William Rogers, Jacob Bigelow, and Endicott, Dalton, and Ross); Cash Book no. 1, January 2, 1867. A short piece on a portrait of Huntington in *Technology Review* (*TR* 43 [June 1941]: 368) refers to a "generous bequest of $80,000 which came to Technology upon his death in 1866," but a review of the Institute records reveals only the $50,000 total, entered as an explanatory note in the cash book when the $17,000 was received, since the legacy tax applied to the entire amount. The $30,000 error in the *Technology Review* article undoubtedly stems from an incorrect assumption that the total figure then appearing in the records was in addition to the $30,000 that Huntington had transferred in 1865, which essentially became a bequest when he died.
63. Government Records 1, June 30, 1863, February 27 & March 17, 1864 (other members of the committee were Erastus Bigelow, Jacob Bigelow, Henry B. Rogers, and William Rogers).
64. Government Records 1, March 17, 1864; Society of Arts Records 1, March 24, 1864.
65. THW to Wyman, April 7, 1866, MIT Letters 1; Government Records 2, October 13, 1866, & March 2, April 20, June 3, 1867.
66. Report of Finances of the Massachusetts Institute of Technology, May 22, 1865, Office of the Treasurer, Reports, 1865–1883, presented at the Annual Meeting, May 25, 1865, Society of Arts Records 2; Cash Book no. 1, June 24 & July 6, 1865.
67. JDR to WBR, June 11, 1865, WBR Papers, folder 50.
68. Notes payable, Ledger no. 1; Cash Book no. 1.

*C*hapter Fourteen   THE BUILDING

1.   Government Records 1, February 21, 1863.

2.   Confusion arises immediately in the official records of the Government and the Museum Committee, in which both are said to have met on February 21, 1863, at the same hour. Government and Museum Committee minutes both indicate the time of meeting as Saturday, February 21, at 7:30 p.m. Rogers is said to have presided at the former and was participating in discussion at the latter. The Museum Committee minutes do not list those present, but several of its members were listed for the Government meeting and thus could have met following the main meeting, but R. C. Greenleaf, secretary of the Museum Committee, makes no note of this.

3.   "Art. II.—MERCANTILE BIOGRAPHY. Erastus Brigham Bigelow," *Hunt's Merchants Magazine and Commercial Review* 30, no. 2 (February 1854): 170.

4.   Museum Committee Records, February 21, 1863. This is the only volume of records for this committee, the last entry being March 11, 1869. Included are loose sheets for meetings on November 22, 1870; February 7, 1871; & February 20, March 2, March 9, & December 18, 1872.

5.   Building Committee Minutes, BSNH, Museum of Science Archives. These minutes are partly a narrative account and partly a record of specific meetings, all without page numbers. The society as a whole approved the selection of the Prestons on November 20, 1861, following a report by Rogers on behalf of the committee. A fragmentary note by Rogers confirms that Bryant and Gilman had been the first choice of the society. WBR Papers, folder 42b.

6.   This conclusion is supported by the presence of relevant drawings bearing 1862 and early 1863 dates in the William G. Preston Collection, Fine Arts Department, Boston Public Library.

7.   Government Records 1, May 6, 1863.

8.   Ibid., June 6, 1864.

9.   MIT Building Committee Minutes, 1863–1867, May 7 & 11, 1863. The subcommittee on the selection of an architect included Eldredge, Davies, and Little.

10.   WBR to MDR, May 24, 1863, WBR Papers, folder 46a.

11.   Ibid.

12.   Museum Committee Records, May 26, 1863.

13.   Government Records 1, June 3, 1863. These minutes refer to the Bigelow committee as the Provisional Committee on Plans and Estimates for the Main or Central Building of the Institute. There is no indication that this enlargement of the Museum Committee ever met.

14.   James F. O'Gorman, *Drawings by Nineteenth Century Boston Architects*, 39; Jean Ames Follett-Thompson, *The Business of Architecture: William Gibbons Preston and Architectural Professionalism in Boston During the Second Half of the Nineteenth Century*, 12.

15.   O'Gorman, 91; Follett-Thompson, 34.

16.   Report of the Building Committee, August 25, 1863, Government Records 1, 80–87; MIT Building Committee Minutes, August 20, 1863.

17. Government Records 1, August 25, 1863.

18. Ibid., September 8, 1863.

19. WBR to HDR, June 15, 1863, *Life and Letters,* 2:166; Alex. Galletly to WBR, July 13, 1863, WBR Papers, folder 46; WBR to HDR, August 4 & 31, 1863, *Life and Letters,* 2:169, 174; HDR to WBR, October 31, 1863, ibid., 180.

20. WBR to HDR, August 4, 1863, & March 2, 1864, *Life and Letters,* 2:169, 189.

21. Loose sheet in Building Committee Minutes, February 13, 1867; WBR to HDR, March 2, 1864, *Life and Letters,* 2:189.

22. Preston to WBR, March 26, 1864, WBR Papers, folder 47.

23. Ibid.

24. MIT Building Committee Minutes, May 7, 1864.

25. Ibid., February 4, 15, 22, 28, & March 25, 1865.

26. Society of Arts Records 2, December 1, 1864.

27. Government Records 1, February 27, 1865.

28. File copy, March 15, 1865, WBR Papers, folder 50.

29. Third Annual Report of the Secretary, May 25, 1865, Society of Arts Records 2, 113–114. The land so reserved from sale never came to the Institute. On April 8, 1873, part of a trapezoidal piece of land at the intersection of Boylston Street and Huntington Avenue was granted to the Institute by the Commonwealth, and on May 8, 1875, the grant was rescinded. The Institute was allowed to locate another site in the Back Bay equivalent to the trapezoidal piece, which would be sold to the city of Boston with the understanding that it be maintained as a public park. The city was required to secure the remainder of the trapezoidal piece, also to be maintained as part of the public park. This area is now Copley Square. Acts of 1873, Chapter 174, and Acts of 1875, Chapter 195, *Acts and Resolves,* 1931, 8–10.

30. MIT Building Committee Minutes, February 28, March 4, 11, & 18, April 1, 3, 5, & 8, 1865.

31. Ibid., April 13, 1865.

32. O'Gorman, 56–57, 118.

33. Government Records 1, April 24, 1865; MIT Building Committee Minutes, May 3, 1865. A loose unsigned drawing of the Institute building with mansard roof in Boston Campus Plans Book 1 (MIT Museum) reveals how inappropriate such a roof would have been. It is not known whether the drawing was done by William Preston or Fehmer, but it does not appear to fit the "sophisticated" and "photographic" style attributed to Fehmer. In view of the difficult circumstances, it may even have been done by Jonathan Preston.

34. MIT Building Committee Minutes, May 17 & 20, 1865; Government Records 1, May 24 & 29, 1865.

35. Government Records 1, June 5, 1865.

36. Ibid.; J. Herbert Shedd to WBR, July 13, 1865, WBR Papers, folder 52.

37. Government Records 1, August 10, 1865. Committee on Warming and Ventilation Report, 231–239.

38. MIT Building Committee Minutes, November 20, 1865.

39. C. H. Dalton, Treasurer, to Prof. Wm. B. Rogers, Chairman, Building Committee, M.I.T. (perhaps the earliest use of the abbreviation by which this institution is now popularly known).

40. MIT Building Committee Minutes, December 6, 1865; WBR to MDR, December 7, 1865, WBR Papers, folder 53. This folder also contains an unrelated piece of correspondence in which Rogers refers to his absence "during the recent holidays." WBR to H. P. Wells, December 15, 1865.

41. Government Records 1, May 29 & December 19, 1865.

42. Undated, but undoubtedly Ross's report of December 6, 1865, WBR Papers, folder 53.

43. Government Records 1, December 19, 1865. Rogers report, 262–269.

44. Government Records 2, February 23, 1866.

45. "Members of the Corporation Deceased," 40; obituary, *Boston Evening Transcript*, February 14, 1889.

46. Report of Edward S. Philbrick, dated January 20, 1866, entered in Government Records 2, February 23, 1866, 7–15.

47. Government Records 2, February 23 & April 12, 1866.

48. Ibid., May 28, 1866.

49. Ibid., August 22, 1866.

50. Ibid., January 11, 1867, 86–90; March 2, 1867. Original copy of the final report in WBR Papers, folder 56.

51. In 1984, in a retrospective look at the first building of the Institute, Dean Emeritus Lawrence B. Anderson of the School of Architecture and Planning described in some detail the "harrowing ineptitude" with which the Building Committee carried out its task. "The project petered out," he said, "with tantalizing slowness, the initial optimism about both costs and time of completion completely unrealizable." He suspected that the records did not reflect probable "recriminations on all sides"—a correct assumption, for the minutes of Thomas Webb, who was Jonathan Preston's brother-in-law, are carefully worded. William Rogers, however, without naming the Prestons but in Jonathan's presence, did not hesitate to imply that they were to blame for the mansard roof fiasco, and Jonathan Preston lost his seat on the Government in 1867 when he was not reappointed to the Committee on the Museum.

    Anderson also pointed out that in 1863 the architectural profession had yet to define the formal procedures and guidelines that exist today with respect to contracts and an orderly process of construction, and building technology was at an early stage of development. William Preston's design for a "handsome building," of brick, sandstone, and granite, had been influenced by "neo-Renaissance" structures in France. There was an "obligatory broad flight of steps" along with a "rather conventional array of windows, arches, and classic orders, with ornamentation appearing in the expected locations." Anderson remarked that Preston appeared to have had a "far greater concern for his envelope than for the elements he had to dispose within it"—laboratories, classrooms, offices, a large lecture hall, an exhibition hall, and a library. In the early stages, however, there remained unresolved questions about the development of the Institute. And a statement by William Rogers as late as the end of February

1865 that the "interior arrangements" required "much reflection and exercise of a great deal of judgment" indicates that two years after the start of the project, Preston probably had received little guidance about the Building Committee's intentions in this regard. Lawrence B. Anderson, "The Rogers Building: 1866–1938," *Places* 1, no. 4 (Summer 1984): 38–46.

52. Anderson, 40–41.
53. Society of Arts Records 2, November 15, 1866.
54. Government Records 2, June 5, 1866.
55. Undated fragment, MDR to WBR, WBR Papers, folder 148.
56. MDR to WBR, October 4, 1864, ibid., folder 48.
57. MIT Building Committee Minutes, November 20, 1865.
58. Government Records 1, September 15, 1865.
59. Government Records 2, June 3, 1867.
60. The Department of Architecture actually moved into the old Rogers Building in 1916. In 1883 it had moved to a new Institute building at the corner of Boylston and Clarendon Streets, in 1892 to a newly built Architectural Building at the corner of Stuart and Clarendon Streets, and in 1898 from those "cramped quarters" to the Institute's Pierce Building on Trinity Place, adjoining the Architectural Building.

    The demolition of the old building in 1938 brought the eclipse of the name of one of the earliest supporters of the Institute of Technology, but the determination of Huntington and his daughter would carry over to a succeeding generation. In 1940 John L. Batchelder, a member of the class of 1890 and the husband of Huntington's grandniece, raised with Karl T. Compton, then president of the Institute, the question of reinstating some form of memorial. In return, Mrs. Batchelder was prepared to present Huntington's portrait to the Institute. A Committee on Fine Arts and Memorials, after considering several options, finally recommended that Room 10-250, the large hall "where every student who goes through the Institute must at some time have had some of his lectures," be named Huntington Hall. The recommendation was approved by the Executive Committee of the Corporation (Executive Committee Records 8, February 13, 1940). The Committee's report, entitled *Huntington Hall*, undated and unsigned, Ralph Huntington file, MIT Museum. The portrait of Ralph Huntington, which came to the Institute in 1941 and hung for many years at the entrance of the new Huntington Hall, is unsigned but may have been painted by Chester Harding. It now hangs in the MIT Museum.

61. Corporation Records 3, May 23, 1883. In connection with a reorganization of the Institute, approved by the legislature in March 1869 (Acts of 1869, Chapter 97), revised bylaws were prepared and adopted on June 23, 1870. Since that time the governing body of the Institute has been called the "Corporation." Government Records 2.
62. On June 6, 1938, a new building at 77 Massachusetts Avenue in Cambridge, designed principally to house the Department of Architecture, was dedicated at the request of the alumni to William Barton Rogers after a farewell ceremony on Boylston Street commemorating "a man, a building, and an idea." The old Rogers Building and the adjacent building designed by Carl Fehmer, named in 1891 for Francis Amasa Walker, were razed to make way for the home office

of the New England Mutual Life Insurance Company. On May 30, 1978, a plaque on that building's façade was unveiled marking the site of the Institute's first home, and Mrs. Franklin W. Hobbs III, great-great granddaughter of James Blythe Rogers, William's elder brother, was present on that occasion. We are grateful to Mrs. Hobbs for her help in locating additional Rogers material—family photographs, manuscripts, and memorabilia—for the MIT Archives and the MIT Museum. Mrs. Hobbs's grandmother, Mrs. Edgar Wright Baird (Mabel Rogers), presented the Jacob H. Lazarus portrait of William Barton Rogers to the Institute in 1955 in her name and that of her great-grandson, William Barton Rogers Hobbs. (Mabel Rogers Baird to James R. Killian, Jr., May 21, 1955, MIT Office of the President, Records, 1930–1959, box 186, folder 13.) The portrait had previously been on loan to the Institute through Mrs. Baird to whom it was willed by the niece of President Rogers, Mrs. C. F. Russell (Mary Otis Rogers), the daughter of Henry Darwin Rogers. It had come to her through a bequest from Emma Savage Rogers. Franklin W. Hobbs III also has close ties to the Institute as the grandson of Franklin W. Hobbs of the class of 1889, who was vice president of the Alumni Association in 1910 and a Corporation member from 1914 to 1919 and again from 1923 to 1955.

*C*hapter Fifteen   THE SOCIETY OF ARTS

1. *Objects and Plan*, 4.
2. Ibid., 28–29.
3. Sir Henry Trueman Wood, *A History of the Royal Society of Arts*, 7.
4. Ibid., 17–19, 26–27, 51.
5. Ibid., 17–19.
6. Ibid., 336.
7. Ibid., 338.
8. Ibid., 332–334, 373–375, 443; Government Records 1, May 24, 1865.
9. Wood, 354–355.
10. *Objects and Plan*, 5.
11. Ibid., 6–7.
12. Ibid., 7–13.
13. Circular letters, November, 1860, & January 7, 1861, WBR Papers, folders 36, 37.
14. James Edward Oliver to WBR, "January 12 or 13 ([1861]-Midnight)," ibid., folder 37.
15. *Account of the Proceedings*, 9–14.
16. First Annual Report of the Secretary, May 11, 1863, Society of Arts Records 1, 137–139, presented at adjourned annual meeting, June 17, 1863; Second Annual Report of the Secretary, May 30, 1864, Society of Arts Records 1, 266.
17. First Annual Report of the Secretary, Society of Arts Records 1, 139.
18. Society of Arts Records 1, April 13, 1863.
19. Annual Report of the Secretary for 1863, 1864, 1865, Society of Arts Records 1, 139, 270; 2, 126.

20. Annual Report of the Secretary, 1864, Society of Arts Records 1, 271.
21. First Annual Report of the Secretary, 1863, ibid., 139–140.
22. Ibid., 140.
23. Society of Arts Records 1, April 8 & 22, May 6 & 20, 1862.
24. Government Records 1, April 8 & 22, July 15, September 23 & 30, December 5 & 15, 1862.
25. Government Records 1, December 15, 1862.
26. Society of Arts Records 1, December 17, 1862.
27. Ibid. The secretary would continue to use the record book started on April 8 for the Institute's first meeting, the volume labeled "Society of Arts Records," a title giving no indication that the first official records of the Institute as the Institute are therein contained. In December 1864, he began to identify the "Ordinary Meetings" as meetings "as a Society of Arts." These early volumes, therefore, set down in a single record meetings of the Institute at which the business of the organization would be transacted; meetings of the Society of Arts; and meetings in which elements of both were included.
28. Ibid.
29. Ibid.; January 14, 1863.
30. Government Records 1, November 24, 1863.
31. Report of the Committee on Publication, February 10, 1864, Government Records 1, 108–120.
32. Government Records 1, March 17, 1864.
33. Ibid.
34. *Objects and Plan*, 7–8.
35. *By-Laws*, 8. For a description of the expected work of these committees, see *Objects and Plan*, 8–12.
36. Society of Arts Records 1, May 25, 1863.
37. Government Records 1, November 24, 1863.
38. Society of Arts Records 1, January 14, 1864.
39. Government Records 1, February 10, 1864.
40. Second Annual Report of the Secretary, May 30, 1864, Society of Arts Records 1, 261–262.
41. Ibid., 260.
42. Paper by Justin Jones, Society of Arts Records 1, February 11, 1864.
43. Society of Arts Records 1, April 14 & 28, 1864.
44. *Economy in Fuel, a Paper Read at the request of Professor Rogers by J. Amory, Before the Technological Institute, and the Report of the Committee Thereon* (Boston, 1864), copy in MIT Archives. A notation on this copy states that Frederic E. Stimpson was a special student for one year, 1865–66. He is so listed in the first catalogue. The registrar's records list his previous address as Lawrence, Kansas, but contain little other information.
45. Society of Arts Records 1, May 25, 1863.
46. Society of Arts Records 2, February 2, March 2 & 16, 1865.
47. Ibid., April 20, 1865.

48. Revised *By-Laws*, 2.
49. Society of Arts Records 1, January 14, 1863.
50. Ibid. 2, February 16, 1865.
51. Letter, William Edson to THW, April 6, 1865, as recorded in Society of Arts Records 2, April 6, 1865.
52. Society of Arts Records 2, April 6, 1865.
53. Third Annual Report of the Secretary, May 25, 1865, Society of Arts Records 2, 93–94.
54. *Objects and Plan*, 8.
55. Society of Arts Records 2, January 4, 1866.
56. WBR to Jacob Bigelow, incomplete file copy, May 29, 1866, WBR Papers, folder 54; pencil markings may indicate that it was considered for possible inclusion in *Life and Letters*, in which it does not, however, appear.
57. Ibid.
58. Society of Arts Records 2, April 19, 1866; *Account of the Proceedings*, 9.
59. WBR to R. Morris Copeland, December 23, 1866, WBR Papers, folder 54.
60. Government Records 2, April 12, 1866.
61. Fourth Annual Report of the Secretary, May 25, 1866, ibid., 274.
62. Society of Arts Records 3, January 3, February 7 & 21, 1867. There is no formal record of the February 28 public meeting. Professor Langley was very likely John W. Langley, a chemist and an 1861 graduate of the Lawrence Scientific School who had been assistant professor of chemistry and natural science at Antioch College for a brief period, returning to Boston in 1867. His interests centered on chemical and metallurgical research, and he would later serve on the faculties of several institutions, including the University of Michigan.
63. Society of Arts Records 3, April 4, 1867.
64. Ibid., December 5, 1867.
65. Society of Arts Records 2, April 19, 1866.
66. Ibid., February 20, 1868.
67. Ibid., April 16, 1868. The report of this committee in printed form, pasted in the record book, appears to be a clipping, not necessarily a newspaper clipping, source unknown.
68. Society of Arts Records 3, May 31, 1867.
69. Fifth Annual Report of the Secretary, May 31, 1867, ibid., 105.
70. Society of Arts Records 2, April 6, 1865.
71. Fourth Annual Report of the Secretary, May 25, 1866, ibid., 219.
72. Society of Arts Records 3, March 7, 1867.
73. Society of Arts Records 3, May 2, 1867.
74. Ibid., April 30, 1868.
75. Ibid., December 6, 1866; December 19, 1867; February 20, May 7, & December 3, 1868.
76. Ibid., May 7, 1868.
77. Sixth Annual Report of the Secretary, May 21, 1868, ibid., 216. Figures for previous years, Fourth Annual Report, May 25, 1866, Society of Arts Records 2, 278; Fifth Annual Report, May 31, 1867, Society of Arts Records 3, 106.

78. Society of Arts Records 3, January 3, 1867.

79. Fourth Annual Report of the Secretary, May 25, 1866, Society of Arts Records 2, 279–280.

80. Society of Arts Records 1, December 24, 1863.

81. Society of Arts Records 2, November 16, 1865.

82. Ibid.

83. Bigelow, *An Address on the Limits of Education*, 6.

84. Ibid., 17, 19.

85. Ibid., 15.

86. Ibid., 15–18.

87. Ibid., 16.

88. Bigelow continued to speak out elsewhere as, for example, at a special meeting of the American Academy of Arts and Sciences on November 21, 1866. His talk, entitled "On Classical and Utilitarian Studies," elicited a sharp response from academic conservatives. At a regular meeting on February 26, 1867, Francis Bowen, Alford Professor of Natural Religion, Moral Philosophy, and Civil Polity at Harvard, launched into a stinging rebuttal in defense of classical studies: "Even if it be granted that the glory of modern times is its mechanical inventions, it may well be doubted whether the study of physical science and the establishment of Technological Institutes will lead to their multiplication or improvement. The fact is notorious, that most of these are the results of accident, or have been made by unlearned men, chiefly by ingenious artisans. Even the disposition which seeks for them, and the course of experiments instituted for their attainment, are unfavorable to habits of scientific research; for gold, not truth, is the object in view; and though some general fact or law of nature may incidentally be developed, the mind was not on the watch for it, and it will probably be overlooked or forgotten. If you would train up inventors, educate your sons at the blacksmith's forge or the carpenter's bench, in watch-factories, cotton-mills, or machine-shops." These arguments, Bowen said, were intended not to "discredit science" but to reveal "the pitiable folly—I had almost said the impiety—of measuring the value of either physics or metaphysics, chemistry or philology, by a low utilitarian standard." Jacob Bigelow, *Remarks on Classical and Utilitarian Studies*, [3], 6. The essay is included in Jacob Bigelow, *Modern Inquiries: Classical, Professional, and Miscellaneous*. See also *Proceedings, AAcadAS* 7 (1865–1868) 237; George E. Ellis, *Memoir of Jacob Bigelow, M.D., LL.D.*, reprinted from the *Proceedings of the Massachusetts Historical Society* (Cambridge, 1880). Francis Bowen, *Classical Studies*, 17.

89. Society of Arts Records 2, December 21, 1865.

90. William R. Ware, *An Outline of a Course of Architectural Instruction* (Boston, 1866).

91. Society of Arts Records 3, May 21, 1868.

92. Government Records 1, May 6, 27, & June 30, 1863; Society of Arts Records 1, May 11 & June 8, 1863.

93. Government Records 1, February 27, March 9 & 17, 1864.

94. Society of Arts Records 1, March 24 & April 28, 1864.

95. Annual Report of the Secretary, 1864, Society of Arts Records 1, 272–273.

96. Society of Arts Records 1, 273. Years later, when Silas Holman was preparing a record of the society's meetings for possible publication, he marked these passages (272–277) for omission.

97. Government Records 1, May 2 & November 28, 1864; January 30 & February 27, 1865; Society of Arts Records 2, April 6, 1865.

98. "Bylaws," 1–7, printed version, n.d., bound into Society of Arts Records 2, April 6, 1865, between pages 48 and 49. The original bylaws also referred to the "Museum of Technology" rather than the "Museum of Industrial Science and Art." An insert bound into this volume between pages 238 and 239 as part of the Secretary's Fourth Annual Report, May 25, 1866, appears to have been prepared later by Silas Holman. This insert states in error that these new bylaws provided for the Society of Arts to elect "its own Executive Committee," a change that did not occur until 1870.

99. Government Records 2, October 13, 1866.

100. Government Records 1, November 24, 1863, April 18, 1865, August 22, 1866.

101. Government Records 2, April 20 & June 3, 1867.

102. Ibid., May 13 & December 3, 1868; February 11, 1869.

103. *Acts and Resolves*, 7–8.

104. Government Records 2, June 23, 1870.

105. *Life and Letters,* 2:259–263; WBR to H. L. Wayland, March 16, 1867, responding to Wayland's letter of November 1, 1866, WBR Papers, folders 54 & 56. *Life and Letters* notes an entry in Rogers's journal (now missing) on the death of Thomas Webb. Henry Rogers and his wife and daughter had been in the United States since the fall of 1865, and he had returned alone to Scotland in April. His wife and daughter accompanied William on his journey to Scotland but returned to Boston later. Robert Rogers also made the trip.

106. Government Records 2, June 27 & August 22, 1866.

107. Ibid., August 22 & September 26, 1866.

108. Ibid., August 22, 1866.

109. Ibid., September 26, 1866.

110. Ibid., September 26, October 5, & November 15, 1866; January 5, April 20, & May 11, 1867.

111. John D. Runkle, "Samuel Kneeland," *Proceedings, AAcadAS* 24 (1888–1889): 438–441. See also *ACAB, DAB,* and *NCAB.*

112. Society of Arts Records 3, November 15, 1866.

113. Ibid., May 16, 1867.

114. Ibid., May 31, 1867. A newspaper clipping pasted in the volume contains Rogers's entire report.

115. Ibid. The "gentle lady" was Mrs. Augustus Hemenway. The "generous friend" was Nathaniel Thayer. Receipt dated April 11, 1867, from Samuel Kneeland to WBR, transmitting $510 "for tuition of certain students for the year 1866–67, in part." WBR Papers, folder 57.

116. *Life and Letters* is incorrect in stating that the legislative resolve was passed in 1867, as an official copy of it, prepared on July 6, 1866, by the secretary of the Commonwealth, is in the Rogers papers and must have accompanied Governor Bullock's first request, which has not been found. WBR Papers, folder 54. Rogers was elected also an honorary commissioner with-

out compensation for the United States but declined because of the press of duties as commissioner for Massachusetts. N. Beckwith, U. S. Commissioner General to WBR, May 10, 1867, and file copy WBR to the Commissioner General, July 16, 1867, ibid., folder 57.

117. WBR to James Savage, June 25, 1867, *Life and Letters,* 2:272.

118. WBR to James Savage, July 27, 1867, ibid., 274–275.

119. Ibid., 276.

120. Oliver, 297–298.

121. Society of Arts Records 3, November 7, 1867.

122. Ibid. Governor Alexander H. Bullock had replaced Andrew as an *ex officio* member following his inauguration early in January 1866.

Chapter Sixteen THE COMMITTEE ON PUBLICATION

1. *Objects and Plan,* 6.

2. Frank Luther Mott, *A History of American Magazines, 1741–1850,* 266–267.

3. Ibid., 151–152.

4. Ibid., 152. Webster was a lecturer on chemistry, mineralogy, and geology at Harvard at the time, who would by 1827 be Erving Professor of Chemistry and by 1850 be hanged for murder; Ware would later be Hersey Professor of the Theory and Practice of Physic at Harvard; and Treadwell would be Rumford Professor from 1834 to 1845.

5. Ibid., 445. In later years, *Mechanic* is said to have focused on woodworking.

6. Ibid., 446.

7. There are many parallels in the organization of the Franklin Institute in Philadelphia and the early plans for the Institute of Technology. Had William and Henry Rogers's 1837 proposal to the Pennsylvania legislature for a school of arts to be connected with the Franklin Institute been successful, the similarities would have been virtually complete.

8. *The Franklin Journal, and American Mechanics' Magazine* 1, no. 1 (January 1826): 1.

9. Sinclair, 196; for a more extended discussion of the *Journal,* see chapter 8 of this source.

10. Ibid., 198–199, 205, 208, 216.

11. *By-Laws,* 9.

12. "John Daniel Runkle and his Share in the Development of Technology," *Technique,* 1901, author unknown. See also Harry W. Tyler (Class of 1884), "John Daniel Runkle," *TR* 4 (July 1902): 278–306.

13. Simon Newcomb, *The Reminiscences of an Astronomer,* 63.

14. Florian Cajori, *The Teaching and History of Mathematics in the United States,* 278.

15. Newcomb, 84–85; JDR to WBR, circular letter, February 13, 1858, typed copy, WBR Papers, folder 33; Cajori (279) states that "in the mathematical notation employed and in the treatment of mathematical subjects, Benjamin Peirce's influence was clearly perceptible. From a scientific point of view, the *Monthly* excelled any of its predecessors."

16. Newcomb, 87.

17. *DAB*, s.v. "Flint, Charles L."

18. *DAB*, s.v. "Hoadley, John C."; Corporation Records 3, February 9, 1887.

19. *DAB*, s.v. "Sabine, Lorenzo," *NCAB*. Lorenzo Sabine, *The American Loyalists; or Biographical Sketches of Adherents to the British Crown in the War of the Revolution; alphabetically arranged with a Preliminary Historical Essay* (Boston: Charles C. Little & James Brown, 1847); *A Historical Essay on the Loyalists of the American Revolution, with a foreword by Benjamin Keen* (Springfield, Mass.: Walden Press, 1957); *Biographical Sketches of Loyalists of the American Revolution with an Historical Essay* (Boston: Little, Brown & Co., 1864; reissued, with a new introduction by Ralph Adams Brown, Port Washington, N.Y.: Kennicat Press, 1966).

20. *DAB*, s.v. "Rice, Alexander Hamilton."

21. Society of Arts Records 1, December 17, 1862.

22. Government Records 1, November 24, 1863.

23. Emerson to JDR, January 5, 1864, JDR Papers.

24. Report of the Committee on Publication, Government Records 1, February 10, 1864, 112. Complete report, 108–120.

25. Ibid., 111.

26. Ibid., 115–116.

27. Ibid., 117.

28. Ibid., 112–113.

29. Ibid., 119–120.

30. Ibid., 112.

31. Ibid., March 17, 1864.

32. Ibid., May 30, 1864.

33. Ibid., June 6, 1864. At this time they were still hoping to open the school in the fall of 1864.

34. Third Annual Report of the Secretary, May 25, 1865, Society of Arts Records 2, 105.

35. Fourth Annual Report of the Secretary, May 25, 1866, Society of Arts Records 2, 271.

36. Ibid., 271–272.

37. Fifth Annual Report of the Secretary, May 31, 1867, Society of Arts Records 3, 104.

38. Society of Arts Records 3, May 31, 1867. Pasted in clipping from unidentified newspaper, an account of Rogers's address.

39. Government Records 2, May 13 & 19, 1868.

40. Ibid., May 19, 1868.

41. Society of Arts Records 3, May 21, 1868. Pasted in clipping from unidentified newspaper, an account of Rogers's address.

42. Government Records 2, December 14, 1870. Society of Arts Records 4, December 15, 1870.

Chapter Seventeen THE MUSEUM OF TECHNOLOGY

1. Conservatory of Art and Science, record of February 18, 1859, meeting, WBR Papers, folder 33.

2. *Boston Advertiser*, October 8, 1860.

3. *Objects and Plan*, 13. The text refers only to "Museum of Industrial Science and Art." The charter of 1861 called it a "Museum of arts." *Officers; Extracts; Objects and Plan; By-Laws*, 7.

4. *Objects and Plan*, 19.

5. Ibid., 4. Included in the Rogers Book Collection in the MIT Libraries are several items showing a plan of the hall of the Museum of Practical Geology and the arrangement of some of the exhibits, together with volumes relating to the School of Mines: *Arrangements of the British Marbles, Alabasters, Serpentines, Porphyries, Granites, Building Stones, &c. in the Vestibule and Hall of the Museum of Practical Geology*, n.d., but internal mention suggests after May 1851; *Arrangement of the Fossils and Rock Specimens in the Galleries of the Museum of Practical Geology*, 1853; *Museum of Practical Geology and Geological Survey, Records of the School of Mines and of Science Applied to the Arts*, vol. 1, pt. 1 & 2 (London: Longman, Brown, Green, & Longmans, 1852 and 1853). Volume 1, part 1, bears the bookplate of Henry D. Rogers, with a notation that it was presented to the Institute by Mrs. Henry D. Rogers. It is inscribed, however, as follows: "Prof. J. B. Rogers on the part of the Professors of the Government School of Mines. London." It seems probable that the inscription was intended for Prof. W. B. Rogers. James B. Rogers, a professor of chemistry in the Medical School of the University of Pennsylvania, died on June 12, 1852, the year of publication for this volume. Its subject matter is far closer to the interest of William and could well have been given to Henry in response to William's request. Volume 1, part 2, bears William's bookplate.

6. The changing of titles has been described as "a favourite British disease"—a tendency that may be reflected in the several titles accorded along the way to the Institute's museum. A. Rupert Hall, *Science for Industry, A Short History of the Imperial College of Science and Technology and its Antecedents*, 4.

7. "Address of Sir Henry de la Beche at formal opening, May 14, 1851, of new building for the Museum of Practical Geology," in Robert Hunt, F.R.S., and F. W. Rudler, *A Descriptive Guide to the Museum of Practical Geology*, 4th ed., 3.

8. Ibid., 4.

9. Sir Henry de la Beche, "Inaugural Discourse, Opening of the School of Mines and of Science applied to the Arts, 6th November 1851," *Records of the School of Mines*, vol. 1, pt. 1, 17.

10. Hunt and Rudler, 4.

11. Ibid., 5.

12. *Records of the School of Mines*, vol. 1, pt. 1, 1 & 3.

13. Ibid., 3–4.

14. Ibid., 12.

15. Ibid., 18.

16. Ibid., 19–20. This volume also contains the Introductory Lectures to the Courses for the Session 1851–52.

17. Ibid., b, d.

18. For a brief account of the evolution of the Imperial College see Hall, chap. 1, "Facing Common Problems," 1–12. See also *Centenary of the Imperial College of Science and Technology, A Short History of the College, 1845–1945* (n.d.), 3–10.

19. *Records of the School of Mines*, vol. 1, pt. 1, 21–22.
20. Edward Forbes, F.R.S. &c., "On the Educational Uses of Museums," *American Journal of Science and Arts*, 2d ser., 18 (November 1854): 340, 341, 343, 345.
21. Hall, 4, 8.
22. Artz, 11–12.
23. Ibid., 143, 147.
24. Ibid., 145–146.
25. Wickenden, 15; House no. 13, 12.
26. *Objects and Plan*, 14.
27. Ibid., 13.
28. Ibid., 14.
29. Ibid., 14–18.
30. Ibid., 18.
31. Hall, 8–12. Hall states that the further development of the institution is a "muddled and complex story"—a statement that might be applied as well to the period which bears most directly on the Institute.
32. "Objects and Plan of an Institute of Technology," *Mathematical Monthly* 3, no. 3 (December 1860): 94.
33. Ibid.
34. Ibid., 19–20.
35. *Boston Advertiser*, January 18, 1861.
36. House no. 171, March 19, 1861, 4–5.
37. *Objects and Plan*, 12.
38. *Officers; Extracts; Objects and Plan; By-Laws*, 9.
39. Society of Arts Records 1, December 17, 1862.
40. *Account of the Proceedings*, 12; "Members of the Corporation Deceased" 2:2; Arthur Emerson Benson, *History of the Massachusetts Horticultural Society*, 341–342.
41. "Members of the Corporation Deceased" 1:35.
42. *Mayors of Boston* (Boston: State Street Trust Co., 1914), 24; "Incorporators," 31; Corporation Records 4, December 14, 1893.
43. "Members of the Corporation Deceased" 1:44; Corporation Records 4, October 9, 1889.
44. "Stephen Preston Ruggles," *Proceedings, AAcadAS* 16 (1880–1881): 433–435.
45. Government Records 1, September 23, 1862.
46. Ibid., 11–12. Rogers's use of the term "alphabet of mechanics" arose in a conversation we (Julius Stratton and Loretta Mannix) had with Dean C. Richard Soderberg of MIT shortly before his death. At that time he called to our attention the "Mechanical Alphabet" now in the Tekniska Museet, Stockholm, part of the collection of models and machines of Christopher Polhem (1661–1751), an important figure in the history of Swedish science and technology, associated with the Swedish Bureau of Mines. Following an extensive stay abroad in the 1690s, during which he visited factories, mills, and universities, observing the machines

and instruments then in use, Polhem advocated the establishment in Sweden of a mechanical laboratory for the construction and demonstration of machines and mechanical devices, a laboratory which might serve also as a school and experimental center. His plan found approval, but it appears that only a *laboratorium mechanicum* was established, its models and machines in 1826 coming under the jurisdiction of the newly founded Tekniska Högskolan. His "mechanical alphabet" consisted of eighty pieces demonstrating mechanical motions. See *Christopher Polhem, the Father of Swedish Technology*, trans. William A. Johnson (Hartford, Conn.: Trustees of Trinity College, 1963).

47. Government Records 1, November 24, 1863.
48. Museum Committee Records 1, December 3, 1863. Ruggles's memoranda were not made a part of the record.
49. Ibid., December 12, 1863.
50. Government Records 1, February 27, 1864.
51. Committee on the Museum Records 1, February 29, 1864.
52. Francis to MDR, April 7, 1863, WBR Papers, folder 45.
53. Government Records 1, June 6, 1864.
54. Secretary's Report, May 30, 1864, Society of Arts Records 1, 258.
55. MDR to WBR, October 4, 1864, WBR Papers, folder 48.
56. Committee on the Museum Records, February 9, 1865.
57. Ibid.
58. Ibid.
59. Ibid.
60. Standing committees for the year 1865–66 were elected at a Government meeting on May 29, 1865, and instructed to meet as soon as possible, organizing themselves by the election of a chairman and secretary. Bigelow's name appeared first on the Museum list on the assumption that he would continue to hold the chairmanship. By the June 5 meeting of the Committee on the Museum, however, he had declined to continue except as a member, and M. D. Ross was elected to succeed him and would serve as chairman for the year 1865–66. Government Records 1, May 29, 1865, and Museum Committee Records 1, June 5, 1865.
61. Society of Arts Records 2, May 25, 1865, 121.
62. *Conservatory Journal* 1, no. 1 (April 9, 1859).
63. Museum Committee Records, October 4 & 5, 1866.
64. Fourth Annual Report of the Secretary, May 25, 1866, Society of Arts Records 2, 270.
65. Ibid., 270–271.
66. Government Records 2, September 26, 1866.
67. Museum Committee Records, October 4 & 5, 1866; Government Records 2, October 5, 1866. In a step unusual for the time, Henry Rogers engaged artist-draftsmen to travel with his surveying party to prepare illustrations for inclusion in his reports. It is not known whether the illustrations given to the Institute at this time included any of their watercolors or other drawings, and if so, what has become of them. See Donald M. Hoskins, "Celebrating a

Century and a Half, The Geologic Survey," *Pennsylvania Heritage* 12, no. 3 (Summer, 1986): 26–31.

68. Fifth Annual Report of the Secretary, May 31, 1867, Society of Arts Records 3, 103. Society of Arts Records 3, February 7, 1867.

69. Fifth Annual Report of the Secretary, 107.

70. Museum Committee Records, January 17, 1868.

71. Ibid.

72. Ibid., March 11, 1869.

73. Sixth Annual Report of the Secretary, May 21, 1868, Society of Arts Records 3, 217; Society of Arts Records 3, May 21, 1868. Newspaper clipping containing Rogers's address pasted in record book. Same clipping, date of May 27, 1868, paper not identified, WBR Papers, folder 247.

74. Government Records 2, November 23, 1867.

75. Ibid., March 23, 1869.

Chapter Eighteen THE SCHOOL OF INDUSTRIAL SCIENCE

1. Government Records 1, June 30, 1863. The committee consisted of E. B. Bigelow, C. H. Dalton, M. D. Ross, S. P. Ruggles, William B. Rogers, and Jonathan Preston.

2. WBR to HDR, September 28, 1863, *Life and Letters,* 2:178.

3. WBR to HDR, November 17, 1863, ibid., 180–181.

4. Government Records 1, November 24, 1863.

5. WBR to MDR, December 9, 1863, *Life and Letters,* 2: 182–183.

6. WBR to James Savage, December 20, 1863, ibid., 183.

7. WBR to Dr. Firth of Norwich, England, September 21, 1863, ibid., 177.

8. File copy, Statement relating to the Mass. Ins. of T: prepared for Gov. Andrew, January 2, 1863, WBR Papers, folder 45; *Address of His Excellency John A. Andrew,* January 9, 1863, Senate no. 1 (Boston, 1863), 65–66, 43–65; Rough Draft of Notice of N. H. Soc: & Institute for Gov.'s Message, January 3, 1864, WBR Papers, folder 47; *Address of His Excellency John A. Andrew,* January 8, 1864, Senate no. 1, 7–8.

9. Marshall B. Dalton, "Edward Atkinson (1827–1905), Patron of Engineering Science and Benefactor of Industry," an address before the Newcomen Society in North America, March 23, 1950, meeting in Boston, in Dane Yorke, *Able Men of Boston,* 220.

10. *DAB,* s.v. "Atkinson, Edward." For further details of Atkinson's long and active life see Thomas Wentworth Higginson, "Edward Atkinson," *Proceedings, AAcadAS* 42 (1906–1907): 761–769; and Harold Francis Williamson, *Edward Atkinson, The Biography of an American Liberal.* Williamson states incorrectly that Atkinson resigned from the Institute Corporation in 1892.

11. Yorke, 63; Hiram F. Mills, "James Bicheno Francis," *Technology Quarterly* 5, no. 3 (October 1892): 274–281. This memorial was read to the Corporation on December 14, 1892. See also W. E. Worthen, "James Bicheno Francis," *Proceedings, AAcadAS* 28 (1892–1893): 333–340.

12. "Augustus Allen Hayes," *Proceedings, AAcadAS* 18 (1882–1883): 422–427; "Incorporators," 25.

13. Corporation Records 3, February 10, 1886; *NCAB.*

14. Corporation Records 3, April 13, 1887. An 1873 gift to the Institute of $25,000 for salaries, now listed in the treasurer's report under the name of Henry Bromfield Rogers, was presumably this fund, but there is evidence of his generosity on several occasions in earlier days. He may be the individual who paid the rent at Summer Street when additional space was needed. In his name also is a 1921 bequest of his daughter, Anna Perkins Rogers, establishing a fund, the income designated for "fellowship or scholarship aid for women graduates of M.I.T. or other colleges" pursuing graduate studies at the Institute. *Report of the Treasurer for the Year ended June 30, 1994*, 278. Rogers was generous also to Harvard, in 1859 providing funds for a gymnasium. When in the 1880s a larger facility was constructed, funds equivalent to his original gift were set aside for a Henry Bromfield Rogers Scholarship Fund. *Endowment Funds of Harvard University*, 147.

15. *DAB*, s.v. "Sherwin, Thomas"; *Proceedings, AAcadAS* 8, 224–226; "Thomas Sherwin," *Biographical Encyclopaedia of Massachusetts*, 223; Government Records 2, July 27, 1869, & October 11, 1871. (Since 1870 the "Government" has been known as the "Corporation." This volume covers February 23, 1866, to May 14, 1873.) *Report of the Treasurer for the Year ended June 30, 1994*, 282.

16. George E. Ellis, *Memoir of Nathaniel Thayer, A.M.* Reprinted from the *Proceedings, MHS* (Cambridge, 1885). This memoir contains no mention of Thayer's association with the Institute of Technology. *DAB*, s.v. "Thayer, Nathaniel"; *Proceedings, AAcadAS* 18 (1882–1883): 438–442; Corporation Records 3, April 11, 1883.

17. "Incorporators," 50.

18. Government Records 1, February 27 and March 17, 1864.

19. WBR to W. J. Walker, April 14, 1863, file copy, WBR Papers, folder 45.

20. WBR to HDR, January 19, 1864, *Life and Letters,* 2:186; Society of Arts Records 1, January 14, 1864. The reference to "Professor" Runkle is an anachronism. When *Life and Letters* was published in 1896, Runkle was a professor, and the title must have been inserted at that time.

21. Committee on Instruction Records 1. The minutes of this committee, its name changed to Committee on the School of Industrial Science in an 1870 bylaw revision, continue through its final meeting on September 29, 1883. It was then superseded by the Executive Committee, which had been created by Corporation action on May 9, 1883, and which held its first meeting on October 22 of that year. Records of both committees are contained in Committee on Instruction and Executive Committee Records 1, with succeeding volumes continuing the series as Executive Committee records. Minutes on loose sheets have survived for meetings on November 14, 1865 (third meeting of the year), April 11, 1866 (fourth meeting of the year), and a special meeting on June 13, 1866.

22. *Historical Register of Harvard University*, 1636–1936, 450; William Watson, "Résumé of the Course of University Lectures on Ponceletic Approximation," delivered during the first term of the academic year 1863–64, WBR Papers, folder 46a.

23. Charles R. Cross, "William Watson, (1884–1915)" *Proceedings, AAcadAS* 52 (1916–1917): 871–873.

24. *Mathematical Monthly* 2 (November 1859): 72; "The Polytechnic School at Paris," ibid. 3, no. 10 (July 1861): 320–324; "The École des Ponts et Chaussées at Paris," ibid., no. 11 (August 1861): 351–353; Society of Arts Records 1, December 24, 1863, & January 28, 1864. These and other papers read by Watson before the Society between 1869 and 1872 were printed for private distribution. William Watson, *Papers on Technical Education* (Boston, 1872).

25. Cross, 871–872.

26. Tenney L. Davis, Watson entry in *DAB*.

27. Prof. Harry W. Tyler (Class of 1884), Memorandum of Conference with Prof. William Watson, June 11, 1902. Harry W. Tyler Papers, folder 3. The memorandum indicated that Watson planned to turn over to Tyler material related to the Institute's early history, but such material has not been found. Watson was appointed to the school's first faculty in September 1865, remaining until he resigned in 1872.

28. *Address of His Excellency John A. Andrew*, January 8, 1864, Senate no. 1, 46–49. *Documents Accompanying Governor's Address*, 1864, "State Military Academy," lxxxiv–cx.

29. *Address of His Excellency John A. Andrew*, January 6, 1865, Senate no. 1, 73–74; *Special Message of His Excellency John A. Andrew*, January 3, 1866, Senate no. 1; *Valedictory Address of His Excellency John A. Andrew*, January 4, 1866, Senate no. 2 (Boston, 1865 & 1866); Government Records 1, May 29, 1865.

30. Government Records 1, February 10, 1864.

31. Ibid., February 27, 1864.

32. Ibid., March 17, 1864.

33. Ibid., May 30, 1864; Society of Arts Records 1, May 30, 1864.

34. *Scope and Plan of the School of Industrial Science of the Massachusetts Institute of Technology* (Boston, 1864), 3.

35. Ibid., 6–8.

36. Ibid., 3–5.

37. Ibid., 5. No correspondence or mention in the records of the Government has been found to support the statement concerning a connection with the Lowell Drawing-school. John Amory Lowell, Trustee of the Lowell Institute and a vice president of the Institute of Technology, was, however, present at the meetings at which the *Scope and Plan* was discussed. He had been a member of the Committee on Instruction in 1862–63.

38. Ibid., 9.

39. Ibid., 10.

40. Ibid., 10–16.

41. Ibid., 17. Admission to the upper years of the regular course required demonstration of knowledge equivalent to a student who had completed the previous year or years. The age requirement was adjusted upwards, e.g., seventeen for the second year.

42. Ibid., 19–28.

43. Ibid., 23–24.

44. Ibid., 17–19.
45. Ibid., 18.
46. Acts of 1868, Chapter 247, *Acts and Resolves*, 1931, 7.
47. WBR to HDR, March 30, 1864, *Life and Letters,* 2:190–191 (excision by Emma Rogers).
48. WBR to HDR, April 13, 1864, ibid., 191–192.
49. WBR to MDR, June 5, 1864, copied with minor excisions into Government Records 1, June 6, 1864; file copy of letter, WBR Papers, folder 47.
50. Government Records 1, June 6, 1864.
51. WBR to MDR, June 5, 1864, WBR Papers, folder 47.
52. Government Records 1, June 6, 1864; Third Annual Report of the Secretary, Annual Meeting, May 25, 1865, Society of Arts Records 2, 100.
53. Government Records 1, June 6, 1864.
54. THW to WBR, June 7, WBR to THW, June 8, and WBR to MDR, June 17, 1864, WBR Papers, folder 47. Dalton to WBR, September 20, with September 13 enclosure, and MDR to WBR, September 20, 1864, ibid., folder 48. Notation by Rogers—received on September 29, answered on October 1, returning the draft, preferring "to adhere to my previous decision—made known to Dr. Webb and Mr. Ross."
55. WBR to MDR, October 1, 1864, as recorded in Government Records 1, November 4, 1864.
56. Government Records 1, November 4, 1864.
57. MDR to WBR, August 4, 1864, ibid., folder 48. Ross headed his letter with this statement: "Day set apart by the President that we may Fast and cultivate *Humility* as a Nation."
58. THW to WBR, August 30, 1864, ibid.
59. Ibid.
60. See Charles W. Eliot, "The New Education," *Atlantic Monthly* 23 (February 1869): 203–220; (March 1869): 358–367.
61. Dalton to WBR, September 20, 1864, WBR Papers, folder 48.
62. MDR to WBR, August 4 & September 9, 1864, ibid.
63. THW to WBR, August 30, 1864, ibid.
64. MDR to WBR, September 9, 1864, ibid.
65. MDR to WBR, October 4, 1864, ibid.
66. WBR to James Savage, July 1 & 22, *Life and Letters,* 2:194, 198.
67. WBR to James Savage, August 5, 1864, *Life and Letters,* 2:201.
68. Ibid. If Rogers kept a complete record of his trip, it has not survived, and some observations may have disappeared through excisions in *Life and Letters.*
69. WBR to HDR, July 23, 1864, *Life and Letters,* 2:200. See also C. H. Wilson to HDR, July 7, 1864, WBR Papers, folder 47. Henry hoped William could meet with Professor Wilson while in Glasgow, but Wilson was away on vacation. In a letter of regret Wilson pointed out that the School of Art in Edinburgh was "perhaps the most complete in many respects in the Kingdom," and offered to write a letter of introduction to the secretary there. He may have done so, since William mentioned two visits to that institution.

70. WBR to James Savage, July 22, 1864, ibid., 199; WBR to Henry Cole, Esq., October 3, 1864, WBR Papers, folder 48; WBR to James Savage, August 5, 1864, *Life and Letters,* 2:200.

71. WBR to RER, August 26, and WBR to James Savage, September 2, 1864, ibid., 205, 206–207.

72. HDR to WBR, August 19, 1864, ibid., 204–205 (second excision by Emma Rogers).

73. Government Records 1, November 4, 1864.

74. *Life and Letters,* 2:216–217.

75. Ibid., 217–218.

76. Fragment, WBR, addressee not specified but most likely William J. Walker, January 1, 1865, WBR Papers, folder 50.

77. Government Records 1, November 28, 1864.

78. MDR to WBR, October 4, 1864, WBR Papers, folder 48.

79. Government Records 1, November 28, 1864.

80. JDR to WBR, January 15, 1865, WBR Papers, folder 50.

81. Society of Arts Records 2, January 19 & February 2, 1865.

82. Printed circular letter, WBR, January 24, 1865, WBR Papers, folder 51o.

83. Advertisement, *Boston Advertiser,* February 6, 1865.

Chapter Nineteen THE SCHOOL OPENS

1. Over the years some have assumed that Rogers's diary figure of 15 students on the first day represents the total registration for the preliminary session. The Institute's first catalogue, covering the year 1865–66, was issued in December of 1865. The names of 72 students were published, identifying those who had attended the "Session of 1864–5," a designation that could only lead to confusion in the future. Except for one unaccountable error, those who had attended that session and were currently enrolled were marked with a star, and those who had not enrolled again, with a dagger. Taking this error into account, it appears that 28 of the 72 had attended the preliminary session, all but 3 of whom enrolled in the fall of 1865, 11 assigned to first-year studies and 14 to the second year. (*First Annual Catalogue, 1865–66,* 5–7.) A marked copy of this catalogue contains pencilled additions to the student list without any indication of prior attendance, these entries probably made by William Atkinson, the first secretary of the faculty. Prescott's figures give the total enrollment as 23 and vary also in the numbers assigned to the first and second years in the fall of 1865 (Prescott, 46). President Francis Amasa Walker presented enrollment statistics in his first annual report in 1883, starting with the fall of 1865, which was the official opening of the regular classes of the school. It would seem that he, too, could find no official records for the preliminary session. Secretary Webb's book listing students and charges paid contains only blank pages for the preliminary session (ASC 2).

   Among those assigned to the second year and not identified with a star was Robert H. Richards. As he would later point out in his autobiography, he was the seventh student to register in February 1865. This is a particularly noteworthy omission because he was a "connection" of William Barton Rogers through his wife, Emma, and the family of her grandmother,

Elizabeth Tudor Savage. Richards was also the grandson of Robert Hallowell Gardiner, the founder in 1822 of the Gardiner Lyceum in Maine. Richards viewed his enrollment in 1865 as the beginning of a new life, and indeed it was. Following graduation in 1868 he remained with the Institute, first as an assistant and instructor and then as a faculty member and head of the Department of Mining and Metallurgy until he retired in 1914. He would maintain an active interest in the Institute until he died in March 1945, in his 101st year. *Robert Hallowell Richards, His Mark,* 34; "Robert H. Richards, 1844–1945," *TR* 47, no. 7 (May 1945): 434–435.

2. *Life and Letters,* 2:224; also Prescott, 45. Often quoted, notably in MIT commencement programs, this may be an abbreviated quotation, for in 1867 in remarks before the Society of Arts, Rogers referred to this often-quoted entry in his "note book" as marking an occasion that "perhaps might prove a memorable day for students in industrial science." Society of Arts Records 3, November 7, 1867.

3. Government Records 1, February 27, 1865. There is no record of Government action with respect to those engaged to teach these preliminary classes, no relevant correspondence in the William Barton Rogers Papers, and no minutes of meetings of the Committee on Instruction for this period. In pressing ahead with the inauguration of a few classes, Rogers apparently acted with power. The first faculty of the Institute would not be presented to the Government for election until September 15, 1865.

4. Government Records 1, February 27, 1865.

5. Ibid., October 23, 1865.

6. Ibid., December 19, 1865.

7. Fourth Annual Report of the Secretary to the Institute, May 25, 1866, 250.

8. Advertisement, paper not identified, September 1, 1865, WBR Papers, folder 238.

9. MDR to WBR, August 24, 1865, WBR Papers, folder 52.

10. Committee on Instruction Records 1, loose sheet for November 14, 1865. No formal entries in this volume until October 29, 1866. Government Records 1, November 14, 1865.

11. Faculty Records 1, November 17, 1865; December 1 & 8, 1866.

12. *Second Annual Catalogue, 1866–67*; *Third Annual Catalogue, 1867–68.*

13. Government Records 1, November 14, 1865. The term "industrial science" was not permanently discarded. A fundamental bylaw change in 1870, clarifying the Institute's governance, resulted in the reappearance of "Industrial Science" through a change of title for the Committee on Instruction to the "Committee on the School of Industrial Science." In the year 1883–84, during the Walker administration, the term "School of Industrial Science" returned to prominence in the catalogue at the head of the list of Officers of Instruction, on nearly all the pages related to the regular program of the school, and in a historical sketch of the Institute. This style was maintained until 1888, when the designation was dropped from the list of officers, and 1889, after which it can be found only in the text, a practice continued through 1917.

14. *First Annual Catalogue of the Officers and Students, and Programme of the Course of Instruction, of the School of the Massachusetts Institute of Technology, 1865–6* (1865).

15. Faculty Records 1, January 20, 1866; Cash book no. 1.
16. *Scope and Plan,* [2].
17. Ibid., 10.
18. *First Annual Catalogue, 1865–66,* 9.
19. Ibid., 11.
20. Faculty Records 1, October 28, 1865; *First Annual Catalogue, 1865–66,* 10.
21. *Seventh Annual Catalogue, 1871–72,* 12–14; *Fourteenth Annual Catalogue, 1878–79,* 13–16; *Eighth Annual Catalogue, 1872–73,* 35; *Ninth Annual Catalogue, 1873–74,* 35.
22. James, 1:166.
23. C. W. Eliot, "The New Education," 219–220.
24. Ibid., 220.
25. Faculty Records 1, September 25 & 26, 1865.
26. *First Annual Catalogue, 1865–66,* 34–35; JAL to WBR, October 26, 1865, *Life and Letters,* 2:251; file copy, WBR to JAL, November 15, 1865, WBR Papers, folder 53.
27. *Fourth Annual Catalogue, 1868–69,* [11].
28. *Objects and Plan,* 20–22, 27; *Scope and Plan,* 10, 17.
29. Advertisement, paper not identified, September 1, 1865, WBR Papers, folder 238.
30. *First Annual Catalogue, 1865–66,* 10–11.
31. Ricketts, 103.
32. *First Annual Report of the Visitors of the Sheffield Scientific School of Yale College* (New Haven, 1866), 18–19. In *Sheffield Scientific School Reports I–VII, 1866–1872.* This volume in the collections of the MIT Libraries belonged to Francis Amasa Walker, inscribed to him as "Professor F. A. Walker, with kind regards of Geo. J. Brush, Jan. 4, 1873." Walker was professor of political economy at Sheffield from 1871 to 1880 and secretary of its governing board for five years beginning in the fall of 1878. (James Phinney Munroe, *A Life of Francis Amasa Walker* [New York: Henry Holt & Co., 1923], 150.) Brush was director of Sheffield from 1871 to 1898.
33. *Catalogue of the Officers and Students of Harvard University for the Academical Year 1865–66,* 75.
34. *Second Annual Catalogue, 1866–67,* 10–11. The decision to drop French as a requirement was taken in December 1866.
35. *Fourth Annual Catalogue, 1868–69,* 12. Several entries in Faculty Records 1 for the fall of 1868 refer only in general terms to discussion of the catalogue.
36. *Fourth Annual Report of the Sheffield Scientific School of Yale College* (New Haven, 1869), 60.
37. Faculty Records 1, October 19, 1868.
38. Day Book, List of Students Attending the School of Industrial Science and Charges Paid, 1865–66, 1866–67 (ASC 2). Pages for those attending the preliminary course beginning in February 1865 are blank.
39. *First Annual Catalogue, 1865–66,* 31; Faculty Records 1, January 30, 1866.
40. *Catalogue of the Officers and Students of Harvard University,* 1865–66, 80.
41. Faculty Records 1, October 20 & 27, 1866. The amounts were never printed in the catalogue: Chemistry, "all-day students": $30 for one month; $50 for two; $75 for three; $100 for four;

$125 for five or six; and $150 for a year. Blowpipe analysis, determinative mineralogy and assaying (including the qualitative analysis if desired): $25 for one month; $40 for two; $60 for three; $80 for four; $100 for five or six; and $125 for a year. Qualitative analysis twice a week with the second-year class: $10 a month or $60 a year. General Chemistry twice-a-week lecture and manipulation with the first-year class: $8 a month or $50 a year. For both chemistry courses: $15 a month or $100 a year.

42. Committee on Instruction Records 1, December 7, 1867, and December 2, 1872; *Fifth Annual Catalogue*, 1869–70, 37; *Eighth Annual Catalogue*, 1872–73, 57; Harvard University Catalogue, 1872–73, 108; *Thirty-Eighth Annual Catalogue*, 1902–3, 193. For comparison, tuition at Rensselaer in 1865 was $150 per year, raised to $200 in 1866, the fee still in effect in 1895 (Ricketts, 105). Sheffield in 1865 charged $100 per year (*First Annual Report of the Visitors of the Sheffield Scientific School of Yale College*, 19), with an additional $75 for those taking Analytical Chemistry to cover chemicals and the use of the apparatus; raised to $125 in 1867 (Annual Report, 1867–68, 52); and by 1870 to $150 (Annual Report, 1869–70, 16).

43. *Second Annual Catalogue, 1866–67*, 26–27. For Harvard, see *Catalogue of the Officers and Students of Harvard University*, 1860–61, 74. The basic bond requirement, with some added alternatives, continued through the remainder of the century, appearing for the last time in the catalogue for 1901–02.

44. *First Annual Catalogue, 1865–66*, 31.

45. *Second Annual Catalogue, 1866–67*, 28.

46. Ibid., 27.

47. Government Records 1, November 14, 1865.

48. Government Records 2, February 23, 1866.

49. Ibid., March 5, 1866.

50. Ibid.

51. Ibid., April 12, 1866.

52. Ibid., May 28, 1866.

53. Ibid., June 27 & August 22, 1866, the latter containing an amendment to the June 27 record.

54. Ibid., October 13 and November 15, 1866; Society of Arts Records 3, November 15 & December 6, 1866.

55. *Report of the Committee of the Massachusetts Institute of Technology, on the Subject of Free Scholarships; also the Indenture of Trust, for the Establishment of a Fund for this Purpose* (Boston, 1867).

56. Ibid., 11–12.

57. *Proceedings, AAcadAS* 24 (1888–1889): 437. In 1877 Charles Pickering Bowditch, son of J. Ingersoll Bowditch, was elected to the Institute's Corporation and served for two years.

58. *Report and Indenture*, 8–12.

59. WBR to [?] (name not legible) regarding a contribution from Mrs. Forbes, WBR Papers, folder 58.

60. Government Records 2, April 12, June 14, and October 11, 1871; MIT Office of the Treasurer, Gift Records, 1868–1947 (AC 53), folder 5; *Report of the Treasurer for the Year Ended June 30,*

1999, 213. The English High School graduate to benefit from the "free scholarship" would be "selected by the Faculty of the Institute in concurrence with the Head Master of said High School for the time being," and there was one further "understanding and agreement." The fund would "revert and be reconveyed or transferred to a board of Trustees for the perpetual benefit of said High School." It appeared in the *Report of the Treasurer of June 30, 1999*, as an endowed fund of the Institute, for "scholarship aid to graduates of English High School, Boston."

61. *First Annual Catalogue, 1865–66*, 34.
62. Ibid.
63. Ibid.
64. *Second Annual Catalogue, 1866–67*, 28–29; *Fourth Annual Catalogue, 1868–69*, 33.
65. *Fifth Annual Catalogue, 1869–70*, 39.
66. *Sixth Annual Catalogue, 1870–71*, 16; President's Report, May 1871–May 1872, 8.
67. JAL to WBR, April 2, 1862, *Life and Letters*, 2:111–112.
68. JAL to WBR, October 26, 1865, as entered in Government Records 1, November 14, 1865. A partial version of this letter appears in *Life and Letters*, 2:251.
69. MIT Treasurer's Statements, 1865–1883 (AC 63), folder 1.
70. In 1931 President A. Lawrence Lowell of Harvard, who was then the trustee of the Lowell Institute, informed President Karl T. Compton of MIT that John Amory Lowell had explored the possibility of carrying out his plan in cooperation with Harvard: "I believe that my grandfather, then the Trustee of the Lowell Institute, originally offered to cooperate with Harvard, which declined to assume the burden; and when Technology was founded he made the same offer to them, which was gladly accepted." A. Lawrence Lowell to Karl T. Compton, March 17, 1931, MIT Office of the President, Records, 1930–1959, box 139, folder 10.
71. Government Records 1, November 14, 1865.
72. *First Annual Catalogue, 1865–66*, 35–36.
73. Ibid., December 19, 1865; Fourth Annual Report of the Secretary, May 25, 1866, Society of Arts Records 2, 246–251.
74. Government Records 1, December 19, 1865.
75. Cash Book no. 1, January 4, 1867.
76. *Fourth Annual Catalogue, 1868–69*, 34.
77. Edward Weeks, *The Lowells and Their Institute*, 82.
78. Government Records 2, August 22, 1866.
79. Ibid., September 11, 1872; *President's Report for the Year ending Sept. 30, 1873* (Boston, 1873), vi.
80. Charles Kastner, "Report Upon the Lowell Course of Practical Design," *President's Report, 1873*, 66. Yet another connection came in 1879 when the Lowell Institute was forced to move its Lecture Series, inaugurated in 1839, from the Marlboro Chapel on Washington Street. Though considered by some to be "quite removed from the lecture centre of the city," MIT's Huntington Hall, deemed the "best available" for their purposes, was leased for a fee of $2,500 per year. The Lecture Series continued to be held there until the Rogers Building was razed

in 1938. Corporation Records 3, May 14, 1879; H. K. Smith, 26; Karl T. Compton to A. Lawrence Lowell, April 13, 1937, and Lowell to Compton, April 14, MIT Office of the President, Records, 1930–1959, box 139, folder 10.

From its earliest days the Institute benefited from the advice and support of members of the Lowell family, beginning with John Amory Lowell as a member of its governing board from 1862 to 1881 and vice president from 1862 to 1870. His son Augustus would serve on the Corporation from 1873 until 1900, and two of his sons would also serve—Percival from 1885 until 1916 and A. Lawrence from 1896 to 1943. John Amory's great-grandson Ralph, descended from his elder son John, served from 1949 until 1978. Three of the above followed John Amory as the sole trustee of the Lowell Institute—Augustus from 1881 to 1900; A. Lawrence from 1900 to 1943; and Ralph, who was appointed "unofficially as co-trustee" in 1938 by A. Lawrence, was the sole trustee until his death in 1978.

81. Augusta R. Curtis to Edward Atkinson, January 30, 1867, WBR Papers, folder 56; also *Life and Letters,* 2:267–268, with minor variations.

82. Edward Atkinson to WBR, February 1, 1867, WBR Papers, folder 56.

83. Anita E. Tyng and Rebecca K. Shepard to Nathaniel Thayer, January 30, 1867, WBR Papers, folder 56; also *Life and Letters,* 2:268.

84. Fragmentary notes, undated, but obviously agenda items for the February 2, 1867, meeting of the Committee on Instruction, WBR Papers, folder 56.

85. Committee on Instruction Records 1, February 2, 1867.

86. A term used in the nineteenth century in the sense of rendering difficult.

87. WBR to Thayer, February 4, 1867, file copy, WBR Papers, folder 56.

88. WPA to WBR, August 18, 1867, WBR Papers, folder 58; *Life and Letters,* 2:275–276.

89. Committee on Instruction Records 1, November 13, 1867; Government Records 2, November 23, 1867.

90. The Institute has been criticized for having admitted Ellen Swallow as a special student when she already had a bachelor of arts degree from Vassar, and for not granting her a master's degree rather than a bachelor's in 1873. For example, see Margaret W. Rossiter, "Women Scientists in America before 1920," *American Scientist* 62 (May–June 1974): 312–323. It is worth noting, however, that it was not uncommon for men to take second bachelor's degrees at MIT.

91. Among major developments at MIT would be the establishment in 1876, with the help of the Woman's Education Association, of the Woman's Laboratory for special instruction in chemical analysis, industrial chemistry, mineralogy, and chemistry as related to vegetable and animal physiology. Ellen Swallow, by then the wife of Professor Robert H. Richards, would play a significant role in the conduct of this laboratory. Women generally represented more than half of the enrollment of the Lowell School of Practical Design also established at the Institute during this period, and direct admission to the regular four-year curriculum would come. Fifty-four bachelor's degrees were awarded to women between 1873 and 1900 in the following fields: architecture, 11; biology, 10; chemistry, 22; geology, 3; general studies, 3; and physics, 5. Among them were ten college graduates, two of whom held both bachelor's and master's degrees. *Twelfth Annual Catalogue,* 1876–77, 20.

92. See "Retirement of Mrs. Stinson," *TR* 14 (January 1912): 46.

93. Transcript of interview of Margaret Dayton Stinson by Ellen Swallow Richards, "Reminisences [*sic*] by Mrs. Stinson. Questions by Mrs. Richards" (MC 460), MIT Archives.

94. Faculty Records 1, October 1 & 20, 1866; Committee on Instruction Records 1, October 29 & November 15, 1866; Government Records 2, June 3, 1867.

95. Committee on Instruction Records 1, December 14, 1870.

Chapter Twenty THE FIRST FACULTY

1. Carlton has sometimes been erroneously referred to as a member of the first faculty. Depending on the source one reads, the Lowell Drawing-school, started in the fall of 1850 by John Amory Lowell, was either "curiously sterile and futile" with a very limited course and vision (see H. Winthrop Peirce, *History of the School of the Museum of Fine Arts, Boston, 1876–1930* [Boston, 1930], 12), or "eminently successful in establishing correct methods of drawing, and had the satisfaction of being imitated all over the country, almost to the entire revolution in the teaching of drawing" (see H. K. Smith, *History of the Lowell Institute*, 28). It should be noted, however, that Miss Smith is inaccurate with respect to other events for which ample proof is available.

2. Cash Book no. 1, 30, 32.

3. Ibid., 45.

4. JDR to WBR, January 15, 1865, WBR Papers, folder 50.

5. WBR to CWE, June 6, 1865, ibid., folder 50.

6. Government Records 1, September 15, 1865. The faculty requested and the Government voted on November 14 that the title of the head of the School be changed from "Principal" to "President."

    There would naturally be some adjustments over the years reflecting the growth of the school and the changing times, but the basic organizational structure of the faculty has remained essentially the same. Through its system of standing committees, the present-day faculty's responsibility for the academic program, admissions requirements, and the general conduct of the school parallels that of the original faculty. The basic pattern proved to be more suitable and durable than the original governance structure of the Institute as a whole, requiring no major change even as the emphasis upon the school increased. As the school became the dominant component, the Committee on Instruction was eventually replaced by an Executive Committee, and the clerical functions carried out by the secretary of the faculty, as well as other routine matters once the concern of the faculty as a whole, would be handled by various administrative offices.

    In the first catalogue issue, the faculty members, all with the title of professor, were listed as "Officers of Instruction." Then, until 1870, under the same heading, the list included also "Assistant Instructors" and "Assistants." Beginning in 1870, the catalogue contained two lists: "Officers of Instruction" and "Faculty." By 1883–84 all "Assistant Professors" were listed as members of the faculty, but it was still possible for an instructor to have a seat on the faculty if so voted. 1884–85 is the first year in which the rank of "Associate Professor" appeared.

7. Government Records 1, September 15, 1865. Storer's first name was Francis, but he was listed as Frank throughout his stay at the Institute.

8. Harvard followed British practice with respect to the master of arts degree. According to Samuel Eliot Morison, "the Master's degree was taken at the traditional space of three years after the Bachelor's; and, as in England, the requirements for it were so slight that a large majority of B.A.'s proceeded M.A. in course. It was not even necessary to reside in college; one only had to return to Cambridge before Commencement in time to discuss a philosophical problem or give a 'commonplace' (sample sermon), to hand in a synopsis of Arts, and to reply to a question (prepared beforehand, and the subject printed) at Masters' Commencement. . . . This practice of taking the second degree in course was rendered progressively easier until in the nineteenth century it was a saying that all a Harvard man had to do for his Master's degree was to pay five dollars and stay out of jail. The sudden falling off of M.A.'s after the Class of 1869 . . . marks the abandonment of this last vestige of the *septennium* considered necessary to make a full-fledged 'Artist.'" From this practice stems the precedent for American universities to consider the "date of the *first* degree as the date of graduation." Morison, *Three Centuries of Harvard*, 26, 34–35.

9. William P. Atkinson, "To the Parents of the Pupils Attending the Brookline High School," n.d., 8, 7.

10. *Report of the School Committee of the Town of Brookline for the Year 1854–55* (Boston, 1855); *Address of Prof. W. P. Atkinson before the Sub-Committee of the Boston School Board* (Boston, 1869). The same address, on a reorganization of the Boston High Schools, reissued in 1870.

11. Memorial to William P. Atkinson, prepared by John D. Runkle, Charles R. Cross, and Davis R. Dewey, Faculty Records 5, April 16, 1890; *Technology Quarterly* 3, no. 2 (May 1890): 89–91.

12. WPA to CWE, March 20, 1862, in James, 1:96–97.

13. WPA to WBR, February 20, 1865, WBR Papers, folder 50.

14. WPA to MDR, August 21, 1865; MDR to WBR, August 24, 1865, ibid., folder 52.

15. Faculty Records 1, September 25, 1865, November 10, 1866, & September 29, 1868; Government Records 4, May 20, 1889. In 1932 the Executive Committee, "as a statement of the distinction between 'Professor Emeritus' and 'Retired Professor'. . . agreed that the title of 'Professor Emeritus' should normally be given to a professor in good standing at the age of sixty-five or over." Executive Committee Records 6, April 5, 1932.

16. Charles H. Grandgent, "The Modern Languages," chap. 3 in *Development of Harvard University*, ed. Morison.

17. Charles F. Read (Class of 1874) et al., "Biographies of Members of the Faculty and Officers of Administration," vol. 1, MIT Archives; *The Harvard Book* (Sketches collected & published by F. O. Vaille & H. A. Clarke, Class of 1874; Cambridge, Mass.: Welch, Bigelow, & Co., University Press, 1875), 1:190; *Historical Register of Harvard University*, 126; Government Records 2, February 8, 1871.

18. James, 1:148.
19. CWE to Arthur T. Lyman, April 18, 1865, ibid., 146–147.
20. WBR to CWE, June 6, 1865, WBR Papers, folder 50.
21. Ibid.
22. CWE to WBR, June 20, 1865, ibid.
23. Ibid.
24. CWE to JAL, June 20, 1865, Lowell Institute Papers, HLHU.
25. JAL to CWE, July 7, 1865, CWE Papers, HUA.
26. WBR to CWE, July 17, 1865, *Life and Letters,* 2:240–243.
27. Ibid.
28. CWE to WBR, July 31, 1865, WBR Papers, folder 52.
29. James, 1:152–153.
30. Ibid., 153.
31. Ibid., 153, 155. In 1869 Eliot was elected to the presidency of Harvard and soon thereafter set in motion its second attempt to annex the Institute.
32. "Biographies of Members of the Faculty and Officers of Administration" 1:20. The sketch of Hague in this volume was written by Robert E. Rogers, Professor of English and History, 1913–1941, and editor of the *Technology Review,* 1917–1922. *DAB*; *NCAB*, s.v. "Hague, James Duncan." Hague is included in a volume of biographical sketches of faculty with a photograph obviously taken late in life and no indication that he was an absent member. His entries in standard biographical sources, however, make no mention of any connection with the Massachusetts Institute of Technology and, it would seem, rightly so.
33. *DAB*; *NCAB*, s.v. "Hague, James Duncan."
34. WBR to Brush, August 2, 1865, file copy, WBR Papers, folder 52.
35. Brush to WBR, August 10, 1865, ibid. Rogers's file copy of his inquiry appears to be a hasty draft, and he may have added but not recorded a note about an offer to Eliot. Brush in his response refers to Eliot as associated with the Institute. Eliot's acceptance was not received until August 17. However, the offer was rather widely discussed in Cambridge and also reached New Haven.
36. WBR to the Reverend Dr. William Hague, September 8, 1865, file copy; Hague to WBR, September 11, 1865, ibid.
37. Government Records 1, October 23, 1865.
38. *First Annual Catalogue, 1865–66,* [4n]; *Third Annual Catalogue, 1867–68,* [4n] (Rockwell's middle initial is incorrect in this entry).
39. *DAB,* s.v. "Henck, John Benjamin"; George F. Swain (Class of 1877), "John Benjamin Henck," *TR* 5 (April 1903): 139–146.
40. J. B. Henck, in *Mathematical Monthly* 1, October 1858 to September 1859: "Ovals and Three-Centre Arches," October 1858, 25–27, & November 1858, 41–45; "On a Simplification in Computing Earthwork," January 1859, 127–129; "The Theorem of Pappus," March 1859, 200–208; "Solution of Prize Problem V., No. VII," September 1859, 390–392.

41. Ibid., "Introductory Note," October 1858, xii.
42. Henck to WBR, November 15, 1860, WBR Papers, folder 36; *Account of the Proceedings*, 10.
43. JDR to WBR, January 15, 1865, WBR Papers, folder 50.
44. WBR to CWE, June 6, 1865, ibid.
45. Faculty Records 1, September 26, 1865.
46. Storer was listed as *Frank* H. Storer in the catalogue during the years of his association with the Institute. Though his first name was indeed "Francis" and so listed in the *Historical Register of Harvard University, 1636–1936*, as well as in an early list of Institute Members, correspondence with William Rogers in the MIT Archives is consistently signed as "Frank." It would appear that among friends and colleagues he used the latter version of his name.
47. Charles W. Eliot, "Francis Humphreys Storer (1832–1914)," *Proceedings, AAcadAS* 54 (1918–1919): 415–418.
48. *DAB* mentions this; Eliot does not.
49. Eliot says (416) that Storer received the S.B. "on examination." *DAB* states that he "completed his chemical course." Harvard's *Historical Register* indicates that the S.B. was *summa cum laude*, with an honorary A.M. in 1870.
50. *DAB*.
51. Eliot, 416.
52. *DAB* indicates that the Boston Gas Light connection continued until 1871.
53. *Account of Proceedings*, 10.
54. Eliot, 416.
55. John Andrew Chewning, "William Robert Ware and the Beginnings of Architectural Education in the United States, 1861–1881" 1:22–29; *DAB*, s.v. "Ware, William Robert."
56. *Account of Proceedings*, 12, 8.
57. Chewning, 1:29–31; Paul R. Baker, *Richard Morris Hunt*, 102, 105. Baker cites A. J. Bloor, "Annual Address," *Proceedings of the Tenth Annual Convention of the American Institute of Architects* (Boston, 1877), 29, as the source of the first quotation.
58. "Members of the Corporation Deceased," vol. 1; Chewning, 1:28 & nn. 59 & 60, 2:296.
59. Chewning, 1:29–31, "The Office Teaching of Ware and Van Brunt." William R. Ware, "On the Condition of Architecture and of Architectural Education in the United States," read at the Ordinary General Meeting of the Royal Institute of British Architects, 28th January, 1867, *Sessional Papers of the Royal Institute of British Architects* (London, 1867), 86.
60. Ibid.
61. Chewning, 1:31–36.
62. WRW to Emma Ware, January 15, 1865, WRW Papers (MC 14), box 2, folder 3; Society of Arts Records 2, February 2 & March 2, 1865; WRW to Emma Ware, March 12, 1865, WRW Papers, box 2, folder 3.
63. WRW to JDR, April 27, 1865, WRW Papers, box 1, folder 2.
64. WRW to Emma Ware, August 2, 1865, WRW Papers, box 2, folder 3. Emma Ware had been contemplating a trip to Richmond and had asked about the location of young Savage's grave.

Ware reported that Rogers did not know just where Savage was buried but proposed to go to Charlottesville himself soon to seek further information.

65. WRW to Emma Ware, September 25, 1865, ibid. See WRW draft of a letter to Francis Amasa Walker, August 1888, "not sent," WRW Papers, box 1, folder 3, for a statement on the terms on which he accepted appointment in 1865.

66. Society of Arts Records 2, December 21, 1865.

67. WBR to CWE, June 6, 1865; WBR to Dr. Hague, WBR Papers, folder 52.

68. Government Records 2, April 12, 1866. The first entry in the Committee on Instruction record book is dated October 29, 1866, and appears on page 43. The prior blank pages would appear to indicate an intention later to record whatever notes may have been available for meetings before that date.

69. Cash Book no. 1, March 19 & April 2, 1866.

70. Cash Book no. 1, April 20, May 1 & 7, June 13 & 30, July 2 & 30, October 8, & December 10, 1866.

71. Government Records 2, April 12, 1866.

72. Ibid., May 19, 1868.

73. "Estimate of the Annual expense of the School of the Institute on the Scale of Organisation which will be necessary at the beging. of the Session of 1866–7," undated, loose sheet in Committee on Instruction Records 1; Government Records 2, April 12, 1866; Committee on Instruction Records 1, February 2, 1867.

74. Committee on Instruction Records 1, November 13, 1867; Government Records 2, November 23, 1867.

75. Ibid.

76. Committee on Instruction Records 1, October 29, 1866.

77. Government Records 2, March 5, 1866.

78. Ibid., April 12, 1866.

79. Ibid., June 3, 1867.

80. History of the Walker Professorship:

   1867–1902   John D. Runkle
   1902–1910   George A. Osborne, retired as Walker Professor, Emeritus
   1910–1930   Harry W. Tyler

   On February 14, 1877, the Corporation granted unanimously the request of Mrs. J. H. Walker that her son, grandchild of Dr. Walker, be entitled to receive tuition and the advantages of the Institute free of expenses. Corporation Records 3, February 14, 1877. A Joseph H. Walker of Cambridge is listed only in 1877–78 and 1878–79 as a student with the first-year class.

   When the last Walker Professor, Harry W. Tyler, retired in 1930, the title seems to have disappeared, and the name of William J. Walker passed into virtual obscurity at the Institute. In 1954 Samuel C. Prescott stated (*When M.I.T. was Boston Tech* [Cambridge: Technology Press, 1954], 40) that Walker's "name is perpetuated in the Walker Professorship of Mathematics," but no such professorship was listed in the catalogue after Tyler's retirement. No correspondence or official records have been found concerning its disappearance. Though Walker's portrait in the collections of the MIT Museum has been restored and he has on occasion been cited as an early and significant benefactor, his name has not been generally known over the years. This is a sad fate for the man who in 1863 saved the Institute from embarrassment and possible extinction, or even amalgamation with Harvard, by preempting the need for a request to the legislature for additional time to secure the guarantee fund. Such a request would have raised serious questions about the viability of an institution that had failed to gain major public financial support in a period of two years.

81. *Account of the Proceedings*, 11.
82. *Proceedings, AAcadAS* 7 (1865–1868): 298–299; Francis B. C. Bradlee, *The Boston and Main Railroad*, 8, 43; Edward Chase Kirkland, *Men, Cities and Transportation*, 1:399; *Historical Register of Harvard University*, 248. *Endowment Funds of Harvard University*, 371, indicates that Hayward's bequest to Harvard for its Astronomical Observatory amounted to $18,000. His 1829 textbook was published by Hilliard & Brown.
83. Cash Book no. 1, August 26, 1866. *The Annual Report of the President and Treasurer*, December 12, 1900 (Boston, 1900), 65, lists "$18,800, Jas. Hayward, for Professorship of Engineering," and the *Report of the Treasurer for the Year Ended June 30, 1999*, 90, carries it simply as "Bequest, the income for salaries."
84. History of the Hayward Professorship:

1867–1881	John B. Henck
1881–1886	George L. Vose
1886–1887	Chair vacant
1887–1909	George F. Swain
1909–1940	Charles M. Spofford

    With the retirement of Spofford in 1940, the Hayward designation disappeared from the rolls of the active faculty, and with his death as Hayward Professor emeritus in 1963, Hayward's "permanent" memorial disappeared completely.
85. William Endicott, Treasurer, to WBR, July 9, 1867, WBR Papers, folder 57; Cash Book no. 1, January 1, 1868. No entry has been found either in the Government records or in those of the Committee on Instruction for 1867 and 1868 with respect to the Thayer pledge or the receipt of the funds.

    Rogers's name was already connected to the Thayer Professorship in the catalogue for 1867–68. He was also professor of geology and unaccountably appeared in that catalogue as Thayer Professor of Physics and Geology rather than as Thayer Professor of Physics and Professor of Geology, an important distinction which eluded recognition at the time. *Third Annual Catalogue, 1867–68*, 4. The Walker and Hayward Professorships also appeared for the first time in this issue.
86. Society of Arts Records 3, May 21, 1868, 190. The Thayer Professorship is listed in the 1999 Treasurer's Report (200) as "Gift, the income for a professorship in Physics." History of the Thayer Professorship:

> 1867–1868   William B. Rogers
> 1868–1877   Edward C. Pickering
> 1878–1917   Charles R. Cross

The Thayer Professorship disappeared following Cross's death as Thayer Professor emeritus in 1921.

87. *Biographical History of Massachusetts*, vol. 9, ed. Samuel Atkins Eliot (Boston: Massachusetts Biographical Society, 1918). The volume contains "opening chapters" by Richard Cockburn Maclaurin, President of MIT, 1909–1920; *More Than Common Powers of Perception: The Diary of Elizabeth Rogers Mason Cabot*, ed. P. A. M. Taylor (Boston: Beacon Press, 1991), 8, 32.

88. Government Records 2, April 1, 1868; WBR memorandum of Government vote, April 6, 1868, WBR Papers, folder 59.

89. William P. Mason [Jr.] to WBR, April 11, 1868, WBR Papers, folder 59. Cash Book no. 1, April 11, 1868.

90. Society of Arts Records 3, May 21, 1868.

91. Executive Committee Records 1, November 27, 1883. Robert R. Shrock in his *Geology at M.I.T., 1868–1965* (1:53–54; 2:344–351) discusses the Mason Professorship at some length, tracing its uncertain history through published Treasurer's Reports and financial records. In 1900 it was listed as a fund for a professorship, with geology specified. Treasurer's Report, December 12, 1900, 65. In the 1994 Treasurer's Report, 266, it appears simply as "Bequest, the income for a professorship."

    Nearly twenty years would pass before the creation of another named chair: the Richard Perkins Professorship of Analytical Chemistry, established in 1887 in recognition of a large bequest. In 1896 the Professorship of Architectural Design was named for Arthur Rotch, also in recognition of a bequest. The William Barton Rogers Professorship of Economic Geology was established in 1912. All have disappeared with no evidence of formal action. There would not be another named chair at the Institute until 1945, when a gift of $350,000 by Alfred P. Sloan, Jr. (MIT class of 1895) made possible the Alfred P. Sloan Professorship of Management. Committee on Instruction Records 1, January 16, 1887; President's Report, December 14, 1887 (Boston, 1888), 33–34; Executive Committee Records 3, May 4, 1896; Executive Committee Records 4, June 10, 1912; Corporation Records 5, October 9, 1912; *TR* 47 (July 1945): 571.

Chapter Twenty-one THE FIRST STUDENTS

1. Refers to a French mathematical text—probably *Elements of Geometry and Trigonometry from the Works of A. M. Legendre* (New York: A. S. Barnes & Co., 1862)—translated and adapted by Charles Davies for use in American schools.

2. Probably Adolphe Ganot, *Traité élémentaire de physique*. Many editions. 8th ed. Paris: chez L'auteur-éditeur, 1859.

3. WPA to WBR, February 20, 1865, WBR Papers, folder 50.

4. For biographical summaries, see Charles Moore, "Daniel Chester French," *DAB*, supp. 1–2; and Leila Mechlin, "William Merchant Richardson French," *DAB* (1928–1936).

5. THW to Stillman B. Pratt [editor, *Bridgewater Banner*], March 14, 1865, MIT Corporation, Office of the Secretary (ASC 22), Letterpress copybook, 1862–1866.

6. Charles E. Barney to WBR, February 23, 1865, WBR Papers, folder 50.

7. James E. Parker to WBR, February 25, 1865, ibid.

8. Edmund J. Hudson to WBR, July 8, 1865, WBR Papers, folder 52.

9. F. P. Appleton to WBR, March 23, 1865, ibid., folder 50.

10. Frederick S. Cabot to WBR, March 27, 1865, ibid.

11. WBR to Cabot, March 28, 1865, ibid.

12. W. C. Chapin to WBR, July 18, 1865, WBR Papers, folder 52.

13. Compiled from the list of students in the *First Annual Catalogue, 1865–66*, 5–7.

14. Eben S. Stevens, "When We Were Freshmen," *TR* 16 (July 1914): 430–431.

15. WPA to WBR, June 4, 1865, WBR Papers, folder 50.

16. WBR to WPA, June 8, 1865, ibid.

17. WPA to WBR, June 25, 1865, ibid.

18. Faculty Records 1, December 4, 1865, January 5 & February 16, 1867.

19. *List of Students of the Lawrence Scientific School,* 45.

20. WBR to E. P. [Elisha Pomeroy] Cutler, July 6, 1865, WBR Papers, folder 52.

21. *Objects and Plan,* 6–7.

22. Albert J. Wright to WBR, October 9, 1865, WBR Papers, folder 53.

23. WBR to Horatio Storer, April 24, 1867, ibid., folder 57.

24. [E. P. Honfort?] to WBR, July 3, 1867, ibid.

25. N. Whitney Conant to WBR, August 10, 1865, WBR Papers, folder 52.

26. H. P. Wells to WBR, December 6, 1865, ibid., folder 53.

27. WBR to Wells, December 15, 1865, ibid.

28. Compiled from the age column in the first register, fall 1865, MIT Office of the Registrar Records (AC 251), box 1, pp. 6–16.

29. From Bowditch notebooks copied by MIT Museum director Warren Seamans for the authors in 1975.

30. William H. Baker was the student from Fitchburg, but it is unclear who Bowditch meant by the student "from Foxboro"; there were three students from Maine in Bowditch's class—Charles B. Fillebrown of Winthrop, Eugene L. Tebbetts of Lisbon, and Charles S. True of Yarmouth.

31. Faculty Records 1, January 18 & February 29, 1868.

32. B. T. Prescott, Jr., to WBR, February 27, 1868, WBR Papers, folder 59.

33. Faculty Records 1, December 21, 1867.

34. Ibid., June 1, 1868.

35. Channing Whitaker to WBR, July 16, 1868, WBR Papers, folder 60.

36. Whitaker to WBR, August 20, 1868, ibid.

37. Faculty Records 1, October 10, 1868, June 5, 1869, & January 4, 1870.
38. Smith and Tilden were both from the MIT Class of 1868, the first set of diplomas awarded.
39. Whitaker to WBR, August 20, 1868, WBR Papers, folder 60.
40. Whitaker to WBR, September 21, 1868, ibid. The part of the letter written after Whitaker's return from work survives in an incomplete form; at least one page is missing, possibly more.
41. Charles S. True to WBR, February 18, 1868, WBR Papers, folder 59.
42. True to WBR, October 19, 1868, ibid., folder 61.
43. JDR to ER, June 6, 1869, ibid., folder 62. The decision not to award William H. Baker a degree is recorded in Faculty Records 1, June 5, 1869.
44. JDR to ER, June 12, 1869, WBR Papers, folder 62.
45. *DAB*, supp. 1–2; for further biographical information on Herreshoff, see Wheeler Preston, *American Biographies* (New York: Harper & Brothers, 1940); John A. Garraty and Mark C. Carnes, eds., *American National Biography* (Oxford, 1999); and *NCAB*.
46. WBR to JDR, February 1, 1870, WBR Papers, folder 64.
47. Faculty Records 1, December 4, 1865 & January 30, 1866.
48. "Memoir of William Edwin Hoyt," *TR* 18 (July 1916): 630–632.
49. "Extracts from Mr. Hoyt's Talk," *TR* 12 (July 1910): 319.
50. Ibid., 320–321.
51. Ibid., 321.

Chapter Twenty-two THE FIRST SIX COURSES

1. Faculty Records 1, September 25, 1865.
2. *Scope and Plan*, 10–16; Faculty Records 1, September 25, 26, & October 21, 1865.
3. *Scope and Plan*, 18; Faculty Records 1, October 28 & November 1, 1865.
4. *First Annual Catalogue, 1865–66*, 10; *Second Annual Catalogue, 1866–67*, 10. In the early catalogues the titles of some of these courses varied within the same issue.
5. *First Annual Catalogue, 1865–66*, 11–19.
6. Faculty Records 1, October 28, 1865; *First Annual Catalogue, 1865–66*, 20.
7. Roy J. Honeywell, *The Educational Work of Thomas Jefferson*, 131.
8. As quoted in Ewing, *Early Teaching of Science*, 11.
9. Bruce 1:331 (1920). This vote was taken prior to the opening of the university.
10. Herbert B. Adams, *Thomas Jefferson and the University of Virginia*, U.S. Bureau of Education Circular of Information no. 1 (Washington: GPO, 1888), 194. Reprinted from *The Andover Review*, April 1886, as chapter 13.
11. "Report from the Committee on Schools and Colleges, Against the Expediency of Withdrawing the Fifteen Thousand Dollars Annuity from the University," Document No. 41, *Journal of the House of Delegates of Virginia, Session 1844–45* (Richmond: 1844), 2. Prepared by W. B. Rogers, Chairman of the Faculty of the University of Virginia, 1844–45. Reproduced in part as Appendix A in *Life and Letters*, 1:399–412.

12. Ibid., 3.

13. Ibid.

14. *First Annual Catalogue, 1865–66*, 20–25.

15. *Second Annual Catalogue, 1866–67*, 16–23.

16. *First Annual Catalogue, 1865–66*, 15.

17. Ibid., 15, 19.

18. *Second Annual Catalogue, 1866–67*, 13, 16; *Fourth Annual Catalogue, 1868–69*, 37–40; *Sixth Annual Catalogue, 1870–71*, 17–25, 47–50.

19. Government Records 1, November 24, 1863.

20. Society of Arts Records 2, December 1, 1864.

21. Prof. Dr. E. Althaus, Prorektor, Universität Karlsruhe (Technische Hochschule), to JAS, November 23, 1983, with catalogue pages covering 1860 to 1865. We owe thanks for help in this regard to the late Dr. Alfred E. Keil, Ford Professor of Engineering and dean of the School of Engineering at MIT.

22. As quoted by Rezneck in *Education for a Technological Society*, 89. Rensselaer's influence on engineering education was emphasized in an extensive study of engineering education published in 1918 by the Carnegie Foundation for the Advancement of Teaching. The study described B. Franklin Greene's curriculum as a "combination" of the studies offered at l'École Centrale and l'École Polytechnique in France and compared it with those of MIT and the University of Illinois, opened in 1867, finding the "general plan" of all three "very much the same... first teaching the necessary theoretical science and then showing how to apply it. This was the plan in the French schools, and it was transplanted without change to America." The report concluded that the "curricula at the Massachusetts Institute and the University of Illinois did not evolve thru a period of years. They were simply adopted in the form given. How much influence the Rensselaer curriculum had in shaping the others [other institutions] it is impossible to say. Internal evidence suggests that this influence was large." Charles Riborg Mann, *A Study of Engineering Education*, 12–14. The Preface to this bulletin was written by Henry S. Pritchett, then president of the Carnegie Foundation and formerly of MIT (1900–1907).

23. *Forty-Second Annual Register of the Rensselaer Polytechnic Institute, Troy, New York, 1865–66*, 14.

24. As quoted in Ricketts, 1895, 78.

25. Ibid., 79.

26. Ibid., 96.

27. Ibid., 130.

28. *First Annual Report of the Visitors of the Sheffield Scientific School of Yale College to the General Assembly of the State of Connecticut* (New Haven: 1866), 17–20. This report, prepared for the General Assembly of the State of Connecticut, included an "Account of the Established Courses of Study"; it was required because of Sheffield's land-grant status.

29. Ibid., 18.

30. Ibid.

31. Ibid.

32. Ibid, 19; *Fourth Annual Report of the Visitors of the Sheffield Scientific School of Yale College, 1868–69* (New Haven, 1869), 60.

33. *First Annual Catalogue, 1865–66*, 15.

34. Eliot, "The New Education," 210.

35. Ibid.

36. Wolcott Gibbs, "Note," February 19, 1869, *Atlantic Monthly* 23 (April 1869): 514.

37. Rudolph, 232.

38. Hector James Hughes, "Engineering, 1847–1929," chap. 26 in Morison, *Development of Harvard University*, 416.

39. *First Annual Catalogue, 1865–66*, 24.

40. Chittenden, 2:302; *First Annual Report, Sheffield*, 32.

41. *First Annual Report, Sheffield*, 32–33.

42. Ibid., [3].

43. Senate No. 108, 43; *Acts and Resolves*, 1931, 5.

44. *First Annual Catalogue, 1865–66*, 32–33.

45. Ibid., 33.

46. "To the Faculty of the Massachusetts Institute of Technology," WBR Papers, folder 58. The petition bears no date but contains a notation by Albert F. Hall, a member of the class, that it was "written by Professor Green [*sic*], probably in 1868." This statement was presumably added in 1872 or later, after Greene had been appointed to the faculty of the University of Michigan. Since the petition was considered by the faculty late in December 1867, Hall's recollection is incorrect.

47. Faculty Records 1, December 21, 1867.

48. *First Annual Catalogue, 1865–66*, 32.

49. Ibid.

50. Faculty Records 1, January 5 & 12, 1867. Eastwood is not listed in the 1866–67 catalogue, published in 1867.

51. Faculty Records 2, May 29, 1875. In 1875 also the faculty voted that twelve graduates of the Lowell School of Design would receive Certificates of Proficiency.

52. WBR to the Honorable Richard H. Dana, Jr., April 29, 1868, WBR Papers, folder 59.

53. WBR file copy of the petition enclosed with letter of April 29, 1868, ibid.

54. Government Records 2, May 13, 1868; *Acts and Resolves*, 1931, 7.

55. Government Records 2, December 7, 1868; Committee on Instruction, December 10 & 23, 1868; *Fourth Annual Catalogue, 1868–69*, 31.

56. Bruce, 2:139, 140.

57. Ibid., 140; 3:64, 387n, and 386.

58. Faculty Records 1, January 20 & 27, 1872, and April 6, 1872; Corporation (formerly Government) Records 2, February 12, 1873. The faculty committee consisted of Professors Atkinson, Henck, and James M. Crafts, the latter appointed professor of chemistry in 1870.

59. Faculty Records 1, May 30, 1868; W. B. Rogers Papers, folder 59. In his 1936 autobiography Robert H. Richards described the nature of the "ordeal" covering every subject in the pre-scribed course, including military drill. He believed that Rogers was following the practice of German institutions "in a somewhat modified form," and said that the plan "was never repeat-ed." He did not know how many had passed these tests, but seemed sure that he had not. And he stated further that "evidently the faculty did not pay much attention to marks," since he was asked to join the instructing staff. Richards, 42–43.

60. "4th Year Annual Examination, 1868" record (AC 251).

61. *Fourth Annual Catalogue, 1868–69,* 30–31; *Sixth Annual Catalogue, 1870–71,* 39; *Ninth Annual Catalogue, 1873–74,* 59; *Twenty-Ninth Annual Catalogue, 1893–94,* 68; Richards, 43.

Chapter Twenty-three A CURRICULAR INNOVATION

1. *Objects and Plan,* 22–23.

2. *Scope and Plan,* 11, 12, 14, 18.

3. Peirce, "Plan of a School of Practical and Theoretical Science," February 27, 1864, College Papers, 2d ser., 13, HUA; Lawrence to Everett, June 7, 1847, ibid., 15; Everett to Peirce, January 31, 1848, College Letters, Edward Everett 3, HUA, also in Everett Letters, reel 28, MHS. No instruction related to architecture would be offered at Harvard until Charles Eliot Norton's fine arts lectures in 1874. The first formal coursework came in 1893, when H. Langford Warren, who had studied under William Ware at MIT from 1877 to 1879, was appointed instructor in architecture. By 1899 he was a full professor in charge of an under-graduate department of the Lawrence Scientific School. George H. Edgell, "The Schools of Architecture and Landscape Architecture," chap. 27 in Morison, *Development of Harvard University,* 443–450.

4. WRW to JDR, April 27, 1865, WRW Papers, box 1, folder 2.

5. Ibid.

6. Society of Arts Records 2, December 21, 1865; Ware, *Outline;* WRW to JDR, October 22, 1869, JDR Papers. How widely the *Outline,* labeled for "private" circulation, was distributed in 1866 is not known. For a full discussion of the *Outline,* see Chewning, 1:38–54.

7. Ware, *Outline,* 5, 3.

8. Ibid., 11.

9. Ibid., 6–7.

10. Ibid., 7, 9, 11.

11. Ibid., 14–16.

12. Ibid., 16, 18–19.

13. Ibid., 27–28.

14. Ibid., 28–29.

15. Ibid., 29–30.

16. Ibid., 30.

17. Charles D. Gambrill to WRW, March 10, 1866, WRW Papers, box 1, folder 2. Gambrill's response was actually two-fold and contained in "A BOOK!" Its title page—"Professor W. R. Ware's Outline DARK LINED by Charles D. Gambrill, No PROFESSOR Egad! but a Member of the American Institute of Architects."

18. Chewning, 1:52. In 1940 Ware's *Outline* appeared in abridged form as "The Teaching of Architecture" in the *Technology Review*: "Professor Ware's essay—one of the earliest plans for formal college courses in architecture and one of the most thoughtful considerations of the art itself—is of historical importance both as record of how professional instruction in the subject began in the United States and as summation of the philosophy of architectural teaching." Prefatory note to William R. Ware, "The Teaching of Architecture," *TR* 42 (April 1940): 237–240, 257. Quotation, 237.

19. H. K. Smith, 57.

20. *DAB, DNB,* s.v. "Reid, David Boswell." The two contain some differing dates, but the *DAB* is likely to be more accurate for his time in the United States. *DAB* states that, following destruction of the Houses of Parliament in 1834, Reid's system was tested successfully in their temporary quarters. Though he was commissioned to oversee ventilation and lighting of the new buildings in 1840, a dispute with the architect brought this arrangement to an end in 1852. His public lectures in the United States are said to have led to his 1859 Wisconsin appointment as professor of physiology and hygiene and director of a museum of practical sciences. The appointment has been cited as the "only contribution to the University" by Henry Barnard, described as a "phantom chancellor" from 1859 to 1861. Reid, however, was "unappreciated by his colleagues," and though a committee was "impressed with his teaching," he was "dismissed in 1860." See Curti and Carstensen, 113, 168–169, 183.

21. D. B. Reid, "A College of Architecture," *American Journal of Education* 2 (December 1856): 630. Reprinted in 1857 as *A College of Architecture, and its relation to professional education and to the improvement of public health* (Hartford: Conn.: F. C. Brownell, 1857).

22. Ibid., 631–633.

23. WRW to WBR, April 24, 1866, WBR Papers, folder 54. Ware, *Outline* (28) contains the paragraph from which this quotation comes. In his letter, he does not indicate the omission of one sentence of the original.

24. WRW to WBR, April 24, 1866, WBR Papers, folder 54.

25. WRW to WBR, May 29, 1866, ibid.

26. Ibid.

27. Loose sheet in Committee on Instruction Records 1, June 13, 1866; Government Records 2, June 27, 1866; Committee on Instruction Records 1, October 29 & November 15, 1866.

28. Faculty Records 1, July 27, 1866.

29. *DAB,* s.v. "Longfellow, William Pitt Preble"; *NCAB* 23:239.

30. "Estimate of the Annual expense of the School of the Institute on the Scale of Organisation which will be necessary at the beging. of the Session of 1866–7." Undated, loose sheet in Committee on Instruction Records 1.

31. WRW draft of a letter to General [Francis Amasa] Walker, August 1888, not sent, WRW Papers, box 1, folder 3. Several other letters in this folder relate to this controversy. Executive Committee Records 1, November 17, 1885, & January 19, 1886; Corporation Records, December 9, 1885.

32. See *Sessional Papers of the Royal Institute of British Architects* (London, 1867), 1–2, 81–90. Ware stated that a portion of his *Outline* would be included in a forthcoming issue of the *Builder*, a British publication.

33. Chewning, 1:58–66.

34. Ibid., 66–71; app. A, "William Robert Ware: European Itinerary, 1866–67," ibid., 2:404–405; Francis W. Chandler, "William Robert Ware—1832–1915," *TR* 17 (July 1915): 424. Chewning (1:68) mentions Ware's stay with Peabody, citing WRW to his sister, June 30, 1867. Since Ware does not refer to McKim and Chandler in that letter, they presumably arrived somewhat later. Ware's later reference to the "unrivalled drawing schools of Paris" suggests that he studied rendering in a drawing school rather than in an atelier.

35. WRW to WBR, March 17, 1867, WBR Papers, folder 56.

36. Committee on Instruction Records 1, April 13 & 20, 1867. This action was never brought to the attention of the Government, at least on the record.

37. WBR to JDR, July 20 or 26, 1867, JDR Papers.

38. WBR to WRW, September 7, 1867, file copy, WBR Papers, folder 58.

39. WRW to WBR, September 9, 1867, ibid.

40. WRW to WBR, September 16, 1867, ibid.

41. *First Annual Catalogue, 1865–66*, 23–24.

42. Government Records 2, August 21, 1868; *A Supplement to the Annual Catalogue of the Massachusetts Institute of Technology.—The Programme of the Courses of Instruction in the Department of Architecture* (Boston, 1868). Published as a supplement to the 1867–68 catalogue.

43. *Supplement to the Annual Catalogue*, 11–14.

44. *Fourth Annual Catalogue, 1868–69*, 27.

45. WRW to WBR, November 2, 1868, WBR Papers, folder 61.

46. WBR to WRW, November 2, 1868, file copy, ibid. Rogers reserved for a postscript information about a payment from John Amory Lowell related to Ware's participation in the Lowell Free Courses and a bill received for printing 1,500 copies of the *Supplement* that he had not paid because he had agreed to pay for only 1,000.

47. WRW to JDR, October 22, 1869, JDR Papers. *Fifth Annual Catalogue, 1869–70*, [4]; *Sixth Annual Catalogue, 1870–71*, 5.

48. In 1888 Chandler rejoined the Institute as head of the Department of Architecture, serving until his retirement in 1911. Roger G. Reed, "Francis W. Chandler, 1844–1926," *A Biographical Dictionary of Architects in Maine* 5, no. 4 (Augusta: Maine Historic Preservation Committee, 1988), n.p.; C. Howard Walker, "An Appreciation of Professor Chandler," *TR* 14 (January 1912): 19–20.

49. Tribute of F. W. Chandler in "William Robert Ware—1832–1915," *TR* 17 (November 1915): 423–425.

50. "Report of the Department of Architecture," *Reports of the President, Secretary, and Departments. 1871–72* (Boston, 1872), 39–40.

51. Chewning, 1:81.

52. *Reports 1871–72,* 40.

53. Committee on Instruction 1, December 21, 1871 (Committee now called the Committee on the School of Industrial Science); Government Records 2, January 3, 1872 (Government now called the Corporation). Since the 1871–72 catalogue was not published until 1872, Létang could be included among the "Officers of Instruction."

54. *Reports 1871–72,* 49–50.

Chapter Twenty-four METHODS OF TEACHING

1. Bruce, 2:129

2. *Fourth Annual Catalogue, 1868–69,* 21.

3. *Objects and Plan,* 25.

4. *Scope and Plan,* 4, 19.

5. *Scope and Plan,* 23–24.

6. WBR to George J. Brush, April 14, 1865, file copy, and Brush to WBR, April 18, 1865, WBR Papers, folder 50.

7. James, chap. 4, 114–147.

8. CWE, "Estimate of Cost of Fittings and Apparatus for the Chemical Laboratories," n.d., MIT Office of the President, Records, 1897–1930, folder 53.

9. *Fourth Annual Catalogue, 1868–69,* 22.

10. *First Annual Catalogue, 1865–66,* 14.

11. Charles W. Eliot and Frank H. Storer, *A Manual of Inorganic Chemistry, Arranged to Facilitate the Experimental Demonstration of the Facts and Principles of Science* (Boston: Rockwell and Rollins, 1867); *A Compendious Manual of Qualitative Chemical Analysis* (New York: Van Nostrand, 1869).

12. *First Annual Catalogue, 1865–66,* 27.

13. Ibid., 28.

14. *Second Annual Catalogue, 1866–67,* 24; *Third Annual Catalogue, 1867–68,* 26.

15. W. A. Nichols to ECP, May 13, 1866, in E. C. Pickering Private Letters, 1850–1883, HUA.

16. Government Records 2, June 3 & November 23, 1867.

17. Ibid., August 21, 1868. It is not certain when Pickering became a member of the faculty. In those days professorial rank did not automatically carry with it membership on the faculty. Since the faculty minutes listed only absent members, they are not a good source on this point. Nor are the catalogues, which prior to 1870 did not distinguish faculty members in the lists from "Officers of Instruction." The first mention of Pickering in Faculty Records occurs in October 1869. By the time he was made fully responsible for physics, however, he must have become a member.

18. This laboratory, established in 1884, has been termed the "first building in the western hemi-

sphere designed for research and teaching in physics." (Edwin H. Hall, "Physics 1869–1928," chap. 17 in Morison, *Development of Harvard University*, 277–291, direct quote, 277; Gerald Holton, "How the Jefferson Physical Laboratory Came to Be," *Physics Today* [December 1984]: 32–37, direct quote, 32.) Neither piece mentions Trowbridge's connection with MIT, his association with Rogers and Pickering, or the establishment of the physical laboratory at the Institute in 1869. Hall states elsewhere that "it was [Trowbridge's] function to bring Harvard over from its old habit of set lectures, demonstrations, and strict text book instruction, to the new habit of laboratory practice, research, and constructive thought," and that "his career may have been determined to some extent by that of his contemporary and friend Edward C. Pickering." (Edwin H. Hall, "Biographical Memoir of John Trowbridge," *NAS Biographical Memoirs* 14 [Washington, D.C., 1932], 186–187.) Hall does not mention, however, the association of either Trowbridge or Pickering with the Institute.

19. E. C. Pickering, *Plan of the Physical Laboratory*, A Supplement to the *Fourth Annual Catalogue, 1868–69*, 3.

20. Edward C. Pickering, *Report on the Physical Laboratory of the Mass. Institute of Technology*, [1870], 1. This is contained in *Compilation of the Papers on Physics Written by Professor Edward C. Pickering, 1865–1877* (Cambridge, 1877, limited edition), 1. From internal textual evidence, and from the fact that a report dated 1871 follows in this volume, it is safe to assume that the report was prepared in 1870, at the end of the laboratory's first year of operation.

21. ECP to ER, March[?] 29, 1869, E. C. Pickering Private Letters, 1850–1883, HUA.

22. Fragment, JDR to ER, April 24, 1869, WBR Papers, folder 62. The remainder of this letter has not been found.

23. Committee on Instruction Records 1, May 11, & Government Records 2, May 14, 1869.

24. JDR to ER, June 12, 1869, WBR Papers, folder 62. Wolcott Gibbs had been appointed to the Rumford Professorship in 1863, with responsibility for the chemical instruction in the Lawrence Scientific School. In 1871, President Eliot transferred such instruction to the Chemical Department of Harvard College under Professor Josiah P. Cooke, moving Gibbs to the Physics Department of the college. Charles L. Jackson, "Chemistry," chap. 16 in Morison, *Development of Harvard University*, 259.

25. JDR to WBR, September 15, 1869, WBR Papers, folder 63.

26. Society of Arts Records 4, November 4, 1869.

27. *Report on the Physical Laboratory of the Mass. Institute of Technology*, 5.

28. Ibid., 2.

29. *Journal of the Franklin Institute* 59 (June 1870): 401.

30. *Report on the Physical Laboratory of the Mass. Institute of Technology*, 8.

31. Government Records 2, January 4, 1870.

32. WBR to Government, May 4, 1872, WBR Papers, folder 67; Government Records 2, May 8, 1872. Although in 1870, following an extensive bylaw revision, the "Government" became the "Corporation," Rogers often used the old term, and records of the Corporation were included in the Government Records book until that volume was filled. The full text of Rogers's

letter appears in Tenney L. Davis and H. M. Goodwin, *A History of the Department of Chemistry and Physics at the Massachusetts Institute of Technology, 1865–1933* (Cambridge, Mass.: Technology Press, 1933), 21–22.

33. See, for example, Florian Cajori, *A History of Physics in the Elementary Branches including the Evolution of Physical Laboratories* (New York: Macmillan Company, 1899); also Frank P. Whitman, "The Beginnings of Laboratory Teaching in America," *Science,* August 19, 1898, and T. C. Mendenhall, *Proceedings, AAAS* 31, 1882, 127–138.

34. Edward C. Pickering, "Physical Laboratories," *Nature,* January 26, 1871, 241.

35. Ricketts, 6.

36. The original notebooks are in the Albert Francis Hall Papers, 1863–1906 (MC 151), box 1.

37. *First Annual Catalogue, 1865–66,* 12–13.

38. "Student Notes: Physics, 1865," Hall Papers, box 1. The title on the notebook cover reads "Albert F. Hall, Physics, Lectures 4th, 5th, 6th."

39. Hall Papers, box 1. While the folder title is "Notebook (Mathematics), 1863," the contents actually include topics other than mathematics.

40. JDR to WBR [via ER], June 25, 1869, WBR Papers, folder 62.

41. *First Annual Catalogue, 1865–66,* 30.

42. *Fifth Annual Catalogue, 1869–70,* 35.

43. On this excursion, one student kept a diary that is preserved in the MIT Archives: Samuel W. Felton Diary, 1872 (MC 452). Felton recorded details about camping out, hunting antelope, and encounters with Indians and buffalo herds, as well as technical notes and sketches of bridges and trusses.

44. Jacob Bigelow, *An Address on the Limits of Education.*

45. *Fifth Annual Catalogue, 1869–70,* 13.

46. *Ibid.,* 18, 21.

47. A[braham] Hun Berry Papers, 1869–1875 (MC 172).

48. Walter H. Sears Papers, 1863–1962 (MC 257), box 1, folder 13.

49. WBR to Alfred P. Rockwell, May 31, 1867, Alfred Perkins Rockwell Correspondence, 1867–1876 (MC 446). The Burat textbook was probably Amédée Burat, *Minéralogie appliquée: description des minéraux employés dans les industries métallurgiques et manufacturières dans les constructions et dans l'ornement* (Paris: Librarie polytechnique de Noblet et Baudry, 1864).

50. Rockwell to "Kate" [Katharine Rockwell], October 15, 1869, Rockwell Correspondence.

51. Edward Charles Pickering Papers, 1867–1869 (MC 457).

52. Bishop, 125–126. Bishop says that White believed that "college students needed strict guidance of their private lives. He thought that military leveling and a common uniform would serve to break down the bulwarks of caste. He was distressed by the 'rustic slouchiness' of many students, and he found them in need of military smartness. He also favored military training for a social purpose." According to Bishop, White further believed that educated men should not be found wanting and "cower in corners" in the event of a "civil commotion." Students at Cornell were strictly regimented, wore uniforms, marched to meals, were required to obtain

a pass to leave the campus, and, when the state delayed the issuing of armaments, drilled with canes and umbrellas.

53. An Act in Addition to an Act to Incorporate the Massachusetts Institute of Technology, approved April 27, 1863, Acts of 1863, Chapter 186, *Acts and Resolves*, 5. The ambiguity surrounding the optional or mandatory nature of military tactics would remain a point of contention in the United States for many years. By the late 1920s pacifist groups in some states were agitating for the abolishment of the "compulsory" nature of this training in the land-grant colleges.

At the same time an interesting argument favoring the "mandatory" intent of Congress was presented in the *Illinois Law Review* by Professor Sveinbjorn Johnson, professor of law and also legal counsel at the University of Illinois. One facet of his argument centered on the act's statement that military tactics must be taught. He contended that if one has a legal duty to teach a particular subject, one has a legal duty to make that subject a requirement for the students, without whom the legal obligation cannot be met. He pointed out in addition that the language of the Act was predicated on the "prevailing educational practices and methods" of the day: "*The leading colleges and universities in the country at that time were either without electives of any sort in their curricula, or the privilege to make a choice of subjects or courses was restricted within very narrow limits.*" Among the institutions cited as examples was the Massachusetts Institute of Technology, whose catalogue "for the year 1866–1867, shows *no electives*, save one specialty in a professional course." It was Professor Johnson's contention that, in the absence of any extensive elective system in existing institutions of higher education, the legislators would have assumed military instruction to be required. Johnson made special note of the action of Massachusetts in amending the Institute's charter to require it to provide military instruction and further cited the Institute as one in which such training was required of all students. Sveinbjorn Johnson, "Military Training in the Land Grant Colleges; Is It Optional or Mandatory?" 271–298.

54. Ross, 61 n. 61, 196–197.
55. Faculty Records 1, January 13 & 20, 1866.
56. *First Annual Catalogue, 1865–66*, 25.
57. Faculty Records 1, January 13, 1866; Committee on Instruction Records, April 11, 1866; *Fourth Annual Catalogue, 1868–69*, [4].
58. *Fourth Annual Catalogue, 1868–69*, 20.
59. A paper entitled "Department of Military Science and Tactics," prepared by Lieutenant Harry L. Hawthorne, who assumed charge of the military instruction in 1892, provides a highly critical account of the Institute's efforts prior to his arrival, particularly so when Moore was in charge. Hawthorne claimed that Moore "left absolutely no impress on the Dept." His assessment may not have been entirely fair, for the third president of the Institute, Francis Amasa Walker, had kinder things to say when Moore returned in 1883, pointing out that the department "is now under admirable control." And again, when Moore was replaced by Hawthorne: ". . . in February, 1892, Lieut. Harry L. Hawthorne, of the 4th Artillery, was assigned for this service. . . . relieving in this duty Gen. Hobart Moore, who had for many years given the

60. Faculty Records 1, February 16, 1867; March 2, 1867 (emphasis in original record).
61. WBR Memorial to the Legislature, January 20, 1867, draft copy, WBR Papers, folder 56.
62. Ibid.
63. *Resolve in Relation to the Issue of Arms to the Massachusetts Institute of Technology*, Resolves of 1867, Chapter 6, Approved March 2, 1867, *Acts and Resolves*, 6–7.
64. Faculty Records 1, October 19, 1868; February 15, March 1, April 19, April 26, October 11, & November 15, 1869.
65. Faculty Records 1, May 13, 1871. The law to which the faculty referred was undoubtedly that passed in 1866 giving the president authority, "upon the application of an established college or university within the United States, with sufficient capacity to educate at one time not less than 150 male students, [to] detail an officer of the Army to act as president, superintendent, or professor of such college or university." By January 6, 1872, shortly before Rockwell submitted his report, the faculty had placed the "whole matter of the Military Drill" in his charge. The idea of seeking help from the War Department was not acted upon until the end of the year, Hobart Moore continuing as instructor.
66. B. F. Edmands to WBR, October 21, 1868, WBR Papers, folder 61.
67. WBR to Edmands, October 22, 1868, ibid.
68. *First Annual Catalogue, 1865–66*, 32–33.
69. Professor Eliot reported on Nelson Conant's thesis, November 7, 1868; Professor Watson on Albert Hall's thesis, November 23, 1868; Professor Henck on the theses by Frank Firth, William Hoyt, Walter Sears, Charles Smith, and Joseph Stone, November 30, 1868; and Professor Rockwell on Robert Richards's thesis, December 2, 1868. In an unusual move, Professor Watson requested (November 14, 1868) that Professors Henck, Ware, and Atkinson read Eli Forbes's thesis, but Watson ended up reporting on it anyway, November 30, 1868. (See the relevant dated entries in Faculty Records.)
70. Faculty Records 1, April 12, 1869.
71. Richards, 35.

Epilogue

1. Faculty Records 1, October 24, 1868. Prescott in *When M.I.T. Was "Boston Tech"* (66) refers to this incident as a "slight stroke."
2. *Life and Letters,* 2:281–282.
3. WBR to JAL, October 31, 1868, WBR Papers, folder 61.
4. *Life and Letters,* 2:282.
5. Ibid., 282–283. M.P.W. refers to Marshall P. Wilder.
6. Ibid., 283.
7. Government Records 2, December 3, 1868.

8. WBR to Jacob Bigelow, December 3, 1868, WBR Papers, folder 61.

9. Government Records 2, December 3, 1868.

10. Samuel Kneeland to ER, December 24, 1868, WBR Papers, folder 61.

11. *Life and Letters,* 2:283–284.

12. WBR to J. Herbert Shedd, July 3, 1868, ibid., folder 60.

13. Kneeland to WBR, September 2, 1868; September 7, 1868, ibid.

14. Government Records 2, December 3, 1868.

15. Bigelow, *Limits of Education,* 26.

$\mathcal{S}$elected $\mathcal{S}$ources

Founding Documents

Objects and Plan of an Institute of Technology. Boston: John Wilson and Son, 1860.

An Account of the Proceedings Preliminary to the Organization of the Massachusetts Institute of Technology; with a List of the Members Thus Far Associated, and An Appendix, Containing Petitions and Resolutions in Aid of the Objects of the Committee of Associated Institutions of Science and Art [sic] (Boston, 1861).

An Act to Incorporate the Massachusetts Institute of Technology, and to Grant Aid to Said Institution and to the Boston Society of Natural History, Approved April 10, 1861, Acts of 1861, Chapter 183. *Acts and Resolves of the General Court relating to the Massachusetts Institute of Technology* (Cambridge, 1931).

[MIT] *Officers. Extracts from Act of Incorporation. Objects and Plan (Abbreviated statement only). By-Laws.* (Boston: John Wilson and Son, 1862).

Scope and Plan of the School of Industrial Science of the Massachusetts Institute of Technology, as Reported by the Committee on Instruction of the Institute, and Adopted by the Government, May 30, 1864. (Boston, 1864).

Ware, William R. *An Outline of a Course of Architectural Instruction.* Boston, 1866.

Catalogues

First Annual Catalogue of the Officers and Students, and Programme of the Course of Instruction, of the School of the Massachusetts Institute of Technology, 1865–6 (Boston, 1865).

Second Annual Catalogue of the Officers and Students, and Programme of the Course of Instruction, of the School of the Massachusetts Institute of Technology, 1866–7 (Boston, 1867).

Third Annual Catalogue of the Officers and Students, and Programme of the Course of Instruction of the Massachusetts Institute of Technology, 1867–8 (Boston, 1867).

Fourth Annual Catalogue of the Officers and Students, and Programme of the Course of Instruction of the Massachusetts Institute of Technology, 1868–9 (Boston, 1868).

Fifth Annual Catalogue of the Officers and Students, and Programme of the Course of Instruction of the Massachusetts Institute of Technology, 1869–70 (Boston, 1870).

Archives and Manuscripts

Harvard University

College Letters. Harvard University Archives
College Papers. Harvard University Archives
College Records. Harvard University Archives
Corporation Papers. Harvard University Archives
Lawrence Scientific School. Faculty Records, 1848–1871. Harvard University Archives
Letters to the Treasurer. Harvard University Archives
Lowell Institute Papers. Houghton Library
Peirce, Benjamin. Papers. Houghton Library

Massachusetts Historical Society

Andrew, John A. Letters.
Andrew, John A. Papers.
Everett, Edward. Diary.
Everett, Edward. Letters.

Massachusetts Institute of Technology

  Institute Archives and Special Collections, MIT Libraries
Class photograph albums, 1870–1895 (AC 319)
Corporation. [Known as the Government until Chapter 97 of the Acts of 1869 was approved on March 20.]
    Corporation. Records, 1862– (AC 278)
    Building Committee. Minutes, 1863–1867 (AC 131)
    Museum Committee. Records, 1860–1869 (AC 131)
    Executive Committee. Records, 1866– (AC 272)

Faculty. Records, 1865– (AC 1)

Finance Committee. Notebook, 1863 (AC 379)

Office of the President.

 Records, 1897–1930 (AC 13)

 Records, 1930–1959 (AC 4)

Office of the Registrar. Student academic records, 1865– (AC 251)

Office of the Treasurer.

 Cash Book, 1862–1872 (ASC 6)

 Ledger, 1862–1882 (ASC 5)

 Treasurer's statements, 1865–1883 (AC 63)

 Annual reports, 1865–1883 (AC 80)

Secretary of the Institute. Records, 1865–1874 (AC 338)

Society of Arts. Records, 1862–1841 (AC 11)

Berry, Abraham Hun. Student notes, 1869–1875 (MC 172)

Cross, Charles Robert. Papers, 1855–1913 (MC 107)

Hall, Albert Francis. Papers, 1863–1906 (MC 151)

Rockwell, Alfred Perkins. Correspondence, 1867–1876 (MC 446)

Pickering, Edward Charles. Papers, 1867–1869 (MC 457)

Rogers, William Barton. Papers, 1804–1911 (MC 1)

Rogers Family. Papers, 1811–1904 (MC 2)

Rogers, William Barton, II. Papers, 1817–1919 (MC 3)

Sears, Walter Herbert. Papers, 1863–1962 (MC 257)

Runkle, John Daniel. Papers, 1853–1880 (MC 7)

Ware, William Robert. Papers, 1826–1917 (MC 14)

MIT. "Incorporators." Compiled by Charles F. Read.

MIT. "Members of the Corporation Deceased." 3 vols. Compiled by Charles F. Read.

MIT. "Members of the Faculty and Officers of Instruction Deceased." Written by Charles F. Read, Robert E. Rogers, Julia M. Comstock, and Robert P. Bigelow.

 MIT Museum

Biographical files

Photographs

Books and Articles

Abbott, Frederick K. *The Role of the Civil Engineer in Internal Improvements, The Contributions of the Two Loammi Baldwins, Father and Son, 1776–1838.* Ann Arbor, Mich.: University Microfilms International, 1979.

Adams, Charles Francis. *The Works of John Adams*, vol. 8. Boston: Little, Brown & Co., 1853.

Ambrose, Stephen E. *Duty, Honor, Country, a History of West Point.* Baltimore: Johns Hopkins University Press, 1966.

Anderson, Lawrence B. "The Rogers Building: 1866–1938." *Places* 1, no. 4, 38–46.

Armes, William Dallam, ed. *The Autobiography of Joseph LeConte.* New York: D. Appleton & Co., 1903.

Artz, Frederick B. *The Development of Technical Education in France, 1500–1850.* Cambridge: MIT Press, 1966.

Ashby, Sir Eric. *Technology and the Academics.* 1958. Reprint. London: Macmillan & Co., 1959.

Bacon, Francis. *Novum Organum.* Vol. 8 of *The Works of Francis Bacon*, edited by James Spedding, Robert Leslie Ellis, and Douglas Denon Heath. Cambridge, Mass.: Riverside Press, 1863.

Baker, Paul R. *Richard Morris Hunt.* Cambridge: MIT Press, 1980.

Beach, Mark. "Was There a Scientific Lazzaroni?" In *Nineteenth-Century American Science: A Reappraisal*, edited by George H. Daniels. Evanston, Ill.: Northwestern University Press, 1972.

Becker, Carl. *Cornell University: Founders & the Founding.* Ithaca, N.Y.: Cornell University Press, 1943.

Bennett, Charles Alpheus. *History of Manual and Industrial Education up to 1870.* Peoria, Ill.: Manual Arts Press, 1920.

Benson, Arthur Emerson. *History of the Massachusetts Horticultural Society.* Boston, 1929.

Bentham, Jeremy. *Chrestomathia.* Vol. 8 of *The Works of Jeremy Bentham.* Edinburgh: William Tait, 1843.

Berman, Morris. *Social Change and Scientific Organization, The Royal Institution, 1799–1844.* Ithaca, N.Y.: Cornell University Press, 1978.

Bevan, Arthur. "William Barton Rogers, Pioneer American Scientist." *Scientific Monthly* 50 (1940): 110–124.

Bigelow, Erastus B. *Remarks on the Depressed Condition of Manufactures in Massachusetts.* Boston: Little, Brown & Co., 1858.

Bigelow, Jacob. *An Address on the Limits of Education*. Boston: E. P. Dutton & Co., 1865.

_____. *Elements of Technology*. Boston: Hilliard, Gray, Little, & Wilkins, 1829.

_____. *Modern Inquiries: Classical, Professional, and Miscellaneous*. Boston: Little, Brown & Co., 1867.

_____. "Remarks on Classical and Utilitarian Studies." Boston: Little, Brown & Co., 1867, [3], 6.

_____. *The Useful Arts*. 2 vols. New York: Harper Bros., 1847.

Bishop, Morris. *A History of Cornell*. Ithaca, N.Y.: Cornell University Press, 1962.

Bowen, Francis. *Classical Studies*. Cambridge, Mass.: Dakin & Metcalf, 1867.

Bradlee, Francis B. C. *The Boston and Main Railroad*. Salem, Mass.: Essex Institute, 1921.

Bridenbaugh, Carl. *Cities in Revolt, Urban Life in America, 1743–1776*. New York: Alfred A. Knopf, 1955.

_____. *Early Americans*. New York: Oxford University Press, 1981.

Brown, Sanborn C. *Benjamin Thompson, Count Rumford*. Cambridge: MIT Press, 1979.

Bruce, Philip Alexander. *History of the University of Virginia, 1819–1919*. 5 vols. New York: Macmillan Co., 1920.

Bullard, John M. *The Rotches*. New Bedford, 1947.

Burns, C. DeLisle. *A Short History of Birkbeck College*. London: University of London Press, 1924.

Cajori, Florian. *The Teaching and History of Mathematics in the United States*. U.S. Bureau of Education Circular of Information no. 3. Washington, D.C.: GPO, 1890.

Cantwell, Robert. *Nathaniel Hawthorne: The American Years*. New York: Holt, Rinehart, & Winston, 1948; New York: Octagon Books, 1971.

Carriel, Mary Turner. *The Life of Jonathan Baldwin Turner*. Privately printed in 1911. Urbana: University of Illinois Press, 1961.

Carson, Joseph. *A Memoir of the Life and Character of James B. Rogers, M.D.: Professor of Chemistry in the University of Pennsylvania*. Philadelphia: T. K. & P. G. Collins, Printers, 1852.

Centennial Celebration of the College of Literature, Science, and the Arts of the University of Michigan, 1841–1941. Ann Arbor: University of Michigan Press, 1943.

"Centennial Commemoration of William Barton Rogers, 1804–1904." *Technology Review* 7 (January 1905): 26–48.

Chewning, John Andrew. "William Robert Ware and the Beginnings of Architectural Education in the United States, 1861–1881." Ph.D. diss., Massachusetts Institute of Technology, 1986.

Chittenden, Russell H. *History of the Sheffield Scientific School of Yale University*. 2 vols. New Haven: Yale University Press, 1928.

Clark, Victor S. *History of Manufactures in the United States.* Vol. 1, 1607–1860. Carnegie Institution of Washington, 1929; New York: Peter Smith, 1949.

Cochrane, Rexmond C. *The National Academy of Sciences: The First Hundred Years, 1863–1963*. Washington, D.C.: National Academy of Sciences, 1978.

Cohen, I. Bernard. "Harvard and the Scientific Spirit." *Harvard Alumni Bulletin* (February 7, 1948): 393–398.

_____. *Some Early Tools of American Science*. Cambridge: Harvard University Press, 1950.

Coles, Harry L. *The War of 1812*. Chicago: University of Chicago Press, 1965.

Commager, Henry Steele. *The Empire of Reason*. Garden City, N.Y.: Anchor Press, Doubleday, 1977.

Conklin, Edwin G. "A Brief History of the American Philosophical Society." *American Philosophical Society Year Book 1975*. Philadelphia, 1976.

Cooke, Josiah P. "Notice of William Barton Rogers: Founder of the Massachusetts Institute of Technology." *Proceedings of the American Academy of Arts and Sciences* 18 (1882–1883): 428–438.

Cross, Charles R. "William Watson." *Proceedings of the American Academy of Arts and Sciences* 52 (1916–1917): 871–873.

Crumbaker, Leslie G. *The Baker Estate or Ridge Hill Farms of Needham*. Needham, Mass.: Needham Historical Society, 1975.

Curry, Leonard P. *Blueprint for Modern America*. Nashville, Tenn.: Vanderbilt University Press, 1968.

Curti, Merle, and Vernon Carstensen. *The University of Wisconsin, 1848–1925*, vol. 1. Madison: University of Wisconsin Press, 1949.

Daniels, George H. *Science in American Society, A Social History*. New York: Alfred A. Knopf, 1971.

Day, Charles R. *Education for the Industrial World*. Cambridge: MIT Press, 1987.

Dupree, A. Hunter. *Asa Gray*. Cambridge: Belknap Press of Harvard University Press, 1959.

Dupuy, Ernest R. *Sylvanus Thayer: Father of Technology in the United States*. West Point, N.Y.: The Association of Graduates, United States Military Academy, 1958.

Eliot, Charles W. "Francis Humphreys Storer (1832–1914)." *Proceedings of the American Academy of Arts and Sciences* 54 (1918–1919): 415–418.

_____. "The New Education." *Atlantic Monthly* 23 (February 1869): 203–220; (March 1869): 358–367.

Eliot, Samuel Atkins, ed. *Biographical History of Massachusetts* 9. Boston: Massachusetts Biographical Society, 1918.

Elliott, Clark A. *Biographical Dictionary of American Science, The Seventeenth through the Nineteenth Centuries.* Westport, Conn.: Greenwood Press, 1979.

_____, comp. *Biographical Index to American Science: The Seventeenth Century to 1920.* New York: Greenwood Press, 1990.

Ellis, George E. *The Life of Count Rumford.* Boston: American Academy of Arts and Sciences, 1871.

_____. *Memoir of Jacob Bigelow, M.D., LL.D.* Reprinted from the *Proceedings of the Massachusetts Historical Society.* Cambridge: John Wilson & Son, University Press, 1880.

_____. *Memoir of Nathaniel Thayer, A.M.* Reprinted from the *Proceedings of the Massachusetts Historical Society.* Cambridge: John Wilson & Son, University Press, 1885.

Ellis, William A. *Norwich University, 1819–1911.* 3 vols. Published by Major-General Grenville M. Dodge. Montpelier, Vt.: Capital City Press, 1911.

Emerson, George B. *Education in Massachusetts: Early Legislation and History.* Boston: John Wilson & Son, 1869.

Endicott, William. "Charles Henry Dalton." *Technology Review* 10 (April 1908): 149–152.

Evans, Oliver. *The Young Millwright and Miller's Guide.* Philadelphia, 1795, 1st edition, being revised over the years with a 15th and final edition in 1860.

Everitt, C. W. F. *James Clerk Maxwell.* New York: Charles Scribner's Sons, 1975.

Ewing, Galen W. *Early Teaching of Science at the College of William and Mary in Virginia.* Williamsburg, Va., 1938.

Ewing, John S., and Nancy P. Norton. *Broadlooms and Business Men.* Cambridge: Harvard University Press, 1955.

Federal Laws and Rulings Relating to Morrill and Supplementary Morrill Funds for Land-Grant Colleges and Universities. Compiled by Division of Higher Education, U. S. Office of Education, Pamphlet No. 91.

Ferguson, Eugene S. *Bibliography of the History of Technology.* Cambridge: Society for the History of Technology and MIT Press, 1968.

Fisher, George P. *Life of Benjamin Silliman, M.D., LL.D.* 2 vols. New York: Charles Scribner & Co., 1866.

Follett-Thompson, Jean Ames. "The Business of Architecture: William Gibbons Preston and Architectural Professionalism in Boston During the Second Half of the Nineteenth Century."

Ph.D. diss., Boston University, 1986.

Fox, Dixon Ryan. *Union College, An Unfinished History*. Schenectady, N.Y.: Union College, 1945.

Franklin, Fabian. *The Life of Daniel Coit Gilman*. New York: Dodd, Mead & Co., 1910.

Franklin Institute. *First Annual Report of the Proceedings of the Franklin Institute*. Philadelphia, 1825. Reprinted with Introduction by Henry B. Allen in *Journal of the Franklin Institute* 247 (April 1949): 289–402.

Frazer, Persifor. "The Franklin Institute." *Journal of the Franklin Institute* 165 (April 1908): 246–247.

Freidel, Frank, ed. *Union Pamphlets of the Civil War, 1861–1865*. 2 vols. Cambridge: The John Harvard Library, Belknap Press of Harvard University Press, 1967.

Frothingham, Paul Revere. *Edward Everett, Orator and Statesman*. Boston: Houghton Mifflin Co., 1925.

Gerstner, Patsy. *Henry Darwin Rogers, 1808–1866: American Geologist*. Tuscaloosa, Ala.: University of Alabama Press, 1994.

Gilman, Daniel Coit. "Our National Schools of Science." *North American Review* (October 1867): 498–499.

Gregory, John W. *Henry Darwin Rogers . . . An Address to the Glasgow University Geological Society, 20th January 1916*. Glasgow: J. MacLehose & Sons, 1916.

Guralnick, Stanley M. *Science and the Ante-Bellum American College*. Memoirs of the American Philosophical Society 109, Philadelphia: The Society, 1975.

Hall, A. Rupert. *Science for Industry, A Short History of the Imperial College of Science and Technology and its Antecedents*. London: Imperial College, 1982.

Hartley, E. Neal. *Ironworks on the Saugus*. Norman: University of Oklahoma Press, 1957.

Harvard University. *Historical Register of Harvard University, 1636–1936*. Cambridge, 1937.

Hatcher, Harlan. *"The University of Michigan," 140 Years from Michigan Wilderness to a World Center of Learning!, 1817–1957*. The Newcomen Society in North America, 1958.

Hawkins, Hugh. *Between Harvard and America: The Educational Leadership of Charles W. Eliot*. New York: Oxford University Press, 1972.

[Henry, Joseph]. *The Papers of Joseph Henry*, ed. Nathan Reingold et al. Washington: Smithsonian Institution Press, 1972–.

Higginson, Thomas Wentworth. "Edward Atkinson." *Proceedings of the American Academy of Arts and Sciences* 42 (1906–1907): 761–769.

Hill, Hamilton Andrews. *Memoir of Abbott Lawrence*. Boston, 1883.

_____. "Memoir of the Hon. Marshall P. Wilder, Ph.D., LL.D." Boston, 1888. Reprinted from the *New England Historical and Genealogical Register*, July 1888.

Hindle, Brooke. *The Pursuit of Science in Revolutionary America, 1735–1789*. Published for the Institute of Early American History and Culture, Williamsburg, Va. Chapel Hill: University of North Carolina Press, 1956.

_____, ed. *Early American Science*. New York: Science History Publications, 1976.

Hofstadter, Richard, and Wilson Smith, eds. *American Higher Education, A Documentary History*. 2 vols. Chicago: University of Chicago Press, 1961.

Holland, James W. *A Eulogy on the Life and Character of Prof. Robt. E. Rodgers [i.e. Rogers], M.D.: Introductory to the Course of 1885–86 at Jefferson Medical College: Delivered September 30th, 1885.* Philadelphia: William F. Fell & Company, 1885.

[Holmes, Oliver Wendell.] "Jacob Bigelow." *Proceedings of the American Academy of Arts and Sciences* 14 (1878–1879): 333–342.

Holton, Gerald. "How the Jefferson Physical Laboratory Came to Be." *Physics Today,* December 1984, 32–37.

Honeywell, Roy J. *The Educational Work of Thomas Jefferson.* New York: Russell & Russell, 1964.

Hughes, Sarah Forbes, ed. *Letters and Recollections of John Murray Forbes*, vol. 1. Boston: Houghton Mifflin & Co.; Cambridge, Mass.: Riverside Press, 1899.

Hunt, Robert, F.R.S., and F. W. Rudler. *A Descriptive Guide to the Museum of Practical Geology.* 4th ed. London, 1877.

In Memory of William Barton Rogers, L.L.D., Late President of the Society [of Arts]. Boston: Society of Arts of the Massachusetts Institute of Technology, 1882.

Jackson, Charles L. "Eben Norton Horsford." *Proceedings of the American Academy of Arts and Sciences* 28 (1892–1893): 340–346.

James, Henry. *Charles W. Eliot*, vol. 1. Boston and New York: Houghton Mifflin Co.; Cambridge, Mass.: Riverside Press, 1930.

Jefferson, Thomas. *Notes on the State of Virginia*. Edited with introduction and notes by William Peden. Published for the Institute of Early American History and Culture, Williamsburg, Va. Chapel Hill: University of North Carolina Press, 1955.

"John Daniel Runkle." *Technology Review* 4, no. 3 (July 1902): 278–306.

Johnson, Samuel A. *The Battle Cry of Freedom*. Lawrence: University of Kansas Press, 1954.

Johnson, Sveinbjorn. "Military Training in the Land Grant Colleges; Is It Optional or Mandatory?" *Illinois Law Review* 24, no. 3 (November 1929): 271–298. Reprinted 1934 by the Civilian Military Education Fund, Washington, D.C.

Kelly, Thomas. *George Birkbeck, Pioneer of Adult Education.* Liverpool: At the University Press, 1957.

Kimball, William Phelps. *The First Hundred Years of the Thayer School of Engineering at Dartmouth College.* Hanover, N.H.: University Press of New England, 1971.

Kirkland, Edward Chase. *Men, Cities and Transportation: A Study in New England History, 1820–1900.* 2 vols. Cambridge: Harvard University Press, 1948.

Kohlstedt, Sally Gregory. "From Learned Society to Public Museum: The Boston Society of Natural History." In *The Organization of Knowledge in Modern America, 1860–1920*, edited by Alexandra Oleson and John Voss. Baltimore: Johns Hopkins University Press, 1979.

Kranzberg, Melvin, and Carroll W. Pursell, Jr., eds. *Technology in Western Civilization.* 2 vols. New York: Oxford University Press, 1967.

Kuslan, Louis I. "Benjamin Silliman, Jr.: The Second Silliman" and "The Rise of the Yale School of Applied Chemistry (1845–1856)." In *Benjamin Silliman and His Circle: Studies on the Influence of Benjamin Silliman on Science in America*, edited by Leonard G. Wilson. New York: Science History Publications, 1979.

Land-Grant Fact Book. Centennial Ed. Washington, D.C.: American Association of Land-Grant Colleges and State Universities, 1962.

Lathem, Edwin Connery, ed. *The Beginnings of The Thayer School of Engineering at Dartmouth College.* Hanover, N.H., 1964.

Latrobe, John H. B. *Picture of Baltimore.* Baltimore: Fielding Lucas, Jr., 1832.

"The Lawrence Scientific School." *Engineering News*, May 5, 1892, 459–461, No. VIII in an extended series, "The Engineering Schools of the United States."

Livingstone, David N. *Nathaniel Southgate Shaler and the Culture of American Science.* Tuscaloosa: University of Alabama Press, 1987.

Lowell, Augustus. *Commemorative Address*, June 3, 1890. Cambridge, Mass., 1890.

Lurie, Edward. *Louis Agassiz, a Life in Science.* Chicago: University of Chicago Press, 1960.

Mack, Edward C. *Peter Cooper, Citizen of New York.* New York: Duell, Sloan, & Pearce, 1949.

Mack, M. P. *Jeremy Bentham.* New York: Columbia University Press, 1963.

Malone, Dumas. *Jefferson the President, Second Term 1805–1809.* Boston: Little, Brown & Co., 1974.

_____. *Jefferson the Virginian.* Boston: Little, Brown & Co., 1948.

_____. *The Sage of Monticello*. Boston: Little, Brown & Co., 1981.

Mann, Charles R. *A Study in Engineering Education*. Prepared for the Joint Committee on Engineering Education of the National Engineering Societies. Bulletin no. 11, Carnegie Foundation. New York, 1918.

Marcou, Jules. *Life, Letters and Works of Louis Agassiz*, vol. 2. New York: Macmillan Co., 1896.

May, Henry F. *The Enlightenment in America*. New York: Oxford University Press, 1976.

McAllister, Ethel M. *Amos Eaton, Scientist and Educator*. Philadelphia: University of Pennsylvania Press, 1941.

McGivern, James Gregory. *First Hundred Years of Engineering Education in the United States (1807–1907)*. Spokane, Wash.: Gonzaga University Press, 1960.

Mellow, James R. *Nathaniel Hawthorne in His Times*. Boston: Houghton Mifflin Co., 1980.

Miller, Lillian B., Frederick Voss, and Jeannette M. Hussey. *The Lazzaroni: Science and Scientists in Mid-Nineteenth-Century America*. Washington, D.C.: Smithsonian Institution Press, 1972.

Mills, Hiram F. "James Bicheno Francis." *Technology Quarterly* 5, no. 3 (October 1892): 274–281.

Morison, Samuel Eliot. *Harvard College in the Seventeenth Century*. Cambridge: Harvard University Press, 1936.

_____. *Three Centuries of Harvard, 1636–1936*. Cambridge: Harvard University Press, 1936.

_____, ed. *The Development of Harvard University, 1869–1929*. Cambridge: Harvard University Press, 1930.

Morison, Samuel Eliot, and Henry Steele Commager. *The Growth of the American Republic*. 2 vols. 3d ed. New York: Oxford University Press, 1942.

Morison, Samuel Eliot, Henry Steele Commager, and William E. Leuchtenburg. *A Concise History of the American Republic*. New York: Oxford University Press, 1977.

Morrison, James Lunsford, Jr. *The United States Military Academy, 1833–1866: Years of Progress and Turmoil*. 2 vols. Ann Arbor, Mich.: University Microfilms, 1971.

Mott, Frank Luther. *A History of American Magazines, 1741–1850*. Cambridge: Harvard University Press, 1938.

Muir, James. *John Anderson, Pioneer of Technical Education and the College He Founded*. Glasgow: John Smith & Son, 1950.

Munroe, James P. "William Endicott." *Technology Review* 7 (January 1915): 18–23.

National Almanac and Annual Record for the Year 1863. Philadelphia: George W. Childs, 1863.

Nevins, Allan. *Abram S. Hewitt, with Some Account of Peter Cooper*. New York: Harper & Brothers, 1935.

Newcomb, Simon. *The Reminiscences of an Astronomer*. Boston: Houghton Mifflin Co., 1903.

O'Gorman, James F. *Drawings by Nineteenth Century Boston Architects*. Philadelphia: University of Pennsylvania Press, 1989.

Oliver, John W. *History of American Technology*. New York: Ronald Press Co., 1956.

Parker, William Belmont. *The Life and Public Service of Justin Smith Morrill*. Boston: Houghton Mifflin Co; Cambridge, Mass., Riverside Press, 1924.

Pearson, Henry Greenleaf. *An American Railroad Builder, John Murray Forbes*. Boston: Houghton Mifflin Co.; Cambridge, Mass.: Riverside Press, 1911.

_____. *The Life of John A. Andrew, Governor of Massachusetts, 1861–1865*. 2 vols. Boston: Houghton, Mifflin & Co., 1904.

_____. *Son of New England, James Jackson Storrow, 1864–1926*. Boston, 1932.

Perkins, Edwin J. *The Economy of Colonial America*. New York: Columbia University Press, 1980.

Perry, Bliss. *Life and Letters of Henry Lee Higginson*. Boston: Atlantic Monthly Press, 1921.

Peterson, Merrill D. *Thomas Jefferson and the New Nation*. New York: Oxford University Press, 1970.

Pfeifer, Edward J. "United States." In *The Comparative Reception of Darwinism*, edited by Thomas F. Glick. Austin: University of Texas Press, 1974.

Powell, Burt E. *Semi-Centennial History of the University of Illinois*. Vol. 1, *The Movement for Industrial Education and the Establishment of the University, 1840–1870*. Urbana, Ill., 1918.

Prescott, Samuel C. *When M.I.T. was Boston Tech*. Cambridge, Mass.: Technology Press, 1954.

"President Eliot and M.I.T." *Technology Review* 22, no. 3 (July 1920): 430–438.

Pritchett, Henry S. Introduction to *Federal Aid for Vocational Education*, by I. L. Kandel. Bulletin No. 10, Carnegie Foundation for the Advancement of Teaching. New York, 1917.

Proceedings and Transactions, Association of American Geologists and Naturalists. Boston: Gould, Kendall, & Lincoln, 1843.

Proceedings at a Banquet Given by His Friends to the Honorable Marshall Pinckney Wilder. Cambridge, Mass.: University Press, 1883.

Quincy, Edmund. *Life of Josiah Quincy of Massachusetts*. Boston: Ticknor & Fields, 1868.

Raymond, Andrew Van Vranken. *Union University*. 3 vols. New York: Lewis Publishing Co., 1907.

Rezneck, Samuel. *Education for a Technological Society, A Sesquicentennial History of Rensselaer Polytechnic Institute.* Troy, N.Y., 1968.

_____. "The European Education of an American Chemist and Its Influence in 19th-Century America: Eben N. Horsford." *Technology and Culture* 11, no. 3 (July 1970): 368-369.

Richards, Robert H. Address, "Centennial Commemoration of William B. Rogers, 1804-1904." *Technology Review* 7, no. 1 (January 1905): 35-40.

_____. *His Mark.* Boston: Little, Brown & Co., 1936.

Richardson, Leon B. *History of Dartmouth College.* 2 vols. Hanover, N.H.: Dartmouth College Publications, 1932.

Ricketts, Palmer C. *History of the Rensselaer Polytechnic Institute, 1824–1894.* New York: John Wiley & Sons, 1895.

"Robert Empie Rogers, M.D., L.L.D., 1842–1852." In Gemmill, Chalmers L., and Mary Jeanne Jones, *Pharmacology at the University of Virginia School of Medicine.* Charlottesville: Department of Pharmacology, University of Virginia, 1966.

"Robert H. Richards, 1844–1945," *Technology Review* 47 (May 1945): 434–435.

Roberts, Joseph K. "William Barton Rogers and His Contribution to the Geology of Virginia." *American Philosophical Society Miscellanea* 1, no. 2 (1935?): 65–68.

Rogers, Emma, ed. *Life and Letters of William Barton Rogers.* 2 vols. Boston: Houghton, Mifflin & Co.; Cambridge, Mass.: Riverside Press, 1896.

Rogers, Henry D. *The Geology of Pennsylvania: A Government Survey: with a General View of the Geology of the United States, Essays on Coal-Formation and Its Fossils, and a Description of the Coal-Fields of North America and Great Britain.* Edinburgh & London: W. Blackwood & Sons; Philadelphia: J. B. Lippincott & Company, 1858.

Ross, Earle D. *Democracy's College.* Ames, Iowa: Iowa State College Press, 1942.

Ross, M. D. *Estimate of the Financial Effect of the Proposed Reservation of Back-Bay Lands.* Boston, 1861.

Rossiter, Margaret W. "Women Scientists in America before 1920." *American Scientist* 62 (May–June 1974): 312–323.

Rudolph, Frederick. *The American College and University.* New York: Alfred A. Knopf, 1962.

Ruffin, William H. "The Brothers Rogers," Virginia Historical Society Library, [1895].

Runkle, John D. "Samuel Kneeland." *Proceedings of the American Academy of Arts and Sciences* 24 (1888–1889): 438–441.

Ruschenberger, William S. W. *A Sketch of the Life of Robert E. Rogers, M.D., L.L.D., with Biographical Notices of His Fathers and Brothers.* Philadelphia: McCalla & Stavely, 1885.

Russell, Foster W. *Mount Auburn Biographies, A Biographical Listing of Distinguished Persons Interred in Mount Auburn Cemetery, 1831–1952.* Cambridge, Mass.: Proprietors of the Cemetery of Mount Auburn, 1953.

Sayre, Mortimer F. "Squire Whipple and Union College." In *Squire Whipple, Class of 1830*, by Mortimer F. Sayre, Shortridge Hardesty, and Carl B. Jansen. Union Worthies no. 4. Schenectady, N.Y.: Union College, 1949.

Schnabel, Franz. "Die Anfänge des technischen Hochschulwesens." In *Festschrift anlässich des 100 jährigen Bestehens der Technischen Hochschule Fridericiana zu Karlsruhe.* Karlsruhe: C. F. Muller Buchdruckerei, 1925.

Schofield, Richard E. *The Lunar Society of Birmingham.* London: Oxford University Press, 1963.

Sellers, Charles Coleman. *Dickinson College: A History.* Middletown, Conn.: Wesleyan University Press, 1973.

Semmes, John E. *John H. B. Latrobe and His Times, 1803–1891.* Baltimore, Md.: Norman, Remington Co., 1917.

Sexton, A. Humboldt. *The First Technical College.* London: Chapman & Hall, 1894.

Shaler, Nathaniel Southgate. *The Autobiography of Nathaniel Southgate Shaler.* Boston: Houghton Mifflin Co., 1909.

Sheridan, Richard C. "William Barton Rogers and the Virginia Geological Survey, 1835–1842." In *The Geological Sciences in the Antebellum South,* ed. James X. Corgan. University, Ala.: University of Alabama Press, 1982.

Shrock, Robert R. *Geology at M.I.T. 1865–1965: A History of the First Hundred Years of Geology at Massachusetts Institute of Technology.* Cambridge: MIT Press, 1977.

Sinclair, Bruce. *Philadelphia's Philosopher Mechanics, a History of the Franklin Institute 1824–1865.* Baltimore: Johns Hopkins University Press, 1974.

Smith, Edgar F. "Biographical Memoir of Robert Empie Rogers, 1813–1884." *Biographical Memoirs, National Academy of Sciences* 5 (1905): 291–309.

Smith, Edgar F. *James Blythe Rogers, 1802–1852, Chemist.* [Philadelphia, 1927].

Smith, George Winston. "Broadsides for Freedom: Civil War Propaganda in New England." *New England Quarterly* 21 (1948): 291–312.

Smith, Harriette Knight. *The History of the Lowell Institute.* Boston: Lamson, Wolffe & Co., 1898.

Snelling, George. *Proposed Modification of the Plan of Building on the Back Bay Territory*. Boston: Damrell & Moore, 1860.

Spencer, Hugh Miller. *The Life of John William Mallet, B.A., Ph.D., LL.D., Hon. M.D., F.R.S.; and the Four Distinguished Sons of Patrick Kerr (1776–1828) and Hannah Blythe (ca. 1775–1820) Rogers*. Charlottesville: Alumni Association of the University of Virginia, 1985.

Stearns, Raymond Phineas. *Science in the British Colonies of America*. Urbana: University of Illinois Press, 1970.

Stellhorn, Chester E., M.D. "Jacob Bigelow, M.D., LL.D." *New England Journal of Medicine* 213 (August 29, 1935): 405–407.

Struik, Dirk J. *Yankee Science in the Making*. Boston: Little, Brown & Co., 1948.

Survey of Land-Grant Colleges and Universities, vol. 2. United States Department of the Interior, Office of Education, Bulletin no. 9. Washington, D.C.: GPO, 1930.

Swain, George F. "John Benjamin Henck." *Technology Review* 5, no. 2 (April 1903): 139–146.

Syrett, Harold C., and Jacob E. Cooke, eds. *The Papers of Alexander Hamilton*, vol. 10. New York: Columbia University Press, 1966.

Talbot, Henry P. "Retirement of Mrs. Stinson." *Technology Review* 14, no. 1 (January 1912): 45–48.

Teller, James David. *Louis Agassiz, Scientist and Teacher*. Columbus: Ohio State University Press, 1947.

Tyler, Harry W. "James P. Munroe, '82 (1862–1929)." *Technology Review* 31, no. 5 (March 1929): 273–274.

———. "John Daniel Runkle." *Technology Review* 4, no. 3 (July 1902): 278–306.

The University of Michigan, An Encyclopedic Survey. Vol. 1 & 2 edited by Wilfred B. Shaw; vol. 3 & 4 edited by Walter A. Donnelly. Ann Arbor: University of Michigan Press, 1942–1958.

Van Doren, Carl. "The Beginnings of the American Philosophical Society." *Proceedings of the American Philosophical Society* 87 (1944): 277–289.

Vital Facts, A Chronology of the College of William and Mary. Williamsburg, Va., 1976.

Vose, George L. *A Sketch of the Life and Works of Loammi Baldwin*. Boston: George H. Ellis, 1885.

Walker, Francis Amasa. "Memoir of William Barton Rogers, 1804–1882." *Biographical Memoirs, National Academy of Sciences* 3 (1895): 1–13.

Ware, Edith Ellen. *Political Opinion in Massachusetts during Civil War and Reconstruction*. New York: Columbia University, Longmans, Green & Co., Agents, 1916.

Ware, William R. *An Outline of a Course of Architectural Instruction*. Boston: John Wilson & Sons, 1866.

Warren, S. Edward. *Notes on Polytechnic or Scientific Schools, in the United States; Their Nature, Position, Aims and Wants*. New York: John Wiley & Son, 1866.

Watson, William. *Papers on Technical Education*. Boston, 1872.

Wayland, Francis. *Report to the Corporation of Brown University, on Changes in the System of Collegiate Education, Read March 28, 1850*. Providence: George H. Whitney, 1850.

_____. *Thoughts on the Present Collegiate System in the United States*. Boston: Gould, Kendall & Lincoln, 1842.

Weeks, Edward. *The Lowells and Their Institute*. Boston: An Atlantic Monthly Press Book, Little, Brown & Co., 1966.

Weiss, John Hubbel. *The Making of Technological Man*. Cambridge: MIT Press, 1982.

Whitehill, Walter Muir. *A Topographical History of Boston*. 2d ed. Cambridge: Belknap Press of Harvard University Press, 1968.

Wickenden, William E. *A Comparative Study of Engineering Education in the United States and Europe*. Bulletin no. 16 of the Investigation of Engineering Education, The Society for the Promotion of Engineering Education, June 1929.

"William Barton Rogers, First State Geologist of Virginia (1835–1841)." *Proceedings of the Virginia Academy of Science for 1934–1935*, 63–67.

"William Johnson Walker." *Technology Review* 1, no. 4 (October 1899): 421–423.

Williamson, Harold Francis. *Edward Atkinson, The Biography of an American Liberal*. Boston: Old Corner Book Store, 1934.

Winsor, Justin, ed. *The Memorial History of Boston*. Boston: James R. Osgood & Co., 1881.

Wolf, A. *A History of Science, Technology, and Philosophy in the Eighteenth Century*. 2d ed. rev. D. McKie. London: George Allen & Unwin, 1952.

Wood, Sir Henry Trueman. *A History of the Royal Society of Arts*. London: John Murray, 1913.

Worthen, W. E. "James Bicheno Francis." *Proceedings of the American Academy of Arts and Sciences* 28 (1892–1893): 333–340.

Wyman, Morrill. *Memoir of Daniel Treadwell*. Memoirs of the American Academy of Arts and Sciences, Centennial vol. 11. Cambridge: John Wilson & Son, University Press, 1888.

Yorke, Dane. *Able Men of Boston*. Boston: Boston Manufacturers Mutual Fire Insurance Co., 1950.

$\mathcal{I}llustrations$

Illustrations used in this work come primarily from the MIT Museum and from collections in the Institute Archives and Special Collections, Massachusetts Institute of Technology. The sketches by Paul Nefflen are reproduced from Frank A. Bourne, "Huntington Hall Frieze," *Technology Review* 7 (1905): 139–149.

Illustrations

Items from the MIT Archives are in various archival and manuscript collections, publications, and other materials, including:

Berry, Abraham Hun. Student notes, 1868–1875 (MC 172)
Cross, Charles Robert. Papers, 1855–1913 (MC 107)
MIT. Building Committee Minutes (AC 131)
MIT. Class Photograph Albums (AC 319)
MIT. Faculty Records (AC 1)

MIT. "Incorporators." Compiled by Charles F. Read.

MIT. "Members of the Corporation Deceased." 3 vols. Compiled by Charles F. Read.

MIT. "Members of the Faculty and Officers of Instruction Deceased." Written by Charles F. Read, Robert E. Rogers, Julia M. Comstock, and Robert P. Bigelow.

MIT. Museum Committee Records (AC 131)

MIT. Office of the Registrar, Student Academic Records (AC 251).

MIT. Society of Arts Records (AC 11)

Rogers, Emma, ed. *Life and Letters of William Barton Rogers.* 2 vols. Boston: Houghton, Mifflin & Co.; Cambridge, Mass.: Riverside Press, 1896.

Rogers, William Barton. Papers, 1804–1911 (MC 1)

Sears, Walter Herbert. Papers, 1863–1962 (MC 257)

Ware, William Robert. Papers, 1826–1917 (MC 14)

Sketches by Paul Nefflen

Paul Nefflen was commissioned in 1870 to create a mural on the frieze panels above the architrave in the lecture hall of MIT's first "permanent" home in the Back Bay, Boston. The work was carried out in 1871 and took Nefflen ten months to complete, part of that time, according to Frank Bourne, "in the bitterest winter weather, with no windows in the hall, as it was in an unfinished condition, the only fire being a tiny stove with just enough heat to keep his colors warm."

Index

Index

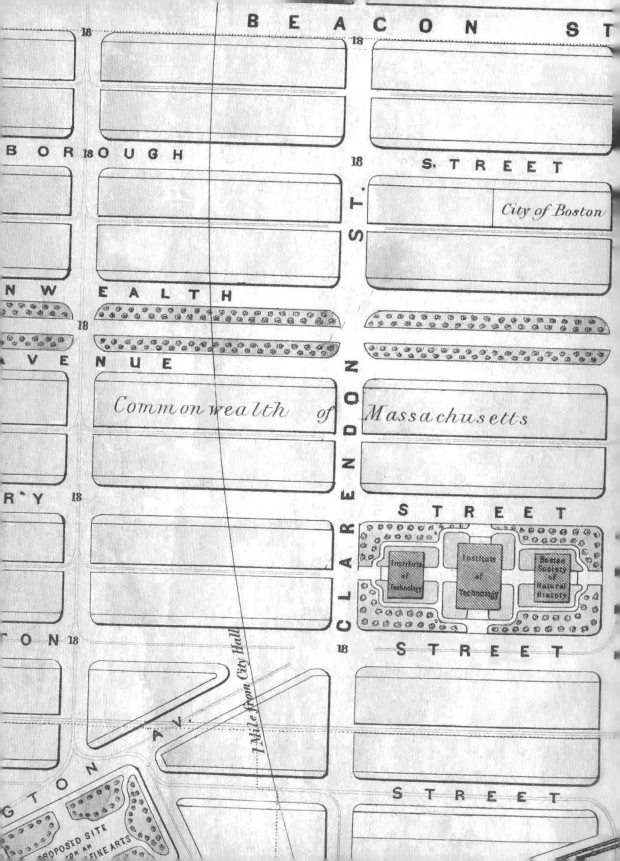

BEACON ST

BOROUGH 18 STREET

S. STREET

City of Boston

NWEALTH

Commonwealth of Massachusetts

AVENUE

CLARENDON ST.

CLARENDON STREET

Institute of Technology

Institute of Technology

Boston Society of Natural History

STREET

1 Mile from City Hall

AV.

PROPOSED SITE FOR AN FINE ARTS